HISTORY, METHOD AND THEOLOGY
A Dialectical Comparison of Wilhelm Dilthey's
Critique of Historical Reason and
Bernard Lonergan's Meta-Methodology

AMERICAN ACADEMY OF RELIGION
DISSERTATION SERIES

edited by
H. Ganse Little, Jr.

Number 010125

HISTORY, METHOD AND THEOLOGY
A Dialectical Comparison of Wilhelm Dilthey's
Critique of Historical Reason and
Bernard Lonergan's Meta-Methodology

by
Matthew L. Lamb

SCHOLARS PRESS
Missoula, Montana

HISTORY, METHOD AND THEOLOGY
A Dialectical Comparison of Wilhelm Dilthey's Critique of Historical Reason and Bernard Lonergan's Meta-Methodology

by
Matthew L. Lamb

Published by
SCHOLARS PRESS
for
The American Academy of Religion

Distributed by

SCHOLARS PRESS
Missoula, Montana 59806

HISTORY, METHOD AND THEOLOGY
A Dialectical Comparison of Wilhelm Dilthey's Critique of Historical Reason and Bernard Lonergan's Meta-Methodology

by

Matthew L. Lamb
Marquette University, Milwaukee, Wisconsin

Dr. Theol., 1974
State University of Münster,
West Germany

Adviser:
Johann B. Metz

Library of Congress Cataloging in Publication Data
Lamb, Matthew L.
    History, method, and theology

    (Dissertation series – American Academy of Religion ;
no. 25 ISSN 0145-272X)
    Originally presented as the author's thesis, State
University of Münster, West Germany, 1974.
    Includes bibliographical references.
    1. Dilthey, Wilhelm, 1833-1911. 2. History—
Philosophy. 3. Lonergan, Bernard J. F. 4. Theology—
Methodology. 5. Christianity and politics.
I. Title. II. Series: American Academy of Religion.
Dissertation Series – American Academy of Religion ;
no. 25.
B3216.D84L35   1978   193   78-18707
ISBN 0-89130-238-7

Printed in the United States of America
1 2 3 4 5

T A B L E   O F   C O N T E N T S

for

my parents

Mr. and Mrs. Matthew C. Lamb

F O R E W O R D

In this study Prof. Matthew Lamb fits together Wilhelm Dilthey's concern with history, the political theology of Prof. Johann B. Metz, and my work in method. It is this conjunction, I feel, that most calls for elucidation. For it rests not, as one might expect, on some genetic dependence, but on an overarching and somewhat complex dialectic. And it is this dialectic that both constitutes the unity of the study and informs the interpretation of the authors under examination.

Now dialectic denotes both conflict and movement. In this case the relevant conflict is between the promise of the Enlightenment and its fulfillment. There was promised that liberation of man under the rule of emancipated reason. But the implementation of that rule was entrusted to modern science; and modern science put its faith far less in the immanent reasonableness of the human spirit, far more in the embodiment of reason in experimental results and mathematical hard-headedness. So extrinsic a criterion and so abstruse a control, it can be argued, have done more for the mechanization than for the liberation of human life.

No less than conflict dialectic implies movement, and the relevant movement has been supplied by the ongoing development of modern science. For in the main it was Newton's achievement that the eighteenth-century Enlightenment celebrated as the inauguration of a new era. But later achievements have kept shifting the meaning and enlarging the horizon of scientific endeavor. Even scientists have been slow to adapt their conceptions of science to real advances of their field. One can hardly be surprised if an even greater lag is discerned in adapting the ideals and norms of the new era to the ever changing embodiments of scientific reason.

One such change and enlargement was seen by Wilhelm Dilthey in the work of the German Historical School. For its technique was not correlation of measurements, and the

coherence of its narratives was not secured by borrowing
mathematical syntheses. If Kant's Critique of Pure Reason
could supply the theoretical foundations that Hume had denied
to Euclidean geometry and Newtonian mechanics, there still
was needed a supplementary critique of historical reason.
Where Kant had grounded an Erklären of things, Dilthey sought
a Verstehen of concrete human living. For concrete human
living was the very stuff of history, and with that stuff one
became familiar only through a heightening of one's own
conscious feeling, knowing, doing.

What Dilthey undertook and carried forward, he did not
complete. At the turn of the century positivist views were
still dominant in accounts of historical method. Even
Dilthey's great follower, Ernst Troeltsch, was unable to
break with historical relativism. Still, Dilthey's quest for
foundations lived on in Husserl's transcendental phenomenology,
while Dilthey's technique of a Besinnung that interprets not
Erfahrung so much as Erlebnis continues in the various forms
of hermeneutic phenomenology.

Meanwhile, however, the very notion of modern science
was being transformed. The success of Einstein's special
theory of relativity transposed the invariants of physics from
the Euclidean image of space to the realm of empirical laws
and theoretical principles. The investigation of the subatomic
order led to ultimates that could be envisaged exclusively
neither as wave nor as particle. Heisenberg's principle of
indeterminacy ran counter to the universal determinism that
had been vindicated by Laplace when he established the
periodicity of the planetary system. The extension of the
relevance of statistical theory from thermodynamics to
quantum theory invited a further extension that introduced
schedules of probabilities to replace Darwin's chance
variations and his survival of the fittest. Finally, these
revolutions in the natural sciences found an echo in rebel-
lions against positivist domination in historical studies.
In Germany there was K. Heussi's Die Krisis des Historismus in
France Henri-Irénée Marrou's De la connaissance historique; in
England R. G. Collingwood's Idea of History; and even before
these three in the United States the penetrating essays of

Carl Becker.

The twentieth-century development of the notion of "modern" science not only has cast a retrospective light on Dilthey's work, but also contributed to the ferment that in Roman Catholic circles prepared the way for the Second Vatican Council. So Lamb finds in my work an instance in which an awareness of contemporary mathematics and science led to a revision of traditional interpretations of Aquinas and of Aristotle. It brought to light, as well, a generalized empirical method that covers the learning process of common sense, the procedures of empirical science, the ways of historical scholarship, and the philosophic grounding of the objectivity of human knowledge. This grounding is placed in authentic subjectivity. It challenges the once seductive implementation of reason through experimental science. It invites thoughtful men and women to the self-understanding and self-appropriation that can follow from a heightened awareness of their own powers of attention, their own intelligence, their own reasonableness, their own conscientiousness. It founds a methodology that not only accounts for the diversity of specializations but also stresses the historicity of their past development and promotes their future interaction and collaboration.

It is the intrinsically practical aspect of my work on method that enables Lamb to relate it to the work of Johann B. Metz. For the latter's political theology has wide-ranging academic implications. Its specific difference seems to be twofold. Where other theology tended to center its attention on its justifying past, political theology would add concern with man's future. Where other theology in its medieval phase ambitioned the role of queen of the sciences and, more recently, has been content to stress the significance of religion for man's inner life, political theology assumes an interdisciplinary role and seeks an interdisciplinary setting. Indeed, its proper Sitz im Leben would be found in the projected Theological Research Center at the interdisciplinary University of Bielefeld, and with that project Metz himself is actively concerned.

Now with such a vision the dialectic of the Enlightenment

moves to a new plane. For an interdisciplinary university
carries on the aspirations for unity and comprehensivenss of
the eighteenth-century Encyclopédie. At the same time the
notion of science, inspired by Galilei, Descartes, Newton,
is sublated by the advances of Einstein, Heisenberg, Darwin.
The natural sciences are complemented by human studies. A
future-oriented theology adds a corrective to a utilitarianism
that denied limits to utility, and so set our activities, our
policies, our institutions on the fatal course of exponential
growth.

In endeavoring to communicate what I consider the overarching idea informing Lamb's study, I had to simplify the
dialectic of the Enlightenment by taking as a base line the
subsequent unfolding of natural science. In his own treatment
of that dialectic, Lamb had to attend to a far larger scope
of historical detail. In doing so he has displayed a great
erudition. If his subject matter and style are at times
difficult, the effort of drawing on his learning and of
entering into his thought is highly rewarding.

Bernard Lonergan

INTRODUCTION

The crisis of historicism has become the crisis of
pluralism. No sooner had christian theologies more or less
come to terms with historical-critical methods, when they became faced with the need to elaborate foundations upon which
to guide the socio-historical praxis of their believing communities. History is not only studied, it is also lived. As
the historico-critical methods effectively challenged pre-
critical assumptions about the past, so the demands of the
present are challenging uncritical assumptions about the
future. Historicism made it evident that theology could not
rely solely on historical-critical methods for its own scientific self-understanding; pluralism is gradually impelling
theologians to find methods adequate to a critical mediation
of theory and praxis. For the profoundly relativizing effect
historicism had on science and reflection, pluralism is now
having on social and cultural praxis. Unless norms immanent
in historical consciousness are found to guide praxis in its
future-constituting present, praxis itself will increasingly
be devaluated into a pluralism of techniques. The significance of Political Theology is both its acute awareness of
this pluralism and its provocative efforts to meet it.

Against the background of the reality of this problem
for contemporary culture and contemporary theology, the present study takes up the writings of Wilhelm Dilthey and
Bernard Lonergan. The reality of the cultural and ecclesial
crisis, the reality of the need for interdisciplinary collaboration, the reality of the demand on the part of thinking
believers that theology offer a positive and critical contribution to that collaboration, the reality of the plea that the
theoretical concerns of theology be grounded on an articulation of authentic religious praxis and be related to intellectual and moral praxis - these are the realities defining the scope and aim of this dialectical comparison.

I do not intend to give an extensive analysis of the

historical influences on, and developments of, the thought of Dilthey and Lonergan. This does not mean that a simple historical account of the development of the two thinkers' positions would not be of value; to some extent this has already been done.[1] I only wish to indicate that the present is a _dialectical_ comparison rather than a _historical_ comparison. The former presupposes the latter, and so the exposition here is open to the judgments of historians on the accurateness of its presentations of the two men's positions. But the former also sublates (in the sense of preserving and relativizing by going beyond) the latter by addressing the texts with questions of more than purely past historical interest, with questions whose interests move beyond the concern with the truth of historical accuracy to the concern with the foundations of truth itself in an age of specialization and crisis.

What are these dialectical questions? J. Habermas, in his study on knowledge and human interest, has pointed out how positivism, as _the_ denial of reflection, has scientistically monopolized methodology by negating the concerns with cognitional subjectivity in its theoretical and practical dimensions, and by concentrating upon an objectivistic theory of scientific inquiry.[2] It has been on the ruins of that forgotten and repressed subjectivity that positivism erected its cult of "pure methodology." Both Dilthey and Lonergan have essayed alternatives to that (mis)conception of methodology. The present work addresses, then, a very specific question to the writings of these two: how can a foundational methodology

---

[1] On Dilthey, cf. P. Hünermann, _Der Durchbruch geschichtlichen Denkens im 19. Jahrhundert_ (Freiburg, 1967), pp. 133-291 on the four periods in Dilthey's thought; regarding his biography, cf. the references in U. Herrman, _Bibliographie W. Dilthey,_ (Berlin, 1969), pp. 131f. R. A. Makkreel, _Dilthey Philosopher of the Human Studies_ (Princeton, 1975). On Lonergan, cf. D. Tracy, _The Achievement of B. Lonergan_ (New York, 1970) which includes a comprehensive bibliography. Also Tracy's unpublished doctoral dissertation, _The Development of the Notion of Theological Methodology in the Works of B. Lonergan_ (Rome, Gregorian, 1969).

[2] Cf. _Erkenntnis und Interesse_ (Frankfurt, 1968), pp. 11-14, 88-92; also H. Schnädelbach, _Erfahrung, Begründung und Reflexion, Versuch über den Positivismus_ (Frankfurt, 1971), pp. 10-130.

be articulated which does justice to a critical mediation from the past into the present and the present into the future, and how would such a methodology apply to theology? The question concerns the mutual mediation of methodology and historicality and how such a mediation would affect theology.

The question asks: (1) how each developed a metascientific methodology capable of providing adequate alternatives to the scientistic claim as the sole legitimate representative of methodological matters; (2) how such a methodology would provide for a critical mediation from the past in the present into the future through a thematization of basic related and recurrent structures constitutive of both history and method; and (3) whether or not such a methodology is also capable of mediating theological performance and, if so, how theology could thereby articulate its own methodological foundations.

These three aspects of the question we are asking of Dilthey and Lonergan necessarily call for a dialectical comparison, and for two reasons. First of all, the question addresses itself precisely to those aspects of the two thinkers' writings where they are most engaged in a dialectical confrontation with other approaches. For they both share a common interest in avoiding the polarity of positions and counterpositions found in the treatment of those problems: such polarities as idealism versus positivism, rationalism versus decisionism, absolutism versus relativism, dogmatism versus historicism, fideism versus liberalism, fundamentalism versus modernism, etc. Both attempted this critique of polarities by seeking to elaborate a new starting point for method within an empirical and transcendental articulation of cognitional theory and praxis.[3] Both saw this starting point

_____

[3]Note that cognitional theory in both Dilthey and Lonergan is not pursued in an abstract transcendentalist manner - they both have extensive critiques of Kant - but in a concrete transcendental manner, seeking to answer the question "What do I do when I know?" Cf. P. Krausser, Kritik der endlichen Vernunft: Wilhelm Diltheys Revolution der allgemeinen Wissenschafts- und Handlungstheorie (Frankfurt, 1968), pp. 62-65; and Lonergan, Collection (New York, 1968), pp. 221-239. Because of the concrete reference and the concern to mediate theory and praxis, the cognitional theory might be referred to as an anthropology of knowledge.

in somewhat similar manners: Dilthey by calling for a radical
"Selbstbesinnung" that would enable one to thematize the
related and recurrent systems in the personal and social constitution of history; Lonergan by calling for a "self-appropriation" of one's own conscious intentionality as an understanding of understanding, enabling one not only to understand
the broad lines of all there is to be understood, but also to
uncover an invariant foundational pattern, opening upon all
further developments of understanding. The elaborations of
these respective stances differ profoundly, so that a comparison of the two authors from the perspective both of their own
common starting points, and from that of the realities discussed above, necessitates a dialectical treatment.

In the second place, a dialectical comparison is recom-
mended by the significance of the thought of the two for the
contemporary crisis. Dilthey was keenly aware of the problems
posed by the emergence of empirical methods and their rapid
spread during the Enlightenment. He saw that the transcendentalism of a Kant was no match for those methods. Yet he
insisted that the human and historical sciences would only
suffer if they failed to develop their own methods based upon
a recognition of the irreducible character of human interiority. M. Riedel has recently called attention to the importance of this central concern of Dilthey.

> The sovereignty of modern historical consciousness has
> receded before a new dogmatism which turns its back
> on history only to plunge once again into the caverns
> of uncritical opinions. These had engulfed philosophical
> thought for centuries. Indeed, philosophy had only
> recently begun to free itself from them. In order to
> break through such dogmatism, other conceptual categor-
> ies are needed than those used in Dilthey's critique of
> historical reason. Yet recalling his critique can be
> instructive in our efforts to keep alive the historical
> imagination of humankind in the face of the present
> threat of a coming "post-historical" era, which seeks
> its legitimacy through a denial of its own past
> history.[4]

It was, as P. Ricoeur has remarked, just this effort of
Dilthey to mediate the concrete being of history to the

---

[4]Cf. M. Riedel, "Einleitung", in Der Aufbau der geschichtlichen Welt in den Geisteswissenschaften (Frankfurt,
1970), p. 80.

sciences by explicating a viable method for the human sciences
that makes his thought worthy of more serious attention than
the ontological turn of hermeneutics has previously allowed.[5]
For the latter turn merely tends to solidify a scientistic
monopoly on method by ontologizing history into an abstract
historicality.[6]

Dilthey, as Riedel observes, does not give us adequate
conceptual means for meeting the problem today which he was
grappling with sixty years ago. The contention of the present
study will be that Lonergan has provided a more adequate means
in his thematization of conscious intentionality, so that the
positivist claim to have dismissed any cognitional theoretical approach through a substitution of a theory of science is
mistaken, at least insofar as the claim is understood to mean
that the sciences can be adequately handled methodologically
through a complete neglect of the constitutive subjectivity
of scientists and scientific communities. Such a claim is
already under fire both in America and Europe - enough so to
dispel, hopefully, an outright dismissal of either Dilthey or
Lonergan as of no more than a past historical significance.[7]
In the light of this questioning of an objectivist equation
of method and mechanism, or logicism, it is particularly
congenial to present Lonergan's meta-method in a dialectical
manner. For that method aims at a meta-logical mode of

---

[5]This was in the course of a lecture on Dilthey at
Chicago University in April, 1970. This tendency can be seen
in Ricoeur's efforts to correlate the hermeneutic problem and
phenomenological method, cf. Le conflit des interprétations
(Paris, 1969), pp. 7-28.

[6]Cf. Hermeneutik und Ideologiekritik (Frankfurt, 1971),
pp. 45-56, esp. pp. 30-32, 120-159. Also Metz in J. B. Metz
and T. Rendtorff (eds.), Die Theologie in der interdisziplinären Forschung (Düsseldorf, 1971), p. 18.

[7]In America one has the work of Thomas Kuhn, cf. The
Structure of Scientific Revolutions, Second Edition, Enlarged
Vol. II/2 (Chicago, 1970) and Imre Lakatos and Alan Musgrave
(eds.) Criticism and the Growth of Knowledge (Cambridge
University Press, 1970). In Europe there is the growing
interest in anthropologies of knowledge, cf. G. Radnitzsky,
Contemporary Schools of Metascience, Vol. II (Lund, 1970),
second revised edition in one volume. Also, R. Bernstein,
Praxis and Action, (Philadelphia, 1971).

communication and comparison both between the reader's own
conscious subjectivity and Lonergan's thematization of conscious subjectivity in an objective method, and between the
meta-method so thematized and all other objectified positions
on knowledge, objectivity, and reality.[8] This is precisely
what distinguishes meta-method from a transcendental-logical
exercise in "Erkenntnistheorie" or "Erkenntnismetaphysik."

Ideally, of course, it would have been better to have
given an exhaustive historical-critical analysis of the
writings of Dilthey and Lonergan before going into a dialectical synthetic account. Space, however, has prohibited this.
As mentioned, nevertheless, my interpretations of the positions of both men are open to the judgments of historians,
and the extensive references to the writings will allow one
to judge the correctness of my interpretations. A metaphor
from Lonergan might be helpful in demonstrating how the dialectical comparison here is intimately related to an historical presentation. The published and unpublished writings of
the two men, along with all of the secondary interpretations
and historical analyses, provide the data as the lower blade
of a scissors. The upper blade is the question with its
three aspects mentioned above. The lower blade of the comparison supplies the materials, rising from the data of the
writings of the two through interpretative and historical
studies to a systematic presentation of Dilthey's critique
of historical reason and Lonergan's meta-methodology. The
upper blade moves downwards from the question on the possible
relevance of their positions for a critical mediation from the
past in the present into the future to a determination of
their methodologies and how the latter would function in the
mediation of historical activity and theological reflection.[9]

---

[8]Cf. Lonergan, Insight: A Study of Human Understanding
(New York, 1957), pp. xxvif., 385-390.

[9]On the scissors metaphor, cf. Insight, pp. 312f., 461,
522f., 577f., 580f., 586f. The lower blade consists in the
materials that are assembled, completed, compared, reduced,
classified, and selected. The upper blade of the dialectic
is the operative questions concerning the adequacy of Dilthey's
critique to methodologically mediate historicality and
theology. Lonergan in Method In Theology (Herder and Herder,
1972), pp. 249-250 briefly enunciates the six phases of

Within such a dialectical context one need not establish

---

assembling, completing, comparing, reducing, classifying, and selecting the materials in a dialectical structure. It is the present writer's contention that sufficient work has been done to allow a dialectical treatment.

First, the materials have been assembled; one has not only the fifteen volumes of Dilthey's Gesammelte Schriften published by Stuttgart/Göttingen, Teubner and Vandenhoeck & Ruprecht; but also the excellent bibliography of primary and secondary literature compiled by U. Hermann, Bibliographie Wilhelm Dilthey (Berlin: Beltz, 1969). On the publications separate from the G.S., cf. Hermann, op. cit., pp. 96f. From the as yet unpublished writing I have only had to have recourse to the important Breslauer Ausarbeitung des II Bandes der Einleitung in die Geisteswissenschaften. I have used a photocopy of the typed manuscript in the University Library at Göttingen, cf., G.S. V, p. xix and 428f. A critical edition and publication of this manuscript are in preparation.

Second, the materials have been evaluatively completed; among the many attempts at this I have found the following especially helpful: E. Stein's Beiträge zur philosophischen Begründung der Psychologie und der Geisteswissenschaften, published in Jahrbuch für Philosophie und phänomenologische Forschung 5 (1922), pp. 1-283; L. Landgrebe's Diltheys Theorie der Geisteswissenschaften, published in ibid., 9 (1928), pp. 237-366; O. Bollnow's Dilthey: Eine Einführung in seine Philosophie (Stuttgart, 1955); H. Hodges' The Philosophy of Wilhelm Dilthey (London, 1952); H. Diwald's Dilthey: Erkenntnistheorie und Philosophie der Geschichte (Göttingen, 1963); and finally, J.-F. Suter's Philosophie et histoire chez W. Dilthey (Basel, 1960).

Third, the materials have been compared by seeking out affinities and oppositions. One has such works as J. Wach's Das Verstehen, Grundzüge einer Geschichte der hermeneutischen Theorien im 19. Jahrhundert in three volumes (Tübingen, 1926/1929/1933) - there has been a reprint in 1966 by Olms in Hildesheim. L. von Renthe-Fink's Geschichtlichkeit: Ihr terminologischer und begrifflicher Ursprung bei Hegel, Harm, Dilthey und Yorck (Göttingen, 1968) and G. Bauer's Geschichtlichkeit, Wege und Irrwege eines Begriffs (Berlin, 1963). Also helpful in this study of the comparative context are P. Hünermann's Der Durchbruch geschichtlichen Denkens in 19. Jahrhundert (Freiburg, 1967), and, with special reference to cognitional theory, G. Simmel, Die Probleme der Geschichtsphilosophie: Eine erkenntnistheoretische Studie, 5th ed. (Munich, 1923), and E. Betti, Teoria generale della interpretazione, 2 volumes (Milan, 1955). If one moves from these broad comparisons to more specific ones there is the comparison of Dilthey with Husserl and Heidegger in G. Misch's Lebensphilosophie und Phänomenologie, 3rd ed. (Darmstadt, 1967); of Dilthey and his teacher, F. Trendelenburg, in J. Wach's Die Typenlehre Trendelenburg und ihr Einfluss auf Dilthey Tübingen, 1926); as well as the many monographs of article

any direct historical link between the two authors, although

---

length comparing Dilthey's position to Kant, Hegel, Nietzsche, Dewey, Jaspers, etc., cf. U. Herrmann, op. cit., pp. 197-205.

Fourth, besides assemblage, completion, and comparison there are also other studies which in comparing either the developmental stages within Dilthey or in reference to other writers seek to reduce the affinities and oppositions by calling attention to their basic components or underlying roots. Within Dilthey's own development I have found P. Hünermann's study in his Der Durchbruch geschichtlichen Denkens im 19. Jahrhundert, on the four periods in Dilthey's developement very helpful, as well as P. Krausser's study on the underlying interest in formal-anthropological feedback structures of learning and inquiry within Dilthey. Cf. P. Hünermann, op. cit., pp. 133-291 and P. Krausser, Kritik der endlichen Vernunft: Diltheys Revolution der allgemeinen Wissenschafts- und Handlungstheorie (Frankfurt, 1968). Within the broader perspective of the development of hermeneutic and historical reflection one has H. -G. Gadamer's reduction of the problem of historicism in Dilthey to a dichotomy in his thought between science and his life-philosophy in Gadamer, Wahrheit und Methode (Tübingen, 1965), pp. 205-228; I. S. Kon, from a Marxist orientation, reduces the difficulty to an identity thought-pattern in Kon, Die Geschichts-philosophie des 20. Jahrhunderts: Kritischer Abriss, Bd. I (Berlin, 1964), pp. 82-108; while Habermas, Erkenntnis und Interesse (Frankfurt, 1968), pp. 178-233, believes the under-lying root of the affinities and oppositions in Dilthey and the period to lie in a covert positivism and contemplative conception of truth in the cultural sciences.

Finally, each of the last three above mentioned studies classifies and selects the basic sources or underlying roots of the affinities and oppositions within Dilthey and the broader context of his period according to their own interests in presenting a dialectical evaluation of Dilthey. Thus Gadamer, op. cit., pp. 218-150, is intent on classifying the basic problem in Dilthey as cognitional theoretical, and selecting the opposition between science and life-philosophy, in order to show the superiority of a phenomenological-existential sublation of cognitional theory in an ontology of historicality. I. S. Kon, op. cit., pp. 99-108, on the other hand, classifies the basic problem as lying in a false identity cognitional theory and so selects the opposition between determinism and freedom in order to show the superior-ity of a Marxist non-identity theory. Lastly, J. Habermas, op. cit., pp. 225-233, classifies the basic problem as a positivistic contemplative stance towards truth, and selects the opposition between the model of participation in communi-cative interaction and the model of empathy in Dilthey, in order to show how the practical interest of the hermeneutic and cultural sciences is itself not ultimate but must be complemented by the emancipatory interest of critical self-reflection.

As one moves from assemblage through completion and

Lonergan has read Dilthey. For the operative question in a
dialectical comparison is not "which of the many interpretations corresponds most closely with the historical evidence?"
where the comparison is a historical-critical one between the
many interpretations and the texts of the authors and descriptions of their historical context. Rather, the operative
question in a dialectical comparison presupposes that the
historical-critical question has been sufficiently answered
to go on to ask "what is the value of the positions of the
two men in regard both to the problems of their own historical
contexts and to the historical context of our time?"[10] Inasmuch as the historical context is reflected in the realities
mentioned above, then one can agree with Hegel that true
dialectical method is "the activity of realities themselves."[11]

Now there are certainly sufficient similarities between
both Dilthey and Lonergan to merit such a comparison. From
very different traditions both sought to elaborate foundational methods which would mediate the constitutive being of
history to empirical scientific methods. Perhaps, then, they
offer viable alternatives to either the logical empiricist
attempts at reducing historical knowledge to formalist laws
of the natural scientific variety, or to the hermeneutic
existentialist efforts of ontologizing historicality into an
almost total non-identity with empirical methods through a

---

comparison to reduction, classification, and selection the
upper blade of the dialectic assumes greater importance. For
while the lower blade consists in the materials operated on,
the upper blade is the operator, i.e., the operative questions
which regard, not the understanding of the texts (as in
interpretation), nor the factuality of historical movements
(as in history), but the value of those movements and understood texts in the light of the dialectician's stance towards
the concrete, dynamic, and contradictory realities of history.
Cf. Lonergan, Insight, pp. 217f., 244, 412f.

[10]Cf. Lonergan, Insight, pp. 217f., 401ff.; Method in
Theology (henceforth M.i.T.), pp. 128-130, 235ff.

[11]Cf. Hegel's Wissenschaft der Logik II (Frankfurt,
1969), pp. 551f.   Lonergan, M.i.T., pp. 249-250, briefly
enunciates the six phases of assembling, completing, comparing, reducing, classifying, and selecting the materials in a
dialectical structure.

Fundamentalontologie or Erkenntnismetaphysik. Both men were
convinced of the need for a differentiation of methods, and,
as well, that an ontology or metaphysics could no longer
provide the foundations for such a differentiation and consequent mediation. Both were dedicated to the methodological
thematization of such a differentiation and mediation, thereby refusing to accept the scientistic monopoly on method since
Descartes. Both would agree with J. Habermas, that the
objectivistic illusion created by that monopoly could be
broken only by grounding method and its objectivity on the
experience of critical self-reflection.[12] If Dilthey was not
as successful as Lonergan in this attempt, still his efforts
in this direction suggest why the later writings of Lonergan
might be defined better in reference to Dilthey than to
Heidegger or Gadamer.[13] For it was only by at least capitu-
lating to a positivistic and scientistic monopoly on method
that the latter two could oppose the truth of historicality
to the objectivism of method. Finally, both Dilthey and
Lonergan were acutely aware of the challenges posed by the
emergence of scientific and historical consciousness to both
philosophy and theology. Neither tried to avoid or blunt the
edge of those challenges by either devaluing science or
ontologizing history.

The goal of this study, then, is defined by the central
question posed to the writings of both men regarding a critical mediation of historicality and method, and the role of
theology in such a mediation. The answers to that question
will not take on the form of some identity-system, as in
Idealism, nor a non-identity pluralism, as in existentialist
ontology, nor a non-identity reductionism, as in empiricism. The answers will seek, instead, to articulate that
unity of identity and non-identity which is the hallmark not
only of any truly critical mediation of historicality but
also of a method for creative collaboration:

> Whenever human subjects speak with one another (and
> not just about objectified matters of fact), they
> encounter one another with the rightful claim to be

---

[12]Cf. Habermas, Erkenntnis und Interesse, pp. 256-262.

[13]Cf. Continuum 2 (1964), p. 26.

> acknowledged as unique individuals in their absolute
> particularity. This acknowledgement demands the
> paradoxical performance wherein, aided by principally
> universal characteristics and through such character-
> istics themselves, the full concreteness of what is not
> identical with those universal characteristics is
> grasped.[14]

Certainly such a dialectical approach is not out of place in
comparing the writings of two men who sought to thematize
methods based on "Selbstbesinnung" and "self-appropriation"
respectively.

The immanent structure of the question regarding the
historical contexts of the two men and its three aspects of
a non-scientistic approach to method, a critical mediation of
historicality, and an application of the methodology to
theology, has provided the mode of procedure in this study.
The procedure will aim at avoiding two extremes. The one
would so let the question dominate the comparison that differences between the two authors would be blurred or compromised. Identity is not confusion. The other extreme would so
stress the individuality of each author that the question
would appear completely extrinsic to two juxtaposed, incom-
municable positions. Non-identity is not isolation.

---

[14] Habermas, Philosophisch-politische Profile (Frankfurt,
1971), p. 192. W. Pannenberg, in his article "History and
Meaning in Lonergan's Approach to Theological Method," Irish
Theological Quarterly 40 (1973), pp. 103-114, correctly sees
how meaning is an act of the subject for Lonergan. But he
fails to see how for Lonergan it is also objective content.
That is, Pannenberg failed to grasp how for Lonergan an approach to the subject was not within the context of identity,
but as a unity of identity and non-identity (subject-ive act
and object-ive content) that can account for both intentional
and non-intentional meaning. The concern of Lonergan with the
subject is not due to an oversight of objective context, but
rather to the need to find critically valid norms for ordering
the objective contexts, as I shall show in Chapter Two. If
the subject is neglected in such a critical and methodical
project, one too easily falls prey to a type of right wing
Hegelian objectivistic "List der Vernunft" that can so easily
be "baptized" into an uncritical "Heilsgeschichte." Pannenberg's assertions that Dilthey's "Verstehen" is not fully
taken into account by Lonergan's "understanding" is traceable
to the above mentioned oversight of how meaning is also
objective context for Lonergan. It also overlooks the problematic of Dilthey's efforts to provide a critically
grounded transition from Erlebnis to the Wirkungszusammenhänge
of history, as we shall see in Chapter Three.

In Chapter One I shall set the context of the study by essaying the hypothesis the Political Theology represents a significant shift in the methodological self-understanding of theology. It represents, in this view, a new type of theologizing that is taking historicality more seriously than those types drawing on ontologies of history. Chapter Two then takes up the first question mentioned above, viz., how Dilthey and Lonergan provide alternatives to the scientistic monopoly on method. It does this by first showing the relevance of this question to the program of political theology, then by showing how both Dilthey and Lonergan propose, in different ways, to critically deal with the modern and contemporary historical situation respectively by moving from metaphysics to cognitional theory (Dilthey) and from cognitional theory to methodology (Lonergan). The Third Chapter addresses itself to the second above mentioned question: how their approaches to the modern and contemporary situations would provide for a critical mediation from the past in the present into the future by explicating a unity of identity and non-identity structurally constitutive of both history and method. There a certain similarity is found insofar as both Dilthey's critique of historical reason and Lonergan's meta-methodology are structured according to the subject-as -subject, the subject-as-object, and the move from the subject to history. Finally, Chapter Four takes up the third question relating to whether or not such approaches to history and method are capable of mediating theological performance and, if so, how theology could thereby articulate its own methodological foundations in a critical fashion. We shall see how Dilthey's approach to religious experience, so fundamental to any understanding of historicality philosophies and theologies, was entirely consistent with his critique of historical reason, and how Lonergan's meta-method provides a very fruitful alternative that is just as concerned with historical religious experience.

I wish to express my gratitude to the Faculty of Catholic Theology at the Westphalian Wilhelms University of Münster, West Germany, for honoring this doctoral dissertation with

the"Universitätspreis" for 1974. Prof. Karl Rahner and Prof.
Peter Hünermann were very helpful in their comments and
criticisms during the course of the work. Gratitude seems
too limp an expression of indebtedness to my director, Prof.
Johann B. Metz, for his assistance and encouragement during
and after my studies at Münster. The same can be said of
Prof. Bernard Lonergan, whose continued friendship and advice
are of a worth beyond measure. Their influence is evident
in whatever is of value in this study. I also want to thank
Prof. David Tracy and Prof. Frederick Lawrence for their
critical collaboration. The State University Library of
Lower Saxony at Göttingen should be acknolwedged for providing me with the unpublished manuscript of Dilthey's projected
second volume in his Einleitung in die Geisteswissenschaften.
A word of special thanks is due to those who have helped me
in preparing this study for publication, Dr. Dennis Doherty,
Sr. Jeannette Martin, Ms. Lorna Rixmann, and Mr. William Sell.

Matthew L. Lamb

Theology Department
Marquette University
October 1977

C H A P T E R   O N E

HISTORY   AND   METHOD   IN   THE   PROGRAM   OF

POLITICAL   THEOLOGY

> Theological pluralism today too
> often expresses no more than a
> mindless capitulation to the
> sorry status of theology itself.
> Pluralism has become more
> encrusted and sterile than all
> the systems so eagerly combatted
> under its banner. If pluralism
> is to become dialectically
> dynamic and the question of
> truth - whose currency has been
> devalued into a matter of
> viewpoints - restored as a
> serious question, then any given
> theological position must strive
> to appropriate precisely those
> elements which other positions
> see as lacking or neglected in
> it, and vice versa.
>
> Johann B. Metz

CHAPTER ONE

INTRODUCTION

Edmund Husserl, in his posthumously published <u>Die Krisis der Europäischen Wissenschaften</u>, documented how the crisis of method in a science is foundational inasmuch as it calls into question the very self-understanding of the science, how it conceives its task and relates itself to the other sciences.

> The crisis of a science denotes nothing less than the fact that its genuine scientific character, the way in which it sets forth its task and constructs its methodology, is cast in doubt.[1]

Few would contend that theology has not been undergoing a profound series of crises over the past decades. If the function of theology is to mediate "between a cultural matrix and the significance and role of a religion in that matrix,"[2] then the series of crises can be studied within the crises of the cultural matrix. Such a study will, I venture, indicate how the political theology articulated by Johann B. Metz is a most serious attempt to come to terms with our contemporary social and cultural crisis.[3]

---

[1]Cf. E. Husserl, <u>Die Krisis der Europäischen Wissenschaften und die Transzendentale Phänomenologie</u> (The Hague, 1962), p. 1. For a critique of the objectivism in Husserl's phenomenological method paralleling Husserl's criticism of the objectivism in modern science, cf. T. Adorno, <u>Zur Metakritik der Erkenntnistheorie</u> (Stuttgart, 1956) and J. Habermas, <u>Technik und Wissenschaft als 'Ideologie'</u> (Frankfurt, 1968), pp. 150-153.

[2]Bernard Lonergan, <u>Method in Theology</u> (New York, 1972), p. xi. Also cf. B. Welte, <u>Auf der Spur des Ewigen</u> (Freiburg, 1965), pp. 410-428; K. Rahner, <u>Schriften zur Theologie</u> IX (Einsiedeln, 1970), pp. 79-126.

[3]This, of course, is understood "sensu positivo non exclusivo." Metz, more than any of the other politicomorphic theologians, has grappled with the theoretical issues of the new mediation of theory and praxis.

When Metz first outlined the notion of political
theology in 1966, few realized that it would mark a turning
point in theological method.[4] A year later Jürgen Moltmann's
call for a political hermeneutics may have seemed to some no
more than another fad occasioned by student unrest and political activism.[5] Such a reaction was understandable in the
United States, where the sixties saw so many theological fads
come and (mostly) go.[6]

A growing number of monographs in Europe, however, are
gradually spelling out the methodological implications of
political theology and the crises to which it is responding.[7]
Instead of simply reviewing this literature, I should like
to propose a typology of modern and contemporary theologies
which will situate the crisis and response of political

[4]Cf. "The Church and the World" by J. B. Metz in The
Word in History. The St. Xavier Symposium (New York, 1966),
pp. 69-85. Also Metz, Zur Theologie der Welt (Mainz, 1968),
pp. 75-89, 99-116. A comparison of the latter essay with its
English translation in Theology of the World (New York, 1969),
pp. 107-124 will show how whole paragraphs and footnotes in
the German have been dropped in the English version.

[5]Cf."Existenzgeschichte und Weltgeschichte, Auf dem
Wege zu einer politischen Hermeneutik des Evangeliums," in
Evangelische Kommentare 1 (1968), pp. 13-20. Reprinted in
Moltmann, Perspektiven der Theologie (Munich, 1968), pp. 128-
146. For an appraisal of the contemporary theological scene
in America, cf. D. Peerman (ed.) Theologie in Umbruch. Der
Beitrag Amerikas zur gegenwärtigen Theologie (Munich, 1968).

[6]For a provocative presentation of the Anglo-American
Crisis cf. Langdon Gilkey, Naming the Whirlwind (New York,
1969).

[7]Cf. especially, H. Peukert (ed.) Diskussion zur "poli-
tischen Theologie" (Mainz, 1969); E. Feil and R. Weth (eds.)
Diskussion zur "Theologie der Revolution" (Mainz, 1969);
P. Neuenzeit (ed.) Die Funktion der Theologie in Kirche und
Gesellschaft (Munich, 1969); M. Xhaufflaire and K. Derksen,
Les deux visages de la théologie de la sécularisation
(Tournai, 1970); G. Sauter, Vor einem neuen Methodenstreit
in der Theologie? (Munich, 1970); J. B. Metz, J. Moltmann
and W. Oelmuller, Kirche in Prozess der Aufklärung (Mainz,
1970); H. -G. Geyer, H. -N. Janowski and A. Schmidt,
Theologie und Soziologie (Stuttgart, 1970); H. Siemers and
H. -R. Reuter (eds.) Theologie als Wissenschaft in der
Gesellsschaft (Göttingen, 1970); A. Hollweg, Theologie und
Empirie (Stuttgart, 1971); M. Xhaufflaire, La Théologie
Politique: Introduction à la théologie politique de J. B.
Metz (Paris, 1972).

theology in as clear a manner as possible. This Chapter
will, accordingly, first set out the general typology of
theologies, then indicate the critique political theology
levels against them, and finally spell out the principal
methodological presuppositions of political theology itself.

A TYPOLOGY OF THEOLOGIES

At a time when other Catholic theologians have rather
comfortably accommodated themselves to the pluralistic conception of theology, Metz has called attention to the dangers
of sterility in such a pluralism.[8] In their own ways, both
Dilthey and Lonergan are also concerned with the sterility
which can result from pluralism - for it should not simply
be accepted to the detriment of the truth intention of theology.[9] Inasmuch as the recognition of pluralism in theology
is related to a prior recognition of a pluralist society and
culture, it is possible to at least indicate how there is an
underlying meta-contextual structure or typology of theological trends.[10] For theology has historically and dialectically been engaged in relating fides and ratio, religion and
culture, religious belief and social reality.[11] This relation
or mediation between religious faith and the cultural matrix
is specifically in terms of the truth of faith. Otherwise
there would be no need for theology as distinct from psychological, sociological, anthropological, or comparative studies

---

[8]J. B. Metz, "Erlösing and Emanzipation," in Stimmen
der Zeit (März, 1973), p. 171.

[9]Cf. Metz, Die Theologie in der interdisziplinären
Forschung (Düsseldorf, 1971), p. 14. Also D. Tracy, The
Achievement of Bernard Lonergan (New York, 1970), pp. 1-21,
266-269.

[10]I am indebted to a discussion with David Tracy where
he put forth the possibility of such a typology. His own
articulation of the typology can be found in his book,
Blessed Rage for Order: The New Pluralism in Theology (New
York, 1975).

[11]Cf. J. B. Metz, "Theologie" in Lexikon für Theologie
und Kirche X Col. 62-71.

of religion.[12] The latter two mediate the significance and
role of religion in and to a cultural matrix, but they avoid
the further question as to whether or not what they mediate
is true and calls for absolute assent and existential
commitment:

> In distinction from other studies of religion, theology
> has its foundation and Logos in faith. Theology assists
> the responsible appropriation of the faith as oriented
> towards its self-articulated consciousness of mission.[13]

The appropriation of the faith as true implies, then, a
mediation of faith to the cultural matrix. And this mediation
is operative both on the level of kerygma - the mission of the
Word to the world - and on the reflective level of theology.
Indeed, the task of theology is within the ecclesial mission of
the Church as proclaimer of the good news.[14] The truth intention of faith must not only be preached and practiced in the
Lebenswelt of personal and social life, it must also be mediated to the scholarly and scientific Wissenswelt.[15] This is especially true at a time when the latter through technology is
having such a powerful influence on the former.[16]

A methodological reflection upon theology - methodological in the sense of methodos as the way toward truth[17] and
so as integrated within fundamental theology[18] - can elaborate
a formal typology of major trends within theology. The basis

---

[12]On the truth intention as constitutive of theology, cf.
Lonergan's analysis in De Deo Trino Vol. II (Rome, 1964), pp.
13-36, and his Method in Theology (henceforth abbreviated
M.i.T.), pp. 267-293.

[13]Metz, "Theologie," L.Th.K. X Col. 67.

[14]Ibid. Col. 68. Also Lonergan, M.i.T., pp. 355-368.

[15]Cf. Metz "Theologie," L.Th.K. X Col. 67-68. Also D.
Tracy, The Achievement of Bernard Lonergan (New York, 1970),
pp. 54-71, 184-205 (henceforth designated Achievement).

[16]Cf. Metz, Die Theologie in der interdisziplinären Forschung (henceforth abbreviated T.i.F.), pp. 10-23. Also Metz,
"Der Zukünftige Mensch und der Kommende Gott," in Wer is das
eigentlich Gott? (München, 1969), pp. 260-275.

[17]Cf. W. Kasper, Die Methoden der Dogmatik (München,
1967), p. 14. Also J. Buchler, The Concept of Method (New
York, 1961).

[18]Cf. K. Rahner, Schriften zur Theologie IX, pp. 81ff. Also

6

of such a typology would be how the various theologies handle
the truth intention in their mediation of faith and culture.
There are four general characteristics of such a typology.

First, the typology is <u>dialectical</u>. Insofar as the
truth intention of faith is taken seriously, there cannot be
a total identification of faith with its cultural matrix.
Historically the Christian faith has been professed and practiced in a vast diversity of cultures, and the theologies
reflecting upon such confession and practice have been equally
diverse. However, this has not meant that the confessions
and practices have been no more than expressions of this
cultural diversity. Indeed, the confessional formulations,
as expressions of the truth intention of faith, have exhibited
a transcultural dynamism non-identifiable with the cultures.[19]
Just how this dialectic of identity and non-identity has
been formulated has varied in theologies but it has always
been present. It will be clear in the following chapter how
the dialectic of identity and non-identity is a central
structure of Metz's political theology.[20]

Second, the typology is <u>meta-contextual</u>. It is a methodological reflection upon theological contexts, seeking to
uncover how these theologies exhibit trans-contextual patterns
in their effort to mediate the truth intention of faith to
the varying cultural contexts or matrices within which they
arise. As meta-contextual such a typology presupposes that
the emergence of historical consciousness and critical consciousness explicate not only the first-order pluralism and
relativism within theology, but also the possibility of a
second-order (or meta-contextual) sublation of any notion of
total relativism. This total relativism has found expression
in historicism and positivism. The latter presuppose that
any confessional formulation, ecclesial practice, or theological system can only be totally identified with its

---

P. McShane (ed.) <u>Foundations of Theology</u> (University of Notre
Dame Press, 1971), pp. 22-59, 76-101, 162-222.

[19]<u>Ibid</u>., pp. 22-40. Also Lonergan, <u>De Deo Trino</u>, pp.
33-61. Also K. Rahner, <u>Schriften</u> IX, pp. 11-33.

[20]Cf. Chapter Two, pp. 64-73 and the references given
there. Also pp. 41-53 of this Chapter.

culturally relative expression. In this view any historical
or critical reflection can only come up with a series of
disparate confessional and theological contexts. Any meta-
contextual intentionality operative within those contexts and
transcending their particularity is denied. In this respect
historicism and positivism are ignorant of their own intentionality, for they posit such a total relativity as a
characteristic of all contexts, i.e., they intend a meta-
contextual attribute inasmuch as they speak of total relativity. Moreover, if there is any one outstanding characteristic of contemporary reflection on science and critical
thought, it is a concern for elaborating the meta-contextual
dynamics which exceed the contextual particularity of first-
order expressions. In mathematics there are the foundational
inquiries initiated by Gödel.[21] Physics and mechanics have
been introduced to meta-contextual reflection by both Einstein and Heisenberg.[22] The biological sciences are beginning to emancipate themselves from reductionism.[23] The human
sciences are overcoming their tutelage to the context of the
physical sciences through attention to and application of
general systems theory[24] and structuralism.[25] Specifically,
psychology and sociology are addressing themselves to explicitly meta-contextual problems concerning their own foundations.[26] Within the philosophy of science as Wissenschafts-

---

[21]Cf. Lonergan, Insight, pp. xxivf., 574. Also H.
Peukert, "Zur formalen Systemtheorie und zur hermeneutischen
Problematik einer politischen Theologie," in Diskussion zur
politischen Theologie (Mainz, 1969), pp. 82-94 and the
references given there.

[22]Cf. P. Heelan, Quantum Mechanics and Objectivity
(The Hague, 1965); "Complementarity, Context Dependence, and
Quantum Logic," in Foundations of Physics Vol. I, 1970, pp.
95-109; "Quantum and Classical Logic: Their Respective Roles,"
in Synthese 21 (1970), pp. 2-33.

[23]A Koestler and J. R. Smythies (eds.) Beyond Reductionism: New Perspectives in the Life Sciences (Boston, 1968).

[24]L. von Bertalanffy, General System Theory (New York,
1968).

[25]J. Piaget, Structuralism (London, 1971).

[26]J. Fabry, The Pursuit of Meaning (Boston, 1968); F.

8

<u>wissenschaft</u> there are very visible tendencies to articulate the dialectic convergence of schools of metascience.[27] Theology, therefore, is by no means abrogating its cultural mission if it attends to the meta-contextual structures or typologies operative within its concern to mediate the truth-intention of faith.[28]

Third, the typology is <u>critical</u> and <u>praxis-oriented</u>. A dialectic meta-contextual analysis of theology is not locked within the limits of abstract theory. It is not guilty of that sociological "functionalism" which neglects the questions of the truth of praxis as a critique of the goals and purposes of the knowledge-system that is theology.[29] The following typology is praxis-oriented because it tries to determine how the mediation of faith and culture actually functions within various theologies. Faith is functionally defined as religious beliefs whose truth-intention transcends normal human verification or falsification processes. This obviously applies to Judaeo-Christian faith.[30] Cultural matrix is functionally defined as those sets of basic assumptions and expectations which underly the common sense, theoretical and practical activities of any particular society or culture. In this sense it is the cognitive and socio-political infra-structure to the common sense, scientific, technological,

---

Goble, <u>The Third Force</u> (New York, 1971); D. Yankelovich and W. Barrett, <u>Ego and Instinct: The Psychoanalytic View of Human Nature - Revised</u> (New York, 1970); C. Hampden-Turner, <u>Radical Man: The Process of Psycho-Social Development</u> (New York, 1971): A. Gouldner, <u>The Coming Crisis of Western Sociology</u> (New York, 1970); G. Winter, <u>Elements for a Social Ethic</u> (New York, 1968).

[27] G. Radnitzky, <u>Contemporary Schools of Metascience</u> Lund, 1970), Second Revised Edition with two volumes in one; G. M. Dobrov, <u>Wissenschafts Wissenschaft</u> (Berlin, 1969).

[28] Metz, <u>T.i.F.</u>, pp. 19-23.

[29] Cf. G. Winter, <u>op. cit.</u>, pp. 116, 152, 183, 186, 190, 249, 283. Also T. Adorno, <u>Stichworte: Kritische Modelle</u> 2 (Frankfurt, 1969), pp. 20-28 on "Vernunft und Offenbarung."

[30] Cf. Lonergan, <u>M.i.T.</u>, pp. 115-124, also Chapter Four of this study, pp. 497-506 and the reference given there.

social, economic, and political suprastructures.[31]

The typology asserts that five fundamental trends can be thematized on the basis of such functional relationships. In terms of the relation of theory and praxis, these five types are not limited to only a cognitive functioning in the mediation of faith and culture. Instead, the types are also seen as illuminating the praxis of both the ecclesial community and the theological community. For the norms that are operative in the various theologies function also in the concrete performance of the believing communities. Moreover, the functioning of the typology is not only meta-contextual but also dialectical. The five types are not presented in some value-neutral fashion. For a critique of the types will be offered in the light of political theology, indicating how the first four types of doing theology are inadequate if theology is to function consciously and criti-cally within the contemporary situation with the questions the latter poses to faith.

Finally, the typology is both _diachronic_ and _synchronic._ Obviously, if the typology is meta-contextual it is not only applicable to a narrowly defined historical period. Indeed, I would maintain that the five types could be fruitfully applied throughout the history of Christian theology. Lim-itations of space and competence, however, have led me to restrict the illustrations of the typology to modern and con-temporary theologies. The diachronic dimension of the typo-logy will, therefore, not extend much beyond the middle of the eighteenth century, with the exception of the reference to classical theology which has a much longer diachronic lineage.[32] The synchronic developments within each type will

---

[31]Cf. P. Heelan, "Quantum and Classical Logic: Their Respective Roles," pp. 20-24 and "Nature and its Transfor-mations," in _Theological Studies_ Vol 33, no. 3 (September, 1972), pp. 486-503. Also Chapter Three of this study, pp. 358-421.

[32]To give an example of how these five typologies might apply to theology in the apostolic age, the Judaic-Christians followed paleomorphic tendencies, the Hellenic Christians represent neomorphism, Peter and the Jerusalem community tended more toward fideomorphism, criticomorphic theology can be found in Paul, whereas politicomorphism issued in Roman

receive greater attention. However, I must again recall the
formal nature of this typology. My aim is not to enter into
a detailed historical inquiry on each of the theologians
mentioned, but to indicate how their efforts at mediating
faith and culture are capable of a meta-contextual analysis
that is both dialectical and functional.

The five basic types might be referred to as paleomorphic, neomorphic, fideomorphic, criticomorphic and politicomorphic respectively. Each will be discussed in succession.
It is crucial to understand that I am not considering all of
the wealth of each type of theologizing, nor am I claiming
to reduce their significance to what they explicitly contribute to the relation of the truth intention of faith to
the mediation of faith and culture. My criticisms of the
first four types accentuate tendencies which I judge important
to discuss in order to clarify the contribution of political
theology to the present theological situation. It would be a
terrible misrepresentation of the theologies discussed if
I maintained - which I emphatically do not - that those
tendencies adequately described the full sweep of the contributions they have made.

1. Paleomorphic Theologies

These theologies are paleomorphic because their mediation of faith and culture is in terms of older (paleo) cultural forms (morphic). The designation is therefore a function of historical process. A theology which may have been
very contemporary at one period of history, if carried over
and preserved within a different cultural context, becomes
paleomorphic. Today Catholic and Protestant theologies which
take their understanding of culture from the classical context of the sixteenth and seventeenth centuries are obvious
examples. Catholic and Protestant scholastic theologies of
those centuries were based upon notions of truth and reason
which typically appealed to the immutable and eternal. As a

---

orthodoxy. The typology could also be applied to patristic
theology, scholastic theology, Reformation theology, and the
Enlightenment period, but such applications diachronically lie
beyond the scope of this study. For a similar effort at
transcultural analysis, cf. H. Richard Niebuhr, Christ and
Culture (New York, 1951).

result they saw the truth intention of faith to consist in propositions revealed by God in scripture and/or tradition. Thus Karl Barth writes of the Protestant theologians of that time as looking upon the Bible as "a fixed total of revealed propositions to be systematized like the sections of a <u>corpus</u> of law."[33] While Avery Dulles writes of the Catholic theologians: "The post-Tridentine scholastics (notably Suarez and de Lugo) shifted the focus of attention from revelation understood dynamically as an immediate communication from God to man, to a static and objective view, which looks upon revelation as a commodity already received."[34] It was in this period that dogmatic theology was introduced, not in distinction from moral or historical theology, but in opposition to the methods of inquiry in the medieval Summae. This dogmatic theology, as Lonergan remarks,

> ...replaced the inquiry of the <u>quaestio</u> by the pedagogy of the thesis. It demoted the <u>quest of</u> faith for understanding to a desirable, but secondary, and indeed, optional goal. It gave basic and central significance to the certitudes of faith, their presuppositions, and their consequences. It owed its mode of proof to Melchior Cano and, as that theologian was also a bishop and an inquisitor, so the new dogmatic theology not only proved its theses, but also was supported by the teaching authority and the sanctions of the Church.[35]

This classical and conceptualistic approach to the truth intention of faith was, at that time, paralleled by an equally classical cultural matrix. Such a matrix is indicated, for instance, in J. Habermas' reference to traditional societies with their "superiority criteria"; K. Rahner refers to them as definite and homogeneous cultures; while Lonergan analyzes them under the rubric of classical cultures.[36] The character-

---

[33] K. Barth, <u>Church Dogmatics</u> I/1 (Edinburgh, 1936) p.156.

[34] A. Dulles, <u>Revelation Theology</u>, (New York, 1972), pp. 51f.

[35] Cf. Lonergan, "Theology in its New Context," in <u>Theology of Renewal</u> (New York, 1968), p. 36.

[36] Cf. J. Habermas, <u>Toward a Rational Society</u> (Boston, 1971), p. 94; K. Rahner, "Theologie," in <u>Sacramentum Mundi</u> Vol. IV, Col. 877-881; Lonergan, <u>Collection</u>, pp. 252-267 and <u>M.i.T.</u>, pp. xi, 124, 301f., 315, 326, 363.

istics of a classical cultural matrix might be summarized as
follows. Cognitively they exhibit static, stable and hierarchical world views providing mythical, metaphysical, or
theological legitimizations of the various institutions constitutive of the culture.[37] This finds powerful expression
in Greek metaphysics and the Aristotelian notion of science
as true, certain knowledge of causal necessity.[38] The socio-
political infra-structure is marked by a centralized ruling
power and an accompanying hierarchical ordering of socio-
economic classes.[39] These cognitive and socio-political
aspects of the infra-structure led to a universalizing of
particular cultural and political systems. This is clear not
only in the normative elitism and superiority of the "cul-
tured" over against the "barbarians" but also in the forms
of political theology operative in such matrices which provided divine sanctions for the hierarchical centralization.[40]
Whatever the significance of these theologies within those
former cultures, it cannot be denied that they no longer
correspond to the realities of contemporary empirical and
pluralist cultures. Nevertheless, such scholastic theologies have been present within European Protestant scholasticism and have predominated in Catholic orthodoxy up to
Vatican II.

Thus a study of the manuals of Catholic theology from
1900 to 1960 reveals the following characteristics. First,
they are written in Latin and are intended primarily for use
in seminaries. These seminaries are almost uniformly isolated

---

[37]Cf. Habermas, ibid., pp. 92-96. Also Chapter Two
of this study, pp. 97-98 and the references given there.

[38]J. Ritter, "Die Lehre vom Ursprung und Sinn der
Theorie bei Aristoteles," in Metaphysik und Politik (Frank-
furt, 1969), pp. 9-33; B. Snell, Die Entdeckung des Geistes
(Hamburg, 1955), pp. 371-439.

[39]Cf. N. Lobkowicz, Theory and Practice: History of a
Concept from Aristotle to Marx (University of Notre Dame
Press, 1967), pp. 3-58, 75-88. Also E. Voegelin, The World
of the Polis Vol II (Louisiana State University Press, 1957).

[40]E. Feil, "Von der 'politischen Theologie' zur 'Theologie der Revolution'?" in Diskussion zur 'Theologie der Revolution' (Mainz, 1969), esp. pp. 113-117 and the references
given there.

from daily contact with the contemporary culture. In this
they reflect the often parallel isolation of the so-called
Catholic Ghetto, either from a surrounding Protestant or
secular society, or, in those countries where Catholicism
is the state-recognized religion, the isolation of those
countries from the mainstream of modern secular nations. [41]
Secondly, the manuals in their very format of theses with
their attendant lists of adversaries, proofs and corollaries,
are pristine examples of deductive classical reason. Such
rigid conceptualism is obvious in their failure to adequately
attend to the advances of historical criticism vis-a-vis
the scriptures and Church history. [42] Their discussions of
science are almost exclusively within the conceptuality of
Aristotelian science as that was translated into decadent
scholasticism. [43] A third characteristic of the manuals is
their defensive and negatively apologetic thrust. Even a
cursory reading of the references of these manuals to modernity would indicate the hostile and negative evaluation of
most things modern. It is not surprising, as Lonergan
remarks, that when Rome wanted to condemn the heresy that
sums up all heresies, they called it modernism."[44]

This manual theology, or as Karl Rahner calls it,
"Schultheologie," was indeed dominant in Roman Catholicism
until Vatican II. And most of the post-Conciliar conflicts
can be traced to the fact that the majority of bishops and
administrators within the Church was formed by such paleomorphic theologies. Thus T. H. Sank's study of the doctrine
of the magisterium taught at the Gregorian University between
Vatican I and Vatican II indicates the profound influence

---

[41] G. Wills, Bare Ruined Choirs (New York, 1971), pp. 38-78.

[42] T. M. Schoof, A Survey of Catholic Theology 1800-1970 (New York, 1970), pp. 14-155.

[43] Ibid., pp. 175-180; D. Tracy, Achievement, pp. 55-56.

[44] B. Lonergan, "Belief, Today's Issue," in The Messenger (June, 1968), p. 8. "One may lament it but one can hardly be surprised that at the beginning of this century, when church-men were greeted with a heresy that logically entailed all possible heresies, they named the new monster modernism."

14

this theology has had on American Catholicism through the
fact that 230 of the 280 American bishops in 1969 had studied
their theology at the Gregorian University.[45]

Needless to say, such paleomorphic theologies performed
a very positive function insofar as they opposed the irrational tendencies of contemporary pluralist cultures. Yet
they were often unable to distinguish the wheat from the
cockle in those cultures to which they had the mission of
bringing Christ's saving message. A summary of the differences between the classical Aristotelian notion of science
and the modern empirical notion of science will illustrate
how conflict was inevitable. First of all, modern science
has moved definitively away from the classical identification
of the scientific ideal with certitude. That ideal had made
any such notion as "scientific opinion" or "scientific
probability" impossible. For it clearly separated science
and opinion, episteme and doxa.[46] The quest for certitude
was not only evident in the various "Notae" attached to each
thesis but also in the attitude of the Roman congregations
bent upon preserving both the "depositum fidei" and their
hierarchical privilege.[47] Secondly, classical theology was
built on eternal, changeless, immobile verities. It considered redemption not so much as an historical process, but
as an achieved fact. Modern science is operational, interested in change, development, process. It is hypothetical,
seeking its verification in the empirical process itself.
Where manual theologies draw a sharp distinction between
theory (dogma) and practice (moral), modern science is
increasingly aware of the interaction between theory and
praxis. The separation of theory and praxis found its ontological ground in the distinction between being and time,
which led to the distinction between wisdom and the theoretical life on the one hand, and the practical and political

---

[45]Cf. T. H. Sanks, Authority in the Church: A Study
in Changing Paradigms (Missoula, 1974).

[46]Cf. Lonergan, Collection, pp. 259-261; also A. Diemer,
op. cit., pp. 24f.

[47]Cf. Sanks, op. cit., pp. 63-102.

life on the other. The necessary and eternal cannot undergo change, hence the proper attitude is not empirical investigation nor revolutionary practice, but contemplation. In classical theology this led both to the priority of the contemplative ways of life over the apostolic, and to the isolation of systematic and dogmatic theology from moral theology.[48] A consequence of this can be seen in the old political theology by which the Church was only too ready to legitimatize unjust social orders as long as these latter did not interfere with her ecclesial (contemplative) functions of worship and teaching.[49]

Thirdly, classical science defined itself primarily in regard to "formal objects," whereas modern science is primarily field-orientated. Thus paleomorphic theologies tend to shun any interdisciplinary collaboration insofar as they see the formal object as exclusively theological. This has also had a detrimental effect on pastoral praxis insofar as it restricted worship and faith to an isolated relationship with God and failed to take into account the total social field of Catholic practice.[50] Fourthly, paleomorphic theologies tend to restrict themselves to an almost exclusive reliance on a classical or Aristotelian logic (or some decadent offspring thereof):

> Indeed, much of what passed for theology in post-medieval Roman Catholicism seems to have found in logic all the science it needed for its "theological" method: one had, it seems, one's certain "Catholic" principles, definitions, axioms and postulates (Scripture, councils, magisterial decrees, consent of the fathers, consensus of theologians, etc.); one next used logic to deduce equally certain conclusions from them; those conclusions were theology.[51]

---

[48]Cf. N. Lobkowicz, op. cit., pp. 59-88.

[49]Cf. H. -J. Vogt, "Politische Erfahrung als Quelle des Gottesbildes bei Kaiser Konstantin d. Gr." in Dogma und Politik (Mainz, 1973), pp. 35-61. Also Ernst Feil as given in footnote 40 above.

[50]Cf. D. Tracy, op. cit., pp. 87-88; also A. Greeley, The Catholic Experience, where he describes the immigrant origins of American Catholicism. Also his The Distant Pilgrim: American Catholicism after the Council.

[51]D. Tracy, op. cit., p. 88.

Nowhere did this centrality of logic at the expense of empirical or historical method become more embarrassing than in
attempting to deal with the development of doctrine. Manuals
have constructed very elaborate, logical structures in order
to articulate the various logical implications of formal
and virtual revelation.[52]

Finally, where modern science is necessarily a communal
venture, classical theology was individualistic, almost
privatized, based upon a Renaissance ideal of "uomo universale." Aristotle had conceived science as a dianoetic virtue
or habit through the application of which an individual, in
conjunction with the practice of other dianoetic virtues,
would find true fulfillment in the theoretic (contemplative)
life.[53] Hence the paleomorphic manuals and the seminary
educational system tried to impart a knowledge "de universa
sacra theologia" to each of the students. This had a very
damaging effect upon priests trained in a dogmatic tradition,
ill suited to the complexities and ambiguities of contemporary
pastoral activity.[54]

One can find this same paleomorphic identification of
theological reflection with past cultural forms in the various
Protestant fundamentalist theologies, e.g., American fundamentalism is as much a product of frontier life and values as
Roman Catholic scholastic theologies are a product of a
classical sixteenth and seventeenth century culture.

2. Neomorphic Theologies

Where paleomorphic theologies identify reason and culture with older forms, the neomorphic theologies identify
reason and culture with their contemporary forms. Theological

---

[52]W. Schulz, Dogmenentwicklung als Problem der Geschichtlichkeit der Wahrheitserkenntnis: Eine erkenntnistheoretisch
- theologische Studie zum Problemkreis der Dogmenentwicklung
(Rome, 1969), pp. 99-223, 171-212.

[53]Cf. the article by J. Ritter in footnote 38 above;
for a fuller treatment cf. E. Voegelin's treatment of science
and contemplation, in his Plato and Aristotle (Louisiana
State University Press, 1957), pp. 293-314.

[54]Cf. A. Greeley, Priests in the United States (New
York, 1972).

reflection is no longer bound to outmoded classical notions of science but rather almost totally identified with modern notions of science and reflection. Protestant forms of neomorphic theology can be found in the various liberal theologies of the nineteenth and early twentieth centuries where the truth intention of faith was rigorously evaluated by the methods of historical criticism.[55] The Catholic response to these theologies on the part of men like A. Loisy and other modernists was equally involved in accepting historical-critical methods as decisive in attaining the truth intention of faith. Where paleomorphic theology tended toward a sectarian or ghetto isolation from the contemporary world, these noemorphic theologies tended very much toward a compromised assimilation to modern secular views so that one could ask what the purpose of theology or of faith was. Why put a Christian label upon ideas and movements which could just as easily be attained or espoused without any faith commitment.[56]

The characteristics of neomorphic theologies are a tendency to an almost uncritical identification with the Zeitgeist of the age, a reductionism which is increasingly embarrassed by any truth intention in faith insofar as the age is secularist, and a pathos for relevancy which seems unable to critically evaluate the dangers present in the particular age with its cultures and social institutions. Examples of these tendencies can be found not only in liberal Protestant or Catholic modernist theologies at the turn of the century, but also in American secular and civil religions as well as in the many forms of secularization and God-is-dead

---

[55]Cf. J. Cooper, The Roots of the Radical Theology (Philadelphia, 1967); also M. Kähler, Geschichte der protestantischen Dogmatik im 19. Jahrhundert (Munich, 1962). B. M. G. Reardon, Religious Thought in the Nineteenth Century (Cambridge, 1966).

[56]Cf. William W. Bartley, The Retreat to Commitment (New York, 1962); James Hitchcock, The Decline and Fall of Radical Catholicism (New York, 1972); Richard P. McBrien, Do We Need the Church? (New York, 1969); Harvey Cox, The Seduction of the Spirit (New York, 1973).

theologies of the 1960's.[57] An increasing number of studies
on secularization theologies shows how the characteristics of
neomorphic theology mentioned above can be found in them.
They are especially unable to distinguish positive and nega-
tive aspects of contemporary culture.[58] Thus, at a time when
American cities were about to erupt in ghetto and race riots,
Harvey Cox was somewhat naively singing the praises of
American city life in his best-selling The Secular City.[59]
Likewise, the Civil Rights and Peace Movements exposed the
naïveté of American civil religions.[60]

At present, perhaps, the most obvious form of a neomorphic
theology can be found in the movement known as "Critical
Catholicism."[61] Where liberal Protestant and Catholic modernist theologies tended to identify their methods with historical
criticism, and where secularization theologies tended to identify their methods of reflection with liberal secular thought,
Critical Catholicism identifies its critique of the former, and
indeed of all theologies, with a Marxist critique of religion.
Such an identification, however, reduces the function of theology to an eventual sublation or negation of any and all theologies. In a somewhat unconscious manner such a theology has
in effect been too uncritical of its own identification with

---

[57] Cf. W. Clebsch, From Sacred to Profane America: The
Role of Religion in American History (New York, 1968); also
R. Richard, Secularization Theology (New York, 1967); also
M. Xhaufflaire and K. Derksen, Les deux visages de la théolo-
gie de la sécularisation (Tournai, 1970).

[58] M. Xhaufflaire, "La Théologie après la Théologie de la
sécularisation," in Xhaufflaire and Derksen, op. cit., pp.
85-129. Also the article by Leo Dullaart on "Institution et
Légitimation," in the same work, pp. 131-153.

[59] Cf. H. Cox, The Secular City (New York, 1965); Frans
van den Oudenrijn, "La Théologie de la sécularisation: une
idéologie religieuse de la société unidimensionnelle," in
Xhaufflaire and Derksen, op. cit., pp. 155-172.

[60] Cf. P. Berger and R. Neuhaus, Movement and Revolution
(New York, 1970); E. Bianchi, The Religious Experience of
Revolutionaries (New York, 1972).

[61] Cf. B. van Onna and M. Stankowski (eds.) Kritischer
Katholizismus Argumente gegen die Kirchen-Gesellschaft
(Frankfurt, 1969).

Marxist reflection and method.[62] Thus Metz can write of such theological attempts:

> According to this model, theology could only maintain itself as a critique of theology within a foundational context of a sociological, psychological, historical, socio-theoretical, or some other type analysis of religion. In my opinion, such an approach would only lead to the liquidation of theology.[63]

What is operative in the clash between various neomorphic theologies, as well as in the conflict between neomorphic theologies and paleomorphic theologies, is their various identifications with different conflicting cultural matrices. As long as there is only an identity thought pattern present - even if this identity is with a non-identity pattern as in Critical Catholicism - there is no way for such theologies to develop precisely those critical methods of reflection commensurate with the critical potentiality of the truth intention of faith. The conflict, therefore, is primarily and almost exclusively one of cultures. No foundations are available for a trans-cultural theological enterprise with the result that the dogmatism of the right is matched by the dogmatism of the left. This will be more evident in the discussions of Marxism in Chapter Two.

3. Fideomorphic Theologies

We have seen how the previous two forms of theologizing tend to identify their reflections on the truth intention of faith with particular cultural understanding of reason or criticism. Against these trends the fideomorphic theologies tend to accentuate the non-identity of faith and culture. The truth claim of faith is not primarily mediated by any historical-critical or philosophical notions. Unlike the paleomorphic theologies, these theologies do not overtly identify their reflections with any past cultural matrix except insofar as those matrices were expressions of revelation and faith. Often the fideomorphic theologies tend to conform with paleomorphic positions insofar as they are

---

[62]Cf. F. van den Oudenrijn, Kritische Theologie als Kritik der Theologie. Theorie und Praxis bei Karl Marx - Herausforderung der Theologie (München/Mainz, 1972).

[63]Cf. Metz, T.i.F., p. 21

dependent upon the Judaeo-Christian amalgamations of faith
and culture in at least the Old and New Testament periods;
or, where Catholic fideomorphic theologies are concerned, with
the patristic and early medieval "ages of faith."

One sees, for instance, how Karl Barth's theology
was a clear fideomorphic protest against the identifications
of faith and culture in the liberal Protestant theologies.[64]
It is only in this light that one can understand the Nein!
of Karl Barth to E. Brunner's attempts at correlating nature
and grace.[65] Barth also represents the difficulty of fideomorphic theologies in their articulation of the critical
potential of the truth intention of faith. The accentuation
of non-identity stood Barth in good stead in the face of the
Arianism of the German Church, thereby showing the potential
for political action within the fideomorphic stance.[66]
However, Barth was unable to articulate the negative potential of his theological position in other than paradoxical
frameworks. Metz has correctly called attention to how
Barthian theology is really more paradoxical than it is
dialectical.[67] For dialectics involve not only contradiction but also a concrete continuity or relation between the
contradictory terms or elements.[68] Yet is was precisely
the Barthian acceptance of the Kierkegaardian infinite
qualitative difference between God and man that led to the
negation of any continuity between the word of God and the
words and actions of men. H. -D. Bastian has convincingly

---

[64]Cf. J. Smart, The Divided Mind of Modern Theology
(Philadelphia, 1967); also Hans Urs von Balthasar, Karl
Barth: Darstellung und Deutung Seiner Theologie (Cologne, 1962).

[65]Walther Fürst (ed.) "Dialektische Theologie" in
Scheidung und Bewährung 1933-1936 (München, 1966).

[66]Cf. T. Rendtorff, Kirche und Theologie. Die system-
atische Funktion des Kirchenbegriffs in der neueren
Theologie (Gütersloh, 1966). Also W. Fürst's book mentioned
in the note above.

[67]Cf. Metz, "Politische Theologie," in Sacramentum
Mundi III Col. 1239.

[68]Cf. Lonergan, Insight, pp. 217ff.; M.i.T., pp.
235ff.

shown how this paradoxical and, at bottom, fideist reliance on obedience to the word of God has had such a detrimental effect on preaching and kerygma.[69]

Within Catholic theology the fideomorphic trend can be seen within various forms of monastic theology with its accentuation of flight from the world and its asceticism with regard to both nature and culture.[70] This is especially exemplified in the early writings of such monks as Eugene Boylan and Thomas Merton.[71] Comparable to Barth one has the towering figure of Hans Urs von Balthasar. Von Balthasar's efforts at elaborating an aesthetic theology have many parallels with Barth's paradoxical theology. Although von Balthasar criticizes the Kierkegaardian denigration of aesthetics, his main purpose in using aesthetic categories is to accentuate the gift quality of revelation.[72] It is this aesthetic quality or element in revelation which underlines the shock character of God's revelation to and transformation of, the mystery of cultural poverty and ugliness in the Old and New Testaments.[73]

---

[69]Cf. H. -D. Bastian, "From the Word to the Words: Karl Barth and the Tasks of Practical Theology," in Theology of the Liberating Word (Nashville, 1971), pp. 46-75.

[70]Cf. G. B. Ladner, "Monasticism as the Exemplary Christian Way of Life," in The Idea of Reform (New York, 1967), pp. 319-340. Also O. Chadwick, John Cassian (Cambridge, 1950); K. Heussi, Der Ursprung des Mönchtums (Tübingen, 1936); Lamy, Agnès, "Bios Angelikos" in Dieu vivant VII (s.a.) 57ff.; H. -I. Marrou, "Civitas Dei, civitas terrena: num tertium quid?," Stud. Patr. II, 342.

[71]It is interesting to note how the Thomas Merton of Seven Storey Mountain and The Waters of Siloe emphasized a non-identity between religious faith and the world, only in his middle period (cf. Sign of Jonas) to discover the presence of the world and a particular cultural stance in monasticism, to go on in his later writings (cf. Conjectures of a Guilty Bystander) to emphasize the need for a critical witness vis-à-vis the oppression and dehumanizing tendencies of contemporary industrial society.

[72]Cf. Hans Urs von Balthasar, Herrlichkeit Vols. I-II (Benziger, 1966-1971).

[73]Cf. von Balthasar, "Revelation and the Beautiful," in Word and Revelation (New York, 1964), pp. 121-163.

22

Another form of fideomorphic theology common to both
Protestantism and Catholicism can be found in the prolifera-
ting pentecostalist theologies. These exhibit many similarities with fundamentalist disregard for cultural and critical
reflection upon religious experience. As with Barthianism,
pentecostalism exerts a very strong attraction on persons
caught within the crisis of cultural relativism and confusion.
It demands obedience if not to the word of God as expressed in
scripture and/or tradition, at least to the authority of
a conversion experience. This experience, however, has
strong tendencies toward a privatized neglect of social and
institutional responsibilities.[74]

The characteristics of fideomorphic theologies are
their tendency toward fideism, their stress upon prayer,
sacrament and worship (if they are Catholic), or upon the
word of God and the obedience of faith (if they are Protestant). Finally, although they may offer many profound reflections on history, science and culture, these reflections
originate primarily from the sources of their own faith
commitment, whether that be scripture or tradition. Because
they attempt to articulate the understanding of faith without
dependence upon an explicit cultural matrix, they are not
as prone to the cultural sectariansim or ghetto mentality
as the paleomorphic. By the same token, however, they often
seem naïve and uncritical vis-à-vis the presuppositions of
their own theological reflection.

4. Criticomorphic Theologies

These theologies attempt to overcome the limitations
of both an identification with culture as found in the
paleomorphic and neomorphic and of a non-identification with
culture found in the fideomorphic. Specifically, criticomorphic theologies are concerned with doing justice to both
the neomorphic concern with modern culture and what faith
has to say to it and the fideomorphic concern with the truth
intention of faith and revelation. They therefore attempt
to articulate a unity of identity and non-identity between

[74]Cf. D. Tracy, "Holy Spirit as Philosophic Problem,"
in Commonweal 89 (1968), pp. 205-213.

faith and culture. I have referred to these theologies as "critico" because they attempt to be critical both in the sense of using the critical-historical methods in their appropriation of the sources and institutions of faith and also because they are critical of many aspects of contemporary culture. Perhaps the most difficult task these theologies have engaged in is their effort at articulating the critical normative unity of identity and non-identity. They do not find that normative unity of critique in classical culture, as does the paleomorphic, nor in the "progressive" elements of contemporary culture as do the neomorphic, nor in an exclusive reliance upon the word of God, as do the fideomorphic. They seek rather to find that normative unity in the interaction between faith and reason, between theology and culture, that will be consonant with both the demands of faith and the aspirations of contemporary mankind.

Criticomorphic theologies seem to predominate in the academic, theological world of today. The primary exemplification of such a theology in Protestantism can be found in Rudolf Bultmann's work. In the 1920's and 30's, Bultmann articulated his theological enterprise as concerned with critically appropriating the advances of liberal theology and the truth claims of Barth's "dialectical" theology.[75] He attempted to formulate the normative unity which would permit him full use of the historical-critical methods while still maintaining the "scandalum crucis" of the Christian kerygma through reliance upon the existential categories of Martin Heidegger.[76] Admittedly, the structure of that normative unity of identity and non-identity was tenuous, as Bultmann had to claim that the only relationship between the level of _Historie_ (factual history open to critical investigation) and _Geschichte_ (existential history constituted by decision and encounter) was in terms of the kerygma.[77] Thus his

---

[75] Cf. W. Schmithals, _Die Theologie Rudolf Bultmanns_ (Tübingen, 1966); A. Malet, _Mythos et Logos: La Pensée de Rudolf Bultmann_ (Geneva, 1962).

[76] A. Malet, _op. cit._, pp. 277-311.

[77] G. Greshake, _Historie Wird Geschichte: Bedeutung und_

24

demythologizing of the New Testament brought on the angry criticisms of the fideomorphic "Kein Anderes Evangelium" movement and the more neoporphic criticisms of Fritz Buri with his reliance upon Karl Jasper.[78]

Within Roman Catholicism forms of criticomorphic theology have been widespread. One may, perhaps, differentiate these forms insofar as they have sought respectively different normative unities of identity and non-identity, i.e., different perspectives out of which to critically appropriate both the sources and institutions of faith and the aspirations of faith and the aspirations of contemporary culture. Thus with some simplification one can say that the theology of Hans Küng finds its critical unity in the New Testament Christian experience; that the theologies of the Lyons Jesuits, H. DeLubac and J. Daniélou found a critical unity in the patristic unity of diversity; that the Le Saulchoir Dominicans, D. Chenu and Y. Congar found a critical unity for their theological reflection in the synthesis of faith and reason of St. Thomas Aquinas; that the theological work of T. de Chardin found its critical unity in the Christian interpretation of the dynamics of modern science; and that the moral theology of such men as B. Häring finds its critical unity in the moral imperatives of Christian action.[79] There is also the outstanding work of Karl Rahner who finds the critical unity of his theological enterprise in the anthropological turn of transcendental reflection.[80] All of these theologies, while often appealing to either past or present

---

Sinn der Unterscheidung von Historie und Geschichte in der Theologie Rudolf Bultmanns (Essen, 1963).

[78]Cf. H. -W. Bartsch (ed.) Kerygma und Mythos III: das Gespräch mit der Philosophie (Hamburg, 1966).

[79]This is not to imply that these theologians, when they draw upon past theological systems or syntheses, uncritically, or even simply in a critical historical fashion attempt to restore those past syntheses. Rather they function as the dialectically normative moment in their critique of contemporary society both inside and outside the Church.

[80]Cf. P. Eicher, Die Anthropologische Wende: Karl Rahners Philosophischer Weg vom Wesen des Menschen zur personalen Existenz (Freiburg, 1970).

cultural matrices, do so only within a critical reflection upon the presupposition of such an appeal.

In order to appreciate the task these criticomorphic theologies have set themselves, especially in relation to such theological enterprises as those of Bultmann and Rahner, it is necessary to understand the historical-cultural situation to which they were responding. In one way or another, they have all sought to integrate the critical consciousness generated by empirical science and historical scholarship with the truth stance of their faith traditions against the extremes of neomorphic rationalism and modernism on the one hand, and paleomorphic scholasticism and fideomorphic fideism on the other. These theologians gradually incorporated the historical-critical methods within their understanding of faith by an appeal to various philosophical analyses of historical subjectivity.[81]

The central issue in this redefinition was the relationship between the competence of the historical-critical methods and the demands of faith with its authority. Could an acceptance of historical methods avoid the pitfalls of liberalism and fundamentalism? Were there not limits to the competence of historical-critical methods which not only "left room for" but actually presupposed dimensions of man's historical being transcending (and grounding) the empirical facticity open to methodical investigation?

In elaborating affirmative answers to these questions, theologians could draw upon the conceptualities of various philosophies of historicality. These philosophies seemed eminently suited to the task of avoiding historicism and dogmatism insofar as they retained vestiges of a Kantian phenomenon-noumenon dichotomy with the inherent limitation on any empirically critical methods such a distinction insured. Thus for W. Dilthey, the inexhaustibility of inner lived experience as the ground of historicality escaped any adequate

---

[81]The following reflections are principally directed toward the German theological context both Protestant and Catholic. For it is in that context that the shift in the methodological self-understanding of theology occasioned by political theology is most evident.

mediation through the methods of rational thought.[82] Dilthey was about as unsuccessful in mediating these polarities of _Erlebnis_ and _Denken_ as E. Husserl was in mediating empirical facticity through his _Epoche_, with its "Weltvernichtung" in an effort to attain transcendental subjectivity.[83] This failure was exposed in M. Heidegger's question to Husserl on how the absolute ego is also the factual "I."[84] Despite the brilliance of Heidegger's own analysis of _Dasein_, the onto-logical difference seemed unable to effectively mediate the ontological and the ontic, so that W. Richardson could ask how _Dasein_ is related to ontic individuals, or Being-as-history with ontic history.[85]

Given this philosophical background on historicality, it is not surprising that these theologians, especially those dependent on Bultmann and Rahner, would articulate the scien-tific self-understanding of theology in reference to historical-critical methods without fear of falling into either liberalism or modernism. For historicality revealed a polarity or dichotomy which set limits to any critical mediation. The designations of the poles or extremes vary in the different theologies: one has Bultmann's _Historie_ as the level of factual history open to critical investigation and his _Geschichte_ constituted by existential decision and encounter.[86] Rahner speaks of _categorical_ history and future

---

[82]Cf. M. Lamb, "W. Dilthey's Critique of Historical Reason and B. Lonergan's Meta-Method," in P. McShane (ed.) _Language, Truth and Meaning_ (University of Notre Dame Press, 1972), pp. 115-166, 321-332, and the references to Dilthey's writings given there.

[83]Cf. T. Prufer, "A Protreptic: What is Philosophy?" in _Studies in Philosophy_ (Washington, D.C., 1963), pp. 13-17 and the references given there. Also cf. G. Brand, _Die Lebenswelt: Eine Philosophie des konkreten Apriori_ (Berlin, 1971), pp. 104ff.

[84]Cf. _Tijdschrift voor Philosophie_ 12 (1950), p. 268.

[85]Cf. W. Richardson, _Heidegger - Through Pheonomenology to Thought_ (Hague, 1963), pp. 634-635; also K. J. Huch, _Philosophie-geschichtliche Voraussetzungen der Heideggerschen Ontologie_ (Frankfurt, 1967).

[86]Cf. G. Greshake, _op. cit._, also A. Malet, _op. cit._,

subject to the causal or functional determinations of scientific explanation, and the <u>transcendent</u> or absolute future identified with the mystery of the Godhead.[87] Or one has G. Ebeling's distinction between considering history as merely factual and considering it as a word-event.[88] W. Pannenberg has already criticized the existentialist and salvation-history approaches to the problems of integrating the historical-critical methods.[89] Yet he himself seeks an integration in terms of a universal history as a tradition-history whose transcendent unity is in God.[90] Parallels might be drawn to Tillich's synthesis of autonomous and heteronomous reason in theonomy.[91]

---

pp. 59-75, 277-311; S. Ogden, <u>Christ Without Myth</u> (New York, 1961), pp. 111-126.

[87]Cf. K. Rahner, "Die Frage nach der Zukunft," in H. Peukert, <u>op. cit.</u>, pp. 247-266, esp. p. 261; on the methodological presuppositions of Rahner's position, cf. P. Eicher, <u>Die Anthropologische Wende</u> (Freiburg-Schweiz, 1970), pp. 50-72, 283-293, 325-332, 388-411.

[88]Cf. G. Ebeling, "Wort Gottes und Hermeneutik," in <u>Z.Th.K.</u> 56 (1959), pp. 224-251; also J. M. Robinson and J. B. Cobb (eds.) <u>The New Hermenutic</u> (New York, 1964), and R. W. Funk, <u>Language, Hermeneutic, and Word of God</u> (New York, 1966), pp. 47-71. On the variations of the bi-dimensionality in hermeneutics, cf. E. Fuch's response in <u>The New Hermeneutic</u>; also S. Ogden, <u>The Reality of God</u> (New York, 1966), pp. 71-98.

[89]Cf. W. Pannenberg, <u>Grundfragen systematischer Theologie</u> (Göttingen, 1967), pp. 22-78, 91-122, 123-158.

[90]Cf. <u>Offenbarung als Geschichte</u> (Göttingen, 1965), pp. 7-20, 91-114. Also J. M. Robinson and J. B. Cobb (eds.) <u>Theology as History</u> (New York, 1966). This problem in Pannenberg is closely related to the philosophical hermeneutics of Hans-Georg Gadamer in his <u>Wahrheit und Methode</u>. The problem might be formulated as: can a universal history that appeals to Gadamer's "Horizontverschmelzung" adequately handle the concrete dialectics operative in history? Is there not only a necessary hermeneutical "merging of horizons" in history, but also a dialectical "conflict of horizons"?

[91]Cf. Tillich, <u>Systematic Theology</u> I (Chicago, 1951), pp. 81-94; also P. Barthel, <u>op. cit.</u>, pp. 152-198 on Tillich's method of correlation. He concludes (p. 196): "Thus, instead of mediating between the positive pole of the symbolic language of lived religion and the critical pole of the philosophical knowledge of Being, Tillich's hermeneutics are

Criticomorphic theologians more dependent upon the French philosophical milieu could draw upon M. Blondel's philosophy of action and E. Mounier's personalism and Bergson's vitalism for categories with which to handle historical process. Such categories, however, were also open to the ambiguity of relating transcendence to immanence, personal commitment to social concern.[92] Likewise, the process theologians in American could appeal to the philosophical categories of Whitehead and Hartshorne in order to do justice to the empirical and historical consciousness. Nevertheless the serious question remained as to how adequate those metaphysical categories were to handle not only the methods of empirical and historical science, but also the demands of the Christian tradition.[93] Common to all these theologies seems to be an attempt at articulating a critical normative unity of identity and non-identity which itself transcends critical mediation. And it is this which keeps theology from either a liberalist or modernist reduction to a psychology, sociology, anthropology, or philosophy of religion. This is not derogatory of theology as a science since the acceptance of the historical-critical methods operates within a reference-frame which allows a critical mediation only from the past into the present. The future is indeed recognized as at least a, if not the, constitutive element in historicality. The eschatological dimension of theology is duly emphasized. But this is done in a manner that places it beyond the pale of critical methods. Hence, Bultmann rejected any dekerygmatization in theology.[94]

---

de facto reduced to a quasi-allegorical interpretation of the ontological cipher of the images, representations, mythologoumena, theologoumena and dogmas of the Christian faith."

[92]Cf. J. Flamand, L'idée de médiation chez M. Blondel (Paris, 1969); also H. Bouillard, Blondel et le christianisme (Paris, 1961).

[93]Cf. J. Moltmann's remarks in E. Cousins (ed.) Hope and the Future of Man (Philadelphia, 1972), pp. 55-59; also W. Pannenberg, "Future and Unity," ibid., pp. 60-78. For a more positive assessment, cf. D. Tracy, Blessed Rage for Order.

[94]Cf. F. Buri, "Entmythologisierung oder Entkerygmatisierung der Theologie," in Kerygma und Mythos II, pp. 85ff.

Ebeling asserted how the "whole which encounters man" is a reality encountered in faith alone.[95]   Rahner insists on theology as a "reductio in mysterium" and sees the theologian's function as the custodian of a "docta ignorantia futuri."[96] Or one has the affirmations of Chardin regarding the movement of the cosmos toward point Omega without any clear criteria for mediating the personalizing forces of Christian faith to the collectivizing trends of modern industrial technology.[97]

This seeming lack of critical reflection upon the articulation of the normative unity within these critico-morphic theologies has had far-reaching consequences for a theological understanding of the concrete praxis of the believer and the Church. For the accent is placed more on historicality constituting man, than on man constituting history. The ground, center, or goal of history was encountered in a moment of existential decision (Bultmann), in a reality-recognizing act of faith (Ebeling), or in an assent to the transcendent mystery of existence with its implicit openness to the divinely willed ecclesial mediation of salvation (Rahner). This implied that praxis was ultimately determined by kerygma, faith, Church, etc., and little attention was given to how such a determined praxis actually functions in contemporary society. Perhaps it is not too far from the truth to suggest that these theologies tended to conceive of the future as a given, or gift, in a way they also thought of the past. Only where the past is given and susceptible of critical investigation, the future is given in a transcendent sense. So, for example, Bultmann:

---

[95]Cf. Ebeling's "Theologie und Wirklichkeit," in Wort und Glaube, pp. 192-202; compare with the article of his on historical-criticism, ibid., pp. 7ff.

[96]Cf. Rahner's "Überlegungen zur Methode der Theologie," in Schriften IX, pp. 79-126, 519-540. There is, of course, a way in which Rahner is hereby insisting upon the need for theology to preserve the non-identity essential not only for the recognition of mystery but also to preserve an openness to the future. Yet in Rahner this is not adequately related to an identifiable praxis.

[97]Cf. Metz, "The Future ex Memoria Passionis," in E. Cousins, op. cit., pp. 117-131.

> The man who understands his historicity radically,
> that is, the man who radically understands himself
> as someone future, or in other words, who under-
> stands his genuine self as an ever-future one, has to
> know that his genuine self can only be offered to him
> as a gift by the future.[98]

There is little room in this understanding of theology for methods aimed at a critical mediation of the present into the future. Invaluable contributions were made by uncovering the centrality of _Existenz_, of decision and conversion. Yet this domain of religious praxis was not integrated methodologically with the concrete historical and social conditions of the faithful and their institutions. The Catholic criticomorphic theologies found their efforts at appropriating a critical "return to the sources" crowned at Vatican II, yet they seemed ill prepared for the further critical questions posed by the crisis that has ensued - a central element of which is how to critically mediate the Christian message to the problems of contemporary society faced with a confusing pluralist present and an ominous future.[99]

POLITICAL THEOLOGY

The fifth and final type of doing theology might be

---

[98]From Bultmann's _History and Eschatology_ (New York, 1962), p. 150. Parallels could be drawn between the present discussion in hermeneutics on the relation of history and critical freedom, and the medieval problematic on grace and freedom. If historicality constitutes man - cf. Gadamer's "In Wahrheit gehört die Geschichte nicht uns, sondern wir gehören ihr." in _Wahrheit und Methode_, p. 261 - then how does one go about a critique of false pre-judgments? Cf. the discussions on this in _Hermeneutik und Ideologiekritik_ (Frankfurt, 1971), and note the limitations of hermeneutics in regard to the dialectics operative in the critique of ideologies: pp. 83-119, 299-317. Cf. also F. Lawrence, "Self-Knowledge in History in Gadamer and Lonergan," in P. Mc-Shane (ed.), _Language, Truth and Meaning_ (University of Notre Dame Press, 1972), pp. 167-217. Note also that I translate _Geschichtlichkeit_ as "historicality" rather than "historicity" since the latter more commonly renders the German "historisch."

[99]Cf. Metz's article referred to in Note 97. Also the book of D. Tracy, _Blessed Rage for Order: The New Pluralism in Theology_ (New York, 1975).

politicomorphic. In many ways this type of theologizing is an extension, or further elaboration, of criticomorphic theologies. Like them it seeks to articulate a unity of identity and non-identity, i.e., it seeks to do justice to the intentions of both the neomorphic identification with contemporary culture and the fideomorphic non-identification of the truth intention of faith with culture. Unlike those theologies, however, the politicomorphic does not rely on philosophies of historicality (German), of immanentism or vitalism (French), or of a metaphysics of process (American) in articulating its normative unity. In general, one might say that the methodological shift in politicomorphic theologies is a shift from concern with a critical mediation from the past into the present to a concern with a critical mediation from the present into the future.[100] Here one has the various theologies of revolution and liberation, which are especially dominant in the developing countries.[101] Within Europe the political theology of Johann B. Metz is especially characteristic of this type of theologizing.

In order to assure a critical mediation not only from the past into the present, but also from the present into the future, politicomorphic theologies cannot rest content with a basically uncritical thematization of the unity. This will be clear from a consideration of the critique the political theology of Metz levels against the previous types of theologizing. Before that, however, a brief sketch of a central feature of Metz's theological development should be made. This will indicate both how the political theologies have arisen within the criticomorphic and how they decidedly differ from them.

In his doctoral work on the philosophy of M. Heidegger, Metz concentrated on the ontological difference between Being

---

[100]Cf. M. Lamb, "Les présuppositions méthodologiques de la théologie politique," in M. Xhaufflaire (ed.) La pratique de la théologie politique (Tournai, 1974).

[101]Cf. esp. F. Herzog, Liberation Theology (New York, 1972). Also R. Alves, A Theology of Human Hope (St. Meinrad, Indiana, 1972); G. Gutierrez, A Theology of Liberation (New York, 1973); E. Feil and R. Weth, Diskussion zur Theologie der Revolution (Mainz, 1969).

32

and beings. The fundamental ontology of the early Heidegger
provided an effort at articulating a unity of identity
(beings) and non-identity (Being) within the horizon of
Dasein.[102] In his doctoral work on Thomas Aquinas Metz saw
a similar unity operative in the anthropocentric horizon of
Aquinas' theology. Although the thought-content of Aquinas'
discussions of God, grace, sin, and redemption were identified within the context of medieval theology, the thought-
form was within the anthropocentric turn of modernity. The
unity of the anthropocentric "Seinsverständnis" was one of
identity and non-identity insofar as it was never totally
"Reflektierbar." Man as the "Inbegriff des gesamten Welt-
Werdens" meant that the theological categories of grace were
both identified with historical man (immanence) and non-
identified with him inasmuch as he is open to Being
(transcendence).[103]

Metz's early explorations of secularization and homini-
zation were within this context defined by K. Rahner's transcendental anthropological turn. The hominized world is the
world denuminized by the transcendence of the Judaeo-Christian
revelation. Man (identity) in his historical becoming is
graced by the transcendent God (non-identity).[104] A theology
of the world indicates how the transcendence of God has
desacralized the world, let it be. God is not the God of the
gaps but allows man to be man. Yet in Christ we have this
non-identity incarnated in the identity (immanence) of the
world. Man is on his own, yet this is possible as an experience of radical secularization only because man can no longer

---

[102]Cf. Metz, "Heidegger und das Problem der Metaphysik"
Scholastik (1953), pp. 1-23, and "Theologische und metaphysi-
sche Ordnung," in Zeitschrift für katholische Theologie 83
(1961), pp. 1-14.

[103]Cf. Metz, Christliche Anthropozentrik (München, 1962).
One notices here how often a Heideggerian identity-in-difference
between the ontic and the ontological emerges in several
different contexts. This is also true of Metz's revisions of
Karl Rahner's Hörer des Wortes: Zur Grundlegung einer Reli-
gionsphilosophie (München, 1963).

[104]Cf. Metz, Zur Theologie der Welt (Mainz, 1968),
pp. 11-45, 51-74.

absolutize the world as god. It was within this context that
Metz began to see how eschatology is the Christian expression
of this unity of identity and non-identity.[105]

Increasingly he became aware of the inadequacy of a
fundamental ontology or a Rahnerian transcendental epistemology to thematize critically this unity. If the anthropological turn was to be taken seriously then it depended upon
the historical praxis of the Christian community, the Church,
to mediate the saving memory of Christ from the past into the
present and the present into the future. The Church, as an
institution of social criticism, must identify herself with
those non-identified with the status quo. Metz showed how
the theological understanding of the eschatological character
of the Church meant that she was the one immanent, historical
institution (identity) whose inner dynamism, as eschatological,
was orientated towards its own sublation in the Kingdom of
God (non-identity).[106]

The main thrust of the criticisms of political theology
has been directed against the deformations in praxis to be
found in ecclesial and social structures and policies.[107]
Any praxis, whether authentic or alienating, has theoretical
presuppositions just as any theory has practical presuppositions and implications. Thus Metz directs telling criticisms
against the types of theologizing mentioned above. Against
the paleomorphic theologies Metz not only directs the usual
criticomorphic critique about its naïveté regarding its own
presuppositions. He specifically sees the often unthematized
realities of the "old political theologies" with their
identification of the Church with the Kingdom of God, and so
their failure to preserve the eschatological nature of the
Church, and their consequent repressive praxis and cunning
identification with political systems.[108] Against the

---

[105]Ibid., pp. 75-88.   [106]Ibid., pp. 99-146.

[107]Cf. Metz, Zur Theologie der Welt, pp. 99-146; and his
Reform und Gegenreformation Heute (Mainz, 1969), and "Kirch-
liche Autorität im Anspruch der Freiheitsgeschichte," in
Kirche im Prozess der Aufklärung (Mainz, 1970), pp. 53-90

[108]Cf. Metz' "Politische Theologie in der Diskussion" in
Peukert (ed.) Diskussion zur politischen Theologie, pp. 268-279.

neomorphic theologies he shows how the almost complete identification of theology with contemporary psychological,
sociological, or philosophical liberal or Marxist thought and
methods only leads to a liquidation of theology and its critical potential for opposing the abstract totalizing operative
in contemporary positivist Liberal and idealist Marxist notions of human emancipation.[109] Against the fideomorphic
theologies he raises the objection that they tend too easily
to identify the historical realities of non-identity with
the mysteries of faith. The paradoxes of Barthianism and
von Balthasar's theology are not adequately dialectical.[110]

Although Metz has not to date published an extensive
critique of criticomorphic theologies, it is possible to
delineate the main lines of such a critique. This is especially necessary in the light of the present inquiry into
the methodological presuppositions of political theology.
Within the limits of the present attempt to clarify the shift
in method implied in political theology, one might ask why
the philosophies of historicality are unable to serve as the
foundations for a critical mediation from the present into
the future. This will then throw light on the implications
for method of the critique by political theology of criticomorphic theologies.

A critical mediation of future orientated praxis implies
a radical critique of any scientistic identification of
method with an objectivistic (Cartesian) rationalist, or
merely logical, calculation.[111] This would identify praxis

---

[109]Cf. Metz, "Erlösung und Emanzipation," in Stimmen
der Zeit (März, 1973), pp. 171-186.

[110]Cf. Metz, Grundlagen des Glaubensverständnisses:
der Glaube und das "Ende der Metaphysik", a Scriptum of the
lectures Metz gave in Münster during the winter semester of
1967-68.

[111]Notice how within the perspective of political
theology the critique of Cartesianism is not restricted to
the specifically hermeneutical phenomena of understanding,
but applies to the inherent limitations of formal system
theories and their logics; cf. Peukert, "Zur formalen Systemtheorie und zur hermeneutischen Problematik einer 'politischen Theologie'," in Diskussion zur "Politischen
Theologie", pp. 82-95.

with technique, and collapse socio-political interaction into a managerial social engineering.[112] On the other hand, a critical mediation implies that method is not totally non-identical with planning and technique. If it were, there would be no alternative to a completely negative attitude towards technology on the part of praxis, i.e., mediation would give way to negation.[113] The success of a critical mediation depends, therefore, on a multi-dimensional approach to method capable of maintaining the unity of identity and non-identity between the many particular methods operative within the spheres of pre-scientific (common sense) social interaction, aesthetic creativity, historical scholarship, scientific theory and technique, philosophical and theological reflection.[114] Such a unity of identity and non-identity presupposes that there are values and interests operative within these various spheres of human theory and praxis, that those values and interests are susceptible of objective (not objectivistic) analysis, and that there are rational and responsible foundations for a critical evaluation of such interests and values.

The philosophies of historicality seemed so involved in rejecting the identification of their methods with either a Hegelian logicism or a positivist empiricism, that they tended

---

[112]Cf. Metz, "Technik - Politik - Religion," in W. Heinen and J. Schreiner (eds.) Erwartung-Verheissung-Erfüllung (Würzburg, 1969), and his "Der zukünftige Mensch und der kommende Gott," in H. J. Schultz (ed.) Wer ist das eigentlich Gott? (Munich, 1969), pp. 260-275. Also the discussion between J. Habermas and N. Luhmann in Theorie der Gesellschaft oder Sozialtechnologie (Frankfurt, 1971).

[113]Cf. the efforts of J. Habermas to mediate the two critically in his Technik und Wissenschaft als "Ideologie" (Frankfurt, 1968), and Erkenntnis und Interesse (Frankfurt, 1968). In a similar vein, cf. Ivan Illich, Tools for Conviviality (New York, 1973).

[114]Note how this methodological perspective provides a framework for political theology which is not immediately tied down to either a practical-critical philosophy of history or an anthropology since it is capable of grounding both. Cf. B. Lonergan, Insight; R. Hanser, W. Lepenies and H. Nolte, Kritik der Anthropologie (Munich, 1971), and the remarks of Metz on p. 63 of Kirche im Prozess der Aufklärung.

towards a total non-identity between historical understanding
and scientific explanation. This led to a growing isolation
of praxis from a society dominated by a rapidly increasing
technology. The concept of historicality (Geschichtlichkeit)
itself arose in German philosophy as a reaction against the
revolutionary momentum of the empirical sciences and the
political programs they inspired, especially in the French
Enlightenment and French revolution.[115]

Positively, the philosophies thematizing historicality
called attention to the errors of mechanistic positivism,
with its objectivistic and scientistic (mis)understanding of
socio-historical realities. They emphasized the constitutive
role of historical tradition and historical subjectivity in
the understanding of specifically human phenomena. Negatively,
however, they were so intent upon delimiting their approaches
from the methods of the empirical sciences, that they ended
up isolating the critical potential of historical subjectivity
from any effective social mediation, thereby privatizing
or ontologizing historicality.[116]

For example, the Kantian context of criticism is
severely hampered by the principle of Anschauung and the
resulting dichotomy between noumenon and phenomenon. As
phenomenal, subjectivity was subject to empirical and critical
investigation, while, as noumenal, the self with its imperatives and regulative ideas transcended empirical facticity.
This seemed to guarantee individual freedom and spontaneity,
but in actual practice it isolated that freedom, depriving
it of any effective critical function in a society more and
more controlled by specialized and technocratized structures.[117] The interests and values constituted by that

---

[115]Cf. L. von Renthe-Fink, Geschichtlichkeit (Göttingen,
1968), pp. 142-144.

[116]Cf. Metz's criticisms of metaphysics in Zur Theologie
der Welt, pp. 89-91; and of privatizing, pp. 99-102. On the
philosophical context of these criticisms, cf. G. Picht,
Wahrheit-Vernunft-Verantwortung, (Stuttgart, 1969), pp. 281-242.

[117]Cf. the criticisms of Kant in Habermas, Erkenntnis
und Interesse, pp. 252-253; in O. Schwemmer, Philosophie der
Praxis (Frankfurt, 1971), p. 175; and in G. Picht, Wahrheit-
Vernunft-Verantwortung, pp. 183-202, 304-317, 427-434.

freedom became less and less relevant to the "objective" sphere of factual scientific knowledge, which then claimed to be the paradigm of knowing.[118]

Similar dilemmas can be traced throughout the philosophies of historicality. Although Dilthey recognized the central role of meaning and value in the constitution of historical experience, his descriptive analytic methods offered no foundations for a critical differentiation of true and false meanings and values.[119] Husserl did indeed recognize how the concrete social world is constituted by praxis, yet the unresolved conflict between his notion of Intuition and that of Intentional Constitution made him unable to relate that praxis to the primordial constitution of the material world, which occurs prior to intersubjective praxis.[120] Heidegger's ontological radicalization of understanding and disclosure was also unable to offer the basis for a critical mediation of praxis. As the early Heidegger seemed more concerned that truth is disclosed in understanding, rather than how it is disclosed, so the later Heidegger sees the mittence of Being in thought as unmediated by an experience.[121] How, then, are we to mediate

---

[118]This was certainly not the intention of Kant, and it is not surprising that Neo-Kantians such as E. Cassirer prefer to drop the phenomenon-noumenon dichotomy, cf. his The Philosophy of Symbolic Forms (New Haven, 1953), pp. 110ff. For a critique of Kant's practical philosophy based on the dichotomy, cf. T. Adorno, Negative Dialektik (Frankfurt, 1966), pp. 281-292.

[119]Cf. H. Diwald, W. Dilthey, Erkenntnistheorie und Philosophie der Geschichte (Göttingen, 1963), pp. 69-71, 76-77, 156-158. Also Habermas, Erkenntnis und Interesse, pp. 178-233.

[120]Cf. E. Tugendhat, Der Wahrheitsbegriff bei Husserl und Heidegger (Berlin, 1970), pp. 252-255 and W. Ryan, "Intentionality in E. Husserl and B. Lonergan: the Perspectives of Intuition - Constitution and Affirmation," unpublished Florida Congress paper. For a critical evaluation of A. Schulz's attempt to expand Husserl's phenomenology to sociality, cf. David Rasmussen, "Between Autonomy and Sociality" in Cultural Hermeneutics Vol. I, No. 1 (April, 1973), pp. 3-45.

[121]Cf. E. Tugendhat, op. cit., pp. 350, 356-362, 376,

38

authenticity - or how will Being mediate itself - in a critical manner to the contemporary social situation?[122] Metz's
eventual rejection of a Heideggerian ontology as the unity
of identity and non-identity finds its philosophical basis
in the dependence of such an ontologizing upon the privatized
autonomy of Kantian noumenal subjectivity.[123]

The pattern in these philosophies of historicality
indicates a limitation on critical methods. They tend towards
an almost exclusive non-identity between reflections aimed
at elucidating the ground of historicality and the new methods
of empirical and critical analysis. They would see in any
affirmation of the possibility of a mediation between the
two as only an effort to reduce the understanding of historicality to a type of objectivistic behavior analysis. This,
however, presupposes that a basically Cartesian interpretation
of scientific understanding and method is the only viable
one.[124] If that were the case, then there could be no unity
of identity and non-identity in a methodologically critical
mediation, and the only alternative would be to delimit the
modes of understanding historicality from the modes of an

399; also W. Weischedel, Der Gott der Philosophen I
(Darmstadt, 1971), pp. 484-489. Also cf. K. J. Huch,
Philosophie-geschichtliche Voraussetzungen der Heideggerschen
Ontologie (Frankfurt, 1967).

[122]Cf. O. Pöggeler (ed.) Heidegger (Berlin, 1969), pp.
41ff.; also T. Adorno, Jargon der Eigentlichkeit (Frankfurt,
1967), and J. Habermas, Philosophisch-politische Profile
(Frankfurt, 1971), pp. 76-92. And, on the neglect of praxis
in Heidegger, cf. G. Brand, Die Lebenswelt, pp. 135-137.

[123]Cf. K. J. Huch, op. cit., pp. 9-42

[124]Cf. Gadamer, Wahrheit und Methode, p. 225: "Die
Gewissheit der Wissenschaft hat immer einen cartesianischen
Zug." And the characterization of method in his Kleine
Schriften I, pp. 49-50. This is not the place to criticize
this interpretation of modern science. Suffice it to note
that B. Lonergan has come up with a very different interpretation of both scientific performance and method, cf.
Insight, pp. 408-411. Moreover, his notion of method has
been fruitfully applied not only to problems in the
interpretation of Physics, but also the contemporary hermeneutical problems, cf. P. Heelan, Quantum Mechanics and
Objectivity (Hague, 1963), and P. McShane (ed.) Language,
Truth and Meaning (Dublin, 1972).

objectivistic and scientistic knowing which would be the domain of empirical science.

The utilization of such an abstract non-identity pattern by the theologies of historicality inevitably led to a serious restriction of even the historical-critical methods. H. Peukert has indicated the incongruity of such restrictions:

> Although historical research, with its appropriate methods, elaborated the historical and social conditions of every statement, understanding (Verstehen) itself was almost exclusively thought of as an ascent out of the domain of socialization into the realm of a transcendent, authentic existence.[125]

The notion of "application," so central to the hermeneutical procedure, was privatized or ontologized, since the critical methods were restricted to the mediation of the past into the present. The eschatological dimension of faith and theology was not critically mediated to the ambiguities of the contemporary world situation, but was reduced to either a call to personal responsibility or, as a realized eschatology, was seen as already having negated the ambiguites with the (equally privatized) arcanum of an existentialist, personalist, or Kantian transcendentalist, converted subjectivity.[126] While a limited critical control was practiced in the archaeological or diachronic dimensions of history, the synchronic and eschatological (or future orientated) dimensions, in which the application concretely occurred, was left without critical methods to guide the concrete, future influencing praxis of the ecclesial community.[127]

This, I believe, is the context for political theology's critique of criticomorphic theologies. Bultmann's existential hermeneutics results in a privatized praxis, with its uncritical acceptance of contemporary man's reality criteria and its inability to disclose the relevance of religious

---

[125]Peukert, op. cit., p. viii.

[126]Cf. Metz in Sacramentum Mundi III, 1232ff.

[127]Cf. Metz, "Politische Theologie in der Diskussion," in Peukert (ed.), op. cit., pp. 268-301.

conversion to the social ills of that reality. Similarly,
Metz criticizes Rahner's transcendental method for failing to
adequately relate its transcendental thematization of
religious experience to the other domains of human experience,
e.g., the scientific and social ones. Rahner realizes the
profound influence these secular domains of experience are
having on the church and theology, but all he does is see
them as part of the pluralistic reality of modernity. Metz
wonders if he does not overlook the very real dangers of an
irrationalism - and a resulting paralysis of praxis - in an
acceptance of pluralism without critically mediating methods
capable of at least distinguishing the wheat from the
cockle.[128]

As Metz can criticize the abstract neglect of concrete
suffering in the emancipation proclaimed by J. Habermas, so
he warns of an almost fideomorphic abstraction of non-
identity into the Christian understanding of God on the part
of J. Moltmann's Der Gekreuzigte Gott, in Hans Küng's talk of
the historicality of God, and in von Balthasar's interpretation of the paschal mystery. What Metz suspects in these
otherwise praiseworthy theologies is an abstract conceptualizing of the concrete reality of non-identity in suffering.[129]

Moltmann himself tended to criticize Ebeling's theology
for being open to the danger of making the gospel a religious
legitimatization and justification of the Establishment,
insofar as Ebeling mystified the real suffering in our social
condition by offering a promise of freedom in faith without
concretizing that freedom in critical methods aimed at bringing freedom to an unfree world.[130] Finally, although W.
Pannenberg has justly criticized the false restrictions of

---

[128]Metz has not yet published his detailed criticisms
of the existentialist, personalist, and transcendental
methods given in his lectures on Fundamental Theology, cf.
the scriptum in note 110 above.

[129]Cf. "Erlösung und Emanzipation," pp. 181f.

[130]Cf. Moltmann, Perspektiven der Theologie, pp. 119ff.,
128-146. This is, of course, a rather pointed summary of
Moltmann's position vis-à-vis Ebeling, cf. the remarks of
H. -N. Janowski on pp. 61-63 in the book cited in note 131
below.

the historical-critical methods by existentialist and
salvation-history theologies, others have asked how Pannenberg's seemingly exclusive reliance on the historical-
critical methods would ever enable him to move from a
hermeneutics of universal history to a critique of ideologies
alienating our own socio-historical situation.[131]

METHOD AND POLITICAL THEOLOGY

The criticisms political theology makes regarding
criticomorphic and the other types of theologizing imply a
profound shift in the self-understanding of theology. For
critically to mediate the Christian message from the present
into the future means that the very foundations of theology
cannot be located in the past - whether in scriptural,
patristic, conciliar, or other ecclesial traditions - and
then mediated theoretically into the present. Rather the
foundations are in the praxis of the present as that praxis
is actually orientated toward the eschatological Kingdom of
God.[132] I should like to spell out briefly some of the
important consequences this shift in foundations has for
theological method.

Firstly, the fundamentally critical problem for theology
is not the problem of integrating dogmatic traditions with
critical-historical scholarship. For this problem is only
one aspect of a far deeper problem of relating the concrete
experiences, understandings, assertions, and decisions of
believing communities to the concrete historical processes
constituted by social praxis.[133] As long as theology concentrated on the historical-critical methods and the resulting
problem of dogma versus history, it could only indicate the
crucial significance of Existenz, conversion, responsibility

---

[131]Cf. H. -G. Geyer, H. N. Janowski, A. Schmidt,
Theologie und Soziologie, pp. 63-65.

[132]That this is similar to Lonergan, cf. Chapter Four,
pp. 497-529.

[133]Cf. Metz in Sacramentum Mundi III, 1234-1235.

for the pre-understanding of history and dogma. In this way
the criticomorphic theologies attempted a synchronism with
the paleomorphic, for they recognized the problem of historical consciousness but tried to tie this in with the older
discussions on the "nature" of the Church and of theology.[134]
They could do this because the philosophies of historicality
allowed them to discuss the "nature" of history. Hence the
criticism leveled against the privatizing or ontologizing
of Existenz, conversion, and responsible decision situations
is that thereby such theologies are not able to handle both
the concreteness of history itself - apostrophized in the
"Leidensgeschichte" and the narratives of history - nor
the concreteness of the historical-critical methods
themselves. For those methods arose not out of classical
concern with nature and substance (nor any of the more
sophisticated conceptualities of the historicality philosophies), but from the specifically modern concern with
empirical historical processes and functions.[135] By restrict-
ing critical mediation from the past to the present within
the conceptuality of the philosophies of historicality,
such theologies could not handle what is actually going forward from the present into the future. To handle that political theology calls attention both to narrative and to
praxis in both its common sense and its scientific forms.

Secondly, just as fideomorphic theologies could not
follow the liberal or modernist route of reducing theology
to no more than the historical-critical methods in the mediation from the past into the present, so political theology
does not maintain that the actual praxis of believing communities can be adequately mediated methodologically by the
methods of psychologies, sociologies, anthropologies, or
philosophies of religious praxis, as with the neomorphic
Critical Catholicism. But where the criticomorphic tend to
assert this non-identity in terms of a supra-historical

---

[134]Cf. D. Tracy, Achievement, pp. 84-91.

[135]Cf. D. Tracy, op. cit., pp. 91-103; also D. R. Kelley,
Foundations of Modern Historical Scholarship (New York, 1970);
and esp. Van A. Harvey, The Historian and the Believer (New
York, 1966) on the differing "moralities" or praxis.

and supra-critical (noumenal) realm of an existentialist, personalist, transcendentalist, or historicalist subjectivity, political theology asserts that an adequately critical mediation of religious praxis demands properly theological methods in order to do justice to the true meanings and values operative within that praxis as eschatological or future orientated.[136]

These meanings and values are not enshrined in some supra-critical monstrance completely non-identical with secular social praxis, as in fideomorphic theologies or the historicality of the criticomporphic, nor are they authoritarianly identified with those programs of secular social praxis which claim to represent an identifiable subject of world history and social process - whether those programs are formulated in secular ideologies (as in orthodox Marxism and Liberal capitalist progress) or in ecclesial ideologies (as in the paleomorphic forms of political theology).[137] For the eschatological proviso as actually immanent in history implies a unity of identity and non-identity which avoids any abstract subject of world or historical process while

---

[136]Metz sees political theology as relating everything to the eschatological message of Jesus by means of the new starting point of critical reason since the Enlightenment, and as this new approach to reason found articulation in Hegel and Marx. Cf. Sacramentum Mundi III, 1234. Metz does not do this by attempting to re-establish the naïve identification of society and religion which critical reason found in pre-Enlightenment social praxis. Instead he fully accepts the challenge of critical reason and through an appropriation of that reason seeks the validity of a theological method and religious praxis which, as a "zweite Reflexion," will respect the post-critical validity of narrative, cf. his "A Short Apology for Narrative," Concilium 85 (1973), pp. 84-96. Compare with P. Ricoeur's "second naïveté" in regard to religious symbolism appropriated through the critical reflection of psychoanalysis, Finitude et culpabilité II, (Paris, 1960), pp. 323-332.

[137]Cf. Metz, "Erlösung und Emanzipation" in Stimmen der Zeit (März, 1973), pp. 171-186. On a unity of identity and non-identity, cf. T. Adorno, Negative Dialektik, pp. 13-64, 161-205, 307-315, 395-398; also J. Habermas, Philosophisch-politische Profile, pp. 184-199. On the dialectical similarities between orthodox Marxism and late Capitalism, cf. Adorno, Aufsätze zur Gesellschaftstheorie und Methodologie (Frankfurt, 1970), pp. 137-166. On the older forms of political theology, cf. E. Feil, op. cit., pp. 113-127.

not falling into relativism or historicism.[138]

Thirdly, just as the eschatological orientation of religious praxis is a dialectical unity of identity and non-identity with the concrete social praxis of secular and ecclesial communities and institutions, so will the methods of a theology concerned with a critical mediation from the past into the present and the present into the future exhibit a dialectical unity of identity and non-identity with the methods operative in the efforts to theoretically and practically understand and guide historical and social praxis.[139] Thus political theology is attentive to both the spontaneous world of narrative and story and the reflective world of scholarship and science. There can be no one-sided effort to sublate story into thought, narrative into argument, nor vice-versa.[140]

This means that in its collaboration with the sciences and philosophies in their methodical efforts to mediate social theory-praxis, political theology is concerned with methods open to both the spontaneous world of narrative and to the non-identity of religious praxis. In this way political theology not only learns from those methods but actively contributes to them insofar as it would liberate them from either a trivializing relativity or a fanaticizing totality. Just as in concrete social praxis there are not only alternative interests and values but also distorted ones, so there is not only a pluralism of methods but also the conflict of opposed methods. Such a dialectic of methods is truncated without theology insofar as it then tends either to trivialize method, reducing it to an end-means calculation without any critical normativity beyond concepts and axioms, or to

---

[138]On the eschatological proviso, cf. Metz, Zur Theologie der Welt, pp. 75-89, 110ff.

[139]This could well be the methodological significance of Metz's determinate negation, cf. Sacramentum Mundi III, col. 1328, for it is this that, among other factors, accounts for his interest in interdisciplinary collaboration.

[140]Cf. Metz, "Erlösung und Emanzipation" as in note 137 above; also his "A Short Apology for Narrative" in Concilium 85, pp. 84-96.

fanaticize method, claiming that the praxis is absolute and without conditions.[141]

Fourthly, this emancipation of the methods of the other sciences and philosophies from trivialization or fanaticization is not done by any direct intervention in their methods by theology. Rather it is done indirectly and heuristically inasmuch as political theology would succeed in interrelating the intellectual praxis of science with the moral praxis of political social life and the religious praxis of ecclesial institutions. Theology would thereby be an instance of socio-critical concern within the academic world just as the church should be one within the political world. For it would oppose any conceptualism that would separate theory from praxis, thought from life. Such an interrelation of intellectual, moral and religious praxis would necessarily be contra-factual, and so critical, insofar as the concrete practices of scientific, socio-political and religious institutions contradict intelligence, responsibility, reverence and love. Within this dialectic of progress and decline, political theology is not immediately concerned with particular programs of reform and revolution. For such programs can at best be ambiguous unless they are carried out within the context of a fundamental appropriation of critical consciousness.[142] Metz is concerned with a theological appropriation of such critical consciousness, and only mediately (i.e., as mediated by that appropriation) with

---

[141]Cf. T. Adorno and M. Hockheimer, _Dialektik der Aufklärung_ (Frankfurt, 1969), on the polarities of trivialization and fanaticization. For more recent examples of this, cf. L. Gilkey, _Religion and the Scientific Future_ (London, 1970), pp. 65-100. On fanaticism in the Enlightenment, cf. _Philosophie_ II, pp. 904-908.

[142]Cf. Metz, _Sacramentum Mundi_ III, 1234. Critical consciousness is not some idea of class but, as Horkheimer pointed out in connection with critical theory, it is the "totality" which, I would suggest, is heuristically anticipated by the transcendental imperatives of attentiveness, intelligence, rationality, and responsibility. Cf. M. Horkheimer, "Traditionelle und kritische Theorie" in _Kritische Theorie der Gesellschaft_ II, pp. 137-191; and Lonergan, _Insight_, pp. 267-270, 348, 639-641, 684-686.

particular programs of change.[143]

Fifthly, how Metz understands the appropriation and articulation of theologically critical consciousness is first of all determined by his understanding of the basic dialectic operative in all spheres of contemporary theory-praxis. That dialectic is the dialectic of the Enlightenment, not in the sense of an unhistorical reproduction of Enlightenment positions and counterpositions, but in the sense of the fundamentally new possibilities of freedom on the one hand, and the enormous threats to human freedom and dignity on the other.[144] The dialectic of the Enlightenment might be characterized as a contradiction between goal and method. The goal was autonomous, free, mature rationality; but the method was increasingly dominated by empirical forms of research which identified rationality with manipulative techque.[145] The growing success of the natural sciences became identified with progress in general, and a scientistic identification of knowing with the procedures of the natural sciences began. Quantification became the canon of exactitude, and the autonomy of the rationally critical subject rapidly was transformed into the anonymity of intensified specialization as theory and technique were put at the service (en-slaved) of industrialization.[146]

---

[143]Cf. Metz's reservations on a theology of revolution, E. Feil and R. Weth, op. cit., pp. ix-x, 112; and H. Peukert, op. cit., pp. 280-282. On the limitations of "practical" common sense, cf. J. Habermas, Technik und Wissenschaft als "Ideologie", pp. 112-113.

[144]Cf. M. Horkheimer and T. Adorno, Dialektic der Aufklärung, esp. pp. ix-x, 1-49; also Metz's article in Kirche im Prozess der Aufklärung, pp. 53-90.

[145]Horkheimer and Adorno, op. cit., p. 36: "...finally it would appear that the transcendental subject of knowledge as the last remembrance of subjectivity itself has been done away with and replaced by the even smoother operations of self-activated mechanisms in our industrialized social order." Cf. also A. Wellmer, Kritische Gesellschaftstheorie und Positivismus, pp. 128-148.

[146]Cf. Horkheimer and Adorno, op. cit., pp. 3, 11, 13, 31-33, where the authors indicate the tendency of the Enlightenment's dialectic as one to human destruction because of the objectivistic quantification as canon of reason.

The critique which the Enlightenment had performed on the systems of belief and value in pre-Enlightenment societies became internalized within industrial society. The apodictic certitude of the mathematico-mechanical methods gradually dispensed with an intelligent discussion of long range goals or purposefulness. Objectivity absorbed subjectivity. Pragmatic utility replaced morality. Technique seemed more appropriate than praxis as theory approximated calculation. While religion was relegated to the free choice of private individuals whose individuality seemed ever more unenlightened and irrational, ecclesial institutions were left with the alternative of either a paleomorphic "orthodox" rejection of, or a neomorphic "liberal" accommodation to, modernity.[147]

What has been the dialectical consequence of this process? If the dialectic of the Enlightenment can be found in the contradiction between its goal and its method, with the gradual usurpation of the former into the latter, then the consequence has been a general disintegration of the unity of identity and non-identity. Thus the apparent dilemma of ecclesial institutions confronted with either a sectarian non-identity with the contemporary situation or a liberal accommodated identity with it is by no means an isolated phenomenon. We have already seen how historicality philosophies sought to articulate a realm of historical subjectivity with methods non-identical with those methods sustaining modern science and technology. Indeed, with the advance of the latter methods, the efforts at mediating historicality and empirical science found in Dilthey and Husserl gave way to more antithetical positions. On the one hand there are Heidegger and Gadamer claiming a complete non-identity between

---

[147]Cf. Ibid., pp. 88-127; also J. Habermas, Philosophisch-politische Profile, pp. 185-199; on the "alternatives" this presented to churches, cf. P. Berger, A Rumor of Angels (New York, 1970), pp. 1-48; and his article "Zur Soziologie kognitiver Minderheiten" in Dialog 2 (1969), pp. 127-132. For Metz's unmasking of this false "alternative" cf. Kirche im Prozess der Aufklärung, pp. 83, 89; Laeyendecker, "The Church as a Cognitive Minority?" in Metz (ed.) Perspectives of a Political Ecclesiology in The New Concilium 66 (1971), pp. 71-81.

historicality and scientificality, and, on the other, contemporary Logical Empiricism and Structuralism claiming an identification of the two to the point of proclaiming the advent
of a post-historical era.[148]

Even the Marxist attempt to reinstate the goal of the
Enlightenment in terms of a fundamental critique of ideology
and alienation found its widespread acceptance through an
objectivistic identification of this goal with a determinis-
tically scientistic interpretation of socio-historical processes in line with positivist methods in science.[149] Hence
one has the practical insignificance with respect to the
expanding advance of science and technology between the socio-
political realities of late Capitalism and established Communism.[150] Late Capitalism tends to stress the non-identity
of historical subjectivity and freedom with the objective
processes of an increasingly technocratic industrialized
society, thereby trivializing freedom to the private sphere
with as little reference to the objective social situation
as the myth of the "free market." Communism, on the other
hand, tends to identify historical subjectivity and freedom
with the attainment of classless society through state ownership of the means of production, thereby determining the
critical normativity of freedom in an objectivistic manner.[151]

---

[148]Cf. G. Bauer, Geschichtlichkeit, Wege und Irrwege
eines Begriffes (Berlin, 1963); G. Brand, Die Lebenswelt, pp.
3-55, 135-137; on linguistic analysis, cf. criticisms by
Marcuse in One-Dimensional Man, pp. 170-199; on structuralism,
cf. A. Schmidt, "Der strukturalistische   Angriff auf die
Geschichte," in Beiträge zur marxistischen Erkenntnistheorie,
pp. 194-265. For a general account of this tendency, cf. R.
Seidenberg, Post-Historic Man (Boston, 1957).

[149]Cf. A. Wellmer, "Der heimliche Positivismus der
Marxschen Geschichtsphilosophie" in his Kritische Gesellschaftstheorie und Positivismus, pp. 69-127; also D. Böhler,
Metakritik der Marxschen Ideologiekritik, pp. 302-328. Cf.
also H. Fleischer, Marxismus und Geschichte, pp. 128-169 for
a more positive interpretation of Marx's position.

[150]Cf. Adorno, "Spätkapitalismus oder Industriegesell-
schaft?" in his Aufsätze zur Gesellschaftstheorie und
Methodologie, pp. 149-166. Also J. Galbraith, The New
Industrial State (Boston, 1967).

[151]Cf. N. Birnbaum, Toward a Critical Sociology, pp.
94-129, 367-392; and R. Garaudy, Die grosse Wende des

A monopoly controlled state or a state controlled monopoly is the cynical choice left when a quantified objectivity sublates subjectivity.

It is within this context of the dialectic of the Enlightenment and its consequences that political theology has called for a new relationship of (1) of religious freedom and ecclesial authority, (2) of morality to politics, (3) of goals, purposes and interests to scientific and technological performance.[152] The appropriation and articulation of critical consciousness, then, does not seek a restoration of any pre-Enlightenment identification between religion and society, morality and politics, philosophical speculation and science. Nor does such an appropriation identify itself with the tendency of the Enlightenment to further a non-identity between critical freedom and traditional authority, between morality and politics, between reflection on goals and scientific procedures. For, as I have already indicated, such a non-identity leads to a type of dialectical absorption or identification which results in an objectivistic reduction of goals into manipulative methods, or moral responsibility into political expediency, while freedom, set simply in opposition to historical tradition, all too easily has become a totalitarianism of tolerance.[153]

In the sixth place, and finally, therefore, it seems

Sozialismus (Wien, 1970); and J. Galbraith, The New Industrial State, pp. 325-406.

[152] Cf. Metz, Kirche im Prozess der Aufklärung, pp. 53-90; Metz, "The Future in the Memory of Suffering," in Concilium 76 (1972), pp. 9-25; and Metz in Die Theologie in der inter-disziplinären Forschung, pp. 10-25.

[153] Thus it is within the perspective of ecclesial community that Metz can avoid the criticism by Rohrmoser of Habermas' program of Enlightenment as a "Reproduktion des Bestehenden." For Metz sees in such a community the answer to Rohrmoser's questions: "But how should one imagine Enlightenment in a society, of which it is said that it has no interest at all in any emancipatory enlightenment about itself? How should one imagine a hoped for enlightenment through non-violent dialogue in that dimension of society affected by such a repressed interest?" in Rohrmoser, Das Elend der kritischen Theorie, p. 101. On the non-identity in the dialectic of the Enlightenment, cf. notes 144-146.

50

to me that political theology as committed not only to a
critical mediation of the past into the present, but also of
the present into the future, is by that very fact involved
in an appropriation of critical consciousness itself in such
a way that this will require a new methodological appropriation of the unity of identity and non-identity. This
appropriation will concretely function in Metz's program
for interdisciplinary collaboration between the sciences
and theology.[154] This program has anticipations which are
both heuristic and critical. Four of them seem especially
relevant to the present discussion.

In the first place, there can be no restriction of
knowledge to the paradigm of science, let alone the natural
sciences.[155] A methodological appropriation of the unity
of identity and non-identity will, therefore, mean that
method cannot be scientistically identified with scientific
theory-technique, but must be capable of elucidating all
forms of human performance. This means that its appropriation
of critical consciousness is differentiated from, yet operative in, the narrative world of common sense and the reflective world of science.[156] In the second place, even within
science the forms of knowing which are concerned with the
control and domination of nature must be correlated (and so
relativized) with a methodical interest in other forms of
knowing, such as the hermeneutical and dialectical.[157]

---

[154]Cf. W. Oelmüller, "Philosophische Überlegungen zu
den Bedingungen eines interdisziplinären Gesprachs mit der
Theologie," in Theologie in der interdisziplinären Forschung,
pp. 93-99.

[155]There are several aspects to this. First, there
are inherent limitations on any systematic knowledge, cf.
the dialectic of Enlightenment section in Chapter Two. Second,
these very limitations imply the need to correlate science
with other modes of knowing, cf. Metz, Theologie in der
interdisziplinären Forschung, pp. 16-17.

[156]Cf. Chapter Two, pp. 156ff.; Chapter Three, pp.
256-260, 431ff.

[157]Cf. Metz, Theologie in der interdisziplinären
Forschung, pp. 17-19; also T. Rendtorff, "Was hiesst
'interdisziplinäre Arbeit' fur die Theologie?" in ibid.,
pp. 52-54. On the methodological implications, cf. H.

Methodologically this implies that there must be an explication of the unity in difference between these various forms
of knowing so that the critique of scientism would not just
be a rear-guard action seeking to preserve certain privileged
areas from the incursion of scientific methods, but rather
an effort to show that scientism itself (or any appeal to
manipulative methods as the paradigm of knowing) cannot
adequately account for the performance of even the natural
sciences themselves. This means a methodological foundation
must be found which is not posited on the separation of the
natural and human sciences but can differentiate and
interrelate them. [158]

In the third place, any metascientific discussion of
the role of theology in interdisciplinary collaboration
raises the question of the universality of theology. But,
as Metz has pointed out, the problems of universality are
inherent in any metascientific discussion. [159] A methodological appropriation of the unity of identity and non-identity
would remove the danger of either a positivist identification
of some universal method with particular methods of the
natural sciences, or an idealist identification of universality with particular hermeneutical traditions; it would
simultaneously avoid the various forms of skepticism which -
in the guise of historicism and relativism - would universalize non-identity to the point of rejecting the very
possibility of any future consensus on true meaning and
value. Only an approach to universality that incorporates
both identity and non-identity can be true to the "known
unknown" of a universal viewpoint. [160]

Finally, the critical anticipations of interdisciplinary

Peukert's article, "Zur Frage einer 'Logik der interdisziplinären Forschung'" in ibid., pp. 65-71; also   the section
on the dialectic of Enlightenment and collaboration in the
following Chapter.

   [158]Chapter Two, pp. 156-208 and references given there.

   [159]Cf. Metz, T.i.F., pp. 21-22, 93-99 and the references
given there.

   [160]Cf. Lonergan, Insight, pp. 531-534, 546-549.

collaboration do presuppose a multi-dimensional approach to method. For, as Metz is careful to emphasize, such collaboration seeks to avoid any canonization of particular paradigms of knowing or methods while also recognizing the imperatives of truth.[161] In this sense the methodological appropriation of the unity of identity and non-identity involves a heuristic openness to all particular methods, which openness is at the same time capable of dialectical criticism.

It seems to me that these six points touch on the main elements involved in a truly critical mediation of both the past into the present and the present into the future. As long as theology depended chiefly upon the historical-critical methods for its scientific self-understanding, it did not need to concern itself with those forces in contemporary society which were involved in transforming social praxis from the present into the future. Tradition and the Christian memory were viewed in an objectivistic manner insofar as they were susceptible of historical-critical analysis, while the preunderstanding and lived experience sustaining the truth of those traditions and memories were privatized or ontologized, i.e., they were effectively removed from the sphere of critical consciousness. This was true not only of the fideomorphic but also the criticomorphic theologies.

Metz, in insisting upon the subversive power of christian tradition and memory in the present praxis as eschatological, is attempting to explicate precisely how the _memoria_, as operative in the present, can be understood only within the horizon of critical consciousness itself. The methodical exigence must, therefore, arise within this exigency for critique. For it is only in this way that the methodological aspects of political theology will contribute to a dialogue with those methods of contemporary scientific and philosophical thought and action aimed at securing man a worthwhile future in our contemporary technological society. Obviously there are many aspects of political theology which are more immediately relevant to the problems facing social and

---

[161]Cf. Metz, _T.i.F._, pp. 14, 18.

ecclesial institutions today. Critical consciousness cannot only be concerned with its own foundations but must also seek to enlighten particular instances of contemporary theory-praxis.

Nevertheless, my purpose in this Chapter was to point out how these more immediate concerns of political theology - with, e.g., ecclesial authority, ecumenism, the meaning of christian dogmas, a narrative soteriology, etc. - are within the context of more fundamentally methodological interests in the critical responsibility for the future of man in a world increasingly dominated by science and technology, and how these interests are now being channeled into the context of methods capable of furthering interdisciplinary collaboration between theology and the sciences. Unless one is aware of the shift which has occurred on this level in political theology, viz., the attempt to provide a critical mediation not only from the past into the present (as the critico-morphic theologies tried) but also from the present into the future, one would fail to do justice to political theology as fundamental theology.[162]

CONCLUSIONS

The aim of this Chapter has been twofold. First, to locate political theology within a typology of forms of theologizing. Then it attempted to outline the main elements in the approach of political theology to contemporary problems

_____

[162]Cf. Metz in Sacramentum Mundi III, 1234, n. 2: "In this way political theology is not the name of a new theological discipline among others, with its own parti-cularized field of investigation. It is not just an 'applied theology,' e.g., theology applied to public opinion and politics. Nor is it simply identical with what has been called 'political ethics' within theology; nor can it be identified with the praiseworthy currents of a Social Theology, as the latter was articulated, for example, in the Social Gospel movement. For political theology appropriates a fundamental characteristic in the elaboration of theologi-cally critical consciousness itself, as that is determined by a new relationship of theory-praxis, according to which any theology by its very nature must be a 'practical' performance-oriented theology."

of relating history and method. The typology itself indicates
how a methodological approach towards history is possible
insofar as the typology is dialectical, meta-contextual,
critically orientated toward praxis, and is both diachronic
and synchronic. Insofar as it more or less adequately outlined contemporary ways or methods of doing theology, it
provided the context for understanding how political theology
involves a shift in the self-understanding of theology. For
it showed how political theology is not dependent upon the
historical-critical methods and historicality philosophies
for its basic methodology. Thus it was especially interested
in discussing the similarities and differences between the
criticomorphic theologies and the politicomorphic as represented by the theology of Metz.

It is within this theological context that the following
study of Dilthey's critique of historical reason and Lonergan's metamethodology will be situated. I hope that this
dialectical presentation of their positions will provide an
approach to method and history capable of answering some of
the key questions raised by political theology. How is
the unity of identity and non-identity to be concretely
understood? Can this be related to the dialectic of the
Enlightenment? How can the dimension of common sense meaning
operative in narrative be dynamically related to the theoretical dimension of analysis and science? How does the exigence
for method arise from the exigence for critique? Can the unity
of identity and non-identity be properly related to intellectual, moral, and religious praxis? Is it possible to have an
approach to method which would be both open to the multiplicity of particular methods and simultaneously critical?

CHAPTER TWO

HISTORY AND METHOD WITHIN THE DIALECTIC

OF THE

ENLIGHTENMENT

> The sovereignty of modern
> historical consciousness has
> receded before a new dogmatism
> which turns its back on history
> only to plunge once again into
> the caverns of uncritical
> opinions. These had engulfed
> philosophical thought for
> centuries. Indeed, philosophy
> had only recently begun to free
> itself from them. In order to
> break through such dogmatism,
> other conceptual categories
> are needed than those used in
> Dilthey's critique of historical
> reason. Yet recalling his
> critique can be instructive in
> our efforts to keep alive the
> historical imagination of
> humankind in the face of the
> present threat of a coming
> "post-historical" era, which
> seeks its legitimacy through a
> denial of its own past history.
>
> Manfred Riedel

C H A P T E R   T W O

INTRODUCTION

In the Introduction it was stated that the present
work addresses three questions to the writings of Dilthey
and Lonergan within the context of political theology. The
first question asked how each developed a metascientific
methodology capable of providing adequate alternatives to the
scientistic claim to be the sole representative of methodological matters. Having established the context of political
theology within a typology of contemporary theologies, it
is now time to address ourselves to that question.

The first section explores the relevance of the thought
of Dilthey and Lonergan to the problematic of history and
method in political theology. The second section goes on to
articulate how the dialectic of the Enlightenment implies a
need for interdisciplinary collaboration. In order to better
understand the foundations upon which such a collaboration
must be built, the third section shows how Dilthey's analysis
of the pathos of the Enlightenment led from a pre-Enlightenment
dependence upon metaphysics to its critique and his own
efforts to elaborate a cognitional theory able to do justice
to the reality of the human cultural and historical sciences.
The fourth and final section then shows how Lonergan has
provided a shift from an individualist cognitional theory to
a metascientific methodology, the exigencies of which are
able to critically interrelate the many contemporary efforts
at articulating a metascientific methodology.

THE RELEVANCE OF DILTHEY AND LONERGAN
TO THE PROBLEMATIC OF POLITICAL THEOLOGY

Within the perspectives of the above outlined methodological presuppositions there seem to be four main areas or

problem-complexes where the present study is relevant to a
foundational reflection on political theology. Those four
are: (1) overcoming the basic dichotomy in historicality
by empirically and critically grounding transcendental
reflection; (2) elaborating a notion of the unity of identity
and non-identity which is methodologically significant;
(3) thereby offering a viable alternative to the Cartesian
interpretation of science and method; (4) providing a real
possibility of articulating the foundations of theology in
a future-orientated present praxis capable of integrating
a critical mediation both from the past into the present and
from the present into the future. I should like to discuss
each of these points briefly.

1. Transcendental Reflection as Empirical and Critical

We have seen how the inability of historicality philosophies to come up with an adequate basis for a critical mediation from the present into the future was due in large part
to their at least implicit reception of the Kantian phenomenon-
noumenon dichotomy. Within the context of Kant's transcendental philosophy, as expressed in his three Critiques, this
dichotomy accounted for the split between regulative and
constitutive principles, between phenomenal necessity and
noumenal freedom, and led Kant to postulate an "intuitus
originarius" or "intellectus archetypus" of God to assure
that the phenomenal effects of a noumenal subject acting in
accordance with the categorical imperative would truly contribute toward the progress of good in history.[1] Yet, as
recent studies have shown, Kant's own more concretely orientated socio-critical writings were not integrated with his
transcendental philosophy.[2] Historicality philosophies, in
drawing upon the transcendental philosophy of Kant,[3] were

---

[1]Cf. Kant's Kritik der Urteilskraft, paragraph 77;
also K. Weyend, Kants Geschichtsphilosophie, pp. 172-185, esp.
pp. 178ff.; also Löwith, Gott, Mensch, und Welt, pp. 70-88.

[2]Cf. W. Oelmüller, Die unbefriedigte Aufklärung, pp.
103-113; and also his "Kants Beitrag zur Grundlegung einer
praktischen Philosophie in der Moderne," Philos. Jahrbuch 75
(1967) pp. 22-55.

[3]This is not the place to enter into the complex

unable to mediate their own thematizations of historicality
with the concrete socio-historical praxis of individuals and
societies. The dimension of memorative narration or story
was disjuncted from reflection and argument.[4] Historical
reason was, so to speak, bifurcated inasmuch as it could not
adequately interrelate its transcendental analysis of historical freedom and subjectivity with the empirical historical-
critical methods. For, as long as the transcendental aspects
of those philosophies suffered from the growing "Diskrepanz
zwischen dem, was angeblich a priori ermittelt wird, und dem,
was sich in der geistig-wissenschaftlichen und gesellschaftlich-
politischen Wirklichkeit der Moderne ausgebildet hat,"[5] there
was no way in which they could empirically and critically
elaborate the heuristic operations of historical subjectivity
in its future-constituting praxis in the present. Metz has,
therefore, rightly called attention to the unfruitfulness of
the reception of Kant's transcendental philosophy, especially
his Critique of Pure Reason, among theologians.[6]

Certainly, if political theology could only turn to the
type of transcendental reflection found in Kant and the
historicality philosophies, then its concern with appropriating critical consciousness would necessarily involve the
rejection of any "Entwurf von Wissenschaft...der im Sinne
der Transzendentalphilosophie beansprucht, Fundamental-
philosophie zu sein."[7] But such a rejection of a Kantian or

---

influence of Kant on the philosophies of historicality. On
the insufficiencies in Kant's position relative to histori-
cality cf. Adorno, Negative Dialektik, pp. 281-292 ; also
R. Garaudy, Gott ist Tot, pp. 128-148; L. Landgrebe, "Die
Geschichte im Denken Kants," in his Phänomenologie und Ge-
schichte, pp. 46-64; and in relation to Heidegger, K. Huch,
Philosophiegeschichtliche Voraussetzungen der Heideggerschen
Ontologie, and H. Declève, Heidegger et Kant (Hague, 1970).

[4]Cf. Metz, "Erlösung und Emanzipation," Stimmen der
Zeit (März, 1973), pp. 171-184.

[5]W. Oelmüller, Die unbefriedigte Aufklärung, pp. 108f.

[6]Cf. Metz in Kirche in Prozess der Aufklärung, pp. 62-
63. Cf. also C. Wild, "Die Funktion des Geschichtsbegriffs
im politischen Denken Kants," in Philos. Jahrbuch 77 (1970),
pp. 260-275.

[7]Oelmüller, Die unbefriedigte Aufklärung, p. 109.

Idealist position must not itself slip into an objectivistic neglect of subjectivity which would belittle or even negate the possibility of historically transcending the structural functionalisms of naturalist, positivist, or historicist determinisms.[8] Such a neglect of subjectivity would surrender reflection to the conceptualist aridity of argumentative logic, severing thought from the sources of story and narrative.[9]

For instance, D. Böhler has tellingly criticized Marx's critique of ideology for its neglect of an adequate reflection on the conditions of its own possibility. Böhler has indicated how such a neglect springs from an implicit acceptance on the part of Marx of the classical dichotomy between theory and praxis. In order to develop a truly heuristic critique capable of application to changing concrete situations, Böhler has found it necessary to develop the complementarity between concrete situational criticisms and the type of transcendental reflection found in Karl-Otto Apel and Jürgen Habermas. For only in this way does he see the possibility of overcoming the dogmatism and objectivism of Marx's critique, and of meeting the need for a new and really critical mediation of theory and praxis.

"Transcendental" reflection would distance the critic of ideology from his contextual analysis of a situation by reminding him of the condition of the possibility of that analysis: his own subjective engagement in a situation. By reason of its

---

[8]Cf. Habermas, Erkenntnis und Interesse, pp. 88-92; K. Huch, "Interesse an Emanzipation," in Neue Rundschau 80 (1969), pp. 534-548. Notice how Habermas has recalled the reflection proper to cognitional theory in order to articulate a critical foundation against the scientistic methodology of positivism and the uncritical ontology of existentialism. For it is only in the praxis of this reflection that one would be able to avoid unreflected appeals to praxis, on the one hand, and on the other an ivory tower speculation either in terms of empiricist methodology or in those of abstract ontologies.

[9]This is the advantage, as will be seen later in this Chapter, of Lonergan's method. Its effective critique of conceptualism aims at revealing the subjectivity operative in both the common sense world (story) and the world of theory (logic, argument).

60

"subjectively" engaged character, any situational
analysis (along with its implicit emancipatory
"project") cannot claim a self-assured, solipsistic,
universal validity. Rather, it must gain an intersubjective validity through dialogue with possibly
competing situational analyses.... Thereby "transcendental" reflection offers itself as an instance
of possible de-dogmatizing in general, and as the
condition of the possibility of an undogmatic critique
of ideology in particular. Such a reflective mentality,
which applies a distancing and de-dogmatizing, is
excluded by the objectivist cognitive attitude of
dialectical materialism's critique of ideology. For
this reason, Marx's "critique" tends from its very
beginning towards dogmatism.[10]

The danger of absolutizing the relative and situational
can only be counteracted by some recognition of transcendence.
It is not surprising that both Metz and Moltmann have called
attention to a relation between future and transcendence,
even if they have not elaborated the methodological implications this relation has in regard to reflection.[11] Metz has
indicated the concealment of the future in the Kantian
transcendentalist position,[12] from which one might conclude
that if a transcendental reflection is going to explicate
the conditions of the possibility of a critical mediation from
the past into the present and the present into the future,
then such reflection cannot be noumenally disjuncted from a

---

[10]D. Böhler, Metakritik der Marxschen Ideologiekritik,
pp. 94-96. It is the oversight of this dimension which is
all too obvious in some of the criticisms of the Frankfurt
School on the part of more orthodox Marxists; cf. esp. "Der
Begriff des Transzendentalen bei J. Habermas," by K. Schrader-
Klebert, in Soziale Welt (1968), pp. 342-359; and Die
"Frankfurter Schule" im Lichte des Marxismus (Frankfurt,
1970), pp. 70-89.

[11]Cf. Metz, "Der zukunftige Mensch und der kommende
Gott," in Wer ist das eigentlich Gott?, pp. 260-275; also his
Grundlagen des Glaubensverstandnisses: Der Glaube und das
Ende der Metaphysik (Manuscript form of his lectures during
the winter semester 1967-1968), pp. 165-179. Also J. Moltmann
Theologie der Hoffnung, pp. 38-43, 210-275.

[12]Cf. Zur Theologie der Welt, pp. 89-91. Cf. Bloch's
notion of "noch nicht-Bewusstsein" as a transcendence without
a Transcendent, Das Prinzip Hoffnung I, 129-203. Notice
how the heuristic character of Lonergan's meta-method in
no way presupposes a Kantian appeal to God in the mediation
of subject and object.

truly empirically verifiable openness to the future. Such
empirical verification of openness would be factually contra-
factual, i.e., it would be verified in the factually ongoing
efforts at understanding and improving one's individual,
interpersonal, and social situations and, insofar as the
heuristic anticipations of such understanding and improvement
contradict the present situation, it would be contra-factual.
This implies that transcendental reflection is not beyond
experience or criticism, that its grounds are not noumenally
unknowable, that such reflection does not reveal some absolute starting point or foundation but the conditions regulating _and_ positively or negatively constituting the socio-
historical process.

Within this context of seeking to interrelate the
heuristic of transcendental reflection with empirical and
critical methods a confrontation of Dilthey and Lonergan
is certainly not out of place. Both thinkers offer novel
approaches to the problems posed by Kant and by the need
to relate experience and criticism to new forms of transcendental reflection. Recent studies on Dilthey, especially
those which draw on his as yet unpublished notes for the
continuation of his _Einleitung in die Geisteswissenschaften_,
indicate how he rejected the Kantian dichotomy between
phenomena and noumena, at least as regards the human sciences,
and how, in his projected critique of historical reason, he
essayed an approach to socio-historical realities which sought
to overcome the rigid and abstract _a priori_ approach of
Kant.[13] In general one might say that the Kantian (and neo-
Kantian) categories were too static and abstract, that its
ideal of theory was too dependent on Newtonian science and
Euclidean mathematics, and that the distinction between pure
and practical reason too much a function of the thing-in-
itself, for a Kantian transcendental method to do justice to
historical and social processes.[14] However, Dilthey did

---

[13]Cf. P. Krausser, _Kritik der endlichen Vernunft_; also
M. Riedel, "Das Erkenntniskritische Motiv in Diltheys
Theorie der Geisteswissenschaften," in _Hermeneutik und
Dialektik_ I, pp. 233-255.

[14]Cf. Krausser, _op. cit._, pp. 223-225; M. Riedel,

not succeed in adequately relating his critique of historical reason, centered on _Verstehen_, with scientific reason as that was developing in the natural sciences, so that, while he criticized scientism, his critical position did not really mediate that criticism to modern science. Hence the criticism of an obscurantism - an arbitrary limitation imposed on empirical inquiry - in Dilthey leveled by those who have claimed, with some justification, that understanding is not the sole prerogative of human studies.[15]

Lonergan, on the other hand, has come up with such a novel version of transcendental method that the present writer has found it advisable to refer to it with the less philosophically loaded expression of meta-method.[16] F. Crowe has mentioned how if Lonergan's "_Insight_ could be defined with

_____

"Einleitung" in the "Theorie Ausgabe" of Dilthey's _Der Aufbau der geschichtlichen Welt in den Geisteswissenschaften_ Frankfurt, 1970), pp. 27-30, 46-52.

[15]Cf. W. Stegmüller, _Probleme und Resultate der Wissenschaftstheorie_ I, pp. 360-375; H. Albert, _Plädoyer für kritischen Rationalismus_, pp. 127-132 where Albert admits the possibility of elaborating a technique of interpretation in Dilthey but overlooks Dilthey's differentiation of outer and inner experience; as the differentiation applies to Habermas' differentiation of interests, cf. H. Albert, _Der Positivismusstreit in der deutschen Soziologie_, pp. 201-205; D. Böhler, "Das Problem des emanzipatorischen Interesses und seiner gesellschaftlichen Wahrnehmung," _Man and World_ 3 (1970), pp. 31-33; N. Lobkowicz, "Interesse und Objectivität," _Philos. Rundschau_ 16 (1969), pp. 263ff.; G. Radnitzky, _Contemporary Schools of Metascience_ II, pp. 12-15.

[16]There are major differences between Lonergan's understanding of transcendental method and the various traditions in Germany associated with _Transzendental-philosophie_. For his differences from Kant, cf. G. Sala, _Das Apriori in der menschlichen Erkenntnis: Eine Studie über Kants Kritik der reinen Vernunft und Lonergans Insight_ (Meisenheim, 1972); for his differences from Husserl, cf. W. Ryan, _Intentionality in E. Husserl and B. Lonergan_ (Louvain, Doctoral Diss., 1972); also the reference in E. Tugendhat, _Der Wahrheitsbegriff bei Husserl und Heidegger_ (Berlin, 1970), pp. 252-255. Of equal significance is the difference between meta-method and the transcendental Thomist trend initiated by Maréchal. On the difference, cf. G. Sala, "Seinserfahrung und Seinshorizont," _Zeitschrift für kath. Theol._ 89 (1967), pp. 294-338; Lonergan, _M.i.T._, pp. 13-14, note 4.

respect to Kant as a correction and completion of his work, so the new phase [of Lonergan's writing] can best be defined with respect to Dilthey."[17] More importantly, in the measure that Lonergan was able to radically correct the Kantian program of transcendental method, to that extent he would also avoid any charge of obscurantism in seeking to relate his transcendental method with the many methods operative in natural and human sciences.[18] For Lonergan's meta-method decisively moves beyond the dichotomies associated with either a scientistic objectivism (as in Logical Positivism or Structuralism) or that abstract subjectivism associated with an Erkenntnistheorie, Epoche, Erkenntnismetaphysik or Fundamentalontologie. The key to meta-method lies in its very cogently formulated invitation to a self-appropriation of the praxis of human understanding and performance in all spheres of human activity whatever they might be. Lonergan, then, could not accept a half-hearted critique of Kantianism; he does not offer a theory of understanding relevant only to certain fields of human experience; there can be no appeal to any noumenal realm totally beyond the ken of inquiry.[19] Nor does he accomplish this by invoking some type of Hegelian absolute knowledge. The key, once again, is self-appropriation which involves not only what factually is (e.g., all the manifold concrete situations resulting from equally diverse social, political, philosophical, scientific, aesthetic, etc., traditions) but also within these factual situations uncovers certain dynamically related and recurrent operations of human historical subjectivity capable of grounding a critical evaluation of those situations.

---

[17] Cf. Spirit as Inquiry, p. 26.

[18] Thus Lonergan derives his preliminary notion of method from consideration of the natural sciences; cf. M.i.T., pp. 3-6; and Insight, pp. 3-172, where Lonergan analyzes certain problems in physics to illustrate the activity of understanding.

[19] Insofar as Lonergan does not approach the subject in a theoretical or conceptual manner he can incorporate the "known-unknown" aspect of the noumenal that effectively checks any tendency toward an identity thought-pattern. Cf. Insight, pp. 531-535.

2. Unity of Identity and Non-Identity

This leads into the second area of possible contributions to political theology, viz., a methodological elaboration of the unity of identity and non-identity. Such a unity is operative in political theology in several manners, e.g., the eschatological Kingdom is both immanent in the future and non-identical with it, determinate negation asymtotically identifies truth and value through the determination of concrete instances of non-identity, the Church can preserve her identity only through sublation of that identity in the Kingdom, fidelity to tradition demands changing that tradition, the "Parteilichkeit" of the Church is her identification with those not identifiable with the establishment, etc.[20] The observant reader will have noticed how a similar unity is operative in the mediation of theory and praxis: there is an identity insofar as there is a praxis of theory and a theory of praxis, but also a non-identity insofar as praxis is not totally "theoretizierbar" and theory is not immediately practical. Likewise, transcendence is identified with experience's own going beyond (or non-identity with) itself; the critical presence of the future in the present is the openness of the present to the radically new.

The appropriation of the truth in the narrative-memorative experience is essential to critical rationality yet non-identified with it. The non-identity of the concrete history of suffering unmasks the abstract totalizing of liberal capitalist, positivist and marxist schemes of emancipation, yet this non-identity can be identified within the mystery of Christ and the Church.

Now, if there were no unity operative in these relations between identity and non-identity, Metz would be dealing with paradox rather than dialectics; he would succumb to his own criticism of Barthian theology as paradoxical rather than truly dialectical.[21] Metz's own formulation of the instances of

---

[20] Cf. Metz, Zur Theologie der Welt, pp. 75-89, 99-116; Reform und Gegenreformation Heute, pp. 13-32, 34-38; Kirche im Prozess der Aufklärung, pp. 80-90, 70-73; Diskussion zur politischen Theologie, pp. 268-301.

[21] Cf. Sacramentum Mundi III, 1239.

identity and non-identity, however, involves an implicit definition of one by the other and so a unitary relationship between them.[22]

How can this unity be determined with due justice to both identity and non-identity? Methodologically one needs to avoid both a scientistic identification of the ideal of knowing with the methods of the natural sciences and any obscurantist privatizing or ontologizing of historicality which would assume methods of reflection on man's socio-historical reality non-identical with other modes of scienti-fic inquiry. What is this evasive unity of identity and non-identity? How could it methodologically function to facili-tate the type of broad interdisciplinary collaboration between the sciences, philosophies and theologies envisaged by political theology? How can memory and narrative be dynami-cally related to critique and argument? There are many options open to political theology in choosing the horizon within which to thematize the unity. The formulation of the dialectical framework of Metz's thought owes much to the Idealist and Marxist traditions, as these traditions have been criticized and applied by E. Bloch, T. Adorno, M. Horkheimer, and J. Habermas.[23] If I have used the unity of identity and non-identity to formulate the dialectic operative in political theology, it is no less evident that in Metz's own articulation of the concrete dialectics operative in society and church, as well as science and thought, he is not concerned with some abstract "Verharmlosung" of the dialectic.

---

[22]On implicit definition, cf. Lonergan, Insight, pp. 12-13, 392, 491f. There is, then, a set of internal relations where the reality of the relation is not distinct from the reality of its terms (cf. ibid., pp. 492ff.). B. Ollman has shown how this approach was central to Marx's social thought; cf. Alienation, pp. 27-43 on Marx's philosophy as one of internal relations, and Metz has adopted this general orientation. On the unity of identity and non-identity in Marx's dialectic, cf. Ollman, op. cit., pp. 52-71.

[23]These philosophical roots of political theology are yet to be adequately articulated; cf. Diskussion zur politi-schen Theologie, pp. 185-216. Metz does, however, mention his indebtedness to Hegel, Marx, Bloch, and the Frankfurt School often; cf. Sacramentum Mundi III, pp. 1232-1240.

There is, however, a common problem for both Metz and, e.g., Habermas, in their (admittedly divergent) receptions and criticisms of Hegel and Marx in relation to the unity of identity and non-identity.

We have seen how historicality philosophies were influenced by the Kantian phenomenon-noumenon dichotomy and how this led to an inability to critically mediate the present into the future. Moreover, this was also related to their failure to adequately mediate a transcendental reflection with empirical methods. The two failures are intimately connected insofar as the latter failure made it theoretically and practically difficult for such philosophies to articulate heuristic anticipations from present praxis which would allow for a critical mediation into the future.[24] A good argument could be made for the extension of the Kantian dichotomy throughout Idealism. Despite Fichte and Schelling's efforts to overcome it through intellectual intuition and Hegel's attempt to correlate the latter with a phenomenologically empirical progression of mind in history, dialectic in Idealism remained under the aegis of a noumenal skepticism.[25] Hegel's "cunning of reason" and self-realization of World Spirit in history prefigured the emphasis on historicality constituting man rather than man constituting history.[26] Marx's sublation of (Idealist) philosophy in revolutionary praxis was an affirmation of man's ability to constitute history, but, as recent studies show, this affirmation was

---

[24]Cf. Chapter One, pp. 30-52. On Hegel, cf. M. Riedel, Theorie und Praxis in Denken Hegels, pp. 204-215; M. Theunissen, Hegels Lehre vom absoluten Geist als theologisch-politischer Traktat, pp. 387-419, 439-440. On the need for a heuristic grounding of theological statements; cf. G. Sauter, Vor einem neuen Methodenstreit in der Theologie?, pp. 63-70.

[25]Cf. W. Becker, Hegels Begriff der Dialektik und das Prinzip des Idealismus, pp. 66-85.

[26]Cf. Adorno, Negative Dialectik, pp. 315-329; Löwith, Von Hegel zu Nietzsche, pp. 227-229, 232-237; M. Theunissen, Hegels Lehre vom absoluten Geist, pp. 60-76; Habermas, Erkenntnis und Interesse, pp. 36-59; F. Schmidt, "Hegel in der Kritischen Theorie der Frankfurter Schule," in O. Negt (ed.) Aktualität und Folgen der Philosophie Hegels, pp. 17-57. Also Ollman, op. cit., pp. 36-37, 119-120.

clouded by a latent positivism and "geschichtsontologischer Objectivismus."[27] Indeed, one could argue that just as in Hegel the skeptical non-identity of self-consciousness with the Absolute led in practice to Hegel's allowing the Prussian monarchy what he did not allow God, so Marx in transposing the unconditionality of the Absolute to the socio-historical and empirically identifiable (setting Hegelianism on its feet) proletariat, minimized those dimensions of consciousness which were not identifiable in terms of work and production, which meant that Marx allowed the relations and forces of production what he did not allow God. By this I mean that he neglected to explicate the subjectivity operative in socio-historical process in the way he had in his critique of religion.[28] Thus Böhler can argue rather convincingly that Marx was as much a prisoner of the classical theory-praxis dichotomy as Hegel, only that he came down on the side of praxis.[29] No wonder, then, that critical theory and political theology, in trying to appropriate the critical consciousness in Hegel and Marx by explicating a new relation of theory-praxis, are accused by some of identifying with

---

[27] Cf. D. Böhler, op. cit., pp. 42-54, 232-250, 328-350, esp. pp. 45f. and p. 248; Wellmer, Kritische Gesellschafts-theorie und Positivismus, pp. 69-127. H. Fleischer's Marxismus und Geschichte offers a less negative judgment in regard to Marx's notion of historical necessity and "objectivity." Yet the type of scientistic objectivism Böhler and Wellmer argue against is all too evident in the Orthodox critique of the Frankfurt School; cf. Die Frankfurter Schule im Lichte des Marxismus, pp. 48-69, 127-132, 134-140.

[28] On Hegel, cf. Theunissen, op. cit., p. 447; on Marx, besides the texts referred to in note 27 above, cf. Adorno, Negative Dialektik, pp. 313-325 where Adorno speaks of "the divinization of history, even by the atheistic Hegelians, Marx and Engel." Also L. Landgrebe, Phänomenologie und Geschichte, pp. 114-134, esp. pp. 124f. It is still too early to adequately assess the impact of K. -H. Ilting's edition and commentary on Hegel's Vorlesungen über Rechts-philsophie: 1818-1831, of which only the first volume has appeared as of this writing.

[29] Cf. Böhler's Metakritik der Marxschen Ideologiekritik, pp. 104-117, 310-328; as Böhler indicates, there was the failure to adequately mediate theory and praxis insofar as praxis, even in Marx, was subsumed under an ultimately objectivistic theory, cf. pp. 320ff.

particular revolutionary groups while they are accused by others of an idealist failure to identify a subject comparable to the proletariat.

This problem such thinkers as Habermas or Metz experience in trying to articulate the unity of identity and non-identity lies in their primarily reflective concern with philosophical issues which are at once profoundly theoretical and fraught with practical implications. Those identified with the Establishment resent their involvement in practical criticism, while those not identified with the Establishment resent their concern with consciousness. To the former they are aiding and abetting anarchy and revolution, to the latter they seem "idealist" and "transcendentalist."[30] The present writer is of the opinion that both of these attitudes miss the real significance of critical theory and political theology in terms of the long range need to thematize the proper relation between theory and praxis in terms of a unity of identity and non-identity. This is not a middle of the road compromise - Metz often quotes Brecht's "Die Wahrheit liegt in der Mitte... begraben!" - but an open-eyed dedication to a rigorous and critical reflection on the presuppositions of changing the established order so that those changes can be promoted consciously and responsibly. This is all the more necessary today, when the complexity of modern society increasingly dominated by scientific technological forces of production have quite literally overwhelmed many critical social theories.[31]

---

[30]A good example of those identified with the Establishment criticizing Metz for implicitly justifying revolutionary tendencies might be found in the articles of the Bavarian Minister of Culture, H. Maier, in Stimmen der Zeit 183 (1969), pp. 73-91, and 185 (1970), pp. 145-171; the criticisms from the left that Metz had failed to concretize the subject adequately and so "idealize" the Church are in K. Derksen and M. Xhauflaire (eds.), Les deux visages de la théologie de la sécularisation, pp. 73-75, and in M. Xhaufflaire, La théologie politique (Paris, 1972). On Habermas, there are the objections institutionalized in the association of German University professors for the freedom of science, on the one hand, and the objections from the left, on the other. Cf. Schrader-Klebert, op. cit., (note 10 above); O. Negt (ed.), Die Linke antwortet J. Habermas (Frankfurt, 1968); J. Habermas, Protestbewegung und Hochschulreform (Frankfurt, 1969).

[31]The key issue here is that science and technology are

A study of Dilthey and Lonergan is a small contribution to the immense task of elaborating that unity of identity and non-identity which could ground the appropriation of critical consciousness and critical action. For both Dilthey and Lonergan have, in different ways, essayed a concrete identification of the unity which would definitively break with the Idealist tradition. Dilthey, for example, was only too aware of the impossible dilemma facing modern man. On the one hand there were the metaphysical systems of identity which had been the bearers of his truth and value systems and could elicit man's undivided assent. But such identity systems, in their very claims to unconditioned acceptance, had always been checked by the non-identity allegiances of the skeptics. Dilthey studied this see-saw alternation of metaphysics and skepticism through history and found it totally inadequate to handle the problems posed to modernity by scientific and historical consciousness. He began to explore a unity which would be beyond a merely theoretical mediation and which could provide an open and ongoing foundation both for the practice of scientific theorizing and socio-historical praxis. This unity he found in inner experience as such. In a sense, he initiated a critique of the foundation of Hegelian dialectic in an absolute self-consciousness. But, as Marxists are quick to point out, Dilthey never succeeded in thematizing this unity in other than an identity fashion.[32] Inner experience as experienced

---

increasingly gaining an independence from economic control and bias, e.g., the pollution problem and the critique against exponential growth in industry are matters forcing the scientific community to assert its own imperatives against the narrower profit interests of business. Cf. D. Meadows (ed.) The Limits of Growth; also A. Touraine, The Post-Industrial Society; N. Birnbaum, The Crisis of Industrial Society, and Toward a Critical Sociology, pp. 393-441; R. Heilbronner, Between Capitalism and Socialism, pp. 3-31, 112-114, 147-164, 259-285; J. Habermas, Technik und Wissenschaft als 'Ideologie', pp. 48-145. There is, then, a need for critical reflection to find means to stem the scientistic monopoly of method if it is to succeed in mediating critical praxis to a society dominated by scientific and technological control centers. Cf. Habermas, Protestbewegung und Hochschulreform, pp. 43ff.

[32] Cf. I. S. Kon, Die Geschichtsphilosophie des 20.

70

70 was a unity for Dilthey which he could not utilize to move from the subject-as-subject to the subject-as-object in a manner that would sublate skepticism. He had, therefore, to leave the methods of the natural sciences outside of his foundational consideration and, failing to offer a critique of Cartesian method and the Kantian dichotomy on that level, found himself in the awkward position of having to hold for the non-identity of historical methods without having adequately thematized a unity. Toward the end of his life he was more and more attracted to Idealism.[33]

Lonergan, on the other hand, has carried through an analysis of the subject which is able to account not only for identity but for non-identity as well.[34] Such a unity can be grasped, he insists, not simply through some transcendental _theory_, but only by the praxis of self-appropriation which elicits an awareness of the subject's own factually contra-factual (insofar as they are alienated by bias) drives toward attentiveness, intelligence, critical rationality, responsibility, and love.[35] For the subject-as-subject is not some Leibnizean monad, not a Cartesian "cogitans me cogitare," not a Kantian transcendentally noumenous

---

Jahrhunderts (Berlin, 1964), pp. 100-108.

[33]Cf. J. -F. Suter, op. cit., pp. 166-171. Hence the qualifications needed in evaluating H.-G. Gadamer's remarks in Wahrheit und Methode, pp. 215ff.

[34]The unity is here interpreted as the subject, identity is then the subject-as-subject and non-identity is the subject-as-object. This is not, therefore, to equate unity with identity - as could be claimed in Idealism - for the subject-as-object is really, and not merely notionally, distinct from the subject-as-subject. But although the distinction is real, one does not end up with an absolute non-identity since the operations of the subject enter into the mediation and/or constitution of the object, i.e., objectivity is self-transcending subjectivity. Cf. Insight, pp. 488ff.; M.i.T., pp. 37f., 265, 292, 338, 179f. This, however, is not an absolute unity since the subject is only virtually unconditioned, i.e., the conditions happen to be fulfilled; cf. J. Habermas, Erkenntnis und Interesse, pp. 44f. on Marx's notion of the unity in the subject; compare with Lonergan, Insight, pp. 336ff.

[35]Cf. Lonergan, Insight, pp. 319-347; M.i.T., pp. 3-25, 53-55, 231ff.

subjectivity nor an Hegelian carrier of absolute knowledge. The subject-as-subject does not correspond to such objectifications insofar as they fail to account for the empirical and heuristic functioning of the subject in its socio-historical development, insofar as they fail to provide an adequate framework within which to meet the further relevant questions and responsible demands for action posed by history.

For Lonergan the subject-as-subject is not some system or theory, not some particular class or group of individuals, not some institution or organization. Yet it includes all these insofar as they have genetically contributed to attentiveness, intelligence, reasonableness, responsibility - or insofar as they have dialectically contributed to inattention, stupidity, irrationality, and irresponsibility. Indeed, Lonergan's approach to the subject is heuristic enough to embrace the entire sweep of human reality, yet it is also normative enough to ground a universal dialectics capable of integrating the many particular dialectics operative in history. This involves, then, both a concrete identification of the subject individually and collectively, and a heuristic non-identification capable of accounting for alienation and ideology as well as for an openness to the future which escapes any complete predictability.

Moreover, in terms of the movement from the subject-as-subject to the subject-as-object, Lonergan makes it abundantly clear that it is no type of transcendental deduction. There is no question of Ursprungsphilosophie. The subject as conscious is not primarily self-conscious but functions within the horizon of the common sense and common nonsense of his particular family, community, national, social, and cultural milieu. With Marx, Lonergan maintains that social life determines consciousness, but, as recent Marx studies also bring out, the possibility of criticism and social change also indicate how consciousness as action can affect and change social life.[36] Social life, meaning social institutions and

---

[36]Cf. H. Fleischer, Marxismus und Geschichte, pp. 51-75, 104-127, 130, 140, 151f. And note how even for Marx, in Habermas' interpretation, the perspective of conceiving the subject under the category of nature still presupposed

orders, is not some force independent of conscious acts of meaning and decision but is the complex resulting from and informed by interlocking sets of such acts as they coalesce into accepted modes of behavior and interests.

The unity, therefore, is defined in reference to the subject, where identity is taken as the subject-as-subject and non-identity as the subject-as-object. The unity cannot be mistaken as an identity, for obviously the subject cannot escape the inherent limitations of concrete historical and social existence. Neither, however, (and this is of the utmost importance due to the objectivistic trend of modern technological culture) can the unity be dispensed with in the name of a total non-identity where the subject would be in the position described by T. Adorno: "Automatically and, indeed, by design subjects are inhibited from knowing themselves as subjects."[37] Objectivism might be defined as the failure to recognize the praxis of the subject in the constitution and mediation of objects. Hence one sees the emphasis in both critical theory and political theology to challenge the spectre of contemporary objectivistic scientism with its scorning neglect of the subject.

Such a thematization of the unity of identity and non-identity is not to overlook the very real differences between critical theory and politcal theology. It is not to seek some half-hearted theological compromise with the dialectic of emancipation, a compromise Metz has warned against.[38] Rather, it is to ferret out those presuppositions and intentions underlying the emergence of the modern and contemporary problematic of which critical theory is one manifestation, as will be shown in the following section on the dialectic of Enlightenment. Thus, while it is possible for critical theory to incorporate Dilthey's critique of

---

that the unity of nature and subject can only be brought about by the subject. Cf. Erkenntnis und Interesse, p. 45.

[37]Adorno, Aufsätze zur Gesellschaftstheorie und Methodologie, p. 146. Cf. Chapter Three on Lonergan's sketch of a meta-sociology.

[38]Stimmen der Zeit (März, 1973), p. 175.

historical reason into its dialectical analysis, Lonergan's meta-method is not so readily assimilated into the intentions of critical theory. The chief reason for this is that, as will be seen in Chapters Three and Four, meta-method is not caught in the problematic of autonomy versus sociality.[39]

3. Overcoming Cartesianism

In the third place, this understanding of the unity of identity and non-identity in terms of the subject sublates the Cartesian notion of method as a generalization from mathematics. Obviously the enormous changes in mathematics from Descartes' day to our own has made such a correlation of mathematics and method more complicated, yet the claims of scientism (that the physical sciences provide the paradigm for verifiable or falsifiable knowing), as well as the quest of logical empiricism for a unified science which would be value-free, indicate the persistence of the correlation.[40] Throughout the changes the Cartesian assumption that the procedures of mathematics provided the canons of clarity and certitude for scientific method remains a constant.[41] If Descartes rejected the idea of a probable science and doubted the possibility of history and politics aspiring to the

---

[39]On the problem of autonomy versus sociality cf. the final section of this Chapter on Lonergan's shift from cognitional theory to method.

[40]This is evidenced in the persistence of the Logical Empirical quest for a reductionist unified science; cf. Radnitzky, Contemporary Schools of Metascience I, pp. 72-92; cf. also J. Mittelstrass, Neuzeit und Aufklärung, pp. 121-132, 207-211, 377-528, where the objectivism in method is shown to move from mathematical logic to analytic logic of language through a Kantian "Vernunftkritik," ibid., pp. 555-578.

[41]Cf. Hegel, Vorlesungen über die Geschichte der Philosophie, vol. 20, p. 145; and E. Husserl, Die Krisis der europäischen Wissenschaft, pp. 83-85; also F. Matson, The Broken Image, pp. 30-110; H. Schnädelbach, Erfahrung, Begründung, Reflexion: Versuch über den Positivismus, pp. 105-130; Horkeimer and Adorno, Dialektik der Aufklärung, pp. 9-49; as an example of this, cf. W. Stegmüller, Probleme und Resultate der Wissenschaftstheorie I, p. 6: "Wichtig ist dabei, dass für jeden einzelnen Schritt einer längeren Ableitung die Überprufung der Korrektheit dieses Ableitungsschrittes auf rein mechanische Weise vollzogen werden kann."

stature of sciences, Leibniz and Spinoza had no such qualms.
For Descartes' method remained fundamentally uncritical as
long as it simply presupposed the correspondence of subject
and object (self and world) in the Mind of God.[42]   Certain
parallels could be drawn between the contemporary debates
on method and those prevalent during the transition from the
Renaissance to the Age of mechanistic Reason.   The Renaissance
approached method according to an analogy with art; knowledge
was to be gained by a familiarity with the Masters of
antiquity.   Vico attempted to articulate the validity of this
approach.[43]   Descartes, on the other hand, was committed
to a notion of method understood according to the analogy of
mathematical science.   This divergence in the understanding
of method runs through not only the nineteenth century disputes between the Naturwissenschaften and the Geistes- or
Geschichtswissenschaften, but also - as Habermas has pointed
out - the disputes today between the logicism of the
critical rationalists and the dialectical hermeneutics of
the critical theorists.[44]   If Descartes succeeded in

---

[42]Cf. Mittelstrass op. cit., pp. 383, 395f.; Löwith,
Gott, Mensch und Welt, pp. 24-40; W. Weischedel, Der Gott der
Philosophen I, pp. 165-175.

[43]Cf. A. R. Caponigri, Time and Idea: The Theory of
History in G. Vico (Notre Dame, 1968), pp. 36-70, 144-187,
esp. 162.   Note that this was not a blind adherence to tradition but a creative affirmation in the meaning and value
of man; Cf. G. Gusdorf, Les origines des sciences humaines
II, pp. 293-306.   On Vico's difference from Descartes; cf.
Gadamer, Wahrheit und Methode, pp. 16-20.   N. W. Gilbert,
Renaissance Concepts of Method (New York, 1960) indicates
the prevalence of the split between art and scientific methods
during the late Renaissance.

[44]On the mechanists'devaluation of memory and tradition,
cf. G. Gusdorf, op. cit., III/II, pp. 333-346, 407-418.   The
differences between method on the analogy of art (affirming
authority and tradition) and method on the analogy of mathematical science is clearly brought out in Gadamer's arguments
for the former; cf. Wahrheit und Methode, pp. 16ff., 209ff.,
260ff.   On the contemporary significance; Cf. Habermas,
Zur Logik der Sozialwissenschaften, pp. 71-125.   Note how
Lonergan derives his notion of method in a third way, neither
through the analogy with art nor through that of science;
cf. M.i.T., pp. 3-25.

differentiating philosophy and science from theology, and
the successive efforts in the eighteenth and nineteenth centuries saw the differentation of science from philosophy, the
contemporary momentum toward interdisciplinary collaboration
calls for a proportionate effort at elaborating a basic
approach to method capable of assuring an open, ongoing, and
critical communication among the increasing specializations.

The foundations for such a methodic collaboration,
however, cannot consist in any one-dimensional insistence
upon science or art, reason or tradition, as the paradigm
for the collaboration. Metz has called attention to this
danger of universalizing a particular, categorical method:

> The danger exists that a particular method, because of
> its categorical successes, would be surreptitiously
> enthroned as universal; and that thereby interdisciplin-
> ary cooperation would be oppressed by a particular
> ideal of method.[45]

The danger will not be averted by any simple-minded concordism. Mere juxtaposition of methods does not insure effective collaboration. Instead, there has to be an effort to
articulate a method of methods - and so in this sense a
transcendental or meta-method - capable of attentively,
intelligently, critically, and responsibly interrelating the
manifold methods actually constitutive of present social,
political, scientific, artistic, philosophical and religious
performance.

There are two aspects to this statement especially
relevant here. First, it takes fully into account that many
of the presently articulated particular (or first-order)
methods are really not adequate to the actual performance
of people operating in any of the just mentioned spheres of
action (social, political, scientific, etc.). Specifically,
I would argue that to the degree that the articulation of
methods in the sciences is influenced by a reductionist ideal
of a unified science (i.e., the goal of reducing all scientific statements to Physics), to that degree the methods
articulated for sciences concerned with fields other than
Physics will not be adequately formulated. This would be

---

[45]Metz, _Die Theologie in der interdisziplinären
Forschung_, p. 18.

76

an example of a particular, categorical method assuming a
universal significance it does not possess. The harmful
effects this has had on methods in biology, psychology, and
sociology have already been extensively documented.[46]   Second,
this attempt to universalize a method which is successful
in a particular, categorical field of inquiry or performance
results from the need for establishing some coherent base
or foundation for interrelating the increasingly specialized
spheres of human activity.

In other words, the transcendental or meta-dimension
is not one which is completely extrinsic to any of the particular and categorical spheres of human activity. The problem
is to determine how that dimension is operative in the categorical spheres of human activity, how it could be properly
articulated and so serve as a basis for an open, ongoing, and
critical correlation of the methods operative in those spheres.
This is not to reverse the historical trend of the differentiation of philosophy from theology, science from philosophy,
art from handicrafts, or theory from common-sense living.
Rather it is to affirm the validity of these differentiations
and specializations of human activity.[47]   In doing so, it
also affirms the need for a higher order integration which
would negatively prevent any particular mode of operation
from imposing itself on any of the others and positively
promote an ongoing collaboration among the specialized
methods.

---

[46]Cf. Radnitzky, op. cit., pp. 86-92, 140-145 of Vol. I;
for a general statement on the harmful effects of this scientistic reductionism, cf. Matson, op. cit., pp. 3-110, and
F. Wagner, Weg und Abweg der Naturwissenschaft (Munich, 1970);
and A. Koestler (ed.) Beyond Reductionism (Boston, 1969);
with regard to special problems in Physics, cf. P. Heelan,
Quantum Mechanics and Objectivity, pp. 57-80; also P.
McShane, Randomness, Statistics and Probability (Dublin,
1970). On biology, cf. F. Wagner (ed.) Menschenzüchtung
(Munich, 1969), pp. 13-49, 95-133; P. McShane, "Insight and
the Strategy of Biology" in Continuum 2 (1964), pp. 74-88.
On psychology, cf. F. Goble, The Third Force (New York,
1970). In sociology one has the problems of positivism
referred to in notes above.

[47]Cf. M. Lamb, "Towards a Synthetization of the Sciences," Phil. of Science 32 (1965), pp. 182-191 and references
to Insight given there.

In regard to meeting these two aspects of the problem,
the present study - as well as the general orientation of
political theology in the matter of interdisciplinary collaboration - is not to enter into the particular debates on
methods within the specialized fields. This demands specialized competence which a theologian does not have for fields
other than his own theological specialties. Nevertheless,
the theologian, as well as any representative from other
disciplines, can object when methods valid and successful
in one field are arbitraily set up as the standard and norm
for other fields. An obvious historical example of such an
attempt was Leibniz's efforts at composing the elements of
philosophy more mathematico, which in turn could provide the
basis for an ecumenical theology formulated according to
mathematical methods, projects to which he alluded in his
small but significantly entitled work Specimen demonstrationum
politicarum of 1669.[48] Less obvious but far more prevalent
is the contemporary scientistic notion that the physical-
mathematical sciences provide the norm for all valid human
knowledge.[49] This will be a constant danger as long as
sufficiently adequate meta-methodological foundations are
lacking. In the absence of such foundations, fluctuations
will continue between the extremes of less successful fields
of knowledge and praxis attempting to ape the methods of the
more successful ones, or of their rejecting those more
successful methods entirely in the name of waning
humanist values.

A variation on this can be observed in the present
disputes on method in Germany. W. Stegmüller argues for
the applicability of logical analytical methods to historical
reality.[50] H. -G. Gadamer, on the other hand, has sharply

---

[48]Cf. G. Gusdorf, op. cit., III/I, pp. 247ff. On the
religious and theological consequences of scientism in the
18th century, cf. ibid. vol. III/II, pp. 17-119, 347-393.

[49]Cf. J. Habermas, "Wozu noch Philosophie?" in his
Philosophisch-Politische Profile, pp. 11-36. Radnitzky,
op. cit., I, pp. 22ff.

[50]Cf. Stegmüller, Probleme und Resultate der
Wissenschaftstheorie I, pp. 335-427. Also P. Gardinier,
Theories of History (New York, 1959).

criticized the scientistic Cartesianism of method, and, in
his philosophical hermeneutics, called attention to the
centrality of art and traditions in the understanding of
historical truth.[51] If some see in this position an obscurantist delimitation of science (e.g., Hans Albert),[52]
there are others who, like K. -O. Apel and J. Habermas, try
to critically mediate both positions by calling attention
to the anthropological and historical presuppositions or
horizons within which these positions have arisen and the
manner in which they have, consciously or unconsciously,
bolstered unenlightened social interests and values.[53] In
America this effort at a critical mediation can be found in
the work of T. Kuhn, who has indicated the interplay between
tradition and creative insight within the process of scientific development.[54]

The criticisms these new discussions imply against Cartesianism is that they attack Descartes' premise regarding
the possibility of reducing all methods to a mathesis
universalis.[55] Insofar as this premise has also been operative in the scientistic notion that eventually all the sciences can be reduced to a unified physico-mathematical science,
it was to be expected that this methodological issue would be at
the heart of the nineteenth and early twentieth century
debates on the relations of the Geisteswissenschaften to the

---

[51]Gadamer, Wahrheit und Methode; also R. E. Palmer,
Hermeneutics (Evanston, 1969), pp. 162-217.

[52]Cf. H. Albert, Traktat über kritische Vernunft, pp.
131-157; and his Plädoyer für kritischen Rationalismus,
pp. 106-149.

[53]Cf. K. -O. Apel and J. Habermas (et al.), Hermeneutik
und Ideologiekritik (Frankfurt, 1971).

[54]Cf. T. Kuhn, The Structure of Scientific Revolutions,
2nd rev. Ed. (Chicago, 1970); I. Lakatos (ed.) Criticism and
the Growth of Knowledge (London, 1970).

[55]Cf. E. Husserl, Die Krisis der europäischen
Wissenschaften, pp. 58-86, on how Descartes began both the
modern idea of a universal mathematical science and an
objectivistic approach to transcendental reflection.

Naturwissenschaften[56] and in the contemporary debates on the
relation of sociology to history.[57] For both of these
debates concern themselves with scientism. Dilthey's
endeavors to thematize methods proper to the human sciences
and history were directed against the empiricist scientism
which, as he saw so clearly, could not be checked by the
transcendentalist-idealist traditions in Germany.[58] In this
respect Dilthey was anti-Cartesian, i.e., he did not hold for
the possibility of a universal scientific methodology according to the analogy of a mathesis universalis. If Dilthey's
model of science was not Cartesian, neither was his cognitional theory or notion of truth.[59] Nevertheless, Dilthey's
differentiation of the cultural sciences from the natural
sciences in terms of a verfiable reference to living experience as the certain ground or foundation for the former
was not without Cartesian connotations. Gadamer objects to
Dilthey's contention that such a lived experience could assure
the Geisteswissenschaften methodological foundations in the
manner in which Dilthey formulated that experience.[60] In
Gadamer's view, Dilthey's reliance upon an introspective
(yet empirical) psychology could not do justice to the
complexities of historical experience as a manifold of
Wirkungszusammenhänge. He sees in Dilthey's position too
little respect for the experience of art and tradition, and
too great an esteem for that ideal of science which, since
the Enlightenment, has sought to articulate its own

---

[56] Cf. A. Diemer, Beiträge zur Entwicklung der
Wissenschaftstheorie im 19. Jahrhundert, pp. 174-223.

[57] Cf. A. Wellmer, Kritische Gesellschaftstheorie und
Positivismus, pp. 7-68, 128-148. Also the issue of Continuum
devoted to Habermas, vol. 8 (1970), numbers 1 and 2.

[58] Cf. Dilthey's G.S. XIII, pp. 83-93, 104-113. Also
the following section on Dilthey's interpretation of the
Enlightenment.

[59] Cf. F. Lawrence, "Self-Knowledge in History in
Gadamer and Lonergan," in P. McShane (ed.) Language, Truth
and Meaning (Dublin, 1972) for a summary of Cartesian models
of science, cognitional theory, and notion of truth according to Gadamer.

[60] Cf. Wahrheit und Methode, pp. 205-217.

foundations apart from (and most often in critical opposition to) historical traditions.[61]

While the present study sharply disagrees with Gadamer's contention that Dilthey's thought was pervasively Cartesian - the next two sections of this chapter indicate how Dilthey criticized Cartesianism - I do admit a less than thorough repudiation of the Cartesian method in Dilthey.[62] Perhaps the greatest contribution of Lonergan to this debate is to have removed meta-methodology from its dependency upon either the analogy of art or the analogy of science. Lonergan is not dependent upon analogy at all in his formulation of the meta-methodological dimension of human performance, nor does he thereby succumb to a univocal approach to method which would, in effect, universalize some categorical method by maintaining its univocal significance for all domains of human historical performance.[63] If, however, Lonergan does not turn to science for an analogy of meta-methodology, he does see the need to focus on the sciences - and specifically the natural sciences - in his preliminary derivation of the notion of method.[64]

His interest in doing so is at once methodical and critical. It is methodical insofar as the natural sciences

---

[61]Ibid., pp. 218-280.

[62]Cf. Lawrence's article referred to in note 59 above, where he adequately presents Gadamer's view of Dilthey but does not advert to possible misinterpretations by Gadamer.

[63]On the limitations of univocity and analogy; cf. Lonergan, Insight, pp. 361f. I cannot enter into the relation between method and the notion of being in Lonergan here; cf. Lonergan's "Metaphysics as Horizon," in Collection, pp. 202ff. and his "Insight: Preface to a Discussion," ibid., pp. 152ff., where he indicates the ontological character of his meta-methodology. Note how for Lonergan meta-method is not a subsection of metaphysics but vice versa; hence he avoids the type of abstract ontologizing of method exemplified in,e.g., W. Hirsch's Über die Grundlagen einer universalen Methode der Philosophie (Berlin, 1969). For a specific application to theology, cf. Lonergan's remarks in Foundations of Theology, pp. 224f.

[64]Cf. M.i.T., pp. 3-6, and, of course, one has the first five chapters of Insight concerned with problems originating in (but whose significance extends beyond) the natural sciences.

exemplify well the success of categorical methods in their
recurrent and related operations of experimentation, observation, hypothesis formation, and verification through further
experimentation and observation. Hence they offer a ready
and highly developed field for deriving a preliminary notion
of method. But Lonergan's interest is also critical. He
realizes that the larger issues raised by the need for the
human sciences and history to develop their own first-order
methods cannot be answered simply by delimiting those methods
from the methods of the natural sciences. For such a
delimitation will not in itself answer the charges of
obscurantism leveled by the proponents of scientism who will
be quick to point out the similarities between the operations
of the natural scientist and those of the human scientist.[65]

Instead of side-stepping the problems, occasioned by
the emergence of modern natural science in the Enlightenment,
through insisting on a rightful differentiation of first-
order methods - whether that side-stepping be done through
Dilthey's distinction of _Erklären_ and _Verstehen_, Habermas'
distinction of technological interests versus hermeneutic
and emancipatory interests, or Gadamer's exposé of the
Enlightenment's prejudice against prejudices - Lonergan sees
in the contemporary advance of science and technology the
need to move beyond a reliance on analogy (whether in terms
of science or art and tradition) in the determination of a
transcendental method of methods or meta-methodology. The
move, he admits, is difficult for it entails a completely new
understanding of method, not as a set of objectivistic rules
or axioms to be followed blindly by the adepts of the method,
but as an appropriation of the creative and critical structures of human subjectivity, whether that subjectivity be
engaged in narration or argumentation, i.e., as the subjectivity is operative in day-to-day common-sense praxis,
political praxis, scientific or technological praxis, artistic
praxis, scholarly historical praxis, religious praxis, or the

---

[65]Cf. for example Hans Albert's response to Habermas'
attempts at delimitation on the basis of transcendental
interests in Albert's _Plädoyer für kritischen Rationalismus_,
pp. 106-149.

praxis of reflection upon all these various spheres of human
performance. In other words - and this is where Lonergan's
thoroughgoing critique of Cartesian or scientistic method
has a special relevance for political theology - Lonergan's
use of modern science as the starting point for deriving a
preliminary notion of method and his consequent elaboration
of a meta-methodology recognize the crucial importance of
meeting head-on the dialectic of the Enlightenment.[66]

4. Foundations for Hermeneutics and Dialectics

This brings us to the fourth and final area of the
possible contributions of the present study to the program
of political theology. From what has been said on the
methodological presuppositions of political theology it should
be well established that Metz's program hinges on the possibility of a critical mediation in theology from the present
into the future as well as from the past into the present,
and on the critical mediation of narrative and argument, of
autonomy and sociality. That implies, as has already been
mentioned, not only a critical hermeneutics and history,
but also a dialectics and communication for theology. It
should also be clear from the previous three areas discussed
that such a critical mediation implies a quest for methodological foundations capable of being both transcendental
and empirical through a thematization of the unity of identity and non-identity, and thereby sublating the Cartesian
ideal of a Science universelle or of a meta-method based on
the reduction of all forms of knowledge and action to those
found successful in the natural sciences and mathematics.

The foregoing discussions are not as extrinsic to theology as they might appear. Descartes' disjunction between
res cogitans and res extensa with their mutual mediation in
the Mind of God was uncritical not only from the viewpoint
of epistemology but also insofar as Descartes excluded
theology from method.[67] Within such a frame of reference it

---

[66]On the dialectic of the Enlightenment cf. Horkheimer
and Adorno, Dialektik der Aufklärung. Cf. also the following
subsection where this is discussed at greater length.

[67]Cf. Oeuvres de Descartes (Paris), p. 1398; also

was to be expected that French positivism under the influence
of Voltaire and d'Alembert, and British empiricism from Hobbes
to Hume, would reject any appeal to the Divine Mind and affirm
the sufficiency of objectivistic methods in the investigation
of all phenomena.[68] The future became a threat man had to
control through the manipulative methods of technological
reason.[69] German thought through Idealism to Marxism reveals
in a more profound manner a somewhat similar pattern. Kant's
response to empiricism and positivism was to re-instate the
primacy of thought; analogous to Descartes he conceived of
method as systematizing principles and sought to establish
the priority of critical method over skeptical and dogmatic
methods.[70] Yet Cartesian overtones were all too apparent in
the dichotomy between noumenon and phenomenon, between
Vernunft and Verstand, the resolution of which in the
"Intuitus Originarius" of God could not suffice to ground the
moral imperatives on which Kant based both his philosophy of

G. Gusdorf, La Révolution Galiléene, vol. I, pp. 244ff.
On the epistemological inadequacies of this position, cf.
Lonergan, Insight, pp. 388-389, 422-423. On the uncritical
mediation of self and world in God for Descartes, cf. K.
Löwith, Gott, Mensch und Welt in der Metaphysik von Descartes
bis zu Nietzsche, pp. 24-40. W. Weischedel, Der Gott der
Philosophen, pp. 165-175, and W. Schulz in Der Gott der
neuzeitlichen Metaphysik have shown how central the notion
of God was to Descartes and German Idealism.

[68]Cf. H. de Lubac, The Drama of Atheist Humanism (New
York, 1963), pp. 75-129. G. Misch, Zur Entstehung des fran-
zösischen Positivismus 2nd ed. (Darmstadt, 1969); F. Matson,
The Broken Image, pp. 6-65; Jacques Maritain, The Dream of
Descartes (New York, 1944); E. Cassirer, Die Philosophie der
Aufklärung, pp. 123-262.

[69]Cf. especially the work of B. Willms, Die Antwort
des Leviathan - Th. Hobbes' politische Theorie (Berlin, 1970),
pp. 105-111, 176-215. For a more general account of this
attitude, cf. Matson's The Broken Image, and H. Blumenberg,
Die Legitimität der Neuzeit (Frankfurt, 1966), pp. 11-200,
405-432,

[70]Cf. Kritik der reinen Vernunft, A 852 - A 856 (B880-
B884). Unlike Descartes, Kant carefully distinguished
between mathematical and philosophical method; cf. F. Kaulbach,
Immanuel Kant (Berlin, 1969), pp. 99-105. On the ambiguity
in Kant's critical method, cf. H. J. Patton, The Categorical
Imperative: A Study in Kant's Moral Philosophy (New York,
1967), pp. 19-31, esp. p. 29.

84

history (from the past in the present into the future) and his philosophical theology.[71] Kant's was not a closed system; the gaps between noumena and phenomena, between reason and understanding, between freedom and necessity, between theoretical and practical reason - these were all an integral part of his thought.[72] Yet non-identity, when it is not related to identity in some heuristic and critical unity, is of little defense against the totalitarian ambitions of a closed identity-system, or against what O. Marquard has aptly designated as "Kontrollvernunft."[73] Through Fichte and Schelling to Hegel, Idealism worked out the implications of intellectual intuition in a brilliant but futile effort to overcome the dichotomies in Kant, revealing in the end its inherent skepticism and the tendency of its genius to compromise with the present-ness of what exists.[74] Unable to thematize a heuristic and critical unity of theory and praxis, of archaeology (past into present) and eschatology (present into future), Hegel could no more account for a contingent affirmation of absolute reality than he could incorporate into this system the ongoing and probable

---

[71]Cf. K. Weyand, Kants Geschichtsphilosophie, pp. 22-39, 137-185; also W. Weischedel, op. cit., pp. 191-213.

[72]Cf. M. Horkheimer, "Kants Philosophie und die Aufklärung," in Kritische Theorie der Gesellschaft Bd. III (Marxismus-Kollektiv, 1968), pp. 306-318; L. Landgrebe, "Die Geschichte im Denken Kants," Phänomenologie und Geschichte, pp. 46-64. On the dangers in Kant's position, cf. Horkheimer and Adorno, Dialektik der Aufklärung, pp. 88-104.

[73]Cf. O. Marquard, Skeptische Methode im Blick auf Kant, (Freiburg: 1958). This is especially evident in Kant's attempts at relating theoretical and practical reason in his Kritik der Urteilskraft; cf. W. Bartuschat, "Neuere Arbeiten zu Kants Kritik der Urteilskraft," in Philosophische Rundschau 18 (1972), pp. 161-189, esp. 184ff.

[74]Cf. T. Adorno, Negative Dialektik, pp. 293-351, esp. 326ff.; W. Becker, Hegels Begriff der Dialektik und das Prinzip des Idealismus, pp. 66-85, on the impossibility of an adequate mediation of subject and object due to Hegel's (and Idealism's) conception of self-consciousness. A similar conclusion is reached from a different perspective in J. van der Meulen's Hegel: Die gebrochene Mitte (Hamburg, 1958), pp. 283-289.

character of modern science.[75]

The breakdown of Idealism was assured by intellectual, moral, and religious exigencies it could not integrate. The exigencies found often completely inadequate and contradictory expressions, and their diverse developments still define much of the contemporary situation. Intellectually, the thrust of modern science and technology with its increasing specialization of knowledge and skills seemed to defy any attempt at synthesis; the empirical methods of historical research and interpretation issued in a historicism which seemed to guarantee that the past would be critically mediated into a present unable to rationally and responsibly guide its

---

[75]Cf. M. Theunissen, Hegels Lehre vom absoluten Geist als theologisch-politischer Traktat, pp. 325-447; also M. Riedel, Theorie und Praxis im Denken Hegels, esp. pp. 204-215. There is still much work to be done in correlating Hegel's congitional theory and his philosophy of history and philosophy of religion. That this is not some obtuse project with little reference to the socio-politcial actuality of Hegel, compare Cassirer's conclusions in Das Erkenntnisproblem in der Philosophie und Wissenschaft der neueren Zeit, vol. III, pp. 362-377, with W. Oelmüller's remarks on Kant and Hegel in Die Unbefriedigte Aufklärung, pp. 269-289. As an example from the area of Hegel's social theory, cf. H. Schnädelbach, "Zum Verhältnis von Logik und Gesellschaftstheorie bei Hegel," in O. Negt (ed.), Aktualität und Folgen der Philosophie Hegels, pp. 58-80. On the present-ness in Hegel's thought, cf. Habermas, "Nachwort," in Hegel, Politische Schriften (Frankfurt, 1966), pp. 351-370; Löwith, Von Hegel zu Nietzsche, pp. 220-229; and W. Weischedel, op. cit., pp. 322-330. The failure to adequately account for the transcendence of subject and object in the sphere of human knowing and doing led to the breakdown of Hegel's conception of God-consciousness cf. W. Weischedel, op. cit., pp. 384-385. Cf. Oelmüller, op. cit., pp. 269f on how Hegel saw no possibility for a renewal of theology through interdisciplinary collaboration with the sciences, but only through a systematic thematization of absolute truth. German idealism never did come to realize the centrality of the shift from classical science, represented in Aristotle's notion of science as knowledge of the per se and necessary, to modern science as empirically contingent and probable; compare Lonergan, Collection, pp. 252-267 with J. Taminiaux, La nostalgie de la Grèce à l'aube de l'idéalisme allemand (Hague, 1967) and A. Diemer, "Die Begründung des Wissenschafts-charakters der Wissenschaft im 19. Jahrhundert: die Wissenschaftstheorie zwischen klassicher und moderner Wissenschaftskonzeption," in Beiträge zur Entwicklung der Wissenschaftstheorie im 19. Jahrhundert, pp. 3-62.

own making of history.[76] Morally, the social and political
praxis of modern man seemed ever more constrained by an
increasingly industrialized technocracy and bureaucratic
polity which allowed the satisfaction of only those needs
consonant with the growth of its own structures rather than
the growth of human freedom and communal responsibility.[77]
Religiously, there was the retreat of religion from the public
to the private, personal sphere of human performance, with
theology attempting to appropriate the critical mediation
of the past into the present, yet unable to articulate the
dialectical significance of religion in a world of increasingly secularist meanings and values.[78]

As the intellectual exigence arose from modern empirical
science and historical studies, so the moral exigence was

---

[76]Cf. Löwith, Von Hegel zu Nietzsche, pp. 65-152;
A. N. Whitehead, Science and the Modern World, pp. 119-141;
G. Iggers, Deutsche Geschichtswissenschaft, pp. 11-162;
K. Heussi, Die Krisis des Historismus (Tübingen, 1932);
R. G. Collingwood, The Idea of History, pp. 86-204; on the rel-
evance of these movements to the present, cf. G. Picht, Mut zur
Utopie and his Wahrheit-Vernunft-Verantwortung, pp. 281-407.

[77]Cf. J. Ritter, "Moralität und Sittlichkeit" in Metaphysik und Politik, pp. 281-309; M. Horkheimer, Kritische
Theorie der Gesellschaft, vol. I, pp. 1-8, 71-109; B. Ollman,
Alienation, pp. 43-51, 131-136; J. Habermas,"Über das Verhältnis von Politik und Moral," in his Arbeit-Erkenntnis-
Forschritt (Amsterdam, 1970), pp. 219-242. From these
studies one can see how the duality of Kant's position on
practical reason and the relation of morality to politics
led through the idealist identity of Hegel to the praxis-
oriented relational   view   of Marx. On Marx's inability,
however, to elaborate a non-classical mediation of theory
and praxis; cf. D. Böhler, Metakritik der Marxschen Ideologiekritik, pp. 9-14, 104-117, 302-328, 328-350.

[78]Cf. the long introduction to Kierkegaard's Philosophical Fragments (Princeton, 1962 - 2nd ed.) by N. Thulstrup,
pp. xlv-xciv; L. Dupré, Kierkegaard as Theologian (London,
1964); Kierkegaard's attack on Christianity was, of
course, against the "old" political theology in the sense
of the alliance between ecclesial institutions and socio-
political structures; cf. E. Feil, op. cit. On the cultural crisis of Christianity in modernity, cf. G. Vahanian,
The Death of God: The Culture of our Post-Christian Era
(New York, 1966); and on the ambiguity of secularization
theology from the viewpoint of political theology, cf.
Metz, Zur Theologie der Welt, pp. 51-71, 99-116, and
M. Xhaufflaire and K. Derksen (eds.) Les deux visages de
la théologie de la sécularization.

highlighted by Marxism and the character of late capitalism, while the religious exigence found expression in existentialist, personalist and secularization theologies. The program of political theology must obviously take these into account, but to do this in a critical manner implies the need for theological foundations which neither Idealism nor these movements have provided. The possible contributions the present study would make to such a task lies in the efforts of both Dilthey and Lonergan to thematize a notion of understanding and reason capable of integrating the three exigencies. Dilthey was keenly aware of the insufficiences of the Kantian transcendentalist approach and the Hegelian idealist system to come to grips with the empirical thrust of modern science. Nor could he accept the positivism and empiricism of his day, especially in the Historical School. He realized full well both the moral dilemma occasioned by scientific and historical consciousness, and the new epoch of religious consciousness initiated in the Christian theology of Schleiermacher. If he did not succeed in carrying out his critique of historical reason and left much to be desired in his theological stance, then from the perspective of Lonergan's meta-method one could ask to what extent Dilthey's theological shortcomings are traceable to an inadequate methodological position vis-à-vis both idealism and empiricism. For, if it is true that in both Cartesianism and Idealism the subject of reason was more divine than human,[79] then the task of articulating an understanding of reason with the exigencies of modernity and contemporaneity requires not only a radical appreciation of the autonomy of human cognitional and practical performance but also, on the basis of that autonomy, a new and critically grounded explicitation of the religious exigence as at once personal and

---

[79]Cf. W. Schulz, Der Gott der neuzeitlichen Metaphysik; W. Weischedel, op. cit., pp. 165-457; the Marxian critique of religion should, therefore, be viewed within the context of Marxist critique of idealist self-consciousness; cf. Böhler, op. cit., pp. 135-139, 152-187. Here Böhler indicates the probable transition in Marx from a synergy of God and man in the "historiosophy" of Cieszkowski to a synergy of man and the logic of history.

social.[80]

Insofar as political theology is committed to take the critical consciousness of modernity seriously, it cannot rest content with any half-hearted attempts at bridging the gulf between the empirico-critical methods of science and the domain of religious belief and practice.[81] A critical mediation from the present into the future cannot be based upon the unquestioned assumptions of both Cartesianism and Idealism regarding the cooperation of man and God; nor can it be based upon the disregard by positivism and empiricism of the orientation to totality underpinning the questioning drive of intellectual and moral performance.[82] The "revolution" Dilthey may have effected in scientific theory and praxis consisted in his recognition of the revolution caused by the modern empirical sciences, the futility of transcendental Idealism to incorporate that revolution, and his steadfast refusal to accept the empiricist interpretations of that revolution.[83] Whatever the shortcomings of his own

---

[80]Such an approach to the problem of religion and theology does not see them in opposition to the scientific thrust of modernity but as grounding that thrust; cf. D. Tracy, "Foundational Theology as Contemporary Possibility," in The Dunwoodie Review (1972), pp. 3-20.

[81]Cf. Metz, Stimmen der Zeit, pp. 171ff.; also M. Xhaufflaire has shown the inconsistency of Feuerbach's positions from the perspective of political theology in his Feuerbach et la théologie de la sécularisation (Paris, 1970), esp. pp. 266-302, 341-383. Note how, in criticizing Feuerbach from the context of Marx, Xhaufflaire did not take into account the ambiguity of Marx himself in this respect; cf. Böhler, as cited in note 79 above.

[82]Cf. T. Adorno (et al.) Der Positivismusstreit in der deutschen Soziologie, on the problem of totality and critique. One does not have to turn to this debate in order to appreciate the problems in the position of critical rationalism; cf. I. Lakatos and A. Musgrave (eds.), Criticism and the Growth of Knowledge where Kuhn illustrates the insufficiency of Popper's critical rationalism with its neglect of the subject of science in history. Cf. also Kuhn's Postscript to the 2nd edition of The Structure of Scientific Revolution (Chicago, 1970), pp. 186ff., 191f.

[83]Cf. P. Krausser, Kritik der endlichen Vernunft; also M. Horkheimer, "Psychologie und Soziologie im Werk W. Dilthey," in Kritische Theorie der Gesellschaft, vol. II, pp. 7-31, 165-240.

interpretation, they cannot be corrected by opting for the objectivism of positivism or empiricism.[84] So, for instance, A. Hollweg characteristically accepts the Lewinian interpretation of modern science as within the Galilean epoch - the human and social sciences are just beginning to enter this epoch - and so criticizes Dilthey for being too concerned with the future-orientation of historicality rather than empirically analyzing the present.[85] In such a framework theology is left with general imperatives regarding the responsibility of faith in technological society but without an elaboration of methods for realizing that responsibility; indeed, the responsibility is relegated to the individual.[86]

Lonergan, on the other hand, sees responsibility as the very foundation of theology as that responsibility has responded to the challenges of intellectual, moral, and religious conversion.[87] He has been able to formulate succinctly and precisely how both the empiricist and idealist traditions have confused the unity-in-difference between subjectivity and objectivity, and how that confusion accounts for the claim that the objectivity of such disciplines as mathematics and science is not attributed to philosophy, ethics, or theology.[88] Moreover, the refusal of both

---

[84]Cf. H. Schnädelbach, Erfahrung, Begründung und Reflexion: Versuch über den Postivismus, pp. 7-31, 165-240.

[85]Hollweg, Theologie und Empirie, pp. 203-231, 234-237. It was to be expected, then, that Hollweg's polemic against the normative grounding of praxis would lead him, as would Lewin's understanding of modern science, to a privatizing of value-judgments, ibid., pp. 301, 325f.

[86]Cf. Hollweg, ibid., pp. 392-403. These negative criticisms should not detract from the value of Hollweg's attempts at correlating theology and the social sciences.

[87]Cf. M.i.T., pp. 130-132, 235-244, 267-293; on conversion in an intellectual, scientific context, cf. T. Kuhn, The Structure of Scientific Revolutions, pp. 149-158; and in the Postscript to the 2nd edition, pp. 202-204: "The conversion experience that I have likened to a gestalt switch remains, therefore, at the heart of the revolutionary process." On the neglected centrality of responsibility, cf. G. Picht, Wahrheit-Vernunft-Verantwortung, pp. 318-342.

[88]Cf. Insight, pp. xxi-xxix, 84-86, 245-254, 319-347, 372-374,401-430; M.i.T., 93-96, 262-265, 314-318, 237-244,

empiricism and existentialism or personalism to accord
authentic subjectivity the status of objectivity springs
from this same context which confuses the experience of the
immediacy of the object in sensation and the critical
mediacy of the object in the horizon of critical rationality.

> Still that context survives only as long as there
> survive the ambiguities underlying naive realism,
> naive idealism, empiricism, critical idealism,
> absolute idealism. Once those ambiguities are
> removed, once an adequate self-appropriation is
> effected, once one distinguishes between object
> and objectivity in the world of immediacy and, on
> the other hand, object and objectivity in the
> world mediated by meaning and motivated by value,
> then a totally different context arises. For it
> is now apparent that in the world mediated by mean-
> ing and motivated by value, objectivity is simply
> the consequence of authentic subjectivity, of
> genuine attention, genuine intelligence, genuine
> reasonableness, genuine responsibility. Mathe-
> matics, science, philosophy, ethics, theology dif-
> fer in many manners; but they have the common feature
> that their objectivity is the fruit of attentive-
> ness, intelligence, reasonableness, and responsi-
> bility.[89]

It is within this totally different context that the question
of God can be critically approached, that the Cartesian
and/or Kantian uncritical appeal to God as mediating subject
and object (as thing-in-itself) is dispelled without
recourse to any (Hegelian) absolute system, because the
autonomy of authentic human subjectivity is grasped in its
open and heuristically related and recurrent operations.
Insofar as this autonomy is attentive, intelligent, reasonable and responsible it yields cumulative and progressive
results in all fields of human theory and praxis; insofar
as those fields are the result of inattentiveness, stupidity,
irrationality and irresponsibility, that autonomy is contra-
factual. The thematization of that autonomy is constitutive
of meta-method, enabling Lonergan to overcome the dichotomies
of the past without sacrificing the real differences between
the many fields of human endeavor and history to the tyranny
of a great idea or an absolute system or a complacent

Collection, pp. 202-239.

[89]M.i.T., p. 265.

tolerance. There is no question of belittling that autonomy, of sublating knowledge in order to make room for faith, but of insisting on the full actualization of it in order to raise the possibility of the question of God.[90]

It is in the light of such meta-methodological foundations that Lonergan can elaborate the many methods of theology as providing not only a critical mediation of the past into the present but also from the present into the future. For theology is not only cast in the _oratio obliqua_ of what tradition has handed on, but also in the _oratio recta_ whereby the believing communities constitute living tradition through their own words and actions. As the functional specialties of research, interpretation, history, and dialectics interrelate the critical methods for mediating the past into the present, so foundations, doctrines, systematics, and communications are concerned with the critical mediating functional specialties from the present into the future.[91] In this writer's opinion Lonergan's application of meta-method to theology in terms of functional specialization does provide a critical and ongoing framework for incorporating the various theological field and subject specialties into the general scheme of archaeology (past into present) and eschatology

---

[90]Note how this understanding contrasts with some of the main personalist and existentialist notions on the need to delimit religious faith and language from the other, more empirical realms of human knowledge and performance; cf. L. Dupré, _The Other Dimension_ (New York, 1972), pp. 13-147. If it is not too gross an oversimplification of Dupré's excellent work, I would say that he overemphasizes in Kierkegaardian fashion the non-identity between religious experience and religious intentionality on the one hand, and man's intellectual and moral experience and intentionality on the other.

[91]It no doubt seems strange to think of doctrines, systematics, and communications as a complex of methods for critically mediating the present into the future. But these are operative within the horizons defined by the foundational reality of intellectual, moral and religious conversion. As such they necessarily participate in the critical mediation process, i.e., they are directed towards the communication of an authentic and liberating message and action to society. On doctrines as critical, cf. Metz's notion of the dangerous memory of Christian doctrine, _Diskussion zur "politischen Theologie"_, pp. 284-296.

(present into future).[92] It is critical because it takes
into account in a foundational way the auto-authenticating
reality of human subjectivity; it is ongoing because it
sets up the various specialized methods in a feedback
pattern.[93]

This is not to assume that Lonergan's meta-method provides all the answers to the questions posed by political
theology. On the contrary. Lonergan himself has only
sketched in the broadest way the social implications of his
approach. In relation to the specific programs of political
theology, one must elaborate the inherently social character
of religious and specifically Christian conversion. This
would have the effect of enabling one to see more clearly
how doctrines are not only historical expressions but also
embodiments of what Metz refers to as the subversive and
dangerous memory of Christian good-news, how systematics in
its quest for a probable and analogical understanding of
doctrines is socio-historically conditioned, and how, finally,
communication is not only a matter of preaching and teaching
but also, and primarily, of doing the Word, of praxis.[94]

---

[92]On the general pattern of archaeology and eschatology and their relation to theory and praxis, cf.
Theunissen, Hegels Lehre vom absoluten Geist als theologisch-
politischer Traktat, pp. 325-429; also P. Ricoeur, De
l'interprétation: essai sur Freud, pp. 444-475.

[93]Cf. Lonergan, M.i.T., pp. 133-145, 364-367.

[94]It is important to note the conception of criticism
underlying these remarks. D. Tracy has been calling for the
explicitation, unless I misunderstand him, of a theoretically
critical grounding of the theological enterprise; cf. his
article in Foundations of Theology, pp. 197-222, and the one
referred to in note 80 above. I fail to see, however, how
this entails any structural revision of Lonergan's position.
True, he has not given us a detailed exposition of meta-
method, for he himself sees method as a framework for creative
collaboration. The critical justification of the entire
theological enterprise is never a completed task (unless one
adopts a classicist notion of criticism) but is a mutual
mediation of theological theory and religious praxis within
the heuristic of mankind's socio-cultural development (and
lack thereof) on this planet. To my mind Lonergan has
brilliantly provided the conditions of the possibility of
thematizing such a critical project. Tracy seems to confuse
this broader issue with a more specific one, viz., whether or
not the thematization of specifically Christian conversion in

These four areas of possible contributions to political theology should be kept in mind in reading the study that follows. They should at least hint at the possibility that the study is not simply some ivory tower exercise in theoretical subtleties. The density of reflection is not meant to obscure the obvious, but to help, hopefully, in bringing the obvious to bear on the complexities of our contemporary situation. For, if it is correct that the basic dialectic operative in that situation is the dialectic of the Enlightenment, then the critical positions of both Dilthey and Lonergan are eminently suited to exposing the fundamental problems of modern and contemporary society.

THE DIALECTIC OF ENLIGHTENMENT
AND INTERDISCIPLINARY COLLABORATION

In order to clarify this point and explicate the aim of the dialectical comparison of Dilthey's critique of historical reason and Lonergan's meta-method, the present section explicitates the above mentioned dialectic of the Enlightenment in relation to collaboration.[95] For that aim is not merely an historical presentation of the two positions but a dialectical confrontation within the context of our contemporary cultural crisis. That crisis might be defined in a variety of ways: the growing paralysis of praxis in the face of anonymous technocratic controls, the "future shock" generated by increasingly rapid change and the resulting disorientation, the intransigence of multi-national corporations in the face of ecological pollution and waning energy resources, the growing poverty in the midst of restricted affluence, the lack of communication and community in the face of ever increasing bureaucratic social structures, the transition from an industrialized to a post-industrialized society, the

---

Foundations explicates a horizon which can and does adopt a critical attitude vis-à-vis the doctrinal traditions of Roman Catholicism.

[95]Cf. Chapter One, pp. 1-53.

persistence of economic and/or national bias (e.g., the
military-industrial complex) in the key decision-making
centers, etc.[96]

Obviously, such a complexity of issues indicates how
the problems of contemporary man and his world are far too
vast for any one mind or specialized research group to effectively handle. If the polarizations in the political,
economic, and academic worlds are any indication, collaboration is not a luxury but an urgent necessity. Yet the pressure of the need seems matched only by the difficulty in
satisfying it. Communication and collaboration call for
some commonly shared ground of understanding and language,
some commonly accepted norms of verification and evaluation,
if communication is to be something more than simultaneous
monologues and collaboration more than the juxtaposition of
efforts. Moreover, it is not only a problem of interdisciplinary collaboration and communication but also of extending
this to cover the execution and implementation of the recommendations arrived at; hence one envisages the need for
ever expanding circles of communication and collaboration
through all sectors of human historical performances on this
planet.

Two questions immediately arise. How would it be
possible to reach a normative understanding helpful for
collaboration across such widely divergent fields of human
historical life represented in the myriad cultural, social,
political, and national groupings - not to mention the
interdisciplinary fields of the arts, natural sciences,
human sciences, philosophies, theologies? Is it not difficult

---

[96]The literature on these subjects is vast. I have
found the following especially helpful: N. Birnbaum, The
Crisis of Industrial Society (Oxford, 1969); N. Chomsky,
American Power and the New Mandarins (New York, 1969);
F. Duchêne (ed.),The Endless Crisis (New York, 1970),
R. Heilbronner, The Future as History (New York, 1961); •
J. Ellul, The Technological Society (New York, 1964);
R. Heilbronner, Between Capitalism and Socialism (New York,
1970); D. Meadows (ed.), The Limits of Growth (Washington,
1972); G. Taylor, The Doomsday Book (New York, 1970);
W. Thompson, At the Edge of History (New York, 1972);
A. Touraine, The Post-Industrial Society (New York, 1971).

enough to attain some type of communication and collaboration among the many particular groups and specializations within each of these fields themselves? Secondly, how could norms be established for a truly <u>ongoing</u> collaboration among the many fields, norms which would positively foster creative new developments within the fields themselves and within the overall collaboration, norms which would be both open and critical?

Why this insistence upon norms? Because the present stage in scientific thought and praxis demands that. All of the formulations of the contemporary crisis could be traced to the contemporary convergence of scientific and historical consciousness in the manifold fields of human performance. Metz has called attention to this in his reflections on the need for a new relationship of politics and morality.[97] Metascience is becoming more aware of the need to reject the idea that values are irrelevant to the praxis of the scientific communities.[98] International congresses on various aspects of the crisis explicitly mention the moral dimensions of their deliberations.[99]

Now there is a central concern in both Dilthey and Lonergan to explicate heuristic and critical patterns of collaboration. Indeed, Dilthey's critique of historical reason has been cogently interpreted as dealing with the

---

[97] Cf. Metz (ed.), <u>New Questions on God</u> (Concilium, 1972), pp. 9-25; also Metz's article in <u>Diskussion zur "politischen Theologie"</u>, pp. 279-284. On the philosophical implications, cf. W. Oelmüller, "Zur philosophischen Begründung des Sittlichen und Politischen," <u>ibid.</u>, pp. 38-71.

[98] For a general discussion, cf. G. Radnitzky, <u>Contemporary Schools of Metascience</u>, vol. I, pp. ix-xl, vol. II, 160-185. It is interesting to note how J. Ellul's conception of "technical morality" or the uses of technique as totally unrelated to ethical morality overlooked the limits of technique in its feedback relationship to both nature and society; cf. <u>The Technological Society</u>, pp. 96-98, 134ff. That is a reality unsuspected when Ellul was writing (1954) but only too obvious now in the spectre of pollution and the problems of cybernetics and the industrial job market.

[99] Cf. the proceedings of the United Nations congress on Ecology in Stockholm, and the 1973 & 1974 meetings of the American Association for the Advancement of Science.

conditions of the possibility of collaboration.[100] He saw
a central task of his generation in the efforts at correlating
empiric scientific activity with the gains of historical
scholarship. The historical traditions which the scientific
revolution had left unquestioned were scrutinized by historians with an increasing array of critical methods. Historical consciousness had broken the last chains of metaphysical or religious absolutes which the scientific revolution had not yet touched. Man was free. But the powerless
subjectivity of Romanticism had shown that the relativity
of historical consciousness must discover its universal
grounds if man could, on the strength of his past, recognize
the real norms for his progress into the future.[101] Yet
there was an ambivalence and pathos in this, for science
and historical scholarship in their positivistic and scientistic interpretations erode the very possibility of those
norms which would underpin an open and critical communication
and collaboration.[102] For the dialectic of the Enlightenment
consists in the illusion generated by the advance of objective knowledge in the sciences dispelling the very subjectivity grounding it in the name of an extroverted "realism."
Hence the disparity, mentioned above, between the goals of
the Enlightenment and its trust in objectivistic methods.[103]

This is the reason why both Dilthey and Lonergan do
not engage in detailing intricate patterns of communication
or collaboration, though their work allows for such. They

---

[100]Cf. P. Krausser, Kritik der endlichen Vernunft:
Diltheys Revolution der allgemein Wissenschafts-und
Handlungstheorie.

[101]Cf. G.S., VIII, 192-193, 204, 225; I, xv, 351-359;
III, 210-268; V, 352-363; VII, 89-117, 335-338; Briefwechsel
zwischen W. Dilthey und Grafen Paul Yorck von Wartenburg
(Halle, 1923), n. 104. Henceforth this will be known as
Briefwechsel.

[102]Cf. F. Matson, The Broken Image; and J. Hellesnes,
"Education and the Concept of Critique," in Continuum vol. 8
(1970), pp. 40-51.

[103]Cf. Habermas' remarks on Adorno's dialectic of the
Enlightenement in Philosophisch-Politische Profile, pp.
184-199, esp. p. 187.

are not primarily interested in working out computer-like
models, though they have uncovered many feedback relations in
human performance. Prior to any such work, they are concerned with thematizing the autonomous, free subjectivity
operative in the questioning drive of modern and contemporary
science. That such an approach is not wholly foreign to the
contemporary problematic might be shown by drawing certain
configurations between the problems Dilthey was confronted
with and those now impelling us toward interdisciplinary
collaboration. The consequences of historical processes
which Dilthey sought to understand have, in the sixty years
since his death, gained a momentum he scarcely could have
foreseen. First, I should like to illustrate this by a
series of configurations indicating both the urgency of
ongoing collaboration and its possible foundations, drawing
certain preliminary conclusions from the position of Dilthey.
Second, I shall then sketch the criticism on Dilthey by
Lonergan in the light of those configurations and the fundamental dialectic they presuppose. These criticisms indicate
how meta-method decisively moves beyond the limits of
Dilthey's critique.

1. Configurations and Collaboration

There are four configurations. First, Dilthey was
keenly aware of the implications of the scientific and
historical revolutions initiated by the Enlightenment. In
cultures and societies prior to these revolutions, myth,
religion or philosophy had the essential functions of providing each community and society with normative value
orientations and world-views which offered at least the outlines of an all-embracing meaning. In the West these functions found a classical and perennial expression in Greek
metaphysics and Christian theology, within which the natural
and human sciences had a subaltern or subcultural status.
The hypothetical, experimental, and explanatory thrust of
modern science effectively dismantled these metaphysical
world-views, reducing their adherents to a subcultural minority status, without supplying any comparable alternatives.[104]

---

[104]Cf. G.S. I, 351-385; VII, 173, 335-345; VIII, 190-196.

This partially accounts for the increasing alienation and distorted communication between scientific communities and other socio-historical groups.[105]

These concerns find a reflection in several currents of contemporary thought. On the surface, there are the discussions about the two-culture problem, about the growing fragmentation within societies, and the status of cognitive minorities.[106] On a deeper level run the arguments on value-free science: the dilemma that, on the one hand, the sciences methodologically avoid the larger issues on their value status within a general orientation toward some ultimate meaning and value, while, on the other hand, the sciences themselves are in need of some normative commitment if they are to avoid irrational and unscientific manipulation by economic-political groups and/or national bias.[107]

Secondly, Dilthey did not accept the scientific interpretations of this movement of modern science. The breakdown of Idealism and the demotion of philosophy from its metaphysical primacy not only freed the empirical sciences to develop their own methods but also allowed philosophy to curtail its speculations on fields taken over by the sciences and concentrate instead on the sciences themselves. This

---

For a contemporary statement of this, cf. M. Riedel, "Die Erkenntniskritische Motiv in Diltheys Theorie der Geisteswissenschaften," in Hermeneutik und Dialektik, vol. I, pp. 233-255; and his "W. Dilthey und das Problem der Metaphysik," in Phil. Jahrbuch 76 (1968), pp. 332-348.

[105]Cf. Dilthey's G.S. V, 145, 356-363; VII, 137f.; I, 372f.

[106]Cf. C. P. Snow, The Two Cultures (London, 1959); F. Matson, The Broken Image; J. Habermas, Technik und Wissenschaft als "Ideologie", pp. 104-119; also his Strukturwandel der Öffentlichkeit, pp. 38-68, 157-198, 257-271; N. Birnbaum, Toward a Critical Sociology, pp. 416-441; P. Berger and T. Luckmann, The Social Construction of Reality, esp. pp. 92-183.

[107]Cf. J. Habermas, Theorie und Praxis, pp. 231-257; G. Picht, Wahrheit-Vernunft-Verantwortung, pp. 343-407; H. Albert, Traktat über kritische Vernunft, pp. 1-79; A. Touraine, The Post-Industrial Society, pp. 193-233; H. Marcuse, One-Dimensional Man, pp. 1-120; E. Fromm, The Revolution of Hope: Toward a Humanized Technology (New York, 1968).

meta-reflection took the form of a theory of theories, a logic of scientific performance, cognitional theory, from the late eighteenth century through the nineteenth.[108] The clear emergence of historical consciousness in Dilthey's era highlighted the need for the tendency of philosophy as a "Besinnung über das Denken" to critically reinforce those who sought to elaborate the specific differences between the human sciences and the natural sciences in terms of a heuristic understanding of man and society.[109]

Today one sees an increasing convergence of scientific consciousness and historical consciousness. Some interpret this convergence in a scientistic sense of a sublation of the latter into the former; they predict the advent of a post-historical age.[110] There are, however, others who cogently argue that the advances in the natural sciences themselves are laying to rest the ghosts of scientism. Those advances seem to be reaching what K. Boulding and M. McLuhan refer to as a "break boundary" situation.[111] The insight of Heisenberg's Quantum Mechanics into the constitutive role of the human scientific observer is paralleled by the praxis of the natural sciences in the formation of new physical and chemical elements and compounds, experimentation in genetic

---

[108] Cf. G.S. V, 356-363, 406-413; VIII, 206-219.

[109] Cf. G.S. I, xv-xx, 116-120; V, 146-153, 361-366, 405f.; VII, 88-120.

[110] Cf. A. Schmidt, "Der strukturalistiche Angriff auf die Geschichte," in Schmidt (ed.), Beiträge zur marxistischen Erkenntnistheorie, pp. 194-265. Also note 54 above.

[111] Cf. F. Matson, The Broken Image on the demise of scientism. On break boundary situations cf. McLuhan, Understanding Media: The Extensions of Man (New York, 1965), p.38. I do not mean to suggest that the natural sciences are transforming themselves into human sciences but that from two directions the natural sciences are being forced to take into account (in a way they previously did not) the constitutive meaning of subjectivity. First, in the intrusion of the subject into the observation process, or rather the recognition that the subject must be taken into account. Secondly, the vast extent of the natural sciences' effective control and transformation of natural processes increases the need to find the norms for this transformation, not in nature, but in mind or constitutive interiority. Cf. my short essay "Science"in Prophetic Voices (New York, 1969), pp. 202-205.

manipulation, the cybernetical alterations in fields ranging from neurology through engineering and industrial production to information systems and aesthetics.[112] Natural scientists are beginning to look to the human sciences for norms capable of guiding the increasing transformation of nature into the man-made world of history.[113] For their part, the human scientists, especially the sociologists and political scientists, are developing a growing interest in the philosophy or science of the sciences.[114] The convergence of scientific and historical consciousness, far from suppressing history, enhances the centrality of history and responsibility insofar as the sciences, in enlarging the sphere of human power and control, are provoking reflection on the till now haphazard and uncontrolled over-all development of the sciences themselves, and on the relation of scientific activity to the other forms of human conscious activity.[115]

Thirdly, at this point the methodological efforts of Dilthey provide instructive insights. The problem is to

---

[112] Cf. Heelan, Quantum Mechanics and Objectivity (Hague, 1965); A. Bucholz, Die grosse Transformation (Stuttgart, 1968); H. Frank (ed.), Kybernetik - Brücke zwischen den Wissenschaften (Frankfurt, 1966).

[113] Cf. Habermas, Technik und Wissenschaft als "Ideologie", pp. 48-103; N. Wiener, The Human Use of Human Beings (New York, 1954), esp. pp. 250 and 280; also Matson, op. cit., pp. 161ff.

[114] Cf. Wolf-Dieter Narr, Theoriebegriffe und Systemtheorie (Stuttgart, 1969); G. Radnitzky, Contemporary Schools of Metascience, vols. I and II on the Anglo-Saxon and Continental schools of metascience respectively. Cf. also the Sociology of Knowledge, e.g., P. Berger, The Social Construction of Reality (New York, 1966) and Wolff, Versuch zu einer Wissenssoziologie (Berlin, 1968); and the need to develop a critical sociology, e.g., N. Birnbaum's Toward a Critical Sociology. This movement has been augmented by the crises mentioned above; cf. note 96.

[115] Cf. note 111 above. This convergence can also be witnessed in the imperatives of planning and coordination in order to overcome the irrationalities of present specialization (e.g., how industrial technology has through uncoordinated specialization led to the spectre of pollution) in order to avert future disaster and in its stead give real human progress a chance; cf. literature in note 96 above, esp. Meadows (ed.), The Limits to Growth.

realize that such totalities as the sciences, societies,
historical processes are parts of a heuristically developing
(or declining) whole. How, then, does one move from the past
and present conditions of these components of the whole to
the functional patterns which could serve as norms to guide
present and future components toward the progress rather than
the destruction of the whole? In the light of Hegelian mis-
takes, Dilthey accepted the impossibility of a deductive
thematization of the whole.[116] For whether the whole was
taken as this concrete universe in all of its as yet unplumbed
ramifications (the objective whole) or as the actuality of
this conscious anticipation of the whole (subjective) one
cannot deduct its normative patterns from the past and present facts or products, but only from how these uncover the
heuristic anticipations themselves. On the other hand,
Dilthey could not accept a positivist rejection of the
whole and a bracketing of the whole to concentrate upon the
individual components. For that approach is unable to account
for the constitutive character of consciousness within those
components, and so it cannot discover the vital sources of
its own conscious activity whereby it could relate the analyzed components to the development of the whole.[117] Dilthey
realized that one could move beyond the impasse of Idealist
concern with a thematic whole and an Empiricist concern with
concrete components by explicating the concrete heuristic
anticipations constitutive of the multiplicity of historical
life-experiences.[118] Such a Lebensphilosophie would seek to
sublate the Kantian Vernunft and Hegelian Geist by articulating the interiority present in the empiricity of historical
life. It would sublate empiricism and positivism through its

---

[116]Cf. G.S., V, 26f., 175, 180, 195, 355f.; IV, 217-228;
VII, 148-152. On the relations of Dilthey and Hegel, cf. H.
Marcuse, Hegels Ontologie und die Theorie der Geschichtlich-
keit, pp. 363-368; and the more nuanced study of J. Suter,
Philosophie et histoire chez W. Dilthey, pp. 156-171.

[117]Cf. G.S., V, 200-240, 400-406; VII, 3-23, 228-245;
VIII, 171-184, 188-189.

[118]Cf. the following section, also G.S., VII, 146-168,
205ff.; VIII, 78-80.

concern with experiential reality - it would be "die Wissenschaft des Wirklichen."[119] In showing the irreducibility of the human sciences to the natural sciences it would maintain the autonomy of <u>historical</u> consciousness, overcoming the historicism of that position by fully accepting the latter as <u>consciousness</u>.[120]

These configurations are reflected today in the growing awareness of the limitations imposed on any purely theoretic or systematic mediation, even in terms of scientific activity itself. This finds expression in the discovery by Gödel of the inherent limitations of any formal-deductive systematic totality, as well as in the questions raised by the persistence of a system in General Systems Theory.[121] At the same time there is a recognition of the constitutive nature of history in the scientific enterprise as such on the part of T. Kuhn's analysis of normal science and revolutionary changes in that enterprise with the limitations such changes imply for scientific paradigms. Historical consciousness is also central in the debates between Structuralism and Marxism, and in those between the logical orientation of the Popper School and the hermeneutic-dialectical trend of the Frankfurt School.[122] While in the sphere of linguistics N. Chomsky has

---

[119]Cf. Chapter Three below, also VIII, 172. Note that in all future references a roman numeral followed by arabic numerals indicates, unless otherwise stated, the volume of Dilthey's <u>Gesammelte Schriften</u> (roman numeral) and the page number (arabic).

[120]Cf. Chapter Three below, also V, 364f.; VIII, 3-9. On the critical potential of cognitional theory vis-à-vis scientistic theories of science, cf. Habermas, <u>Protestbewegung und Hochschulreform</u>, pp. 43-46; and A. Wellmer, <u>Kritische Gesellschaftstheorie und Positivismus</u>.

[121]On Gödel's theorem cf. J. Ladrière, <u>Les limitations internes des formalismes</u> (Louvain, 1957); H. Hermes, <u>Aufzählbarkeit, Entscheidbarkeit, Berechenbarkeit</u> (Berlin, 1961) and the interesting applications to theological hermeneutics by H. Peukert, "Zur formalen Systemtheorie und zur hermeneutischen Problematik einer politischen Theologie," <u>Diskussion zur politischen Theologie</u> (Mainz, 1969), pp. 82-95. On General Systems Theory, cf. Narr, <u>op. cit.</u>, pp. 170-182.

[122]On Kuhn's metascientific position, cf. <u>The Structures of Scientific Revolutions</u> and Lakatos (ed.), <u>Criticism and</u>

indicated the unresolved issue of consciousness.[123] Common
in varying degrees to each of these discussions are the
problems of totality, of the limitations on its logical,
systematic mediation, and of the possible sources of other
mediations and their relations with other forms of mediation
and evaluation in social historical life.

Fourthly, Dilthey realized that the limitations of
systematic mediations meant that any "Besinnung über das
Leben" must take into account the artistic and the religious
mediatory functions in society and history. There could be
no Hegelian sublation of the artistic imagination or religion
through systematic logical thought.[124] He saw a certain
transcultural dimension operative within religious interiority both in terms of the ability of historical religions to
assimilate divergent worldviews and in terms of the transcendent in Schleiermacher's dialectic.[125] His own studies on
literature had convinced him of the "typical" significance
of the artistic as creator and carrier of meanings constitutive of worldviews.[126]

Contemporary theologies, especially in the West, indicate a massive effort at critically confronting their

---

the Growth of Knowledge for his debate with Popper. On the
debates between Structuralism and Marxism, cf. note 110
above, also L. Sebag, Marxisme et Structuralisme (Paris,
1964) and L. Althusser, Pour Marx (Paris, 1965). On the
Popper-Frankfurt debate, cf. E. Topitisch (ed.), Logik der
Sozialwissenschaften (Cologne, 1965); T. Adorno (et al.),
Der Positivismusstreit in der deutschen Soziologie and W.
Hochkeppel (ed.), Soziologie zwischen Theorie und Empirie,
pp. 75-93, 135-153; also Narr, op. cit., pp. 45-83. For
Dilthey's possible contributions in this debate, cf.
Krausser, op. cit., pp. 210-219.

[123]Cf. J. Lyons, Chomsky (London, 1970), pp. 83-108;
also J. Searle, "Chomsky's Revolution in Linguistics,"
The New York Review of Books XVIII (June 29, 1972), pp.
16-24.

[124]Cf. V, 378-398; VI, 144-157, 288-305; VIII, 172f.

[125]Cf. VIII, 172f.; XIV, 100-147; also his projected
theory of dogma reviewed in Renthe-Fink, op. cit., pp. 99-
110. Cf. also Chapter Four below.

[126]Cf. VI, 185-188; VIII, 172f. Also F. Rodi, Morpho-
logie und Hermeneutik: Diltheys Ästhetik, pp. 80-115.

religious traditions with the insights and challenges of the
secularist, atheistic, revolutionary, and scientific currents
of thought and action. Of paramount importance here is to
what extent these theologies must contribute to the dialectic of survival and progressive emancipation on which the
future of mankind depends.[127] For its part, a comparison of
the contemporary artistic imagination with its historical
predecessors typifies the direction of the dialectic. The
art forms of previous ages conformed to certain easily
identifiable patterns, e.g., Romanesque, Gothic, Baroque. The
freeing of the individual imagination in Impressionism and
Expressionism, and the shift toward psychic automism in
Surrealism, liberated the artistic and poetic imagination
from set patterns. The creative variety and polyvalence
of art forms today seem to insist that pattern has value only
to the extent that it reflects the process itself; meaning
must somehow contain its own controls.[128]

This very brief sketch of parallel problematics in
Dilthey and our own present situation as within the dialectic
of the Enlightenment suggests two interrelated sets of provisional conclusions. The first infers the need for broad
interdisciplinary communication and collaboration. The
emergence of scientific consciousness in the Enlightenment,
combined with that of historical consciousness which Dilthey
recorded in philosophy and the Geisteswissenschaften, has
today affected almost every facet of living. This demands
that the constitutive character of scientific consciousness
be properly thematized and appropriated in a critical meta-
method so that, on the one hand, the historical praxis of

---

[127]Cf. J. B. Metz, Stimmen der Zeit (1973), pp. 171-182;
also Zur Theologie der Welt, pp. 99-146 and Diskussion zur
politischen Theologie, pp. 217-301; also G. Picht, Mut zur
Utopie, pp. 131-154. The significance of meta-method lies
in its ability to appropriate both modern scientific-historical
consciousness and religious consciousness; the question is
how intellectual and moral conversion is related to religious
conversion and how all three are ongoing processes; cf.
M.i.T., pp. 237ff.

[128]Cf. W. Hoffmann, Grundlagen der modernen Kunst
(Stuttgart, 1966), pp. 143-496; T. Adorno in Aspekte der
Modernität (ed. Steffen, Göttingen, 1965), pp. 129-149.

the sciences can responsibly constitute its own present and
future activity by promoting projects germane to human historical development (thereby avoiding irrational and "unscientific" manipulation by group or national bias), and,
on the other hand, so that through meta-method the scientific
components of our world situation could be mediated to other
historical components, such as the artistic or religious.

The collaboration such a program requires would be
possible only if history itself, in its spontaneous and
reflective manifestations, is grounded in certain open and
dynamic structures of conscious intentionality. For only on
the basis of such an approach to history would one be able
to do justice to both the spontaneous history of the Lebenswelt and the reflective knowledge of history in research,
interpretation, critical history, and dialectics. Only then
would one be able to relate dynamically the differentiations
of narrative and argument. And one would do this, not by
appealing to the success of the particular methods of historical research in disregard of the problems of historicism (as in the Historical School), nor by so concentrating
upon the meaning uncovered in historical interpretation that
one would either identify that meaning with its logical
expressions (as in the early Husserl and the linguistic
analysts) or assert an almost total non-identity of that
meaning from the meaning found in the natural sciences
and mathematics (as inchoatively in Dilthey and developed
in Heidegger's ontological hermeneutics), nor by so emphasizing the possibility of critical history that one would
overlook the constitutive character of traditions (as in the
Enlightenment's "Vorurteil gegen Vorurteile"), or assume
that criticism could only be grounded in a decisionistic
faith (as with Popper and Albert), nor by erecting some
categorical phenomenon as the criterion for the dialectics
in history (as with Marxism in regard to economics).
Instead, one would ground a meta-methodological approach to
all historical performance on the open, ongoing, and critical
appropriation of conscious intentionality as this is operative
in the related and recurrent operations of common-sense
Lebenswelt and in the methods of research, interpretation,

historical criticism, and dialectics.

The second set of provisional conclusions asks to what extent Dilthey's critique of historical reason could provide the guidelines for elaborating the foundations of such a collaboration. Positively, there is his recognition of the irreducible nature of inner experience: the vital self-presence-in-world (conscious intentionality) which grounds all historical objectifications and is ongoing. Dilthey did not retreat into a vague Romanticist hermeneutics; with the conceptual tools available to him he tried to work out the basic functional patterns or structures operative in spontaneous history and the reflective mediation of history in historical scholarship. Negatively, he did not succeed in overcoming historicism, or in articulating a dialectic based on Verstehen, or in offering an adequate position on theological method. A fundamental problem in the present study of his thought, then, will be to what extent his shortcomings in theology are due to a failure to criticize properly the "autonomous" subjectivity he saw as the result of historical consciousness; to what extent he did not criticize sufficiently presuppositions common to both idealism and empiricism; to what extent the perceptualism he allowed in the natural sciences was simply "interiorized" in his treatment of inner experience, and if this, in turn, kept him from adequately relating science to life.

For the key issue in a confrontation between Dilthey and Lonergan is that the latter does not introduce theological elements or implications immediately into his thematization of meta-method. In this sense he fully respects the autonomy of reason so central to "the history of freedom in the modern epoch."[129] Indeed, it is precisely this autonomy which must be fully respected if meta-method is to be both empirical and transcendental. Lonergan's method does not fall into the abstract totalizing of autonomy found in existentialism or the equally abstract totalizing of sociality in orthodox

<hr>

[129]Cf. Metz, "Kirchliche Autorität im Anspruch der Freiheitgeschichte," in Kirche im Prozess der Aufklärung, pp. 53-90; and W. Oelmüller, "Probleme des neuzeitlichen Freiheits-und Aufklärungsprozesses," ibid., pp. 91-143.

Marxism and liberal neo-Marxism.[130] For, although Lonergan does not immediately introduce theological elements or implications into his methodological articulation of the subject, his study of self-transcending subjectivity as a unity of identity and non-identity does indicate how both the individual and societies are faced with a non-identity of evil and suffering which cannot be abstractly forgotten or repressed.[131]

Hence, the arguments with Dilthey, from the framework of Lonergan's meta-method, will be critically grounded in the experience of cognitional self-appropriation. It is this perspective which gives the present study a range beyond the immediate interest in Dilthey and Lonergan. For it presents a basic stance or horizon which seeks to uncover the dialectic between the aspirations of modernity toward freedom and responsible autonomy and the failure of modernity to thematize that freedom and autonomy in a free and autonomous fashion. The perceptualism in Dilthey's critique of historical reason was, and is, symptomatic of an understanding of freedom and autonomy in their relationships to knowing which seem incapable of thematizing the unity of identity and non-identity.

2. Critique and Method

I believe, therefore, that a confrontation of Dilthey and Lonergan is not without relevance to an understanding of later thinkers whose criticisms of Dilthey remain more or less within the limits defined by Anschauung, not as a figure of speech but as a stance toward the real.[132] For the fundamental problem in Dilthey formulated above concerns the bifurcation of the phenomenal and noumenal, which is by no means absent in more recent philosophers.[133] Only by overcoming this bifurcation would we be in a position to ground

---

[130]Cf. Metz, Stimmen der Zeit, pp. 171ff. Also the final section of this Chapter.

[131]Cf. Insight, pp. 619-633, 687-703, 721ff.

[132]Cf. the final section of this Chapter.

[133]Cf. T. Prufer, "A Protreptic: What is Philosophy?" Studies in Philosophy (Washington, D.C., 1963), pp. 1-19. And W. Oelmüller, Die Unbefriedigte Aufklärung, pp. 9-34.

meta-method on responsible autonomy and to handle the long
range problems of our present historical situation. The
emergence of modern science and historical consciousness
in the Enlightenment, their increasing differentiations and
contemporary convergence force into the open a need for a
basic dialectic to liberate man from a fundamental alienation.
As basic the dialectic was always operative, but the classical
forms of culture and traditional societies rendered its
thematization impossible by their arbitrary standardizations
of man and his historical activity. The dissolution of those
classical forms and traditional societies[134] has faced
contemporary man with the dilemma of recognizing his own
radical historicality and simultaneously finding the critical
norms with which to counteract the repressive irrationality in
himself and society, with which, in other words, to guide his
own constituting of history in a truly free and responsible
manner. The dilemma goes to the heart of the dialectic of
the Enlightenment. The various forms of the phenomenon-
noumenon dichotomy, both in their cognitional theoretical,
epistemological, and ethical implications, at bottom have
failed to come to terms with the dilemma and dialectic.

The significance of Lonergan's meta-method, it seems
to me, consists in its ability to confront and sublate the
dilemma insofar as it overcomes the dichotomy through its
thematization of the basic horizon of historicality.[135] The
invitation to a self-appropriation of basic horizon is not to
reach above or behind history, not to autocratically impose

---

[134]On classical culture, cf. Lonergan, Collection, pp.
252-267; M.i.T., pp. xi, 124, 300-302, 315, 326, 338f., 363;
on traditional societies, cf. J. Habermas, Technik und
Wissenschaft als "Ideologie", pp. 65-73.

[135]On basic horizon, cf. D. Tracy, The Achievement of
Bernard Lonergan, pp. 133-182; that this approach is protean,
notice its import for eschatology, D. Tracy, "Horizon Analysis
and Eschatology," Continuum 6 (1968), pp. 166-179, and its
relevance for fundamental problems in physics, cf. P. Heelan,
"Horizon, Objectivity and Reality in the Physical Sciences,"
I.P.Q. (1967), pp. 375-412. Historicality is not ontologized
but rather understood in a manner open to meta-method as the
ongoing process of conscious intentionality; cf. M.i.T.,
pp. 325, 235-253, 302-318.

some pattern on it, nor to ontologize history through abstract references to historicality, but to discover in one's self the open and dynamic structures of one's own concrete consti- tuting of history; and, through collaboration, to gradually interrelate the complications, concretizations, amplifications, and differentiations of consciousness in its manifold arti- culations within the course of history.

An appropriation of the basic structures of conscious intentionality as empirical, intelligent, critical, and responsible does not allow one to turn immediately to spe- cialized problems. The latter must be handled by autonomous methods suitable to their fields. The importance of meta- method as the appropriation of conscious intentionality con- sists in its ability to order the cumulative complexity of multiplying specializations, and to do so in a way that is both open and critical. It is open inasmuch as it succeeds in bringing to light the dynamic and creative drive of the human mind, structuring its fundamental meta-method on that drive. It is also this open character of meta-method that assures the possibility of mediating the future:

> Now it becomes apparent that this world-horizon itself
> has the character of a project. It must have the
> character of a project, since "world" itself is in
> time, is openly oriented into the future.[136]

It is critical because it goes to the heart of the dialectic of the Enlightenment through exposing the false ultimacy of manipulative and objectivistic reason which has gained such a mastery over man and society through techno-

---

[136]This is the conclusion of G. Picht in his article on "Die Kunst des Denkens" in Wahrheit-Vernunft-Verantwortung, p. 434. Picht is arguing for the primacy of poetic reason over theoretical and practical reason. But note that he has accepted the Kantian understanding of the latter two and ends his article where the difficulty begins for Kant, who was unable to effectively interrelate his critique of pure reason and his critique of practical reason in his critique of aesthetic reason in Kritik der Urteilskraft; cf. note 73 above. But insofar as creative reason grounds the entire range of patterns of performance (whether those patterns be theoretical, practical, or aesthetic) then certainly a thematization of the heuristic structures of creative reason (Welthorizont als Entwurf) is within time and as such open to the future; cf. Lonergan, Insight, pp. 105-139.

logy.[137] It effectively removes method from being the prerogative domain of scientism, while it also refuses to disparage method in the name of an ontologizing historicality.[138]
Thus it effectively offers an alternative to the either-or
dilemma of positivism versus idealism, empiricism versus
existentialism. For the orientation of meta-method is the
adoption of a moving viewpoint which, through collaboration,
could elaborate the concrete dialectics operative in all
patterns of historical performance: whether those be common-
sense, artistic, political, scientific, philosophical, or
theological.[139] Meta-method sets up the obvious but overlooked dialectic of the basic horizon that breaks through
the phenomenon-noumenon bifurcation without resorting to an
exclusive identity or non-identity pattern. Men, groups,
classes, societies, nations are either attentive, intelligent,
reasonable, and responsible in their constituting of history,

---

[137]Cf. Adorno and Horkheimer, _Dialektik der Aufklärung_;
note how meta-method does not succumb to any possible accu-
sation of resignation in the face of objectivistic scientism
because it has seen through the "objectivistic illusion" in
the identification of method with objectivistic technique.
Cf. G. Rohrmoser, _Das Elend der kritischen Theorie_ (Freiburg,
1970) and W. Post, _Kritische Theorie und metaphysischer_
Pessimismus (Munich, 1971).

[138]Cf. J. Habermas, _Philosophisch-Politische Profile_,
p. 31; yet Habermas himself realizes the need to sublate
this false identification of reason with manipulative technique;
cf. _Technik und Wissenschaft als "Ideologie"_, pp. 48-103;
Horkheimer, "Zur Kritik der instrumentalen Vernunft," in
Kritische Theorie der Gesellschaft, vol. III, pp. 118-279.
Yet this does not lead critical theory to renounce the need
to develop scientifically acceptable alternatives to scientism; cf. Habermas, _ibid._, pp. 112-113; and his _Protest-_
bewegung und Hochschulreform, p. 44: "Die Kehrseite der
Positivimuskritikist nämlich die Einsicht, dass sich jede
Theorie der Gesellschaft am Forschungsstand der empirischen
Wissenschaften und vor dem Forum der zeitgenössischen
Wissenschaftstheorie rechtfertigen muss." On the possibilities of Lonergan's meta-method in this context, cf. final
section of this Chapter.

[139]Cf. Lonergan, _Collection_, pp. 219-220; _Insight_, pp.
390-396; _M.i.T._, pp. 3-25. Note how meta- or transcendental
method provides the possibility of a _critical_ metaphysics as
the integral heuristic structure of proportionate being by
indicating how metaphysics is not the ultimate instance of
criticism but rather meta-method itself, _ibid._, pp. 120,
261, 343; _Collection_, pp. 202-220.

or they are inattentive, stupid, irrational, and irresponsible.

This foundational dialectic defines the basic positions and counter-positions, and it does so by appealing to the inherent open and dynamic structures of human freedom. There is no skirting of the dialectical issue, as in empiricism and positivism; nor is there any appeal to a Kantian faith in the "Intuitus Originarius" of God, to an Hegelian absolute knowledge, or to a Marxian "Träger der Geschichte."[140] Meta-method is not an Husserlian epoche with its "Weltvernichtung" in an effort to attain a transcendental subjectivity, only to be asked by Heidegger in what sense the absolute ego is also the factual "I"; nor is it some form of Heideggerian "Daseinsanalyse" where the ontological difference does not clarify how Dasein is related to ontic individuals or how Being-as-history is related to ontic history, thereby leaving its speculations on historicality open to the charge of abstract ontologizing of history.[141]

It is understandable how the effort at recovering those dimensions of historical existence, society, and the future minimized or discounted by the advance of objectivistic methods would appeal to the "forgotten" traditions of onto-logical reflection.   Yet the failure to bring this ontological dimension into a practically critical relation to our "scientized" and technological society (in order to unmask the destructive, repressive, and irrational practices of that society) has led, as M. Horkheimer has indicated, to an ontologizing equally as objectivistic as the manipulative

---

[140]Cf. Prufer, op. cit., pp. 13-16. On Kant see the references in notes 29, 30, 68, 69, 70, 133, 134, 135 above; on Hegel, cf. notes 88, 89, 90, 92, 136, 137 above; the reference to Marx's position in notes 91, 92, 93, 99, 139, 141 above. Note how for Marx the Kantian noumenal Ding-an-sich reappears under the name of nature prior to human history; cf. Habermas, Erkenntnis und Interesse, p. 47.

[141]On Husserl and Heidegger, cf. references in final section of this Chapter; also the question posed by Bormann to Gadamer: "Doch wie erfahren wir diese Verbindung von Object und Subject, von Sein und Verstehen?" in Bormann's "Die Zweideutigkeit der hermeneutischen Erfahrung," Philos. Rundschau 16 (1969), p. 118. On the ontologizing of his-toricality, cf. Adorno, Negative Dialektik, pp. 132-134.

methods it belittled.[142]   Nor does one have to turn only to
German existentialism to witness this tendency; the counter-
culture in the United States amply illustrates the frustration
of those unable to humanize a growing technocratic anonymity.[143]

The dialectic set up by the Enlightenment cannot be
met by simply delimiting the modes of knowing, by trying to
reinstate the ontological validity of subjectivity. Such an
approach fails to get at the heart of the matter insofar as
it tries to establish a "sacred grove" or noumenal domain
inaccessible to scientific investigation. As such, it does
not have the ability to offer a truly radical critique of
scientism but is merely a privatized appendage, a metaphysical
curiosity, which can well be tolerated as a minority opinion
within technocratic rationality. The relevance of Lonergan's
meta-method is that it goes to the core of the dialectic
of the Enlightenment. It challenges the scientistic monopoly
of method as a mere assemblage of rules or protocol axioms,
not by asking the metaphysical question concerning what it
is that we know, nor even primarily by asking the epistemological question of why or how reliable knowledge is possible, but by asking the praxis-oriented cognitional theoretical question of what the sciences do when they know.[144]
It is within this critical perspective that meta-method is
able to relate the basic structures of knowing and action in
the sciences with those in the other spheres of human historical activity. Insofar as meta-method articulates a dialectic in terms of those structures of human activity it would

---

[142]In Kritische Theorie der Gesellschaft, I, pp. 17ff.;
II, pp. 84f. The juxtaposition of mechanism and mysticism, of
positivism and metaphysics, is by no means unintelligible; cf.
J. Habermas, Erkenntnis und Interesse, pp. 103-104.

[143]Richard King, The Party of Eros: Radical Social
Thought and the Realm of Freedom (Univ. of North Carolina
Press, 1972) presents a sympathetic but cogently critical
account of the counter-culture in the United States. The
counter-culture is a symptom of the dilemma within our
society, not a solution for it.

[144]On the differentiation of these three fundamental
questions, cf. Lonergan, M.i.T., pp. 25, 83, 261, 286f.,
316. Also the final section of this Chapter.

provide a meta-dialectical framework for interrelating
particular dialectics and liberate them from the bias generated by the tendency to universalize the particular.[145] This
is especially necessary today as we become more aware of the
complexity of the socio-historical changes and revolutions,
and the insufficiency of particular dialectics to account
thematically for their own functioning when the thematization
of the dialectic is treated in isolation.

Politically, the absurdity of the arms race and the
threat of total nuclear destruction have ruled out national
sovereignty or class warfare as ultimate dialectical criteria.
This realization, however, must not minimize the dialectical
tensions created by politico-economic exploitation and
colonialism.[146] Economically, the scandal of increasing
poverty in the midst of affluence and the concentration of
capital reveal the ideological aspects of the free enterprise
system, while the momentum toward a post-industrial society
proportionately narrows the applicability of dialectics
based upon ownership of the means of production.[147] Scientifically, the point was made by Norbert Wiener that to live
successfully in an increasingly man-made world "we must know
as scientists what man's nature is and what his built-in
purposes are." Yet this implicit recognition of the end
of the ivory tower myth of value-free science must not, in its
turn, give way to a new objectivistic myth by reducing praxis

---

[145]Cf. Lonergan, M.i.T., pp. 20-25, 137; Insight, pp.
230-232, 747 on the social consequences of this tendency.
Thus the dialectics in meta-method no more sublate the particular dialectics than meta-method would the manifold of
particular methods; cf. ibid., pp. 222-242, 380f., 393, 685f.

[146]Cf. N. Chomsky, American Power and the New Mandarins,
pp. 221-404; G. Picht, Mut zur Utopie, pp. 35-70; R. Heilbronner, The Future as History, pp. 61-114; M. Raskin, Being
and Doing: Colonialism in America (New York, 1971).

[147]Cf. R. Heilbronner, The Limits of American Capitalism
(New York, 1965) and his corresponding, "Reflections on the
Future of Socialism," in Between Capitalism and Socialism,
pp. 79-114; F. Lundberg, The Rich and the Super-Rich (New
York, 1969); W. Brus, Funktionsprobleme der sozialistischen
Wirtschaft (Frankfurt, 1971). R. J. Barnet and R. Müller,
Global Reach (New York, 1975).

to manipulative technique.[148] In meta-science this is reflected in the tension between recognizing the inherent limits of
formal deductive and inductive logics, and the futility of
vague or non-verifiable appeals to the pre-logical.[149] These
dialectical problems are, perhaps, summed up on the level of
philosophy where, on the one hand, the growing acknowledgment
of a tyranny in tolerance and a new irrationalism under the
guise of pluralism is matched, on the other, by an abhorrence
of any restriction of freedom or arbitrary imposition of
particular systems.[150] Theologically, there arise the
problems associated with the mounting irrelevance of ecclesial
traditions and institutions in the face of these contemporary
dialectical tensions, and, on the other hand, the need to
explicate theological foundations which will not negate those
traditions and institutions through some uncritical
secularization.[151]

In meeting these dialectics the advantage of meta-method
consists in its exclusion of the noumenon-phenomenon dichotomy,
which means that it moves beyond the dilemma of immanentism
versus extrinsicism. For all forms of extrinsicism are
radically criticized without falling into the pitfalls of

---

[148]This was the intention of Wiener in his The Human
Use of Human Beings, pp. 250-280; G. Picht, Wahrheit-
Vernunft-Verantwortung, pp. 343-407; F. Matson, The Broken
Image, where he concludes: "When man is the subject, the
proper understanding of science leads unmistakably to the
science of understanding." (p. 247). Also J. Habermas,
Technik und Wissenschaft als 'Ideologie,'"pp. 48-168; and
his Arbeit-Erkenntnis-Fortschritt (Amsterdam, 1970), pp.
335-355.

[149]Cf. W. -D. Narr, Theoriebegriffe und Systemtheorie
(Stuttgart, 1969), pp. 63-65, 79-83; Radnitzky, op. cit.,
pp. xiv-xxi, xxiv-xl. On the American scene, cf. T. Kuhn,
"Logic of Discovery or Psychology of Research?" in Criticism
and the Growth of Knowledge, pp. 1-23, 259-266.

[150]This is the problematic of relativism versus dogma-
ticism as it has been articulated in myriad manners since
the breakdown of classicist culture. Cf. Lonergan, Collection, pp. 252-264; H. Marcuse, One-Dimensional Man, pp.
203-257.

[151]Cf. K. Derksen and M. Xhaufflaire, Les deux visages
de la théologie de la sécularisation on the ambiguity of
secularization; also cf. the references in note 53 above.

immanentism.[152] This may appear remote from the concerns hinted at in the outlines of the dialectics above until one reflects on the centrality of structure versus consciousness, of fact versus value, of price versus labor, of logic versus intuition, of institution versus freedom, of a hermeneutical tradition versus a critique of ideology, of a system of beliefs versus a criterion of criticism - polarities which are intrinsic to the debates occasioned by the particular dialectics dealt with above. It is in the light of them that I believe one must situate the relevance of meta-method, the basic dialectic of which is grounded in the open and dynamic sources of human activity, leading everyone to desire and claim some measure of attentiveness, intelligence, reasonableness, and responsibility in the historical activities constituted by his personal, group, and national practices - whether that practice be in the spontaneous worlds of common sense, economics, and politics, or in the reflective worlds of science, philosophy, theology. For in terms of meta-method the fundamental alienation of men and societies is from these sources of human praxis.

In order to clarify the historical similarities and differences between the contexts of Dilthey and Lonergan, however, it will be necessary to explore in more detail how they respectively analyze the shifts that have occurred. The next two sections will accordingly differentiate Dilthey's understanding of modernity as defined in relation to the shift from metaphysics to cognitional theory, and Lonergan's understanding of the contemporary problematic as a shift from cognitional theory to method.

THE PATHOS OF THE ENLIGHTENMENT:
FROM METAPHYSICS TO COGNITIONAL THEORY

Georg Misch has documented how seriously Dilthey was committed to the ethos of the Enlightenment, to the mediation

---

[152] Cf. Lonergan's De Methodo Theologiae (Unpublished Scriptum, Rome, 1962), pp. 28-35.

of scientific and historical, empirical and critical, consciousness.[153] If this was "the passionate impulse" of the
young Dilthey, it was just as vibrant in the evening of
Dilthey's life, even though he then realized the fragmentary
character of his contributions to such a mediation.[154] In
the last year of his life Dilthey recalled how, despite his
admiration for the natural sciences and the revolutions they
were effecting in human awareness, he realized that their
methods could not adequately do justice precisely to the
world of historical awareness they were so strongly influencing. He was, in a sense, a man without an intellectual
country or integrating and ordering worldview which could
coordinate his many historical interests. Although he was
disgusted with the attempts to artificially restore a theological worldview, he could not rest content with a merely
hypothetical character of a contented postivist worldview.[155]

The ethos of the Enlightenment, then, was not without
a pathos. P. Hünermann has shown how, for Dilthey, the poetic
was the "organ and prototype of the epochal new self-
understanding of modernity."[156] And F. Rodi has studied the
enigma of Dilthey's aesthetics - an enigma that consisted
in the attempt to do justice to both the genetic and gener-
alizing methods of morphology and also to the more historical,
individualizing approaches of his _Verstehen-Hermeneutik_.[157]
He sees the enigma of the aesthetics as the enigma of Dilthey
himself - "that enigmatic old scholar" whose immersion in
the philosophical, aesthetic, and scientific currents of his
time had stamped his mind with a resignation, a pathos for
totality and detail, which he could never resolve.[158] It

---

[153]Cf. Misch's long introduction to Volume V of the _G.S._,
pp. xi-xxx. The same point is made by J. -F. Suter, _op. cit._,
pp. 13-48.

[154]Cf. _G.S._ V, ix-xii.

[155]Cf. _G.S._ V, 4.

[156]Cf. Hünermann, _op. cit._, pp. 148-152.

[157]Frithjof Rodi, _Morphologie und Hermeneutik: Diltheys
Ästhetik_ (Stuttgart, 1969), pp. 9ff.

[158]_Ibid._, pp. 9-10.

was, however, more than simply a personal characteristic of
Dilthey - for in his own eyes it was the fate of the Enlightenment itself. His earliest diary entries attest to the
pathological literature of the eighteenth and nineteenth
centuries; the "Weltschmerz" arising from the mounting tension
between individuality and universality, between "life" and
"ideal."[159]

Dilthey was not only concerned that "the period of the
Enlightenment is the foundation of our scientific culture and
of my education."[160] He also was only too aware of the profound difference between the Enlightenment in Germany and
its counterpart in France and England.[161] As the real force
of the empiricism, characteristic of the Enlightenment in the
latter countries was beginning to be felt in the Germany of
his time, Dilthey saw how the skepticism it would bring with
it would make the skepticism of antiquity appear like "a
syllogistic game."[162] For the Enlightenment was the beginning
of a whole new control of meaning and value which would make
itself felt in every domain of human thought and action. The
classical control had found its expression in metaphysical
worldviews claiming to offer universally valid systems of
meanings and values.[163] The Enlightenment had solidified the

_____

[159] Der junge Dilthey: Ein Lebensbild in Briefen und
Tagebüchern, 1852-1870, edited by Clara Misch (nee Dilthey),
2nd edition (Stuttgart, 1960), pp. 2-5. From henceforth this
work will be referred to as D.J.D. In later life, 1898 to
be exact, Dilthey formulated the dilemma and contradiction
even more strongly; cf. G.S. VIII, pp. 193-194.

[160] Leben Schleiermachers I, p. 83. Cf. also Das Erlebnis und die Dichtung, pp. 219ff., and G.S. VIII, 191.
This, of course, is the guiding motive for Dilthey to under-
take a critique of historical reason, cf. I, pp. xvff. Henceforth Leben Schleiermachers will be abbreviated to L.S.

[161] L.S. I, pp. 85-87; also G.S. III, pp. 19-25, 86-205
(esp. pp. 142-157).

[162] L.S., p. 86; also G.S. VIII, p. 194. It was the
Enlightenment that rendered futile any dreams of a "modern
metaphysics" which could provide a mediation of meaning
comparable to pre-Enlightenment metaphysics, Cf. G.S. II,
pp. 498-499.

[163] Cf. G.S. I, pp. 150-158; 215-235; II, pp. 494-499.
As these references make clear, Dilthey distinguished between

gradual emancipation (begun during the Reformation and Renaissance) of religious subjectivity, scientific investigation, and political praxis from the domination of the medieval metaphysical epoch.[164] Yet Dilthey was of the opinion that a thoroughgoing modern control of meaning and value had not yet been found. He could not share the mechanistic optimism of the positivists or the rationalistic deductivism of the Neokantians; both were equally abstract.[165] Neither could handle the concrete socio-historical processes set in motion by the Enlightenment. The new control had to be empirical but it could not be empiricist or idealist. For Dilthey knew all too well where the latter two would lead: "there would remain only a choice between a total submission to authority or a total cynicism."[166]

In order to appreciate Dilthey's understanding of the Enlightenment, one has to realize the extent to which he - more than any of his philosophical contemporaries - grasped the centrality of the scientific revolution in all domains of modern man's social historical life.[167] He saw the

---

the metaphysics of the Greeks and the metaphysics of the emerging European peoples, with the latter exhibiting an uneasy alliance with Christian interiority.

[164]Cf. G.S. I, pp. 351-359; II, pp. 16-18, 48, 53, 110-144.

[165]Cf. G.S. I, pp. 123-124: "Indeed, empiricism is not less abstract than pure speculation. The notion of man as a combination of impressions and sensations, from which influential empiricist schools construct man, as from atoms, contradicts that inner experience from the elements of which the image of man really emerges. Their machine (idea of man) would not have the ability to provide for itself in the world. The structure of society, which follows from this empiricist notion of man, is just as much a projected construction of abstract elements as those constructions of speculative schools of thought.... Against the dominant empiricism, as well as against pure speculation, we must strive to uncover the historical and social reality of man as fully as possible."

[166]L.S., p. 86. It is noticeable how Dilthey saw in German Idealism and the transcendental philosophy of Kant a corrective to empiricism only if the more experiential framework of Schleiermacher could be made fruitful for the grounding of the cultural sciences. Cf. ibid., pp. 94-113.

[167]M. Riedel, Einleitung, p. 14.

significance of the increasingly specialized empirical methods of the natural sciences in the dissolution of fundamental metaphysical concepts and the speculative systems built on those concepts.[168] More important still, he saw the dangers in the wholesale adoption by the human sciences of those natural scientific methods; how the pragmatism, positivism, and utilitarianism of the social sciences were as unable to handle the historicality of social reality as the transcendental approaches of the Neokantians.[169] The pathos of the Enlightenment for Dilthey consisted in its healthy skepticism vis-à-vis the antinomies of metaphysics linked to its unhealthy bewilderment regarding its own foundations and the trust it put in the progress of the natural sciences. Under the pressure of the resulting "anarchy of convictions" it was all too easy to either resign oneself (and the social process) to a laissez-faire experimentation in hypothetical reason, or to blindly throw one's trust to a metaphysics (and resulting social order) "which would seductively promise to provide the power for reshaping practical life."[170]

In order to appreciate the task Dilthey set himself in attempting a critique of historical reason, it is important to see how he criticized the philosophies of science, seeing in both French positivism and British empiricism and German Neokantianism common shortcomings, and was able because of these criticisms to avoid the naive "critique of metaphysics" which, as Habermas mentions, soon was to turn on the "critique of knowing" of those very philosophies of science.[171] Here Dilthey was committed to taking modernity and its critical spirit in total seriousness in order to ground that very spirit, not leaving it to a hypothetical utilitarianism nor a

---

[168]Cf. G.S. VIII, 191, 199-201 where Dilthey discusses the pathos of modernity as that of the Enlightenment.

[169]Cf. Hodges, op. cit., pp. xix-xxi, 18-20, 28-31, 53-55, 72-76, 104f., 108f., 147f., 162-164. For a summary of Dilthey's remarks in this connection, cf. G.S. I, pp. xv-xx.

[170]G.S. I, pp. xvif., 407.

[171]Cf. Habermas, Erkenntnis und Interesse, pp. 88-92.

totalitarian decisionism. A similar attitude is to be seen
in Dilthey's critical evaluation of the theological situation
in modernity: a refusal to identify Christianity with its
dogmatic expressions and a quest for an adequate expression
of the religious impulse, rather than a simple rejection.

This section will seek to establish this context of
Dilthey's critique by first discussing his critique of the
philosophies of science prevalent in his time, and will then
take up his understanding of the critique of metaphysics and
the need to take metaphysical questions seriously in any
critique of historical reason.

1. Metascience: A Critique

Dilthey himself never used the term "metascience" to
designate the philosophy of science. But he recorded well
the shift occurring within philosophy from the seventeenth
century onwards as it moved from metaphysical concerns to
concentrate its attention on the sciences themselves. As
the sciences became ever more privileged mediators of a
valid knowledge and objectivity, philosophy had little choice
but to differentiate itself from an exclusive priority given
to metaphysical reflection. The philosophies of Descartes,
Spinoza, or Leibniz had sought to provide the basis for a
new identity-affirmation of metaphysics with their "constructive" methodologies - Dilthey's designation of the deductive
identity thought-patterns which essayed a new articulation of
certain principles as first or basic, and on which one would
then construct a rationalist world through deduction.[172]

Such methodologies, however, came under the sharp
critique of those who saw philosophy as dedicated instead to
a cognitional theory, a logic of science, or theory of scientific theories - taking the sciences and mathematics as the norm
of knowledge.[173] Cognitional theory, at the hands of a Comte,
Locke, Hume, or Kant replaced metaphysics by declaring it an

---

[172]Cf. G.S. I, pp. 351-359, 386-397; II, pp. 246-296,
452-471; III, pp. 25-40.

[173]Cf. G.S. I, pp. 14-21, 359-373; II, pp. 453-458;
V, pp. 356-363, 406-413: VIII, pp. 206-219. On the theological implications of this shift as exemplified in Leibniz,
cf. III, pp. 62-68.

unfounded futility.[174]   Identity systems gave way - despite
the Hegelian interlude - to non-identity. Dilthey was not
about to choose sides; he did not see either identity or
non-identity as capable of adequately mediating the reality
of historical life. It is central to an understanding of
his critique of historical reason to clearly situate his
criticisms of the transcendentalist, positivist, and empiricist philosophies of science, or, as they might be called
today, schools of metascience. For it is only in the light
of these criticisms that we would be in a position to appreciate how Dilthey's seemingly cognitional theoretical approach
does not fall under the verdict of "der Überschwenglichkeit
und der Sinnlosigkeit" which contemporary scientistic positivism and empiricism have passed on the older traditions of
transcendentalism, positivism and empiricism - just as the
latter had done regarding metaphysics.[175]

First, I shall briefly characterize, according to Dilthey,
the three schools of metascience in his day, then go on to the
three main criticisms he leveled against them.

Within this context I have not explicitly treated Dilthey's notion of the "naturalist systems" which, in the
seventeenth and eighteenth centuries, preceded and made
possible the three schools of metascience. Instead I have
concentrated on the cognitional theoretical and practical
implications of naturalism as these affected the positions
of Kantian transcendentalism, Comtean positivism, and British
empiricism.

A.   Three Forms of Metascience. There are three main
forms of this unmetaphysical approach to the philosophy of
science, or metascience. The first was the cognitional
theoretical stance of Kant and his followers. He initiated
a transcendental methodological analysis of the a priori
conditions of the possibility of knowledge, where the latter
was defined in terms of the mathematical and natural sciences

---

[174]Cf. G.S. V, 356-363; also I, 377f., 394f.

[175]Cf. reference in note 20 above; also J. Mittelstrass,
Neuzeit und Aufklärung, pp. 377-410, and E. Cassirer, Die
Philosophie der Aufklärung, pp. 160-177.

of his day. While this offered a critique of the constructive methods operative since Descartes, it nevertheless
sought to provide a new basis for a metaphysics within the
limits of transcendental subjectivity.[176] It was not
surprising, therefore, that pure reason soon diminished the
efficacy of criticism, that the empirical was soon smothered
by purely hypothetical speculations within the successive
attempts to elaborate a new metaphysics.[177]

The second form rejected any concessions to a transcendental cognitional theory. It sought to remain strictly
within the boundaries of the empirical sciences and their
results. The center of this philosophy of science or metascience was in the givenness of experience, as that was
defined by the particular sciences. The task of philosophy
was to criticize thoroughly all efforts of reflection to
uncover universal validity and to content itself with an
ongoing correlation of the manifold results of the sciences.[178] Thus it became an "encyclopedia of sciences," finding
its basis in the inner relations of the sciences and restrict-
ing itself to the objective knowledge - however hypothetical -
of those sciences.[179] Here we have the positivist

---

[176]On Dilthey's relation to Kant, cf. J. -F. Suter, _op._
cit., pp. 49-44; P. Krauser, _op. cit._, pp. 37-40; H. Krakauer,
Dilthey's Stellung zur theoretischen Philosophie Kants.
(Doctoral dissertation in Erlangen, 1913.) On Dilthey's
critique of Kant, and its relation to the constructive
methods of metaphysics, cf. _G.S._ V, 354ff. Compare this to
Dilthey's presentation of Schleiermacher's dependence on, and
criticism of, Kant in _L.S._ pp. 94-118. On Herbart and Lotze,
who influenced Neokantianism, cf. Dilthey's "Erfahren und
Denken: Eine Studie zur erkenntnistheoretischen Logik des 19.
Jahrhunderts "(1892), _G.S._ V, 74-89; VII, 191f.

[177]Cf. _G.S._   V, 356 and 358, where Dilthey is refer-
ing to the Neokantians as continuing many of the positions of
thinkers like Herbart and Lotze. Cf. also V, 242f. On the
influence of Lotze on the Baden Neokantians, cf. I. M.
Bochenski, _Europäische Philosophie der Gegenwart_ (Bern,
1947), p. 103, and T. Yura, _Geisteswissenschaft und Willens-_
gesetz: Kritische Untersuchung der Methodenlehre der Geistes-
wissenschaften in den Badischen, Marburger und Dilthey-Schule
(Hamburg, Diss., 1938).

[178]Cf. _G.S._ V, pp. 356-363.

[179]Cf. _G.S._ V, pp. 359f.; also I, pp. 104ff.

methodologies which include and go beyond those developed
by Comte and his followers. There are, for example, the
voluntaristic methods of political and legal sciences which
are closely related to positivism,[180] or the mechanistic
ideals of a unified social science.[181]

The third form of metascience was an empiricist
(Dilthey occasionally referred to it as phenomenalist) method.
It accepted the failure of metaphysics to provide a foundation
for scientific objectivity, but it also realized the ahistorical insufficiency of both the transcendental and the positivist methodologies.[182] For both of these previous methodologies had failed to do justice to the empirical reality of
human historical consciousness itself, to the factuality
of minds in their countless and manifold objectifications in
history.[183] Inner experience was the starting point for this
cognitional theoretical approach, but it was inner experience
as handled by an explanatory psychology, i.e., a psychology
based upon a transposition of the objectivistic methods of
the natural sciences.[184] As long as this tutelage remained
such empirical methods could not answer the questions posed
by the transcendental methods regarding the universal validity
of knowledge, nor could they collaborate in the task of the

---

[180]Cf. G.S. V, pp. 360f. Also X, pp. 13-17; and I, pp.
86-112. On Dilthey's critique of positivism and especially
Comte, cf. J. F. Suter, op. cit., pp. 13-37, 137-144.

[181]Cf. G.S. I, pp. 86-115, 420-423; III, pp. 176f., 200;
for a contemporary analog to Dilthey's observation that
modern society "is comparable to a massive mechanized factory"
(I, p.1), cf. L. Mumford, The Myth of the Machine: The
Pentagon of Power (New York, 1970), pp. 230-299, esp. p.
240: "The effect of this regimen has become plain. What
social reformers like Condorcet, Saint-Simon, Auguste Comte
learned from the Napoleonic era was the efficacy with which
military technique can be applied to social behavior. These
prophets envisaged a 'revolution so final and complete that
it would render all legal and political institutions absolute.'
That goal identifies the new megamachine, and this revolution
is now in process."

[182]Cf. G.S. V, pp. 361f.

[183]Ibid. V, p. 362; I, p. 377.

[184]Cf. G.S. V, pp. 158-168. Also Hodges, op. cit.,
pp. 16ff.

positivist methods to correlate the many individual scien-
ces.[185] In general, the third form represents the Anglo-
Saxon empiricist positions from Hume through Adam Smith,
Bentham, and James Mill to John Stuart Mill and Bain.[186]

These three forms of metascience, or the philosophy
of science, corresponded to the three main orientations of
the Enlightenment in Germany, France, and England respectively. In his own time Dilthey saw the need for a communication and confrontation among these three orientations or
"schools" of metascience.[187] Indeed, his own work was an
anticipation of such a confrontation since he realized that
"die ungeheure Kraft" of empiricism and positivism would
challenge the entire spectrum of the German Enlightenment
thought from Leibniz to Schleiermacher and Hegel.[188] More
than that, his own studies of these schools had convinced
him that they had certain common failures which led them to
misrepresent the empirical significance and performance of
the sciences themselves. There were three failures common to
these metascientific orientations: a too exclusive reliance on
the methods of the natural sciences, a too objectivistic
approach to the problem of a scientific mediation of the

---

[185] Cf. G.S. V, p. 362.

[186] Ibid. Dilthey mentions the influence of Herbart on
these trends; on the relation of the Neokantians and English
empiricism, cf. W. M. Simon, European Positivism in the 19th
Century (Ithaca, New York, 1963).

[187] Cf. J. -F. Suter, op. cit., pp. 4ff.; H. A. Hodges,
op. cit., pp. 1-25; G. Iggers, Deutsche Geschichtswissenschaft
(München, 1971), pp. 163-198; H. I. Marrou, De la connaissance
historique (Paris, 1954), pp. 19-23.

[188] Cf. G.S. V, p. 3; L.S., pp. 85f.: "The limits and
characteristics of the German Enlightenment can be fully
grasped only if its profound opposition to the British
and French scientific movements is considered. The historical abstraction of a common philosophy of the Enlightenment, for which we must thank a totally false theological
point of view, has prevented historians from gaining an
important insight. During the eighteenth century, the
scientific movement in England and France took a direction
which contradicts that taken by a whole series of German
thinkers, from Leibniz to the deaths of Schleiermacher and
Hegel." Also M. Riedel in Hermeneutik und Dialektik I, pp.
236f.

totality of reality, a resulting inability to mediate methodologically scientific theory and social praxis.

B. Reduction to Natural Scientific Methods. First of all, there was an excessive dependence upon the methods of the natural sciences. Dilthey was well aware of the massive proportions of the scientific revolution brought about by the spread of mathematics and the exact natural sciences. He traced their gradual institutionalization in the academies, their influence on European societies, and their increasing specialization.[189] While the natural sciences were eroding the metaphysical conceptions on objectivity, knowledge, and reality without falling into the skepticism which had always shadowed metaphysics, it was understandable that meta-scientific reflection would base itself upon the methods of those sciences. Copernicus, Galileo, and Kepler had initiated these methods in their correlations between empirical observation and mathematical-mechanical measurement. The latter represented the a priori elements which went into scientific construction of experience.[190] The subjectivity of sense impressions was checked by the objectivity of the logical-mathematical constructions of experience, British empiricism turned to an analysis of the phenomenality of the perception of the external, given, physical world. The methods of analysis and synthesis in Hobbes, the simple and complex ideas of Locke, or the association psychologism of Hume - these were all efforts to critically ground scientific knowledge via the external experiences of phenomena.[191] The ordering of the sciences was based upon mathematics and mechanics.[192]

---

[189] Cf. L.S., pp. 84ff., 98; II, pp. 257f.; III, pp. 15-40, 111-127; B.A., p. 41. For a contemporary historical treatment of this cf. P. Gay, The Enlightenment: An Interpretation vol. I, pp. 3-27.

[190] Cf. G.S. I, pp. xviii, 14-21, 360f., 375-377; II, pp. 259ff. Also L.S., pp. 100f., 111; and H. Schnädelbach, op. cit., pp. 133-143.

[191] Cf. ibid., pp. 13-31; B.A., pp. 60, 70-72, 88; V, 74-89, 158-168.

[192] Cf. G.S. II, p. 375 where Dilthey quotes from Hobbes'

The French positivists were less prone to ground their metascience on the analysis of perception; they chose instead to ground it on the generalizations from the natural sciences.[193] Similar to the empiricists, however, "the external world, the knowledge of physical regularities, is also for them the sole object of strict scientific knowledge."[194] Here too, metaphysical speculation is rejected and the intellectual history of man is seen, as Turgot outlined in anticipation of Comte, as culminating in positive sciences.[195] The same process of generalization from the natural sciences is articulated in Comte's methods of induction and deduction, assuring as they did the key role of the natural sciences in sociology.[196] If British empiricism broke with Comte in some respects under John S. Mill, it still maintained the supremacy of the natural sciences and their methods in determining the philosophy of science and all critically grounded knowledge.[197]

If Kant and the transcendental-idealist methods marked a turn to the subject and the a priori conditions of the possibility of knowledge, still the principle of intuition guaranteed a place of priority to the methods of mathematics and the natural sciences in determining what was objective

---

Examinatio et Emendatio Mathematicae Hodiernae (Opp. lat. IV, 26).

[193]Cf. G.S. II, pp. 312ff.; also G. Misch, Zur Entstehung des französischen Positivismus in Archiv für Philosophie Bd. XIV (1901), pp. 1-39; reprinted by Wissenschaftliche Buchgesellschaft, 1969.

[194]G.S. II, p. 313.

[195]Cf. G.S. II, pp. 314ff.

[196]Cf. G.S., pp. 104-109 where Dilthey argues against the positivist sociology of Comte.

[197]Ibid., p. 105: "If Stuart Mill repudiated the more flagrant errors of Comte, the more subtler ones continued in his works. The sociology of Comte emerged from the tendency of eighteenth century French philosophy to subordinate the historical world under the system of our knowledge of nature. The subordination of the method of studying cultural and mental realities under the method of the natural sciences was at least defended and maintained by Stuart Mill."

knowledge.[198] Thus in a pattern similar to Comte's rejection
of inner observation, Kant's transcendental apperception with
its refutation of idealism tried to show how inner experience
is possible (or grounded) because of outer experience; this
coincided with the necessary relation of empirical consciousness to transcendental consciousness, or consciousness of
self as originating apperception prior to all experience.[199]
So for Kant, the "Ego that thinks" and the "Ego that intuits
itself" is similar to the relation we have to any object
of intuition, so that the inner perception knows the subject
as appearance of phenomenon and not "in itself."[200] In
line with this, Dilthey brought out how Kant's entire critical
project appealed to mathematics and the natural sciences.
Kant had " - as he often with pride emphasized - justified
the dignity of mathematics, the validity of natural science,
and the immense structure of law-like truths in the
positive sciences."[201]

  C. Objectivistic Scientism. Secondly, Dilthey's studies
of the seventeenth and eighteenth century naturalist systems
uncovered the presuppositions of this dependence on the
logical methods of mathematics and the natural sciences.
From Descartes on, there was an increasing identification
of method with logic, which identification was especially
noticeable in the cognitional theoretical grounding of scientific knowledge.[202] There were two presuppositions to such

---

[198]Cf. G.S. I, xviii, 134, 308, et passim where Dilthey
discusses Kant's unhistorical reference frame. Also P.
Krausser, op. cit., 46, 224f.; G.S. I, 418; V, 5, 195f.;
VIII, 174f., 182.

[199]Cf. Kant's Kritik der reinen Vernunft B, pp. 275-279;
A, p. 117. Compare this with Dilthey's remarks on Comte in
B.A., p. 256; also G. Misch, Zur Entstehung des französischen
Positivismus, pp. 24ff.

[200]Cf. Kant, ibid., B 156. On Dilthey's criticism of
this, cf. G.S. I, xviii, 10, 418; V, 11, 145, 171f., 238,
362; VI, 314f.; VII, 26f.; VIII, 174f.; B.A., pp. 192-196.

[201]L.S., p. 102; also G.S. III, 172f.; VIII, 174f.

[202]Cf. G.S. II, 452-479. Also cf. H. Schnädelbach, op.
cit., pp. 13ff.; and N.W. Gilbert, Renaissance Concepts of
Method (New York, 1960), pp. xiiiff.

128

a position on method as at once objectivistic, empirical, and logical. The first was a critique, in the light of the natural sciences, of the objective validity of metaphysical notions in favor of the autonomy of thought (Kant), of the forms of perception (British empiricism), of the positive sciences (Comte).[203] From this perspective one could say that "all knowledge of nature is only a symbol of an unknown and ultimately unattainable realm,"[204] as evidenced in the Kantian noumenal thing-in-itself, in Humean skepticism, in Comte's restriction to positive phenomena.[205] How could this avoid the pitfalls of metaphysical skepticism? The second presupposition was a carry-over from the natural law speculations of the seventeenth and eighteenth centuries.[206] It grounded the certainty that appearance (Erscheinung) was not illusion (Schein) because the sciences could inductively discover immediate truths and logically deduce general laws from them.

This notion of immediate truths enabled Dilthey to uncover the objectivistic tendency in the methods of all three schools of metascience; how they could bracket the question of ontological validity, while still affirming the validity of objective scientific knowing. For immediate truths do not assert reality, rather they assert that if a reality is there, then the emergence of another reality is related to it. It is immaterial whether this relationship is one in the realm of perception (Locke, Hume) and thought (Kant), or in the realm of nature (Comte).[207] Thus the objectivism of method had nothing to lose from the hypothetical character of natural scientific explanation.[208] Similarly, a logical necessity could be coupled with

---

[203]Cf. G.S. X, p. 21.   [204]G.S. X, p. 21.

[205]Cf. L.S., p. 101; G.S. II, p. 313; B.A., p. 60; G.S. I, p. 104ff.

[206]Cf. G.S. II, pp. 439ff.; III, pp. 7-24, 147-157, 222ff.

[207]B.A., p. 46.

[208]Cf. B.A., pp. 18, 21, 41, 49, 111; G.S. I, pp. 14-21.

empirical verification, for the conception of law and regularity was maintained without recourse to the rationalism of the naturalist systems of Leibniz or Spinoza.[209]

The hypothetical character of the natural sciences did not diminish their objectivity, for objectivity referred to the validity of the hypothetical explanatory constructions rather than to their correspondence with reality. The empirical data was supplied by the Kantian principle of intuition, the Empiricist perception, and the Comtean phenomenal observation.[210] The validity of the a priori synthetic judgments in Kant, of Hume's perceptual associations with "the scientific theories and methods as genuine logical facts" as its object - these were all valid insofar as they manifested the immediate truths whose objectivity depended upon a logical necessity. Hence the notion of law as intelligible relation, was alienated from the real: "Inasmuch as these logical necessities seemed to be superimposed on reality as an alien necessity, there emerged the notion of law."[211] On the other hand, this conception of law was not the consequent rationalism of a Leibniz or Spinoza. For the bracketing of reality or ontological validity left the immediate truths as "an unknowable fate."[212] In a profound insight Dilthey saw how this approach to method as an

---

[209] Cf. G.S. I, pp. 358ff., 386-408; II, pp. 465f.

[210] On Comte, cf. B.A., pp. 254f.; G.S. I, pp. 86ff.; on Kant, cf. L.S., pp. 94-113; B.A., pp. 20, 192, 233-236; on the empiricist tradition, cf. G.S. I, pp. xvi, 90, 105ff.; V, pp. 74f., 160-163.

[211] B.A., p. 45.

[212] Ibid., p. 45 where Dilthey reflects on how the doctrine of immediate truths blocked any reflection on the real origins of thought. "...the image of a thought appears to us as something foreign to mind itself, as though thought were preceded by an unknowable reality under whose control beings emerged - just as each new generation of men are born under the power of the State and the constrictions of its laws. As just such an unknowable fate has the doctrine of immediate truths, dressed up as a law of thought, dominated our world of thought as a law of nature does nature itself." For a contemporary confirmation of Dilthey's analysis of the naturalist systems, cf. P. Gay, The Enlightenment: An Interpretation, pp. 297ff.

130

objectivistic logical cognitional theory tied together Neo-kantians, Hegelians, and other contemporary efforts at grounding the sciences.[213] It was this false objectivistic identification of method and logic, based upon an inverted and ungrounded conception of natural and historical laws, which led to the efforts of universal histories in Germany, of a universal Sociology in France, and the laissez-faire Utilitarianism in England.[214] Common to all were unfounded generalizations which paid too little attention to the concrete procedures of the particular natural and historical sciences, and did so in the name of an objectivistic identification of method and logic which allowed for an objectivistic mediation of the totality of the sciences in the name of constitutive a priori structures and regulative ideas (Kantianism), of the general and fundamental laws of human evolution (Comteanism), of the perceptualist reductionism to associations and customs (British Empiricism).[215]

_____

[213] B.A., pp. 45f.: "This analysis of the characteristics of immediate truths contains two important consequences for the grounding of all science. It explains the tendency both to place the law of thought as an unknowable fate before and above all reality, and to place its beginning with Science. And it makes all too clear the fatal inversion that is present in the role which Herbart and Hegel gave to logic. The former made logic into the highest judge over the given, over reality. The latter, indeed, dissolved the whole of reality into logicism. From this came the consequence, that in the works of both reality is subordinated under the law of necessity, and a single structure of necessary links embraced both nature and the human spirit. This same orientation determines the construction of some of the more important attempts at grounding science in our day. And yet our analysis shows how such a positing of immediate truths dressed up as laws of thought really inverts the natural order of things, and how it subjects the entire view of the world to such a fate."

[214] On the universal histories in Germany, cf. G.S. I, pp. 86-92 where Dilthey sees a common error in terms of the universalizing tendencies of the philosophy of history in Germany and the positivist sociologies in France and England. Similar criticisms of the three tendencies can be found in Dilthey's work of 1875, "Über das Studium der Geschichte der Wissenschaften vom Menschen, der Gesellschaft und dem Staat," in G.S. V, pp. 31-73, also III, pp. 222-237. On British Utilitarianism, cf. X, pp. 11ff. For Dilthey's later reflections on a correct understanding of universal history, cf. VII, pp. 252-294.

[215] Cf. the notes 113-124 of Chapter One above. This

Lest one imagine that this concern of Dilthey with scientistic objectivism was unresponsive to the political and economic realities of scientism, it should be pointed out that he was not oblivious to these latter. The mechanistic naturalist systems, Dilthey saw, were vulnerable to a reductionism which would leave society wide open to technocratic and economic manipulation. Meaning and value would be equated with material objects. Perhaps it was the genius of Dilthey, that he saw how this reductionism was operative in both socialism and capitalism. Thus of socialism he could say that it was the logical outcome of an uncritical dependence upon natural scientific methods, i.e., of scientism:

> Socialism has thus developed. It disputes that property, marriage and family might henceforth be seen as an unchangeable foundation of society and its action. It can make use of the ultimate consequences arising from the very powerful orientation of the natural sciences as its own foundation. Only with such presuppositions could one establish that natural selection, heredity, or human animality are the real and sole principles for transformations in the forms of social life.[216]

Even more critical is Dilthey's evaluation of capitalism. He saw it as an economic consequence of the naturalism underpinning the Enlightenment. It is surprising that he wrote comparatively little on this subject, when he ended his study of the naturalist systems of the seventeenth century with the stark words:

> The naturalist system had the terrible consequence, within the economic sphere, of capitalism. Movable capital is as unlimited in its power within the modern legal system as it was long ago within the system of the Roman Empire. It can reject whatever

---

led to their inability to critically mediate theory and praxis, as Dilthey states in G.S. V, p. 33: "Moral philosophy carries on its present meagre existence only within certain faculties of philosophy - and even there it is beginning to die." It is not surprising that a renewed interest in overcoming scientism is linked also with the re-emergence of the importance of practical philosophy, cf. W. Oelmüller, "Probleme des neuzeitlichen Freiheits- und Aufklärungs- prozess," in Kirche im Prozess der Aufklärung, pp. 91-143.

[216] G.S. X, p. 15.

> it wants, and can grab whatever it wants. Capitalism
> is like a beast with a thousand eyes and tentacles
> which can turn itself wherever it wants without
> any conscience.[217]

D. Theory and Praxis Unmediated. Thirdly and finally,
Dilthey found a common failure in these three schools of
metascience to adequately mediate theory and praxis. In his
own grounding of the cultural sciences, he had called attention to the interdependence of three categories or types
of statement: the factual, the theoretical, and value-
judgments. All three types are operative within the human
sciences.[218] Yet methods drawing too exclusively from the
natural sciences, and caught within the confines of an
objectivistic identification of logic and method, cannot
critically relate these three types. They tend to confine
the human sciences "in the strait jacket of a knowledge of
recurrent regularities according to the analogy of natural
sciences."[219] As a result, none of the three schools of
metascience were in a methodological position to appreciate
the problems for praxis which the natural sciences were
posing, and which methodologically grounded human sciences
could master. In actual practice the modern sciences had
broken down the classical separation of theory and praxis
- at least in the form of technology.[220] If this was the
enthusiastic spirit of Renaissance and Enlightenment society
for science, Dilthey knew the autonomy it promised was not
a reality.

More accurately than any of his contemporaries, Dilthey
saw how the specialization in the sciences was leading away
from autonomy to a new anonymity in the megamachine society:

> Modern society is similar to an immense, mechanized
> factory which is kept in operation through the services
> of innumerable persons. Each is equipped with the
> isolated technique of his own particular profession.
> No matter how perfectly he has made this technique
> his own, he is in the situation of a worker, who spends
> his entire life laboring in a particular point of this
> factory. He does not have the powers to know what

---

[217] G.S. II, p. 245.   [218] Cf. G.S. I, pp. 26f.

[219] Ibid., p. 27.

[220] G.S. II, pp. 257f. Also L.S., pp. 91ff.

> puts the whole factory in motion. Indeed, he cannot even imagine all the other components of this factory, and how they work together towards the goal of the whole. He is a service instrument of the society, not a conscious organ collaborating with others in its formation.[221]

In general, one might say that Dilthey was dissatisfied with the lack of concern on the part of the three schools of meta-science with precisely this problem. The roots of this unconcern lay in the objectivistic approach to method, out-lined above, which led the schools to reject classical or dogmatic metaphysics <u>without</u> sufficient reflection on the role that metaphysics played in the mediation of theory and praxis in traditional societies.

In those societies metaphysics, or first philosophy, transcended the domain of experience: "it fills out what is given in experience through an <u>objective</u> and <u>universal</u> inner system or structure."[222] While the particular sciences were related to particular domains of experience, metaphysics sought to articulate their objective ground in being as being. "Metaphysics contains the grounds for particular horizons of experience, and it controls the whole realm of human action through those grounds."[223] Both theory and praxis - the true and the good - were object-ive.[224] This objectivism accounted for the skepticism, which was the inseparable shadow of classical metaphysics.[225] The revolutionary impetus of the modern natural sciences was

---

[221] <u>G.S.</u> I, p. 3; also III, p. 131f. where Dilthey sees reason in the Enlightenment as conceived mechanistically.

[222] <u>G.S.</u> I, pp. 130f. Thus it is the loss of subjecti-vity proportionate to the objectivity of technical reason. W. Oelmüller has called attention to this, as has also the Frankfurt School; cf. <u>op. cit.</u>, pp. 102-116, 125-131.

[223] <u>G.S.</u> I, p. 129.

[224] <u>G.S.</u> I, p. 188: "For the hellenic mind all knowing is a type of seeing; for it both theoretical and practical activity are related, by means of intuition (<u>Anschauung</u>), to Being standing over against it and presupposed to it. For that mentality knowledge as well as action is a touching of intelligence with something external to it, and, indeed, knowing is a picture of what stands over against it."

[225] Cf. <u>G.S.</u> I, pp. 125f, pp. 235-241.

given an objectivistic interpretation in the natural law theories of the eighteenth century.[226] Yet they were unable to integrate the contingent and voluntaristic aspects stemming from Christianity, and the consequences they had for historical and moral praxis.[227] The logical approach to cognitional-theoretical method, then, presented an interiority form of the classical cosmological objectivism. Thus Dilthey can remark of Kant: "There is a tendency towards conceptual constructions out of mathematical elements, which are very different from their temporal emergence. While this procedure was cosmological in Plato, it is subjective in Kant."[228]

In depending upon the natural sciences and the implicit logicism of naturalist systems since Descartes, all three schools of metascience attempted an objectivistic grounding of the natural and human historical sciences, i.e., an objectivistic grounding of the mediation of theory and praxis. This kept them as it had kept the adherents of classical metaphysics, from recognizing the true locus of the differentiation of theory and praxis as methodologically grounded. For it is only in thematizing methods based upon interiority as such, i.e., lived historico-social experience, that one can differentiate and interrelate theory and praxis:

> The solid point for all knowledge, even of the objective world, lies in interiority, in the turn to interiority.... Only when this clear insight is present, does the moral world, and the solid point of all action in it, enter into the all-embracing context of the human sciences. With it the false dichotomy between theoretical and practical science is overcome, and the true differentiation of the natural sciences and the cultural sciences can be grounded.[229]

In trying to ground the philosophy of science in an objectivistic manner, the schools of metascience prior to Dilthey were unable to handle the human, historical, and social

---

[226]Cf. G.S. I, pp. 198, 223, 236ff.

[227]Cf. G.S. I, pp. 251ff., 319f.

[228]G.S. I, p. 424; also I, p. 188.

[229]G.S. I, p. 225.

sciences and realities in a proper way. The a priori of
Kant, and the psychologisms of Locke, Hume, and Comte, were
all "rigid and dead."[230] The objectivistic methods of
induction and deduction in Comte, Mill, and Spencer were no
more than a mechanistic "rattling" to Dilthey.[231] They were
all guilty of metaphysical objectivism in their efforts at a
critical grounding of the sciences. Dilthey thus turns the
tables on these schools by claiming that they had not sufficiently criticized metaphysics!

It is not surprising, therefore, that their theories
were unable to mediate theory and praxis. Nature and science
were objectivistically "de-souled," for the regularly
recurrent relations between facts were "a completely apa-
thetic afterthought as far as praxis was concerned."[232]
Kant's replacing of the explicit dogmatism of metaphysics
with an implicit dogmatism of an objectivistic critique of
reason grounded in a phenomenon-noumenon dichotomy resulted
in an empiricist triumph over the very subjectivity Kant
thought he was protecting.[233] A similar verdict is passed
in the Breslauer Ausarbeitung of 1880 against both the
positivist and the empiricist ideal of an objectivistic and
reductionist unified science, a verdict that applies as well
to the false idealism of the transcendentalist cognitional
theory:

A generation of sophists has arisen who theoretically

---

[230] B.A., pp. 59f.; also G.S. I, xviii.

[231] B.A., p. 60, pp. 268f. Krausser, op. cit., pp.
224-226.

[232] L.S., p. 86.

[233] L.S., p. 104: "An a priori metaphysics of nature,
next to it an understanding of the human spirit divided
between empirical facticity and the application of miserable
teleological hypotheses, moral reflection totally cut off
from it because of its own a priori; teleological principles
thrown together with aesthetic intuitions, etc. In brief,
if one grasps the end product of these sciences relative
to that general conception, it is as if one saw before
him an organic body decaying from poison." For Dilthey the
critical method of Kant (cf. G.S. I, p. 133f.) was too short
on criticism insofar as his cognitional theory was too objectivistic, accepting, as he did, the natural sciences as the

deny the reality of objects, and who claim that the
final goal of all knowledge is to construct a unity
among all the data of consciousness. Practically,
this results in once again allowing for the reality
of objects, so that they make a bad joke of philosophical reflection. They insist as a Shylock on
their false opinion, according to which every thing
and every person external to them are only their own
images. These objects exist only because they are
images, so long as they exist for the perceivers.
Philosophy has gotten a bad name for itself through
these people. For, while they guard the entrance to
philosophy as a dull doorman with offensive pretensions,
they alienate the positive sciences from philosophical
research. They split theory from praxis, thereby
condemning the former to sterility, and the latter to
a narrow-minded popularity.[234]

The central issue in both these criticisms is how objectivism is no more than another manifestation of the split
in methodological consciousness between reality and thought,
objectivity and subjectivity, since its failure to come to
terms historically with metaphysical objectivism.[235] Such
an objectivism fails to take into account the concrete
historical dimensions of human interests and motives; it
seeks rather to construct everything (including subjectivity)
in a theoretical fashion.[236] Theory usurps attention to
praxis and critique is assimilated to the ideals of logic.
Reason, then, is reduced to "pale thought-activity," and
the world of scientific theory is not only seen as differentiated from, but actually opposed to, the world of concrete
social praxis, which is treated as a world of prescientific
appearance, if not illusion.[237]

---

norm for knowing.

[234]B.S., p. 11; also p. 19. M. Riedel has correctly
called attention to the import of this indictment; cf. his
Einleitung, pp. 27-32.

[235]Cf. G.S. II, pp. 453-471, where Dilthey gives a
very perceptive analysis of the Cartesian dichotomy between
subjectivity and objectivity; also V, pp. 352-363.

[236]Thus compare the constructive methods of metaphysics
in G.S. V, pp. 353ff. with those of German Geschichtsphilosophie and English and French sociology, I, pp. 86-112.

[237]Cf. G.S. I, pp. xviii, 372f. Also M. Riedel, Hermeneutik und Dialektik I, pp. 238f.

In summary, the metascientific position of Dilthey's critique of historical reason would, within the context of the three schools, have a threefold task. First, the human sciences had to be clearly differentiated from the natural sciences; secondly, the methodological implications of this differentiation demanded a differentiation of logic and method in order to, thirdly, provide a framework within which the concrete domain of historical and social praxis could be related to the sciences.

The implications of this project can, however, only be properly understood within the philosophical contexts of Dilthey's work. For a metascientific method can avoid objectivitism only if it is aware of the sources and power of metaphysical objectivism.[238]

2. Philosophy: From Metaphysics to Meta-Physical Consciousness

Recent studies on Dilthey, especially the monographs of M. Riedel, have been pointing out how Dilthey's critique of historical reason was not only a quest for the methodological grounding of the cultural sciences, but also a critique of that pure reason which had found its historical expressions in a multiplicity of metaphysical systems.[239] Indeed, Dilthey was aware that the former could never be adequately achieved until the "queen of the sciences," standing as she did at the very entrance to the human sciences, was dethroned.[240] This was not to be done simply by disclaiming metaphysics, simply by exposing the contradictory systems and their antinomies throughout the two thousand year history of metaphysics. Nor was the task a negative one, for it had as its goal the removal of those deep shadows of skepticism, which were the inseparable companions of metaphysics.[241] In order to properly understand this aspect

---

[238]Cf. the final section of this Chapter. For the results this nad for Dilthey's approach to religion, cf. Chapter Four.

[239]M. Riedel, "W. Dilthey und das Problem der Metaphysik," Phil. Jhbk. 76 (1968/69), pp. 334ff.; also P. Krausser, op. cit., pp. 37-45.

[240]Cf. G.S. I, pp. 125f.   [241]Ibid., pp. 125, 235ff.

of Dilthey's critique it is necessary to discover what, for Dilthey, was the central enigma in the pathos of the Enlightenment.

The sharpest formulation of this enigma was given in 1903 on the occasion of his seventieth birthday. He ended this talk with the sobering remark:

> I was finally driven through this task [of a critique of historical reason] to an all-encompassing problem. An apparently insoluble contradiction emerges when historical consciousness is followed out to its ultimate consequences. The last word of the historical world-view is the finitude of every historical phenomenon, whether it be a religion or an ideal or a philosophical system. Thus one has the relativity of every type of human apprehension of how things are. Everything seems passing in a process, nothing remaining stable. And yet against this there emerges the need of thought, and the striving of philosophy, for a universally valid knowledge. The historical world-view is the liberator of the human spirit from the final chains, which natural science and philosophy had not yet broken. But where do we find the means to overcome the anarchy of conflicting convictions that threaten to inundate us?[242]

Nor was Dilthey exaggerating when he confessed that he had labored on the solution of this central dilemma his life long. Thirty-three years earlier the same concern echoes in the pages he wrote on Schleiermacher and the Enlightenment in his Life of Schleiermacher.[243] He realized then that the sublation of metaphysics could not be effective unless the need for rationality, inherent in any metaphysical mediation of totality, was sufficiently respected.[244] The critique of the history of metaphysical reason demanded that the needs and motives which found expression within that history be properly recognized. Otherwise one ran the danger, as was evident in the three schools in metascience treated above, of simply denouncing the previous objectifications as metaphysical while falling into new forms of metaphysics, which were all the more perilous insofar as they were uncritically thought of as unmetaphysical.

---

[242] G.S. V, 9; also VIII, p. 290.

[243] Cf. L.S., pp. 83-93.   [244] L.S., p. 98.

My purpose here is not to enter into Dilthey's detailed
critique of metaphysics in the second book of his Einleitung
in die Geisteswissenschaften. Instead, I am interested in
this only inasmuch as it throws light on the emergence of
post-Enlightenment metaphysics. For it was Dilthey's insight
into the role and function of metaphysics in this context
which convinced him of the need to preface his cognitional
theoretical grounding of the human sciences with a "phenomenology of metaphysics."[245] This calls for a discussion of
three areas in the thought of Dilthey: first, his analysis
of his post-Enlightenment situation; secondly, how the
elements of metaphysics would appeal to that situation; and
finally, the forms metaphysics took within that situation.

A. Enlightenment and Modernity. In general, Dilthey
saw his age as having three fundamental characteristics,
each of them profoundly influencing the philosophies of his
day.[246] The first two characteristics arose from Enlightenment science, giving rise to the importance of the philosophy of science, or metascience, and the problems this
occasioned mentioned in the former subsection. The first
characteristic was the effect the natural sciences were
having on man's relation to nature. They effectively denuminized the world of nature and seemed to open the possibility of an unlimited control and domination of nature by
man.[247] More importantly, they gave the example of a type
of knowing whose methods could achieve a type of universal
acceptance and, through their successes in this, provide
models for scientific knowledge and validity in general.[248]
Of special relevance in such methods were the hypothetical
character of their investigations, and methods of empirical
verification which did not appeal to any knowledge of totality.

---

[245]M. Riedel, "W. Dilthey und das Problem der Metaphysik,"
pp. 339f.; also D.J.D., p. 274.

[246]Cf. Dilthey's essay "Die Kultur der Gegenwart und
die Philosophie" of 1898, G.S. VIII, pp. 190-205.

[247]G.S. VIII, p. 192; on the denuminization, cf. also
VII, pp. 335-338; III, pp. 40-46.

[248]Cf. G.S. VIII, p. 192.

These were the main reasons, according to Dilthey, why the modes of explanation in the natural sciences were not metaphysical.[249]

Correlative to this was the denuminization of culture and society. The Enlightenment eroded the metaphysical and religious foundations of society. "The faith in an unchangeable order of society has vanished, we are now situated in the transformation of that social order according to rational principles."[250] Several components went into this new attitude toward social structures. Increasing industrialization and commerce set in motion the formation of new centers of economic power and the resulting tensions between the bourgeoisie and the working class.[251] These tensions initiated the emergence of new forms of political organizations which sought to mediate the conflicting interests involved in the growing awareness of individual freedoms, on the one hand, and on the other, the demands of national and class consciousness.[252] Social sciences and human studies took on an increasingly empirical quality, emancipating themselves through the theories of natural law and progress from the metaphysical presuppositions of the old order.[253] The French Revolution proved the praxis-orientated dimension of the new self-reliance of man reflected in the social historical sciences.[254]

The third basic characteristic of his contemporary culture consisted for Dilthey in its particular "Wirklichkeitssinn" or stance toward reality. As this manifested itself in the poets and writers of his time, it was no longer the idealist pathos of a Goethe, Fichte, or Schelling, but that mixture of historical challenge and immersion in life

---

[249]Cf. _G.S._ I, pp. 365-371.

[250]_G.S._ VIII, p. 192; also III, pp. 217ff.

[251]Cf. VIII, p. 192; also X, p. 13-17.

[252]_G.S._ VIII, p. 192.

[253]Cf. _G.S._ I, pp. 379f.

[254]Cf. _G.S._ I, pp. 83-85; VIII, p. 193; X, pp. 13-17; _E.D._, pp. 250f.

found in a Voltaire, Schopenhauer, or Nietzsche.[255] The
pathos of Enlightenment was, as Georg Misch put it, "the
pathos of this-worldliness" where the sciences seemed to
increase the power to change in inverse ratio to their
powerlessness in agreeing upon the values and purposes
grounding such change.[256] In destroying the traditional
religious and/or metaphysical foundations of all previous
theory and praxis, the Enlightenment had begun to extend
"the anarchy of thinking" into ever more presuppositions of
human thought and action.[257]

> Insofar, however, as the present generation asks
> wherein the final goal of individual or general
> human striving lies, a profound contradiction
> appears within it. This generation is no wiser than
> a Greek in the Ionic or Italian colonies, or an Arab
> at the time of Averroës, when it comes to the great
> riddle about the origin of reality, about the value
> of our existence, or about the ultimate worth of
> our actions. Precisely today, surrounded by the rapid
> progress of the sciences, we find ourselves more
> puzzled by these questions than any previous
> generation.[258]

The historical Enlightenment, in revealing the relativity
of all systems of values and purposes, had a profoundly
"tragic" aspect to its striving for knowledge. "There
appears to us a tragic dimension in the human effort at
attaining knowledge, a contradiction between willing and
ability."[259]

For Dilthey this central enigma of any post-Enlightenment society went to the very core of the problem of grounding
the cultural sciences.[260] As we have seen in the previous

---

[255]Cf. G.S. VIII, p. 191.

[256]Cf. G. Misch, Lebensphilosophie und Phänomenologie,
p. 308; also G.S. I, pp. 3f.

[257]Cf. G.S. VIII, p. 194. [258]G.S. VIII, p. 193.

[259]G.S. VIII, p. 194; cf also E.D., p. 16: "...the
society of the Enlightenment also contained tragic instances
enough in the conflict of the ruling classes and the middle
class, of the hierarchical order and the freedom of conscience, of despotism and political rights."

[260]Cf. the analysis of Chapter Two, the section on the
dialectic of the Enlightenment and interdisciplinary

142

section, the major trends in the philosophy of science in Dilthey's time were, in his judgment, incapable of properly interrelating theory and praxis. Yet the actual influence of both the natural and human sciences in their modern empirical forms were, as the first two basic characteristics indicated, de facto changing the entire stance of man to himself and to his world. They were upsetting the classical distinctions between theoretical philosophy and practical philosophy.[261] Moreover, both the natural and the human sciences are activities of the human subject, so that any critically grounded approach to them could not retreat from the "turn toward the subject" established by Kant.[262] Hence the crucial significance of grounding the human sciences consisted in the explicit necessity of coming to grips with the activities of the human subject in history - a necessity which need not have arisen as long as one concentrated on the natural sciences and their object. This, however, could not be achieved without, to a certain extent, overcoming the dichotomy between philosophical and empirical human studies.[263] Only in sublating that dichotomy would one open up the possibility of uncovering the ground of human thought and action preceding the differentiation into theory and praxis, or into factual judgment and value judgment.

B. The Critique of Metaphysics. Dilthey seemed to be playing the Enlightenment against itself.[264] For he

---

collaboration, pp. 88-109. The "post-Enlightenment" is used here to designate how the modern (i.e., Dilthey's) and our own contemporary situation has still not come to terms with the Enlightenment. Cf. the essays of J. Moltmann, J. B. Metz and Oelmüller in Kirche im Prozess der Aufklärung.

[261]Cf. M. Riedel, op. cit., pp. 340-343. Also J. Habermas, Theorie und Praxis, pp. 231-257.

[262]Cf. Dilthey's recognition of this in G.S. V, p. 1 at the end of his career, and compare it with his early remarks in his journal (D.J.D., pp. 79f.).

[263]Cf. G.S. I, pp. 126, 357; II, 257f.

[264]This can be seen by comparing Dilthey's remarks on the emergence of modern man and society in G.S. I, p. 354f. with his introductory statements on I, p. 3. Where in the latter place he sees the anonymity of modern industrialized

pointed out how the independence of reason (Selbststandigkeit der Vernunft) is itself dependent upon social historical development. To overlook this dependency and attempt an abstract assertion of reason's independence of metaphysical and religious traditions was, for Dilthey, simply substituting one set of dogmas for another. The substance of his criticisms of the three schools of the philosophy of science was that they had failed to take both philosophy (and metaphysics) and modern science seriously enough.[265] Dilthey's own thought on this subject never achieved a final and completely coherent articulation. Nonetheless, it is possible to sketch the general lines of his historical analysis and critique of metaphysics. A careful study of Book Two of the Einleitung in die Geisteswissenschaften reveals, I believe, a fundamental pattern. The thrust of his critique of metaphysics is that it is an objectivistic identity thought pattern attempting to mediate the totality of reality. The inseparable companion of metaphysics was a skepticism which could be defined as an objectivistic non-identity thought pattern denying the possibility of any total mediation.

With Kant, Dilthey holds that metaphysics transcends the domain of experience and that the phenomenon of metaphysics is linked with the moral dimension of human existence.[266] But in a way peculiarly his own, Dilthey insists that a distinction must be drawn between the ground of all metaphysical objectifications or systems in an inner experience of moral and religious truth - what Dilthey calls meta-physical consciousness - and its systematic objectifications.[267] Meta-physical consciousness is the depth of "Selbstbesinnung," the

---

society, with its submersion of the individual under a technocratic system, in the former text he is showing how modernity began with hopes of emancipating the individual from repressive feudal systems. Cf. also G. Misch's comments in G.S. V, pp. cxivff. Thus he saw the frightful consequences of emerging capitalism, cf. II, p. 245.

[265] Cf. L.S., p. 86.

[266] Cf. G.S. I, pp. 130f., 384.

[267] Cf. G.S. I, pp. 384-386; also G. Misch, Lebens-philosophie und Phänomenologie, pp. 312f.

144

experience of dedication to self-transcending values and goals which indicates how freedom is not completely conditioned by nature, that we as persons are orientated toward the totality of the universe.[268] In this sense, meta-physical consciousness does not transcend experience but is inner experience itself in its self-transcending totality:

> The entire phenomenology of metaphysics has shown that metaphysical concepts and propositions do not emerge out of the pure status of knowledge towards perception. Rather, they emerge from the activity (Arbeit) of knowing on a context constituted by the totality of the human spirit. In this totality, there is present with the ego another independent of ego; with the will something other that resists it, whose impressions the will cannot change; with feeling something else from which it suffers. These are present, therefore, immediately, not through a syllogistic conclusion, but as life.[269]

This is the core and ground of human selfhood, the lived unity of identity and non-identity which is inner experience.[270] One might term this the subject as subject, prior to and grounding any and all objectifications. Yet this subject as subject is not monadic, its own auto-experience (identity) is simultaneously allo-orientated (non-identity) in experience of suffering and resistance.[271] This lived unity is "as reality there" and is the origin of specifically human facticity, value, and purposefulness.[272]

This unity of identity and non-identity in lived inner experience is never susceptible of total objectification. "For what is present in the totality of our essential being can never be completely articulated in thought."[273] Dilthey's

---

[268]Cf. G.S. I, pp. 385-395f.   [269]G.S. I, p. 305.

[270]M. Lamb in McShane (ed.) Language Truth and Meaning, pp. 128f.

[271]Cf. G. Misch, ibid., pp. 118-120; also G.S. I, pp. 395f.; V, pp. 90-138, esp. 98-114, 130; also cf. Metz, "Erlösung und Emancipation" in Stimmen der Zeit (March, 1973), pp. 171-184 where he shows the concrete subjectivity present in the history of suffering.

[272]Cf. G.S. I, pp. 395f.; also my article in Language Truth and Meaning, pp. 131-133 and the references to Dilthey's writings given there.

[273]G.S. I, p. 396; also I, pp. 137, 139.

phenomenology of metaphysics was a careful historical analysis
of the origins and development of metaphysical systems as
objectivistic transferrals or projections attempting logically
valid generalizations about reality.[274] In this respect he
was within the nineteenth century current of the anti-
metaphysical critique of independent "pure" reason represented
by such philosophers as Feuerbach, Marx, and Nietzsche. He
differed from them as well as from the critiques of metaphysics given by the Kantian, empiricist, and positivist
positions, inasmuch as his psychological-anthropological
critique was coupled with extensive historical analysis.[275]
The guiding insight of Dilthey was provided by the epochal
shift in the notion of science from its classical metaphysical
ideal of necessary and universal causes to its modern notion
as an ongoing empirical and specialized investigation of
contingent natural and historical intelligibility.[276] Within
this frame of reference there are six stages in Dilthey's
critique which call for a brief analysis here.

First, the origins of metaphysics in the West are to
be found in the experience of interiority grounding religion,
and the efforts to demythologize the expressions of this
grounding-religious-experience through the demands of a
rationality defined in terms of the Greek conceptions of
science.[277] The totality of lived inner experience (found in
the religious dimensions of life prior to any of its objectifications) was, for Dilthey, interiority as the "totality
of all the powers of the human spirit" differentiating itself
according to historical circumstance into myth, poetry, metaphysics, and the sciences.[278] This interiority provided the
dynamics of all historical development inasmuch as it is

---

[274]Cf. G.S. I, pp. 395, 401; also M. Riedel, "W. Dilthey
und das Problem der Metaphysik," p. 345.

[275]Cf. G.S. I, pp. 126, 134; also Riedel, op. cit., pp.
342f.

[276]Cf. G.S. I, pp. 365-368.

[277]Cf. G.S. I, pp. 127-179, esp. p. 136.

[278]Cf. G.S. I, p. 137.

latent in all human experience and cannot be fully objectified. "For never will knowing, as exemplified in the sciences, be able to master that primordial experience (Erlebens), which is present in the immediate awareness of the human spirit."[279] This, however, was never articulated in any of the Greek metaphysics insofar as its ideal of knowing was not patterned on this immediate awareness but on the object-ive knowing of the external world:

> Indeed, this structure was ultimately grounded in consciousness. It constituted, with the historical world, the totality of reality. Nevertheless the metaphysical thought of the Greeks had interpreted this structure in terms of a study of the external world.[280]

Variations of this can be seen in Socrates, Plato and Aristotle.[281] The projection process in metaphysical thinking occurs, then, from interiority as operative but unknown to constructions which attempt to articulate an objective and universal world-context. Inner totality is projected into a cosmic totality. The "In-sich-sein" of experienced interiority is projected as substantial forms into the external world.[282]

Second, the development of metaphysical thinking led to an identity thought pattern or "Denkform." Correlative to the mathematics and astronomy of the time, the ideal of science realized in metaphysics was to be a knowledge of necessary and first causes.[283] The homogeneity of substantial form not only ruled out a properly scientific knowledge of contingent change,[284] but also assured an objectivistic conception of the true and the good.[285] This accounted for both the Platonic notion of ideas and the

---

[279] Ibid.

[280] Cf. G.S. I, pp. 151, 205f.

[281] Cf. G.S. I, pp. 176-179; on Plato, pp. 182, 185, 187,; on Aristotle, pp. 195-201, and esp. 201-211.

[282] Cf. G.S. I, pp. 202-204; B.A., p. 58; M. Riedel, op. cit., pp. 343-346.

[283] Cf. G.S. I, pp. 193-196, 201ff.

[284] Cf. G.S. I, p. 206.

[285] Cf. G.S. I, pp. 188-190.

Aristotelian substantialist approach to psychology and society.[286]   The metaphysical intelligibility of knowing and doing corresponded to the metaphysical intelligibility of being as true and good, grounded in the contemplative appreciation of the highest intelligibility of divinity.[287] The objectivism of such constructive metaphysical methods did not concern itself with the cognitional theoretical grounding of this correspondence between knowing and reality.[288]   Instead, the identity principle was dogmatically affirmed throughout the history of Greek metaphysics.[289] Dilthey could articulate the inner structure of metaphysical systems according to the identity of "similes a similibus cognoscantur":

> The logical character in nature was conceived as a given, human logic as the second given, and the third datum constituted the correspondence between these two: the divine Reason as producing the nexus between the logical character of nature grounded in it and human logic that emerged from it.[290]

As long as the problems of reality, objectivity, and value or good were posed in terms of _Logos_ and reason, instead of _Leben_ and interiority, a necessary knowledge of the ground of world-process had to be dogmatically affirmed as the condition of the possibility of the correspondence between reason and world, subject and object.[291]

Third, it was inevitable that the dogmatic assertion of identity in metaphysics would be plagued by the non-identity

---

[286]Cf. _G.S._ I, pp. 191, 210, 229.

[287]Cf. _G.S._ I, pp. 199-208.

[288]Cf. _G.S._ I, pp. 197-199.

[289]_G.S._ I, p. 194:"This development was completed by Aristotle's following theorem. The _Nous_, as the divine Reason, is the principle and end through which the rational order of things is at least in a mediated way conditioned. Thus human reason, insofar as it is related with the divine, can know the universe to the degree that it is rational. Metaphysics, as the science of reason, is possible because of this correspondence." Cf. _G.S._ I, pp. 193-199.

[290]_G.S._ I, pp. 387f., 193-196; also M. Riedel, _op. cit._, p. 344.

[291]Cf. _G.S._ I, p. 198f.

148

thought patterns of skepticism. Skepticism effectively
criticized the objectivism in metaphysics by insisting on
the relativity of perception and thought.[292] The two sources
for truth in Aristotle, perception and the immediate principles of reason, were criticized and found wanting.[293] In a
variety of ways, skepticism indicated how metaphysical positions really presupposed the ultimate truth or good and the
possibility of man's limited attainment of the true or good
was grounded uncritically on that presupposition.[294] But the
non-identity thought pattern of skepticism was in fact only
a half-hearted critique of metaphysics. For like metaphysical
identity-thought, skepticism maintained that the true and the
good had to be grounded object-ively. Only, unlike metaphysics, it denied any such object-ive foundation of knowing
and doing. Correctly, skepticism denied the possibility of
any grounded knowledge of what lay behind relative phenomena:
"It correctly denied the validity of every type of knowledge
about the objective substratum of phenomena: Kant's thing-
in-itself."[295]

Fourthly, what neither the identity of metaphysics nor
the non-identity of skepticism realized was how the unity of
identity and non-identity in human historical interiority
sublated both their positions.

> The limits of their thought are most evident in a
> very peculiar debate. The skeptics say: everything
> is false; so the metaphysicians explain: then even
> that conviction is false and it is thereby sublated.
> The best grounded reply of the skeptic is: we express
> with such words only our own condition, without
> concern for its consequences and without making a
> statement about anything. In order to settle the
> debate, the cognitional theorist must enter it to
> explain how even in the skeptics' own condition a
> true knowledge is present, and how it is the starting
> point of all philosophy.[296]

[292]Cf. G.S. I, pp. 235-239.   [293]Cf. G.S. I, p. 197.

[294]G.S. I, pp. 240f.

[295]G.S. I, p. 236. That Dilthey was striving to reject
the Kantian noumenon, cf. M. Riedel, Einleitung, pp. 27ff.

[296]G.S. I, p. 237.

> But they have no idea that in themselves, that the
> inwardness of their condition, which the skeptics
> do not deny, is itself a knowledge. Indeed, it is the
> surest knowledge, so that from it is derived the
> certainty in any other form of knowing.[297]

Hence, although skepticism seemed victorious in respect to
metaphysical knowledge, it overlooked the reality of interiority which cannot be denied. "Knowledge itself is not
radically undermined.... The disjunction (either external perception or thinking) opens a third possibility. This openning
was overlooked by both the skeptics as well as Kant."[298] The
emergence of Christianity contained within it the possibility
of thematizing such interiority, but the efforts on the part
of Christian thought to communicate its message to Greek and
Latin cultures led its "Selbstbesinnung" into metaphysical
rather than cognitional theoretical modes.[299] There resulted
the antinomies between inner experience and presentational
thought, between the contingency of freedom and the necessity
of Divine Will, which eventually brought about the disintegration of medieval metaphysics as empiricism had Kant's
position.[300] What the skeptics and Kant overlooked, and what
the antinomies in medieval thought brought into sharp focus,
was the need for a new mediation of meaning and value rooted
in the immediate reality of human interiority.

Fifth, before this new mediation could be articulated,
however, a secularization of nature and society had to be
achieved. And it was precisely this that the naturalist

---

[297] G.S. I, p. 236.   [298] G.S. I, p. 240.

[299] Cf. G.S. I, pp. 261, 272-275.

[300] G.S. I, p. 327: "So emerges the inner character of
medieval metaphysics as full of contradictions. The objective and necessary thought-structure of the world is confronted with free will in God, which is expressed in the
historical world, in creation from nothing, and in the moral-
religious order of the society. Here we encounter the first,
still incomplete form of a contradiction which will destroy
metaphysics from within, and which will eventually demand
that the human sciences become independent of the natural
sciences. Indeed, Kant's critique of metaphysics received
its orientation from this task: to try to think through
simultaneously the necessary causal relationships and the
(free) moral world." Cf. G.S. I, pp. 279-283, 317-320,
323, 327f.

systems and natural law thought of the seventeenth and eighteenth centuries effected. The Greek and Medieval systems had constructed their identity systems through the mediation of the Unmoved Mover and God as the divine Logos mediating cosmic intelligibility and human intelligibility. In the naturalist systems of Descartes, Hobbes, Spinoza and Leibniz, the mechanic-mathematical methods of the natural sciences were linked to a natural law conception of the historical political sciences by means of logical-methodical deductive systems.[301] The theistic grounding was sublated and immanentized in Spinoza's "connexio idearum idem est ac ordo et connexio rerum."[302] Leibniz's principle of logical reason was at once the apogee and disintegration of metaphysics.[303] For the advance of both the natural sciences and the human sciences was clearly demonstrating that - even accepting a mechanistic interpretation of natural science - no principle of the logical identity between _Denken_ and _Sein_ was necessary.[304] Although the naturalist systems had challenged the previous metaphysics, their quest for a universal and objective identity revealed the same projection process mentioned in the second and third points above:

> It makes no difference whether Hegel makes the world reason into the subject of nature, or Schopenhauer a blind will, or Leibniz presentational monads, or Lotze an all embracing interactive mediating consciousness, or whether the most recent monists see psychic life revealed in every atom. All these are images of their own self, images of psychic life. These guide the metaphysician as he decides what can be reasonably asserted. And it is their secretly working power that guides him as he transforms the world into an immense and phantastic reflection of his own self.[305]

Clearly, the positive gains of the naturalists - their trust in rationality, the progress of humanity, their concern for

---

[301]Cf. _G.S._ I, pp. 223ff., 387ff., 379 (note); II, pp. 440-442, 452ff.

[302]Cf. _G.S._ I, pp. 387f.   [303]_G.S._ I, pp. 388 and 390.

[304]Cf. _G.S._ I, pp. 365-408, esp. 402-405.

[305]_G.S._ I, p. 405; also I, p. 379ff.

man and his world - these gains of the Enlightenment had to be preserved.[306] But they could not be critically grounded in a metaphysics, no matter how "new," which merely substituted abstractions about substance, cause, etc., with equally abstract approaches to human nature, society, history. The measure of the abstraction could be gauged by their efforts to identify the center and ground of human nature and history, to reduce their multiplicity and relativity to some absolute standard and norm.[307] In doing this they seemed unaware of how their absolute abstractions were but reflections of their own contingent subjectivity. In immanentizing the ground of identity and developing an anthropology (no matter how mechanistic) they assured metaphysics its own sublation: "The transformation of the world into the knowing subject through these modern systems is simultaneously the euthanasia of metaphysics."[308]

Sixth, Dilthey's analysis of the origins, growth, and decline of metaphysical thinking revealed the remnants of metaphysical objectivism in the transcendentalist, empiricist, and positivist schools of metascience. Precisely because they each dismissed metaphysics in the name of the natural sciences of their day, they were unable to appreciate how the real critique of metaphysics can only occur in a critical grounding of the human sciences and historical studies, which grounding includes their differentiation from the natural sciences. In themselves, the methods of the natural sciences were profoundly non-metaphysical.[309] But when they were taken as the ideal of all science and knowledge, then the fundamental stance of mind to reality was conceived according to the experience of the external world - a stance which, when generalized, is precisely that of metaphysical thinking.[310]

---

[306]Cf. G.S. I, pp. 380ff.; II, 452ff.

[307]Cf. G.S. I, pp. 382-386; II, 458-471; V, 353-356.

[308]G.S. I, p. 405.

[309]Cf. G.S. I, pp. 368ff.

[310]Cf. the references in notes 283-289 above.

152

The three schools were each aware of the three fundamental characteristics of post-Enlightenment man: the denuminization of nature, of society, and the need to overcome the anarchy of values without hindering, but rather being completely faithful to, the freedom of responsible rationality. In dismissing metaphysics too glibly however, they had overlooked its deep roots in metaphysical consciousness and fell victim to a typically metaphysical objectivism.[311]

C. Meta-Physical Consciousness. For Dilthey there was no question of negating metaphysical consciousness; it was inherent in man's striving to attain meaning and value and it was manifested in the essential function of philosophy in society.[312] But metaphysics as a science was passé, to be replaced by a critical "Selbstbesinnung" capable of grounding the human historical sciences. For such a grounding revealed the unity of identity and non-identity in lived inner experience as the source and ground of all historical objectifications. Such a source is never capable of total objectification, it can only be lived and understood, and finds its articulation in an endless succession of historical and social objectifications.[313] It demands a close attention to the specialized sciences aiming at a knowledge of particular phenomena.[314] The tasks facing metascience and philosophy in his time, then, were to ground those sciences, to interrelate

---

[311]Cf. G.S. I, pp. 134, 377.

[312]Cf. G.S. I, pp. 384-386: "However, the meta-physical of our life as personal experience, i.e., as moral-religious truth remains. Metaphysics...which retraced the life of men towards a higher order, did not have its power - as Kant in his abstract and unhistorical thought patterns assumed - because of some conclusions of theoretical reason. Nor would have such conclusions produced the idea of the soul or of a personal God. Rather such ideas were grounded in inner experience, with this experience and the reflection on it did such ideas develop.... This is the meta-physical, which is only faintly reflected in the numberless images of the history of metaphysics. For metaphysics as a science is a historically limited phenomenon - the meta-physical consciousness of the person is eternal." Also cf. V, p. 365.

[313]Cf. G.S. I, pp. 76-86, 383-385.

[314]Cf. G.S. I, pp. 94f.

their specialized methods, and to overcome thereby, the pathos of the Enlightenment.[315] These could be adequately achieved only by attempting a mediation of the immediate knowing of historical interiority, whose unity of identity and non-identity grounded both theory and praxis, meaning and value.[316]

Instead of truly sublating metaphysics in a cognitional theory grounded on "Selbstbesinnung," the three schools of metascience attempted a purely theoretical sublation in terms of, on the one hand, a cognitional theory concerned too exclusively with perception and thought, and, on the other hand, a generalized philosophy of history and sociology. The objectivism of the approaches to perception and thought have already been discussed.[317] It was on the basis of such approaches that they tried to ground and interrelate the sciences, using as their ideal the methods of the natural sciences. But in their efforts to come to grips with the central enigma of the Enlightenment, the relativity of meaning and value coupled with the practical need for change, they predictably turned to an extension of objectivism in terms of theoretical constructions which Dilthey could only brand as a new form of "metaphyscial fog."[318]

The problem was how to mediate the specialized sciences with a truly scientific understanding of the total context of historical social reality, thereby relating factual knowledge with that of general laws and of values and imperatives.[319] In Germany there were various philosophies of history, from Lessing to Hegelian and Kantian varieties, whose origins lay in the Christian conception of historical process. In England and France there were generalized forms of sociology, from Saint-Simon and Comte to J. Stuart Mill and H. Spencer, whose origins could be traced to the revolutionary

---

[315]Cf. G.S. VIII, pp. 195-201, 378.

[316]Cf. G.S. I, pp. 4-14, 27-86, 94f., 109.

[317]Cf. the section on Objectivistic Scientism in this Chapter and the references given there; also notes 59f. M. Riedel makes a similar point in his Einleitung, pp. 32ff.

[318]G.S. I, p. 112.   [319]Cf. G.S. I, pp. 87-89.

upheavals during the last third of the eighteenth century.[320]

The main import of Dilthey's critique of both these tendencies was that they simply illustrated the dichotomy between a philosophical approach to history and society and the specialized approach of the positive sciences; which dichotomy was "the corrupting inheritance of metaphysics."[321] Instead of realizing that the only possible approach to totality, which would be in line with the specialized sciences, was the introrsive methods aimed at an ongoing interrelating of the various specialized sciences - what Dilthey called "the method of experience" - they attempted to abstract some principle, ideal, or formula representative of the overall progress of history and society with their multiple meanings and values.[322] They essayed secularized answers to the questions previously within the domain of theology: "Where does the exhausting advance of mankind lead? Why such world suffering? Why is progress limited to such a small number of humans?"[323]

But such problems, if answerable at all, could only be approached asymptotically through the collaboration of many specialized sciences as a far distant goal: "Universal history, to the extent it is not something beyond human abilities, would only be attained as the final stage of all the cultural sciences collaborating together."[324] If the task they set themselves was impossible, so also the methods they used were wrong. From limited historical and social studies they attempted to construct theories which those studies could not support.[325] Comte's and Mill's sociologies

---

[320]Cf. _G.S._ I, pp. 89f.; II, 244f.; for the later qualifications of Dilthey regarding his critique of Comtean sociology, cf. I, pp. 420-422; on the philosophy of history, cf. L. von Renthe-Fink, _Geschichtlichkeit_, pp. 121f.

[321]_G.S._ I, p. 113.

[322]Cf. _G.S._ I, pp. 110, 95-104.

[323]_G.S._ I, pp. 100.

[324]_G.S._ I, p. 95; also VII, pp. 252-291.

[325]Cf. _G.S._ I, pp. 104-112; note also how the methods of metaphysics were "constructive," _ibid._ V, 353-356.

were not based so much on the positive sciences as they were
on a naturalist metaphysics (Comte) or a subordination of
social to physical phenomena (Mill).[326]

Thus, for Dilthey, the problems facing a post-
Enlightenment society could be adequately handled only by
overcoming both all forms of metaphysics and skepticism by
articulating a whole new control of meaning and value in
terms of lived inner experience. We see here how for Dilthey
the task of grounding the human sciences and the task of
philosophy confronted with the pathos of the Enlightenment
converge and unite. The critique of metaphysics is, at
bottom, the sublation of any philosophical speculation that
cannot prove its mettle by confronting the problems posed
to the modern mind in the scientific revolution.

> The origin and highest task of philosophy consists
> in heightening to a consciousness of itself the
> objective thinking of the empirical sciences, which
> produce from appearances an order of laws. Phil-
> osophy justifies it before itself.... But the time
> is drawing to an end, in my opinion, when there will
> be a separate philosophy of art, and of religion, of
> law, or of the state. This is the highest function
> of philosophy: grounding, justifying, critical
> consciousness, organizing power which embraces all
> objective knowledge, all determination of value,
> all establishing of purpose.

Dilthey was not unaware of the epochal significance this had,
for he continued:

> This so emerging powerful connection is destined
> to guide the human race. The empirical sciences
> of nature have transformed the external world.
> Now the epoch of world history has begun, in which
> the sciences of society will gain an increasing
> influence.[327]

The recognition of meta-physical consciousness, and the
critique of the metaphysical objectivism in the philosophy of

---

[326]Cf. G.S. I, pp. 86-92, 104-115; VIII, pp. 222ff.,
245-248.

[327]G.S. VIII, pp. 224f., also 172; Briefwechsel, p. 220;
also G. Misch, Lebensphilosophie und Phänomenologie, p. 66.
Compare this with Habermas' evaluation of the contemporary
task of philosophy in his essay "Wozu noch Philosophie?" in
Philosophisch-Politische Profile, pp. 11-36.

history and Comtean sociology, indicate how the new mediation could not be an objectivistic and scientistic negation of the past. He saw the destructive influence such negations had on man and society, not to mention science itself.[328] The pattern in his critique of metaphysics is the same as in his criticisms of the transcendentalist, positivist, and empiricist schools of metascience: sublation by a critique of objectivism in the name of interiority.

But to what extent did Dilthey's reliance on the Kantian notion of _Anschauung_ and the consequent noumenon-phenomenon dichotomy within the natural sciences render his cognitional theoretical foundation for the cultural sciences untenable? It certainly did not initiate a viable metascience. We must now inquire whether Lonergan's metamethod is capable of entering into the contemporary metascientific debates in a critical fashion.

THE CONTEMPORARY CRISIS:

FROM COGNITIONAL THEORY TO METHOD

Dilthey's critique of historical reason, while it had some influence upon the development of education and pedagogy in Germany and on the philosophy of Husserl and Heidegger, by no means stemmed the increasing advance of empiricist and positivist science.[329] Indeed, one could claim that until recently, Dilthey has only received attention from those interested in establishing an ontological island securely protected from the tides of empiricism and behaviorism sweeping across the intellectual mindscape.[330] Dilthey's insight into the futility of Kantian transcendentalism in the face of empiricism was prophetic of his own efforts.[331]

---

[328]Cf. _G.S._ I, pp. 3f., 113, 222-224; X, 11f., 113ff.

[329]Cf. Habermas, _Erkenntnis und Interesse_, pp. 204-234.

[330]Cf. Hans Albert, _Plädoyer für kritischen Rationalismus_ (München, 1971); Hans Albert, _Traktat über kritische Vernunft_ (Tübingen, 1968).

[331]On Dilthey's early aspiration to give a new critique

Nevertheless the contemporary crisis in human thought and action sketched above does indicate how Dilthey himself did foresee many aspects of the post-Enlightenment situation.[332]

Although Lonergan is not historically dependent upon Dilthey inasmuch as it was not the German but the Anglo-Saxon and Thomist context out of which he came,[333] still Lonergan is dialectically related to Dilthey. For the concern with conscious interiority in a fashion that sublates Idealist and Empiricist counterpositions is as central to Lonergan's method as it is to Dilthey's project.[334] Yet the different historical contexts do imply rather important differences. While Lonergan would agree with the critique Dilthey leveled against the Kantian, Positivist and Empiricist trends in the metascience of his day, and while he would agree with the fundamental assertions of Dilthey regarding meta-physical consciousness, still Lonergan would not agree with Dilthey's solution, viz., that the subject-as-subject should be enthroned within the confines of the cultural sciences but not the natural sciences. The advance in modern natural science since Dilthey's death made it imperative to take that performance more seriously than even Dilthey himself did. The differences that resulted from this must now be spelled out in regard to metascience and philosophy.

1. Metascience: From Differentiation to Critical Integration

The previous section showed how the root of Dilthey's metascientific critique of Kantianism, positivism and empiricism was to be found in their too excessive reliance upon natural scientific methods. It was this that led to their reductionism, scientistic objectivism and the resulting failure to mediate theory and praxis. Lonergan agrees with the general lines of the diagnosis of Dilthey, but he does not

---

of reason, cf. D.J.D., pp. 79-81; on Kant's inability to stem the Enlightenment's position, cf. pp. 120ff. of this Chapter.

[332]Cf. pp. 93-114 of this Chapter.

[333]On the context of Lonergan's development, cf. D. Tracy, The Achievement of Bernard Lonergan (New York, 1970).

[334]Cf. Insight, pp. xvii-xxx.

158

believe that the solution is to be found in separating the cultural sciences from the natural.[335] His "use of the terms, insights, understanding, is both more precise and has a broader range than the connotation and denotation of Verstehen. Insight occurs in all human knowledge, in mathematics, natural science, common sense, philosophy, human science, history, theology."[336] Lonergan has effectively dealt with the convergence of scientific consciousness and historical consciousness discussed above.[337] Mindful of the Hegelian critique of Kantian cognitional theory,[338] he has not attempted to elaborate a cognitional theory isolated from the actual performance of the sciences. It is such an elaboration that would transform cognitional theory into method, and transform method from its classical Cartesian concern with axioms and rules of procedure (technique) into an appropriation of the inner dynamics of human performance in all those domains mentioned by Lonergan (praxis).[339]

A. Schools of Metascience and the Exigencies of Meaning. In his contemporary book, Contemporary Schools of Metascience, G. Radnitzky has provided a rather accurate overview of the Anglo-Saxon and Continental schools of metascience, what he respectively designates as the Logical-Empirical and Hermeneutical-Dialectical Schools.[340] Although Lonergan has not addressed himself to the problem of metascience as Radnitzky has formulated it, anyone familiar with Lonergan's own development cannot fail to see how his elaboration of meta-method has unique possibilities of integrating the differentiations operative within contemporary schools of metascience.[341] What one finds is that the trends associated

---

[335]Cf. M.i.T., p. 212. [336]M.i.T., pp. 212-213.

[337]Cf. pp. 97-108 of this Chapter and references given there.

[338]Cf. Habermas, Erkenntnis und Interesse, pp. 14-35; Tracy, The Achievement of Bernard Lonergan, pp. 91ff.

[339]Cf. M.i.T., pp. xi, xii, 3ff.

[340]Cf. Radnitzky, Contemporary Schools of Metascience Vols. I & II (Lund, 1970).

[341]Cf. Heelan, "Towards a Hermeneutic of Pure and

with Logical-Empiricism are the metascientific correlative of Lonergan's _systematic_ exigence. The Hermeneutical-Dialectical trends, on the other hand, are the metascientific correlative of what Lonergan terms the _critical_ exigence. Making such correlations, however, is not a facile type of syncretism. For it raises the question of the dynamic orientation of the systematic and critical exigencies to the _methodical_ and _transcendental_ exigencies, thereby indicating how the errors within both the Logical-Empirical and Hermeneutical-Dialectical schools of metascience arise from their failure to grasp the limitations of their respective perspectives. The following discussion will indicate how the four exigencies are operative within the metascientific debates today.

First, the _systematic exigence_ arises inasmuch as the quest for meaning is not content with the common-sense meanings of everyday discourse.[342] Common-sense discourse is concerned with the persons and things as their meaning is related to us. It is the sphere of ordinary language, where the self-correcting process of learning is not controlled by scientific knowledge but by the day-to-day usage common to the linguistic group in which we are born and grow.[343] The systematic exigence of meaning can intervene within this process to give rise to a world of theory distinct from, yet related to, the world of common sense. Lonergan sees two primary exemplifications of the systematic exigence. The first gave rise to Hellenic scientific theory. Its emergence is illustrated in the early Platonic dialogues where Socrates

---

Applied Science: An Essay in the Phenomenology of Scientific Activity," in The European Philosophy Today (Dublin, Sept., 1971); Tracy, The Achievement of Bernard Lonergan, pp. 105-113; Insight, pp. 70-139.

[342]Cf. M.i.T., pp. 81-83; Tracy, op. cit., pp. 224-228; also Chapter Three of this study, pp. 424-431 and references given there.

[343]Cf. Insight, pp. 189-191; M.i.T., pp. 70-73, 86-90; P. Berger uses this notion of common sense to define the social character of reality in P. Berger and T. Luchmann, The Social Construction of Reality (A Doubleday Anchor Book, New York, 1967).

is depicted as inquiring after universal definitions of
such commonly ascribed attributes as justice, courage,
temperance, etc. The Athenians knew within the common-sense
world of discourse what they meant when referring to individuals as just, courageous, temperate; but they were hard
pressed to come up with the universal definitions Socrates
was after.[344] The shift from the Platonic dialogues to
Aristotle's Nicomachean Ethics indicates that the answers to
Socrates' questions could not be found within the context
of common-sense language but within the context of a
theoretical treatment of virtue and vice; indeed, the theoretic context goes beyond the common-sense questions to
establish its own control of meaning.[345]

Moving to the Aristotelian corpus and the entire
thrust of Hellenic and Medieval theory - what has aptly been
termed classical scientific theory - common characteristics
can be found.[346] The ideal or criterion for scientific theory
was certain knowledge through necessary causes or principles.
The necessary, immutable and eternal was the norm for
ἐπιστήμη and scientia.[347] The universal was its presupposition and goal.[348] Corresponding to these classical criteria
were the insistence upon logical deduction and induction, the
concern for essential definitions, and, because a knowledge
of first principles allowed deduction, the possibility of
individual minds to grasp the totality of classical

---

[344]Cf. Lonergan, Collection, pp. 256-257; Snell, Die
Entdeckung des Geistes (Hamburg, 1955), pp. 246ff., 371-400.

[345]Cf. Collection, pp. 257-263; M.i.T., p. 82; Eric
Voegelin, Order and History Vol. III: Plato and Aristotle
(Louisiana State University Press, 1957), pp. 304-314,
323-331, 355-357.

[346]Cf. Collection, pp. 252-267; Tracy, The Achievement
of Bernard Lonergan, pp. 82-91; A. Diemer, Beiträge zur
Entwicklung der Wissenschaftstheorie im 19. Jahrhundert
(Meisenheim am Glan, 1968), pp. 4-32.

[347]Cf. A. Diemer, op. cit., pp. 15-29; Joachim Ritter,
Metaphysik und Politik: Studien zu Aristoteles und Hegel
(Frankfurt, 1969), pp. 9-33; Snell, Die Entdeckung des
Geistes, pp. 412-421.

[348]A. Diemer, op. cit., p. 25.

science.[349] As we shall see in the following chapter, these characteristics of classical science originated in a cosmo-centric description object-ifying control of systematic meaning.[350]

Modern scientific performance, despite the tendency to interpret itself within classical categories,[351] effectively moved beyond the limitations of the classical conceptions of the systematic exigence. Beginning with Galileo, the natural sciences no longer sought universal and certain knowledge through immutable and necessary principles. The criterion became the quest for a de facto intelligibility, admittedly hypothetical and probable.[352] Aristotelian logic and the quest for essence gave way to more precise measuring devices whereby physical properties were correlated systematically by plotting their interactions on the number field to obtain mathematical functionals.[353] There occurred a shift from deductive reasoning to methods of ever more exact empirical observation, hypothesis formulations with the aid of mathematico-mechanical models, and verification through controlled experimentation and further observation. The self-correcting process of learning took on a specialized context, expressed by technical languages, which can no longer be mastered by any one individual.[354] The classical ideal of the Renaissance uomo universale rapidly gave way to increasing

---

[349]Cf. Tracy, The Achievement of Bernard Lonergan, pp. 84-90; A. Diemer, op. cit., pp. 24-32.

[350]Cf. Chapter Three, pp. 272ff.; also Chapter Two, pp. 142-152.

[351]Cf. G. Picht, Wahrheit, Vernunft, Verantwortung (Stuttgart, 1969), pp. 135-140; Habermas, Theorie und Praxis (Berlin, 1967), pp. 231-259.

[352]Cf. Hans Blumenberg, Die kopernikanische Wende (Frankfurt, 1965), G. Gusdorf, La révolution galiléenne (Paris, 1969), pp. 236-278.

[353]Cf. Heelan, "Horizon, Objectivity and Reality in the Physical Sciences," International Philosophical Quarterly, VII (1967), pp. 375-412; Jürgen Mittelstrass, Neuzeit und Aufklärung: Studien zur Entstehung der neuzeitlichen Wissenschaft und Philosophie (Berlin, 1970), pp. 207-308.

[354]Lonergan, Collection, pp. 261-266.

collaborative ventures of specialized communities of scientists, technologists, and scholars.[355]

In summary then, the systematic exigence has led to the differentiation of the worlds of theory and technical languages from the worlds of common sense with their everyday languages. The meta-scientific dimension of the exigence is evident in the fact that it accounts for not only the classical theory of Greek and Medieval science, but also for the modern scientific achievements.[356] Within this very broad perspective it is possible to situate the general characteristics of Logical Empiricism and, one can add, the concerns of French Structuralism. There is a way in which all of these groups are dependent upon the further development and confluence of the three schools of metascience operative in Dilthey's time.[357] Thus one can see the concern with the common-sense world in the groups concerned with ordinary language.[358] The Formalists' use of the linguistic analysis of Russell and Moore to develop an ideal or improved theoretic-technical language comes down on the side of the world of theory.[359] The dependence of the latter on classical elements of theory is clearly explicated in the Reconstructionists who concentrate more on ontology after the linguistic turn.[360] The Pragmatists show a greater concern with the subject of two worlds, seeing man as the user-of-language and

---

[355]Cf. Alvin W. Weinberg, Probleme der Grossforschung: Wissenschaftspolitik und Organisationsformen der Forschung. Die Forschungspolitik der BRD (Frankfurt, 1970).

[356]This is illustrated by J. Mittelstrass who sees a first Enlightenment in the Hellenic period and a second Enlightenment in the modern world; cf. op. cit., pp. 15-130. On the medieval world of theory, cf. Tracy, op. cit., pp. 54-60.

[357]H. Schnädelbach, Erfahrung, Begründung und Reflexion: Versuch über den Positivismus (Frankfurt) 1971).

[358]Eike von Savigny, Philosophie und normale Sprache: Texte der Ordinary - Language - Philosophie (München, 1969); Radnitzky, op. cit. Vol. I, pp. 51-54.

[359]Ibid., pp. 22-39 and references given there.

[360]Ibid., pp. 40-47 and references given there.

the producer-of-science.[361] On the other hand, the Structuralists are, like the Formalists, so concerned with the intelligibility of structure that they tend to reject any concern with the subject.[362] _ Finally, those who adopt Popper's notions on the growth of scientific knowledge, as well as those who appeal to systems-analysis and cybernetics, are aware of the break between classical and modern science and are thereby highly critical of the tendencies of logical empiricism.[363]

Why are all of these trends, from the perspective of Lonergan's meta-method, within the systematic exigence? There are several reasons. In one form or another all of these trends attempt to find a metascientific unification within either the world of common sense (ordinary language) or, more predominantly, within the world of theory: This can be seen in the Formalists' ideal of an improved language and their quest for an ideal unified science in terms of the ideal concept formation, ideal confirmation patterns, ideal attributes of empirical languages, and ideal explanatory procedures.[364] Inasmuch as they are dependent upon the Principia Mathematica, they strive to conform to classical (Aristotelian) two-valued logic, so that the problem of probability and statistical methods are at best problematic to their "eternalistic" a-historical frame.[365] Hence emerges the reductionist tendency within these schools: physics and mathematics provide the best systematic coordination of

---

[361]Ibid., pp. 48-51 and references given there.

[362]Claude Levi-Strauss, Structural Anthropology (New York: 1967); Günther Schiwy, Der französische Strukturalismus (Hamburg, 1969); Jean Piaget, Structuralism (London, 1971).

[363]Karl R. Popper, The Logic of Scientific Discovery (New York, 1968); Radnitzky, op. cit. II, pp. 139-146; Hans Albert, Traktat über kritische Vernunft; Ludwig von Bertalanffy, General System Theory (New York, 1973).

[364]Radnitzky, op. cit. I, pp. 112-169.

[365]Cf. Radnitzky, op. cit. I, p. 101; Heelan, "Quantum and Classical Logic: Their Respective Roles," Synthese 21 (1970), pp. 2-23; Insight, pp. 35-46.

knowledge. Methodology is thereby conceived as laws or
axioms or syntactical procedures (this is especially so in
earlier phases) descriptive of logical or structural regularities; or method is, especially in Popper, seen as prescrip-
tive of the effort to attain ever closer ideal approximations
within a criticist frame.[366] Praxis within such a context
takes on the function of hypothesis-checking.[367]

Second, the differentiation caused by the systematic
exigence between the world of common sense and the world of
theory, and the limitations of both, leads to what Lonergan
calls the _critical_ _exigence_.[368] There is no simple transition
from common sense to theory or vice versa. There is an
inclination to regard science as value-free and superior to
the common (non)sense of pre-scientific discourse.[369] Where
such elitism is less evident, there is still the expectation
on the part of what we might call the "systematic" schools of
metascience to assume that only the precision and order of the
world of theory can bring order into the chaos of common sense.
This tendency is evident in the reductionism whereby the
human sciences are denied a methodology specifically their
own, in the utopias of social engineering, in the disrepute
of the political.[370] As long as classical metaphysics was the
dominant framework for integrating the world of theory, the
world of common sense could be left to the direction of a more
or less privatized phronesis.[371] The emergence of modern
scientific theory, however, rendered the man of practical

---

[366]Radnitzky, _op. cit._ I, pp. 57, 99-101, 117.

[367]_Ibid._, p. 98.

[368]Cf. _M.i.T._, pp. 83-85; also Chapter Three of this
study pp. 424-431 and the references given there.

[369]Radnitzky I, pp. 72-91; also _M.i.T._, p. 248; F.
Matson, _The Broken Image_, pp. 3-65.

[370]Cf. J. Habermas, _Strukturwandel der Öffentlichkeit_
(Berlin, 1965), pp. 157-198, 231-156; Matson, _op. cit._,
pp. 66-112.

[371]Pierre Aubenque, _La Prudence chez Aristote_ (Paris, 1963).

common sense obsolete.[372]   Metaphysics was increasingly less
relevant, until the Kantian "Wendung Zum Subject" replaced
it with an objectivistic epistemology which, in turn, was
sublated by scientistic positivist methodologies.[373]   The
latter were, in effect, a resignation in the face of the
critical questions and a one-sided option for theory.[374]

Indeed, since Kant awoke from his dogmatic slumber
there has been a massive effort to do justice to the critical
exigence.   According to Lonergan the main characteristic of
the critical exigence is the need to properly interrelate
the worlds of common sense and the worlds of theory.[375]   After
an extensive study of conscious performance in both, Lonergan
concluded there could be no sublation of one into the
other.[376]   They are as different as Eddington's two tables.[377]
If there is such a profound differentiation how can a critical
integration be effected?   Must one choose between one or the
other and use it as the norm of critique, as the Ordinary
Language does in opting for common-sense usage and the
Formalist linguistics does for its improved language and
ideal of unified science?[378]   The problem runs deep, for the
particularity of common-sense worlds of discourse is grounded
in the concreteness of <u>historical</u> contexts, whereas theoretical worlds of discourse tend towards the abstract and

---

[372]Cf. Lonergan, <u>Collection</u>, pp. 260-261; Hans F. Fulda
"Theoretische Erkenntnis und pragmatische Gewissheit," in
<u>Hermeneutik und Dialektik</u> Vol. I (Tübingen, 1970), pp. 145-165;
Bernard Murchland, <u>The Age of Alienation</u> (New York, 1971).

[373]Cf. Habermas, <u>Erkenntnis und Interesse</u>, pp. 234ff.

[374]Cf. G. Picht, <u>Wahrheit, Vernunft, Verantwortung</u>,
pp. 135-140; Matson, <u>op. cit.</u>, pp. 56ff.; J. Habermas, <u>Technik
und Wissenschaft als "Ideologie"</u>, pp. 48-119.

[375]Cf. <u>M.i.T.</u>, pp. 83-85.

[376]Cf. Lonergan, <u>M.i.T.</u>, pp. 83-85; also <u>Insight</u>, pp.
289-299, esp. pp. 293-299.

[377]Cf. Sir A. Eddington, <u>The Nature of the Physical
World</u> (University of Michigan Press, 1948), pp. 273-292.

[378]Cf. Radnitzky I, pp. 22-54.

universal.[379]   Is metascience bound to remain within the world
of theory - Popper's "third world" of objective structures?
Are the only metascientific norms for understanding history
to be gleaned from a systematic effort at historical
explanation?[380]

If that were so, Structuralists like M. Foucalt would be
correct in announcing the "death of man," the advent of a
post-historic era.[381]   The transformations of the world of
common sense through technology - the seemingly limitless
production of similar goods - seem to re-enforce the notion
that "technique" can succeed in absorbing the worlds of history
and common sense into the worlds of theory and science.
L. Mumford has charted this tendency towards a megamachine
sublation of society and history.[382]

Against this trend, however, the Hermeneutical-
Dialectical schools of metascience have insisted that the
critical exigence cannot be subsumed into the systematic.
In one way or another they have called attention to how the
critical exigence demands attending to a subjectivity which
transcends total mediation by the worlds of common sense or
theory.   In the discussion of the dialectic of the Enlightenment we have seen how the inherent limitations of formal
systems - e.g., the theorem of Gödel - indicated the need for
discovering a world which would be capable of critically
integrating both common sense and theory.[383]   Lonergan sees
the critical exigence as opening up the world of interiority,
of the subject-as-subject.   It is this world of interiority
which, as a unity of identity and non-identity with the worlds

---

[379]Cf. G. Gusdorf, La révolution galiléenne Vol. II
(Paris, 1969), pp. 433-460; Lonergan, M.i.T., pp. 175-196.

[380]Radnitzky, op. cit. I, pp. 170-187.

[381]Cf. Michel Foucalt, The Order of Things: An Archaeology of the Human Sciences (New York, 1970), pp. 367-373,
386-387; L. Mumford, The Transformations of Man (New York,
1972), pp. 120-136.

[382]Cf. L. Mumford, The Myth of the Machine: The Pentagon
of Power (Columbia University Press, 1970).

[383]Cf. to this Chapter pp. 93-115 and the references
given there.

of common sense and theory, provides the norms for a proper
mediation of theory and praxis and keeps metascience from
an infinite regression into meta, meta, etc., theoretical
systems.[384]   As Lonergan stated in 1957:

> The subject-as-subject is reality in the sense that
> we live and die, love and hate, rejoice and suffer,
> desire and fear, wonder and dread, inquire and doubt.
> It is Descartes' "cogito" transposed to concrete living.
> It is the subject present to himself, not as presented
> to himself in any theory or affirmation of conscious-
> ness, but as the prior (non-absence) prerequisite to
> any presentation, as a priori condition to any stream
> of consciousness (including dreams).
> The argument is: the prior reality is not object-as-
> object nor subject-as-object; there only remains the
> subject-as-subject; and this subject-as-subject is
> both reality and discoverable through consciousness.
> The argument does not prove that in the subject-as-
> subject we shall find the evidence, norms, invariants,
> principles for a critique of horizons; it proves that
> unless we find it there, we shall not find it at all.[385]

It is this prior presence to which the Hermeneutical-
Dialectical   in metascience refer when they point out
that all science originates in a _Lebenswelt_.[386]   It was this
priority that Marx affirmed in saying that life determines
consciousness and not vice versa.   It was this, as we have
seen, that led Dilthey to differentiate the _Naturwissenschaf-
ten_ and _Geisteswissenschaften_ in order to overcome the pathos
of Enlightenment.

Lonergan's _Insight_ and his subsequent work attempt to
articulate how the critical exigence does in fact enable us
to uncover the evidence for invariant norms within the
subject-as-subject. He sees the critical exigence as defined
by three fundamental questions, which I shall here cast in
their metascientific terms. The first is the cognitional

[384]Cf. H. Peukert, "Zur formalen Systemtheorie und zur
hermeneutischen Problematik einer 'politischen Theologie'"
in _Diskussion zur 'politischen Theologie'_, pp. 85-91;
Lonergan, _Insight_, pp. xxiv-xxvi.

[385]Lonergan's unpublished _Notes on Existentialism_
(Boston College, 1957), p. 28.

[386]Cf. W. Marx, "Vernunft und Lebenswelt," in _Hermeneu-
tik und Dialektik_, pp. 217-232. Also cf. G. Brand, _Die
Lebenswelt: Eine_ Philosophie des konkreten Apriori (Berlin,
1971), pp. 3-34.

theory-praxis question: what does science do when it knows?
Then there is the epistemological question: why is doing that
knowing? And finally the metaphysical or ontological question: what does science know when it does it?[387] For Lonergan,
the second and third questions can only adequately be answered
when the first is. Moreover, it is only in the light of
the first question that one could critically integrate history
and science, common sense and theory, the natural and human
sciences, without derogating from the very different epistemological and ontological procedures and objects they are
concerned with.[388]

If we look at the origins and present trends of the
Hermeneutical-Dialectical schools of metascience we can see
how they attempt critical responses to these questions.
Indeed, from insufficient answers to the first there is a
progressive concentration on the second and third until, in
the work of, e.g., Karl-Otto Apel, there is a renewed
interest in the first.

The origins of the H-D trends of metascience cannot
simply be placed in Kant and his shift to the subject. As we
have seen in previous sections, there is an objectivism in
Kant's approach which is really more suited to the Logical
Empirical forms of metascience.[389] Idealism necessarily puts
system and thought as the criteria of critique. Against
this both Dilthey and Marx protested. Although largely
ignorant of one another's work, it is within them that the
origins of the H-D trends in metascience can be traced.[390]
Nor would it be too great an oversimplification to find in
Dilthey the origins of the hermeneutical interests, and in

---

[387]Cf. Lonergan, M.i.T., pp. 25, 83, 261, 287, 316; also
D. Tracy, op. cit., pp. 227ff.

[388]Cf. Lonergan, M.i.T., pp. 20-25 and Chapter Three
of this study, pp. 424-452.

[389]Cf. pp. 121-132 of this Chapter. H-D is an abbrevia-
tion of Hermeneutical-Dialectical.

[390]Cf. Lorenz Kruger, "Über das Verhältnis der hermeneutischen Philosophie zu den Wissenschaften," in Hermeneutik
und Dialektik Vol. I, pp. 3-30; Paul Lorenzen, Szientismus
versus Dialektik in ibid., pp. 57-72.

Marx the concern for dialectics. While both exhibit a concern to move beyond the worlds of commonsense and theory in order to find the norms of their critical work, Dilthey remained within the framework of science, seeking to differentiate the human sciences from the natural, whereas Marx sought to dialectically expose the role of science within the totality of socio-historical reality. A brief survey of the "Wirkungsgeschichte" of these hermeneutical and dialectical origins of the Continental schools of metascience will indicate how they fall within the critical exigence of Lonergan.

Dilthey's differentiation of the Geisteswissenschaften from the Naturwissenschaften was within the critical concern of the cognitional theory-praxis question of what the sciences do when they know. The pathos of the Enlightenment, the increasing anarchy of convictions regarding norms for man's free constitution of history, led Dilthey to seek those norms within the experience of conscious interiority grounding the human historical sciences. For the latter had emerged from the social life-praxis of man.[391] Nevertheless, the hermenutics of Dilthey tended to immunize this experience of the subject-as-subject within the realm of the human sciences; it did not essay a critical integration with the natural sciences.[392]

E. Husserl's phenomenology attempted to overcome this deficiency by stressing the intention of objects in consciousness. The critical exigence in phenomenology concentrated upon the epistemological question of why what the sciences do is knowledge. In this epistemology Husserl was primarily dependent upon the natural sciences and mathematics and their logics for paradigms of knowledge. Yet his failure to clear up the ambiguities of the cognitional theory-praxis question led to an irreconcilable conflict between his analysis of intentional constitution and his reliance on intuition in

---

[391]Cf. Dilthey, G.S. I, pp. 3-21; and the references given in note 386 above.

[392]Cf. M. Lamb, "W. Dilthey's critique of historical reason and B. Lonergan's meta-methodology," in Language Truth and Meaning, pp. 115-166; also Chapter Three of this study, pp. 219-236.

determining the epistemological criteria of verification.[393]
As a result, phenomenology was unable to adequately correlate
the concrete Lebenswelt of commonsense and the concept of
world constitution derived from intentionality.[394]   There
emerged an increasingly conceptualist Wesenschau which
bracketed through Epoché a truly critical grounding of the
empirical sciences - much as Popper was hampered from such a
grounding because of his failure to correlate world two
(subjective minds) with world three (the objective structures
of theory).[395]

From the breakdown of the epistemology of phenomenology,
the critical exigence turned, in M. Heidegger, to an affort
at a foundational ontology of Dasein. The Heidegger of Sein
und Zeit projected an analysis of "der Ursprung der Wissenschaft aus der eigentlichen Existenz."[396] Yet this project
was abandoned, along with the fundamental ontology, in
Heidegger's later work. According to Lonergan the underlying
reason for this can be found in Heidegger's failure to criticize the Kantian notion of intuition, i.e., his failure to
work out the prior cognitional theory-praxis question.[397]
Instead Heidegger attempted to immunize his profound insights
into the being structures of existence by labeling the history
of Western intelligence as a forgetfulness of being, the
apotheosis of which could be found in the technicity of

---

[393]Cf. W. Ryan, "Intentionality in Edmund Husserl and
Bernard Lonergan: the Perspectives of Intuition-Constitution
and Affirmation," in Essays in Methodology (University of
Notre Dame Press, 1974).

[394]Cf. G. Brand, op. cit., pp. 104-117.

[395]Cf. W. Marx, op. cit., pp. 224-231; T. Adorno, Zur
Metakritik der Erkenntnistheorie: Studien über Husserl und die
phänomenologischen Antinomien (Stuttgart, 1956); on Popper cf.
J. Habermas, "Gegen einen positivistisch halbierten Rational-
ismus," in Der Positivismusstreit in der deutschen Soziologie
(Berlin, 1969), pp. 155-192.

[396]Cf. Heidegger, Sein und Zeit (Tübingen, 1963), pp.
356-364, esp. p. 363. Also E. Tugendhat, Der Wahrheitsbegriff bei Husserl und Heidegger (Berlin, 1970), pp. 292-298.

[397]Cf. Lonergan, Insight, pp. xxviiif.; also his Notes
on Existentialism, pp. 14-17; G. Brand, op. cit., pp. 133-137.

modern science.[398]   Unable to distinguish between how the
sciences actually perform and the positivist or empiricist
accounts of what is known by science, method is left to the
latter.[399]   The merging of horizons seems inadequate to the
task of the critique of horizons; hermeneutical reflection,
as Gadamer himself remarks, "vermittelt nicht selbst ein
Wahrheitskriterium."[400]

A similar pattern can be found in the critical development of Marxism. Where the failure to articulate a proper
cognitional theory-praxis in Dilthey led to an epistemology
in phenomenology which could not critically ground the sciences to an ontology in philosophical hermeneutics which could
only isolate itself from the sciences, there is an opposite
trend in Marxism. The dialectical position of K. Marx was
clearly within the critical exigence in terms of the shift
from commonsense and theory to consciousness. Only this
concern with consciousness was not an abstract preoccupation
with cognitional theoretical questions, but an effort to
overcome the opposition between Idealism and Materialism in
the self-conscious action of the proletariat.[401]   A dialectical, and so non-idealist, "Wendung zum Subject" is seen in
Marx's critique of Feuerbach:

> that the object, reality, material existence is only
> grasped under the form of an object or of an intuition.
> They are not understood as subjective, as material,

---

[398]Cf. M. Heidegger, Die Technik und Die Kehre (Tübingen,
1962); W. Richardson, Heidegger: Through Phenomenology to
Thought, pp. 256-258, 284, 326, 396-399.

[399]Cf. H. G. Gadamer, Kleine Schriften I (Tübingen,
1967), pp. 46-58; E. Tugendhat, op. cit., pp. 360, 376, 399;
C. V. Bormann, "Die Zweideutigkeit der hermeneutischen
Erfahrung," Phil. Rundschau, 16 (1969), pp. 92-119.

[400]Cf. Gadamer, "Replik," in Hermeneutik und Ideologiekritik, p. 300; J. Habermas, Philosophisch-politische Profile,
pp. 76-92.

[401]Cf. A. Schmidt (ed.), Beiträge zur marxistischen
Erkenntnistheorie (Frankfurt, 1969); A. Schmidt, Der Begriff
der Natur in der Lehre von Marx (Frankfurt, 1962); Irving
Fetscher, "Die Überwindung des Gegensatzes von Materialismus
und Idealismus in der selbstbewussten Aktion des Proletar-
iats," in Karl Marx und der Marxismus (München, 1962), pp.
127-132.

human activity, praxis. Hence, idealism develops the active aspect in an abstract way since it does not recognize the real, material activity of men - in contradistinction to materialism.[402]

In his Economic and Philosophical Manuscripts Marx saw that having "one basis for life and another for science is a priori a falsehood," since both are grounded in the transformation of nature through the historical life action of man.[403] This cognitional theory-praxis basis or foundation has been well outlined by A. Schmidt. Marx was aware of the need to stress the unity of identity and non-identity - "Thought and being are indeed distinct, but they also form a unity." - yet this did not lead him to a dualism of methods for knowledge of nature and history.[404] Thus he wrote in Die Deutsche Ideologie:

> We acknowledge only one science, the science of history. History can be viewed in two ways: as the history of nature and as the history of humankind. Both aspects are not to be dichotomized. As long as humans exist, the history of nature and the history of humans will condition one another.[405]

Had Marx explicated this unity in the cognitional theory-praxis more, had he shown how a nomological approach to history is not to neglect the anthropological and praxiological approaches, he would not be so susceptible to the criticisms of encouraging an abstract reification of history.[406]

As it was both Engels and Lenin turned from Marx's original insights to a more epistemological orientation that was not so concerned with what a scientific knowing does as with why it is a knowing. Engels' "dialectic of nature"

---

[402] Karl Marx, Theses on Feuerbach (1845), MEGA I/5, p. 533.

[403] Karl Marx, The Economic & Philosophic Manuscripts of 1884 (New York, 1972), pp. 170-193.

[404] A. Schmidt, Der Begriff der Natur, pp. 38-41 and also the references given in note 403 above.

[405] K. Marx, Deutsche Ideologie, MEGA V/1, p. 567.

[406] Helmut Fleischer, Marxismus und Geschichte (Frankfurt, 1969), pp. 13-43; Dietrich Böhler, Metakritik der Marxschen Ideologiekritik (Frankfurt, 1971).

transformed Marx's subject-oriented history into an objective process of nature. A theory of evolution replaced the unity of historical praxis with a unity of nature: "Die Dialektik ist...die Wissenschaft von den allgemeinen Bewegungs- und Entwicklungsgesetzen der Natur, der Menschengesellschaft und des Denkens."[407] Hence the emergence one finds of an epistemology in Engels and in Lenin of how the sciences mirror or reflect ("Abbilden" and "Wiederspiegeln") the objective dialectic of nature. A study of Lenin's Erkenntnistheorie would show how he was not aiming at advancing the dialectical critique of Marx as he was essaying an epistemological appropriation of the advancing natural sciences.[408] The naive realism that resulted undermined the unity of nature and history in the field of praxis, replacing it with an objectivistic unity in material process.[409]

This involution of Marx was completed in the writings of J. Stalin, whose almost total identification of dialectics with the evolutionary process of nature sought to satisfy the critical exigence by turning to a metaphysics (however crypto-) of nature: "die sogenannte subjektive Dialektik (die Entwicklung unseres Denkens) eine Widerspiegelung der objectiven Dialektik (der Entwicklung der Erscheinungen der materiellen Welt) ist."[410] There is an analogous insight in Engels and Popper regarding the impossibility to truly ground the critical exigence with a resulting option for belief in

---

[407] F. Engels, Anti-Dühring, p. 173; also A. Schmidt, Der Begriff der Natur, pp. 41-50.

[408] The notion of "abbild" can be found, before Engels, in J. Dietzgen's Das Wesen der menschlichen Kopfarbeit (1869). Lenin expanded on the ideas of Dietzgen and of Engel in his "Erkenntnistheorie des dialektischen Materialismus" in his major work Materialismus und Empiriokritizismus (1908). For a summary account of this cf. G. A. Wetter, Sowjetideologie Heute (Frankfurt, 1962), pp. 53ff.

[409] Cf. I. Fetscher, Karl Marx und der Marxismus, p. 132 and the reference to A. Schmidt given in 407 above.

[410] J. Stalin, Osnovy markisistskoj Filosophii, here quoted from the German translation Grundlagen der marxistischen Philosophie (Berlin, 1960), p. 323.

scientific progress.[411] But whereas this led Popper to opt for an "open society" of competing beliefs, it led Stalin to solidify the Leninist doctrine of absolute party fidelity. The analogue with Comtean positivism is obvious, leading to a "geschichtsontologischer Objektivismus" where the Party has a premium on knowing what the "laws" of history are.[412]

It is not surprising, therefore, that the contemporary schools of metascience are involved once again in a return to the cognitional theory-praxis question. There has been a critical re-evaluation of the metascientific implications of the hermeneutical trend from Dilthey through Husserl to Heidegger and Gadamer. The same has occurred in the field of dialectics both within Communism and in the Neo-Marxist trend of the Frankfurt School.[413]

Space does not permit an extensive comparison between what Radnitzky calls the Hermeneutical-Dialectical school of

---

[411]Cf. I. Fetscher, op. cit., p. 87: "Der Marxismus wird damit zu einem genauen Analogon von Comtes Positivismus. Dass hier der Stalinismus in der Engelsschen Tradition steht, beweist ein Zitat aus Engels Schrift 'Ludwig Feuerbach und der Ausgang der klassischen deutschen Philosophie', das Schdnow in diesem Zusammenhang bringt. Wenn man eingesehen hat, dass die Philosophen vergeblich nach der absoluten und allumfassenden Wahrheit streben, meinte Engels, 'lässt man diesem Wege und für jeden einzeln unerreichbare absolute Wahrheit laufen und jagt dafür den erreichbaren relativen Wahrheit nach auf der positiven Wissenschaften und der Zusammenfassung ihrer Resultate vermittelst des dialektischen Denkens."

[412]Cf. I. Fetscher in note 411 and to D. Böhler in note 406 where he shows how there was the possibility of this reification of history implicit in Marx's own development. The consequences of this abstract metaphysical approach to history have been formally outlined in J. B. Metz's "Erlösung und Emanzipation" in Stimmen der Zeit (March, 1973), pp. 171-178.

[413]Thus one has the writings of M. Riedel and Karl-Otto Apel dealing with the problems of an anthropology of knowledge from the hermeneutical perspective, whereas J. Habermas is attempting the same from both the hermeneutical (Hegel, Dilthey, Husserl, Heidegger and Gadamer) and the dialectical perspectives (Marx and Marxism). These two trends or perspectives are constitutive of the Frankfurt School; cf. Martin Jay, The Dialectical Imagination: A History of the Frankfurt School and the Institute of Social Research 1923-1950 (Boston, 1973).

metascience and the method of Lonergan. It is clear,
however, that Lonergan's treatment of the critical exigence
does provide a framework for understanding why those representing this school are presently engaged in developing an anthropology of knowledge to meet the cognitional theory-praxis
question in a way that would avoid the epistemological and
ontological dead-ends of previous hermeneutical and dialectical thought and action. The point of the previous
discussion was to show that Lonergan's raising of the cognitional theory-praxis question is by no means a falling
behind the present "status quaestionis" of contemporary
metascience, either as regards the Anglo-Saxon or the
Continental schools.

B. The Methodical and Transcendental Exigencies. If
the systematic exigence has led to a differentiation of
theory from common sense, then the critical exigence is concerned with uncovering a realm of meaning and norms which
underlies both common sense and theory. Where the Logical-
Empirical Schools of metascience seek an ordering and
grounding of the sciences within the context of the systematic
exigence, the Hermeneutical-Dialectical are more aware of
the inherent limitations of such a context and seek to base
their metascience on what Lonergan would term the critical
exigence. Regarding both of these schools of metascience,
they would be seen as attempting to come to grips with the
contemporary crisis as outlined in the previous section on
the dialectic of the Enlightenment.[414] Lonergan does not
see the resolution of the crisis in terms of a cognitional
theory as theory - he claims that the problems raised by the
systematic exigence cannot be answered within theory or
system.[415] Nor does he subscribe to the critical hermeneutical or dialectical attempts outlined above insofar as they
proceed from insufficiently appropriated critique. The
increasingly recognized insufficiency of phenomenological
epistemology and Heideggerian ontology in hermeneutics, and
of a naive materialist epistemology and naturalist ontology

---

[414]Cf. Chapter Two, pp. 93-114.

[415]Cf. Lonergan, M.i.T., p. 83.

in dialectics, has reopened the question of a prior cognitional theory-praxis.

It is precisely here that the critical exigence becomes,
for Lonergan, the methodical exigence. If the critical
exigence uncovers the worlds of interiority (Dilthey) and
history (Marx) as distinct from the spontaneous world of common
sense   and the reflective world of theory, this distinction
is not a separation. The heightened consciousness of the
subject-as-subject is not an illusory isolation within a
Leibnizian monad, a Kantian noumenon, a Hegelian absolute
concept, a Marxist nature prior to history, nor even Dilthey's
immediate self-awareness grounding only the cultural sciences.
For Lonergan the critical exigence reveals the subject-as-
subject in the conscious praxis of experiencing, understanding,
judging, deciding, acting. And it is this conscious praxis
which can methodically ground all human and historical activity, whether scientific or otherwise, since these structures
of praxis are the fundamental related and recurrent operations yielding progressive and cumulative results.[416]

Lonergan does not hesitate to designate this methodical
exigence as based upon cognitional theory and issuing in a
transcendental method.[417] But the designation is not to be
taken in the usual Kantian sense, except in the broad sense
which,   for example, Karl-Otto Apel uses when he writes:

> Anyone who wants to know at all must entrust himself
> with the truth as a subject of knowledge. And that
> also means: he must presuppose himself as a critical
> instance of valid reflection. In my opinion we cannot
> retreat from this emancipation of the knowing subject
> gained in the cognitional theory of modernity.[418]

Thus Lonergan speaks of the rational appropriation of one's
own rational self-consciousness as a heightening of awareness
so that one appropriates the open and dynamic a priori
related and recurrent operations of experiencing,

---

[416] Cf. Chapter Three of this study, pp. 357-453; also
Lonergan, M.i.T., pp. 3-25.

[417] Cf. Lonergan, M.i.T., pp. 83-85 and the references
given to M.i.T. in note 416 above.

[418] K.-O. Apel, "Sprache als Thema und Medium der transzendentalen Reflexion," in Man and World (1970), p. 327.

understanding, judging, and deciding.[419] This appropriation is not, however, caught in the illusion of the privatized knowing subject:

> The withdrawal into interiority is not an end in itself. From it one returns to the realms of common sense and theory with the ability to meet the methodical exigence. For self-appropriation of itself is a grasp of transcendental method, and that grasp provides one with the tools not only for an analysis of common sense procedures but also for the differentiation of the sciences and the construction of their methods.[420]

So Lonergan is able to show how the activity of the knowing subject, i.e., cognitional praxis, is operative within the classical and statistical methods of the natural sciences.[421] The complementarity between classical and statistical procedures is assured, and on that basis P. Heelan has been able to offer a very novel interpretation of Quantum Mechanics and begin to elaborate a Quantum Logic which aims at overcoming the limitations of the classical logic of the _Principia Mathematica_.[422] Now the two-valued truth-functional propositional logic of the _Principia Mathematica_ had a profound influence on the development of the mainstream of Logical-Empirical schools of metascience, leading the Formalists to restrict their program to the formalizations of meta-mathematics and the logic of science, viz., physical or "exact" science.[423] Yet it is precisely this ultimately classical reliance on system which Lonergan calls in question by his attention to the creative novelty of the non-systematic and random.[424]

---

[419] Cf. Lonergan, _Insight_, pp. xxviii, 319-347.

[420] Lonergan, _M.i.T._, p. 83.

[421] Cf. Lonergan, _Insight_, pp. 33-172; also to Chapter Three of this study, pp. 388-409 and the references given there.

[422] Cf. P. Heelan, _Quantum Mechanics and Objectivity_ (The Hague, 1965); also P. Heelan, "Quantum and Classical Logic: Their Respective Roles," in _Synthese_ 21 (1970), pp. 2-33.

[423] Cf. Radnitzky, _op. cit._ I, pp. 22-39.

[424] Cf. Lonergan, _Insight_, pp. 51-68.

On the one hand, the Formalist approach to the non-systematic and statistical is to see it only as a provisional ignorance ultimately to be sublated in classical laws - hence the debate over the indeterminacy principle of Quantum Mechanics. On the other hand, thinkers like Jacques Monod see in chance and probability the refutation of any fundamental intelligibility or meaning within the universe. The denial of classical laws seems to issue in a totalization of randomness.[425] In contrast to both of these positions, Lonergan elaborated a methodical complementarity of both classical and statistical methods of inquiry in terms of conscious interiority. Classical procedures arise from questions for intelligence (subject-ive aspect) which through observation, hypothesis formation, and verification issue in the knowledge of conjugates (object-ive aspect).[426] Statistical procedures arise from questions for reflection (subject-ive aspect) which observes the occurrence of conjugates, sets up the probability of recurrent schemes, and verifies these through an inverse insight into the non-intelligibility of random divergencies from probability scales, thereby issuing in a knowledge of events (object-ive aspect).[427]

The complementarity is not, therefore, concordism. There is no way that Lonergan is merely tampering with the results of classical or statistical investigative procedures. Instead he is calling attention to what scientists do when they know laws of the classical or statistical type. And he is doing this by adverting to related and recurrent operations yielding progressive and cumulative results, i.e., he is transforming method from its Cartesian classicism to its transcendental and empirical foundations. Thus he can go on to elaborate the canons of empirical method;[428] and he can

---

[425]Cf. Jacques Monod, Chance and Necessity (New York, 1972).

[426]Cf. Lonergan, Insight, pp. 35-53.

[427]Cf. Lonergan, Insight, pp. 53-68; and also Chapter Three of this study, pp. 401-409.

[428]Cf. Lonergan, Insight, pp. 70-102.

develop the complementarity of classical and statistical methods into a complementarity in the knowing (subject-ive) aspects and of the known (object-ive) aspects, where the former are seen in their heuristic structures of observations, data, formulation, and verification, and the latter in terms of emergent probability.[429]   Not only does this allow Lonergan to essay a solution to the problems of space and time, thereby showing how his linking of metamethod with related and recurrent operations of interiority is not dependent upon Kantian a priori forms of sensibility, but he can also address himself squarely to the truth intention in mathematics and empirical science.[430]

By showing the difference between analytic propositions and analytic principles in reference to the sources of meaning and judgment as a grasp of the virtually unconditioned, he can situate the functional relevance of mathematical logic and the Formalist concern with linguistic analysis.[431]   This might be stated in semiotic fashion by extending the idea of functional specialization where the operations of conscious interiority operate in a related manner toward an end or goal established by one level of operation. Thus:

experience   -   syntactics
understanding -   semantics
judging   -   sigmatics
deciding   -   pragmatics

The syntactic level is concerned with the formal relations between symbols or signs. Grammatically syntax is concerned with the relations between conventional parts of speech; logically syntax involves the laws of formation and transformation pertaining to analytic propositions.[432]   In

---

[429] Ibid., pp. 103-139.

[430] Ibid., pp. 140-172, 281, 287, 299-315; also Lonergan's unpublished Notes on Mathematical Logic (Boston, 1957).

[431] Cf. Lonergan, Insight, pp. 304-315.

[432] Cf. Lonergan, Notes on Mathematical Logic, p. 10; Georg Klaus, Wörterbuch der Kybernetik Vol. II (Frankfurt, 1969), pp. 564, 569, 632-634. Note how this correlation of Lonergan's basic related and recurrent operations of the subject-as-subject with the fields of semiotics provides

metascience the Logical–Empirical ideal of unified science
and, more recently, Structuralism are primarily operative
in this syntatical sphere.[433] For both are concentrated
upon the formulated products and the axiomatic relations
between them. Semantics deals with the meanings of symbols
and signs, where that meaning is not restricted to syntactical
relations but adds the further dimension of meaning itself.
Grammatically there is the shift to philology and lexico-
graphy; logically one has the formal terms of meaning and
provisional analytic principles where one, for example,
moves beyond a Bloomfieldian emphasis upon syntactical relations to the semantic logical relations evident in Chomsky's
work.[434] Metascience has evinced this semantic shift in
general systems theories, as well as in the more Husserlian
phenomenological concerns of a general hermeneutics of
mathematical and scientific (natural) systems.[435] Sigmatics,
usually included within semantics, deals with what is meant,
signified or symbolized. This corresponds to Lonergan's
full terms of meaning and analytic principles, implying as
they do judgments of fact.[436] Logic comes close to a sig-
matic function in its discussions of the truth value problematic, and it is here that Heelan's concern with a Quantum

---

a very fruitful position analogous to that taken by K.–O. Apel
in his article "Szientismus oder transzendentale Hermeneutik?
Zur Frage nach dem Subjekt der Zeicheninterpretation in der
Semiotik des Pragmatismus," in Hermeneutik und Dialektik Vol.
I, pp. 105-144.

[433]Cf. Radnitzky, op. cit. I, pp. 72ff.; on Structuralism cf. P. Ricoeur, Le conflit des interprétations (Paris,
1969), pp. 31-100.

[434]Cf. G. Klaus, op. cit., pp. 561-564; Lonergan,
Insight, pp. 304-309; J. Lyons, Chomsky (London, 1970), pp.
27-46, esp. pp. 34-35.

[435]Cf. L. von Bertalanffy, General System Theory (New
York, 1968), pp. 30-86; G. Brand, op. cit., pp. 65-103; W.
Stegmüller, Probleme und Resultate der Wissenschaftstheorie
und Analytischen Philosophie, Band I: Wissenschaftliche
Erklärung und Begründung (Berlin, 1969), pp. 1-71.

[436]Cf. G. Klaus, op. cit., p. 565; Lonergan, Insight,
pp. 304-309, 357-359.

Logic and meta-contextual language functions.[437] From a metascientific standpoint Lonergan sees here the role of a critical metaphysics as the integral heuristic structure of proportionate being.[438] As critical, however, such a metaphysics is subordinate to metamethod and so necessarily addresses itself to the questions of a philosophical hermeneutics centered on "die Sache selbst."[439] Finally, pragmatics gets into the relations between the symbols and signs and their users. Grammatically there is Chomsky's generative grammatics; in logics one sees the various attempts at a performative logic.[440] In metascience this dimension is seen both in the praxiologists and in the dialectical concern with how science is actually used, its guiding interests and political-ethical aspects.[441] This is also seen in Lonergan's metamethodical extension into ethics.[442]

If Lonergan's discovery of a metamethodical complementarity of classical and statistical methods indicates the relevance it has for metascience as a shift from a privatized cognitional theory to a concern with method, it does so in

---

[437] Cf. P. Heelan, "Quantum and Classical Logic: Their Respective Roles," in Synthese 21 (1970), pp. 1-6, 10-24.

[438] Cf. Lonergan, Insight, pp. 385-430 where he shows the necessity of a critical-dialectical method in metaphysics

[439] Cf. Lonergan, Collection, pp. 202-220; G. B. Sala, "Seinserfahrung und Seinshorizont nach E. Coreth und B. Lonergan," in Zeitschrift für katholische Theologie (1967), pp. 294-338. It is evident that Lonergan's basic disagreement with Coreth, and indeed with all forms of Thomist transcendental metaphysics, stems from the fact that Lonergan can not see how any metaphysics can be critically and dialectically grounded except insofar as metaphysics relinquishes its foundational position to a metamethodology articulating cognitional praxis.

[440] Cf. N. Chomsky, Aspects of the Theory of Syntax (Boston, 1965); also his Language and Mind (New York, 1968); on performative logic, cf. D. Evans, The Logic of Self-Involvement (London, 1963); Lonergan, M.i.T., pp. 74-75.

[441] Cf. Radnitzky, op. cit. I, pp. 48-51; II, pp. 78-100, 160-176; also the article by Apel referred to in note 432 above.

[442] Cf. Lonergan, Insight, pp. 595-633; also D. Johnson, "Lonergan and the Redoing of Ethics," in Continuum V (Summer, 1967), pp. 211-220.

ways other than the semiotic references. For Lonergan's methodical approriation of the non-intelligibility of random occurrences is a very technical affirmation of non-identity within even the physical sciences. It shows that the unity of identity (classical anticipations) and non-identity (randomness) is unavoidable even in Physics. But the unity as a complementarity can only be established through a methodical exigence which moves from conscious interiority back to the methods of commonsense and theory. In this way Lonergan's metamethod does not end up identifying the natural sciences with only a technical interest, as Habermas' does.[443] Heelan, relying on metamethod, can speak of the hermeneutics and dialectics of Physics, and especially Quantum Mechanics. For the methodical concern with what scientists do when they know indicates how prior to the transcendental interest in technical control is the transcendental interest in explanatory knowledge itself.[444] From that prior horizon one can move on to explore technology as bodily extensions for measurement and control, where the natural sciences are seen as indeed prone to a positivistic and mechanistic self-(mis)understanding through the Industrial Revolution.[445] Yet, if Habermas tends - in a manner similar to Dilthey - to

---

[443]Cf. J. Habermas, Technik und Wissenschaft als 'Ideologie', pp. 48-103.

[444]Cf. P. Heelan, "Towards a Hermeneutic of Pure and Applied Science: An Essay in the Phenomenology of Scientific Activity," in European Philosophy Today (Dublin, Sept., 1971). The explanatory thrust of an unrestricted desire to know (cf. Chapter Three, pp. 388-409) incorporates Fichte's unrestricted desire to know and (cf. Habermas, Erkenntnis und Interesse, pp. 244ff. on Fichte's pure interest to know) and does so within a context of method that allows it to critically offset the technical interest in control insofar as the latter would tend towards a mechanomorphism that would exclude the subject. Thus the significance of Quantum Mechanics consists precisely in its discovery within natural science of the impossibility of complete control.

[445]Cf. Heelan's article referred to in note 444 above, pp. 15-18; also his notion of measurement in "Horizon, Objectivity and Reality in the Physical Sciences," Internat. Philos. Qrtly., 7 (1967), pp. 375-412; L. Mumford, The Myth of the Machine: The Pentagon of Power; Jacques Ellul, The Technological Society (New York, 1964).

leave the natural sciences to the positivists, Lonergan's
metamethod does not.

The non-systematic and the random of an instance of
non-identity and an integral component of the methodical
exigence for Lonergan have enabled him to give common-sense
meaning and action its rightful place in method. Without
going into the two chapters in Insight dealing with common
sense as subject and as object, it is important to realize
how this dimension of human activity is central to metascience. The Ordinary Language philosophers, as well as the
revised pragmaticism of someone like Apel, have indicated
how the avoidance of an infinite regress of meta-languages
can only be accomplished by recognizing the prior everyday
communication out of which the scientific community and its
technical languages spring and to which they return.[446] It
is within this context that Metz's interest in interdisciplinary collaboration has led him to a concern with narrative
and story as prior to argumentation and theory.[447] Obviously,
as has already been mentioned in the first chapter, the two
forms cannot be isolated into an either-or option. To neglect
this dimension of story and narration would, as Metz has
indicated, lead to a negation of historical knowledge and
historical reason.[448]

It is this that Lonergan refers to when he affirms,
with Vico, the priority of poetry,[449] and the matrix of
history in the existential history and narrative history:

> It [the historical being of man] may be named, if
> considered interiorly, an existential history -
> the living tradition which formed us and thereby
> brought us to the point where we began forming
> ourselves. This tradition includes at least
> individual and group memories of the past, stories
> of exploits and legends about heroes, in brief,

[446]Cf. Apel's article in Hermeneutik und Dialektik
in note 432; also Radnitzky, op. cit. II, pp. 34ff.

[447]Cf. Metz, "A Short Apology of Narrative," in
Concilium 85, pp. 84-96.

[448]Cf. to Metz's article in note above; also his article on redemption and liberation in Stimmen der Zeit (1973).

[449]Cf. Lonergan, M.i.T., p. 73.

enough of history for the group to have an identity as a group and for individuals to make their several contributions towards maintaining and promoting the good of order.[450]

It is this dynamic structure of common sense and story which underlies the process of hi-story, as both Lonergan and M. Novak elaborate.[451] Story is a narrative structure of time, and prior to the narration it is lived in meaningful or meaningless action.[452] There is an intellectuality in the dramatic subjects living out their hi-story - to it Aristotle referred when he assigned the centrality of phronesis to moral life. And it is in discovering this lived hi-story as experiencing, understanding, judging, deciding, and acting that Lonergan has been able to uncover the unity grounding metamethod and the total range of human activity, whether in common sense, science, politics, economics, philosophy or theology.[453]

Moreover, it is within both the dramatic subject and community that Lonergan sees the basic unfolding of dialectic. For the transcendental imperatives of Be Attentive, Intelligent, Critical, Responsible as operative in experiencing, understanding, judging, deciding and acting are not some iron laws of history but the structure of freedom. Individuals and groups can be inattentive, stupid, irrational and irresponsible.[454] So dialectics is not some abstract process - as it tends to be in both Marxist and Liberal versions - but concrete, dynamic, and contradictory.[455] Lonergan understands the dialectic of progress and decline, of understanding and bias, as calling for a critique of history that would sublate

---

[450]Lonergan, M.i.T., pp. 182; also Chapter Three of this study, pp. 422ff. and compare with pages 256-260 of that chapter and with pages 497ff. of Chapter Four.

[451]Cf. M. Novak, Ascent of the Mountain Flight of the Dove (New York, 1971), pp. 44-88.

[452]Cf. Lonergan, M.i.T., pp. 175-184.

[453]Cf. Chapter Three of this study, pp. 254-281, 357-453.

[454]Cf. Lonergan, M.i.T., pp. 52-55; Insight, pp. 209-244.

[455]Cf. Lonergan, Insight, pp. 217ff.

the Liberal thesis and the Marxist antithesis.[456] He names
this cosmopolis and sees foreshadowings of it within the
historical consciousness operative in both the liberal idea
of progress and Marxist class warfare. Yet "it comes at a
time when the totalitarian fact and threat have refuted the
liberals and discredited the Marxists."[457] Reading Lonergan's
reflections on cosmopolis indicates the need for the methodical exigence to elaborate a metamethod which does not shun
the critical task of self-appropriation.

For metamethod, like the method of philosophy and unlike
the methods of the empirical sciences, is not independent
of particular results nor prior to praxis.[458] What this leads
to, however, is a growing realization of a profound inadequacy
which neither method nor philosophy can correct on their own:

> But if the need of some cosmopolis makes manifest
> the inadequacy of common sense to deal with the
> issue [of scotosis and bias], on a deeper level it
> makes manifest the inadequacy of man. For the
> possibility of cosmopolis is conditioned by the
> possibility of a critical human science, and a
> critical human science is conditioned by the
> possibility of a correct and accepted philosophy.
> However, as the intervening chapters have attempted
> to explain, and as the history of philosophy rather
> abundantly confirms, the polymorphism of human
> consciousness loses none of its ambivalence because
> men have turned to philosophy.[459]

The methodical exigence, precisely if it is true to itself,
must recognize the seemingly intractable character of evil
and suffering, of alienation and the social surd.[460] Should
one wish a concrete example of this, one need only turn to
the genesis, development, and present decline of the Frankfurt

---

[456]Cf. Lonergan, Insight, p. 241.

[457]Cf. Lonergan, Insight, p. 241; on cosmopolis ibid.,
pp. 238-242.

[458]Cf. Lonergan, M.i.T., pp. 3-25.

[459]Lonergan, Insight, p. 690; note that for Lonergan
"cosmopolis is above all politics," ibid., p. 239; on the
limits of human liberation cf. Chapter Four of this study,
pp. 480-485.

[460]Cf. Lonergan, M.i.T., pp. 52-55; Insight, pp. 225ff.

School of Critical Theory.[461]

The transcendental exigence is initially simply the fact of raising further questions. There will be no time when the source of questions will dry up in history. There can be no retreat to obscurantism, no relevant questions can be dogmatically or arbitrarily brushed aside. It is this drive to question that underpins both the exigencies of meaning and the movement from experiencing through understanding and judging to decision and action.[462] Transcendence is not some absolute knowledge or ego or a priori innate forms; it is struggle and search, it is as concrete as the vast efforts of human beings on the planet in the slow and painful discoveries and setbacks they have endured throughout history, the differentiations and lack thereof they have experienced.[463] The cognitive self-transcendence that has given rise to the vast sweep of mankind's intellectual achievements, its art, literature, sciences, philosophies, is one aspect of transcendence in history.[464] Then there is the more painful process of moral self-transcendence that occurs under the aegis of questions for deliberation. It is the quest for value and is as concrete and real as mankind's struggles for personal and social human values and goods. It is expressed in the achievements of social and political justice, and its absence is etched in the blood and pain of repressed, alienated, maimed, broken and destroyed human lives.[465]

But are these the only forms of transcendence? If so, it is understandable why modern man based his autonomous identity upon success (hi)stories. Cognitive self-transcendence would indicate a virtually endless progression of technological and scientific advances, each successive one

---

[461]Cf. Martin Jay, The Dialectical Imagination: A History of the Frankfurt School and the Institute of Social Research 1923-1950 (Boston, 1973).

[462]Cf. Lonergan, M.i.T., pp. 83-85; Insight, pp. 634ff.

[463]Cf. Lonergan, Insight, pp. 634-657; M.i.T., p. 84.

[464]Cf. Lonergan, M.i.T., pp. 85-99.

[465]Cf. Lonergan, M.i.T., pp. 27-55; also Chapter Four of this study pp. 480-485 and references given there.

going beyond some of the limitations of the previous. Moral self-transcendence would aver a progression in moral sensitivity, at least in the general sense of more humane and just social, economic, and political orders. Indeed, it is precisely the restriction of transcendence to these cognitive and moral dimensions which has characterized secular thought and society since the Enlightenment. Gradually having recognized his own inherent genius and freedom, man released himself from the static constraints of the old order and began exploring his own abilities to transcend accepted custom, established theories, encrusted technologies. With all the gusto of Prometheus unbound in a new world, modern man affirmed his dedication to the _quest_ for knowledge, wealth, comfort, justice, rather than to any particular achievements. Science and technology provided the model for this exhilarating experience of "transcendence without a Transcendent" (E. Bloch) in their promise of an exponential growth-without-end of knowledge, material progress, economic benefits, etc. The _extrorsive_ thrust of his transcending quest would continually fashion new heavens and new earths. _Unbounded visible progress became the foundations of modernity_.[466]

Now those foundations are beginning to crumble. As Lonergan states it, man's capacity for continuous development is limited genetically and dialectically.[467] Genetically, nature is unable to sustain unlimited material progress. Whatever corrections and qualifications to the M.I.T. and Club of Rome reports on _The Limits of Growth_ must be made, no one can deny that its critique of exponential growth as based upon the false presupposition of endless resources marks the end of an epoch.[468] Human history also could not find

---

[466] Cf. H. E. Richter (ed.), _Wachstum bis zur Katastrophe?_ (Stuttgart, 1974), pp. 7-31, 72-127. It is possible to see exponential growth as resulting from the unrestricted drive of the human spirit catastrophically projected into an unrestricted extroversion into material production.

[467] Cf. _Insight_, pp. 634-730.

[468] Cf. Robert Heilbronner, _An Inquiry into the Human Prospect_ (N.Y., 1974); Dennis L. Meadows (ed.), _Limits to_

adequate meaning and value in continuous genetic development.
That would mean that the significance and value of any given
generation of men would consist in contributing materials
for succeeding generations to surpass: human meaning and value
would be condemned to continually die in the waiting room of
the future. Yet it was these false genetic presuppositions
of progress that have led to the dialectical opposite of
progress. In trying to quench the boundless thirst of man's
Promethean fire, the cancerous growth of the megamachine
threatens to pollute the planet beyond repair. Having
equated cognitive transcendence with extrorsive quantification
and mechanization, technology has been both trivialized and
fanaticized in the competition for "progressive success."
While millions are condemned to subhuman life and death,
the successful industrialized nations scavenge the earth
for the resources to fuel their production of the endless
trivia of luxury and the expansion of their ever more lethal
weaponry. Lest men question the value of their total dedication to megamechanistic productivity, "work ethics" from
Calvin to Marx and Hitler assured them that the moral
asceticism of labor offered transcendent rewards of increased
freedom and material prosperity.[469]

Today as never before we must ask, with W. Benjamen:
"Is it progress when cannibals use knives and forks?" Were
not Horkheimer and Adorno perhaps correct in their analysis
of the horrors of the Third Reich as only symptomatic of what
is intrinsic to the perversion of cognitive and moral transcendence in modernity? Could it be - shades of Soylent
Green - that the Nazi extermination camps with their portals
proudly proclaiming Arbeit macht frei cynically symbolize the

---

Growth (Washington, 1972); J. Habermas, Legitimationsprobleme
im Spätkapitalismus (Frankfurt, 1973); W. Oelmüller (ed.),
Fortschritt Wohin? (Düsseldorf, 1972). For a concrete
illustration of the totalitarianism spawned within mechanomorphic industrialism, cf. R. Barnet and R. Müller, Global
Reach (New York, 1974).

[469]Cf. Max Weber, Wirtschaft und Gesellschaft (Tübingen,
1922), pp. 227-356, 642-678, 753-817; also A. Neusüss (ed.)
Utopie (Berlin, 1972), pp. 178-234 for the relevant
analyses of Horkeimer, Bloch, and Marcuse on this problematic.

fate of modernity's much vaunted autonomy? How long can the human holocaust in the Promethean fires of exponential productivity last? Is there not a danger that the multinational corporations of today, with their profit charts and power curves, are becoming clean efficient cults of a megamachine Idol?

Clearly, if mankind's cognitive and moral transcendence is to overcome the bias and scotosis of its mechanomorphic perversions, then empirical human science is going to have the difficult task of becoming truly critical, and moral reflection must recognize the disastrous consequences of accepting man alone as the ultimate moral norm in the universe. Man's self-encapsulated autonomy seesaws between a fanatical absolutizing of relative meanings and values and a trivializing cynicism or indifference towards any ultimate meaning and value. In either case man ends up destroying his own effective freedom, his own ability to extend the sphere of attentativeness, intelligence, rationality, and responsibility. Hence it is that Lonergan sees the methodical exigence as necessarily leading to the transcendent exigence if one is to seriously appropriate "the eros of the human spirit."[470] For it is only in the context of an experience of the transcendent exigence that the unrestricted character of human quest(ion)ing can attain an intimation of its limitless sweep without in any way jeopardizing the finitude of human being-in-the-world:

> This lack of limitation, though it corresponds to the unrestricted character of human questioning, does not pertain to this world.[471]

Lonergan indicates how in questions for intelligence, in questions for reflection, and in questions for deliberation, the question of God is implicit: if mankind is the only instance of conscious attentiveness, intelligence, rationality, and responsibility then its quest for meaning and value cannot reach beyond the possible historical attainments of meaning and value; if that is the case, then all (so circumscribed) meaning and value is ultimately negated by

---

[470] Cf. M.i.T., pp. 12f.; also Insight, pp. 657-677.

[471] Insight, p. 671.

the finitude and non-identity of historical suffering, guilt, death. Developing human autonomy as ever more capable of attention, insight, reasonableness, responsibility and love shatters on the massive heteronomy of "the butcher's block of history" (Hegel). Yet our very ability to recognize and painfully experience heteronomy as heteronomy, absurdity as absurd, intimates that the autonomous subject-as-subject in its individual and collective quest(ions) for meaning and value goes beyond all particular historical instances of meaning and value in its very experience of those limited instances. Otherwise we would be unable to experience the latter as limited; because we do so experience them then a questioning of our quest(ions) for meaning and value includes an orientation to (a quest-ioning of) unlimited meaning and value.

> Such is the question of God. It is not a matter of image or feeling, of concept or judgment. They pertain to answers. It is a question. It rises out of our conscious intentionality, out of the a priori structured drive that promotes us from experiencing to the effort to understand, from understanding to the effort to judge truly, from judging to the effort to choose rightly. In the measure that we advert to our own questioning and proceed to question it, there arises the question of God.[472]

There are several aspects of this transcendental exigence which should be discussed in relation to metascience. First, the God-question of the transcendental exigence recognizes the validity of religious experience, but it does not thereby legitimatize all religious expressions. Insofar as historical religions tended to oppose the unfolding of human attention, intelligence, reasonableness, and responsibility they have been guilty of alienating religious expressions from an authentic experience of the God-question. God is not experienced in history as an answer, for the God-Answer would sublate all history. Rather He is experienced as Question and Mystery, as the assurance that the ultimate quest(ions) of meaning and value are real questions and so answerable only in going beyond the limitations of any finite achievement. Thus the critique of religion in, e.g., Freud

---

[472]M.i.T., p. 103.

and Marx could be correct insofar as religion failed to express the unity of immanence and transcendence in the God-question. But such a critique undermines its own intentionality it if thereby dismisses the God-question, for it would thereby be opposing the meaning and value of a further unfolding of human attentiveness, intelligence, rationality, and responsibility.[473] The transcendental exigence guarantees human autonomy, or the subject-as-subject, that no matter how overwhelming the heteronomies and non-identities of existence are, they do not finally extinguish the autonomy and identity of meaning and value. The God-question does not, therefore, abolish heteronomy or non-identity, but preserves the unity of identity and non-identity that allows man to experience his gifted finitude, and so removes the illusory defense mechanisms of modern man's encapsulated autonomy based on success (hi)stories.

Second, the transcendental exigence allows human autonomy to be and become because it does not interfere with the unfolding of the previous exigencies. The God-question is not introduced in the systematic exigence, as it was by the Rationalist such as Spinoza, with his "scientia intuitiva" of infinite substance as "natura naturans," or Leibniz, with his geometric a priori proofs, or Hegel, with his "Begriff des Begriffes" as absolute knowledge.[474] Such an approach to the God-question tends to liquidate the validity of all pre-systematic experience, religious or otherwise, and absolutize finite systems - consequences only all too evident in the post-Enlightenment modern period. Nor is God introduced into the critical exigence in order, as with Kant, to have a divine "intuitus originarius" mediate phenomenon and noumenon in history, or, with Schelling, to account for a self-grounding

---

[473]For a metacritique of Freud in this regard, cf. P. Ricoeur, Freud and Philosophy (Northwestern Univ. Press, 1969); for a relevant critique of Marx, cf. D. Böhler, Metakritik der marxschen Ideologie-Kritik.

[474]On Spinoza, cf. his Ethica more geometrico demonstrata, I, definitio 6; and II, propositio 47, nota. On Leibniz, cf. his Philosophische Schriften, vol. IV, pp. 403ff. On Hegel, cf. W. Weischedel, Der Gott der Philosophen, vol. I, pp. 290-305, 356-360.

of intellectual intuition.[475] For this would imply an
uncritical God-of-the-gaps (Kant: "knowledge must give way to
faith") ill-suited to grapple with the critical issues of
human and religious knowledge. Nor is the God-question
handled in the methodical exigence's concern with the subject
as it is in Schleiermacher's dialectic and in existentialist
and personalist philosophies.[476] For then there is a tendency
to short-circuit the properly methodical reflection on the
subject's own autonomous development. Lonergan, on the other
hand, investigates the autonomous operations of the systematic,
critical, and methodical exigences, and only in the context
of their critical appropriation does the God-question become
a _real_ question.

Finally, the transcendental exigence unmasks the element
of abstract totalization of emancipation in the metascience
of J. Habermas and K.-O. Apel. Metz has rather pointedly
called attention to the "dialectic of emancipation" that can
cleverly reproduce the dangers of the dialectic of Enlightenment by failing to be aware of the defense mechanisms
operative in the success (hi)stories of the history of
emancipation.[477] Both Habermas and Apel have contributed
much to the methodical elaboration of a critical complementarity between contemporary schools of metascience. They have
done so on the basis of a new, and in many ways successful,
articulation of a critical theory-praxis mediation. Nevertheless, their rather broken relation to the possibility of
theology could jeopardize their entire project.[478] On the
one hand, their articulation of the competence for consensus

---

[475]Cf. W. Weischedel, _op. cit._, pp. 191-213, 264-281;
also K. Weyand, _Kants Geschichtsphilosophie_, pp. 22-39, 137-
185. On the late Schelling, cf. W. Kasper, _Das Absolute in
der Geschichte_ (Mainz, 1965), pp. 187-215.

[476]Cf. F. Wagner, _Schleiermachers Dialektik: Eine
Kritische Interpretation_ (Gütersloh, 1974), pp. 156-172. On
existentialism and personalism, cf. Metz's scriptum, _Glaube
und Geschichte: Das Ende der Metaphysik_ (Münster, 1967-68).

[477]Cf. Metz, "Erlösung und Emanzipation," pp. 127-137.

[478]Cf. M. Theunissen, _Gesellschaft und Geschichte_
(Berlin, 1969); also W. Oelmüller, _Was ist heute Aufklärung?_
(Düsseldorf, 1972), pp. 54-143.

within an ideally unlimited community of investigators (as constitutive of a properly critical scientific enterprise) correctly preserves the unity of identity and non-identity within rational discourse. On the other hand, however, Habermas concedes the secularist restrictions of communicative interaction by excluding the possibility of attaining a consensus on the meaning and value of the ultimate non-identities of human life, namely, suffering, guilt, death - "with these we must on principle live on without hope."[479] Such a restriction on the competence for consensus tends to be an arbitrary limitation of further relevant questions; if allowed to stand it can develop into the defense mechanisms analyzed by Metz. For if precisely _those_ questions are not faced, there is a fatal susceptibility to a nihilistic cynicism which would see in any creative activity of man only "a neurotic activity that diverts the mind from the diminution of time and the approach of death."[480] Metascience can dismiss the possibility of theology only at the risk of _truncating_ its own commitment to attentive, intelligent, rational, and responsible science. The positivist "truncated reason" against which Habermas has rightly argued is not unrelated to that deeper scotosis which refuses to acknowledge the answerability of non-identity. As Lonergan remarked: "...the relentless modern drift to social engineering and totalitarian controls is the fruit of man's effort to make human science practical though he prescinds from God...."[481]

If the universe is not to be degraded to the status of energy reservoir and junk yard at the service of a cold and calculating megamachine whose exponentially cancerous growth is the materialist perversion of transcendence, if men themselves with their achievements and histories are not to be degraded into means used by, and pawns used for, the "success" of scientistic technocracy, then the God-question must be

---

[479] J. Habermas, _Legitimationsprobleme_, p. 165.

[480] R. Heilbronner, _An Inquiry into the Human Prospect_, p. 140.

[481] Lonergan, _Insight_, p. 745.

194

critically dealt with in metascience. For it is only that
theological question that can give the meaning and value of
a Cosmic Word to the universe and can gift human autonomy
with a sacredness promoting the full unfolding of man's
transcending quest for meaning and value.

It is within this concrete historical context of
achievement and failure that religious self-transcendence
arises:

> To deliberate about deliberating is to ask whether
> any deliberating is worth while. Has "worth while"
> any ultimate meaning? Is moral enterprise consonant
> with this world? We praise the developing subject
> ever more capable of attention, insight, reasonable-
> ness, responsibility. We praise progress and denounce
> every manifestation of decline. But is the universe
> on our side, or are we just gamblers and, if we are
> gamblers, are we not perhaps fools, individually
> struggling for authenticity and collectively endeavor-
> ing to snatch progress from the ever mounting welter
> of decline? The questions arise and, clearly, our
> attitudes and our resoluteness may be profoundly af-
> fected by the answers. Does there or does there not
> necessarily exist a transcendent, intelligent ground
> of the universe? Is that ground or are we the primary
> instance of moral consciousness? Are cosmogenesis,
> biological evolution, historical process basically
> cognate to us as moral beings or are they indifferent
> and so alien to us? Such is the question of God.
> It is not a matter of image or feeling, of concept
> of judgment. They pertain to answers. It is a
> question.[482]

This God-question is manifested as differently as the vast
historical array of different religions. But to ignore it,
to cast aside those traditions as naive projections, is to
open history to the trivialization we now witness in the
consumerist ethos of Western societies, a trivialization of
man that has so easily flipped over into a fanaticization
of some abstract system, ideal, or hero that usurps the boundless questions with some finite answer.[483]

History, then, does not have some immanent subject. For
man himself in his own immanence is impelled towards

---

[482]Lonergan, M.i.T., pp. 102f.

[483]Cf. Chapter One, pp. 44-46 and the references given
there. Metz has tellingly articulated this dialectic of
trivialization and fanaticization in regard to redemption
and liberation.

transcendence. Unless the fact of religious transcendence
is accepted the very source of cognitive and moral striving
and questioning begins to dry up. Whatever the perversions of
the religious question when religious institutions and
traditions have cut off the question by absolutizing its
social or cultural expressions, it still remains. To reject
religion because of its abuse would be just as stifling as
to reject human sexuality because of its constant abuse, or
knowledge because of its, or moral quest because of its abuse.
There is, then, a theological dimension to history and method.
It lets them be insofar as it is genuine for it prevents any
absolutizing of particular achievements or lack thereof. It
affirms the ultimate worth whileness of the universe and
the pain of historical growth since:

> Bad will is not merely the inconsistency of rational
> self-consciousness; it is also sin against God. The
> hopeless tangle of the social surd, of the impotence
> of common sense, of the endlessly multiplied philo-
> sophies, is not merely a cul-de-sac for human progress;
> it also is a reign of sin, a despotism of darkness;
> and men are its slaves.[484]

There is, then, no systematic implication which postulates
a necessary connection between methodical exigence and the
transcendental exigence. For method itself, as we have seen,
is not something systematic but based upon human freedom or
the lack thereof. The transcendental exigence witnesses to
this concrete historical freedom either to be attentive,
intelligent, critical and responsible or not. This means that
history and method are not some idealist abstraction but are
implicated in the contingent and particular processes of
human historical consciousness with its achievements and
failures. Religious transcendence is simply the recognition
that mankind's cognitive, moral and historical striving for
intelligence, wisdom and love is in harmony with the
universe.[485]

2. A Functional Feedback Method for Metascience

If the contemporary crisis as outlined in the section on

---

[484]Cf. Lonergan, Insight, p. 692; also M.i.T., pp.
117f.

[485]Cf. Lonergan, Insight, pp. 101-105.

the dialectic of enlightenment and as seen in the pluralism
of schools of metascience - if this crisis is to be met,
Lonergan does not propose some fideist flight into religious
faith. The recognition of the transcendental exigence at
the heart of the methodical exigence impels him as a theologian to a critical yet open attempt at overcoming the pluralism of metascientific schools insofar as that pluralism leads
to the sterility of irrationality which Metz has uncovered.
Thus, in Insight, Lonergan essayed a critique of philosophies
based upon the extent to which they respected or hindered the
effective development of experience, understanding, reason and
responsibility.[486] The task of philosophy in the light of
meta-method is precisely to express this critical concern.
We have seen how the systematic, methodical, and transcendental
as well as the critical exigencies offer a perspective capable
of integrating the multiplicity of metascientific positions
and counter-positions.

In order to concretize this open and critical integrating function of meta-method, a feedback model elaborating a
methodological correlation of the steps toward overcoming an
irrational pluralism can be articulated within the framework
of Lonergan's notion of functional specialization. The model
offers, on the broad spectrum of metascience, an instance of
the self-correcting process of learning.[487] This model is not
based on some kind of privatized, armchair synthesizing. It
presupposes and orders a vast collaboration aimed at directing
the cognitive, moral and religious efforts at attaining human
and historical self-transcendence. The model seeks to
establish the metascientific meaning of the open and dynamic
criteria of attentiveness, intelligence, reasonableness and
responsibility - that is, it is based upon an appropriation
of the unity of identity and non-identity which is the basic
horizon of historical subjectivity.[488]

The question is, how in the light of past and present

---

[486]Cf. Lonergan, Insight, pp. 401-430.

[487]Cf. Lonergan, Insight, pp. 174-175, 286-287, 289-
291, 300, 303, 448f., 706, 713-718.

[488]Cf. Chapter Three of this study, pp. 422ff.

scientific and historical development, do we go about a
responsible, critical, intelligent and attentive correlation
of the human and scientific enterprise in such a way that it
will contribute toward a progressive humanization of mankind
in the future, rather than its dehumanization or, in the
limit, its annihilation? Like functional specialization,
therefore, such a model involves both an orientation toward
the past and an orientation toward the future. It has an
archaeological and an eschatological dimension.[489]

In Figure One world complex denotes the concrete totality of natural and human - historical phenomena investigated
by (and so affected by) the natural and human sciences.
Because nature in its physical, chemical, and biological
components (and the subcomponents of these such as the
physio-chemical, geological, geo-chemical, geo-physical,
ecological, etc.) can only be considered in continual interaction with mankind, nature is here termed environment.[490]
World complex in its socio-historical reality is represented
by four main divisions of possible institutional interaction.
The political systems include both intra-national and national
political groupings, as well as the international institutions
of a political or military nature such as the U.N., N.A.T.O.,
etc. Political systems would also include smaller social
units aimed at the integration of those units within a good
of order.[491] The economic systems include the total range of
business institutions such as banks, industries with

---

[489]Cf. Chapter Four of this study, pp. 506-529 and
references given there. For a concise treatment of the two
phases in functional specialization, cf. Lonergan, M.i.T.,
pp. 133-135. On the fact that Lonergan envisages functional
specialization as a dynamic model operative in any attempt
to move from data to result within sciences that investigate
the past and confront the future, cf.   Foundations of
Theology, p. 233.

[490]The fact of pollution has rather strikingly reminded
us of the unity-in-difference between nature and history; cf.
P. Heelan, "Nature and its Transformations," in Theological
Studies Vol. 33 n. 3 (Sept., 1972), pp. 486-502.

[491]On the good of order, cf. Lonergan, Insight, pp.
211-217, 596ff.; also Chapter Three of this study, pp.
441-448.

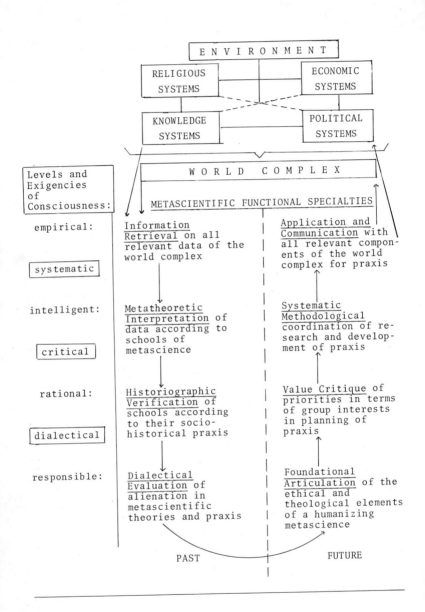

Figure One: Metascientific Functional Specialties
in a Theory-Praxis Mediation within the
World Complex and Systems

management and labor, stock markets and regional or international monetary regulating agencies. The knowledge systems
involve the vast panoply of institutionalized school systems,
universities, research centers, think tanks, etc. They also
would include the many systems involved in the communications
media insofar as those systems disseminate the entire range
of information. Finally, the religious systems comprise all
world religions with their respective organizational structures, rituals, doctrines and theologies.

This fourfold differentiation of institutional systems
does not claim any ahistorical universality. In archaic
society all four systems were often undifferentiated in one
person or group.[492] The ancient high civilizations witnessed
a hesitant differentiation of the political-economic systems
from the knowledge-religious systems.[443] Medieval Western
civilization brought about a differentiation of the knowledge
systems from the religious systems, as seen in the emergence
of the Medieval universities from the monastic communities.[494]
In the later Middle Ages and the Renaissance the emergence of
capitalism from feudalism introduced a sharp differentiation
of economic systems from political systems.[495] These historical processes of differentiation have challenged mankind with
all of the social and political tensions, conflicts and
ambiguities reported each day in our contemporary communications media. The dotted lines between these four systems
indicate how their differentiation can never be a complete
separation. Late capitalism manifests all of the problems
and repressions of an economic system covertly and overtly
dominating the other systems. The Marxist-Communist solution
in terms of collapsing the difference between economic and

---

[492] Cf. A. Marshack, The Roots of Civilization (New York, 1972), pp. 109-147.

[493] Jacquetta Hawkes, The First Great Civilizations (New York, 1973).

[494] H. S. Denifle, Die Entstehung der Universitäten des Mittelalters bis 1400 (Berlin, 1885); D. M. Chenu, Nature, Man and Society in the Twelfth Century (Chicago, 1968).

[495] Cf. Karl Marx, Capital Vol. III (New York, 1967), pp. 325f., 332, 334-336.

political systems tends too much toward the undifferentiation of former historical civilizations.[496] As Adorno and others have documented, there is little difference between a state-owned monopoly and a monopoly-controlled state.[497] The present feedback model, if implemented in practice, could lead to a new social order which would respect the differentiations and avoid simplist solutions through regression to undifferentiation. It is, then, a metascientific extension of cosmopolis.[498]

As with functional specialization, the four levels of consciousness each operate for goals defined by one of the levels. The four levels differentiate into eight metascientific specializations: the first four specializations deal with the movement of appropriation of the present and the past; the last four specializations move from that appropriation to an articulation of the steps which must be taken in order to move from the present into the future. The systematic exigence operates between the empirical and the intelligent levels; the critical exigence operates between the intelligent and rational levels; while the dialectical aspects of the methodical exigence operate between the rational and responsible levels. The transcendental exigence is operative in the dialectic and consequent foundational specializations in the movement from past to future.[499] A brief indication of the eight metascientific specializations will be sufficient to show how this feedback model would function. It is important to realize that it is a _feedback_ model. As the specializations articulate the past and present

---

[496] Cf. Karl Marx, _A Contribution to the Critique of Political Economy_ (New York, 1970), pp. 21, 34, 125-128, 134-135.

[497] Cf. T. Adorno, "Spätkapitalismus oder Industriegesellschaft?" in _Aufsätze zur Gesellschaftstheorie und Methodologie_ (Frankfurt, 1970), pp. 149-166.

[498] Cosmopolis for Lonergan is primarily socio-cultural as a unity-in-difference with the intellectual and the moral dimensions of politics; cf. _Insight_, pp. 238-242.

[499] The transcendental exigence must be operative within the dialectical and foundational specialization for the reasons given in Chapter Four of this study, pp. 480-485.

elements constitutive of the world complex, and as they move toward a future constituting praxis which changes the world complex, these changes are fed back into the metascientific specializations and so the process continues.[500]

First, on the empirical level of data research, there would be approximations to a complete informational retrieval system on all of the particular aspects of human historical praxis, on the components of the world complex. Such a wide assemblage of data would, of course, never be complete. It would first be made according to the hypothetical expectations of what data would be relevant. An approximation to such a data collecting specialization can be found in the Massachusetts Institute of Technology's development of non-linear feedback computer models for assembling the relevant data on world dynamics.[501] The feedback functional structure within the metascientific specialty, Information Retrieval, would assure an asymptotic advance toward the ideal of complete information retrieval.

Second, the metascientific specialty of interpretation would aim at explicating all of the theoretical systems regarding scientific knowledge of the systems operative within the world complex. Many of these theories have already been discussed. Metascientific interpretation would be principally concerned with systematizing these theories and their inter-relations. It would also be structured according to the three questions operative in the critical exigence. What do scientists do when they know? Why is that knowing science? What do they know when they do that? These critical questions would investigate each of the present metascientific theories in regard to (1) theories on research and researchers, (2) theories on science as a knowledge system, (3) theories on the effective and constitutive functions of (1) and (2). An example of this specialization can be found in Radnitzky's

---

[500]The feedback character is a system analytic affirmation of the unity of identity and non-identity. This is also operative in Dilthey; cf. Peter Krausser, Kritik der endlichen Vernunft (Frankfurt, 1968).

[501]Cf. Jay W. Forrester, World Dynamics (Cambridge, Mass., 1971).

studies on the contemporary schools of metascience.[502]

The third metascientific specialty is history. For the theories discussed in the second have constituted communities, influenced scientific research, been related to political and socio-economic processes, have affected social communities, and in general have had repercussions on each of the components of the world complex. The purpose of this specialization would be to study the effects of scientific theory and praxis on the plane of historical process. Although he has not provided such a study, Radnitzky refers to its necessity as the historiography of science. There have been many studies of this in reference to technologies and the individual sciences. An example of this type of historiography in regard to technology can be found in Lewis Mumford's The Myth of the Machine.[503] A historiography of the human sciences can be found in Georges Gusdorf's Les sciences humaines et la pensée occidentale.[504]

The fourth metascientific specialization is dialectics. For the historiographies indicate how the historical development of societies and scientific communities vary according to basic philosophical world views. For example, there are the studies of I. Kon and G. Dobrov from a Marxist perspective, there is the pragmatist perspective in general systems theories, the empiricist perspective of the Formalists, the empirical criticist framework of K. Popper.[505] The

---

[502]Cf. Gerard Radnitzky, Contemporary Schools of Metascience.

[503]Cf. L. Mumford, The Myth of the Machine Vol. I: Technics and Human Development (New York, 1967); Vol. II: The Pentagon of Power (New York, 1970).

[504]Cf. Georges Gusdorf, Vol. I: De l'histoire des sciences à l'histoire de la pensée (Paris, 1966); Vol. II: Les origines des sciences humaines (Paris, 1967); Vol. III: La révolution galiléene, tome I (Paris, 1969); Vol. III: La révolution galiléene, tome II (Paris, 1969).

[505]The difference in historiographies of metascience reveals therefore, the presence of dialectical horizons whose concrete dynamic and contradictory character cannot be sublated by a metascientific reliance solely upon the systematic exigence or the critical exigence epistemologically or metaphysically formulated. Thus I have shown in the previous

purpose of metascientific dialectics is to map out the concrete contradictions among these historiographies. It also can indicate how the historiographies overlook relevant historical influences and practical repercussions in the developments of sciences and societies, thereby exposing dialectical tensions within those societies. For example, to what extent are the values the respective theories claim are concretely realized actually realized in the praxis those theories motivate? This type of work has been rather effectively done in an admittedly limited sphere by the Frankfurt School. There is also G. Picht's unmasking of the presuppositions of classical scientific theory in the postivist, empiricist approach to science in the West, with its consequent disregard for the overall effects of technological advance on both society and nature.[506] Hence we now have the contemporary dialectics of pollution and exploitation versus industrialization. Of course the present study is also an example of metascientific dialectics for it is attempting to show how both Dilthey and Lonergan have developed their positions in a dialectical confrontation with other theories of knowing found in philosophies of science.

Fifth, this dialectic is not a value-free exercise for it operates on the level of responsibility. In order to provide for the transition to a future oriented (prognostic) planning and ordering of the scientific enterprise, it is necessary to find adequate, open, yet critical norms. The present study is also concerned with such foundations. Yet the metascientific specialty of foundations would require a vast collaborative effort to articulate those ethical and theological foundations upon which an adequate critique of history could be based. It would have to work out the relation of the intellectual conversion required by science to the moral conversion required by socio-political life to the religious conversion required by the affirmation of an

---

subsection (pp. 151-179 above) how Lonergan's dialectical formulation of the methodical exigence can properly handle a dialectics of horizons.

[506]Cf. Georg Picht, _Wahrheit, Vernunft, Verantwortung_, pp. 343-407.

204

ultimate meaning and value. To what extent, for example, has the atheism of Marxist communism helped or hindered the realization of its own humanitarian goals? Other limited examples of this type of foundational inquiry can be found in the ethical and theological implications of K. Jasper's notion of unbounded communication, in J. Habermas' notion of communicative interaction free from dictatorial constraint, in K. Popper's regulative principle of critical enlightened reason.[507] It is precisely such foundational reflection insofar as that reflection articulates an appropriation of the open and dynamic structures of human consciousness that the dialectic between normal and revolutionary science exposed in T. S. Kuhn's studies would not lead to a complete relativism or fideism.[508]

The sixth metascientific specialty of planning critique would proceed on the basis of such ethical and religious foundations to a criticism of the interests and value judgments operative in scientific theory and praxis. This specialty would seek to establish a metascientific doctrine of interests and values aimed at best realizing the foundational goals. An example of this specialty can be found in Habermas' critique of the interest and value judgments in positivism, pragmatism, and historicism, as well as his own sketch of the values or interests involved in his unity of

---

[507]J. B. Metz has rather provocatively shown how any purely philosophical approach to ethical problems of human liberation is involved in a degree of abstraction incapable of handling the concrete processes of liberation and its limitations; cf. his article "Erlösung und Emanzipation" in Stimmen der Zeit (March, 1973), pp. 171-184; for Lonergan's formulation of a similar need of ethical reflection to issue in specifically theological reflection on praxis as foundational, cf. Chapter Four of this study, pp. 480-485 and the references given there.

[508]Notice how Lonergan's dynamic correlation of intellectual, moral, and religious conversions properly preserves the unity-in-difference between these patterns of experience; cf. Chapter Four, pp. 485-506. Such a correlation would provide the continuity in change which would, as a metacontextual heuristic, overcome the dangers of relativism of which Kuhn has been accused; cf. Imre Lakatos & Alan Musgrave (eds.), Criticism and the Growth of Knowledge, pp. 25-58, 91-230.

knowing and interest in self reflection.[509] This metascientific doctrine of values would imply taking a stand with regard to the profit motivation in capitalism as well as the party motivation in communism as these affect the establishment of priorities for planning and research. It would critically seek, in the light of the foundations, to shift planning and research away from the destructive priorities and interests in weapons research and development to more positive human values such as the need for agricultural production, medical planning and research, anti-pollution, etc. Just as metascientific foundations do not identify with the status quo but rather seek a unity of identity and non-identity, so the critique of planning aims at effecting those changes in present practice which are required by the goals set in the fifth specialty.[510]

The seventh metascientific specialty would aim at elaborating a new general systematic methodology capable of adequately correlating the value and interest priorities uncovered by the sixth specialty. This specialty of general systematic metascientific methodology would attempt to integrate all that is positive in the present schools of meta-science, but also of eliminating the negative elements which have been uncovered in the historiography, dialectics, foundations and planning critique of those theories and their practices. An example of the beginnings of such a metascientific methodology might be found in the methodological work now being done at the Institute for Interdisciplinary Collaboration and Research at Bielefield.[511] Another rudimentary example might be found in the International Congresses for Ongoing Collaboration sponsored by those interested in the meta-methodology of Bernard Lonergan.[512]

---

[509]Cf. J. Habermas, Erkenntnis und Interesse.

[510]Cf. Chapter Three of this study, pp. 441-448 and the references given there.

[511]Cf. J. B. Metz and T. Rendtorff, Die Theologie in der interdisziplinären Forschung (Düsseldorf, 1971).

[512]Cf. Joseph Collins, "Foreword" in Foundations of Theology, pp. xiii-xx; J. Navone, "Ongoing Collaboration: The

Eighthly, a metascientific research application specialty would guide the actual application of such general
methodological planning to the ongoing research projects now
in operation. Such an application involves a wide collaboration with a manifold of political, academic, business and
religious institutions. It also involves the development
of an ongoing communication between these systems and the
metascientific planning groups. Even more important, such a
metascientific specialty of application involves an effort
at communication, not only between those institutions and
the planning groups, but an effort at communicating the
required changes to the social communities at large. An
example of such application and communication can be found
in such institutions as Common Cause in the United States,
the various groups connected with Consumer Advocate R. Nader,
the many governmental agencies aimed at application and communication of policy in planning, research, and development,
and the countless smaller political action groups which aim at
realizing changes within the varied components of the world
complex.[513] In the Third World such groups are often
underground, attempting revolutionary change within a
repressive socio-political order.[514] The aim of this
metascientific specialty of communication and application
would be to promote those forces for change which are most
conducive to genuine human and social development. The
empirical nature of this specialty arises from the need to
attend to local and national differences in communication and application.[515] A real freedom of the communications

---

First International Lonergan Congress," in Gregorianum (1970),
pp. 541-560.

[513]There is need for a metacontextual communications
systems analysis; cf. L. von Bertalanffy, op. cit., pp.
41-44. A somewhat inadequate example of this being applied
to the Roman Catholic Church can be found in P. Granfield,
Ecclesial Cybernetics (New York, 1967).

[514]Cf. I. L. Horowitz et al. (eds.), Latin American
Radicalism: A Documentary Report on Left and Nationalist
Movements (New York, 1969); Piero Gheddo, Why is the Third
World Poor? (New York, 1973).

[515]This results from the fact that empirically the

media is important in this specialty insofar as they are thereby able to counteract official corporate or governmental propaganda.

This is a feedback model. With the communication and application of coordinated plans for the research and development of programs for change the world complex is altered. This change is then fed into the informational data research specialty and its scope and consequences can be processed through the eight functional specialties in order to improve upon the particular change. The following Chapter will discuss this at greater length in regard to Lonergan's model of the human good.

The metascientific feedback model is, of course, within the knowledge systems of the world complex - hence the arrow from knowledge systems to the first specialty. Yet it is not a question of remaining within a value-neutral conception of knowledge. Through information research, interpretation, historiographic verification, and dialectical evaluation of all present and past relevant data, the model goes on to the future constituting development of praxis through foundations, value judgment critique, systematic planning of praxis to the communication and application of that praxis. Here the political systems become important. The tendency to minimize the political and sidestep it in favor of economic models of social engineering and calculation is a woeful consequence of the dialectic of the Enlightenment. Lonergan has pointed out how even in regard to technology itself the manifold of technological possibilities cannot all be applied. Many are economically unfeasible and so must be shelved. But the process of selection cannot be allowed to stop there. Among

---

socio-cultural and socio-historical Contexts are widely divergent. Hence the need for subsidiarity; cf. Lonergan, Insight, p. 234: "There is such a thing as progress, and its principle is liberty...for the ideas occur to the man on the spot, their only satisfactory expression is their implementation, their only adequate correction is the emergence of further insights; on the other hand, one might as well declare openly that all new ideas are taboo, as require that they be examined, evaluated, and approved by some hierarchy of officials and bureaucrats." On subsidiarity, cf. M.i.T., pp. 366-367, where Lonergan explains its need within the context of communications.

the many economic probabilities of application the political
must come in to chose those more suited to the common good
of the entire social order.[516] Thus the political should
exercise a critique of values that will offset the bias
of established economic interests. The frightful spectre
of the military-industrial complex is the result of the
political making itself subservient to established economic
interests.[517]

The feedback model is, therefore, aimed at a massive,
collaborative effort at a critical mediation of theory-
praxis. It reflects the fact that the contemporary crisis
in the world complex of societies, nations, cultures, civilizations is occasioned by the need for critical planning and
praxis aimed at overcoming the bias and repression of present
political, economic, religious, and knowledge systems. Thus it
is a further concretization of Lonergan's call for an
effective cosmopolis.[518] The model graphically illustrates
how there can be no appeal to some identifiable human or
supra-human subject of history and method. If Dilthey
poignantly expressed the pathos of the Enlightenment as a
confusion regarding norms at the very time scientific and
historical consciousness has given mankind tremendous power,
then Lonergan's efforts at elaborating a methodological
response to this dilemma should merit serious consideration.
For, in Lonergan's phrase, mankind must be made conscious
"of its responsibility to the future of mankind," where that
responsibility is concerned, "to adapt a phrase from Marx,
not only with knowing history but also with directing it."[519]

Just as technical, economic, and political development

---

[516]On the ordering of technological possibilities by
economic probabilities, and of economic probabilities by
political needs, cf. J. Habermas, Theorie und Praxis, pp.
231-260; G. Barden & P. McShane, Towards Self Meaning, pp.
105-116, and esp. pp. 84-88.

[517]Cf. L. Mumford, The Pentagon of Power, pp. 321-377;
J. Bosch, Der Pentagonismus oder die Ablösung des
Imperialismus? (Hamburg, 1969).

[518]Cf. Lonergan, Insight, pp. 238-242, 633, 690.

[519]Lonergan, Insight, p. 227.

> gives man a dominion over nature, so also the advance
> of knowledge creates and demands a human contribution
> to the control of human history.[520]

This is not just technique but praxis. For the challenge
of history is "for man progressively to restrict the realm
of change or fate or destiny and progressively to enlarge
the realm of conscious grasp and deliberate choice.[521] The
human scientists must begin to learn how to master the social
surd of decline and dehumanization with the skill and mastery
with which the mathematician and physicist have mastered such
inverse intelligibilities as primes, surds, imaginaries,
continua, infinities, statistics.[522] That calls not for
more technique, but "for human science to become critical and
normative," capable of being contra-factual when the "facts"
are the result of inattentiveness, stupidity, bias, and
irresponsibility.[523]

CONCLUSIONS

This Chapter has attempted to answer the question
whether or not the critical positions of Dilthey and Lonergan
effectively challenge the scientistic monopoly on method. It
has, I hope, demonstrated that they do. As such they offer
very relevant contributions to the methodological presuppositions of political theology, as well as to overcome the
antinomies set up by the dialectic of the Enlightenment.
Specifically, they indicate the possibility of overcoming
an idealist transcendental versus a positivist empirical
dichotomy by thematizing a unity of identity and non-identity

---

[520]Ibid. This control of human history is not in terms
of technique but of the open and dynamic related and recurrent operations of human praxis; cf. Chapter Three of this
study, pp. 441-448, and the references given there.

[521]Lonergan, Insight, p. 228.

[522]Cf. Lonergan, Insight, pp. 234-236.

[523]Cf. Lonergan, Insight, pp. 226-232; on the basic form
of human alienation, cf. M.i.T., p. 55; also Chapter Four of
this study, pp. 409-415, 480-485.

in terms of the subject-as-subject. If Dilthey correctly saw the inadequacy of the philosophies of science in his day, and the need to find other than metaphysical foundations for the emerging scientific and historical consciousness, still he could only point towards the need to find those foundations in conscious interiority. Lonergan has carried out this need by definitively breaking with the Cartesian objectivism in method. And Lonergan did this not by erecting some barrier between the natural and human sciences, but by adverting to the related and recurrent operations of experiencing-understanding-judging-deciding underpinning both. For the methodical exigence cannot be identified with the systematic but only is possible if the critical exigence is duly respected. Thus Lonergan has moved from an individualist cognitional theory to a framework for method capable of handling the pluralism of schools of metascience.

It now remains to determine precisely how both Dilthey and Lonergan approach the subject-as-subject in the critique of historical reason and metamethod respectively. For interiority will be effective as a methodological foundation only if it is not seen as some privatized or ontologizing reflection on interiority, as a merely theoretical "Begriffspiel," but if it is experienced in its related and recurrent operations yielding progressive and cumulative results, if it is appropriated as the open and dynamic praxis of subjects-as-subjects in history.

C H A P T E R   T H R E E

THE STRUCTURES OF HISTORY AND METHOD IN

W. DILTHEY'S CRITIQUE OF HISTORICAL REASON AND

B. LONERGAN'S META-METHOD

> Dilthey's critique of historical reason
> is not, as its name might suggest, a mere
> annex to Kant's "Critique of Pure Reason."
> Rather, it is a new and unique theory over
> against Kant, the Positivists, and all
> metaphysics of history. At its core is his
> structural theory.... For it deals with a
> formal, anthropological theory of the
> particularly dynamic historicity and capacity
> to learn within human beings.

> Peter Krausser

> Thought on method is apt to run in some one
> of three channels. In the first, method will
> be conceived more as an art than as a science.
> There are, however, bolder spirits. They
> select the conspicuously successful science
> of their time. They study its procedures.
> They formulate precepts. Finally, they pro-
> pose an analogy of science. Science properly
> so called is the successful science they have
> analyzed. Clearly enough, these approaches
> to the problem of method do little to advance
> the "less successful" subjects. Some third
> way, then, must be found even though it is
> difficult and laborious. It will go behind
> the procedures of the natural sciences to
> something both more general and more funda-
> mental, namely, the procedures of the human
> mind.

> Bernard Lonergan

CHAPTER THREE

INTRODUCTION

The previous chapter has answered the first question
formulated in the Introduction by affirmatively stating that
both Dilthey and Lonergan do provide adequate alternatives
to the scientistic monopoly of method. It is now time to
move on to the second question concerning the structures
of history and method in Dilthey's critique of historical
reason and Lonergan's meta-methodology. These structures must
provide an approach to history and method which will avoid
the extremes of either an idealist appeal to some world
mind or other total subject of both history and method, and
an empiricist appeal to a total relativity or historicism
where there are no norms for guiding a critically methodological approach to history.

The first section of this chapter will delve into the
notion of conscious interiority or self-awareness as the
proper realm within which to find such an approach to history
and method. The second section will then take up the basic
structures of Dilthey's critique of historical reason in
terms of both the subject-as-subject and the subject-as-
object. The third section will then explicate the basic
structures of Lonergan's meta-method and the subject-as-
object. Such a dialectical comparison of Dilthey's and
Lonergan's work should indicate how the danger of a privatized
cognitional theory can be overcome inasmuch as one adverts
to the self-transcending character of conscious interiority.
For the approach toward method and history within the context
of conscious interiority clearly accentuates that lost
subjectivity neglected and repressed by the mechanistic
objectives of modern scientistic reason. As we have seen
in the last chapter, the context of Dilthey's movement from
metaphysics to cognitional theory for the foundations of
his approach toward history and method is further complemented

and criticized by Lonergan's movement from cognitional
theory to transcendental method for such foundations.

THE FOUNDATIONAL CONTEXTS OF DILTHEY'S CRITIQUE
AND LONERGAN'S META-METHOD

The starting points of Dilthey's critique of historical
reason and Lonergan's methodology are both common and diverse.
Their similarity may be found in their common concern with
conscious interiority as the foundational reality of any
functionally structural approach to history and method.
They are diverse, however, inasmuch as Lonergan is both more
critically aware of the self-transcending character of
conscious interiority and is more concerned with showing
the relevance of this interiority to the procedures and
methods, not only of the human historical-cultural sciences,
but also to the procedures and methods of the natural sciences. These foundational contexts are in the true sense of
the term, historical, for two reasons. The first reason has
already been discussed in the previous chapter where it was
shown how the dialectic of the Enlightenment and the resulting
crisis of critical normativity in our contemporary situation
called for an approach toward history and method which would
transcend the idealist and empiricist extremes. The second
reason may be found in a properly transcendental and empirical
understanding of history as constituted by conscious human
meanings and actions.

This section will explore that starting point. First,
it will indicate how Dilthey saw the need for new foundations.
Second, it will show how the starting point for Dilthey's
critique was within lived consciousness. Third, it will show
how he expanded that starting point in a methodological move
from experience to understanding. Fourth, the differentiation
of natural sciences and cultural sciences within Dilthey's
method will be discussed. Fifth, the foundations of Lonergan's
approach to method will be explicated in terms of recurrent
patterns of experience. Finally, those foundations will be
discussed in terms of the ongoing discovery of mind in history.

1. The Need for New Foundations

The previous chapter has already indicated how Dilthey could not feel satisfied with any of the metascientific theories prevalent in his day. Here, then, I would like to emphasize certain aspects of his criticisms of those theories as they relate to the grounding of the cultural sciences. First the importance of that grounding will be touched upon, then how it must go beyond both Kantianism and Empiricism.

A. "The Life and Death Question for Our Civilization". The pathos of the Enlightenment was, for Dilthey, its healthy skepticism regarding all previous religious and metaphysical systems linked to its very unhealthy bewilderment regarding the foundations of its own criticism.[1] The scientific revolution in the Enlightenment began overthrowing the religious and/or metaphysical worldviews and normative value-orientations which had provided the foundations of pre-Enlightenment societies and cultures. In the West such foundations had found their classical expressions in the systems of Greek metaphysics and Medieval theologies within which systems the natural and human sciences and studies had a subaltern or subcultural status.

The hypothetical, empirical, and specialized thrusts of modern science - both natural and cultural - began effectively dismantling these worldviews, reducing their adherents to a subcultural minority status. Yet they were not supplying any comparable alternatives to those religious or metaphysical worldviews.[2]

This had become a "survival question for our civilization" insofar as the sciences were de facto supplying men with the power to transform both nature and society.[3] Not only were the empirical sciences overthrowing theological and metaphysical systems, but they were profoundly influencing

---

[1]Cf. pp. 115ff., of Chapter Two.

[2]Cf. G.S. I, pp. 351-385; VII, 173, 335-345; VIII, 190-196. For a comparable contemporary analysis, cf. J. Habermas, Technik und Wissenschaft als Ideologie, pp. 48-103; specifically I am referring to his notion of traditional societies, pp. 65-73.

[3]Cf. G.S. I, pp. 3ff.

politics and literature.[4] Dilthey could not side with either
the nihilistic skeptics, who like Nietzsche tended toward a
solipsistic voluntarism, nor with those who sought to restore
the old foundations through some new conception of metaphysics
more in (a compromised) harmony with modern science.[5] Where
the former emphasized the non-identity almost to the point of
irrationalism, the latter tended to stress identity to the
point of a rationalist logicism. For Dilthey the negation
of metaphysics as a foundation for the sciences did not
sublate the need for foundations, quite the contrary. The
specialized sciences were making the question of scientifically
valid foundations ever more acute as they were contributing to
the disintegration of the old.[6] The French Revolution illustrated how modern science was not only transforming our
theoretical knowledge but also our social and political
praxis.[7] For there is no more a presuppositionless science
than there is a presuppositionless philosophy.[8] The presuppositions of Enlightenment science which at once emancipated society and science from the ancien régime of the
previous metaphysical (monarchical) systems and yet failed
to provide the basis for the new science and society - those
presuppositions were in the naturalist systems:

This older system of the eighteenth century and of the

---

[4]For the influence of Enlightenment science on literature and politics, cf. G.S. III, p. 155f., 170-275 (esp.
199-200); E.D., 7-17.

[5]For the relation of Dilthey to Nietzsche, cf. G.S.
VIII, pp. 199-201, 226; also J. -F. Suter, op. cit., pp. 145-
155. On the new conceptions of metaphysics, cf. V, pp. 353-356.

[6]Cf. M. Riedel, Einleitung, p. 27; J. Habermas,
Erkenntnis und Interesse, pp. 88-178; H. Schnädelbach,
op. cit., pp. 185ff.

[7]Cf. G.S. I., p. 4; X, p. 29; IX, pp. 176-178; III, pp.
199, 224ff.

[8]B.A., pp. 78a-78b: "The analyzed relationship
[between philosophy and science] implies that there is no
presuppositionless foundation for science. The full support
of this judgment becomes clearer when it is combined with the
development of the scientific mentality, as the latter is
revealed in the history of the sciences."

> Enlightenment had its classic representatives in
> Leibniz, Locke, Rousseau, Kant, and Lessing.
> However much they differed from one another, they
> did agree in one thing: a reason dwells in the
> systems of human culture which can be developed
> in a rational context and which contains principles
> for practical action. This system wrought havoc
> on the feudal, absolute, catholic social order in
> France. It proved itself capable, in the French
> Revolution, of destroying the old order; but it
> was bankrupt when it came to attempting a new social
> regulation.[9]

We have already seen how those systems influenced the three
schools of metascience with which Dilthey was chiefly concerned, how the naturalist systems involved the schools in
the bracketing procedure of immediate truths in order to
reconcile the hypothetical processes of science with
objectivity. The objectivistic identification of method
and logic(ism) which resulted could not, however, provide
the necessary new foundations for theory and praxis.

B. Beyond Kantianism and Empiricism. The only way that
a Hegelian panlogicism could be avoided was through a
dogmatic assertion (unverifiable in experience) of the
noumenal ground of inner freedom. This found classic
expression in the Kantian phenomenon-noumenon dichotomy,
which ended up restoring the metaphysical distinction between
positive science and rational philosophy, between theoretical
and practical reason. For, as noumenal, the ground of praxis
was not capable of any empirical and critical mediation.
Dilthey saw how the transcendentalist position did not really
counter Humean skepticism and so left the door open to empiricism and positivism.[10] Empiricism and positivism were

---

[9] G.S. X, p. 29.

[10] M. Riedel, Einleitung, p. 29: "The Kantian critique
of reason did not hinder the natural sciences from interpreting their categories as no more than constructive tools
with only hypothetical value. Much less did Kant halt the
application of natural scientific methods to the ethical
and political sciences. The result was the renewal of Humean
empiricism in the positivistic philosophies of Comte and Mill.
The latter reduced the whole of human knowledge to the study
of a law-like coexistence and succession of mental facts, so
that, in the name of scientific laws, knowledge itself became
no more than an indifferent and meaningless event."

equally unable to critically ground theory and praxis, for they also were dependent upon the notion of immediate objectivistic truths and so could not come up with the experiential ground of theory-praxis:

> This modern empiricism is not an experiential philosophy, but a construction of experience working with unverifiable hypotheses. It is just like the modern apriori rationalism of transcendental philosophy, that is no less hypothetical and constructive in its methods of procedure.[11]

If the only possible methods are objectivistic - whether in terms of thought (Kantian) or of perception (empiricist and positivist) - then there could be no way of avoiding hypothetical and constructive procedures. It was the merit of Dilthey to have uncovered the tendency of empiricism and positivism toward the ideal of a reductionist unified science which would provide foundations in terms of protocol axiomatic formulae, _and_ to have seen that the evidence on which they were based was as incapable of critical verification as the objective a priori approach of Neo-kantiansim. Thus Dilthey could bring out how the Neo-kantians were, no less than the empiricists and positivists, conceptualistic atomists and mechanists.[12] The "shift toward the subject" could not ground the positive sciences as long as the subjective presuppositions of philosophy and science were treated as objectivistic abstractions.[13] In his own way, then, Dilthey was concerned with foundations which would put the "natural method" on its feet, which would cut through the objectivistic abstractions common to the transcendentalist, empiricist, and positivist efforts to handle the breakdown

---

[11]M. Riedel, _op. cit._, pp. 34-35.

[12]Cf. _B.A._, pp. 87-88. Dilthey goes on to describe Lotze's position. For Herbart and Lotze's influence on Neo-kantians, cf. E. Cassirer, _Das Erkenntnis-Problem_ III, pp. 1-16, 378-410; also the references in note 177 of Chapter Two.

[13]Cf. _B.A._, p. 88. On the objectivistic approach to the a _priori_ in Kant, cf. Sala, G. _Das Apriori in der menschlichen Erkenntnis_ (Meisenheim, 1972). On Dilthey's rejection of a presuppositionless science of philosophy, cf. _B.A._, pp. 71-72; cf also _ibid._, p. 41 and Riedel, _Einleitung_, p. 40f.

of Hegelian Idealism.[14]

2. The Starting Point: Lived Consciousness

For Dilthey the emergence of the positive historical
and human sciences heralded not only the end of the old
classical differentiation between theoretical and practical
reason, but also indicated the new reference-frame of the
differentiation.[15] As we shall see, the natural sciences
could not provide the methods capable of a sure grounding
- "der feste Punkt" - of theory-praxis insofar as they could
not exceed the limits of a hypothetical constructive approach
to reality. The pathos of Enlightenment could lead to a
catastrophe, which Dilthey and Yorck saw as imminent, if the
mechanism and "mindless materialism" continued to determine
the relation of theory and praxis. If Yorck saw "that the
age of Mechanism (Galileo, Descartes, Hobbes) is virtually
our own," so Dilthey indicated its roots:

> If one seeks the ultimate basis for our present
> situation, it lies in the fact that now the natural
> sciences have drawn the final consequences from the
> position they took in the seventeenth century....
> The important question is which energies can be
> mobilized to overcome this influence.[16]

Dilthey then continued, situating the importance of his
grounding of human studies:

> Now my book came out of the conviction that the

---

[14]Cf. references in note 188 of Chapter Two. That this
is not a problem of "purely" historical interest, but one
that dialectically engages us, cf. M. Theunissen, Hegels
Lehre vom absoluten Geist als theologisch-politischer
Traktat, pp. 3-59.

[15]G.S. I, p. 225: "The split between theoretical and
practical philosophy indicates the limits inherent in the
Hellenic mentality. The assertion that in interiority, in the
turn towards interiority, lay the solid foundation for all
knowledge, including that of the objective world - such a
thought lay beyond the horizon of a Socrates. Only when
such a clear insight is present does the moral world, and
the solid foundation of all actions in that world, enter
into an all embracing structure of human science. Only with
such an insight is the false differentiation of theoretical
and practical science overcome, and the true differentiation
of the natural sciences and the human sciences can be grounded."

[16]On Yorck's statement, cf. Briefwechsel, p. 68; on
Dilthey's, ibid., p. 156.

autonomy of the cultural sciences, and the knowledge
of historical reality they contain, would contribute
to this mobilizing. Put another way: the historical
world leads through a consciousness raising (Selbstbesinnung) to a victorious, spontaneous capacity for
life, which is not able to be formulated in thought,
but can be analytically indicated in the structure
of individual lives and in their mutual interaction.
This leads, finally, to a higher structure of a special
kind, which surpasses natural scientific mediation. It
is necessary to bring this into sharp relief and
articulate it energetically, if it is again to come to
a thematized self-conscious validity.[17]

There was, therefore, a need to confront empirical scientific
consciousness with historical consciousness. The latter
had, indeed, broken the last chains of metaphysical or
religious absolutes which the former had not already destroyed.
Man was supposedly free. But the "powerless subjectivity" of
Romanticism, as well as the faltering efforts of an
objectivistic transcendentalism, empiricism, and positivism,
were showing that the relativity of historical consciousness
had to discover its universal grounds if man could, on the
strength of his past, recognize the real norms of his progress
into the future.[18] Scientific consciousness was not degraded.
Yet Dilthey saw that the momentum and clarity of method in
the natural sciences were not matched by the human sciences.[19]
As long as the human sciences merely copied the procedures
of the natural, they could not fully perform as they should
if they were to be empirical. That is, if they were to
adequately deal with the experience grounding socio-historical
reality.[20] For "all science is experiential science."[21]

Dilthey never had a fixed expression for the experience

---

[17]Briefwechsel, pp. 156-157.

[18]Cf. G.S. VIII, pp. 192f., 204, 225; I, xv, 351-359;
III, 210-268; V, 352-363; VII, 89-117, 335-338; Briefwechsel,
p. 104.

[19]Cf. G.S. V, pp. 31-73, especially 31-36, 189; VII,
pp. 79-88, 148.

[20]Cf. G.S. I, pp. 8-14, 14-21; VII, 3-19; Renthe-Fink,
op. cit., p. 107.

[21]G.S. I, xvii; cf. also Riedel, Einleitung, pp. 34f.

central to the human sciences and history. He variously referred to it as awareness (<u>Bewusstheit</u>), consciousness (<u>Bewusstsein</u>), self-presence (<u>Selbigkeit</u>), interiority (<u>Innerlichkeit</u>), mental fact (<u>geistige Tatsache</u>), spontaneity (<u>Lebendigkeit</u>). In his earlier writings it is usually referred to as inner experience (<u>innere Erfahrung</u>), while in the later the term lived experience (<u>Erleben</u>) is more frequent.[22] Without this inner presence of self - "Inner-werden, Für-mich-dasein des Zustandes" - there could be no history, no science, no art, no philosophy or religion.[23] This is historical life (<u>Leben</u>) whose free spontaneity (<u>Lebendigkeit</u>) is historicality (<u>Geschichtlichkeit</u>).[24]

Philosophy in its historical forms had never sufficient-ly grounded itself on this "total, full obvious experience."[25] Indeed, they could not until the advance of the empirical human studies had begun to show up the deficiencies of all constructive (and so hypothetical) foundations for human theory-praxis. Insofar as this inner experience was the source of all philosophies, Dilthey's explicitation of it would be tantamount to a philosophy of philosophies.[26] And since historicality embraces all historical reality, such a thematization of inner experience would be "the science of reality."[27]

The starting point of lived consciousness was the key insight of Dilthey regarding the grounding of the human sciences. For it cut through the conceptualism of Kantian

---

[22]Cf. <u>G.S.</u> I, xvii-xix, 9, 15, 27; VII, 26, 261-262, 255; VIII, 186.

[23]<u>G.S.</u> I, pp. 38, 42, 49, 51, 61, 64-70; V, 136, 196, 265f.; VI, 62, 188-190, 228-305; VII, 3-23, 79-88; Renthe-Fink, <u>op. cit.</u>, pp. 106-113, 120-129.

[24]Cf. <u>G.S.</u> VII, pp. 228f., 256, 261f.; Renthe-Fink, op cit., pp. 82, 90, 107, 115-117, 120-125.

[25]<u>G.S.</u> VIII, p. 171; cf. also I, 86-115; and Diwald, <u>op. cit.</u>, pp. 204-220.

[26]<u>D.J.D.</u>, p. 80; <u>G.S.</u> V, pp. 88f., 339-416; VIII, pp. 171, 206-219.

[27]<u>G.S.</u> VIII, p. 172; V, p. 136f.

transcendentalism, Comtean positivism and British empiricism; and it did so, not by entering into all the subtlety of argument which those positions represented, but by calling attention to an experience of life which underpins and goes beyond any argument. That lived experience was the conscious self-presence any merely theoretical or argumentative method would necessarily tend to overlook. For Dilthey, the science of the real was science liberated from the unreality of imagining that science alone attained the real.

3. Method: From Experience to Understanding

Dilthey is careful to distinguish this starting point in a "Selbstbesinnung" from both the Cartesian perspective of the positivists and empiricists, and the Kantian perspective of the transcendentalists. It is difficult to correlate the many diverse attempts of Dilthey to articulate his own position. The fact that he never completed his Einleitung was in no small measure due to his dissatisfaction with all previous cognitional theories and his consequent pioneering efforts at elaborating one that would be truly foundational. It is not surprising, then, that his successors and critics have often failed to understand his position.[28]

In order to bring out this hitherto rather neglected import of Dilthey's starting point and critical theory of knowledge, I would like in this section to first indicate how this "Selbstbesinnung" of Dilthey was a unity of identity and non-identity, then show how he differed in this approach from the objectivistic cognitional theories and criticized them. Finally I shall spell out some of the elements in a methodological elaboration of this starting point in terms

---

[28]M. Riedel, Einleitung, p. 30: "Against this background, the philosophical position of Dilthey appears somewhat differently than we are accustomed to view it from the perspectives of either the Dilthey school or that of Heidegger or Carnap. For Dilthey himself it was not just an issue of the rather questionable task of elaborating an isolated cognitional theory for the cultural sciences. Instead, at issue for him was the full implications of the experience and knowledge in those sciences for philosophy, and how to bring that experience and knowledge to bear on the grounding of an autonomy of human reason." Note how the neglect of this central thrust of Dilthey's thought was in no small measure due to the lack of attention given the unpublished Breslauer Ausarbeitung.

of Dilthey's philosophy of science or metascience.

A. The Subject as Unity of Identity and Non-Identity. The novelty of Dilthey's starting point as a self-reflection of inner experience consisted in his efforts to thematize this starting point in a manner which would avoid both the absolutism of an identity philosophy and the skeptical relativism of a non-identity philosophy. Moreover, this task Dilthey proposed to accomplish, not by isolating philosophy from modern science, but by fully accepting the task imposed on philosophy by modern science, viz., to seek to ground the scientific enterprise in a critical and not a metaphysical manner. As critical, the grounding had to be achieved in an empirical and ongoing manner if it was to be consonant with empirical science. Yet also as critical, it had to find its empirical foundations in such a way that they would provide a basis for criticizing all the historically relative philosophical and scientific positions. This implied that the sought after foundations had to go beyond both the formally unconditioned absolutes of identity thought patterns and the totally conditioned hypotheses of non-identity thought patterns.

As we have seen in handling the schools of metascience, the merit of Dilthey's criticisms of those schools was in his insight into their common objectivistic roots. The unity of identity and non-identity is not susceptible to any total objectification. That unity can, for Dilthey, only be had in inner experience as experienced. It was this discovery of Dilthey that cut through the Cartesianism and logicism of all previous cognitional theories. For conscious interiority is not mediated conceptually; the metascientific grounding is not in terms of "immediate truths" or other axiomatic formulae, it is not any theoretic construction or objectification, but the immediate reality of the subject as subject, where one has the unity of consciousness (identity) and being (non-identity), of subject (identity) and object (non-identity):

> So is being or reality, along with being-for-me and
> consciousness, different from one another and yet
> related to each other. In actual performance I do

not experience a relationship but a unity.[29]

Whenever any interiorizing of the process in the act of perception leads to a consciousness of the object, consciousness possesses its content as mediated by the relationship between subject and object in self-awareness, as a factual reality of completely similar immediacy and evidence.[30]

One need not direct one's awareness to this conscious interiority, one can "lose oneself" in the objects and concerns of theory or praxis, but the ground of the concerns is still there as conscious interiority. "Thus an object is only present for a subject, an objective reality for a common reality."[31] Thus it is this experience of inner experience or conscious interiority which opens up "an immeasurable realm of reality" inasmuch as it is the unity of existence and act in the subject as subject:

For I do not need to be conscious of my consciousness, nor to feel my feelings; rather, in the very occurrence of consciousness I am aware of it. The existence of the psychic act and the knowledge of it are not two different things. Here there does not exist the difference between an object seen and the eye which sees it.... The psychic act is, because I experience (erlebe) it.[32]

This is not some type of Cartesian dualism, for the certainty of self-presence is not only auto-centric but allo-centric as well. "And the certainty with which objective reality is attained is first of all every bit as immediate as that certainty with which I am certain that any act of consciousness is consciously present to me."[33]

It is important to emphasize that this unity of identity and non-identity is in conscious interiority as experienced. The "Selbstbesinnung" which is Dilthey's starting point is simply the turning of one's attention to this lived experience of subject-as-subject without yet trying to objectify that lived experience in a subject-as-object:

---

[29] B.A., p. 7.   [30] B.A., p. 19.

[31] B.A., pp. 4-5. On the immediate certainty of objective reality in inner experience, cf. B.A., p. 12.

[32] B.A., pp. 5 and 8.   [33] B.A., p. 12.

> ...there is no observation of inwardness or its
> content. Rather, the orientation of attention
> here only produces a heightening of the degree of
> awareness with the tension of its effort.[34]

For Dilthey there was a type of inner perception which does
not objectify in the manner of external perception.[35] It
is this inner experience which is the ground, and Dilthey
seemed to find it especially in feeling. The awareness
concomitant with sorrow is not a feeling of sorrow as of an
object; it is a sorrowful awareness. Thus it is conscious
interiority as experienced which is Dilthey's interpretation
of the "Judgment (Satz) of Consciousness as Phenomenality."[36]

B. Beyond an Objectivistic Cognitional Theory. With
the novelty of the starting point there also came the necessity of articulating it in a new way. Dilthey was aware
of the Socratic-Platonic, the Augustinian, and the Cartesian
forms of "Selbstbesinnung."[37] The first two failed insofar
as they became articulated in objectivistic metaphysical
contexts, while the Cartesian form issued in a logico-
mathematical approach to cognitional theory. The philosophy
of consciousness under the aegis of Cartesianism could spill
over, either into the reductionist associational-psychological
methods of the empiricists and positivists, or into the
absolutism of transcendental idealist reflection. Where the
former correctly emphasized the need to respect the empirical

---

[34] B.A., p. 14. Cf. also G.S. V, p. 197.

[35] G.S. V, p. 197.

[36] B.A., p. 1-26. Note how this interpretation of
Dilthey's notion of "feeling" is not exactly that given by M.
Redeker in his preface to vol. XIV of Dilthey's writings.
Redeker rightly draws the parallels to Fichte's notion of
feeling as the unconscious "Urakt des Geistes" prior to
knowing and willing. Cf. XIV, p. liii. It is clear from
Dilthey's usage here, however, that it is not unconscious
in the sense of non-awareness, but only in the sense that it
is a consciousness which is not objectified, what I refer to
as the subject-as-subject. Cf. B.A., pp. 190ff. On the
"Satz der Phänomenalität," cf. B.A., pp. 13-14, 190-192. On
the need to relate such categories as multiplicity-unity,
whole-part, to the experience of the subject, cf. G.S. I,
p. 31.

[37] Cf. G.S. I, pp. 186ff., 260-267; II, 452-479.

methods of modern science, the latter realized that such methods were unable to offer the foundations needed to articulate the constitutive character of consciousness. Dilthey attempted to sublate both positions by calling attention to lived inner experience as at once empirically relative and foundationally normative.[38] Thus he could oppose his method based on "Selbstbesinnung" to all forms of cognitional theory which, laboring under Cartesian presuppositions, sought a purely objectivistic theoretical ground for theory-praxis.[39] Thus he rejected any notion that would place his foundational concerns within a "vicious circle of empty theory."[40] For none of the previous cognitional theories - whether of an idealist, transcendentalist, empiricist, or positivist character - had adequately overcome the dichotomy between subject and object. In one way or another they had all tried to construct objectiv(istic) theories to account for the spontaneous activity of the subject-as-subject. But, as Herbart had pointed out in reference to Fichte, if the duality of subject and object is accepted as ultimate, then one cannot possibly attain the subject in itself through objective, theoretical thought processes.[41] One falls into either a skeptical resignation in the face of relativism which would hold to an unending succession of "more adequate" theories (if one held onto the ultimately rational structure of the universe) or simply of other theories; or one would posit a type of intellectual intuition as revealing some sort of absolute ground, whether in terms of a Kantian synthetic apperception, a Fichtean self-positing Ego, or a Hegelian

---

[38]Cf. Riedel, Einleitung, pp. 27-52; also G.S. VII, pp. 92f.

[39]B.A., p. 33; cf. also p. 53: "I call the foundations which philosophy must achieve 'Selbstbesinnung' rather than 'cognitional theory.' For it must be a foundation of human action as well as of thought and knowledge." That Dilthey is not here excluding the possibility of a praxis-oriented cognitional theory according to Lonergan, cf. note 73 of this Chapter.

[40]Cf. B.A., pp. 11f.; G.S. VII, pp. 89-93.

[41]Cf. B.A., pp. 190f., 195ff.

absolute knowledge.

The process of history had itself refuted the claims of the transcendental idealists, but Dilthey also saw how an empiricist or positivist relativism failed to account for the belief in progress - an attitude which could only end in the nihilism of Nietzsche.[42] Against both, Dilthey affirmed the truth and reality of the subject-as-subject.[43] This unity of content and act is a "self-feeling" as the ground of self-consciousness, prior to its articulation in concepts and language.[44] "It is the primary reality of being-for-itself, which as conscious life itself has no separation of subject and object, rather it constitutes the foundation for any such differentiation."[45]

Now, if according to the "Judgment of Phenomenality" reality as lived is conditioned by conscious interiority, and the latter is a unity of identity and non-identity between self and world, then the main task of elaborating a meta-science or "Grundwissenschaft" is to articulate a cognitional theory faithful to the lived reality of the subject-as-subject. Such a metascientific method would be foundational inasmuch as it sublated the dichotomy between theory and praxis, between philosophy and positive science. Thus Dilthey could criticize the cognitional theories based either on the

---

[42] Cf. G.S. VIII, pp. 199-201.

[43] B.A., p. 191: "No matter how one turns - there must be a point at which the content of consciousness and the act of consciousness are inseparable for consciousness itself, that is, where the content and act are not separated as subject and object. Whatever the fact of self-awareness demands for its own explanation, we can find it within self-awareness itself. Only in this way can whatever is required for the conditions of self-awareness be verified in the truth [of self-awareness]. This process is nothing else than the simple fact of the interiority (Innewerdens) or inner quality present in any conscious human condition of a self: an act of will and its energy, an act of reflection and its inner tension, an act of feeling."

[44] B.A., pp. 200 and 217.

[45] B.A., p. 200. Note that this immediate consciousness as "Being-for-itself" can also refer to reflection as a "turning-inward." Cf. ibid., the marginal record by G. Misch.

objectivism of a Kantian transcendentalist method or on the
objectivism of an empiricist associational psychologism.[46]
This was the "missing link" between perception and thought
which neither the skeptics nor Kant could discover because
it is the lived practice of inner experience itself.[47] The
new foundations would not be constructed on "immediate
truths" or other hypothetical attempts at constructing
experience, but on an attention to, and understanding of,
the reality of inner experience. The certainty of this inner
experience does not arise from any theoretical efforts at
constructing a priori laws of thought or forms of perception.
That would set logic over reality, thought over experience.
Contrary to such an inversion, Dilthey held that "the
foundation of the sciences is not constituted by the airy
evidence of thought but by reality - that reality which is
fully interior to us and all important for us." A cognitional
theory based on this reality would then "render understandable
to us the achievements of thought by adverting to this
immediate knowledge of reality."[48]

Because Dilthey effectively shifted the meaning of
cognitional theory from simply objectivistic theory to an
articulation of inner experience as the ground of theory-
praxis, he realized that a cognitional theory true to his
notion of "Selbstbesinnung" had profound consequences for
philosophy. Just as the classical dichotomy between theory
and praxis was rooted in the dichotomy between philosophy
and empirical science, so the new foundation of theory-praxis
required the sublation of that latter dichotomy.[49] This

---

[46]B.A., p. 223: "A cognitional theory which proceeds in
such a fashion can only discover a world of theoretical
understanding that stands in an unbridgeable opposition to
the real world. It is precisely the sublation of this
opposition through a real grasp of the factual presence
[of self-consciousness] that is the condition which alone
can provide the foundations for the sciences of history
and of society."

[47]Cf. G.S. I, p. 240. Also pp. 82ff of Chapter Two.

[48]B.A., p. 41.

[49]Cf. B.A., pp. 11-12, 246-247; G.S. I, 225; and B.A.,
p. 53.

Dilthey saw as a sublation of the dichotomy between philosophy and psychological science.[50]

Dilthey's efforts to meet these requirements are to be found throughout his writing career. The main steps he took can be traced in his yet unpublished lectures of 1865 on the "Logik und System der philosophischen Wissenschaft" and his notes on the cognitional theoretical continuation of his Einleitung in die Geisteswissenschaften known as the Breslauer Ausarbeitung of 1880, through his published writings of the nature of our belief in the external world (1890) and his notion of a descriptive and analytic psychology (1894 to 1896), to his final attempts at expounding his position on the grounding of the human sciences and the structures of the historical world from 1905 to 1910.[51]

It has sometimes been asserted that the last period of Dilthey's writings, from about the turn of the century till his death in 1911, marked a shift in his cognitional theoretical position. The influences of Husserl's Logischen Unterschungen (1900-1901) and Dilthey's own work on the young Hegel are cited as decisive in opening his eyes to the "Unangemessenheit der erkenntniskritischen und psychologischen Fragestellung."[52] This, however, has recently been questioned by M. Riedel and the present writer agrees with him that the work of the later Dilthey is more of a continuation of his

---

[50] G.S. VIII, pp. 174-175. In B.A., p. 73 Dilthey criticizes Kant for his failure to take into account the contributions of the positive sciences in articulating the genesis of knowing.

[51] Cf. Volumes V and VII for the published material. A publication of the Breslauer Ausarbeitung is being prepared. On the lectures of 1865, cf. Riedel, Einleitung, pp. 19f. and Krausser, Kritik, pp. 45-49.

[52] P. Hünermann, op. cit., pp. 240f. Also K. -O. Apel, Das Verstehen, p. 174 who makes the highly ambiguous statement that the later Dilthey moved "away from psychology as the foundational science and gave his theory of understanding an objective turn, without thereby surrendering his basic position." Notice the opposite opinion of P. Krausser in his Kritik der endlichen Vernunft, pp. 15-18, 23.

earlier phases than a break with them.[53] It is true that in his last period Dilthey was more concerned with articulating a theory of knowing which would realistically and critically thematize his notion of lived experience. He himself thanks Husserl for this.[54] But he had no intention of abandoning his critique of objectivism; indeed, he saw a danger of this in the "psychological scholasticism" of Brentano and Husserl.[55] Moreover, the Breslauer Ausarbeitung of 1880 shows how aware Dilthey was of the need to develop a theory of knowing congenial to his insight into lived experience.[56]

   C. The Elements of the New Methodology. For Dilthey there was, then, a threefold task in assembling the elements of the new metascientific methodology. First, he had to trace the history of philosophical-foundational thought through its metaphysical and theological emergence and decline. Such an "exaltation of the thinking subject through the stages of history" led, as we saw in the last chapter, to the pathos of the Enlightenment. The autonomy of historical reason was faced with the need to find its own immanent norms of progress from the present into the future.[57] This autonomy manifested itself on the one hand in the shift to the subject character- istic of transcendentalist metascience, and on the other hand, in the increasing spread of empirical specialized science. The dominance of the methods of natural science as the model of knowing in both the transcendentalist and the empiricist and positivist schools of metascience meant none of these trends were able to do justice to the historical spontaneity of the subject-as-subject. This was only too obvious in the empiricist Anglo-Saxon and French positivist traditions, with

------

[53]Cf. Riedel, Einleitung, pp. 53f.

[54]Cf. G.S. VII, p. 14, note.

[55]Cf. G.S. VII, p. 237.

[56]Cf. B.A., pp. 38-51. Also cf. Dilthey's remarks on his own system prior to 1900, i.e., around 1896 to 1897 in G.S. VIII, pp. 176-184. That Dilthey was still involved in a cognitional theoretical grounding in 1910, cf. G.S. VII, pp. 117-120.

[57]Cf. G.S. VIII, pp. 176ff.

their objectivistic reductions of the subject's operations
to associational perceptualisms; but it was no less true
of any Kantian effort to discover the a priori structures of
a pure reason divorced from the spontaneous activity of
historical subjectivity.[58]

Secondly, Dilthey had then to proceed to his own
thematization of that historical subjectivity. This meant
that the full range of inner experience as cognitive-emotive-
volitional had to be articulated not as static a priori forms
but as dynamic evolutive structures. The descriptive,
"verstehende" psychology aimed, not at some "definitive"
solution of the problem of knowing - as with Kant, Hume,
Locke, or Fichte - but at uncovering the open and ongoing
structures which would make possible a progressive historical
solution.[59] As empirical, such a descriptive psychology or
"an anthropology of knowing and action" involved a shift in
the meaning of "empirical" from the empiricist and positivist
concentration on external experience to inner experience.[60]
As foundation, such a cognitional theory involved an approach
to the subject-as-subject which maintained the unity of
identity and non-identity which accounts for the continual
interaction between self and world, so that the dynamic
structures of conscious interiority are articulated according
to the actual patterns of historical growth and change.[61]

---

[58]Cf. Krausser, Kritik, pp. 37-45; Riedel, Einleitung,
pp. 49ff.

[59]Cf. M. Riedel, ibid., p. 50.

[60]Cf. Krausser's Kritik, pp. 210ff. Note that when I
use cognitional theory in reference to Dilthey's own position
I do so in contra-distinction to the purely conceptualistic
cognitional theories of previous transcendentalist, empiricist,
and positivist positions. Thus one might refer to it as a
cognitional theory-praxis, or use Krausser's "anthropology of
human knowing and acting." This however, is not purely
formal; cf. Krausser, op. cit., p. 93.

[61]B.A., pp. 60-61: "The a priori of Kant is stiff and
dead; but the real conditions of consciousness and its
presuppositions, as I understand them, are living, historical
processes. They are in development and have a history; and
the unfolding of this history consists in the adaptation of
consciousness to an ever more accurately known multiplicity
of inductive experience." Also, ibid., pp. 268-269.

This means that the dynamic structures found in the subject-as-subject as a "living unity" are not privatized a priori forms of some transcendental "knowing subject," but the at once individual and collective structures of conscious "life itself."[62] The particularity of historical research and the universality of scientific research are thereby seen as complementary. This also accounts for the possibility of understanding objectifications of lived experience which we ourselves have not experienced,[63] as well as allowing for the possibility of a critical grounding of the sought-after cognitional theory since the particularity of historical reality is itself part of an ongoing total process.[64] One does not thereby go behind life to some absolute originating knowledge, but manifests the open and ongoing structures of life itself.[65]

In the third place, if the dynamic structures of conscious interiority - what Dilthey referred to as "Seelenleben" - are not privatized but in fact the structures of socio-historical life-contexts, then the descriptive psychology of Dilthey should provide a metascientific base for understanding and interrelating the many specialized sciences dealing with particular aspects of that life-context.[66] Here also we can see the peculiarity of Dilthey's position. He criticized both the Kantian transcendentalist methods and the Hegelian idealist ones for being unable to integrate the procedures and results of the positive sciences.[67] On the

---

[62]Cf. M. Riedel, Einleitung, pp. 44ff., and references given there.

[63]Cf. G.S. VII, pp. 118ff., also Apel, Das Verstehen, pp. 173-175; Diwald, Dilthey (Göttingen, 1963), pp. 130ff.

[64]On the life-contexts or "Lebenszusammenhang" cf. Diwald, op. cit., pp. 113ff.; Bollnow, Dilthey, pp. 48ff.; Hünermann, op. cit., pp. 246ff.; Landgrebe, Theorie, pp. 250-255, 277ff.

[65]Cf. G.S. V, p. 5; VIII, pp. 184, 193; I, pp. 418f.; Briefwechsel, p. 221.

[66]G.S. VIII, p. 172.

[67]On Kant, cf. B.A., p. 73; G.S. I, pp. 308f.; V, p. 27; VIII, pp. 171, 174f. On Hegel, cf. IV, pp. 219-220. Dil-

other hand, he also criticized the empiricists and positivists for attempting to work out an interrelation of the sciences in a reductionist mechanistic manner.[68] Dilthey's own foundational studies of the cultural sciences consisted in an effort to articulate the extensions and complexifications of the dynamic structures uncovered by his descriptive analysis of conscious interiority. The method did not undergo any radical revision; P. Krausser has shown how Dilthey's structural feed-back approach was first discovered in reference to hermeneutics.[69] This indicates two important factors in Dilthey's approach. First, the dynamic structures were not conceived of as privatized a priori forms necessitating an apodictic grounding in individualized consciousness. Second, what Dilthey referred to as the "Lebenszusammenhang or life-context was the ground, not only of the pre-scientific "life-world," but also the ground of science - at least of the human sciences. This is of crucial significance. It shows how for Dilthey the grounding of the cultural sciences was meant to restore to its rightful primacy the reality of socio-historical life over any conceptuality. The foundational importance of Verstehen over Erklären was Dilthey's attempt to stem the tide of scientistic objectivism and re-orientate the metascience of his day toward its own forgotten and repressed subjectivity. The narrative of life had to re-establish its primacy over the conceptualism of a purely argumentative or deductivist methodology.

4. The Differentiation of Natural Sciences and Cultural Sciences

Had Dilthey in fact explicated fully his own methodological position thoroughly he would have seen how the

---

they criticized Humbolt and his followers for attempting an artificial synthesis between historical research and the transcendental-idealist philosophies from Kant to Hegel; cf. VII, p. 115.

[68]Cf. Krausser, op. cit., pp. 40-45; also G.S. I, pp. 90-92, 370-386; V, pp. 359-360: note here how Dilthey indicates the lack of historical awareness on the part of positivism.

[69]Cf. P. Krausser, op. cit., pp. 27-36.

intersubjectivity he found in the cultural sciences was also, in its basic structures, applicable to the natural sciences. That he did not enter into the natural sciences and the interiority operative there is due, to a great extent, to his own conception of the subject-as-subject, his dependence upon the mode of feeling as offering the key to that consciousness which is operative prior to any objectification of itself. As it was, Dilthey made it clear from the start that he considered his efforts directed solely at the grounding of the cultural sciences. Thus the proper place to discuss his differentiation of the natural and cultural sciences is within the context of his starting point in lived consciousness, rather than as a consequence of his analysis of that consciousness itself, which is the topic of the following section of this chapter. The differentiation of the two forms of knowing constitutes, for Dilthey, the prologomenon to his critique of historical reason, defining, as it does, the type of experience he refers to as grounding the cultural sciences. First I shall discuss the unity of experience grounding the differentiation, then the differentiation itself, and finally present a difficulty that threatened Dilthey's unity.

A. The Unity of Experience. We have seen how Dilthey saw the subject as providing a unity of identity and non-identity insofar as the subject was defined as the locus of conscious experience as such. There was not any effort to conceive of this unity as an identity; Dilthey maintained that such inner experience of conscious interiority was not some transcendental self-consciousness but that both self and world, subject and object, were simultaneously given in consciousness. Such an approach to consciousness is not abstract or theoretical but concrete and practical:

> Both are present to us simultaneously and together; we find things present with our self, our self with things.... And indeed when our self and reality or things, self-consciousness and world-consciousness, are only both sides of a total consciousness, then this is not grounded in a theoretical process. Instead, we are interiorly aware of our self and things because in this continuous act of life the

totality of our essence is operative.[70]
There then follows a description of walking, touching, willing,
pain and desire - actions where self and thing, subject and
object, are both operative in a continuous feedback correlation between themselves. The subject, concludes Dilthey,
is not simply "ein Zuschauer, das Ich, der vor der Bühne der
Welt sitzt" but an actor or agent who is also acted upon. It
is against the abstract conceptualizing approach of the
transcendentalist philosophies that Dilthey attempts to
clarify this concrete and empirical description of conscious
action-in-world which he terms "Leben" and "Erlebnis":

> Reality is nothing else than this experience.... This
> is the continuous fact which is the foundation of
> self-consciousness. Without a world we would have
> no self-consciousness, and without this self-
> consciousness no world would be present to us. What
> happens in this act of so-called encounter is life
> itself - not a theoretical process, but what we express
> with the term experience (Erlebnis).[71]

The unity of experience, therefore, is the unity of
consciousness as a totality which is both a consciousness
of self (identity) and of world (non-identity). There is
no effort to deduce one from the other, as with the conceptualism of Fichte, whom Dilthey criticizes.[72] As we shall
see in the following section, Dilthey is not at all interested
in simply giving another theory, another hypothetical construct, in regard to consciousness. He is rather attempting
to describe what it is that man does as a consciously alive
being. The starting point for Dilthey's critique of historical reason, the grounding unity of experience, is not an
epistemological question of why knowing, feeling, or willing
can or cannot attain objectivity; nor is it the meta-physical
question regarding what we can ultimately know or constitute

---

[70]B.A., pp. 187f. This is discussed at greater length
in his essay on the reality of the external world in G.S. V,
pp. 126-135.

[71]Cf. B.A., pp. 188-189 and 90-94. On the feedback
character of this relation, cf. P. Krausser, op. cit.,
pp. 95-100.

[72]Cf. B.A., pp. 13, 21-26, 191; G.S. VII, pp. 109-111.

in our knowing, feeling and volition. Rather he is interested only in as exact a description as possible of what it is that we do when we know, feel, will.[73]

Such a unity of experience is operative not only in the individual conscious living of persons but is also a constitutive element in the more complex realities of socio-historical systems: groups, communities, societies, nations. Correlative to the "self-feeling" of a conscious interiority of the individual, there are the "communal feelings" of a community, of many communities within a nation, and so on. Dilthey refers to these as "psychic facts of a second order" with the relations of identity and non-identity articulated in notions of "community feeling, a feeling of being-for-itself (a reality for which we have no word), control, dependence, freedom, need."[74] Moreover, the basic thrust of this approach is not changed in the later works of Dilthey, as the writings of 1905 and 1910 attest.[75] In the latter writings the notion of structure and the movement from the spontaneous life-world to reflection on it in the cultural sciences is more pronounced, but the basic approach is still

---

[73]On the importance of the questions, cf. Lonergan, M.i.T., pp. 25, 83, 261, 287, 316; D. Tracy, Achievement, pp. 227f. Note also that when Dilthey contrasts, as in B.A., his own method of "Selbstbesinnung" to "Erkenntnistheorie" in order to bring out the theoretical and practical import of his approach vis-à-vis Neokantian and positivist cognitional theories, he is not excluding the possibility of a praxis-oriented cognitional theory concerned with what we do when we know and act, as in Lonergan. Thus in G.S. VII, p. 117, Dilthey speaks of his method as "erkenntnistheoretisch" while also stating how he opposed the "intellectualism" of the then predominant theories of knowing. For Dilthey's notion of "erkenntnistheoretische elbstbesinnung" cf. G.S. I, pp. 95, 116ff. Cf. references to B.A. in note 39 above. On the differences with Kant, cf. Landgrebe, Diltheys Theorie der Geisteswissenschaften, pp. 247-250.

[74]Cf. G.S. I, pp. 64-70. Note how Dilthey is attempting to get at the conscious constitution of social realities without the objectivistic categories of a Neokantian transcendentalist analysis. Hence the notion of "feeling." The quote is from p. 68.

[75]Cf. G.S. VII, pp. 70-88; also P. Krausser, op. cit., pp. 107-161.

236

in terms of "Erlebnis" and the conscious interiority constituting that unity of experience.[76] Thus it is not surprising
that for Dilthey the fundamental problem in a methodological
founding of the cultural sciences was summed up in terms
of an adequate knowledge of this unity of experience and how
the social organizations of meaning, value, and purpose were
related to the individual:

> The center of all problems associated with the grounding
> of the cultural sciences is as follows: the possibility
> of a knowledge of the psychic unities of life, and
> the limits of such a knowledge. It concerns, then,
> how this psychological knowledge is related to second
> order facts, through which relation one could decide
> about the nature of these theoretical sciences of
> society.[77]

It was against both empiricism and speculative transcendental systems that Dilthey sought to ground his critique
of historical reason in an experience that would be empirical
(without being empiricist) whose unity would be transcultural
(without being transcendentalist).[78] Yet it was also to
enable Dilthey to account for the indispensable similarity
between the methods of the natural sciences and those of
the cultural sciences. There was no intention on the part
of Dilthey to create some type of total non-identity between
the two realms of science. Indeed, his quest for the differentiation of the two in terms of experience indicates that he,
more than most of his contemporaries, was aware of the subjectivity operative in the methods of the natural scientific
community. Perhaps the evaluation of P. Krausser is not
completely off the mark when he sees the clear relevance
of Dilthey's position to our own scientific theoretical
situation.[79]

---

[76]G.S. VII, p. 83. Dilthey is here contrasting the
natural and cultural sciences with the two centers of
"Aussenwelt" in nature and "Innenwelt" of history.

[77]G.S. I, p. 68. Cf. also VII, pp. 71, 119-120.

[78]Cf. G.S. V, 259ff., 434; VII, 80.

[79]Cf. P. Krausser, op. cit., pp. 210-219, esp. 218-219:
"It seems to be that the structural theory of Dilthey proves
itself superior to the comparably one-sided or incontrollably
many-sided theories presently available. Dilthey's theory

B. The Differentiation of Natural and Cultural Sciences. Running through all of the treatments by Dilthey of the differentiation of the natural sciences from the cultural sciences is the effort to ground their differentiation in terms of the differentiation of experience as extrorsive and introrsive. Dilthey did not attempt a logical or formalist differentiation; to him this was insufficient inasmuch as it misplaced the real difference by seeking some objectifiable ground.[80] Moreover, he did not see the differentiation as primarily one of nature-society or nature-history. For such differentiations were too open to the objectifications of both society and history, as exemplified in the writings of Comte and Hegel. Comte was led to a mechanistic reductionism of society, with its attendant sublation of any difference between the natural and social sciences; while Hegel offered an alternative to historicism only by an unexperiential absolute knowledge which tended to sublate the natural sciences into those of mind coming to itself.[81] For Dilthey the proper differentiation was that between man's experience of nature and the experience of his own conscious living or, as Rothacker

---

is not vague regarding the fundamental thesis against either the possibility or indeed the necessity of a value-free science or scientifically controlled action - which is more than can be said for either the dialectical theory of science (Adorno, Habermas), or the analytic theory of science (Popper), or the hermeneutical theory (Gadamer). Dilthey's theory escapes the many criticisms leveled against the other theories. Habermas criticizes Gadamer's notion of prejudice as overlooking the necessity and possibility of a critical correction and control of prejudgments. Popper criticizes the dialecticians for promoting a 'doubly entrenched dogmatism' while Habermas objects to the analytic positions for their inflated dualism, which leads them to 'eliminate questions of life-praxis from the horizon of science altogether.'"

[80]The objects considered by common sense and by empirical science are generally the same; cf. Lonergan, Insight, pp. 289-299.

[81]On Comte, cf. notes 196, 205, 231 of Chapter Two, and the references given there, esp. G. Misch, Zur Entstehung des französischen Positivismus, pp. 67, 86-93; and Dilthey's critique in G.S. V, pp. 50-56. On Hegel, cf. G.S. IV, pp. 238-247, 247-251. For a general critique of both Hegel and Comte by Dilthey, cf. G.S. I, pp. 86-112, esp. 104ff.

defines it, between nature and mind.[82]

In order to situate Dilthey's differentiation of the sciences, I shall first outline his criticisms of both the sociology of Comte and the philosophy of history, predominantly Hegelian, in their failures, from Dilthey's point of view, to ground and adequately differentiate the natural and cultural sciences. Then I shall sketch the differentiation Dilthey himself offers. There are four main points, the first two will deal with the insufficiency of Comtean sociology and Hegelian philosophy of history, the next two will then develop Dilthey's position.

In the first place, we have seen how for Dilthey the grounding of the cultural sciences depended upon the possibility of articulating an approach to the totality of what he terms human-social-historical reality. With the demise of the metaphysical mediations of totality there was a vacuum of meaning and value which had to be critically taken over by a basic approach to totality which would not conflict with, but be structured according to, the advance of the sciences. In this, Dilthey felt that both positivism and idealism were dead ends. The positivists had, indeed, seen the central significance of the empirical methods and the irrelevance of metaphysics. Yet, in their admiration for the success of the natural sciences, they had overlooked the need for a critical enlightenment of the very presuppositions of scientific knowledge and how this was especially necessary in regard to the sciences dealing with mankind. As a result they tended to either reject such sciences as truly scientific or they accepted them only on the basis of draining the value-judgments in them to the status of relative factual judgments.[83] Positivism, in minimizing the need for a critical methodological analysis of knowledge and value,

---

[82]Cf. Rothacker, _Logik und Systematik der Geisteswissenschaften_, pp. 12f.

[83]G.S. I, p. 5. Note the similarity of this judgment on positivism with that of Habermas in _Erkenntnis und Interesse_, pp. 88-92. It shows that Dilthey was aware of the tendency in positivism to denounce cognitional theoretical procedures as meaningless just as it had earlier rejected metaphysics.

tended itself to a totalitarian view which saw all of reality as reducible to natural scientific methods and the consequent ideal of a unified physical science.

It was in this manner that Dilthey conceived the need to ground the cultural sciences as being at once a need to articulate a cognitional theoretical foundation for them and, simultaneously, to differentiate those sciences from the natural sciences. For, while positivism claimed that any effort to articulate a methodological approach to the totality of historical reality was illusionary, a hang-over from metaphysics, still in fact by their setting up the natural scientific methods as the criterion for all knowledge, they projected such a totality.

In this respect the philosophies of history were more honest; they openly admitted the need for somehow dealing with totality. But where positivism had "totalized" the natural sciences and given them the status of absolute criterion, the philosophies of history which came out of idealism tended to the same type of "totalization" from the viewpoint of history and mind. No wonder, then, that Hegel would represent this tendency so well, completely overlooking his own historical conditionedness and elaborating an absolute knowledge on the basis of "Begriff." In doing this he failed to take account of the concreteness of the totality which the cultural sciences handle. "Eine Theorie, welche die gesellschaftlich-geschichtlichen Tatsachen beschreiben und analysieren will, kann nicht von dieser Totalität der Menschennatur absehen und sich auf das Geistige einschränken."[84] As a result the idealist philosophies of history had to attempt to define historical progress either by taking the criterion from some particular social context and proclaiming it the norm for all societies and cultures, or by seeking to elaborate a formula for historical process which would account for the changes within the entire "Totalzusammenhang der Gesellschaften in der Geschichte." This, however, was impossible.[85]

---

[84] G.S. I, p. 6; also G.S. VII, pp. 107-112.

[85] G.S. I, p. 110.

In the second place, therefore, Dilthey's criticism of both a sociology as grounding all the human sciences, after the manner of Comte in France or of Stuart Mill and Spencer in England, and the philosophies of history in Germany[86] could be summarized in two points. First, they both resulted from the naturalist secularization of theological totalizations regarding society and history. Yet the contents of the theological versions of this total view of history were concrete, i.e., such theologies of history concentrated upon certain ecclesial communities or traditions as embodying or incarnating the religious experience grounding the entire scope of history and of society. Once this concrete religious experience is severed from its concrete historical embodiment however, not only do the ecclesial institutions "dry up and decay" but the attempt to restore a secularized version seems bound to merely substitute abstract metaphysical surrogates such as "Reason," or "World Spirit," or "society as a unity."[87] For Dilthey this was no more than a "metaphysical shadow game" - shadows replacing the "massive reality" of what the Mystical Body meant in Medieval theological interpretations of history and society.[88] In the place of a christian eschatology, the secular utopias could offer only an uncertain future.[89]

---

[86]G.S. I, pp. 89-90; notice how this parallels Dilthey's criticisms of the French positivist, British empiricist, and German transcendental idealist traditions of the philosophy of science or metascience given in Chapter Two.

[87]Cf. G.S. I, pp. 98-104.

[88]Cf. G.S. I, pp. 99-100: "The idea of a unifying plan within world history radically shifted during the 18th century inasmuch as such a plan was maintained (in a secularized form) cut off from its firm premise in systematic theology: a massive theological reality is reduced to a metaphysical shadow game."

[89]G.S. I, p. 100. "From the darkness of an unknown beginning, the complex and enigmatic events of world history stumble onwards into a future equally shrouded in darkness. For what purpose this exhaustive striving of the human race?... Within the horizon of an Augustine, it could well be understood; from the viewpoint of the 18th century, it is an enigma without any clear indications for a solution. Thus every attempt during the 18th century to demonstrate

The problem which these secularized transformations of religious themes were all struggling with was how to give the increased individualism that had resulted from the Enlightenment a meaning and direction vis-à-vis society and history; how to relate the consciousness of individuals to the broader scope of social and historical awareness. Dilthey sees this as an "Ersatz" for the doctrine of the Mystical Body and hence is not suprised that in Hegel and Comte there were explicit efforts at transforming their methods into a secularist sublation of religion.[90]

As a result, the second point in Dilthey's criticisms of Comtean sociology and Hegelian philosophy of history is that in their effort either to reduce the cultural sciences to the natural sciences (Comte) or vice versa (Hegel), they failed to take into account the empirical methods of both types of science sufficiently. In their efforts at grounding the sciences they tended to treat the sciences themselves as giving only data or raw material to be subsumed under their general laws and categories. Dilthey compares them to the alchemists.[91] What Dilthey sees as the major weakness of the positivist and idealist approach to a grounding of the sciences in terms of either a differentiation of nature-

---

a plan or meaning within human history is only a transformation of older systems: Lessing's education of the human race, Hegel's self-evolution of God, Comte's shifts in hierarchical organizations - that's all they are."

[90] Cf. G.S. I, pp. 100-101. Note that Dilthey's interpretation does not fall under the criticisms of H. Blumenberg in his Die Legitimität der Neuzeit inasmuch as Dilthey is careful to distinguish the legitimacy of modern science from the metaphysical reflections on progress. What Blumenberg overlooks is that, although it is perfectly true that the secular idea of progress puts the responsibility for the future in man's hands rather than as an expectation of salvation from God, and so differs profoundly from a christian eschatology (cf. ibid., pp. 24f., 32, 35-37, 44, 57), nonetheless there was precisely a neglect of this autonomous and free responsibility of men in favor of "Vernunft," "Weltgeist" or "die Gesellschaft" on the part of 18th century thinkers. This is what Dilthey criticizes.

[91] Cf. G.S. I, pp. 91-92. Note the importance of Dilthey's interpretation of Goethe (the Faustian motif is strong in this comparison with the dream of the alchemists) regarding the emergence of Enlightenment science, cf. E.D., pp. 11-17, 124-127, 170-186.

242

society or of nature-history is that such differentiations
are not equipped to take into account the need man has to
mediate the singular and the universal, the concrete and
the recurrent patterns by means of the individual sciences
themselves.[92] The positivist and idealist differentiations
did not enable their proponents to come up with a concrete
and heuristic methodological framework which would enable
them to remain critically open to the advance of the
individual sciences. Their systems tended to suppress rather
than facilitate those particular investigations which alone
could asymptotically move toward a clarification of the many
elements in the ongoing realities of societies and history.[93]
Thus Dilthey can conclude that the tasks which such projects
set themselves, as well as their methods, were false.[94]

In the third place, then, Dilthey argued for the need
to differentiate and ground the cultural sciences through a
cognitional theoretical "Selbstbesinnung." There are three
reasons which he advances for this. First, the need to take
the scientific revolution since the Enlightenment seriously
demands that one's foundation not be dependent upon
unverifiable generalizations stemming from an effort to find
surrogates for theological or metaphysical systems. The
secularized versions of the Mystical Body in either a
Comtean sociology or an Hegelian philosphy of history failed
to respect the autonomy of man, tending to make him an
instrument of the "cunning of reason" or "the organizing
forces of society." Dilthey's differentiation and grounding
in terms of nature-mind guaranteed for him that the autonomy
of man as an individual would be not only respected but
seen as the foundation of the entire scientific process.[95]

---

[92]Cf. G.S. I, p. 92; also P. Krausser, op. cit.,
pp. 37-45.

[93]Cf. G.S. I, pp. 109-112.

[94]Cf. G.S. I, pp. 93-109. This shows the importance
of Dilthey's handling of these two approaches together,
how they both spring from opposite but related false differentiations of the sciences. Hence Hodges' criticisms
are not apropos, cf. his The Philosophy of W. Dilthey, pp. 186ff.

[95]G.S. I, p. 100 "What someone lives through in the

Moreover, the objectivism in making either the nature-society or nature-history differentiations foundational led, for Dilthey, to a notion of theory-praxis mediation where praxis was seen as a deduction from (or application of technique based on) a passive observation of certain "laws" of history or society. Against this his insistence upon experience saw the development of mankind as leading to precisely that inner experience which is the autonomous source of theory and praxis: "the end result of the development of mankind can only be appropriated in lived experience (Erlebnis), not in a passive contemplation."[96]

The second reason for the need of a cognitional theoretical self-reflection as grounding and differentiating the sciences was that this approach not only gave autonomous individuality its due, but also was able to handle the totality of history in a heuristic and openly critical fashion, thereby giving the individual sciences their rightful place in the gradual elucidation of society and history.[97] Not only would this allow for an interrelation of factual judgments and value judgments, but also for the possibility of a heuristic anticipation of universal history based upon the cumulative and progressive results of the individual sciences.[98]

The third reason consists in the possibility of such an approach to mediate via method between a critical philosophy

---

solitude of his own soul, his struggles with fate in the depths of his conscience, these are realities for him, not for a world-process or for some organism of human society. Yet this reality of conscious living is only glimpsed as a shadowy outline in the metaphysics of Comte or Hegel."

[96] Cf. G.S. I, p. 104.

[97] G.S. I, pp. 95, 97-98: "...every formulation in which we express the meaning of history is only a reflection of our own lived interiority.... The meaning of history is, therefore, an extraordinary combination of realities. Thus there would also be here the same task of coming to self-awareness (Selbstbesinnung), which researches within inner life the origin of value and norm, and their relation to being and reality, thereby analyzing carefully and slowly this aspect of the complex, historical whole."

[98] Cf. G.S. I, p. 95; and XI, pp. 139-164.

and the particular sciences. This is central to a correct
understanding of Dilthey's entire project of a critique of
historical reason. He sees the expansion of logic from a
mere formalist approach, concerned with the products of
the sciences, to a dynamic expression of the ongoing
cognitional praxis of the sciences, occurring through an
elaboration of the dynamic structures of human knowledge
and action. This demands a rejection of the neat boudaries
between philosophy and science:

> There is here a movement within science in our
> century that cannot be stopped, a movement to tear
> down the boundaries which a narrowly constrained
> professionalism had erected between philosophy and
> the specialized sciences.[99]

This "logic as doctrine on methods" takes seriously the form
which philosophy in Germany had adopted as critical, seeking
to uncover the dynamic cognitional basis for both concept and
judgment in the process of knowing itself, i.e., in the
concrete psychic acts themselves.[100]

The fourth and final point in situating Dilthey's
differentiation of the natural and cultural sciences is to
understand how the central idea in this differentiation is
grounded in the difference between an outward-oriented
(or extrorsive) experience and an inward-oriented   (or
introrsive) experience. As there is a differentiation of
experience into inner and outer, so there is a differentiation
of science into natural and human or cultural. For the
natural sciences the empirical methods of observation and
hypothesis formation find their verification, their relation

---

[99] G.S. I, p. 117.

[100] Cf. G.S. I, p. 118: "Thus the demands of logic
regarding concepts and propositions lead back to the central
problem of every cognitional theory: the nature of our
immediate knowledge (Wissens) of conscious reality
and its relation to the progress of knowledge..." Note how
this conception of method is not the logistic conception
of Descartes inasmuch as it places the criterion, not in
certain self-evident principles or axioms, but in the
factual process of immediate knowing and doing itself.
Cf. also G.S. I, pp. 116-120 on the task of a cognitional
theoretical grounding of the cultural sciences.

to reality, in the extrorsive experiences of the outer world.[101] The natural scientist's object is always mediated by some type of sense perception: "only through the senses is a reality independent of the self present to us. Thus only sense-impressions can be combined into an object." There is not only the correlation of subject and object, but also a priority of experience, which, however, the natural scientist need not reflect upon as such.[102]

Now this unity of experience was not, as it was for Kant, the synthetic unity of apperception. Kant's refutation of idealism tried to show how inner experience is possible because of outer experience, which coincided with the necessary relation of empirical consciousness to transcendental consciousness, or consciousness of self as originating apperceptive unity prior to all experiences.[103] Thus for Kant the "Eye that thinks" and the "Ego that intuits itself" is similar to the relation we have to any object of intuition and inner perception, so that the inner perception knows the subject as appearance and not "in itself."[104] Dilthey's motives for rejecting the Kantian critique might be summarized in two reasons. First, it did not correspond to either the anticipations of the natural scientists nor to the convictions of common sense. Second, this was so because Kant failed to grasp the immediate reality of inner experience as a unity, so that his a priori is "rigid and dead" insofar as the real conditions and presuppositions of consciousness must account for precisely this living unity grounding historical experience.[105] The unity of experience is nothing else than the self-presence interior to all and any historical activity, whether spontaneous or reflectively

---

[101]Cf. G.S. I, pp. 14-21; V, pp. 169, 223, 237, 242-258; VII, pp. 88-93, 125.

[102]Cf. G.S. V, pp. 248f.

[103]Cf. Kant, Kritik der reinen Vernunft, A p. 117, B p. 275-B 279.

[104]Cf. ibid., B 156.

[105]Cf. G.S. I, xviii, p. 418; VIII, pp. 175f.; B.A. pp. 192-197; also Krausser, op. cit., pp. 46, 224f.

scientific. That unity is immediately real and certainly there.[106]

It is this unity, moreover, which accounts for the possibility of differentiating the natural and cultural sciences. In both scientific realms are to be found methods of comparison, analysis, explanatory construction. In both hypothesis formation plays an important role.[107] The natural scientist classifies and measures, by comparing objects and analyzing their various components. In doing this he is experiencing objects, the reality of which is testified to by the fact that his experience of impression and resistance does not originate in his own inner experience.[108] In its spontaneous form, it is this which grounds our common sense awareness of the reality of an external world.[109]

But the entire thrust of the natural sciences is to structure this experience within the measuring contexts which allow for explanatory constructs on the cause-effect relations between objects. As this becomes more pronounced in the natural sciences they have become more involved in "thought structures" which cannot exceed the status of hypothesis.[110] For this is to move beyond the experience of reality to conceptual constructions.[111] This is why any methodology based upon the natural sciences cannot ground the factuality of the real, nor overcome a hypothetical

---

[106]Cf. G.S. I, pp. xvii, 10; V, pp. 11, 145, 171f., 238, 362; VI, pp. 314f.; VII, pp. 26f.

[107]Cf. G.S. V, pp. 171-175, 210, 238, 253f.; also Krausser, op. cit., pp. 34, 42, 60-65.

[108]Cf. G.S. V, pp. 95, 98-105, 108-111; VII, pp. 32-35.

[109]Cf. G.S. V, pp. 95, 98-105, 133.

[110]Cf. G.S. I, pp. 363-373, 392-395, 404; V, pp. 91f., 242-258; VII, pp. 32-35, 275, 295-303.

[111]G.S. I, p. 369: "When one leaves the realm of experience itself, one has only to do with thought out concepts, not with reality." Also VII, p. 275: "Rather are primal truths as the first expressions for reality least of all hypothetical; the further one moves towards generalities, the more pronounced is the hypothetical aspect."

approach to the real.[112] The extrorsive movement of the
natural sciences away from experience implies that they cannot
know or conceptualize real objects themselves but only
experience them:

> There does not exist a truth of the external object
> as a correspondence of the image with a reality, for
> this reality is not present in any consciousness,
> and thus is beyond any comparison. One cannot will
> to know how the object appears when no one subsumes
> it in his consciousness.[113]

The reality of the human sciences, the objects they
seek to understand, is quite otherwise. Social and historical
realities are expressions of living human awareness, of
human interiority.[114] Hence, while the "Geisteswissenschaften"
might make use of explanatory-constructive methods, still
they could be grounded in a certain, and not just hypothetical manner.[115] This grounding will be in terms of
introrsive experience, i.e., the "objective reality" for
these sciences is not attained by hypothetical constructions
but through a description and analysis of human interiority.[116]
The grounding and differentiating of the sciences, therefore,
is not a question of going "behind" inner experience, to
some noumenal realm, but rather of letting interiority become
aware of itself. "Conscious life here grasps life" - Kant's
treatment of inner experience or "life" as mere appearance
was a "contradictio in adjecto."[117] Just as man experiences
the certainty of his own self-presence, so the reality of
social and historical life is experienced (erlebt) and
understood (verstanden) rather than just hypothetically

---

[112] G.S. I, p. 10.

[113] G.S. I, p. 394; cf. also I, p. 198.

[114] Cf. the references given in notes 22 and 23 above.
Also G.S. V, pp. 265, 332, VII, pp. vii, 19, 157, 146f.,
191, 237, 309; VIII, p. 178.

[115] Cf. G.S. I, p. 9; V, p. 153; VII, p. 125.

[116] Cf. G.S. V, pp. 136f., 151f., 156f., 170-173, 175-
179, 191-195; VIII, pp. 179ff.

[117] Cf. G.S. V, pp. 5, 195f.; VIII, pp. 174f.; also
Diwald, op. cit., p. 48.

explained (erklärt).[118]

There is doubtless, for Dilthey, a problematic associated with the inevitable dependence of man and nature, and consequently of the relevance of natural sciences for human sciences. He was aware of the contradiction between the transcendental philosophies, which saw the knowledge of nature dependent upon consciousness, and the empirical perspective, which reduced the mental to natural processes. As far as the human sciences and their grounding was concerned, Dilthey was convinced that a satisfactory solution was possible.[119] Inasmuch as the human sciences "have grown from the praxis of life itself," it is possible to uncover the reality grounding them through a cognitional theoretical "Selbstbesinnung" which would describe and analyze the functional relationships and structures operative in individuals (Lebenseinheiten) and determine how the larger acquired patterns or contexts (erworbene Zusammenhänge) are related to, and differentiate, those structures.[120]

There is a basic circular character in this procedure: the human sciences reflect upon the many acquired contexts in history, and to ground them one begins with the dynamically lived interiority of the individuals and thence proceed to interrelate the results of the many sciences regarding the acquired contexts.[121] The circle is not a logically vicious one, since the attention to the individual is itself a result of the Enlightenment and the demands of our historical epoch

---

[118]Cf. G.S. V, pp. 145, 171-175, 363; VIII, pp. 15-19, 180-182.

[119]Cf. G.S. I, pp. 20f.

[120]Cf. G.S. I, pp. 21, 128f.; V, pp. 151f., 197-201, 180; VII, pp. 3-23, 82f., 135, 279; VIII, pp. 13, 39, 176ff.; Briefwechsel n. 58; on basic structures and acquired contexts, cf. V, pp. 176-184, 200-226. It is necessary to see how for Dilthey the acquired contexts always enter into the cognitional self-reflection, so that it is not merely some type of transcendentalist self-introspection, cf. VII, p. 279: "Man knows himself only in history, never through introspection." And the remarks of Diwald, op. cit., pp. 152f.

[121]Cf. G.S. V, pp. 228f; VII, vii, pp. 152, 262f., 277, 255-258.

to respect the autonomy of human freedom and mediate that autonomy to the sciences.[122] This circular process from the acquired contexts to the individual and then back to the acquired contexts to interrelate them methodologically contains many hypothetical elements. But insofar as the descriptive-analytic elaboration of human interiority provides a methodological foundations, the circle has a certain basis within inner experience itself.[123]

The differentiation between the natural and the cultural sciences, then, parallels that between outer and inner experience. The former are extrorsive, seeking correlations in nature; the latter are introrsively oriented, seeking the correlations of meanings, values, goals constitutive of man in his social and historical reality.[124]

It is in this perspective that Dilthey saw the necessity of an anthropological and psychological description of the dynamic structures of man's constitution and mediation of history. He wavered in his designation of the grounding insofar as he would refer to it as descriptively psychological (to differentiate it from a hypothetical explanatory psychology which remained objectivistic), or as cognitional-theoretical (to emphasize its methodological import), or as philosophical-anthropological (to bring out its foundational interest in truth). Yet in all these designations there is the central fact of the foundational importance of inner experience grounding the differentiation of the cultural sciences from the natural sciences.

C. The Noumenal Residue. M. Riedel has remarked how the ambivalence of Dilthey's critical position is that it is secretly dependent upon the very positions it criticizes.[125]

---

[122]Cf. G.S. I, pp. 14-39; VII, pp. 335-345, 345-347. On the non-logical character of this circular process, cf. Habermas, Erkenntnis und Interesse, pp. 215ff.

[123]Cf. G.S. V, pp. 136f., 142-145, 173-175, 178f., 193f., 197-200, 206, 237-240; VI, p. 145.

[124]Cf. G.S. VII, pp. 79-88, esp. 82f.; also B.A., pp. 251ff.

[125]Cf. M. Riedel, Einleitung, p. 33.

This is certainly true of Dilthey's criticism of Kant's noumenal thing-in-itself. Dilthey energetically criticized the Kantian thing-in-itself as noumenal from the perspective of common sense and its anticipations.[126] This common sense approach was less metaphorically elaborated in Dilthey's 1890 essay on the origins of our belief in the reality of the external world. There too, one sees the intense sensitivity of Dilthey for the anticipations of common sense, and his efforts to articulate this in terms of feeling and action. The experiences of impression and resistance ground our awareness of the transcendent character of their objects.[127] Dilthey experienced the immediate reality of his own self-presence and realized the artificiality of the Kantian construction of pure reason and its ungrounded assertion of an unknowable thing-in-itself. For the anticipations of conscious feeling and willing give us a certainty of the reality of other objects and persons besides ourselves; and this immediate certainty of consciousness in its common-sense anticipations gives the lie to an over intellectualized conceptuality which seeks to give some type of general argument for the existence of things as though it had to. To Dilthey this is a less critical stance inasmuch as it fails to accept the critical significance of experience over thought.[128] This is an effort to "correct" our experiences from the abstractions of our conceptions instead of realizing that the proper critical procedure is just the opposite.[129]

In an essay two years later, 1892, Dilthey traced the relations of experiencing and thinking in the cognitional theoretical logics of the nineteenth century. He found in

---

[126]B.A., p. 20. Cf. Riedel, Einleitung, pp. 38ff.

[127]Cf. G.S. V, pp. 90-138. Cf. H. A. Hodges, op. cit., pp. 51ff.

[128]G.S. V, p. 126: "This expectation of necessarily deducing the existence of something transcending consciousness from the reality of consciousness itself has arisen within insufficiently critical thought."

[129]Cf. ibid., p. 127.

such quasi-Neokantian positions as Sigwart's and Lotze's
a dichotomy between experience and thinking: "This school
of Kant acknowledges the infeasibility of empiricism. It
replaces the latter with a primordial duality between perceptions and the activity of thought."[130] Dilthey sees how,
for these Kantians, the relation between experience and
thought can only be grounded through an external postulate –
which postulate is a telelogical order grounded in God.[131]
This Dilthey rejects as just another, indeed more subtle,
form of metaphysically uncritical thought-patterns. It is
an attempt to counteract empiricism with <u>hypothetical</u>
<u>constructions</u> instead of with the reality of inner experience,
i.e., the immediate self-presence of conscious life.[132]

This is precisely the crucial point in Dilthey's
own position: did he manage to uncover the genetic relation
between experience and the level of concepts and judgments?
His very differentiation of the natural and cultural sciences
contains elements of a rift between thought and experience
insofar as he emphasized the impossibility of grounding the
natural sciences since they were explanatory constructs of
objective realities which could be experienced in impression
and resistance, but could only be hypothetically known as

---

[130] Cf. <u>G.S.</u> V, p. 79. The essay is pp. 74-89.

[131] Cf. <u>ibid.</u>, pp. 79-81, 80-81: "And as with the
self-certainty of thought, so also that of willing leads
to the presupposition of a metaphysical structure. We are
led to demand a harmony between the imperatives of duty and
the laws of nature: a postulate which implies the idea of
a rational teleological order grounded in God."

[132] <u>G.S.</u> V, pp. 83f.: "Conscious life itself, living
spontaneity, behind which I cannot penetrate, contains the
structures with which all experience and thought is
explicated. <u>Herein lies the decisive point for the entire
possibility of knowledge.</u> Only because in life itself and
in experience is the entire structure contained, which then
emerges in the forms, principles and categories of
thought - only because in conscious living and experience can
these be analytically demonstrated - is there a knowledge
of reality.... If there is more than merely hypothetical
knowledge, then a genetic relationship must exist between
perception and thought - a relation which sublates the
duality of the foundations of knowledge, and so changes merely
hypothetical, presupposed, and postulated relationships
into objectively valid ones."

constructs. Despite his polemic against Kant, then, there are strong overtones of the thing-in-itself in Dilthey's statement:

> There does not exist a truth of the external object as a correspondence of the image with a reality, for this reality is not present in any consciousness, and thus is beyond any comparison. One cannot will to know how the object appears when no one subsumes it in his consciousness.[133]

This acceptance of the rift between subject and object, self and world, in terms of the natural sciences would break down the unity of experience, of identity and non-identity, unless Dilthey was able to show how for the human sciences there is a real and true mediation of the immediate experience of self-presence in conceiving and judging and deciding. But if he showed this in terms of the human sciences, why not apply it also to the natural sciences and the knowing operative in them? As we shall see, Dilthey did not fully succeed in this. He was apparently overpowered by the reality of immediate self-awareness, but seemed unable to articulate this for knowing. Instead, he referred to that immediacy as a "self-feeling" and centered his description of immediacy around feeling.

It is not surprising that in his later writings there emerges a tension, a contradiction, between science and "life." In the measure that Dilthey was unable to mediate the immediacy of living consciousness in his cognitional "Selbstbesinnung," to that degree he would find it difficult to integrate - or genetically relate - the human sciences to life. He could masterfully criticize the implicit metaphysical objectivism in the transcendentalism, positivism, and empiricism of his day; but he himself seems to fall into an objectivism of his own since he is unable to conceptually and judgmentally mediate the truth of immediacy. Hence the difficulty in explicating the demand for "general validity" on the part of the cultural sciences with their immediate relation to life.[134] Dilthey explains how the cultural scientist is

---

[133]Cf. references in note 113 above.

[134]Cf. _G.S._ VII, p. 137.

conditioned by his acquired contexts and how this goes contrary to the demands of science.[135]

The efforts of Dilthey to develop a theory of empathy to handle the relation of the cultural sciences to life is understandable from the centrality of feeling in his notion of inner experience. Yet it was inadequate as a mediation between the immediacy of conscious interiority and the performance of science, whether natural or cultural. As a result one has a tendency in Dilthey to insist upon the validity of experience, but to be incapable of critically mediating that validity to the sciences.

It is important to keep this aspect of Dilthey's position in mind when discussing the cognitional theoretical self-reflection of Dilthey's critique of historical reason. It indicates how Dilthey and Lonergan can both insist upon the centrality of the subject in elaborating a critical method, yet how they differ in the fulfilling of that program. Both Gadamer and Habermas have called attention to the disparity between science and life in Dilthey's position. But where Gadamer criticizes the attempt of Dilthey to mediate science and life, Habermas praises Dilthey for the attempt but sees it hampered by an implicit positivism in its notion of objective truth.[136] My own position is closer to Habermas' than Gadamer's in this regard. However, if I am correct in tracing the contradiction between science and life to the noumenal residue in Dilthey's notion of the unity of experience, then there is more than a need to see, as Habermas puts it, "that the objectivity of understanding is possible only within the role of a reflective participant in an ongoing communications process."[137] For the problem becomes one, not simply of differentiating interests (as with Habermas), but of critically grounding those interests in a praxis-oriented articulation of the subject. For it is only in that way that one could sublate the noumenal without falling

---

[135] Cf. ibid.

[136] Cf. Gadamer, Wahrheit und Methode, pp. 218-228; Habermas, Erkenntnis und Interesse, pp. 224-233.

[137] Habermas, ibid., p. 227.

into either an absolute knowledge or a critical reflection
unable to mediate its own foundations.[138]

Such a metacritique of Dilthey's position would be in
the name of the beginnings he initiated in his own critique
of objectivism. It would emphasize the centrality of the
subject-as-subject more than Dilthey himself did, and it
would do this without falling into the abstract ontologism
of Gadamer's criticisms, nor into the equally abstract
naturalism of Habermas. In this aspect at least, the
methodological position of Lonergan corresponds to the
theological position of Johannes Metz in the latter's
criticism of abstractions in the false objectivism of both
technocratic positivism and liberal marxism.[139] The noumenal
residue in Dilthey, as in Kant, is theologically no more
than a secularized shadow of the massive reality of mystery
in the subject. But this mystery, if it is not to be
uncritically affirmed, must be based upon a thorough critique
of any appeal to the noumenal as an arbitrary limitation of
human knowing and acting. Theology must not seek to uncover
some "gap" in the foundations of the natural or cultural
sciences in the hope of thereby restoring its own prestige. On
the contrary, only a fully autonomous foundation can truly
serve as a foundation for the sciences and theology. The
dialectic of the Enlightenemnt must not be short-circuited.
In this task Lonergan's notion of the exigencies of meaning
as not only systematic, critical and methodical but also
transcendent is a fruitful approach to articulating the
subject of both history and method.

5. Patterns of Experience as the Foundation for Meta-Method

The final section of the previous Chapter has already
indicated how, for Lonergan, the methodical exigence cannot
base itself upon an exclusive analogy of science. It must
seek to integrate the complexities of both the narrative
world of common sense and the systematic world of the

---

[138]Cf. R. Bubner's "Was ist kritische Theorie?" in
Hermeneutik und Ideologiekritik, pp. 160-209.

[139]Cf. J. B. Metz, "Erlösung und Emanzipation,"
Stimmen der Zeit 191/3 (März, 1973), pp. 171-184.

sciences. In order to do justice to such complexities within the context of the subject-as-subject, it was necessary for Lonergan to uncover the dynamic relationships between experience and conceptualization, between consciousness and knowing.[140] For knowing does involve experiencing, and although the notion (of experience) is, as Gadamer has remarked, the most ambiguous notion of contemporary philosophy, nevertheless Lonergan has striven to go behind such notions to the experiencing itself.[141]

Lonergan did not begin his effort at grounding method by differentiating the natural and human sciences. For he clearly saw how any scientific activity is itself the result of activities of conscious intentionality as experienced. He was fond of quoting Albert Einstein's dictum that one should pay more attention to what scientists do rather than to what they say.[142] That scientific "doing" involves highly complex patterns of experiencing. The "saying" however, is more often than not the result of scientists appealing to untenable philosophical notions of experience and knowledge in order to communicate in a nonscientific way what they are doing. Lonergan, while accepting a basic differentiation between the natural and human sciences in terms of mediated (natural) and constitutive (human) meaning, nonetheless cannot accept that differentiation in terms of Dilthey's analysis of extrorsive and introrsive experiencing.[143] Such a dichotomy of experiencing is traceable to a naive understanding of the experiences involved in the acquisition of knowledge. It leads to the Kantian verdict of the unknowability of the thing-in-itself with its consequent phenomenon-noumenon

---

[140]Cf. Chapter Two, pp. 158ff.; M.i.T., pp. 6-25; Insight, pp. 3-32.

[141]Cf. Gadamer, Wahrheit und Methode, pp. 329-344.

[142]Cf. Albert Einstein, Essays in Science (New York: 1934), p. 12: "If you want to find out anything from the theoretical physicists about the methods they use, I advise you to stick closely to one principle: don't listen to their words, fix your attention on their deeds."

[143]Cf. Chapter Three, pp. 233-249 and references

bifurcation.[144] This is of central importance, not only for the human sciences, but also for the natural sciences. A proper methodological articulation of the unity of identity and non-identity, of self and world, of subject and object must be set in a context that is neither one of complete identity nor one of complete non-identity. The context as a true unity must instead be one of reality; for "we know the real before we know such a difference within the real as the difference between subject and object."[145] The bridge building, which Dilthey complained philosophers had been doing since Descartes' dichotomy between self and world, vanishes.[146] Admittedly, the self-appropriation of conscious experience to which Lonergan devotes his method, is only a beginning, yet:

> It is a necessary beginning, for unless one breaks the duality in one's knowing, one doubts that understanding correctly is knowing. Under the pressure of that doubt, either one will sink into the bog of a knowing that is without understanding, or else one will cling to understanding but sacrifice knowing on the altar of an immanentism, an idealism, a relativism. From the horns of that dilemma one escapes only through the discovery (and one has not made it yet if one has no clear memory of its startling strangeness) that there are two quite different realisms, that there is an incoherent realism, half animal and half human, that poses as a half-way house between materialism and idealism and, on the other hand, that there is an intelligent and reasonable realism between which and materialism the half-way house is idealism.[147]

A. <u>Consciousness and Knowledge</u>. The experience of consciousness is, of course, identical insofar as experiencing is necessarily in some fashion conscious. For Lonergan it is by adverting to this conscious quality of all experiencing that he can erect the foundations of his method. There is an immediacy of the subject to himself in all conscious

---

given there.

[144]Cf. Chapter Three, pp. 249-254 and references given there.

[145]Cf. Lonergan, <u>Verbum: Word and Idea in Aquinas</u>, p. 88.

[146]Cf. <u>Briefwechsel</u> note 48.

[147]Cf. <u>Insight</u>, p. xxviii.

activity; it is so immediate that calling attention to it
often seems strange. Relying upon the genetic psychology
of J. Piaget, Lonergan shows how the world of immediacy
common to infants is a world bounded by the narrow horizons
of what the infant can immediately experience.[148] But such
an immediacy is not static, it is a formally dynamic structure
open to further differentiations of operations and integrations of those differentiations. The unity of the subject-as-
subject may be called a self-assembling, self-constituting
formal dynamism. Thus to the immediate operations of seeing,
hearing, smelling, touching and tasting of the infant,
there accrues an inquiring, imagining, understanding and
conceiving as the child begins to learn language and is
thereby gradually introduced into the far wider world
mediated by the meaning of language. Within this world,
however, the child is still unable to differentiate fairy
tales, myths, and other imaginative stories from the human
historical realities of day-to-day living. The differentiation of consciousness and knowledge is still inchoate.
Gradually the conscious experience of reflecting, weighing
the evidence, and judging enables the growing human person
to distinguish fact from fancy. This process of differentiation and integration leads, in the young adult, to an
increased reliance upon the conscious experiences of deliberating, deciding, and acting as he or she begins to move from
the world mediated by meaning to the world of his or her
history which will be constituted by those actions.[149]

This admittedly schematic presentation of the complexities involved in the formally dynamic structures of conscious
experiencing, highlights recurrent structures within human
consciousness. Those structures of experiencing-understanding-
judging-deciding are common to every human historical subject
as he or she is a subject. They are also involved in the
acquisition of knowledge. For the context of unity as one
of reality means that the subject is within a world and that
that world occupies the subject's attention much more commonly

---

[148]Cf. _M.i.T._, p. 76; _Collection_, pp. 221-239.

[149]Cf. _Collection_, pp. 240-267.

than the subject's own subjectivity.[150]

Knowing is also a formally dynamic structure as is consciousness. By and large, the structures of knowing and consciousness are not adverted to and so the intentional presence of the objects (world) is the presence of a spectacle to the spectator: "taking a good look at the object."[151] This extroverted, naive notion of knowing does not only influence common misconceptions of what knowledge is all about, but it also, according to Lonergan, underpins both the empiricist analyses of human and scientific knowledge and the idealist analyses. Where the empiricist believes that knowing is possible through an actual or highly sophisticated "good look," the idealist realizes that the things-in-themselves cannot be so intuited and therefore restricts knowledge to either the phenomenal world of appearance or an immanentist world of ideas.[152]

Lonergan's analysis of human consciousness and knowing in his book Insight, effectively cuts through the full range of such misconceptions. Indeed, he holds that once the open and formally dynamic structures of consciousness are properly understood, the resulting self-appropriation of one's own conscious intentionality can ground a critique of all other philosophies whether those philosophies concern the world of common sense or the world of science and theory.[153] Even more directly than Dilthey, Lonergan holds that such self-appropriation does not involve any mode of introspection in the sense that the subject, instead of looking outward, would look inward and discover the a priori forms of his own intuiting. "Any such effort is introspecting, attending to the subject; and what is found is, not the subject as subject, but only the subject as object; it is the subject as subject that does the finding."[154] It was such introspection which led Kant to conclude that introspection could only give us

---

[150]Cf. Insight, pp. 352-356.

[151]Cf. Insight, pp. 250-254; Collection, pp. 223-236.

[152]Collection, p. 235.   [153]Insight, pp. 3-347.

[154]Collection, p. 227.

knowledge of phenomena rather than of the reality of self.[155]
What is required in order to know self-consciousness is a
heightening of consciousness.

> To heighten one's presence to oneself, one does not
> introspect; one raises the level of one's activity.
> If one sleeps and dreams, one is present to oneself
> as the frightened dreamer. If one wakes, one becomes
> present to oneself, not as moved but as moving, not
> as felt but as feeling, not as seen but as seeing. If
> one is puzzled and wonders and inquires, the empirical
> subject becomes an intellectual subject as well. If
> one reflects and considers the evidence, the empirical
> and intellectual subject becomes a rational subject,
> an incarnate reasonableness. If one deliberates and
> chooses, one has moved to the level of the rationally
> conscious, free, responsible subject that by his
> choices makes himself what he is to be and his world
> what it is to be.[156]

The experiences of knowing are the experiences of conscious
activity itself and the latter is known inasmuch as a heightened attention of the subject-as-subject discloses the related
and recurrent operations of experiencing, understanding,
judging, deciding and acting. It is only insofar as these
operations are known that the subject-as-object is truly
a knowledge of the subject-as-subject.

For Lonergan to base his meta-methodology upon the
subject-as-subject does not involve any Hegelian appeal to
some absolute knowledge or subject of world process as
Geist. The relation of knowing to consciousness as an
ongoing, open and formally dynamic structure implies that
there is no purely objective term of subject of knowledge.
Lonergan expresses this ongoing dynamism of consciousness
as the unrestricted desire to know. There will be no end to
the questions arising within individual lives and within the
total history of mankind. For every question answered, more
questions emerge, and it is upon the basis of this questioning
drive or unrestricted desire to know, that Lonergan bases the
central thrust of his entire methodology rather than upon some
particular answers or concepts.[157]

---

[155]Cf. Kant, Kritik der reinen Vernunft, B 275-279;
Ibid., A 117; Ibid., B 156.

[156]Collection, p. 227.

[157]Cf. M.i.T., pp. 13-20, 11, 105, 110, 116-119; Insight,

B. The Patterns of Experience. Attention to conscious experiencing means that Lonergan is well aware of the limitations of knowledge as knowledge. Human consciousness is not some computer-like apparatus concerned only with processing conceptual or perceptual inputs and acting upon them as outputs. Rather, the human subject is capable of many varied patterns of conscious experiencing. We have already seen how the dialectic of the Enlightenment has tended to reduce human praxis to mechanistic forms of technique.[158]

Lonergan has called attention to the fruitfulness of the humanist psychologies associated with the third force in psychology initiated by A. Maslow.[159] Maslow has shown how in a highly technocratic industrialized society like our own, there is a tendency to reduce human intersubjective relationships to roles. Human subjects are increasingly led to experience themselves as fulfillers of certain roles within a megamachine society concerned only with the smooth functioning of its own structures. Like cogs in a machine the roles are dispensed and fulfilled by subjects increasingly inhibited from truly knowing themselves as subjects. A schizoid condition results inasmuch as the subject renounces his or her own subjectivity in order to function properly within the objective realm of social relationships. This objective realm is defined by an increasingly artificial satisfaction of basic deficiency needs such as those for food, shelter, sex, security, belongingness, and esteem. The growth needs of the human subject such as needs for meaningfulness, order, justice, wholeness, individuality, beauty, goodness, truth and love are neglected or are cynically identified with deficiency needs.[160] The problem faced by third-force

---

pp. xi, xiv, 4, 9, 74, 220-222, 348-350, 380-381, 528, 550, 596, 599-600, 623-624, 636-639, 642, 682, 701-702, 738.

[158]Cf. Chapter One, pp. 46-49; Chapter Two, pp. 93ff and references given there.

[159]Cf. M.i.T., pp. 38-39; Frank Goble, The Third Force (New York, 1971); on the socio-political dimension of Maslow, cf. Charles Hampden-Turner, The Radical Man.

[160]Cf. Frank Goble, The Third Force, pp. 37-53.

psychologies is how roles and the deficiency needs can be integrated within patterns of experience which give at least equal importance to the growth needs of the human subject. Lonergan's treatment of the patterns of experiencing offers a fruitful heuristic integration of such roles within growth patterns.

If by experience we refer to the stream of activities performed in our waking hours, then the patterns are revealed in the conation, interests and purposes which give the stream of experience its direction. Such direction is not total or univocal since there are a multiplicity of conations, interests and purposes. By patterns is meant the intelligible relations that link together sequences of sensations, memories, images, conations, emotions, inquiries, insights, conceptions, judgments, decisions and human movements and actions.[161] Lonergan sees six such basic patterns of conscious experiencing.

First, there is the _biological_ pattern of experience. Here the sequences of activities all converge toward the satisfaction of physiological and security deficiency needs. These center about the activities of intussusception and reproduction or, when the organism is threatened, self-preservation.[162] When the physiological needs for air, water, food, sleep, shelter, sex cover the predominant interests of a group, then belongingness and esteem are measured according to how individuals contribute to the safety and security with which those needs are met. One had here not only the Darwinian criterion of the survival of the fittest, but also its more sophisticated counterpart in contemporary social criteria based upon how well individuals contribute to the secure functioning of industrial and mechanistic processes.[163] Hence the tendency, all too evident today, to reduce the sexual dimension to ever more elaborate

---

[161] Cf. _Collection,_ pp. 221-239; _M.i.T.,_ p. 6-13.

[162] Cf. _Insight,_ pp. 181-184.

[163] Cf. Lewis Mumford, _The Myth of the Machine--The Pentagon of Power_ (New York, 1970), pp. 51-76, 300-320.

techniques of mutual manipulation.[164] Extroversion is a basic characteristic of the biological pattern of experience. There is little concern with the immanent activities of living.

Second, there is the _aesthetic_ pattern of experience. When physiological needs are sufficiently met, human experience can readily skip into that symbolic activity associated with the play of children, the sports of youth, the catchiness of a tune, the rhythms of a dance, the wonder at beauty. Art liberates experience from both the drag of physiological purposiveness and from the wearying constraints of factual knowing.[165] Art is the objectification of the purely experiential pattern as S. Langer's _Feeling and Form_ illustrates.[166] It is an escape from the conventional and routine to allow experience to create its own rhythms and cadences, shapes and forms. The spontaneity of experience in the aesthetic pattern witnesses to an inherent thrust of experience beyond the biological; the discipline that spontaneity must undergo if it is to express good art witnesses to the inherent intellectuality of human experience - if by intellectuality one means the "significant forms" of aesthetic experience.[167]

In the aesthetic pattern, sequences of conscious activities converge toward the expression in symbols of all facets of experience itself. Langer calls this a purely experiential pattern because the experience in question is not functioning primarily in an instrumental manner, i.e., sensation and imagination are not geared to aid in fulfilling various roles, but rather toward expressing their own spontaneity. Those expressions, however, can all too easily become routine as they are separated from the creative aesthetic experience itself and are increasingly integrated

---

[164]Cf. R. May, _Love and Will_; George F. Gilder, _Sexual Suicide_ (New York, 1973).

[165]Cf. _Insight_, pp. 184-185; _M.i.T._, pp. 61-69.

[166]_M.i.T._, pp. 61-62.

[167]S. Langer, _Feeling and Form_, pp. 3-44.

within a process of mechanistic reproduction.[168]   Adorno
has called attention to this devaluation of the aesthetic
pattern in the mass produced culture industries of contemporary society.[169]

Third, there is the _intellectual_ pattern of experience.
The liberation from biological routines in aesthetic experience is heightened even more in the intellectual pattern.
Here the inherent intellectuality of human experience
emerges. Sense and imagination, even the unconscious,
become an adaptive collaborator with the spirit of inquiry
and reflection.[170] So, for example, a scientist or philosopher bent upon a solution to a problem illustrates
how senses and imagination have been trained over the years
of study and observation to become absorbed in the questions
at hand. In this pattern of experience the sequence of
activities of sensing, remembering, imagining, feeling,
inquiring, understanding, conceiving, judging, deciding and
acting all converge on the expression of questions and their
solutions. The joy of discovery not only follows the long
hours of investigation, but is also tempered by the responsibility and further questions posed by the discovery
itself.[171]

It is within the intellectual pattern of experience
that the systematic exigence moves the human subject beyond
the familiar sights and sounds of common sense living, away
from the immediacy of sense into worlds of obscure insight
and complicated theories. Patterns of perception change and
new universes of discourse open up. Symbolism loses its
ties with perceived objects and forms to become an adaptive

---

[168]Cf. T. Adorno, _Ohne Leitbild: Parva Aesthetica_
(Frankfurt, 1969), pp. 60-70; 168-192.

[169]Cf. T. Adorno, "Kultur und Verwaltung," in _Kritische
Theorie der Gesellschaft_ (Frankfurt Beiträge zur Soziologie,
Band 10, Frankfurt 1962); Max Horkheimer and Theodor Adorno,
Dialektik der Aufklärung (Frankfurt, 1969), pp. 128-176.

[170]Cf. _Insight_, pp. 185-186.

[171]Cf. _Insight_, pp. 596-604; G. Picht, _Wahrheit,
Vernunft, Verantwortung_ (Stuttgart, 1969), pp. 318-342.

instrument of observation, hypothesis formation and verification of intelligible (but non-perceivable) correlations.[172] Reality is no longer synonymous with body and knowing is no longer a question of intuition but rather a verification. Lonergan has called attention to how it has taken modern science several generations to free itself from perceptualist illusions. This is dramatized in the invariant four dimensional interval of space-time in Einstein's Special Relativity Theory ($ds^2 = dx^2 + dy^2 + dz^2 - c^2dt^2$), where the correlation of space ($x + y + z$) with time (t) is highly intelligible and explanatory yet cannot be imagined in any perceptual Euclidean geometry.[173] The worlds of sub-atomic physics and Quantum Mechanics have only accentuated the difference between reality as perceived and reality as understood and explained.[174]

The emergence of these two notions of reality within the systematic exigence gives rise to the critical exigence: how to relate the world of common sense experience and its reality to the world of scientific theory and explanation. Is one really real and the other not? Does the sun really rise in the east? Or, to use Eddington's example, is this table colored, solid, bulky, or is it a multitude of colorless wavicles so small that the table is mostly empty space? This critical problem is not only apparent in the natural sciences of physics, chemistry and biology, but also in the human sciences like psychology and sociology. For example, do I act for the reasons I give, or from some to me unknown, and so unconscious, motivations.[175] Such critical questions can only be answered by properly attending to the open and

---

[172]Cf. Insight, pp. 7-19, 250-254; M.i.T., pp. 81-85.

[173]Cf. Heelan, Quantum Mechanics and Objectivity, pp. 3-22, 169-179.

[174]Patrick Heelan, "Towards a Hermeneutic of Pure and Applied Science: An Essay in the Phenomenology of Scientific Activity," European Philosophy Today (Dublin, 1971); Insight, pp. 254-267.

[175]The notion of the unconscious in Freud is within Lonergan's understanding of empirical consciousness, cf. Insight, pp. 456-458; M.i.T., pp. 33-34.

formally dynamic structures of human consciousness and human knowing.[176] The desire to know within the intellectual pattern is accompanied by a certain fear of knowing.[177] For knowledge not only creates the critical questions about reality but also gives power, creating the danger of a destructive hubris, as the stories of Prometheus and Faust poignantly illustrate, and the dialectic of the Enlightenment now confronting technocratic society frighteningly demonstrates.[178]

The fourth pattern of experience is the ethical or moral pattern. Not only do the growth needs in man lead him to artistic play and intellectual inquiry, but also to decision and action. Within this pattern the sequence of conscious activities converges on the problems of deliberation, decision and action.[179] The dialectic of Enlightenment has led to a crisis of will in the moral pattern of responsibility. Freud in psychology, along with Marxism and liberal behaviorism in sociology, have reduced all decisions to unconscious determinisms. Not even the behaviorists or human scientists can agree - let alone the person on the couch or in the street - how men should decide. Yet every day we are confronted with the need to choose. Most people tend to let emotive standards of pleasure and pain act as norms for their decisions and actions. The results are an increasing disregard of growth values and a regressive reliance upon defensive deficiency needs and their values.[180] People tend to follow the crowd, lose any self-direction, experience a powerlessness and drifting at the core of their own living.[181]

---

[176]Cf. Chapter Three, pp. 409-412 and the references given there.

[177]Cf. Chapter Three, pp. 412-415 and the references given there.

[178]Max Horkheimer and Theodor Adorno, Dialektik der Aufklärung, pp. 50-87.

[179]Cf. M.i.T., p. 286; Insight, pp. 607-619.

[180]Cf. Chapter Three, pp. 409-412 and the references given there.

[181]Cf. R. May, Power and Innocence (New York, 1972).

If this is the denial of the moral and ethical pattern within common sense experience, such a denial is no less evident within the world of technology and science. Pollution, limits of natural resources, limits to growth, along with the specter of nuclear war, mean that men must become aware of the necrophilic tendencies within contemporary technocracy and convert its technology to more consciously biophilic purposes.[182] But where can we find the moral norms for such a re-humanization? The ethical dilemma of contemporary man leads to the same conclusion as the critical dilemma discussed in the intellectual pattern of experience. For such norms cannot be found in extrinsic nature but only within ourselves, within conscious intentionality and the dynamisms which foster creative self-transcendence.[183] When pleasure and pain become the ultimate standards then emotions and feelings become warped and dead, as is evident in the paradox of sex without passion, pleasure without enjoyment.[184] When the structures of technological efficiency become the norm, then human action is reduced to an arid conceptualistic mechanism of roles and manipulative techniques.

The fifth basic pattern of experience is the _religious_. Implicit in the previous three patterns has been how the need for growth within experience involves a dynamic "going beyond" or transcendence. The aesthetic pattern involves going beyond the biological routines, the intellectual pattern involves going beyond common sense expectations, the moral pattern involves going beyond emotive criteria. What is gone beyond, or transcended, is not left behind but is rather integrated within a higher pattern of experienced meaning and value. So aesthetics transforms the fulfillment of physiological needs into the symbolic activities of meals, courtship, dance, story. Intellectual activities transform common sense operations into the intricate patterns of observation,

---

[182]Erich Fromm, The Revolution of Hope: Toward a Humanized Technology (New York, 1968).

[183]Cf. Insight, pp. 601-602; M.i.T., pp. 34-41.

[184]Cf. references in note 164 above; also Insight, p. 596; M.i.T., pp. 34-36.

hypothesis formation, and experimental verification. Moral deliberation transforms human actions into quests for worth and value.[185] The religious pattern of experience emerges when man's sequence of activities converge on the wonder and thrust grounding such a process of transcendence. Humankind is oriented into mystery, into the known unknown.[186]

Within this context religion is not a deficiency need, a mere projection of unfulfilled wishes, but an integral dimension of human growth.[187] It is a recognition that man's striving for freedom, meaning, value, love is not running counter to the universe. That there is an ultimate life, goodness, beauty, and truth grounding all conscious striving.[188] Even the experiences of atheism, of absurdity and nausea, bear witness to this religious dimension. For, if there was not any ultimate meaning, value and goodness somehow present within the conscious depths of man, how could he possibly experience nausea or absurdity? It would be like asking that man experience hunger without conceding that he has any digestive system oriented towards food.[189]

The religious pattern of experience allows the full sweep of elemental wonder to well up from the depths of human becoming; it experiences that wonder and mystery of living as ultimately good and holy and creative. Man, as the threshold where the universe emerges into consciousness, is not alone. A dimension of peace and joy pervades his being; in prayer and quiet he is invited to experience an ultimate goodness, gentleness, and loveableness in the universe. The enigma of evil, of suffering and death call out for the reality of a redemption which would affirm the meaning and

---

[185]Cf. Insight, pp. 636-639.

[186]Ibid., pp. 531-534, 639-644.

[187]Cf. M.i.T., pp. 104-105; A. H. Maslow, The Farther Reaches of Human Nature (New York, 1973), pp. 269-279.

[188]Cf. M.i.T., pp. 101-103.

[189]Cf. R. D. Laing, The Divided Self (New York, 1969), pp. 27-65; 147-220.

and value of his growth.[190]

Thus religion, despite its many perversions in history, is not contrary to man's striving for aesthetic creativity, his vast quest for scientific knowledge, or his moral search for meaning and value. Instead it is at one with the drive for further growth and the unrestricted desire to know that underpins human historical experience.[191] Quietly man is beckoned to become fully himself so that he may ultimately transcend or go beyond even his present stage of consciousness.[192] The transcendental exigence is not inimical to the methodical, critical, or systematic exigencies; it is instead the ultimate affirmation of their worth and value.[193]

The sixth pattern of experience is the _dramatic_. None of the above patterns of experience are continuous in human living. Indeed, many do not even experience one or another pattern in any appreciable degree. Prior to art and science, to morality and religion, there are the tasks set by everyday living. Those tasks are endowed by men with a certain artistry and knowledge, a certain goodness and mystery. These life styles vary from culture to culture, from one group to another within a society or culture. It is in such daily living that we find the primordial drama glimpsed in theater and film, in novels and poetry.[194] In the dramatic pattern the sequences of activities of sensing, imagining, inquirying, understanding, judging, deciding, and acting converge on the tasks to be accomplished. And the quality of the life drama will depend upon how differentiated the participants are in the other patterns of experiencing.[195]

In the previous chapter we have already discussed how

---

[190]Cf. _Insight_, pp. 688-696.

[191]Cf. _M.i.T._, p. 108.

[192]Langdon Gilkey, _Naming the Whirlwind: The Renewal of God-Language_ (New York, 1969); Sebastian Moore, _God Is a New Language_ (London, 1968).

[193]Cf. _Insight_, pp. 83-85.

[194]Cf. _Insight_, pp. 187-189.

[195]Cf. _Insight_, pp. 189-191.

the dramatic pattern of living in contemporary societies is marked by the dialectic of the Enlightenment, on how the tendency toward mechanization and manipulative calculation tends to reduce human interaction to role playing, minimizing the humanizing growth of freedom and responsibility. For there is within the drama of group living not only the possibility of attentiveness but of inattentiveness not only the possibility of intelligence but of stupidity, not only the possibility of rationality but of irrationality, not only the possibility of responsibility but of irresponsibility. As the latter possibilities are realized bias and scotosis result.[196] Individual and group bias is all too evident in racism and sexism, exploitation and repression, in the prejudice with which one group seeks its own advantage over another.

If the descriptions of the other patterns have appeared somewhat idealistic, it is because they are all too easily infected by dramatic bias and scotosis. Artistic symbol and play can sell its soul to the highest bidder, so that the costumes are gorgeous and the lighting superb, but there is no real play. Science and technology can mask its own refusal of insight and responsibility in the trappings of a reductionist positivism only too ready to dance to the tune of greedy mandarins.[197] Morality can become the prerogative of a bigoted puritanism which all too easily can collapse into hedonism and consumerism. Religion seems a facile prey to legitimatizing group and national political and economic biases, as is evident in crusades, religious wars, colonialism, and the sanctioning of capitalism.[198]

Lonergan mentions the functions of satire and humor in

---

[196] Cf. Insight, pp. 191-203.

[197] Cf. Noam Chomsky, American Power and the New Mandarins (New York, 1969); also references given in notes 168-169 above.

[198] Carl Amery, Die Kapitulation oder Deutscher Katholizismus heute (Hamburg, 1963); Helmut Gollwitzer, Die reichen Christen und der arme Lazarus (München, 1969); David O. Moberg, The Great Reversal - Evangelism versus Social Concern (Philadelphia, 1972).

attempting to counteract bias and scotosis.[199] The longer
cycles of decline generated by alienation from attentiveness,
intelligence, rationality, and responsibility in general bias
can only be met by a cosmopolis committed to the demands of
attentiveness, intelligence, reasonableness, and responsibility.[200] He sums up what he means by cosmopolis:

> It is a dimension of consciousness, a heightenend
> grasp of historical origins, a discovery of historical
> responsibilities. It is not something altogether new,
> for the Marxist has been busy activating the class-
> consciousness of the masses and, before him, the liberal
> had succeeded in indoctrinating men with the notion of
> progress. Still, it possesses its novelty, for it is not
> simpliste. It does not leap from a fact of development
> to a belief in automatic progress nor from a fact of
> abuse to an expectation of an apocalyptic utopia reached
> through an accelerated decline. It is the higher syn-
> thesis of the liberal thesis and the Marxist anti-
> thesis. It comes to minds prepared for it by these
> earlier views, for they have taught man to think
> historically. It comes at a time when the total-
> itarian fact and threat have refuted the liberals and
> discredited the Marxists. It stands on a basic analysis
> of the compound-in-tension that is man; it confronts
> problems of which men are aware; it invites the vast
> potentialities and pent-up energies of our time to
> contribute to their solution by developing an art and
> a literature, a theatre and a broadcasting, a journalism
> and a history, a school and a university, a personal
> depth and a public opinion, that through appreciation
> and criticism give men of common sense the opportunity
> and help they need and desire to correct the general
> bias of their common sense.[201]

In the previous chapter the final section showed how Lonergan's notion of cosmopolis, together with the basic related
and recurrent operations of conscious intentionality, can
form the elements of a metascientific feedback model.[202] It
would be the task of the functional metascientific specialty
of communications to attend to the development of what Lonergan refers to as a post-scientific literature which would impart the insights of science and scholarship to contemporary
cultures, a task already called for by C. P. Snow and

---

[199]Insight, pp. 624-626.

[200]Cf. Insight, pp. 225-244.

[201]Insight, p. 241.

[202]Cf. Chapter Two, pp. 195-210.

F. Matson.[203]

6. The Ongoing Discovery of Mind in History

One might ask, however, if the attention to consciousness and to patterns of experience is really capable of providing a socio-historical framework. Does it not seem to be just another variant of a privatized cognitional theory? If consciousness does have certain related and recurrent operations and as such underpins knowledge, can this be an effective method for understanding the vast cultural shifts that have occurred in mankind's history? Lonergan has developed notions from Karl Jaspers and Bruno Snell regarding the ongoing discovery of mind. The elements are present in his sketches for a thorough critique of the Hegelian position. Just as Hegel had to presuppose an absolute knowledge in order to construct his phenomenology of mind because he had to eventually sublate all experience in concept, so Lonergan's reversal of the priority from concepts to experience enabled him to avoid such uncritical presuppositions.[204] The third section of this chapter will indicate how the subject-as-subject is able to critically ground its own appropriation. There I shall also enter more into detail regarding the social and historical dimensions of the subject-as-subject.

Now I should indicate how the conscious experiencing at the starting point of Lonergan's methodology is open to disclosing an ongoing discovery of mind, not as an exercise in some logic of history (Hegelian, Marxist, or otherwise), but as a hermeneutic mediation from the past into the present in such a way that the dialectical task of the present vis-à-vis the future is not only possible but required. To date, Lonergan has not extensively treated the ongoing discovery of mind and the differentiations of consciousness except in connection with theological doctrines.[205] However, his development of the patterns of experience can be used to

---

[203]Cf. M.i.T., pp. 97-99; C.P. Snow, The Two Cultures (London, 1958); F. W. Matson, The Broken Image (New York, 1966).

[204]Cf. Collection, pp. 252-267; Insight, pp. 372-374.

[205]M.i.T., pp. 305-318.

elaborate a functional typology of historical differentiations. The typology is not dealing with consciousness (in Lonergan's understanding) but with knowledge, i.e., when we say that the moral or intellectual patterns of experience were in very rudimentary stages in primitive or ancient high civilization societies, this does not imply that people in those societies were not intelligent or moral in their conscious living. What it states is that knowledge of, or an expressed reflective inquiry into, those patterns was rudimentary. What we are dealing with here is not the subject-as-subject but the subject-as-object in history.

A. A Historical Typology of the Patterns. Although Lonergan has not delved into such a typology other than in passing references within unpublished materials and a few remarks in his published writings, I do believe that it is in line with his thought to develop a historical typology. The main functional relation is between the dramatic pattern and the one which tended to provide the control of meaning by the dramatic pattern. If we were to take the dramatic pattern as expressive of the socio-historical system as a whole, then we can determine which of the other five patterns, in the fashion of social sub-systems, were functionally primary in the determination of the dramatic pattern.[206] This would give us five basic historical types.

In primitive societies the biological pattern enjoys a functional primacy within the dramatic pattern. Deficiency needs within the biological pattern tend to determine both the aesthetic and the religious patterns of experience. This can be seen in such aesthetic and religious phenomena as cave paintings, ritual burials, fertility rites, fetishes and totems.[207] The biological pattern's functional primacy within the dramatic pattern is especially evident in the time-factoring stories and rituals which measured time within the context of mating, hunting, agricultural seasons and other

---

[206]Cf. T. Parson, The Social System (New York, 1968), pp. 68-112 for an account of social sub-systems.

[207]Cf. Ruth Benedict, Patterns of Culture (New York, 1960); L. Mumford, The Transformations of Man (New York, 1972), pp. 23-35.

activities aimed at meeting the basic needs of the biological pattern.[208] The moral and intellectual patterns are in very rudimentary stages within primitive societies - rudimentary in the sense explained above. Thus we have the following configuration:

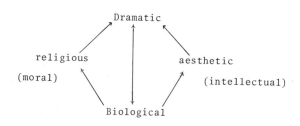

In the <u>Ancient High Civilizations</u>, such as those in Babylon, Egypt, Crete, the Incas and Mayas in Central and South America, and those which sprang up along the Indus and Yellow river valleys of Asia, the biological pattern was no longer functionally primary. The increase in population and food supply had led to a high degree of specialization and we find that the cooperation of these many specialized social activities depended greatly upon writing and tabulation. The ancient forms of writing indicate how it had emerged from the aesthetic pattern of experiencing.[209] The importance given to those who could write, as well as the gradual emergence of codified or written stories outlining the functions and relations within the societies, indicate how the aesthetic pattern of experience had functional primacy within the dramatic. The activities of the aesthetic pattern were geared toward commerce, as a highly complex form of satisfying biological needs, and toward religions, which in their myths, rituals and stories became increasingly concerned with moral and intellectual questions although even here those questions had not emerged with sufficient autonomy to form

---

[208]A. Marshack, <u>The Roots of Civilization</u> (New York, 1972).

[209]Cf. Jacquetta Hawkes, <u>The First Great Civilizations</u> (New York, 1973), pp. 4-16, 38, 41-45, 214-224, 279, 435-437.

an expressed knowledge of the moral and intellectual patterns of experience.[210]   Hence the configuration:

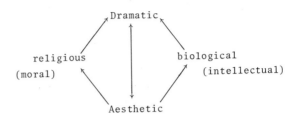

In what K. Jaspers has termed the <u>Axial Period</u> from about 800 to 200 B.C. there seems to have occurred a shift in which various civilizations moved from an aesthetic functional primacy in their dramatic pattern - which could not distinguish between myth and magic on the one hand, and history and science on the other - to an explicit concern with the intellectual and moral patterns of experience.[211] Thus the moral and intellectual patterns became explicit and decisively important in Greece, Israel, Persia, India and China. While there were those philosophers who advocated giving predominance to the intellectual pattern, e.g. Plato's philosopher king, still the dramatic pattern seems to have been dominated by the functional primacy of the moral pattern of experience as explained above. This does not mean that axial civilizations were more moral than others, but that the objective and expressed concern with moral issues played a key role, or was functionally primary, within their dramatic structuring of day-to-day living. So the religious patterns were purified by the Jewish prophets who called attention to the moral dimensions of Yahweh's demands on Israel.[212]   In Hinduism the Law of Karma was developed to show how men lived

---

[210] Cf. Hawkes, <u>The First Great Civilizations</u>; Bruno Snell, <u>Die Entdeckung des Geistes</u> (Hamburg, 1965).

[211] K. Jaspers, <u>Vom Ursprung und Ziel der Geschichte</u> (München, 1964).

[212] F. Heiler, et al., <u>Die Religionen der Menschheit</u> (Stuttgart, 1969), pp. 578-584.

in a moral world. In China, Taoism and Confucianism emphasized
the moral precepts to be followed.[213] In Greece and later
in Rome morality was not only related to the religious, but
was seen in its own right as grounding the socio-political
realm. Thus Plato and Aristotle emphasized the importance
of _phronesis_ as moral prudence in the conduct of personal and
public affairs.[214] In Rome this emphasis can be found not
only in Stoicism but also in the codified legal systems of
Roman Law.[215] Lonergan sees in this axial period the emergence of the systematic exigence, but since we are dealing
with the functional primacy within the dramatic pattern,
the moral rather than the intellectual pattern is primary.

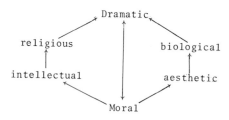

In Western _Medieval_ _Civilization_: the breakdown of
Greco-Roman civilization was accompanied by a resurgence of
religious cults and philosophies, e.g., the introduction into
the west of oriental mystery cults. Christianity prevailed
and gradually formed the basis for a culture which would
integrate the various patterns of experience according to the
functional primacy of the religious pattern. In the high
Middle Ages the religious pattern was articulated with a
heavy reliance upon the legal systems of the Romans, initiated
by the Justinian code, and the philosophical heritage of

---

[213]_Ibid._, pp. 117-127, 228-259, 323.

[214]Eric Voegelin, _Plato and Aristotle_, Vol. III
(Louisiana State University Press, 1957), pp. 315-357; B.
Snell, _Die Entdeckung des Geistes_, pp. 218-257.

[215]Lewis and Reinhold, _Roman Civilization_, Vol. I: _The
Republic_ (New York, 1967), pp. 439-514; Vol. II: _The
Empire_, pp. 532-550.

both Greece and Rome.[216]   Inasmuch as the functional primacy of the religious pattern had to differentiate itself from the moral pattern of socio-political systems, there was the beneficial effect of gradually differentiating church and state. However, this had also a detrimental effect insofar as the Church was conceived on the analogy of the state. This is seen in the reliance of canon law on Roman law, the theories of the "two swords," the Church legally conceived as a "perfect society," the Pope assuming the role of Pontifex Maximus.[217] The functional primacy of the religious pattern within the intellectual is evident in the massive creative emergence of the schools of theology with their systematic quest for an "intellectus fidei."[218] The influence of the religious pattern on the aesthetic can be found in the mystery plays, chant, rituals, architecture and paintings of the time.

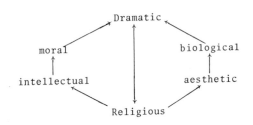

In the late Renaissance there was a breakthrough of the natural sciences toward an explanatory theoretic control of meaning. In the _Enlightenment_ and _Modern Periods_ the rapid expansion of an explanatory control of meaning through plotting physical events on the number field led to an increasing domination or functional primacy of the intellectual pattern of experience. We find this, for instance, in Galileo's

---

[216]Cf. Lewis & Reinhold, _Roman Civilization_, Vol. II: _The Empire_, pp. 552-610.

[217]Cf. Roland H. Bainton, _Christendom_, Vol. I (New York, 1964), pp. 182-223.

[218]Y. Congar, "Théologie" in _DTC_, Vol. XV, col. 346-447; Lonergan, _Verbum: Word and Idea in Aquinas_.

distinction between primary and secondary qualities.[219] But, as we saw in the previous chapter, there also emerged a dialectic of the Enlightenment whereby intelligence itself became assimilated to its own products, i.e., was conceived in mechanomorphic rationalistic terms.[220] Religion came under heavy and in some instances justifiable attack, and decreased in its cognitive and social importance. Morality was grounded on a more or less mechanistically conceived natural law.[221] Thus the Medieval respect for revelation was replaced by a respect for reason, and Divine law was replaced by natural law. The satisfaction of biological needs became increasingly dependent upon the forces of industrial production. Medieval salvation history was replaced by a notion of progress equated with an increasing availability of material goods.[222] Artificial material needs, linked to deficiency needs, became increasingly inculcated by a capitalist consumer advertising so that industrial production could profitably continue to increase.

The aesthetic pattern also came under the influence of rationalist forms (e.g., French classical drama) until the

---

[219] For the telling critique the implications of Relativity give to the widely accepted distinction between primary and secondary qualities, cf. Insight, pp. 84-86, 99, 252-254, 388-389, 413. Descriptive and explanatory conjugates are not other names for these qualities since both conjugates are verifiable. Indeed, descriptions mediate explanations, ibid., pp. 247, 345.

[220] Cf. Chapter One, pp. 46-48 and the references given there; L. Mumford, The Myth of the Machine - The Pentagon of Power.

[221] Peter Gay, The Enlightenment: An Interpretation, Vol. II (New York, 1968); E. Cassirer, Die Philosophie der Aufklärung (Tübingen, 1932), pp. 214-243; E. Block, Naturrecht und menschliche Würde (Frankfurt, 1961); Paul Hazard, European Thought in the Eighteenth Century (London, 1954).

[222] Henri de Lubac, The Drama of Atheist Humanism (New York, 1971), pp. 128ff.; Charles Frankel, The Faith of Reason: The Idea of Progress in the French Enlightenment (New York, 1948); Paul Hazard, European Thought in the Eighteenth Century.

278

Theater of the Absurd heralded a dead end.[223] Indeed, we might say that the scientific revolution was quickly co-opted by the industrial revolution. Positivism, materialism (whether of Marxist or capitalist vintage), determinism and behavioristic reductionism are all hallmarks of a dramatic pattern based upon a mechanomorphic conception of intellect and reason.[224] The gradual absorption of "enlightened" religious attitudes into moral considerations can be found not only in Kant but also in Deism and a Golden Rule American religiosity.[225] Thus we have the following pattern:

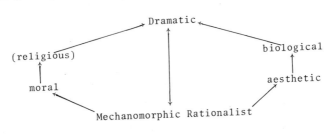

This historical typology of the patterns of experience shows why it was necessary for Lonergan to ground methodology, not upon a differentiation of the human sciences from the natural sciences, but upon an appropriation of the related and recurrent operations of conscious intentionality as those operations can be found in all spheres of human knowing and doing. Especially with the increasing primacy of a mechanomorphic rationalism from the Enlightenment onwards, it would do little good - as German idealism, Dilthey's Lebensphilosophie, phenomenology and existentialism have illustrated - to attempt to isolate some sphere of human subjectivity and immunize it against the increased

---

[223]H. N. Fairchild, Religious Trends in English Poetry Vol. VI: 1920-1965 (New York, 1968); Eugene Goodheart, The Cult of the Ego (Chicago, 1970), Martin Esslin, The Theatre of the Absurd (New York, 1971).

[224]Cf. Chapter One, pp. 46-48 and the references given there.

[225]P. Hazard, op. cit., pp. 377-460; William A. Clebsch, From Sacred to Profane America (New York, 1968).

dominance of empiricism, positivism, or behaviorism. Instead
Lonergan seems to have gone to the crux of the contempoary
crisis by showing how the methods of the natural sciences
are the result of the basic operations of the subject-as-
subject. So in Insight, Lonergan ranges through the fields
of mathematics, geometry, classical physics, quantum
mechanics, biology and some of their major problems in order
to illustrate the presence of the basic related and recurrent
operations of the subject-as-subject, and how a knowledge of
that presence can effectively contribute to the solution of
those problems.[226]

This also clarifies why, in the final section of the
last chapter, I was concerned to show how Lonergan's notion
of functional specialization and his development of the
exigencies of meaning make significant contributions to
present debates in the philosophy of science or metascience.
It will do little good to attempt to offset the dialectic
of the Enlightenment by some insistence on praxis or a
critical philosophy unless one incorporates those concerns
into a thoroughgoing understanding of the natural sciences and
the effect they are having through technology on contemporary
society. This can be seen in the schematic presentation of
the above outlined typology in relation to the emergence and
expansion of human history. Figure 2, adopting some aspects
of Jaspers' diagram of the axial period, offers this overview.

The purpose and main orientation of Lonergan's meta-
methodology seeks to appropriate reflectively the dynamics
of conscious intentionality in such a way that the intellectual pattern of experience might be liberated from mechanomorphic rationalism.[227] For a true self—understanding within
the intellectual pattern applies as well to the natural
sciences and technology as to the human and historical
sciences.[228] As with cosmopolis, the dialectic effects of such

---

[226] Insight, pp. 3-316.

[227] Insight, pp. 238-242; Lewis Mumford, The Myth of the
Machine - The Pentagon of Power; Garrett Barden & Philip
McShane, Towards Self Meaning (Dublin, 1969).

[228] M.i.T., pp. 20-25.

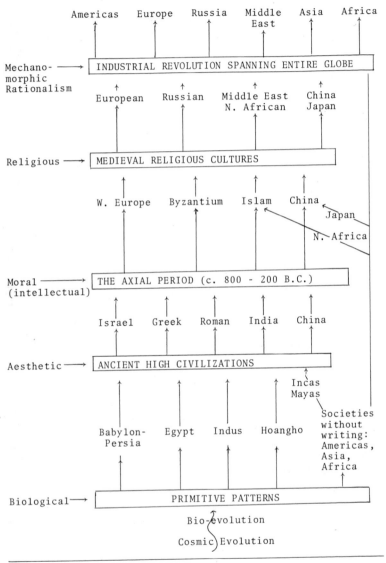

Figure Two: A Historical Overview of the Typology

self-appropriation would be to halt the profit-at-expense-
of-persons ideology which today makes science and technology
the slave of industrial interests. This would also mean a
gradual end to sprawling military-industrial complexes.
L. Mumford has forcefully documented how such a complex
can arise within a society which correlates the cooperation
among specialized groups according to mechanomorphic
models.[229] Cosmopolis cannot be linked to a military force
aimed at protecting economic investments in underdeveloped
countries, where those investments do nothing to liberate
and humanize their people but rather keep them in a state
of dire poverty inasmuch as their natural resources are used
to fuel the production of luxury and destructive items in
the wealthy nations.[230]

Such a methodological self-appropriation within the
intellectual pattern would be the exact opposite of an
objectivistic, conceptualist homogenization of individual
cultures and societies into a mechanized uniformity of life-
style. For it seeks not a worldwide megamachine society
but a creative collaboration within the plurality of cultures
and histories.[231] Lonergan is aware of the dangers in the
present industrialized countries in terms of pollution and
limited natural resources; he sees both as a result of uncoordinated specialization. Insofar as men repress the transcendent exigence through recognition of only materialist
values, there is a tendency to seek an infinity within the
production of material goods - a tendency nature cannot sustain.
For that tendency can only find fulfillment within the subject-
as-subject. To seek it elsewhere is either to trivialize
human existence or to fanaticize it, not to free it.

---

[229] Insight, pp. 238-242; L. Mumford, The Myth of the
Machine - The Pentagon of Power. Note that I use mechanomorphic
in a sense different from Mumford. It means in my context a
machine-like or mechanistic self-misunderstanding. Mumford
usually uses the term to describe alienated agrarian production.

[230] Insight, pp. 241, 632; R. Barnet and R. Müller,
Global Reach: The Power of the Multinational Corporations
(New York, 1974).

[231] Cf. Insight, pp. 207-218, 232-238.

THE STRUCTURES OF DILTHEY'S

CRITIQUE OF HISTORICAL REASON

0. Introduction

The task of presenting a brief analysis of the structures of Dilthey's critique of historical reason is difficult,
and for two reasons. First of all there is the peculiarity
of his position. This has been emphasized by Dilthey himself
as well as by most of the secondary literature.[232] There is
a strange and baffling combination of psychological, historical, and phenomenological currents in Dilthey's grounding
of the cultural sciences. The second difficulty consists in
the admittedly unfinished character of Dilthey's own life
project. Precisely because his position sought to elaborate
a somewhat novel approach to the foundational issues of
both philosophy and the cultural sciences, he found it
increasingly difficult to coordinate his reflections on the
many diverse fields where he perceived a relevance of his
critique of historical reason.

In Chapter Two I indicated how Dilthey differentiated
his task from the other currents of the philosophy of science
in his time. In the first section of this chapter I went on
to show how he developed the starting point of his position
as a "Selbstbesinnung" capable of respecting the unity of
identity and non-identity necessary to avoid the extremes of
empiricism and idealism. Now I shall try to indicate how
he developed this starting point into the foundations for
the cultural sciences. In line with the foundational
significance of Dilthey's presentation of the unity of inner
experience as experienced I have attempted to correlate the
many different writings of Dilthey on topics related to the
critique of historical reason within the framework of the
subject-as-subject, the subject-as-object, and the unity of

---

[232]So, for example, P. Krausser's _Kritik der endlichen
Vernunft_, pp. 210ff. Also M. Riedel, _Einleitung_, pp. 9-32;
P. Hünermann, _Der Durchbruch geschichtlichen Denkens im 19.
Jahrhundert_, pp. 284-291. On Dilthey's own appraisal of
his approach as new, cf. _Breslauer Ausarbeitung_, p. 86.

the two in historical hermeneutics.[233] The advantage of such a framework lies in its ability both to systematize the unfinished critique of historical reason and to show the development in the chronological progression of Dilthey's writings.

To take the latter first, the framework exhibits the basic continuity between the early, middle, and late periods in the classification of Dilthey's work.[234] The early period covers those writings from 1857 to 1883 when Dilthey was elaborating the related and recurrent operations and structures which could overcome the dichotomy between an empirical and a transcendental (Kantian) idealist approach to a grounding of the cultural sciences. The main writings in this period relative to his foundational concerns are his Breslauer Ausarbeitung and his first volume of Einleitung in die Geisteswissenschaften.[235] The second period, extending from 1884 to 1896, saw Dilthey attempt to articulate in some detail the dynamic structures of inner experience in relation both to the question of what it is man does when he experiences and understands, and how that activity gives a knowledge of the external world. The chief writings here were those centered about his treatises on a descriptive psychology and our belief in an external world.[236] In his last period,

---

[233]Cf. Chapter Three, pp. 232ff.

[234]I have here placed the fourfold division of Dilthey's development elaborated by Hünermann in a threefold schema. For the appearance of the Einleitung in die Geisteswissenschaften of 1883 is not really a period in itself, especially in view of the work Dilthey did in 1880 on this same project. Hence I believe it more accurate to follow a threefold division of early, middle, and late; all the more so inasmuch as Hünermann gives no reasons at all for his singling out of 1883, cf. his op. cit., pp. 135f., and p. 169 where he admits the continuity of the Einleitung in die Geisteswissenschaften with the early period: "Bringing together the many tentative beginnings of his earlier writings, Dilthey presented a first major outline of his question and the projected answer in 1883."

[235]Cf. G.S. Vol. I for the Einleitung in die Geisteswissenschaften; I shall quote extensively from the unpublished Breslauer Ausarbeitung (as B.A.).

[236]Cf. G.S. V.

1897 to 1911, Dilthey was more interested in the intentionality character of the basic structures and how the subject as
unity provides the foundations for a historical and hermeneutical knowledge. It is here that one sees the indirect
influence of phenomenology on Dilthey. The central writings
of the period have been collected in his Der Aufbau der
geschichtlichen Welt.[237] Running through the last two periods
of his writings were also the efforts of Dilthey to both
elaborate the expansion of the basic structures in the fields
of philosophy, aesthetics, pedagogy, and ethics, and to work
out the historical and cognitional theoretical foundations
of the emergence and spread of the cultural sciences.

If we move from the chronology of Dilthey's writings
to his own projected divisions of his introduction to the
cultural sciences we can see how the framework of the subject-
as-subject, the subject-as-object, their unity and the
expansion arising from that unity, provide a significant
correlation capable of integrating the key fourth and
fifth books of that introduction. In Figure Three I have
outlined the five books of Dilthey's projected introduction
to the cultural sciences. It should be clear that the sections most relevant to his critique of historical reason are
the first, second, fourth and fifth. The third section, on
the emergence of modern cultural sciences and a concomitant
history of cognitional theories, has been incorporated into
the relevant discussions within Chapter Two and the present
chapter. This seemed dictated by the very different historical situation of our own time, as well as by the very incomplete nature of those studies by Dilthey.

The relevant insights from the first and second
editions of the introduction to the cultural sciences have
been touched upon in previous sections. In Dilthey's
own description of the projected fourth and fifth books of
his Einleitung in die Geisteswissenschaften he tells us only
that they would present his own "cognitional theoretical
grounding of the cultural sciences."[238] The plausibility

---

[237]Cf. G.S. VII.

[238]G.S. I, p. xix. That Dilthey did not alter his

INTRODUCTION TO THE CULTURAL SCIENCES

I. The Need of New Foundations for these Sciences

    G.S. I, pp. 3-120.

II. The Rise and Fall of Metaphysical Scientific Foundations

    G.S. I, pp. 123-408.

III. The Emergence of Modern Cultural Sciences and the
Concomitant History of Cognitional Theories

    G.S. II; III; IV; and V, pp. 31-89.

IV. The Basic Structures of a Cognitional Theoretical
Grounding of the Cultural Sciences

1. The Subject-as-Subject: Breslauer Ausarbeitung;
    G.S. V, pp. 139-316.

2. The Subject-as-object: G.S. V, pp. 90-138; VII,
    pp. 3-251, 295-347.

3. The Unity of Subject and Object in History: G.S.
    VII, pp. 252-291; VIII, pp. 3-71.

V. Differentiations of the Basic Structures:

1. Philosophical: G.S. V, pp. 339-416; VIII, pp.
    75-234.

2. Aesthetics: G.S. VI, p. 90-287, 313-321; Das
    Erlebnis und die Dichtung.

3. Ethics: G.S. VI, pp. 1-55; X, pp. 13-124.

4. Pedagogics: G.S. VI, pp. 56-89; IX.

Figure Three: A Possible Correlation of Dilthey's Own
Writings to his Projected Introduction
to the Cultural Sciences (G.S. I, p. xix).

of dividing the two according to his studies of the basic
structures of inner experience and the differentiations of
those structures in philosophy, aesthetics, ethics, pedagogics
can be found not only in the fact that he de facto performed
in this manner, but also in his realization that the basic
structures of interiority provided heuristic anticipations
of the totality of historical and social experience.[239] The
core of Dilthey's critique of historical reason consisted .
in his efforts to thematize the related and recurrent
operations of inner experience in terms of certain basic
structures.

In this section I shall seek to integrate these elements
of the critique. The first sub-section will deal with the
subject-as-subject, explicating the basic structures of lived
inner experience. The second sub-section will go on to discuss the subject-as-object, defining the intentionality thrust
of inner experience as capable of explicating the non-identity
of objectivity. The third sub-section can then take up the
unity of the two in Dilthey's move from interiority to
history, with its larger contexts and social systems. These
three sections correspond to the general themes associated
with the notions of experience (Erlebnis), expression
(Ausdruck), and understanding as re-experiencing (Verstehen
als Nacherleben) respectively. The first sub-section will
be the more detailed inasmuch as it provides both an excellent
introduction within the German philosophical context to the
approach of Lonergan to meta-method, and indicates how the
unity of identity and non-identity in history (third sub-
section) is subject to the critique of not adequately overcoming historicism.

1.   The Subject-as-Subject
Dilthey himself never used the terminology I have used in

---

position in this regard, cf. VII, pp. 4ff., which is his
Erste Studie der psychische Strukturzusammenhang of 1905.
Then in his Der Aufbau der geschichtlichen Welt in den
Geisteswissenschaften of 1910 he showed emphatically how he
is building on his cognitional theoretical analysis, cf. VII,
p. 117.

[239]Cf. Misch's introduction in G.S. V, p. ciii.

order to correlate the unity of identity and non-identity with
the subject, identity being the subject-as-subject and non-
identity the subject-as-object. Nevertheless, in Dilthey's
exposition of Schleiermacher's philosophy he did work through
corresponding notions. In Schleiermacher's dialectic, as
Dilthey interpreted it, there is a unity of identity and
non-identity between subject and object, between _Denken_ and
Sein, between self and world. But where Schleiermacher places
the unity in God, Dilthey is more interested in the manifestation of that unity in man. The method of the dialectic
concentrates upon the subject; it is an "Organon of Knowledge"
which is more of an "aesthetic theory" than a systematic
science since it originates in, and is structured according
to, a "Selbstbesinnung:"

> This would, then, constitute the inner core of this
> teaching: a becoming, processive knowledge-structure
> of the whole of reality in the physical and ethical
> sciences. Dialectic is the raising of consciousness
> regarding it (the Platonic _phronesis_).[240]

Insofar as such a self-reflection goes beyond the merely
objective or subjective dichotomy, its goal is to provide a
self-awareness capable of judging all philosophical systems.[241] There is no absolute system which can conceptually
capture the spontaneity of the subject which the "aesthetic
theory" appropriates.[242] Instead the self-reflection reveals
a heuristic anticipation of rationality, a desire for the
true and the good, which cannot be fully realized in any
conceptual or social system.[243]

It is in such a "Selbstbesinnung" that the non-identity
in identity, the _Sein_ in _Denken_, is seen by Dilthey to occur
within the unity of the subject:

> Here, thinking is primordially one with being. They
> are not separated from one another; rather they
> are originally for, with, and through one another.

---

[240]_G.S._ XIV/1, p. 73.   [241]Cf. _G.S._ XIV/1, p. 78.

[242]Cf. _ibid._, pp. 85f. where the comparative method results in structural similarities, yet note Dilthey's ambiguous
remarks on p. 86. On the non-deductive character of
Schleiermacher's dialectic, cf. _ibid._, pp. 91-93.

[243]Cf. _G.S._ XIV/1, pp. 91, 95-99, 217-220.

> Nonetheless, we distinguish in self-consciousness the knowledge of our self and that self as such. The self and consciousness of it develop with and through one another in reflection and in willing. From this it follows that in self-consciousness a being is present to us. This being is different from thinking, which has it as an object. Simultaneously, however, there is a living relationship of each to the other; they cannot be viewed as incommensurable to each other.[244]

It was, moreover, from this insight into the possibilities of a unity in the subject that led Dilthey to envisage the possibility of going beyond Schleiermacher's notion of the architectonic unity of a "world-knowledge" only from the side of the object (and so as ultimately grounded in the transcendence of God).[245] Indeed, Schleiermacher's own insistence upon the relation of God-consciousness to self-consciousness and world-consciousness indicates the need for a unity on the part of <u>consciousness</u> or the subject.[246] Thus Dilthey sees how the dialectic of Schleiermacher leads from an "aesthetic theory" to a fulfillment in science insofar as the less rigorous knowledge of a subject-oriented "aesthetic theory" has, in the development of science, led to the sciences dealing with socio-historical realities. For the differentiation of natural science and human science or history emerges from the opposition of the real and the ideal. Schleiermacher saw how the natural sciences contributed to the process of making the real (nature) ideal (science), and how the cultural sciences were part of that process of converting the ideal (of consciousness) into the real (of constituted history). Thus the division of method

---

[244] <u>G.S.</u> XIV/1, p. 107.

[245] Cf. <u>G.S.</u> XIV/1, pp. 143-147.

[246] Cf. <u>G.S.</u> XIV/1, pp. 138-142; 196: "There is [in Schleiermacher] the notion of a dynamic, living whole, which objectifies itself in all relationships... And it is this that distinguishes Schleiermacher from every phase of Schelling's development, that he proceeds from man, rather than from nature. Just as his cognitional theory attains the highest principles from an analysis of human knowing, so also does he ground his method within the oppositions between self-activity and receptivity, between subject and object, between soul and body, and within the further differentiation of the ethical world."

which saw the natural sciences as predominantly empirical
and the cultural sciences as predominantly speculative;
this division Dilthey sees as gradually sublated "in the
idea of knowledge" which contains "the unity of these two
only relatively different methods of investigation."[247]

This should indicate how Dilthey, in his own development
of a foundational cognitional theory was actually using a
schema or framework which can be articulated as a unity in
the subject of identity and non-identity, where the identity
is the subject-as-subject and the non-identity is the subject-
as-object.[248] Using this framework, the following sub-section
will draw upon the phenomenologically descriptive accounts
which Dilthey gave of the basic structures of the subject.
There are two units to this sub-section. The first will
clarify how Dilthey intended his approach to the subject to
be in a mode capable of revealing the subject-as-subject.
The second will then outline the related and recurrent
structural operations of the subject.

A. Becoming Aware of Conscious Interiority. A problem
confronts us immediately in any talk about the subject-as-
subject. The problem is that any such talk is objectifying,
and so how do we avoid the difficulty of simply referring
to objectifications in such talk and never getting to the
subject-as-subject? This problem was a central one in
Dilthey's Breslauer Ausarbeitung. He was bent upon breaking

---

[247] Ibid., pp. 224-227. It is essential not to give an
abstract or idealist interpretation to the unity. The unity
is the subject, is Leben. Thus in G.S. I, p. 31, Dilthey
warns against using such constructions as unity and multiplicity, whole and part, in a manner that would detract
from the originating Erlebnis.

[248] Cf. G.S. XIV/1, pp. 187-194 on the subject-object
relation in Schleiermacher. Notice that it was about the
time that Dilthey was working on this (cf. B. Groethuysen's
remarks in G.S. VII, pp. 357f.) that Dilthey also described
his own critique of historical reason in terms of the subject:
"The structure of the cultural world is absorbed into the
subject.... Thus, on the one hand, is this cultural world the
creation of the acting subject, and, on the other hand,
is the movement of the human spirit directed towards it in
order to gain an objective knowledge.... The subject of
knowledge is here at one with its object, and this applies
to every dimension of its objectification."

290

through the false problems set by both empiricism and
idealism. For Dilthey the entire development of idealism,
from Descartes' cogito and Berkley's esse est percipi through
Kant and Hegel to Fichte's absolute Egology overlooked the
factual experience of consciousness as inner experience.[249]
The movement was dealing with abstractions of Denken and
Sein, substituting "metaphysical chimeras" for the reality
of understanding and being.[250] This was clear for Dilthey
both in regard to consciousness and in regard to self-
consciousness.

The argument against both has a similar structure.
Although Dilthey never acknowledged it, his argument is a
variant of Aristotle's notion that there is a unity of the
understanding and the understood in act.[251] The argument for
the unity in regard to consciousness runs as follows: if
the act of a state (Zustand) was different from the act of
consciousness of that state, then the effect of the state
upon consciousness would not be the state itself but a third
act (Z') and insofar as this third act was itself a state,
one would have to posit yet another act (Z'') as resulting
from the consciousness of it, and so on indefinitely. Dilthey
can conclude: "real consciousness would eternally elude
us."[252] In other words, there must be an experience of
consciousness as a state which is its own act of awareness
(the subject-as-subject) grounding all mediations in terms
of the object.

---

[249]Cf. B.A., pp. 232-233a.

[250]Cf. B.A., p. 233: "In this theory one sees...the
submission to a method of abstraction that severs being from
thinking and so creates metaphysical chimeras, since
thinking is as much an abstraction as being. However, this
metaphysical abstraction cannot be regarded as an explanatory ground for the general tendency to assume the existence
of things or objects."

[251]This is expressed by Aquinas in "Sensibile in actu
est sensus in actu, intelligibile in actu est intellectus
in actu." Cf. B. Lonergan, Verbum: Word and Idea in Aquinas
(University of Notre Dame Press, 1967), pp. 82f., 147-149,
163f., 171-175, 184, 188f.

[252]Cf. B.A., p. 241.

All mediations must finally arrive at an end in which the knower and the object are one, and thus an interiorization occurs. If such a point does not appear, there would be no consciousness. Suppose there is a state of affairs and, different from it, a knower. As soon as the knower lets himself be influenced by this state of affairs, it is a state of affairs within him.[253]

It is precisely "interiority" which is the defining characteristic constitutive of the subject-as-subject.

The same basic argument is taken over from Herbart's critique of Fichte's idea of an absolute positing of the ego in self-consciousness. Kant prepared for Fichte's dilemma insofar as he distinguished the unity of the "I" from the concomitant awareness of self. Thus perceiving the self is like perceiving any other object.[254] Fichte's efforts to place the identity of subject and object in the subject-as-object failed since it sought to explicate the relation of the subject to itself as to an object. If self-consciousness was a case of the self considering itself as an object, then a consideration of this object (self-consciousness) would also constitute another object, and one would never arrive at an originating and grounding self-consciousness. "So emerges an unending series, and, instead of the reality of a performative positing of the self, we have only an eternal question about the self."[255] The solution is clear enough for Dilthey: one cannot explain self-consciousness by appealing to subject and object since self-consciousness is presupposed and experienced in any such appeal.[256] To break this hold of an objectifying approach to the subject, Dilthey proposed the notion of "Erlebnis" and an attention to it that

---

[253] B.A., p. 242.

[254] Cf. references in note 117, 118, 142, 143 of Chapter One; in notes 1-3, 70-73 of Chapter Two and in notes 103-106 in Chapter Three.

[255] B.A., p. 197.

[256] Cf. B.A., p. 198: "The inversion is clear enough. An opposition between subject and object cannot explain self-consciousness, for they presuppose self-consciousness, i.e., what is constitutive in self-consciousness, namely the union of self and will."

292

was not objectifying.

At first sight it seems a rather obvious and simple notion. It is the factual experience of awareness, of not being in a deep and dreamless sleep, but of living and so spontaneously performing the activities associated with, indeed constitutive of, human life. No matter how preoccupied we are with the objects of our attention and concern throughout the day, such preoccupation is possible because it is a <u>conscious</u> preoccupation. Objects are "there" for us because we are ourselves "here," present to ourselves.

> To-be-for-oneself is as interiority the simple nature of psychic process, inasmuch as this always is not a mere immersion in an object, but is experience (Erleben). This is the foundation of what we call life itself, its most primal seed, which includes in itself the recurrent conditions of self-consciousness. Such an interiorization, in which an individual appropriates his own state of affairs, could also be termed "self-feeling," even if its development includes more. In this fact is included the core of self-consciousness.[257]

It is interesting to notice how Dilthey refers to the inner self-possession of the subject, his self-awareness, as a certain self-feeling. It was to underline the falsity of Fichte's starting with the difference of subject and object and attempting to arrive at their unity.[258] But there are other reasons also. I should like to discuss the three main reasons as they were formulated by Dilthey in his <u>Breslauer Ausarbeitung</u> of 1880. For those reasons indicate how even in his early period he was aware of the novelty and scope of his approach to the grounding of the cultural sciences, and how the intentionality thrust of his later period was by no means lacking in his earlier work.

The first, and primary reason why Dilthey referred to the subject-as-subject as a "self-feeling" was that he seems to

---

[257] B.A., p. 199.

[258] Cf. B.A., p. 195, where Dilthey acknowledges that Fichte overcame the onesidedness of Kant's theoretical reflection on consciousness insofar as Fichte emphasized action and will. Yet Dilthey also remarks marginally: "Fichte set a false task for himself at the start of his philosophy: to move from the difference of subject and object to their identity."

have hit on this designation of self-awareness as overcoming the objectivistic notions of consciousness prevalent in idealism. This was undoubtedly due to Schleiermacher's own understanding of "feeling as the primal act of the human spirit" as the unity of Denken and Sein, of understanding and willing.[259] So Dilthey can write that the immediate self-consciousness, prior to any self-reflection or conceptualization, is feeling: "Feeling is always the unity of that being which thinks as it wills and wills as it thinks."[260] This was in direct contradiction to the notion of consciousness and self-consciousness propagated by the idealist tradition which, with Reinhold would define consciousness as "the presentation of the presenter and the presented as distinct and yet related to each other,"[261] or with Hegel where "consciousness generally is the relation of the ego to an object be it inner or outer."[262]

Against such conceptions of consciousness as defined only in terms of the subject-object dichotomy, Dilthey presented his own emphasis upon living awareness prior to any differentiation of subject and object. Indeed, he saw that in this respect the positivism of Comte was little different from idealism. For Comte also accepted an ultimate dichotomy between subject and object, claiming that the mind could not directly be aware of its own operations as it could of all external things. Contrary to this, Dilthey showed how even direct acts of observation would be impossible without the concomitant living awareness of the subject-as-subject.[263] Hence there was, for Dilthey, a radical difference between a natural event and a conscious event:

Consciousness or interiority or inwardness are only different expressions for the same elementary fact.

---

[259] Cf. G.S. XIV/1, p. liii; XIV/2, p. 523.

[260] G.S. XIV/2, p. 523.

[261] Cf. K. L. Reinhold. Versuch einer neuen Theorie des menschlichen Vorstellungsvermögen (1789), p. 235.

[262] Hegel, Propädeutik (Theorie Werkausgabe, Bd. 4), p. 204; also p. 73, 74.

[263] Cf. B.S., pp. 254-258.

> In any event, intelligence is immediately aware of
> itself; if one understands thereby that intellectual
> activity of consciousness includes in itself an
> interiority or awareness of and for itself. This is
> precisely the difference between a process of conscious-
> ness and the natural processes known to us. In the
> latter an image in the eye would, indeed, need a second
> eye to be seen. In the former, on the contrary, there
> is no need of an external perceiver, since the process
> of consciousness includes an awareness of itself in
> itself. Critically understood, this reality is just
> the opposite of how Comte imagined it.[264]

We could not be immediately aware of the neural base of our
thinking, feeling, and willing. That base would be only
slowly discovered. However, that did not mean that such a
reductionist base could, even if truly discovered, provide
a critical standpoint from which to ground all the conscious
activity of man. Quite the contrary. For it would only be
by means of our consciousness, and not directly by any normal
base, that we would discover the neural base to begin with:
hence the originating and fundamental character of consciousness.[265]

The second reason leading Dilthey to refer to consciousness as feeling indicates how Dilthey himself discovered
the subject-as-subject. The question is how do we become
aware of consciousness in such a way that we do not _ipso_
facto objectify that "becoming aware?" He himself seems to
have hit upon it in the event of feeling and willing rather
than in the event of a conceptual knowing. There is a
difference between the observation of a natural event and
the self-observation of a conscious event.[266] Inasmuch as
the conscious event is immediately given, there is not
primarily an object-ive "seeing" of consciousness distinct
from the awareness itself:

> The existence of the psychic act and the knowledge of
> it are not two different things. Here there does not
> exist the difference between an object seen and the
> eye which sees it.... The psychic act is, because I

---

[264] B.A., p. 259.

[265] Cf. the argument given in B.A., pp. 255-256.

[266] Cf. B.A., p. 259; G.S. V, p. 197.

experience (erlebe) it.[267]

And the experiencing of the act, as the act itself, is conscious so that consciousness itself can only be loosely defined, in terms of this self-presence or "the being-for-me of a state or mood."[268] If this is so, then the feeling and willing is not perceived as an object:

> A state of affairs is there for me inasmuch as it is conscious. When I feel myself sorrowful, this feeling of sorrow is not my object, but insofar as this state of affairs is conscious to me, it is there for me as one state of consciousness. I interiorize it.[269]

Undoubtedly the feeling, just as the willing, might have an object or an objective; yet the feeling and willing themselves are simply "there" as conscious. Hence the manner in which we advert to them is an entirely different kind of observation than that associated with external events:

> When one designates as observation the orientation of attention to something placed before me, then there is no observation of inwardness or its content. Rather, the orientation of attention here only produces a heightening of awareness with the tension of its effort.[270]

It is only in this sense of a heightening of awareness in a reflection upon itself that one can speak of an inner observation. This interiority of awareness is "the simplest form in which psychic life emerges," and, indeed, does not as feeling carry with it a differentiation of inner and outer, rather it is the ground from which any such differentiation would occur.[271] Hence Dilthey can speak of a series of degrees in feeling as one moves from feelings of inner states (sorrow, pain, joy, etc.) to those of smell, taste, hearing and touching where the object plays an increasing

---

[267] B.A., p. 8. Notice, then, how this subject-as-subject is constitutive of Erlebnis.

[268] B.A., pp. 2 and 259.

[269] G.S. V, p. 197; also the recurrence of this theme in pp. 1-14 of B.A.

[270] B.A., p. 14; also G.S. V, p. 197.

[271] Cf. B.A., pp. 14f., 18.

role.[272]

Dilthey would refer to a cognitional theory which failed to account for this immediate self-awareness, and the heightening of consciousness needed to become aware of it, as "uncritical and unpsychological."[273] For such theories do not take into account the conscious acts which are the very condition for any awareness of the object.[274] To counteract such a false approach to consciousness, we must begin "from the self-feeling, from those emotions, those tensions of the will, through which we also discover how their elements are always united with some consciousness of the external world."[275]

The third reason for Dilthey's designation of feeling as the mode of becoming aware of consciousness had to do with his difficulty with the objective character of thought. He did not find the subject-as-subject so clearly operative in thought as in feeling and will. He certainly was aware that thinking was an inner experience; that, like feeling and willing, thinking also had both the acting subject and the orientation of the acts to an objective content (Inhalt-lichkeit).[276] But he saw a special predominance of the subject in feeling which he could not find in thought.[277] There are ways in which we speak of feelings with an aware-ness of their primarily subjective character so that feeling indicates "the merging of a content with interiority, in which an object cannot be dissociated from our self."[278] Dilthey was aware that he was not giving us a feeling of this immediacy of consciousness in his analysis, but that he was reflecting upon that immediacy. In this sense the truth of his analysis had to conform to the "conditions of our

---

[272]Cf. B.A., p. 15f.

[273]Cf. B.A., p. 17. This implies that for Dilthey "critical" is defined in relation to verification in exper-ience, and the grounding of all critical awareness is in terms of Erlebnis.

[274]Cf. B.A., p. 18.   [275]B.A., p. 19.

[276]Cf. B.A., pp. 111f.   [277]Cf. B.A., p. 112.

[278]Ibid.

reflective consciousness."[279]

Nevertheless, by reflecting upon the immediacy of consciousness and doing so in such a manner that Dilthey was simply describing the immediacy, he was able to confer the certainty of the immediacy on the descriptions themselves. For no matter how skeptical one might be, he must at least be conscious if he is even to be skeptical.

> Accordingly, the starting point and object of our analysis is inner perception as immediately certain. Our hoping and fearing, our wishing and willing, this inner world holding together our self-consciousness, is as such the reality itself, is immediate certainty and the realm of truth.[280]

Thus, while it would be "childish" to claim that thought could be compared to the external object thought about, without using thinking itself for the comparison,[281] it is necessary to admit that a self-reflection (Selbstbesinnung) upon inner experience allows precisely such a comparison and "so puts an end to the game of skepticism."[282] Dilthey can conclude:

> My thinking, willing, wishing, desiring - these exist, they are facts of consciousness present in inner awareness and in memory. Thus a comparison [between them and knowing] can be performed.[283]

In Chapter Two we saw how Dilthey was convinced that some way had to be found which would break through the merely hypothetical status of all conceptual systems without, however, appealing to an absolute which would belie historicality.[284] In the previous section we saw how Dilthey's "Selbstbesinnung" offered the possibility of just such a breakthrough.[285]

In order for such a starting point as "Selbstbesinnung" to become adequately worked out into a critique of historical reason, it was necessary for Dilthey to sublate the rift

---

[279]Cf. B.A., pp. 266f.   [280]B.A., p. 266.

[281]Cf. B.A., p. 267. Compare this with B. Lonergan, Verbum: Word and Idea in Aquinas, pp. 59f.

[282]B.A., p. 267.

[283]Ibid. (Emphasis in original).

[284]Cf. Chapter Two, pp. 120-142.

[285]Cf. Chapter Three, pp. 214-231.

between experience and thought, between empiricism and idealism, so that the articulation of the subject would not be simply another "theoretical" system but actually thematize the activity of the living subject experiencing historical-social life. It was in pursuit of just such a unity that Dilthey himself turned to in several chapters of the Breslauer Ausarbeitung, and then more fully developed in his 1890 essay on Erfahren und Denken and in the studies of the next few years (1894 to 1896) on a descriptive psychology.

Dilthey formulated the crucial issue of this problem in his essay on experience and thinking: how can one articulate the genetic relation between experience (the lived awareness we have in experiencing outer and inner perceptions) and thinking. Only such an awareness of a genetic relationship would overcome the dichotomy between experience and thought, life and logic, empiricism and idealism. For it would end a reliance on the merely hypothetical without introducing idealist absolutes but rather by attending to the structures of living consciousness.

> If there is not to be just a merely hypothetical knowledge, then a genetic relation must exist between perception and thinking. This relation sublates the duality at the foundation of knowledge and transforms the merely hypothetical, postulated, and presupposed relationships [in knowledge] into objectively valid ones.[286]

The procedures Dilthey appealed to in attempting to articulate such a genetic relationship between perception and thought can be found in rudimentary form in his sketches of the Breslauer Ausarbeitung, and then in fully explicated form in his essays on an analytic and descriptive psychology.

In the Breslauer Ausarbeitung Dilthey discussed the impossibility of explanatory psychology to really explain self-consciousness.[287] It was not a question of presenting a subject introspecting upon itself (after the manner of a subject-object split) in order to "see" itself as subject.

---

[286]G.S. V, pp. 82f. Note how Dilthey is interested in finding the origin in the subject of authentic objectivity. Hence it is not a question of equating objectivity with logical products; cf. B.A., pp. 44ff.

[287]Cf. B.A., pp. 185ff.

Such an approach would attempt to uncover the unconscious causes of consciousness in a typical cause-effect frame of reference found in the natural sciences.[288] It corresponded to the character of natural events, of which we have no immediate consciousness and so must necessarily devise hypothetical constructions in an effort to explain our experience of them.[289] Against this, as we saw in the previous section, Dilthey set the immediacy of experience as inner consciousness. Becoming aware of this inner experience was not a question of some type of inner "looking" at what was there - after the manner of external perception.[290] To uncover the genetic relation between perception and conception one had simply to direct one's conscious attention to the awareness concomitant with all experiencing in order to describe the structures and functions operative in, or constitutive of, inner experience.[291] Because it is a self-reflection of self-consciousness itself, the fact that one's attention is turned to this consciousness does not introduce a duality of subject and object into consciousness, but instead reveals the unity of self and consciousness.[292]

By stressing this attention to inner experiencing

---

[288] Cf. B.A., pp. 190ff. The cause-effect approach to consciousness is equated with the reductionist "myth" of being able to explain consciousness through physiological or neurological processes. Cf. M. Lamb, "Ascent from Human Consciousness to the Human Soul," in Insight; A Quarterly of Religion and Mental Health Vol. 3 (1964), pp. 18-28.

[289] Cf. B.A., pp. 257ff.

[290] Cf. B.A., pp. 8, 259; also pp. 19-26.

[291] Cf. B.A., p. 189; also G.S. V, pp. 139-158

[292] Cf. B.A., p. 190: "...the unity of consciousness has as its consequence the consciousness of the unity present in everything that emerges in consciousness. Theoretically this implies that even a consciousness of the self as an object exists as a single conscious act united with the act of the self, so that the object of self-consciousness (or the self with the conscious act in which the self is posited) is really a unity." Dilthey goes on to ask how this unity is given in experience - and not just "theoretically" - and introduces the "self-feeling" as the only adequate approach; cf. B.A., pp. 190-192.

itself, Dilthey was also emphasizing the critical nature of his thematization of historical reason. There was undoubtedly a relativity of all conceptual systems in history, of all viewpoints and frames of reference. This implied, as was mentioned in Chapter Two, that the only proper grounds of criticism could be found in experience as the arbiter of systems and viewpoints.[293] In this sense, any metascientific or philosophical grounding of the sciences had to be both critical and experiential.[294] For the descriptive approach would not start out from a piecemeal dissection of the elements of awareness - as the explanatory approach of the natural sciences - but would rather start from the totality of self-awareness and seek to describe the interrelations of the dynamic structures and functions of that totality.[295] Hence Dilthey claimed that his philosophy is grounded in a universal experience insofar as all experience is conscious.[296] And it is precisely this experiencing as conscious which defines reality itself:

> Reality is the object of experience. We designate as experience (Erfahrung) the process in consciousness through which a real thing emerges for consciousness. This reality can be an external thing, an external event, or a fact of psychic life; no matter which, as factual realities they are objects of experience.

He then continues with the affirmation of how this attention to inner experience is just that link between perception and conception which is the key to his overcoming of the dichotomy between empiricism and idealism:

> Therefore, prescinding from their place in the thought

---

[293]Cf. Chapter Two, pp. 137-155.

[294]Cf. B.A., pp. 249-251; here Dilthey shows how empiricism is not "Erfahrungsphilosophie" since it cannot handle the experience of consciousness. "The starting point and foundation of science is an analysis of the essence of experiences insofar as these are present in consciousness..."

[295]Cf. B.A., pp. 28, 133, 248f.

[296]Cf. B.A., pp. 250-251: "Originally is truth for the philosopher found only in experience. Philosophy is grounded on universal experience.... Thus the philosopher's task is an analysis of experiences."

process, there are no concepts or propositions, no matter how abstract, that cannot be presented by us as objects of experience, inasmuch as we interiorize them as psychic facts.[297]

There were three steps in Dilthey's elaboration of the subject as inner experience. The first consisted in his efforts to articulate a descriptive psychology which would concentrate upon the basic structures and functions of conscious interiority as experienced. The second step attempted to explicate how such structures were self-mediatory, while the third was concerned with how the basic structures are complicated and differentiated in the larger fields of social and historical realities. These three steps correspond to the three sub-sections of this section.

Before continuing however, it is imporant to clarify why Dilthey's critique of historical reason developed in this manner. As already indicated, these three steps correspond roughly with the chronology of Dilthey's writings. From the perspective of our own time, we might be inclined to hold that the second step should have phenomenologically preceded the first, that the self-mediation of inner experience (as oriented towards its extended objects) should critically precede any elaboration of the inner structures themselves. That they do not shows how Dilthey's phenomenological stance is radically different from that of Husserl or Sartre. Since Husserl, phenomenology has been chiefly concerned with how consciousness constitutes objects. Husserl himself, in his earlier work, was mainly interested in consciousness as manifested in the constitution of logical and mathematical objects; and in his later works, where he was more interested in subjectivity as such and borrowed much from the notions of Lebensphilosophie, he was still concerned with the intentionality relations of subjectivity as transcendental.[298] It was not suprising, therefore, that both Heidegger and Sartre would reject the Husserlian notion

---

[297] B.A., p. 249.

[298] Cf. Robert Sokolowski, The Formation of Husserl's Concept of Constitution (The Hague, 1964), pp. 195-217.

302

of subjectivity as transcendental by claiming that either
the _Dasein_ of the subject is being-in-world (Heidegger) or
that the ego of consciousness was present _to_ or for consciousness as any object in the external world was
(Sartre).[299]

Dilthey's descriptive or phenomenological psychology,
on the other hand, did not in any way deny the intentional
thrust of consciousness and how the world or object enters
into the constitution of the subject. Yet he was primarily
concerned with the subject-as-subject and the description
of the activity of the subject in its lived experience.
This subject-orientation was to emphasize the fact that our
self-consciousness as spontaneously active was not simply a
presence to self in no way different from our presence to
any other object. Only when this immediate and certain
character of consciousness was fully recognized could one hope
to overcome a complete relativity without falling into an
absolute subjectivity - however that absolutizing might be
designated.[300] Dilthey, then, was first of all concerned
with establishing the need for an approach to the subject
which would be descriptively close to the immediacy of inner
experience. Only in the light of such a descriptively empirical method could he then move on to handle the intentionality
of inner experience in its constitution of objects. It is
this prior concern with an empirically descriptive elaboration
of the subject which makes Dilthey's critique of historical
reason peculiarly his own, differentiating his notion of
experience (_Erlebnis_) from the subsequent phenomenological
and existentialist traditions, as well as from the prior

---

[299]Cf. M. Heidegger, _Sein und Zeit_, pp. 114-117, 326-323; J. -P. Sartre, _The Transcendence of the Ego_ (New York, 1971), pp. 31-106.

[300]Hence the central importance of finitude, as P. Krausser has brough out in his _Kritik der endlichen Vernunft: Diltheys Revolution der allgemeinen Wissenschafts- und Handlungstheorie_ (Frankfurt, 1968). On the later Dilthey's use of intentionality in a Husserlian manner; cf. L. Landgrebe, _W. Diltheys Theorie der Geisteswissenschaften_, pp. 303ff.

Kantianism and contemporaneous Neo-Kantianism.[301]

B. Basic Structures and Functions of Interiority. In Dilthey's essay Ideen über eine Beschreibende und zergliedernde Psychologie of 1894 he left no doubt that he was not simply seeking a new form of "psychology" but that his principal aim was to provide a psychological grounding of the cultural sciences.[302] This inevitably led to a great deal of misunderstanding both in his own life and in subsequent studies of just what he was about. Ebbinghaus criticized Dilthey's essay a year after its publication for, at bottom, a wrong-headed interference in psychology. Dilthey subsequently showed how Ebbinghaus misunderstood the basic interest in the article with the structural systems (Strukturzusammenhänge) of conscious life.[303] Ebbinghaus hit at the core of Dilthey's effort in claiming that the basic structures could not be directly experienced and thereby go beyond merely hypothetical constructions. Fifty-seven years later, H. A. Hodges felt that Dilthey himself later backed off from his position, and in this he was merely voicing the common assumption that the later period of

---

[301] For Dilthey "Erfahrung" is correlative to "Erleben" and so defined primarily in reference to the subject-as-subject. This is not, then, in opposition to science, but underpins all conscious activities of man. This is clearly not the position of H. -G. Gadamer in his Wahrheit und Methode, pp. 329-344.

[302] Thus the first chapter of the essay reads: "The task of a psychological grounding of the cultural sciences." Cf. G.S. V, pp. 139-153.

[303] For Ebbinghaus' article, cf. Zeitschrift für Psychologie Bd. IX (Okt. 1895), pp. 161-205. For Dilthey's rejoinder, cf. G.S. V, pp. 238-240. That Dilthey was upset at the misunderstanding of Ebbinghaus can be gathered from his correspondence with Graf Yorck. For in 1883 he writes that he went walking every week with Ebbinghaus, finding his knowledge of psychology helpful (Briefwechsel, p. 38). In the following year, the summer of 1884, he sees a certain lack of philosophical depth in Ebbinghaus' position (ibid., p. 46). Once Ebbinghaus' article is published, Yorck tells Dilthey that he can remember no argument so "malicious" since that between Jacobi and Schelling (ibid., p. 195). Dilthey apparently missed the psychological Congress in Munich in the fall of 1896, even when he knew William James would be there, because of his feelings regarding Ebbinghaus (ibid., p. 210).

Dilthey's writings retreated from his concern with a descriptive psychology in his middle period.[304] I have already indicated that this view of the relation between the early, middle, and later periods is now being called into question.[305] Indeed, I shall argue here that it misses the central thrust of Dilthey's critique of historical reason. For what Dilthey was trying to establish in the course of his work was a new control of meaning in terms of living experience or conscious interiority.[306]

In the previous section we have seen how Dilthey began his critique with a differentiation of the methods of natural science from those of the human or cultural sciences. In the first chapter of his _Ideen_ he returns to this within the context of setting the task for a psychological grounding of the cultural sciences. Those who would see in this a type of "psychologism" which would reduce all manifestations of human historical and social living to certain obtuse psychological processes miss the central meaning of Dilthey's _Ideen_. For the mistake of psychologism was precisely its reductionist tendency, its failure to realize that conscious living was before all else a totality which could not be reduced to unconscious motives or elements.[307] Dilthey was no more concerned with establishing psychology as the foundation of all the cultural sciences than, in our own day, J. Habermas or T. Kuhn could be accused of such when the former draws upon psychology as typifying a self-reflection central to his critique of knowledge and human interest, or when the latter refers to a psychology of research to account for paradigm changes in science which K. Popper's "science without a subject" could not.[308]

---

[304]Cf. Hodges, _op. cit._, pp. 213ff.

[305]Cf. the references on pp. 221-229 of this Chapter.

[306]This is the entire thrust of Chapter Two; cf. especially pp. 115-155 on Dilthey.

[307]On the character of psychologism, cf. E. Husserl, _Logische Untersuchungen_, Ed. I, pp. 50ff. Also W. Moog, _Logik, Psychologie und Psychologismus_ (Berlin, 1919).

[308]Cf. J. Habermas, _Erkenntnis und Interesse_, pp. 262-

It was to counteract the excessive objectivism of the
philosophy of science of his day, that Dilthey moved beyond
the hypothetical constructions of a purely empiricist
or logicist approach. Thus Dilthey saw that if the
cultural sciences simply transferred methods of the natural
sciences they would be involved in "hypotheses everywhere
hypotheses!"[309] To those who maintain that the scientificality
of psychology depends upon an exclusive use of natural scientific methods, Dilthey counters that the true disciples of
the pioneers in the natural sciences would not merely copy
their methods but creatively find methods suited to the very
different field constituted by specifically human phenomena.[310] Because they have not done this:

> Contemporary science has thereby fallen into the
> following dilemma that has contributed extraordinarily
> to a massive increase of the skeptical spirit, and to
> a superficial, sterile empiricism, as well as to the
> increasing separation of life from knowledge.[311]

The dilemma consists in science, on the one hand, providing
the possibility of a growing consensus and public verification,
while on the other, it has resulted also in the skepticism di-
vorcing knowledge from human living. It was in light of
these metascientific problems, and not simply to "psycho-
analyze" the works of literature or other cultural manifestations, that Dilthey elaborated a descriptive and analytic
psychology. He stated explicitly that a descriptive psychology
does not in any way pretend to come up with a causal explanation of cultural manifestations - which would be to mis-
interpret his approach as simply a variant of explanatory
psychology - but rather to mediate the totality of human
awareness (experienced in the genial manifestations of culture)
to the problems of the philosophy of science.[312]

364; on Kuhn, cf. I. Lakatos (ed.) Criticism and the Growth
of Knowledge for Kuhn's lead-off article "Logic of Discovery
or Psychology of Research?" (pp. 1-23) and his replies, pp.
231-278.

[309] Cf. G.S. V, p. 143.   [310] Ibid.

[311] G.S. V, p. 145.

[312] Cf. G.S. V, pp. 153, 303ff.

Before going into Dilthey's description of conscious interiority there is another problem to handle besides that of psychologism. The problem is the relation of his descriptive psychology to cognitional theory. In the Breslauer Ausarbeitung of 1880 he spoke of a "cognitional theoretical grounding of the cultural science." In the Ideen of 1894 he refers to a "psychological grounding." The reasons for this shift of terminology are given in the Ideen, and they are twofold. First of all, Dilthey was of the opinion that cognitional theory, while occupying a very different position within the complex of scientific reflection than the cultural sciences, was also in need of a psychological grounding. By this he meant precisely that type of experiential base which would deliver cognitional theory from the vicissitudes of competitive, contradictory systems.

> Indeed, cognitional theory arose from the need to secure some section of solid land, commonly valid knowledge of whatever extent, amid the ocean of metaphysical fluctuations. If cognitional theory now were to become uncertain and hypothetical, it would betray its own purpose. Thus the same unhappy dilemma exists for cognitional theory, as exists for the cultural sciences.[313]

Dilthey had, namely, perceived the process that was eroding the primacy of cognitional theory just as the latter had dethroned that of metaphysics.[314] That process was empiricism and positivism with their recourse to a "banal empiricality" restating the objectivism which cognitional theory and the "Shift to the Subject" had criticized in metaphysics.[315] An empiricism which denies the experiential reality of conscious interiority condemns the empirical to a barren objectivism.[316]

The second reason for the change in terminology was Dilthey's conviction that the Neo-Kantian insistence upon a complete independence of cognitional theory from psychology

---

[313]G.S. V, p. 146.

[314]Cf. Habermas, Erkenntnis und Interesse, pp. 88-92.

[315]Cf. G.S. V, pp. 146f.; also the references given in pp. 125-137 of Chapter Two.

[316]Cf. G.S. V, p. 147.

was based on the false dichotomy in Kant between intuition
and thought. Cognitional theory became too exclusively
concerned with knowing in isolation from feeling and willing,
so that the total context of conscious interiority was
sacrificed. Yet such an approach overlooks the "living
consciousness" of the cognitional theorist and "no magic
of a transcendental method" can wipe away this presupposition.[317] The process of knowing presupposes the totality of
inner experience, and so, while cognitional theory need not
develop in conjunction with a descriptive psychology, still
it is an illusion to pretend that a presuppositionless
cognitional theory was possible.[318] Again we see that the
central intention of Dilthey's critique, as a concern with
the totality of inner experience and so a restoration of the
relation between experience and thought, is at the bottom
of both his criticism of a Kantian cognitional theory and
his turn to a descriptive and analytical psychology.[319] Thus
the terminology in Dilthey indicates that he is interested in
locating cognitional theory within a broader context of
living consciousness, to purify it of an excessively logical
or idealist preoccupation. In turning attention to that
living consciousness as the basis of cognitional theory
(as it is the basis of the cultural sciences), he sees the
starting point as "Selbstbesinnung."[320]

Having established that Dilthey's descriptive psychology
is not psychologism nor a Kantian type cognitional theory, we

---

[317] G.S. V, pp. 148f.; also cf. VII, pp. 333f.; VIII, pp.
174f. For Dilthey, as these texts indicate, the appeals to
psychology were not in the name of some obtuse psychologism
(cf. VII, p. 19) but to come up with a cognitional theory
which thematized actual conscious performance or practice.

[318] Cf. G.S. V, pp. 150f.

[319] Cf. pp. 216ff. of this Chapter and the references
given there.

[320] Cf. G.S. V, pp. 151f.: "Cognitional theory is
psychology in movement, and, indeed, in movement towards
a particular goal. In the act of self-awareness
(Selbstbesinnung), which embraces the entire, vibrant scope
of conscious inner life, cognitional theory finds its
foundation."

can turn to his notion of descriptive and analytic psychology itself. There are three main topics to cover in presenting this. First there is the differentiation from an explanatory and constructive psychology; second, the method of descriptive analysis, and finally, the results of the method as revealing the basic structures and functions of conscious interiority.

The differentiation of what Dilthey calls explanatory and constructive psychology from descriptive and analytical strikes the contemporary reader as strange, to say the least. There is no recorded remark that would substantiate whether or not Dilthey was aware of Freud's work. The psychology Dilthey was referring to was academic rather than remedial or clinical. Explanatory psychology referred to a psychology which patterned its basic methodological stance according to the methods of the natural sciences. It treated consciousness as any object would be treated, by attempting to discover certain basic elements and deducing (or constructing) the phenomenon from those unconscious elements.[321] Dilthey briefly traced the history of such an explanatory psychology from Descartes, Spinoza and Leibniz through Hume, James and John Stuart Mill, to Christian Wolf's rational psychology, Comte, Spencer and Herbart and Taine.[322] He also saw elements of it in Wundt, James and Sigwart.[323] It would take the present study far afield, but it should be noticed that Dilthey's presentation of a psychology that attempts to explain conscious living by constructing it from a small set of unconscious elements applies equally well to Freud's main orientation.[324] Indeed, it would be interesting to trace

---

[321]Cf. G.S. V, p. 158.

[322]Cf. G.S. V, pp. 154-165; also VIII, p. 262. Notice how Dilthey criticizes the lack of respect for experience in Wolf's dichotomy between rational and empirical psychology.

[323]Cf. G.S. V, pp. 165-168; his attitude was not simply negative, thus on p. 177 he mentions his debt to Spencer and James.

[324]Cf. Paul Ricoeur, De l'interprétation: essai sur Freud (Paris, 1965), pp. 81-90; also Richard Wollheim, Freud (London, 1971), pp. 20-64. The friend and correspondent of

similarities (as well as differences) between Dilthey's descriptive and analytical psychology and Jung's analytical psychology or Frankl's more consciousness oriented Logotherapy.[325] Yet the very suggestion indicates the disparity between Dilthey's quest for metascientific foundations for the cultural sciences and the more specific goals of psychology as a particular science. Dilthey was not interested in coming up with explanatory schemas for man's conscious activity; he wanted instead to describe that conscious activity as it is experienced. This alone, in his view, would provide a critically experiential base capable of overcoming the merely hypothetical nature of any construction which would presuppose that conscious activity was to be investigated simply like any other object.[326] He was not, therefore, aiming at a revision of psychology itself, but at calling attention to the empirical psychological facts of consciousness which cannot be explained away by a reductionist concern with unconscious physical processes or elements. Thus he quotes a representative of explanatory psychology to the effect that all psychic events must be reduced to neurological and physiological processes which mediate them, concluding: "Herewith is the bankruptcy of an independent explanatory psychology evident. Its tasks would be taken over by physiology."[327]

Freud, Ludwig Binswanger, finds several positive correlations between Freud and Dilthey, cf. his Grundformen und Erkenntnis Menschlichen Daseins, 4th ed., (Munich, 1964), pp. 672, 678.

[325]Thus L. Binswanger notes how Jung's "archetypal images" could be related to Dilthey's notion of the "typical" and "symbolical," cf. ibid., p. 652. Perhaps a key issue on which to compare Dilthey and Jung would be in regard to their notions of "type," cf. C. Jung, Psychological Types (volume 6 of his Collected Works); for Jung's analysis of the extroverted and introverted types is a psychological correlate of Dilthey's meta-scientific distinction between extrorsive and introrsive experience. On Victor Frankl's Logotherapy, cf. J. Fabry, The Pursuit of Meaning (Boston, 1968.

[326]Cf. B.A., p. 251; G.S. V, pp. 140-153.

[327]G.S. V, p. 166.

Contrary then to hoping for a complete sublation of an explanatory psychology, Dilthey was interested only in pointing out that without a descriptively analytical approach which would mediate the immediacy of self-awareness - and as such would provide the basis for the human sciences - an explanatory psychology itself would be sublated in neurology or physiology. Within such a process, moreover, he saw how the number of (hypothetical) explanatory elements would increase in an effort to approximate the living reality of consciousness.[328] This has as a result, however, the increasingly hypothetical character of explanatory psychology, so that the very purpose for which the explanatory elements were invoked, namely, to act as a norm for the verification of hypotheses, is missed.[329]

Having established this seemingly contradictory character of explanatory psychology, Dilthey goes on to discuss the method of a descriptive and analytical psychology and its relation to explanatory psychology. In articulating the aims and methods of descriptive-analytic psychology Dilthey clearly differentiates it from explanatory-constructive psychology. In general one might say that there were two aims Dilthey had in mind for his descriptive psychology.

First of all, there was a rather negative aim, namely to expose the inadequacy of explanatory psychology as a prime example of a human or cultural science handicapped by its complete dependency upon the methods of the natural sciences. Thus Dilthey not only sought to point out the deficiencies and contradictions within an explanatory (i.e., natural science oriented) psychology, but also how such a psychology adversely influenced the study of history and criminal law - not to mention the study of political economy and literature.[330] Indeed, his arguments here have a marked similarity with those today against a behavioristic psychologism.[331] Dilthey realized that a key argument against his

---

[328]G.S. V, pp. 167f.   [329]G.S. V, p. 168.

[330]Cf. G.S. V, pp. 191-193; VII, p. 19.

[331]For example, compare Dilthey's arguments, referred to in the previous note, with those of R. Wellek and

differentiation of the <u>Naturwissenschaften</u> and <u>Geistes-</u>
<u>wissenschaften</u> in terms of extrorsive and introrsive experi-
ence would appeal to psychology as practiced in a positivistic
reductionist manner.[332]   If the core of grounding the cultural
sciences in a "Selbstbesinnung" was not to be immediately
misunderstood, Dilthey realized that the relation of his
critique of historical reason to psychology had a foundational
importance, whereas the relation to historical and/or
sociological studies would be derivative.[333]

Secondly, the positive aim of Dilthey's critique called
for a thematization of inner experience which would sublate
the extremes of empiricism and idealism, experience and
thought.   Such a sublation could only occur if Dilthey could
succeed in developing an approach to inner experience which
would not only respect the unity of the subject but would also
be grounded on, and structured according to, that "originating
and omnipresent unity in the process of conscious living."[334]
Instead of beginning with unconscious components, which could
only be put forward hypothetically, and from them attempting
to explain conscious behavior and living experience, Dilthey
sought to remain within the unity of conscious experience
as a whole.   This whole was immediately present in the spontaneous self-presence of conscious living:

> The psychic process of life is primarily and completely,
> from its most elementary to its highest forms, a
> unity.   The inner life (<u>Seelenleben</u>) does not grow
> together from parts.   It is not constructed from

A. Warren against psychologism in literature; cf. their <u>Theory</u>
<u>of Literature</u>, 3rd ed., (London, 1963), pp. 81-93.

[332]Cf. <u>G.S.</u> V, pp. 255f.

[333]Cf. Dilthey's uncompleted essays, "Grundgedanke
meiner Philosophie" (c. 1880) and "Übersicht meines Systems"
(1896) in <u>G.S.</u> VIII, pp. 171-173, 176-184.   Making social and
historical frameworks derivative is by no means without
parallel in contemporary critical thought.   Cf. Charles
Hampden-Turner, <u>Radical Man: The Process of Psycho-Social</u>
<u>Development</u> (New York, 1971); also F. Matson, The Broken
Image, pp. 30-65, 161-230.   As the work of men like T. Kuhn
and J. Habermas illustrate, such an approach can counteract
the objectivistic tendency of reflection on science and
society, cf. note 308 of this Chapter.

[334]<u>G.S.</u> V, p. 211.

elements; nor is it a composite, nor a result of converging atoms of impressions or of feelings. It is primordially and always an all-embracing unity.[335]

It was the intention of Dilthey to make this "ganze unverstümmelte Erfahrung" the starting point and basis of his critique of historical reason.[336] This unity - or as Dilthey also referred to it, this "totality"[337] - is what is primary and given: a descriptive method would begin from it (rather than from elements, as in an explanatory approach), and seek to differentiate thematically the various functions of the unity. "Out of this unity do the various inner functions differentiate themselves, while remaining within its strucutre."[338] The unity, therefore, was the unity of self-presence as experienced; and the immediacy of this unity is spontaneously differentiated into various functions. The positive aim of a descriptive and analytical psychology would be to articulate the unity and its foundations.

The method of such a psychology is patterned upon the reality it investigates. Dilthey was of the opinion that even the unity we try to hypothetically posit in natural, external objects is a projection of the inner unity of our own self-experience.[339] Unlike explanatory psychology, a descriptive approach would begin with, and remain within, the whole or unity of this self-presence. This is possible since that unity is not some blind unconscious process but has an inherent intellectuality capable of intelligently attending to itself in an experiential (and not merely abstractly logical) manner.[340] Intelligent attention is not an

---

[335]Ibid.

[336]Cf. G.S. VIII, p. 171; also I, pp. 86-115.

[337]Cf. B.A., pp. 90, 94, 187f.; G.S. V, pp. 170-172.

[338]G.S. V, p. 211; also V, p. 170.

[339]Cf. G.S. V, pp. 169f. Also M. Riedel, "W. Dilthey und das Problem der Metaphysik," Phil. Jhbk. 76, pp. 344ff. on projection.

[340]Cf. G.S. V, pp. 171-172: "...the first characteristic of our understanding of inner states, which conditions the psychological research, is the intellectuality of inner

explanatory experience but understanding as <u>Erlebnis</u> for it is not simply an intellectual exercise, but "an activity of the whole soul."[341]

> We explain through purely intellectual processes, but we understand through the collaboration of all the powers of the human spirit.... The experienced structure of inner life must remain the solid, lived and immediately secure foundation of psychology, no matter how deeply it also enters into experimental, specialized research.[342]

Understanding then, as rooted in the experience of self-presence encompasses and extends beyond any purely intellectual explanatory interests. The descriptive approach is committed to a heightening of awareness whereby the experience of self-reflection would be identical with the experience of self-presence (hence my designation of this process as the subject-as-subject).[343] It is this introrsive movement of the descriptive method which is essential to Dilthey's method and clearly differentiates the observation it entails from that of the natural sciences. For although there is a descriptive movement within the latter, it is not directed toward experienced self-presence, nor does it remain within that presence:

> But the notion of a descriptive science has a much deeper meaning in psychology than it could have in the natural sciences.... In psychology this structure of functions within lived experience is present interiorly. All specialized psychological knowledge is only an analysis of this structure.[344]

The analysis of this totality as experienced interiority is not abstract nor transcendental, in the sense that it would aim at capturing the whole in some type of <u>a priori</u> concepts. By remaining within the context of inner experience the priority of <u>Erlebnis</u> is assured, as well as immediacy and objectivity of the structure of that inner experience.[345]

---

perceptions."

[341] Cf. <u>G.S.</u> V, p. 172.

[342] <u>Ibid</u>.; Cf. also Chapter Three, pp. 229-232.

[343] Cf. <u>G.S.</u> V, pp. 197-200.   [344] <u>G.S.</u> V, p. 173.

[345] Cf. <u>G.S.</u> V, pp. 173-176.

The antinomies which Dilthey uncovered in the Kantian transcendentalist approach were traceable to the attempt to conceptually construct the subject, deducing all categorical functions or structures from conceptual a priori analysis. This Dilthey rejected as simply another variant of an explanatory psychology.[346] Whereas such an approach is forced to begin with hypothetical constructions in order to explain subjectivity, a descriptive method begins with the certainty of self-presence, seeks to analyze the structures and functions given immediately within that self-presence, and only in its later stages does it allow of certain hypothetical constructions when the immediacy of understanding is not sufficient to uncover or decide an issue.[347]

Dilthey divides the three main tasks of a descriptive and analytic method into (1) uncovering the basic structures, (2) determining the development of the structures, taking into account the goals and values of the structures, and (3) showing how such developing structures are articulated into acquired contexts (erworbene Zusammenhänge).[348] Inasmuch as P. Krausser's Kritik der endlichen Vernunft has provided a somewhat detailed discussion of these tasks, I shall not go into them here.[349] It is important to realize, however, that each of these stages are meant to be descriptively analytic, i.e., Dilthey is concerned with the reader understanding them by relating them to his own inner experience. This is accomplished, not by some type of purely objectivistic introspection, but by that heightening of awareness and attention to self-presence whereby that self-presence reveals its own immediacy:

> The inwardness of inner processes or states are different from the observation of the same through a heightened mode of consciousness brought about by the will. As always, we must avoid the confusion of the presuppositions for natural knowledge with those for the knowledge of cultural (geistiger)

---

[346] G.S. V, p. 175.

[347] Cf. ibid., pp. 175- 176.

[348] Cf. G.S. V, pp. 176-180. In B.A. this is the "objective context," cf. pp. 166-168 of B.A.

[349] Cf. Krausser's Kritik der endlichen Vernunft, pp. 69- 161, especially his Figures four, five, six, and seven.

realities. Thus we must guard against the transposition of what happens in observing external objects into the attentive perception of inner states.[350]

In Figure Four I have outlined the basic cognitive-emotive-volitional functions of conscious interiority as they occur in various writings of Dilthey. Dilthey saw Kant as the classical proponent of this threefold division; but he was also influenced by his teacher, F. A. Trendelenburg.[351] Even more than the latter, however, Dilthey dropped any connotation of a faulty psychology, emphasizing their quality as dynamic functions and structured events. As Dilthey uncovered the basic structures, four general characteristics emerged.

First of all, the cognitive-emotive-volitional structures are not hypothetical constructions. They are functional differentiations within the totality of conscious interiority. Thus Dilthey often refers to the totality of inner experience as "the totality of our inner life, the activity of the entire willing-feeling-thinking man."[352] This is, therefore, an instance of functions differentiated within the unity of the whole context (Zusammenhang) of inner experience, so that the functional structures are themselves experienced in their reality.[353]

Secondly, these structures or basic functions are not reducible to one another. Imagination and knowing - Dilthey interchangeably refers to the cognitive functions as

---

[350]G.S. V, pp. 197f.

[351]Cf. B.A., pp. 95f. Trendelenburg showed Dilthey the socio-historical import of the division, cf. his Über den letzten Unterschied der philosophischen Systeme, second ed. (Berlin, 1955). Here one notes the circular character of Dilthey's procedure: he experiences the cognitive-emotive-volitional structures, and this not only individually but historically and socially; cf. J. Wach, "Die Typenlehre Trendelenburgs und ihr Einfluss auf Dilthey" in Philosophie und Geschichte II (1926).

[352]G.S. V, pp. 11, 200f., 263-265; VII, pp. 22f.; B.A. pp. 94, 173, 225-228. That Dilthey was not proposing a faculty psychology, cf. B.A., 92-95 where he rejects the notion of "substance" as applied to soul and goes on to emphasize the dynamic operational notion of knowing-feeling-willing.

[353]Cf. G.S. V, pp. 206, 211.

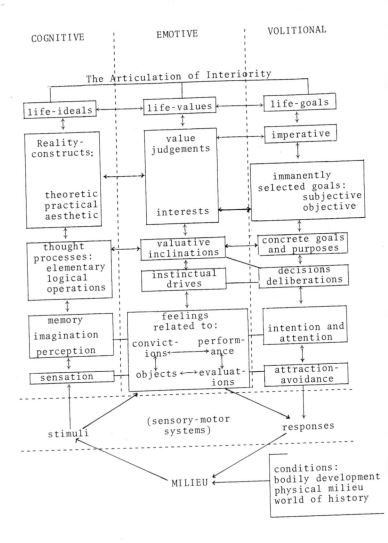

COGNITIVE   EMOTIVE   VOLITIONAL

The Articulation of Interiority

life-ideals ↔ life-values ↔ life-goals

Reality-constructs:

theoretic
practical
aesthetic

value judgements

imperative

interests

immanently selected goals:
subjective
objective

thought processes:
elementary logical operations

valuative inclinations

concrete goals and purposes

instinctual drives

decisions deliberations

memory imagination perception

feelings related to:
convict-ions ↔ perform-ance
objects ↔ evaluat-ions

intention and attention

sensation

attraction-avoidance

stimuli   (sensory-motor systems)   responses

MILIEU

conditions:
bodily development
physical milieu
world of history

Figure Four: Basic Structures and Functions of Interiority
(G.S. I, 64-70; V, 90-316; VI, 139-157;
VII, 3-23; VIII, 15-24.)

"Vorstellen" or "Denken"[354] - are not reducible to feelings and emotions, nor are the latter reducible to deciding and willing, etc.[355] There cannot be a question, then, of merely reducing any of these functions to certain unconscious elements and constructing them according to models in the natural sciences in their determinations of cause-effect relationships.[356] This is again the application here of Dilthey's insight into life as inner experience or conscious interiority. As thought cannot go behind life inasmuch as thinking itself is a function of living experience, so consciousness cannot go behind consciousness to deny the reality of its own factuality or there-ness.

> The science of inner life cannot go behind the structure as it is present in inner experience itself. Consciousness cannot get in back of itself. The structure in which thinking itself is operative, from which it proceeds, and on which it depends, is a presupposition for us that cannot be sublated. Thinking cannot get behind its own reality, the reality in which it comes into being.[357]

This is not, of course, to deny that unconscious motives and elements cannot be investigated and explanatory constructions put forward for verification. The point is that such procedures are not the foundations of a critical stance toward the cultural sciences but rather derivative from the foundations actually given in conscious living.[358] The self-evidence of consciousness as given does not mean for Dilthey that these cognitive-emotive-volitional structures are known as such from the first dawning of awareness. Quite the contrary. The structures are operative without any reflective attention to them. Hence Dilthey's designation of them as

---

[354]Thus for Dilthey Denken was primarily an activity of the subject related to Wahrnehmen and Vorstellen and through these to the Gegenstand, cf. B.A. pp. 33f., 68f., 94f., 198f.

[355]Cf. G.S. V, pp. 212-213.

[356]Cf. G.S. V, p. 212.

[357]G.S. V, p. 194; also V, p. 136.

[358]Cf. G.S. V, pp. 194f.

life:

> ...we have not little by little and tentatively
> discovered the living structure of the human spirit.
> It is life, it exists before any knowledge. Its
> characteristics are spontaneity, historicality,
> freedom, development. When we analyze this inner
> structure, we never come upon reified or substantial
> objects, we can never fit it together from elements.
> There are no isolated elements, everywhere they are
> inseparable from the functions. Normally these
> functions do not come into consciousness for us.
> Differentiations, levels, distinctions are indeed
> there, although we are not aware of the processes
> by which they are ascertained.[359]

This is precisely the difficulty of cognitional theory, and
Dilthey realized that an exact thematization of conscious
living had to do with the "thousand year task" whereby mankind
has gradually come to a point where exact expression of its
inner experience could be possible.[360] Indeed, as was argued
in Chapter Two and the previous section, it was the emergence
of historical consciousness which has necessitated the thematization of interiority as a foundation for a scientific
understanding of man's cultural, historical, and social
processes.[361]

Thirdly, the correlation evident in Figure Four is that
between the milieu and the self, even though the "Umwelt" is
not as extensively represented as conscious intentionality is.
This is important; Dilthey was not about to fall into an
idealist concern with subjectivity in his efforts to counteract empiricism in psychology. Instead he was working on a
notion of what we now term a dynamic feed-back system
embracing man and world. This has been sufficiently studied
by P. Krausser in his Kritik der endlichen Vernunft where he
shows the gradual development of feedback models in Dilthey's
writings and their characteristics as self-correcting

---

[359]G.S. V, p. 196.

[360]Cf. G.S. VII, p. 18. Dilthey was always concerned
to situate his own efforts at a descriptive and analytical
psychology within the historical perspective. This should
be abundantly clear from Chapter Two of this study, which
sketched the historical context for Dilthey's critique of
historical reason.

[361]Cf. Chapter Two, pp. 93-114, 137-156; Chapter Three
pp. 214-221.

processes of learning.[362] It would be a gross misunderstanding of Dilthey to see in his critique of historical reason a subjectivist minimalizing of objectivity or of externality. For although Dilthey saw the methods of the natural sciences as mainly hypothetical in their efforts at explaining the world of nature, still he tried to establish clearly that the _experience_ of the external world in terms of the experiences of impression and resistance gave us a certainty regarding its existence and influence. He tried to demonstrate this in an essay of 1890, "Contributions toward resolving the question of the origin of our faith in the reality of the external world."[363]

Since Heidegger's remarks in _Sein und Zeit_ and Gadamer's _Wahrheit und Methode_ it is customary to see in this essay a locus classicus for Dilthey's basic Cartesianism.[364] A closer study of Dilthey would have shown, however, how his critique of empiricism and idealism presupposed a radical critique of Cartesianism. For to begin with the Cartesian notion of subjectivity as not intrinsically related to objectivity, to begin with a primal dichotomy between self and world, meant that (as Dilthey put it in a letter to Graf Yorck) one could only succumb to the conclusions of a Hume, a Kant, and their followers, that "we would finally remain encapsulated in the Cartesian Ego."[365]

It was to counter such an abstract transcendentalist approach to subjectivity that Dilthey insisted upon the fundamental reality or there-ness of experience. The unity

---

[362]Krausser, _op. cit._, pp. 27-208.

[363]Cf. _G.S._ V, pp. 90-138.

[364]Cf. M. Heidegger, _Sein und Zeit_, pp. 205-206. Also H. -G. Gadamer, _Wahrheit und Methode_, pp. 218-228. For a complete presentation of Gadamer's understanding (and to my mind, misunderstanding) of Dilthey in this regard, cf. F. Lawrence, "Self-Knowledge in History in Gadamer and Lawrence," in P. McShane (ed.) _Language Truth and Meaning_, pp. 167-174, 210-217.

[365]_Briefwechsel_, p. 55 (letter number 48). It was also in this letter that Dilthey complained of the senseless "bridge building" between self and world which philosophers had been attempting since Descartes.

of the subject was not encapsulated, as it was a unity which could ground both the identity of the subject-as-subject and the non-identity of the subject-as-object. For Dilthey the _experience_ of material objects was certainly of the object-as-object, even if our knowledge of the object would be conceptually mediated through the hypothetical constructions of the natural sciences. This is somewhat similar, then, to Lonergan's distinction between consciousness and knowledge. The cognitive functions, for Dilthey, could not attain the object in an immediate manner, but only through conceptual constructs.[366] But in the volitional and emotive functions there is clearly the experience of the object:

> The self and the objects both lie within consciousness.
> For external energy is present in its influences on
> the will and feelings. Furthermore, the object has the
> same essential structure as the self. For it is not
> constructed in a vacuum through thought, but has its
> own life and independent essence in the lived experience
> of the will.[367]

In thematizing the structures and functions of the subject-as-subject, therefore, Dilthey had no intention of treating them in isolation from world. As Krausser has documented, Dilthey conceived of conscious interiority as part of a dynamic total system in constant feedback relation with the natural, historical, social, and cultural environment. During the period he was working on the _Breslauer Ausarbeitung_ he became engrossed in neurological studies and Krausser has given us a schematized model of the feedback systems he outlined.[368] In Figure Four these are reduced to a simple mention of the action-reaction, stimuli-response, input-output correlations. Dilthey studied the growing complexity of interiority, i.e., the functional processes between input and output, as one ascended from lower to higher animal forms.[369] Nevertheless, these biological, physiological,

---

[366]Cf. _G.S._ V, pp. 126-130. On Lonergan's distinction, cf. previous section.

[367]_G.S._ V, pp. 132f.

[368]Cf. P. Krausser, _op. cit._, pp. 90ff.

[369]Cf. _G.S._ V, pp. 207-211; 98-100; also the quotations

and neurological studies were by no means central to his
descriptive psychology. They were not the foundations or
core but only the periphery: that region where hypothesis
and explanatory constructions had their rightful place.[370]
In the Figure, therefore, I have reduced Dilthey's studies
of the spinal cord and brain to a simple indication of the
sensory-motor systems operative in the constant exchange
between self and world.[371]

The fourth point leads to a discussion of the basic
structures and functions themselves. The many two-headed
arrows indicate the continual complex interplay between the
spheres of imagining, feeling, and willing. The circular
patterns of this interplay are evident. Of primary importance
in mediating the cognitive and volitional is the centrality
of the emotive functions. I have already analyzed how
Dilthey's "Selbstbesinnung" of the subject-as-subject tended
to concentrate on the reality of self-presence as a "Selbst-
gefühl."[372] This was, in effect, an effort within the
context of German Idealism and Schleiermacher to attain that
creative and living subjectivity which Henry Newman attempted,
from a very different perspectives, with his notion of the
illative sense.[373] In his <u>Breslauer Ausarbeitung</u> Dilthey was

---

from <u>B.A.</u> in P. Krausser, <u>op. cit.</u>, pp. 229-233.

[370] Cf. <u>G.S.</u> V, pp. 175f.; 210, 238; VII, p. 23. This
is because of the hypothetical nature of Darwin's evolutionary theory, cf. subsection on emergent probability
in this Chapter.

[371] For a more detailed account of Dilthey's neurological
investigation; cf. P. Krausser, <u>op. cit.</u>, pp. 95-100, 229-235.

[372] Cf. pp. 289ff. of this Chapter and the references
given there.

[373] Thus Newman refers to the Aristotelian notion of
<u>phronesis</u> in determining the nature of the illative sense,
mentioning how he goes beyond Aristotle insofar as the
illative sense pertains to both theory and practice, cf. J. H.
Newman, <u>A Grammar of Assent</u> (New York, 1955), pp. 276ff.
Dilthey also saw his "Selbstbesinnung" as related to the
Socratic-Platonic-Aristotelian notions of <u>phronesis</u> cf.
<u>G.S.</u> I, pp. 178f. I have not found any evidence to
substantiate M. Riedel's claim that Dilthey appeals to the
Socratic-Platonic <u>phronesis</u> in contradistinction to the
Aristotelian, cf. <u>Hermeneutik und Dialektik</u>, vol. I, p. 234,

322

struggling to articulate the _experience_ of thinking and judging; acknowledging in feelings of conviction and objectivity the subjective emotive dimension of intellectual activities. This was to counteract the Idealist separation between mind and will, as well as the empiricist idea that the mind simply reflects (_Abbildtheorie_) objective reality:

> What we call reality is something different than this dead and passive objectivity of an image in a mirror. It is the inwardness revealing an activity outside of me through the impression of feeling and a resistance met by the will.[374]

It was in this context that he would later see how the activities of knowing and doing were intimately related in a living commitment to feeling and value. In the _Breslauer Ausarbeitung_ he had complained of the way in which both Idealist and Empiricist cognitional theories had propagated a destructive separation of theory (knowing) and praxis (doing).[375] And in his _Ideen_ he put forward the description of moving from knowing to doing through the mediation of feelings of value and a striving to realize them. By themselves imagination and knowing do not provide any adequate motivation for action. The life-value that unites knowing and doing, that carries forward the process of living, need not be known in order for us to act.[376] Why? Because value as motivational is not simply theoretical.[377] For Dilthey the theoretical activity of thinking could not uncover the subject-as-subject. "Since in the process we label as theoretical, the content becomes an

---

note 6. True, in _G.S._ XIV/1, p. 73 he refers to only the Platonic, but in _G.S._ I, p. 179 he says of the _Selbstbesinnung_ "It is only the return to the cognitive ground of knowing, so that logic emerges from it as scientific theory, somewhat as Plato envisioned it and Aristotle carried it out." Dilthey would thus see the self-reflection as the origin of both logic and ethic, but still emphasized the shortcomings of the Greek position in their failure to thematize conscious interiority as such.

[374]_B.A._, p. 205.

[375]_B.A._, pp. 11f., 246f.; on the theoretical and practical significance of his own "Selbstbesinnung," cf. _B.A._, p. 53.

[376]Cf. _G.S._ V, pp. 204.   [377]_G.S._ V, p. 205.

object, standing over against the one who grasps it."[378] The judgment of value that reveals the subjectivity and liberates it from a mere cause-effect (stimulus-response) pattern is grounded in the emotive functions as central to conscious interiority, uniting the functions of cognition and volition:

> A bundle of instincts and feelings, that is the center of our inner structure. Out of the welter of impressions attention focuses on perceptions, as this center dictates, through the participation of feeling in it. The perceptions are linked with memories, a series of thoughts are formed. To this is joined an enhancement of our there-being (Dasein) or pain, fear, anger. So are all depths of our being moved. And from this comes the transition from pain to desire, from desire to longing, or to some other series of inner states, resulting in arbitrary actions.[379]

Although the emotive functions do not of themselves provide a scientific analysis of interiority, they are the foundations of any such analysis.[380] As central and foundational, not only did Dilthey see the emotive structures as capable of relating the cognitive and volitional structures, but of doing so in that spontaneous, living manner of the subject-as-subject.[381] The thought processes, as elementary logical operations, make possible a certain self-determination which, through distinct valuations and volitional purposes, liberates the subject from the tyranny of a spontaneity at the mercy of sense stimuli.[382]

---

[378] B.A., pp. 198-199.

[379] G.S. V, p. 206; cf. also V, p. 185.

[380] Cf. G.S. V, pp. 206ff. "And this is decisive for the entire study of the human spirit's structural context: the passage from one state to another, the force that leads from one to another, falls within inner experience. Because we experience (erleben) this passage and force, because we become interiorly this structural context, which embraces all passions, sufferings and destinies of human life, we can understand human life, history, all the depths and abysses of human existence... The lived structural context is the foundation."

[381] Cf. G.S. V, pp. 197, 190, 196; B.A., p. 14.

[382] G.S. V, 112; VII, 42-43. Note how the two-headed arrows indicate the growing complexifications of the circular

The upper section of Figure Four schematizes the main developmental structures of interiority, the functions present in its articulation into the acquired patterns (erworbene Zusammenhänge) constituting individuality.[383] Physical development, environment and, especially, the socio-cultural differences of history (geistige Welt) are the outer conditions leading to different constructions of reality, different ideals, values, purposes in the myriad articulations of interiority.[384] This is especially true of the finalistic selectivity (Zweckmässigkeit) whereby different individuals go about realizing both subjective and objective purposes.[385]

Each of these structures and functions are realized differently in different individuals, societies, cultures. But the variety of realizations does not lead to a sublation of its own presuppositions, history does not sublate its own basic structures.[386] If men were to cease being cognitive-emotive-volitional there would be no history. Because the basic structures are both experienced and of this inner experience they share the latter's certainty and universality.[387] In one stroke, so to speak, they ground both the relativity of historical consciousness and the universality of scientific consciousness. Hence the unity of identity and non-identity in the subject-as-subject: the basic structures

---

process from stimuli to response from reflex-machanisms through elementary learning processes to the gradual articulation of an individual's ideals, values, goals.

[383] G.S. V, 177-183, 217, 226-237, 241-316.

[384] G.S. V, 185-190, 214-217.

[385] Cf. G.S. V, pp. 215-219; VII, pp. 8-9, 324-331.

[386] Compare Dilthey's remarks in 1880 (Krausser, op. cit., pp. 224-225) with those in 1896-1897 (VIII, p. 182). Krausser totally overlooked the intention of Dilthey to overcome the hypothetical basis of the Geisteswissenschaften in his descriptive-analytic psychology. Put in terms of Krausser's own elaboration of the recurrent structures of finite reason - are these structures themselves aufhebbar? For Dilthey they were not.

[387] G.S. V, pp. 171-176, 206, 221, 223-224. These three basic structures are not reducible to one another; cf. G.S. V, pp. 212-213; VII, pp. 137-138.

of interiority in their realization constitute individuality "while simultaneously relating the individual to other human beings."[388] History does not sublate a certain fundamental similarity between men;[389] if there were a total heterogeneity there would be no possibility of any understanding at all.[390]

2.   The Subject-as-Object

Besides knowing, feeling and willing there is also the known, felt, willed. It is this shift of attention from acts to contents that defines Dilthey's transition from the subject-as-subject to the subject-as-object. In the grounding of the human sciences in a descriptive-analytic psychology, the inner experience is self-mediating. From 1900 until his death in 1911 it was this self-mediation that especially interested Dilthey. His pyschological and historical "Selbstbesinnung" leads to a philosophical one as "consciousness about every consciousness and a knowledge of all knowing."[391] If self-presence in its spontaneous historicality is not an awareness of the self as object but as subject,[392] then how would a method based on the self-mediatory subject-as-subject attain objective knolwedge? Dilthey confessed both his own personal desire, and that of the human sciences in general, to attain "an objective knowledge of the correlations of human experiences in the human-historical-social world."[393] Dilthey had claimed, against Kant, that we do experience the reality of the external world through the emotive and volitional functions of interiority; he agreed with Kant that the cognitive functions were not able to attain reality-in-itself. But the reality-in-itself which the human sciences seek to know is within inner experience

---

[388] G.S. VII, p. 309; also G.S. V, pp. 226-237.

[389] Cf. G.S. I, p. 395; V, pp. 226, 223-230, 251; also Diwald, op. cit., pp. 145-153.

[390] G.S. VII, pp. 210-216, 225, 237-239, 257, 262-264.

[391] G.S. VII, p. 7; VIII, p. 13.

[392] G.S. VII, pp. 26-27; V, pp. 190, 196-197.

[393] G.S. VII, pp. 3, 103, 295, 304-305, 309, 313-314; VIII, p. 233.

itself, and so Dilthey had to explain how the cognitive
functions attain an objectively valid knowledge of this
inner reality. He did this by working out the notions of
objective comprehension and possession, relating them to
the basic structures of interiority.

In Figure Five I have schematized these notions. Here
I shall limit myself to discussing some important aspects
of each.

A. Objective Mental Comprehension. Objective mental
comprehension is a unity of diverse operations (attention
to mental facts, observation of them, relating them to their
conceptual contexts, judging this relation) aimed at grasping
cognitively the experience.[394] This experience is inexhaus-
tibly varied and complex, as history demonstrates. Dilthey
was extremely cautious on the subject of an objective
knowledge. He saw clearly the mistake of Hegel in trying
to mediate historical life conceptually.[395] The historian
or philosopher will never know "the essence of life"; there
would always be "the inexhaustibility of lived experience."[396]
Yet "the human spirit must bring about a valid knowledge from
its own resources," and such self-mediation should be understood as systematic knowledge representing the myriad aspects
of historical life. There is no one science of historical
life.[397] The many scientific efforts at understanding build
a "second-order mental world," a world of theory, which
strives to adequately represent the world of spontaneous
history and inner experience.[398] The notion of representation
guarantees that the normative would not be in the mediation

---

[394]G.S. VII, pp. 6-9, 22-23, 121-129.

[395]G.S. IV, pp. 219ff.; VII, pp. 3, 31, 150, 157, 258,
271; VIII, p. 12.

[396]G.S. VII, pp. 194-195; p. 29.

[397]G.S. VII, pp. 6-7, 331.

[398]G.S. VII, pp. 300, 307; V, p. 45; VII, pp. 146, 219,
254. Note that Dilthey was ultimately unable to ground the
transition from spontaneous historicality to the world of
theory since, while Erleben was not perceptualist (not of the
subject-as-object but the subject-as-subject), Erkennen and
Wissen, as representative, were.

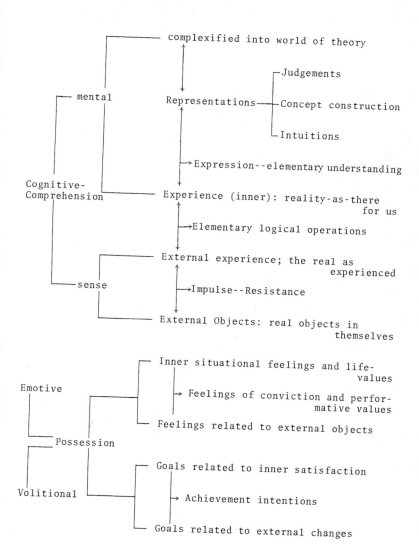

Figure Five: Objective Comprehension and Possession
(G.S. V, 90-138; VII, 3-69, 121-129, 207-213, 295-303, 307.)

but in the self; not in the concepts and judgments of theory, but in inner experience. A fundamental error in all metaphysical systems, Hegel's included, was to maintain that their worlds of theory had an objectivity independent of spontaneous history (<u>Lebendigkeit</u>).[399]

Dilthey's cognitional theoretical grounding of the human sciences, then, did not have its starting point and norm within the world of theory - as Kant's did in terms of the natural sciences and mathematics - but in the spontaneous historical world.[400] The human sciences themselves sprung from the praxis of life, they are a complex of historical and systematic contexts, so that there is a continuous interaction between "experience and concepts."[401]

> Concepts and generalized judgments are the middle terms between the events and the grasping of their connection. These concepts and judgments arise primarily in the praxis of life. The slow progress of insight into the interconnection (<u>Zusammenhang</u>) of history is, therefore, dependent upon the development of the analytic sciences dealing with the specialized purposive structures which, as cultural systems, run throughout history.... Finally, historical understanding and the systematic cultural sciences are not only based on conclusions from historical, social life, but also they presuppose certain insights into the development of lived human interiority.[402]

The key to the self-mediation of the basic structures of interiority is to determine how the mediating concepts and judgments function as representations, first within spontaneous historical life and then in reference to an objective comprehension of interiority.

The experience of comprehension (<u>Auffassungserlebnis</u>) is a structural unity through the relations of its components among themselves and to their objects. Elementary understanding grasps <u>what</u> someone is experiencing in his

---

[399] G.S. VIII, p. 51; cf. I, pp. 150-350.

[400] G.S. VII, pp. 332-333; VIII, pp. 174-175.

[401] Cf. G.S. V, pp. 21, 341; VII, pp. 160, 164, 316.

[402] G.S. VII, pp. 316-317.

[403] G.S. VII, pp. 30-31, 326; V, pp. 319, 332.

expressions; spontaneous interiority achieves a partial
transcendence in its expressions, an object-ifying of itself,
especially in linguistic expressions. In this spontaneous
knowing we are not aware of the acts themselves but of their
contents which determine the object.[404] The latter does not
change as the various acts bring its various aspects to
consciousness: "without a change in the object, the type and
kind of consciousness of the object changes, as one moves
from intuition to memory or to judgment."[405] This accounts
for the structural unity among the representative acts, also
proving the normative element as "intuited or experienced."[406]
The reality itself of the object is intuitively related to
the subject in true judgments. Judgments do not grasp
the thing itself but representatively determine its
essence.[407] "The reality itself" is "intuitively present."
The representative functions of concepts and judgments are
not clearly distinguished.[408] As long as the experienced is

---

[404] G.S. VII, p. 37.   [405] G.S. VII, p. 38.

[406] G.S. VII, pp. 38, 42-43.

[407] G.S. VII, pp. 38-39; cf. p. 25: "The modifications,
which differentiate various experiences by an objective
character, indicate that here there is not only a content
within inner experience (Erlebnis), but also a type of
consciousness. Such are the data, as they characterize
perceptions, or the acknowledgment of a fact, as this occurs
in the imaginative presentation of a painter or poet, or the
positing of reality in a judgment. No matter what psychological differences may exist between an imaginative presentation
and a perception relative to the same object or content -
structurally there is no difference in the type of consciousness relative to the objective." Thus perceptions, imaginative representations and judgments are structurally similar
in objective comprehension.

[408] G.S. VII, pp. 38, 316-317. Note also the influence
of Schleiermacher here, XIV/1, p. 133: "In the order of concepts is expressed what is persistent and essential. On the
contrary, the system of our judgments is concerned with how
the change of conditions, the interplay of causes and effects,
produces contingent and mutable states relative to the
persistent and essential." Thus concepts and judgments presuppose one another in circular fashion (121-122) but concepts
themselves have an "ursprüngliche Identität" with the objects
(122) and knowing occurs both in the form of concepts and
of judgment (125). Concepts dominate speculative knowing and
judgments empirical and historical knowing (133). On

not fully represented, a drive exists to ever more adequate
knowledge, constitutive of the move from experience to the
universal. The realization of all the relations contained
in the experienced or intuited would be "the concept of the
world."[409]

Turning to the objective comprehension of inner experience itself, or the self-mediation of "Geist," one finds
similar functions or acts unified by the object, in this
interiority. The only difference here is that the reality
is already there:

> Indeed, the comprehension grounded in lived experience
> corresponds with that founded in sense intuition inas-
> much as both contain a relation to an object....
> The comprehension of the psychic structure is just
> as much an unending task as that of external objects.
> But it consists in discovering what is already contained
> in lived experience. Thus the reality of the psychic
> object is simultaneously always possessed and ever to
> be conceptually explicated.[410]

Attentative observation must be careful not to destroy the
spontaneity of inner experience.[411] The definitive establishing (festigen) of the object is attained in the positing of
judgments which refer to the inner experiences and determine
their essence within a context of representations.

> Judgment means lived experience (Erlebnis). It is a
> representative connection that is conditioned by the
> nature of signs and relates to lived experience.[412]

What is meant in judgment, then, is really not the inner
experience but its "essential determination":

> What is meant in a judgment, therefore, is a fact which
> transcends lived experience and refers to the psychic
> structure according to its essential determination,
> or a series of essential determinations. And these
> essential determinations are not referable back to

Dilthey's interpretation as a whole, cf. XIV/1, pp. 105-135.

[409]G.S. VII, pp. 38, 41.   [410]G.S. VII, p. 32.

[411]G.S. VII, pp. 19, 194. Here one notices the
perceptualism of knowing as contrasted with the awareness
of feelings as experienced.

[412]G.S. VII, p. 30.

lived experience through correspondence.[413]
As judgments, the conceptual constructions of interiority
are representative. Historically they are manifold; Dilthey
gives four (an objective universal, an empirical, a causal
and a religious) besides his own conceptual construction of
interiority as structurally dynamic. "Each of these directions
is grounded in the nature of this [interiority] and the manner
of its presence. . . . Each of these objectifications of
experience grasps one aspect of the psychic reality."[414]
These different, sometimes contradictory, conceptualizations
of interiority made possible entire historical epochs, thereby
expressing an aspect of interiority and, through such conceptual expressions, affected (einwirken) the interiority
itself. As the conceptualizations, so the other modes of
objective comprehension or interiority, attentative observation and judgments, all express in their own way some reality
insofar as they are concerned with inner experience. "Since
at every turn we have only to do with representations of
the experienced."[415]

Dilthey's elaboration of the objective comprehension
and the self-mediation of interiority, therefore, could arrive
at no inherent justification of his own conceptualization of
inner self-presence as imagining-feeling-willing. Or rather,
its justification implied the verification of all other
conceptualizations as well. Because interiority as experienced is alone normative and the inexhaustible ground of
all historical expressions, any representation that occurs
must express some aspect of interiority. Any statement
about the experienced is objectively true insofar as it is
brought into "correspondence" with the experienced; which
means, through an understanding as a re-experiencing
(nacherleben) of the statement-as-expression, one relates the

---

[413] G.S. VII, pp. 30f., 125, 244; cf. note 416 below.

[414] G.S. VII, pp. 31f.

[415] Cf. G.S. VII, pp. 32, 139-140. On p. 9 Dilthey did
formulate a principle of selection in terms of better and
more conscious representations of the total Zusammenhang, but
his own further elaboration reduced the principle of selection
to one of classification.

statement to the inner reality of self-presence from which
it originated.[416] Thus Dilthey would indirectly show the
advantages of his conceptualization of interiority insofar as

---

[416]G.S. VII, pp. 13, 18: "The necessity of the relation
between a determinate experience and its corresponding psychic
expression is immediately experienced (erlebt). It is the
difficult task of structural psychology to make judgments
which reproduce the structural experiences with the
consciousness of a correspondence that stands in some
adequate relation to particular experiences." Also pp. 26-27:
"Every statement about an experienced is objectively true, if
it is brought into correspondence with the experience... it
states only the occurrence of the perceptual relationship
itself." Also VII, 125-127, 213-216, 38, 44. Now the
"Wesensbestimmungen" in judgments cannot as such be brought
into correspondence with experience since they transcend
experience (cf. note 413 above) but, Dilthey seems to maintain,
insofar as they occur within the there-ness of self-presence,
they are brought into correspondence with experience, not as
determining the objectivity of their content, but simply as
occurring. Five years later Dilthey was a bit more nuanced,
cf. VII, 125: "The relationship of representation extends
throughout the entire structure of discursive thought in objective comprehension, as this occurs through judgments. The
given in its concrete intuitiveness (Anschaulichkeit), along
with the representative world of images, are themselves represented in every form of discursive thought through a system
of relations of fixed thought-components. And conversely,
a return to the object corresponds with that system when it
verifies the judgment or the concept in the complete fullness
of the object's intuitive there-being (anschaulichen
Daseins)." Here the object as being-there in its intuitive
fullness verifies the judgments or concepts if it preserves
them. In any case, the important point for Dilthey is that the
reality-itself of inner experience consisted in that experience itself prior to any objective mental comprehension.

The result is obvious: since he did not thematize knowing
as immediately given experience, the experience itself takes
on a noumenal character to such an extent that Dilthey cannot
judge any other conception of interiority or inner experience
as false. Because it is Unerschöpflich and the normative is
only in the empirically given, any expression must reveal
something of interiority. On a similarity with Heidegger's
ontological notion of truth, cf. sections on the noumenal
residue in Chapter Three. Also Tugendhat, op. cit., 344:
"Heidegger's position fails to distinguish between the
factual act of dis-covering and what is dis-covered in
specie...resulting in a position according to which truth
does not distinguish an adequate demonstration from an
inadequate one, but a demonstrated being from a hidden
one; a being becomes true, when it is factually shown or
demonstrated (aufzeigt)." Also ibid., pp. 331-356.

he could relate any historical expression to his conception of the totality of interiority as imagining, feeling, willing.

B. Objective Emotive Possession. If objective mental comprehension is orientated to a knowledge of reality, and mirrors the ambiguity of the Kantian noumenon, objective possession (Gegenständliches Haben) in feeling and willing show how Dilthey was seeking a way out of conceptualism.

> What is at stake here is to prepare a comparative method of investigation for the theory of knowledge. What must be done is to disengage logic and the whole theory of knowledge from their preponderant relation to knowledge of reality. Then logical and theoretical scientific statements must be constructed that refer equally well to knowledge of reality and to determination of value, to the positing of purpose and to the determination of norms.[417]

The aim of Dilthey's description of the objective possession of emotive structures is to sketch the immanent teleology within the emotive living of subjects that accounts for the contents as objective. There are five main aspects in Dilthey's treatment of objective possession in feeling.

First, feelings are differentiated from both knowing and willing. Both of these latter are primarily directed to objects in the sense that knowing is an experience of the comprehended object and willing seeks to attain or realize an object-ive.[418] This brings out a second difference insofar as as feelings are objectively less capable of predictive ordering:

> Feelings are different from objective comprehension and volitional attitudes in that the lived experiences in those two are interrelated in a more regulated way. The interrelations of feelings in the course of an affect or a passion seem irregular and fortuitous. It is this difference that gives emotive acting its special character.[419]

We have already seen how Dilthey's notion of the subject-as-subject was rooted in his notion of "self-feeling" or emotive self-presence. This difference of the emotive from the cognitive and volitional presupposes a relation. The basis of the emotive as objective is to be found in the acts of

---

[417]G.S. VII, p. 45.   [418]G.S. VII, p. 47.

[419]G.S. VII, pp. 48, 54.

objective comprehension:

> The acts of objective comprehension form the basis
> for feeling. Everything that belongs to these acts
> can serve as such a basis. The relation of subject
> and objective world, that arises in these acts as a
> consistent schema of comprehension, is also the
> objective basis of our feelings and our willing.
> Emotive lived experience is emotive conduct towards
> the objectively given, or towards possible or imagined
> situations or objects.[420]   .

The emotive mediates the cognitive and volitional, while the
cognitive shares in the mediation inasmuch as the "relation
between feelings occur only insofar as representations act
as mediators."[421] The relation-in-difference to the volitional can be seen in how feelings may motivate decision and
action, but also may not, especially those feelings related
to aesthetic enjoyment.[422]

Second, the emotive objective possession is experienced
(Erlebt) insofar as the subject thoroughly experiences, in an
either painful or pleasurable fashion, the object of its
feelings. The experience of emotion allows us to enter into
the thoughts, feelings and projects of other individuals;
it creates that world of sometimes weak, sometimes powerful
feelings which only poetry and music can even begin to
express.[423] There can be a withdrawal in feeling from the
objects-in-themselves to the attitude (Verhalten) of the
subject. This can be found both in the phenomena of mood
(Stimmung) and of the sequence of many moods in the emotive
psychic orientation or form of the subject as Gemüt:

> Insofar as the subject maintains the firm relationships
> of objects and humans to itself by means of representa-
> tions of past emotive lived experiences, and similarly
> maintains a system of felt relations to things,
> individuals, communities and humankind itself - insofar
> as the subject lives in these firm relationships, and
> not in a theoretical or practical mode, we call this
> manner of living Gemüt.[424]

Thus there occurs a structuring of representations, memories,

---

[420]G.S. VII, pp. 49-50. [421]G.S. VII, p. 54.

[422]G.S. VII, pp. 56-57. [423]G.S. VII, p. 48.

[424]G.S. VII, p. 48.

commitments and intersubjective relations that constitute
the subject in its objective possession of a horizon or
world. The emotive provides a depth not attainable by
cognition:

> In it [feeling] depths appear that knowledge cannot
> attain. A turn toward these depths occurs on the basis
> of objective comprehension, which determines the object
> by feeling, just as feeling drives toward reaching the
> object. In the midst of the interaction between
> ourselves and objects, feelings measure the energy,
> the pressure of the world, the energy of people
> around us.424a

Third, of special importance in the structuring of
objective emotive possession is the differentiation between
object-orientated feelings (Gegenstandsgefühle) and situational feelings (Lagegefühle). It is a distinction that
arises from the distinction in objective comprehension between
subject and object, self and world. The situational feelings
emphasize the emotive appropriation by the subject of other
persons and objects. These latter are only indirectly
present in such feelings inasmuch as they alter the conditional situation (Zuständlichkeit) of the subject. Object-
oriented feelings are more directly related to objects
or persons. They arise from perceptions and judgments of
objects or persons and so lead to an emotive evaluation in
terms of pain and pleasure, beauty or ugliness, value or
disvalue. In this fashion both the subject himself as well
as others can be objectified:

> Let us consider the nature of object-oriented feelings.
> In judging by these feelings, the objective has the
> attributes of beauty, meaning, value. We enjoy, in
> the approval of ourselves and in feeling pleased
> about ourselves, the qualities of our person. These
> give our own existence value, meaning, beauty - and
> thus a self-evaluation occurs. The same transition from
> pleasure or approval to a judgment about an objective
> quality of the object occurs in the judgment about an
> object of sense or another person.424b

Thus the "Gegenstandgefühl" is an even more emphatic instance
of the subject-as-object than the "Lagegefühl" which is more

424a G.S. VII, pp. 52-53.

424b G.S. VII, p. 53; also cf. VII, 51, 53.

undifferentiated. Dilthey describes the latter by Hegel's
remarks on the "muffled inner movements of the human
spirit."[425]

Fourth, Dilthey sees the objective possession in emotive
interiority as grounding the aesthetic transformation of
nature and the human world. Feelings as "objective" do not
need other feelings in order to arise. They can be evoked
by objects and forms in nature.

> Empathy towards nature is the emotive interpretation
> of the same; it is a re-feeling of something related
> in nature by the mood of whoever is contemplating it.
> And this projective feeling is based on our mood
> reacting to the already accomplished interpretation of
> a natural phenomenon, such as a shimmering sea or a
> dark forest. Even here the object-oriented feeling is
> not tied up with a feeling about a feeling.[426]

There is a gap between nature and subjectivity so that nature
appears as alien, strange. The unity is broken: "Man in his
Ego-ness becomes alien to nature, the unity is destroyed."[427]
This duality impels man to strive to achieve a higher unity
in the aesthetic; "works of art are created in which the
divergence between the inner regularities of emotion and
external ones are sublated."[428] These aesthetic products
represent a whole, a totality of feeling that strives to
express a totality of world.[429] An example of this emotive
aesthetic transformation of nature might be found in the
attribution of human emotions and attitudes to natural things
and animals in fables, fairy tales, animated cartoons, etc.
This totality constituted by objective emotive possession is
also realized in the aesthetic transformation of intersubjective relationships. The "Umwelt" of aesthetically
transformed nature is paralleled by a "Mitwelt" of positive
and negative fellow feelings arising from shared "situational
feelings" of compassion, joy, sorrow, envy, etc. Representative presentations call forth these fellow feelings and, if
the "Mitwelt" is to find a totality on the emotive level, it

---

[425] G.S. VII, p. 53. [426] G.S. VII, p. 52.

[427] G.S. VII, p. 58. [428] G.S. VII, p. 58.

[429] G.S. VII, pp. 58f.

must be in the unifying act of a great passion:

> The inner legitimacy of a mature mood finds its ful-
> fillment in art. Thus it should be the task of man
> to form the course of his affective reactions into a
> completed unity, that they become a rounded off
> affective unity. History shows us the ever renewed
> efforts of man to stylize himself.... Only in the
> unity of a great passion could he attain that unity
> for himself.... Great artists brought to consciousness
> for humankind different types of feelings and emotive
> situations. They impel men to seek a new affective
> unity on the basis of different affective elements.
> Affective types for entire epochs or whole peoples
> emerge; similarly, each individual seeks to realize
> his own affective unity. On the basis of this emotional
> unification, the affective modes of expression take on
> their particular form. In the plastic arts, in the
> style of theater acting, in the living interaction of
> men among themselves, there emerges a certain unifica-
> tion of external movements as expressive of the inner,
> affective unity.[430]

Hence the subject-as-subject moves from the subject-as-object
to the subject-to-subject of a "Mitwelt."

Fifth, objective emotive possession not only leads to
an aesthetic transformation but also to the structuring of
moral values. Here too the distinction of "objective and
situational feelings" enters into a differentiation of values.
Situational feelings give rise to life-values (Lebenswerte)
that express the tendency to unify the inner emotive
dynamisms of the subject.[431] Object-oriented feelings lead
to the effective values (Wirkungswerte) that express the
evaluation of persons and things according to object-oriented
value judgments.[432] The experience of value is the foundation
for volitional goals and purposes.[433] Both of the values,
life and effective, tend toward an objective universal system
of values. The universe is evaluated as ultimately good, bad,
or indifferent, for it depends upon the subjective attitudes
of individuals how they will objectively systematize values.
"According to the inner connections among the various relations of the Ego, the larger emotive evaluations take on their

---

[430]G.S. VII, pp. 59f.   [431]G.S. VII, p. 49.

[432]G.S. VII, p. 49.   [433]G.S. VII, p. 55.

own tonality."[434] As with objective comprehension, so here
Dilthey seems to end in a "pathetic" relativism of values
- pathetic inasmuch as men strive for some objective reference.

> Man seeks for objective contexts of value, in which
> the multiplicity of his evaluative feelings, his
> approval and disapproval, his feel for the beautiful
> and the ugly, for the good and the bad, and all his
> other feelings of value, will find their expression
> in their gradations and nuances.[435]

C. Objective Volitional Possession. In volitional
expressions, as was the case with knowing and feeling, an
objective relation with the willed content is grounded in the
subject's experience:

> As the other two modes of acting, so willing
> exhibits a relation to content. This content is
> the objective that is willed, and the process is
> related to it. As a behavior or act, however, it
> can only be experienced (erlebt), and not presented
> in concepts.[436]

There are three main aspects of Dilthey's description of
volitional objective possession - a description that is
necessarily sketchy due to the fragmentary nature of his
remarks.[437]

The first characteristic is that the experience of
willing is always constituted by an orientation to content
or an "Inhaltlichkeit" whereby a series of stages in objective
possession from instinct through striving and deciding to
goals can be mapped out. It is in attempting to satisfy
such volitional orientations that the individual, or group,
experiences the pressure of external objects and other persons and groups as either recalcitrant (objects of nature)
or of diverse strivings, interests and purposes (other groups
of persons).[438] Here, then, it is a question of the object
to be possessed (Haben).

The second characteristic is how objective possession

---

[434]G.S. VII, p. 60.   [435]G.S. VII, p. 60.

[436]G.S. VII, p. 61.

[437]Dilthey's only analysis is in the fragments published
in G.S. VII, pp. 61-69.

[438]G.S. VII, p. 64.

moves from representation through deliberation to decision and action regarding determinate goals. These goals comprise both those immanent within the subject, aimed at satisfying more or less distinct needs and goals (<u>Befriedigungszwecke</u>), and those goals which concern changes to be made in the external environment of the "Umwelt" and "Mitwelt."[439] The emotive situation evaluates these goals either positively or negatively.[440] The divergence of values, mentioned above, is also present in regard to goals and purposes. When the diversity of emotions and evaluations can be unified in terms of a great passion, along with the value judgments and interests flowing from it, the diversity of intentions and goals can be unified in striving to attain those emotive value-judgments, out of which striving arises the unifying imperatives of a life.[441] It is within such a context that <u>choice</u> (<u>Wahl</u>) and <u>decision</u> (<u>Entschluss</u>) emerge to put an end to the (in itself endless) process of deliberation.[442]

The final characteristic of objective possession as volition involves the social dimension of purposes, goals, imperatives. For Dilthey, Kant's categorical imperative is an effort to internalize the external imperative of command and obedience within the subject through its neglect of the emotive dimensions discussed in the second point above.[443] However, this leaves the phenomena of command and obedience in a radically uncritical condition since neither are in themselves necessarily rational or responsible. The objective possession of imperatives and goals in society must not be left in such a decisionistic context. Dilthey attempted to overcome such restrictions by integrating the social dimensions of striving and willing, and the concomitant aspects of cooperation through command and obedience, within the larger framework provided by the cognitive and emotive structures of interiority. This guaranteed that the social processes of volition would occur within the context of

---

[439] <u>G.S.</u> VII, pp. 54, 63-65.

[440] <u>G.S.</u> VII, pp. 63f.   [441] <u>G.S.</u> VII, p. 65.

[442] <u>G.S.</u> VII, p. 64.   [443] <u>G.S.</u> VII, p. 67.

a communicative interaction whereby individuals and groups
could set about determining the ideals and values which they
wished to realize through volitional cooperation.[444]

We have seen how Dilthey conceived of _Erleben_ as recurrent structurally interrelated functions or acts in which the
individual experiences impulses and information from his
physical and socio-cultural environment, assimilates them in
ever more complex inner patterns, and is thereby capable
of ever more decisive action within and on his environment.
The circular action-reaction patterns progress from the
automatic reflex mechanism through elementary learning
processes up to the intricate articulation of interiority
in adulthood, where the individual's many activities in
various acquired contexts or systems (_Zusammenhänge_), e.g.,
family, community, profession, nation, church, etc. are
more or less unified in the progressive effort to realize
short or long term ideals, values, goals. The present
section has been concerned with _Ausdruck_, with how interiority
expresses itself. Objective possession deals with spontaneous
and ever more nuanced and sophisticated expressions of
emotion and conation, of aesthetic feelings and willed
projects, of values and purposes. Objective mental comprehension explicated the patterns or structures aimed at
cognitively grasping (_auffassen_) interiority, whether on the
spontaneous level of ordinary expressions or language, or
on the level of a reflective grasp of the spontaneous level
in the human sciences' respresentative world of theory which
culminates in the effort to express representations of the
inner patterns of interiority itself. In this sphere of
objective comprehension and possession the circular patterns
are also present. Dilthey explicated human reaction as the
recurrent processes operative in the cognitive-emotive-
volitional reaction of individuals within their environments
- a reaction made possible only by a continuous interaction
with, and assimilation of, its cognitive-emotive-volitional
expressions.

---

[444]_G.S._ VII, pp. 64-65.

3. From Interiority to History

The final step in Dilthey's critique of historical reason is to move from the acts of the subject-as-subject and the contents of the subject-as-object to the unity of both within historical process. For history is not only an objective reality to be studied and analyzed in a manner similar to the analysis of nature. Doubtless history involves an almost unlimited number of objectifications, but those objectifications are of human subjects, who in their personal and social life express their consciousness.[445] In this sub-section I shall briefly touch upon the main aspects of Dilthey's methodical approach to history. There are three main topics to be considered. The first asks to what extent Dilthey essays a meta-history. The second shows how understanding (Verstehen) is the unity of identity (Erleben) and non-identity (Ausdruck) in history. The third will then outline how Dilthey's notion of world view is related to his understanding of interiority. Finally, a critical appraisal of the positive and negative aspects of Dilthey's critique of historical reason will provide the transition to the structures of Lonergan's meta-methodology.

A. A Meta-History? Dilthey was convinced that his approach to "Erleben" as the subject-as-subject would allow him to thematize the differentiation of conscious acts and contents within a totality of conscious life itself. As he wrote regarding his critique of historical reason, "this critique indicates that the factual findings correspond with the otherwise grounded assumption: we proceed from the totality."[446] The differentiation of the life-process into acts of imagining and knowing, of feeling and evaluating, of willing and acting - this differentiation was not one which would itself change. For if humans would not imagine, know feel, evaluate, will and act, they would not be human. History, in its finitude, could not sublate its own presuppositions: if humans did not perform such actions as these,

---

[445]G.S. VII, pp. 191-225. Also Landgrebe, op. cit., pp. 333-359.

[446]B.A., pp. 180-181.

there could be no history. From the perspective of the contents of such acts, humans certainly have changed and are limited by their historical period. But the structural similarity of the acts leads to a discovery of a fundamental similarity of inner life or consciousness, so that Dilthey can speak of human living out of "a common interior (seelischen) structural context";[447] out of a "similar structure of the whole human (geistigen) life,"[448] Indeed, without such a fundamental similarity of process and act there would be a complete heterogeneity of men and cultural epochs which would undercut the possibility of any understanding at all.[449] Dilthey sees the articulation of such fundamental similarities as the key task of a grounding of the cultural sciences - not hesitating to use the term transcendental method:

> And throughout these cultural sciences it is demonstrable how the similarity of lived interiority (des geistigen Lebens) provides a foundation for the interaction of outer experience, inner experience, transcendental method and the transposition of inner experience into objects. Everywhere thought uncovers a similar structure of the whole cultural life as the foundation on which the cultural sciences rise.[450]

It was precisely such a concrete factual similarity that was at the basis of the false metaphysical abstractions concerning the identity of reason in Hegel and Schleiermacher, and the identity of will in Schopenhauer.[451]

This does not mean that the cognitive-emotive-volitional functions are some static a priori structures - any more than the continuity in the life-process itself was unchanging. Rather they are the dynamics of historical change.[452] The aim of Dilthey's critique was not to find some vantage point

---

[447] G.S. V, p. 226.

[448] G.S. V, p. 251. Cf. H. Diwald, op. cit., pp. 145-153.

[449] Cf. G.S. VII, pp. 210-216, 225, 237ff., 257, 262ff.

[450] G.S. V, p. 251.   [451] G.S. V, p. 226.

[452] Cf. G.S. I, pp. 38, 42, 49, 51, 61, 64-66; V, pp. 136, 196, 265f.; VI, 62, 188-190, 228-305; VII, pp. 2-23, 79-88; Renthe-Fink, op. cit., pp. 106-113, 120-129.

above the flux of history; the unity of the subject was not a closed identity but a unity of continuity in change:

> The continuity of the course of life corresponds to the unity of consciousness. Accordingly a context of facts have a duration, the past aspects of which disappear in darkness, while those coming enter into its bright horizon. Within this continuity of a changing, and in the changes of a self-same "I," we distinguish changes of feelings, of willing, and of knowing.[453]

Historical change, therefore, implies both the continuity of identity and the difference of non-identity, i.e., it is a unity of identity and non-identity. Because of the dramatic character of the unity, Dilthey warns against any mechanistic understanding of the changes in the cognitive-emotive-volitional functions, as though the unity of the self was a product of the unified operations of knowing, or feeling, or willing.[454]

The historical finitude of the intentionality structures led Dilthey to his position regarding self-consciousness as a unity of identity and non-identity. It might be argued that Dilthey's distinction between act and content, between continuity and difference, provided him with a conceptual framework which, from the viewpoint of continuity and act, transcended the historical finitude of contents and objects. Was Dilthey not advocating, then, a metahistorical standpoint for his critique of historical reason - a standpoint outside of history and its finitude? Such an objection overlooks, however, what I think to be a major contribution of Dilthey to our understanding of historical temporality. The objection presupposes that history is constituted by discontinuity, that the finitude of history is the ultimate triumph of non-identity. It presupposes that the only continuity operative in historical change is the physical continuity of an objectivistic measurement of time. It was just such presuppositions that underlay the crisis of historicism, as K. Heussi has shown.[455]

---

[453] B.A., p. 173. [454] Cf. B.A., pp. 173-175.

[455] Cf. Karl Heussi, Die Krisis des Historismus (Tübingen, 1932), pp. 20, 37, 103, where Heussi shows the crisis of historicism was occasioned by the simple-minded

This naive stance toward continuity - a stance easily occasioned by natural scientific methods - was criticized by Dilthey. For the full understanding of the objective context of history could only occur "when the contemporary abstraction from self-consciousness is sublated and this consciousness is brought into the investigation."[456] Dilthey's position could be termed "meta-historical" only if one confined history to discrete units in constant flux with no more continuity than an extrinsic physical progression. From such a relativist and historicist affirmation of non-identity, any effort to investigate the identity aspects of conscious living could only be denigrated to the counterposition of an Idealist identity thought-pattern. Against this Dilthey maintained that an adequate understanding of historical change had to unify both continuity and difference, where both the identity of the former and the non-identity of the latter are constitutive of the historical finitude of intentionality. Thus Dilthey was by no means succumbing to a meta-historical approach after the fashion of the Idealist or Kantian transcendentalist positions. History does not sublate its own presuppositions.

The emphasis upon conscious process and acts within the unity of the objective context of history (as a unity of identity and non-identity) led Dilthey to assert the key role of freedom and action in the changes operative within the continuity. The temporal continuity was not put in some abstract identity framework like "World Spirit" or "Bearer of History," nor in a relativistic non-identity framework like "noumenal subjectivity." We are both determined by the historical life-process and in some way determine it. Insofar as we are determined by it, we have the experience of necessity; as we are able to determine it, we experience the consciousness of our freedom.[457] Our will to change and determine the process is a complex matter, dependent upon our interests and will to do so, along with our power to

_____

approach of historians towards the nature of an objectivity divorced from subjectivity.

[456]Cf. B.A., p. 167.   [457]Cf. B.A., p. 172.

implement those interests and will.[458] This was the element which led Dilthey to interpret the relation between self and world, between subject and object, not in a mechanistic manner of input-output, but within the context of freedom and conscious interiority.[459] The open endedness of the historical process, and Dilthey's own interpretation of the significance of the Enlightenment, led him to see the importance of an appropriation of conscious interiority in order for modern man responsibly to act. No longer relying upon metaphysical world views or theories, man had to find in his own free interaction with others and the world the norms for his decisions.[460] The new relation of theory and praxis meant that his critique of historical reason had to thematize human freedom in historical finitude, for "this is the factual reality which, as action, provides the foundation for what we term psychic act."[461]

B. Verstehen. Much work has already been done on Dilthey's notion of understanding as a hermeneutical and historical category.[462] Here I should like to call attention to certain essential aspects of understanding insofar as it attempts to express, in the domain of history, the unity of identity and non-identity. For by it, Dilthey tried to show how the related and recurrent functions of interiority provide a basis for understanding the myriad expressions of consciousness in the total self-mediation of interiority that is human history. Through "Verstehen" he tried to avoid the extremes of an idealist absolutism and an empiricist

---

[458]Ibid.

[459]Cf. Chapter Three, pp. 216-218 and references given there.

[460]Cf. Chapter Two, pp. 56-114, 137-155; Chapter Three, pp. 214-231.

[461]B.A., p. 172; also cf. B.A., pp. 11-12, 246-247. M. Riedel, "Das Erkenntniskritische Motiv in Diltheys Theorie der Geisteswissenschaften," Hermeneutik und Ideologiekritik I, pp. 233-244.

[462]Cf. A. Stein, Der Begriff des Verstehens bei Dilthey (Tübingen, 1926); L. Landgrebe, W. Diltheys Theorie der Geisteswissenschaften, pp. 277-332.

relativism. He tried to initiate a reflection on history
that would be commensurate to the spontaneous constitution
of history.

For a grounding of the human sciences must show how
the objects they deal with are in fact expressions whose
meaning, value and purpose is constituted by interiority:

> The method of understanding is really grounded in the
> difference of its external object from the object
> of the natural sciences. The human spirit objectified
> itself in the former, purposes are formed in it,
> values have been realized in it. And understanding
> grasps precisely this inner human dimension informing
> its object.[463]

There are two characteristics of the understanding which
concern Dilthey's attempt to interrelate historical and
scientific consciousness. First of all, understanding
"always has an individual for its object."[464] This was
because understanding involved a re-experiencing, a
"Sichhineinversetzen" in the historical expressions,[465] made
possible by the similarity of interior basic patterns in all
individuals. Thus Dilthey continues in the above quotation:

> A living relationship occurs between me and it [the
> object]. Its purposiveness is grounded in my positing
> a purpose, its beauty and goodness in my bestowal
> of value, its intelligibility in my intelligence....
> The cultural sciences integrate in an opposite way [to
> the natural sciences]. Primarily and principally,
> they translate the vast and expanding human-historical-
> social external reality back into the inner spontaneity
> from which it emerged.[466]

Thus the human sciences are involved in the introrsive movement of interiority itself. This accounts for the importance
of individual biography as the expression of the "life history
of life-unities" in historical studies.[467]

---

[463]G.S. VII, p. 118; also pp. 3, 71, 79, 82-83.

[464]G.S. VII, p. 212. Note that Dilthey was not advocating what is known as a strictly psychological interpretation
of expression in understanding, cf. VII, pp. 19, 85.

[465]G.S. VII, pp. 213-216.   [466]G.S. VII, pp. 118-120.

[467]G.S. VII, pp. 196-204, 246-251.

On the other hand, Dilthey was aware that the majority of historical expressions were contexts or systems (<u>Zusammenhänge</u>) whose complex interrelations could never be found in any one individual's inner experience. Thus the systems of laws, the involved relationships that make up a state or nation, the sciences, periods or epochs - in understanding these the historian or human scientist is not re-experiencing the interiority of an individual but of many individuals, in none of whom the totality of the expression was present. These expressions of the "objective spirit" were real but they could not be inferred from the reality of the experienced self-presence of any one individual.[468] Did this mean that there could be no objectively true knowledge of them since they could not be grasped as the expression of experienced interiority?[469] Dilthey rejected any Hegelian hypostatization of objective spirit as a solution.[470] Nor could he be content with branding them as subjective constructions of historians. Somehow they had to be related to the basic structures of interiority.[471]

Dilthey saw that understanding is always <u>of</u> correlations or systems.[472] History could be understood as an operational-system (<u>Wirkungszusammenhang</u>) in which there was a continual interaction between individuals and the larger contexts or systems so that in seeking to understand the individuals we are led to ever larger contexts:

> The mystery of the person stimulates for its own sake ever new and deeper attempts at understanding. And in this understanding is opened the realm of individuals, embracing men and their creations. Herein lies the most proper contribution of understanding for the cultural sciences. The objectivation of interiority (<u>der objektive Geist</u>) and the power of the individual determine together the cultural world. History rests on the understanding of both of these.[473]

---

[468]<u>G.S.</u> VII, pp. 163-188, 251.

[469]<u>G.S.</u> VII, p. 308.

[470]<u>G.S.</u> VII, pp. 150-152, 271.

[471]<u>G.S.</u> VII, p. 150, 308, 251.

[472]Cf. <u>G.S.</u> VII, p. 257.   [473]<u>G.S.</u> VII, pp. 212-213.

The individual was a "cross roads" of the many systems
operative in community, profession, nation, epoch.[474] So
that the individual is the bearer and representative of these
systems.[475] As a result,

> ...the understanding of the individual is only possible
> through the presence of a general awareness in him, and
> this general awareness has its presupposition in
> understanding. Finally, the understanding of a part
> of the historical process reaches its completion only
> through the relation of the part to the whole, and the
> unversal historical overview of the whole presupposes
> the understanding of the parts that are united in
> it.[476]

This was illustrated in attempts to understand Bismarck.[477]
Dilthey thought he had found the principle for overcoming
the tension between historical understanding's concern for
the particular and scientific consciousness' quest for the
universal - just as the basic recurrent structures did.[478]
Because the individual is born and develops in a complex
of operational-systems understanding him sublates the
"limitations of individual experience." Each of his
objectifications represents or expresses something which can
be understood only in reference to those operational-
systems.[479] This meant that the larger systems had reality
only insofar as they were related to individuals, only then
could they be re-experienced and understood. Dilthey seemed
to hesitate to go quite that far:

> Now the question arises, how can a system that was not
> as such produced in any one mind - and so can be neither
> directly experienced, nor traced back to the experience
> of a person - be formed in the historian through its
> expressions and statements about it? This presupposes
> that there are logical subjects which are not psycho-
> logical subjects. There must be a means to delimit
> these; there must be a proper basis to grasp them as
> unities or systems.[480]

> We must turn towards new categories, gestalts, and forms
> of life that do not appear in the individual life. The
> individual is only the crossing point for cultural

---

[474]_G.S._ VII, p. 135.   [475]_G.S._ VII, p. 151.

[476]_G.S._ VII, p. 152.   [477]_G.S._ VII, pp. 141-143.

[478]Cf. _G.S._ VII, pp. 137-138, 141.

[479]_G.S._ VII, pp. 141, 146-147.   [480]_G.S._ VII, p. 282.

systems and organizations that are interwoven in this
existence. How could they possibly be understood
starting from him?[481]

Yet his own positing of reality in the experienced self-
presence of interiority left no alternative to Dilthey.

C. Worldviews. In his unfinished efforts to elaborate
such categories there is no set terminology employed in
designating the larger systems. It is not difficult, however,
to find the basic structures of interiority in his references
to meaning-systems (cognitive), value-systems (emotive) and
operational-systems (volitional); although Dilthey himself
never explicitly derived them in this manner and more often
referred to history as an operational-system.[482] It must be
kept in mind that such systems are differentiated only by
the predominance of either the cognitive, emotive, or volitional; in any individual all of the basic functions are
operative in his participation in each of the larger systems.
This is also true of his correlating the various philosophical
world-views where the predominance of the cognitive as a
striving for a knowledge of external reality leads to a
materialism, positivism or naturalism (e.g., Democritus,
Lucretius, Hobbes, French encyclopedists, modern materialists
and positivists). Where the emotive-valuational predominates,
one sees all of reality as the expression of interiority,
from which one has the world-views of objective idealism
(e.g., Heraclitus, Spinoza, Leibniz, Schelling, Hegel,
Schaftsbury, Goethe, Schleiermacher). When the volitional
is ascendant the independence of man over nature is stressed
and one has the idealism of freedom or dualistic idealism
(as in Plato, the Christian theologians, Kant, Fichte, Schil-
ler, Carlyle).[483] A study of the characteristics of objective

---

[481]G.S. VII, p. 251. The "Formen des Lebens" indicates
that the Realitätscharakter of Leben extends to Lebensverlauf
(VII, p. 140) but beyond this individual sphere Dilthey is
very vague.

[482]G.S. VII, pp. 152-188, 228-245; cf. Diwald, op. cit.,
pp. 221-248.

[483]On the types of world-views, cf. G.S. V, pp. 402-403;
VIII, pp. 75-118, 140-156. On their methodological presuppositions, VIII, pp. 3-25, 157-162. Note that as Dilthey could

idealism reveals Dilthey's own position as falling within its world-view.[484]

Although Dilthey could not account for the reality status of the larger systems he saw clearly that historical understanding was essentially a movement from part to whole and whole to part. Indeed, this was the most common characteristic of the structure of the human sciences.[485] Our knowledge of the basic structures of interiority is dependent upon the historical expressions or objectifications of that interiority, and the understanding of the expressions is possible only because of the structures:

> Thus emerges at every point and time in cultural scientific work the same circulation of lived experience, understanding, and representation of the cultural world in general concepts.[486]

Dilthey remarked on the presence of this circular process in the interpretation of texts, in historical criticism and scientific research.[487] It was this circular movement from individual to larger systems and back that promised to reconcile historical and scientific consciousness in understanding.[488]

The ground of this circularity lies in man's finitude which is "tragic" because united to an insatiable desire to overcome his present limitations:

> There would be a simple exit from this circle if there were unconditioned norms, purposes or values which could serve as a measure for historical

---

only classify the many representations of interiority, so his effort to overcome the antinomies of the many philosophical systems could only achieve a classification of the antagonists without any hope for a lessening of the conflict, cf. G.S. VIII, pp. 75-76, 220-235.

[484]Cf. E. Rothacker, Logik und Systematik der Geisteswissenschaften, (Munich, 1927), pp. 52-67; Diwald, op. cit., pp. 210-211. This is evident insofar as Dilthey centered his entire analysis of interiority upon the emotive-valuational experience.

[485]G.S. VII, p. 153.   [486]G.S. VII, pp. 145, 152.

[487]G.S. VII, pp. 161-162; XIV/2, pp. 657-659, 708; Krausser, op. cit., pp. 73-92.

[488]Cf. notes 474-478 above.

investigation and comprehension.[489]

The emergence of scientific and, especially, historical consciousness sounded the death-knell for any such absolutes.[490] Relative to this consciousness the uncondi- tioned is now in the process itself of striving for an ever fuller understanding:

> Herein lies the fact that thinking progresses from relation to relation without ever reaching its goal, as far as we can see....[491]

We cannot know "the essence of life," inner experience is inexhaustible so that its explicitation is an "unending task," representations are inadequate and need ever to be corrected; these are the tensions that lead the human sciences back and forth from whole to part in a self- correcting process of understanding.[492] The meaning of history is in the recurrent structural relationships between part and whole, between interiority and the interlocking operational-systems of history:

> The evident meaning of history must first be sought in the ever present, ever recurrent structural relations and operational systems, the formation of values and purposes in them, the inner order in which these relate to one another. This stretches from the structure of the individual life up to the final all- embracing unity. This is the meaning history always and everywhere has, it rests on the structure of the individual life, and reveals itself in the objectifica- tions of life through the structure of assembled systems.[493]

This circular method of all historical understanding assured that the meanings, values and purposes of each individual, community, society, culture, epoch could be

---

[489]G.S. VII, p. 262.

[490]G.S. VII, pp. 173, 335-338.

[491]G.S. VII, p. 300; VIII, p. 172.

[492]G.S. VII, p. 9, 32, 38, 81, 128, 142-143, 145, 150, 153, 157, 161-162, 191, 211, 331. Note the parallel to Gadamer's dialectic of finitude and infinitude, cf. Wahrheit und Methode, pp. 434, 444-449; and also Kleine Schriften I, (Tübingen, 1967), p. 111, where Gadamer sees the move to unlimited possibilities through finitude.

[493]G.S. VII, p. 172, also pp. 232-236.

352

grasped both in their individuality and their interrelated generality.[494] What is present structurally in the recurrent patterns of cognitive-emotive-volitional interiority ramifies out in ever growing circles until the entire sweep of mankind and history is anticipated.[495]

D. A Critical Appraisal. If I am not mistaken, the importance of Dilthey's critique of historical reason for laying the foundations of vast inter-disciplinary collaboration might be summed up in four points. First, his discovery was of the factual and irreducible character of self-presence, or the subject-as-subject, as an awareness concomitant to and constitutive of all conscious historical activity. Second, this interiority was not amorphous but openly and dynamically patterned in structurally recurrent and related functions or operations whose unity came from their aims of assimilating from, and contributing to, the patterns and processes of the physical and historical world insofar as those operations are of the subject-as-object. Third, the world of history as a unity of the subject-as-subject and the subject-as-object is effected and constituted by the interactions of many instances of interiority so that any historical objectification is the expression of that interiority, and as such is understandable. Grounding the human sciences consists in thematizing the basic and recurrent structures common to all men for this structured interiority is a unity of identity and non-identity. Fourth, the possibility thereby arises of inter-relating all the manifold of contexts or systems of human activity since, insofar as they are products of consciousness, their correlation according to the basic patterns of interiority would integrate them in an open and dynamically revisable way.[496] For one would have uncovered

---

[494] G.S. VII, pp. 154-155, 191.

[495] G.S. VII, p. 171.

[496] Cf. Dilthey's own attempts to ground the human sciences in this way (volumes I, VII, VIII passim), to inter-relate all systems of philosophy (volumes V and VIII), to work out a poetics and aesthetics (vol. VI), a pedagogies and ethics (vol. VI, IX), and his desire to apply the method to religion (Renthe-Fink, op. cit., pp. 94-110).

the recurrent and related operations of human freedom itself.

Given the inherent limitations of any system or systems, the only way to ground interdisciplinary collaboration on a large scale is to venture a thematization of the pre-systematic open and dynamic operations of the subject-as-subject which account not only for today's systems but will also develop, correct, and eventually replace them. This applies not only to scientific but also to political, social, cultural, aesthetic, philosophical and theological systems. If Dilthey offers a very fruitful starting point in such an undertaking, I should also like to point out where the new control of meaning he was trying to explicate needs to be corrected.

First of all, his notion of conscious interiority as experienced was primarily discovered in relation to feeling. Thus he attempted to correlate the cognitive and volitional structures via the emotive; as a result reality was defined in terms of an experienced "being there for me" as a self-presence prior to all questions and answers. The inner reality-itself is simply given, there. "Selbstbesinnung" aimed at articulating this there-ness of self-presence which alone could be certain and normative. Objective comprehension with its observations, concepts, and judgments had no more than a representative function whose verification consisted in their occurrence, i.e., they must be there as self-presence is there. This implicated Dilthey in a series of dilemmas.

First of all, he had to admit that the representations were both expressions of the reality-itself of interiority (subject-as-subject) and also transcended experienced interiority as he conceived it. Interiority itself as experienced was not self-transcending. The relation between subject and object, world and self, became ultimate. Dilthey accepted this for the natural sciences, their object's reality-itself fell under the Kantian noumenon. This did not apply to the reality-itself of interiority as experienced, as given, in the myriad instances of conscious human beings. Yet the expressions of this interiority were brought into "correspondence" with this inner reality by their occurrence and not by their content. This was a norm that could apply to any, even contradictory, expressions so that in the end we cannot know the experienced reality-itself, it too falls under the Kantian noumenon. The difference is that here the noumenal is possessed, is present and there as our immediate self-presence.[497]

Dilthey did not intend such a conclusion but he did not know how to avoid it. He saw no structural difference in objective mental comprehension between knowing external objects and knowing inner experience. Instead of working this out into a criticism of Kant's notion of knowledge, applicable to the natural as well as human sciences, he simply stated that the elements, regularities and inner structural relationships of the latter are contained in inner experience itself.[498] Five years later even this relation of objective knowing to inner experience is rejected inasmuch as any scientific objectification of interiority, such as concepts-judgments-thought constructions, transcend the inner experience from which they emerge so that their understanding cannot help one in grasping the depths of interiority.[499] Ironically, in the same pages Dilthey sees the self-transcending character of the great works of art as a truthful guide to understanding interiority.[500]

Secondly, because interiority as experienced was not self-transcending for Dilthey, he could not adequately handle the larger systems in history which could not be understood as expressing a given individual's self-presence. On the other hand, he realized how no individual could be understood apart from these larger historical systems.

Thirdly, the mere there-ness of inner experience was not able to ground a dialectic when taken as the normative moment in interiority. For the only way to falsify a conceptualization of interiority or a world-view, according to Dilthey's criterion, would be to show that it did not occur. This is what accounts for his inability to overcome the relativism of

---

[497]Cf. G.S. VII, pp. 32-33.   [498]G.S. VII, p. 32.

[499]Cf. G.S. VII, pp. 205-206.

[500]G.S. VII, p. 207; cf. also pp. 19, 85.

historicism. He saw correctly that any historical activity
expresses some aspect of interiority, that the meaning-values-
purposes of history have their ground in the recurrent basic
structures of interiority; but his own formulation of those
structures as centered in feeling, and normative only as given
in the there-ness of self-presence, left him with no more
than an interiorized form of positivism.[501] He could not
effectively move from a "consciousness-raising about life"
(subject-as-subject) to a "consciousness-raising about
thinking" (subject-as-object), inasmuch as he had not
grasped interiority as self-transcending. Knowing was at
bottom not experiencing but perceiving the experienced and
representing it in concepts and judgments. These latter
were not the reality-itself of interiority and their correspondence with that reality remained, for Dilthey, "completely nebulous."[502] Unwilling to impose an arbitrary
conception or norm on historical spontaneity, he was left
with no effective criteria for determing truth and error.[503]

---

[501] Compare this criticism with that of Habermas in
Erkenntnis und Interesse, pp. 224-226.

[502] Cf. I, p. 198; VII, p. 206; VII, p. 18 and note
416 above.

[503] For Dilthey the reality-itself of interiority is
that given there-ness of _Selbigkeit_ or _Innerlichkeit_ and any
statement about this experienced is "objektiv wahr" insofar
as it utters the occurrence of the experience (_Erlebnis_) -
i.e., any expression is true insofar as either through
experience or re-experience (_Nacherleben_) it manifests the
given there-ness of interiority, the "für-mich-dasein eines
Zustandes." This meant that all expressions, insofar as
they occur, must express some aspect of interiority and
therefore be understandable through re-experience. Now
Heidegger's ontological radicalization of understanding and
disclosure seems to curiously reflect a similar pattern. In
Sein und Zeit, number 44 the main concern of Heidegger is _not_
how truth discloses but _that_ it discloses, so that _any_ manner
of disclosure is related to truth and the luminosity of
"there" is seen as the "ursprünglichste Phänomen der
Wahrheit." But when all understanding is characterised as
truth one no longer inquires into the truth of understanding
since as disclosure it already is truth. Cf. Tugendhat,
op. cit., pp. 350, 356-362, 399. Compare Tugendhat's
complaint that Heidegger gives no concrete formal regulatives
(_op. cit._, pp. 360, 376, 399) with Diwald's remarks on the
lack of criteria for veracity in Dilthey (_op. cit._, pp. 157,
69-71, 76-77, 156-158.).

356

His critique of historical reason had to sacrifice reason in
the name of historicality, unable to overcome historicism
it tended toward the skeptical avowal of the ultimate
irrationality of historical life.[504]

Does this failure mean that reason is unable to appropriate the sources of its own historical activity? I think
Lonergan's transcendental method has achieved what Dilthey's
critique did not. Historicism is overcome, not by renouncing
the claims of scientific objectivity as Gadamer proposes,[505]
but by relating them to the open and dynamic structures of
interiority. This is possible if the normative is not in the
experienced there-ness or givenness of interiority but in
the experienced operations of direct and reflective understanding. So far as I can see, this is the only way of
destroying the bifurcation of phenomenon-noumenon that has
haunted almost all reflections on historicality, and from
which Dilthey could not finally escape. For the only manner
in which he could successfully unite continuity and discontinuity in history would be by adequately accounting for them
within a notion of the subject-as-subject which could
critically ground its own transition to the subject-as-object.
In Chapter Two we have already seen how Lonergan sees the need
for the critical exigence to move into the methodical exigence
by attending to the subject-as-subect. If Dilthey did not
succeed in carrying through such a program, at least he pointed
the way towards it. The historical starting point had to
develop from cognitional theory to method and the discovery
of the subject-as-subject had to lead to a more radical
critique of any noumenal left-over of Kantianism. The
noumenal residue found in Dilthey's differentiation of the
natural and the cultural sciences infected his critical
attempt to elaborate a cognitional theory upon which to base
the cultural sciences.

---

[504]Cf. G.S. VII, pp. 151, 288-289; Bollnow, op. cit., pp.
26-33; Diwald, op. cit., pp. 160, 185, 187, 222; and G. Lukács,
Von Nietzsche zu Hitler (Frankfurt, 1966), pp. 113-135.

[505]Cf. Wahrheit und Methode, pp. 218-228, 477-512.

THE STRUCTURES OF LONERGAN'S
META-METHODOLOGY

0. Introduction

I have already had occasion to remark how Lonergan did
not base his efforts at elaborating a transcendental or
meta-method upon a differentiation of the natural and
cultural sciences.[506] As he states in Method in Theology,
thought on method usually runs in one of three channels. Some
attempt to envisage method as an art to be communicated more
by example and re-experiencing, others try to elaborate method
on the analogy of science where the successful science
provides the paradigm for all knowing.[507] In the subsection
on overcoming Cartesianism, it was shown how Dilthey attempted
to get beyond the notion of method as art versus science by
appealing to the subject-as-subject, so emphasized in the
aesthetic approach to method, in order to ground the cultural
sciences. Yet, as we also saw, the very fact that he allowed
the natural sciences to keep their scientistically conceived
notions of method, meant that he was only able to create an
island of subject-ive awareness in the raising tide of
scientism.[508] Lonergan has tackled the issue more directly
in advocating a third approach to method by thematizing the
operations of the subject-as-subject that are as applicable
to the natural sciences as to the human sciences, and that
are as applicable to spontaneous common sense living as to
the scientific and scholarly activities.

In presenting Lonergan's third way of approaching
method, viz., to go behind the operations of science and
common sense to the related and recurrent operations of the
subject-as-subject, I shall follow somewhat the same divisions
as in treating the structures of Dilthey's critique of historical reason. The first subsection will deal with the subject-
as-subject; the second will take up the subject-as-object,
while the third will go into the socio-historical dimensions

---

[506]Cf. below pp. 254ff.; also Chapter Two, pp. 157ff.

[507]Cf. M.i.T., pp. 3ff.   [508]Cf. Chapter Two, pp. 73ff.

of the unity of the subject-as-subject (identity) and the subject-as-object (non-identity).

It should be kept in mind both that I am not here attempting to give a full exposition of Lonergan's methodology and that, insofar as he has succeeded in thematizing the unity in the subject, the subject-as-subject is not some theory or idea but the living self-awareness grounding all objectifications. Those interested in a more detailed exposition of Lonergan's development might refer to the excellent work of David Tracy, The Achievement of Bernard Lonergan.[509]

1. The Subject-as-Subject

At the end of his as yet unpublished lectures on existentialism in 1957, Lonergan stated in concise fashion the conclusion we have reached in Chapter Two.[510] The immense proliferation of theories in the emergence and expansion of scientific consciousness, and the recognition of the historical conditionality of all human horizons through the emergence of historical consciousness, means that if any norms are to be found for a new control of meaning and value in man's constitution of history, they will only be found within the subject-as-subject. For "the prior reality that both grounds horizons and the critique of horizons and the determination of the field [of all human activity] is the reality of the subject-as-subject."[511] We have seen how a formally systematic control of meaning falls under the limitations of all formal systems spelled out by Gödel, and how a critical control of meaning, if it simply relies on cognitional, epistemological, or metaphysical theories, cannot handle the problems raised by the sciences and history.[512] The reason is that all such approaches are objective and so fall under the inherent historicity of objects with their

---

[509]Herder and Herder, New York, 1971. Tracy's work concentrates on the theological development of Lonergan.

[510]Notes on Existentialism mimeographed by the Thomas More Institute (1957). On the dialectic of the Enlightenment, cf. Chapter Two, pp. 93ff. below.

[511]Notes on Existentialism, p. 28.

[512]Cf. Chapter Two, pp. 93-115, 156-209.

consequent inability to attain the creative source of
their own objectifications. Thus we have seen how even
Dilthey was unable to critically justify his own conception
of interiority as cognitive-emotive-volitional without
justifying all worldviews because he had not critically
moved from the subject-as-subject to the subject-as-object.
In the end the criticisms Dilthey leveled against Kant came
back to haunt his own critique insofar as he ended up with
the shadow reality of experienced noumenal subjectivity.
Lonergan intimates this dilemma when he writes of the
subject-as-subject:

> It is not any object known objectively and it is not
> the subject known objectively, for all objects are
> known within some stream of consciousness and so
> within a horizon; and it has been contended that such
> objects cannot justify any horizon without thereby
> justifying all horizons.[513]

Against all of these efforts at finding some critical
norm within a systematic or critical appeal to objects or
to subjects objectified in theories, Lonergan shows the
possibility of presenting the subject-as-subject as a reality
"in the sense that we live and die, love and hate, rejoice
and suffer, desire and fear, wonder and dread, inquire and
doubt. It is Descartes' _cogito_ transposed to concrete
living."[514] It is this concrete experience of self-presence,
or the subject-as-subject, that is the reality prior to any
theories or affirmations of it, or of any objects. As
Lonergan concludes:

> The argument is that the prior is not object as object
> or subject as object; there only remains the subject
> as subject, and this subject as subject is both reality
> and discoverable through consciousness. The argument
> does not prove that in the subject as subject we shall
> find the evidence, norms, invariants, and principles
> for a critique of horizons; it proves that unless we
> find it there, we shall not find it at all.[515]

To show how Lonergan has developed the thematization of the

---

[513] _Notes on Existentialism_, p. 28.

[514] _Ibid._, p. 28. Naturally such a transposition of
Descartes' "cogito" sublates the Cartesian framework for
method, cf. Chapter Two, pp. 73-82.

[515] _Notes on Existentialism_, p. 28.

subject-as-subject, I shall first say something about the polymorphism of consciousness, then go into the related and recurrent operations of consciousness, and finally discuss the invariance of those operations.

A. The Polymorphism of Human Consciousness. Awareness of consciousness is a common enough reality to all people who are not in a deep and dreamless sleep. It is this simple presence of self that is operative in all of our dreaming, and the massive variety of our waking activities. Usually it is simply taken for granted. Spontaneously we go about our daily chores and tasks attending to the multiplicity of other persons and objects which flood our waking life. In our knowing and doing we rarely pay attention to the prior consciousness which, in its own intentional spontaneity, is the reality of our self-presence-in-world, where "world" refers to the common assumptions, beliefs, meanings, values, languages, expectations, and so on that we are born into and gradually appropriate in our growing and learning.[516] This is the reality Lonergan refers to as the subject-as-subject. It includes all human conscious activity and is not by any means limited to what human beings know. For knowledge is but a very thin slice of the reality of living consciousness.[517] In this broad meaning of consciousness as living self-presence in world it is equivalent to experience, if by that we mean that experience is not necessarily objectified in understanding. Thus we consciously experience the "unconscious" in dreams, and we experience the totality of our activities in waking life. Most often we do not know what it is that we are experiencing, and the entire history of human knowledge is a gradual expansion of the thin slice of knowing into ever more fuller aspects of experiencing - an expansion which increases our experiencing and so raises new questions.

A first approximation toward uncovering some of the fundamental patterns of conscious experiencing has already

---

[516] Cf. G. Brand, Die Lebenswelt: Eine Philosophie des Konkreten Apriori (Berlin, 1971).

[517] Cf. pp. 256ff. of this Chapter.

been made. We have seen how experiencing falls into certain basic patterns.[518] There is the _biological_ pattern of experience dominated by extroverted conation, emotion and bodily movement aimed at satisfying biological needs. Then there is the _aesthetic_ pattern in which consciousness slips beyond stimulus-response functions to the liberation of symbolic creativity. In the _dramatic_ pattern the many patterns blend and succeed one another in the interest of realising the practical objectives set by one's intersubjective "world." The _intellectual_ pattern sets conscious experience the task of being a supple, active collaborator in intelligent inquiry and critical reflection aimed at satisfying the exigencies of the desire to know. The _moral_ pattern impels us towards an appreciation of good and value beyond the instinctual level of desires and fears. But desire outstrips achievement so that the _religious_ pattern evolves in which man's dynamic orientation toward the known unknown finds sensitive integration in the symbols, mysteries, and rituals of the religious imagination.[519]

These varied patterns Lonergan describes as the polymorphism of human consciousness which becomes a critical tool for him in showing how the myriad forms of philosophizing down the ages can come up with such diverse understandings and misunderstandings regarding such key issues as reality, objectivity, and subjectivity. For "the polymorphism of human consciousness is the one and only key to philosophy" if one is going to work out a meta-contextual critique of such diverse views.[520] Rather than repeating the detailed expositions of how this key is used in _Insight_ and Lonergan's other philosophical writings, it may be well to show how he defines the perimeters of its use. Just as Metz attempts to cut through the proliferation of systems on redemption and liberation by recalling attention to a narrative memory of redemption, so Lonergan seems to have rather effectively cut

---

[518]Cf. pp. 260-272 of this Chapter.

[519]Cf. _Insight_, pp. 181-189; 385-387; 530-549.

[520]_Ibid_., p. 427.

through the welter of philosophic speculations by recalling attention to lived consciousness and its spontaneous operations.

Human consciousness is polymorphic because it does not "ab ovo" know the multiplicity of the patterns in which its stream of conations, emotions, interests move. The patterns may alternate, blend or mix. The patterns can interfere with one another - as when a scholar is distracted from his intellectual pursuits by the countless chores of his or her dramatic day to day living. They may conflict to a point of break down. These patterns are operative in man's spontaneous constitution of history, he need not reflect on them any more than his own self-presence consists in a self-perception. He experiences them as he experiences his own awareness concomitant to all his conscious historical activity. Yet the conation, interest, attention, purpose of these patterns indicate that they objectify themselves in familial and community structures, in customs, works of art, languages, societies, cultures, scientific treatises and movements, philosophical writings and schools, religious doctrines and churches. Just as the patterns themselves admit enormous variations, such as the sexual, musical, poetic, literary, social, political, scientific, philosophical, theological, so the objectifications of the patterns admit of myriad diversifications. As the patterns, so these objectifications can develop and decline, flourish and be thrown into crisis. We have already seen how they provide an insight into entire historical epochs.[521]

Anticipating the following sections somewhat we can see how the polymorphism of consciousness provides a critical meta-contextual key for Lonergan. Neither philosophers nor scientists are exceptions to the possibility of allowing the patterns to interfere with one another. Such interference was common enough between, say, the intellectual and religious patterns in the disputes over the historical-critical methods and revelation. An even more recalcitrant interference is what Lonergan puts his finger on when he shows how the biological extroversion to bodies can blend with the

---

[521]Cf. pp. 272-282 of this Chapter.

intellectual notion of a thing, so that the resulting confusion leads one to imagine that objectivity is extroversion,
that reality is the "already-out-there-now" real, so that
knowing is a matter of "taking a look" at it. Lonergan
maintains that one of the fundamental themes in the unfolding
of modern philosophy is precisely this conflict between
objectivity as extroversion and intelligence as knowledge.[522]
It can also be found as a major issue in the methodological
discussions involved in the development of Quantum
Mechanics.[523]

So the many forms of positivism and empiricism and
materialism attempt to show how the data and facts are really
"out there" and devise many ways of structuring knowing so
that it can really "look at" or "attain" that reality. The
various forms of Idealism on the other hand, more or less
correctly see that this is a hapless if not hopeless project
and so either concede that reality is unknowable in itself
(Kantian noumenon) or transform all reality into the idea
and concept (Hegelianism). Thus Lonergan can summarize the
dilemma:

> Cartesian dualism had been a twofold realism, and both
> the realisms were correct; for the realism of the extro-
> verted animal is no mistake, and the realism of rational
> affirmation is no mistake. The trouble was that, unless
> two distinct and disparate types of knowing were recog-
> nized, the two realisms were incompatible. For rational
> affirmation is not an instance of extroversion, and so
> it cannot be objective in the manner proper to the
> "already out there now." On the other hand, the flow of
> sensible contents and acts is neither intelligent nor
> reasonable and so it cannot be knowledge of the type
> exhibited by science and philosophy. The attempt to fuse
> disparate forms of knowing into a single whole ended in
> the destruction of each by the other; and the destruc-
> tion of both forms implied the rejection of both types
> of realism. The older materialism and sensism were
> discredited, but there was room for positivism and
> pragmatism to uphold the same viewpoint in a more
> cultured tone. German Idealism swung through its magni-
> ficent arc of dazzling systems to come to terms with
> reality in relativism and Neo-Kantian analysis. But if
> a century and a half have brought forth no solution,

---

[522]Cf. _Insight_, p. 413.

[523]Cf. P. Heelan, _Quantum Mechanics and Objectivity_
(The Hague, 1965).

> it would seem necessary to revert to the beginning and
> distinguish two radically distinct types of knowing in
> the polymorphic consciousness of man.[524]

Lonergan proceeds to show how Husserlian phenomenology and
existentialism did not meet the issue. My own analysis of
the philosophies of historicality draws upon this polymorphic
key.[525]

Admittedly, this is already getting into the problem of
knowing and so is moving beyond the subject-as-subject in
terms of consciousness. Nevertheless, it shows how Lonergan
bases his critical stance on the latter. It also is necessary
in order that no misunderstanding of an appeal to the subject-
as-subject will arise insofar as someone would maintain that
what Lonergan is doing is advocating a form of subjectivism.
For subjectivism comes from the same oversight as objectivism.
Only where the latter tends to put all the critical emphasis
upon externality as the "already out there now real,"
subjectivism appeals to some obtuse mode of introspection
whereby the subject can look into the "already in here now
real" of his mind or subjectivity. But Lonergan is as
stringent in his criticisms of this type of introspection
as Dilthey was. For "to heighten one's presence to oneself,
one does not introspect; one raises the level of one's
activity":

> I have been attempting to describe the subject's pre-
> sence to himself. But the reader, if he tries to find
> himself as subject, to reach back and, as it were,
> uncover his subjectivity, cannot succeed. Any such
> effort is introspecting, attending to the subject; and
> what is found is, not the subject as subject, but only
> the subject as object; it is the subject as subject that
> does the finding.[526]

If the patterns of human consciousness provide a first
approximation to the polymorphism of the subject-as-subject,
it is necessary to delve into the related and recurrent
operations of consciousness in order to find what Lonergan
means by raising the level of one's activity.

----

[524] _Insight_, pp. 414f.

[525] Cf. pp. 30-41 of Chapter One; and pp. 107-115
158-195 of Chapter Two.

[526] _Collection_, pp. 226f.

B. __The Basic Structures of Consciousness__. Similar to
Dilthey, Lonergan is convinced of the fundamental importance
of self-presence-in-world or conscious intentionality as
the meta-context for adequately relating both scientific
consciousness and historical consciousness. We have seen how
Dilthey ultimately failed to correlate consciousness as
experienced with knowing and how, as a result, the reality-
itself of interiority became, so to speak, an experienced
noumenon. The circle from experienced there-ness to expression to re-experience was broken and the bifurcation of the
phenomenon-noumenon reemerged as that between experience
and representation. This accounted not only for Dilthey's
difficulties with the larger systems in history, but also
for his inability to overcome historicism.[527]

Meta-method, on the other hand, is grounded in a
self-appropriation which is a heightening of consciousness,
a making aware of the basic patterns and structures operative
in any instance of human conscious activity. The recognition
of the polymorphism of consciousness avoids the inadequacy
of Dilthey's conception of "Erleben" and its relation to
knowing. For the self-appropriation Lonergan calls for is
a discovery neither in the world of common sense nor in the
world of theory but in the world of interiority disclosed by
the methodical exigence.[528] In this sense it is a discovery
of the sources of meaning and truth "beyond the sciences,"
as Gadamer requests.[529] But, unlike Gadamer, it is a
discovery which can return to the worlds of common sense and
of scientific theory in a critically methodical manner inasmuch as the self-appropriation occurs within the intellectual
pattern of experience.[530]

---

[527] Cf. pp. 249-253, 352-356 of this Chapter.

[528] Cf. Chapter Two, pp. 158ff.

[529] Cf. Gadamer, __Kleine Schriften__ I, pp. 51-54.

[530] The self-appropriation can, of course, occur in other
patterns than the intellectual. Thus Lonergan refers to the
self-appropriation of one's emotions in psychotherapy, cf.
__M.i.T.__, p. 34. Cf. also P. McShane and G. Borden, __Towards
Self Meaning__ (Notre Dame, 1970).

I need not list all the glories and torments conferred by the scientific and techno-industrial revolutions on our time to show that the intellectual patterns of experience today are profoundly altering human experience in the other patterns as well. The discussion of an historical typology based upon the patterns of experience indicated how our present time is still under the influence of a mechanomorphic conception of intelligence, and the discussion of the dialectic of the Enlightenment in Chapter Two went into some of the consequences of that conception.[531] Historical consciousness, no less than scientific, arose within the intellectual pattern. Only through historical studies did man become aware of the relativity of all social, cultural, and religious contexts. Humans always constituted history, just as they always had certain biological processes, but it was only when they became reflectively aware of this historical spontaneity that the massive problems associated with historicism appeared. Spontaneous historicality can no more cope with the highly differentiated problems of the human constitution of history than common sense can handle the problems of, say, genetic manipulation. For the basic issue here is the relation between consciousness and know-ledge. Hence it is critically important to mediate the sources of this spontaneous making of history within the intellectual pattern, where scientific and historical con-sciousness operate, in order that this creative spontaneity as methodologically mediated could provide the norms for both interrelating the many fields of specialization within the intellectual pattern, and for dialectically criticizing the interference and pseudo-problems within this pattern caused by the polymorphism of human consciousness.

Dilthey's program of a radical _Selbstbesinnung_ which would transform the Socratic _phronesis_ and attain the sources of both theoretical and practical reason fell far short of its goal.[532] Lonergan has gone further than Dilthey and, to my

---

[531]Cf. Chapter Two, pp. 93-115. Chapter Three, pp. 272-281.

[532]Cf. M. Riedel, "Das Erkenntniskritische Motiv in

knowledge, further than any of the present adherents of philosophical hermeneutics, by showing how the entire classical distinction between theory and practice can no longer be maintained.[533] He has sought to deepen the Socratic _phronesis_ into a new notion of wisdom.[534] For in the measure that one moves beyond the world of theory and establishes a new control of meaning in terms of conscious intentionality, one can begin the slow process of applying the new control of meaning throughout all phases of human conscious activity. Hence the refrain throughout _Insight_:

> Thoroughly understand what it is to understand, and not only will you understand the broad lines of all there is to be understood but also you will possess a fixed base, an invariant pattern, opening upon all further developments of understanding.[535]

The appropriation of consciousness within the intellectual pattern enables one to experience how the related and recurrent operations of human consciousness are operative within all the patterns of human experience; and understanding those operations, one can begin to lay the foundations for the type of attentative, intelligent, reasonable, and responsible collaboration required of our time.

Figure Six outlines the related and recurrent operations of consciousness. The operations occur within different related levels of consciousness. Lonergan is not, however, interested solely in offering another cognitional "theory" but rather in having the reader appropriate, or come to know in his or her own conscious experience, the activities described.

Diltheys Theorie der Geisteswissenschaften," in _Hermeneutik und Dialektik_ I (Tübingen, 1970), pp. 233-239. Also cf. _G.S._ V, pp. 151-152, 197-201, 180; VII, pp. 3-23, 82-83, 135, 279: "Der Mensch erkennt sich nur in der Geschichte, nie durch Introspektion." (Cf. Diwald's objection, _op. cit._, pp. 152-153); _G.S._ VIII, pp. 13, 39, 176ff., _Briefwechsel_ n. 58; on basic structures and acquired contexts: _G.S._ V, pp. 176-184, 200-226.

[533]See _Collection_, pp. 252-267; also the lectures: "Theology and Man's Future," and "The Absence of God in Modern Culture" in _Second Collection_ (Philadelphia, 1974), pp. 101-116, 135-148.

[534]Cf. _Insight_, pp. 306, 407.

[535]_Insight_, pp. xxviii and 748.

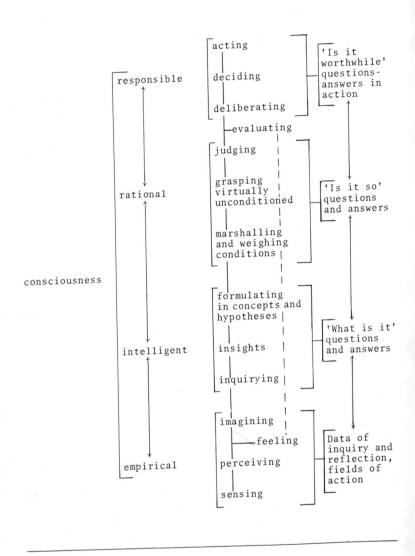

Figure Six: The Basic Levels and Structures of Consciousness

The empirical level of consciousness is that defined by
the acts of sensing, perceiving, imagining, feeling. It is
the level where consciousness is rooted deeply in the rhythm
and processes of nature and the collective neurological and
psychic past.[536] It is the level that emerges dimly in our
night dreams and more forcefully in the dreams of the day.[537]
It is fully operative in wide-awake sensing and perceiving
and imagining. Perceptions are the flow of sensations as
complemented by memories and directed by imaginative acts of
anticipation.[538] Imagination is the matrix of intelligence,
providing the images and associations and memories that give
rise to insight. It is not identical with intelligence since
we do not understand everything we imagine, any more than we
do everything we perceive or sense.[539] This is the level of
given data for inquiry, the realm where conditions must be
fulfilled for judgments of fact concerning objects, and the
field of human action. Lonergan has not studied the nervous
system deeply since it is not crucial to his understanding
of how consciousness relates to objects. Rather he is content

---

[536]Cf. G. Durand, Les structures anthropologigues de
l'imaginaire (Paris, 1963); S. Gooch, Total Man (Holt,
Rinehart and Winston, 1972); J. Jacobi, The Psychology of
C. G. Jung (Yale University Press, 1962).

[537]Cf. Lonergan's reliance on Biswanger M.i.T., p. 69.

[538]On the cultural determinants in perception cf. A. I.
Hallowell, "Culture, Personality, and Society," in Anthropology Today: Selections, (Chicago, 1962), pp. 362-363. Referring to J. J. Gibson, Perception of the Visual World (Boston,
1950), Hallowell points out how a completely relativistic
account of perception is as untenable as a purely absolute one.

[539]Data for inquiry are not only to be found in the
experienced but also in the experiencing, as the psychological
sciences demonstrate. Here too, sensations and images only
potentially contain the knowledge of the intelligible relations which intelligence seeks. Besides the direct mode of
inquiry there is the introspective mode where inquiry and
reflection investigate their own nature, cf. Insight, p.
274. Note that in this essay insight not only refers to
the rare moments of understanding which common usage applies
to it, but to every act of understanding and the habits it
forms in the mind, cf. ibid., p. 6. I have not discussed
here the role of insight and common sense in ordinary understanding, cf. ibid., pp. 173-181.

to leave that to the relevant physiological and neurological sciences.[540] For there is a key shift insofar as empirical consciousness does not directly integrate neural processes but psychic contents: a central distinction for Lonergan.[541]

We are not content, however, with empirical consciousness, with empirically experiencing life. Questions emerge slowly at first, then in torrents - education might be defined as learning the art of how to ask relevant questions.[542] Lonergan distinguishes three generically different set of questions which define the three other levels of consciousness and their operations. Questions for direct understanding are the "what is it" type that can also include "why" type questions. E.g., "why did this happen?" means "what caused it to happen?", "why is this hot?" means "what causes this to be hot?". "How" type questions are also a variant of the "what" type, e.g., "how do you feel?" means "what are your feelings like?". The "what" questions inquire into the data provided by empirical consciousness. Men not only just experience experiencing, they want to know what it is about. They also experience the urge to question, i.e., their experiencing is by definition problematic.[543] Insights come as the release to the tension of inquiry. They grasp intelligible correlations in the data. These insights are then formulated in concepts and hypothetical formulations. Thus concepts do not precede understanding but are the expression of it, a central fact overlooked by the many forms

---

[540]For how he would integrate them, cf. section on Emergent Probability below. Also Insight, pp. 467-469.

[541]Cf. Insight, pp. 266, 467-479, 514-520. Also M. Lamb's "Ascent from human consciousness to the human soul," in Insight, A Quarterly Review of Religion and Mental Health, volume 3, number 2 (Fall, 1964), pp. 18-28.

[542]Cf. Piaget, Genetic Psychology; on the self-correcting process of learning cf. Insight, pp. 174-175, 286-287, 289-291, 300, 303, 706, 713-718 passim.

[543]On the unrestricted desire to know, cf. Insight, pp. xi, xiv, 4, 9, 74, 220-222, 348-350, 380-381, 528, 550, 596, 599-600, 623-624, 636-639, 642, 682, 701-702, 738; on the similarity to Dewey, cf. Robert O. Johann, "Lonergan and Dewey on judgement" in Language Truth and Meaning, pp. 79ff.; also p. 310.

of conceptualism.[544] The intelligible correlations are hypothetical conceptions, they could be the relevant descriptions or explanations of the data.

Insights always involve what Lonergan calls enriching abstraction. Rather than offering an impoverished replica of empirical data, insight anticipates intelligibility through its questions and enriches the data:

1) by setting in motion, through insight, the circuit of observation, hypothesis formation, and verification to disclose what is relevant, significant, important, essential, formal in the data and so will be immanent in all other similar data;

2) by formulating this intelligibility, which formulations relegate the irrelevant, insignificant, negligible, incidental to the empirical residue from which intelligence always abstracts.[545]

This enrichment by abstracting insight is not only appreciated in the man of intelligence who can go to the relevant core of any common sense problem or issue. The irrelevancy of the empirical residue is not only annoying in the endless trivia of a consumerist ethos, but is seen in the most powerful scientific technique, generalization, illustrating the enrichment to be gained by abstracting from it.[546] Scientists are expected to explain the different kinds of sub-atomic elements, chemical elements and compounds, cells, organs, sensations, emotions - in short, every type of existent.

---

[544] On the oversight of insight in conceptualism, cf. Insight, pp. xxvi ff.; also Lonergan's discovery of this in Aquinas, Verbum: Word and Idea in Aquinas, pp. 142, 144-147, 151-152, 155-156, 168, 180-181, 186-189.

[545] Cf. Insight, pp. 87-89, 311; on the empirical residue, cf. ibid., pp. 25-32, 65, 311, 663, 382.

[546] Cf. Insight, pp. 25-30, 87-89. "Properly, then, abstraction is not a matter of apprehending a sensible or imaginative Gestalt; it is not a matter of employing common names just as it is not a matter of using other tools; finally, it is not even a matter of attending to one question at a time and, meanwhile, holding other questions in abeyance. Properly, to abstract is to grasp the essential and to disregard the incidental, to see what is significant and set aside the irrelevent, to recognize the important as important and the negligible as negligible." ibid., p. 30.

Gratefully, however, they can be spared the need to offer
different explanations for each of the billions upon billions
of purely individual differences among the same types. For
difference of time and place in itself does not give rise
to different measurements or experimental results. Something
different in the places and at the times produces significant
variations. Otherwise each place and time would require its
own complete retinue of sciences whose laws and principles
and methods could not apply to any other place or time.[547]
This same enriching abstraction can be found in critical
historical scholarship as it sifts through what is relevant
and irrelevant to the understanding of a particular event or
person or epoch.[548]

Human consciousness is not satisfied with insights
and hypothetical conceptions - as the saying goes, insights
are a dime a dozen. As critically or rationally conscious we
want to know if the understanding grasped by insights and
formulated in concepts expresses correctly the immanent
intelligibility of empirical data or experience. There is a
marshalling and weighing of the evidence and we go about
determining what conditions must be fulfilled if in fact
the hypothetical understanding is correct. Questions of
the "what" type are followed, when answered, by questions
for reflective understanding: "Is it so?" Critical rationality
submits the most brilliant systems and ideas to the rigors of
this question. These type questions can be answered by a
"yes," "no" or "maybe," depending on whether or not the
conditions are fulfilled. The marshalling and weighing of
the evidence leads to a grasp of the virtually unconditioned
inasmuch as one knows that the conditions are or are not
fulfilled.[549] The general form of reflective understanding
involves a grasp of the virtually unconditioned, so that a
prospective judgment will be virtually unconditioned, if

---

[547]For an examination of the problem this poses for
Physics cf. *Insight*, pp. 141ff.

[548]Cf. *M.i.T.*, pp. 187ff.

[549]Cf. *Insight*, pp. 280-281 on general form of reflective insight and judgment.

(1) it is the conditioned; (2) its conditions are known; (3) the conditions are fulfilled. The ferreting out of conditions and the determining if they are fulfilled leads to a grasp of whether or not they are, which is then formulated in judgments.

Common to all judgments is the contextual aspect which Lonergan casts in a historical perspective. Judgments occur only within the context of past judgments and accepted beliefs; in the present there is the dialectic between those judgments which complement and balance previous judgments and those which conflict with the habitual context; and because knowing is a dynamic structure, there is the orientation beyond our habitual context.[550] Lonergan goes into the particularities of concrete judgments of fact, common sense judgments, probable judgments (so extensive in the sciences), and mathematical judgments.[551] The grasp of the virtually unconditioned in concrete judgments of fact occurs in a reflective insight which at once grasps:

(1) a conditioned, the prospective judgment that a given direct or introspective insight is correct,
(2) a link between the conditioned and its conditions, and this on introspective analysis proves to be that an insight is correct if it is invulnerable and it is invulnerable if there are no further, pertinent questions, and
(3) the fulfillment of the conditions namely, that the given insight does put an end to further, pertinent questioning and that this occurs in a mind that is alert, familiar with the concrete situation, and intellectually master of it.[552]

This is schematized in Figure Seven. Notice how Lonergan is not giving some computer blue print of knowing but is continually calling attention to the subject's conscious abilities as decisive. He is careful to point out the differences in the subject's operations within common sense and empirically scientific judgments, probable judgments and mathematical ones.[553]

Between judgments and deliberations are the processes of

---

[550]Cf. _Insight_, pp. 277f.; on beliefs, cf. pp. 703-718.

[551]_Insight_, pp. 279-318.   [552]_Insight_, p. 287.

[553]_Ibid._, pp. 289-315.

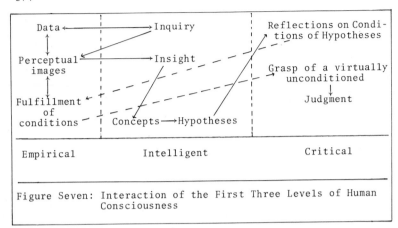

Figure Seven: Interaction of the First Three Levels of Human
Consciousness

evaluation. There is the apprehension of value in feelings
and critical refinement of those moral feelings in judgments
of value whereby real values are distinguished from apparent
values in terms of the degree of cognitive and moral growth
in the persons.

> The judgment of value presupposes knowledge of human
> life, of human possibilities proximate and remote, of
> the probable consequences of projected courses of action.
> When knowledge is deficient, then fine feelings are
> apt to be expressed in what is called moral idealism,
> i.e., lovely proposals that don't work out and often
> do more harm than good. But knowledge alone is not
> enough and, while everyone has some measure of moral
> feeling for, as the saying is, there is honor among
> thieves, still moral feelings have to be cultivated,
> enlightened, strengthened, refined, criticized and
> pruned of oddities. Finally, the development of know-
> ledge and the development of moral feeling head to the
> existential discovery, the discovery of oneself as a
> moral being, the realization that one not only chooses
> between courses of action but also thereby makes one-
> self an authentic human being or an unauthentic one.
> With that discovery, there emerges in consciousness
> the significance of personal value and the meaning of
> personal responsibility.[554]

Similar to Dilthey, then, Lonergan recognizes the importance
of feelings in the determination of value and the mediation
between the cognitive and volitional spheres of interiority.
Feelings are not isolated from the latter in terms of the

---

[554]_M.i.T._, p. 38.

subject-as-subject since, for Lonergan, the cognitive exhibits the same centrality of the subject in insight (mediating empirical experience and concepts) and in the grasp of the virtually unconditioned (mediating the marshalling of evidence and judgment). There is no need, therefore, to rely so heavily upon a "self-feeling" in the discovery of the subject-as-subject.[555]

Moral feelings and judgments of value in evaluation lead into the fourth level of consciousness defined by questions of the type "Is it worthwhile?". Deliberation is conditioned by the development of practical insights and practical reflections in the process of evaluation. Decision intervenes to put an end to the deliberation, and that decision will be in conformity with the growth of consciousness if it is responsibly made by:

1) demanding conformity of the subject's doing to his knowing,

2) acceding to that demand by deciding reasonably.[556]

The decision is then expressed, not in some immanent activity, but in action whereby rational consciousness becomes responsibly rational self-consciousness.[557]

This all too brief sketch of the related and recurrent operations of experiencing-understanding-judging-deciding and their respective levels of consciousness as empirical-intelligent-critical-responsible should be complemented by a few observations.

First of all, the activities coalesce into unities that are both subjective (acts) and objective (contents). What is sensed is what is perceived and imagined; what is sensed, perceived and imagined is what is inquired into, grasped in an understanding insight; what is understood is what is formulated in concepts and hypotheses; what is so formulated is what is reflected on in terms of the conditions for its being true or false; what is so reflected on is what is grasped as virtually unconditioned; what is so grasped is what is formulated in judgments; what is so known is what is

---

[555]On feelings, cf. M.i.T., pp. 30-41; Insight, pp. 608f.
[556]Cf. Insight, pp. 612-616. [557]Ibid., pp. 614-616.

evaluated and deliberated upon as to whether or not it is worthwhile; what is so deliberated upon is what is decided upon, and on the basis of that decision acted out. This objective unity is isomorphic to the subjective unity of the acts themselves. Consciousness is a unity of diverse acts or related and recurrent operations yielding cumulative and progressive results. Sensing, perceiving, imagining, inquiring, understanding, conceptualizing, weighing the evidence, grasping a virtually unconditioned, judging, deliberating, deciding, and acting occur within the formally dynamic unity of the subject-as-subject.[558] Hence there is the unity of identity and non-identity within the operations of the subject.

Secondly, Lonergan is able to show how these related and recurrent operations are present within the natural sciences. In Insight he begins his investigation into the activity of human consciousness with an extensive foray into classical and statistical scientific methods. Some of the results of this will be treated in the following subsection. Here it might be well to see how he summarizes the results of that investigation. For it shows how method for Lonergan is grounded in the subject and can simultaneously pattern itself on the operations of the natural sciences. We have seen how human consciousness is a normative pattern of recurrent and related operations yielding cumulative and progressive results. Now this is precisely how Lonergan defines method:

> A method is a normative pattern of recurrent and related operations yielding cumulative and progressive results. There is a method, then, where there are distinct operations, where each operation is related to the others, where the set of relations forms a pattern, where the pattern is described as the right way of doing the job, where operations in accord with the pattern may be repeated indefinitely, and where the fruits of such repetition are not repetitious, but cumulative and progressive.[559]

He then goes on to derive this preliminary notion of method from the functions of methods in the natural sciences. There

---

[558]Ibid., pp. 322-328; Collection, pp. 221-239.

[559]M.i.T., p. 4.

is a recurrence of inquiries, observations and descriptions, discoveries, formulations of discoveries in hypotheses, deductions from hypotheses and experiments to verify if the deductions check out in empirical facts. These operations are related, as he amply demonstrates in his articulation of the canons of empirical method.[560] And they yield cumulative and progressive results, as we shall see when discussing emergent probability.[561] Thus at one sweep Lonergan removes method from the sole monopoly of the positivists and overcomes its Cartesian identification with rules or axioms to be blindly followed by trained "Fachidioten":

> Method is often conceived as a set of rules that, even when followed blindly by anyone, none the less yield satisfactory results. I should grant that method, so conceived, is possible when the same result is produced over and over, as in the assembly line... But it will not do, if progressive and cumulative results are expected. Results are progressive only if there is a sustained succession of discoveries; they are cumulative only if there is effected a synthesis of each new insight with all previous, valid insights. But neither discovery nor synthesis is at the beck and call of any set of rules.[562]

The reliance upon prescriptions and objectivistic methods is especially challenged in times of revolutionary discoveries in science when the normal paradigms are upset and eventually replaced.[563]

The final observation regarding the levels and structures of human consciousness deals with the sublation that is operative between the levels. The empirical is sublated in the intelligent, in the sense that it is elevated, preserved, gone beyond. The intelligent is sublated in the rational, the rational in the responsible.[564] There is a transcending

---

[560] Cf. _Insight_, pp. 70-102.

[561] For a summary of this; cf. _M.i.T._, p. 5.

[562] _M.i.T._, p. 5-6.

[563] Cf. T. S. Kuhn, "The Structure of Scientific Revolutions," in the _International Encyclopedia of Unified Science_ 11/2 (Chicago, 1970).

[564] On the similarity to Hegel's _Aufhebung_, cf. _Insight_, pp. 421-422.

378

operative in the sublations insofar as the intelligent transcends (sublates in the threefold sense) the empirical, the rational transcends the intelligent, and the responsible transcends the rational. Hence the self-transcending character of the subject-as-subject is another way of saying that it is open to ever fuller growth and development as it moves from past awareness through the present into the future.[565] For the unity of the subject as conscious is the unifying thrust of the unrestricted desire to know which acts as the operator restlessly moving from sensation, perceptions and images through inquiry, with its insights and formulations, to grasping a virtually unconditioned and judgment, only to demand a consistency of deliberation and decision in actions consonant with knowing.[566]

C. Invariance and Freedom. The significance of the basic levels and structures of human consciousness consists in the fact that their formally dynamic nature is also critically self-mediating. Human historical interiority is not any one of the levels taken in isolation from the others.[567] The there-ness of self-presence, to use Dilthey's phrase, as experienced is not content simply with the empirical acts and contents of consciousness. There is the experience of questioning, understanding, formulating this understanding in concepts, weighing the evidence, judging, deliberating, evaluating, deciding, and acting. And these experiences are just as real as those of sensing, perceiving, imagining. In common sense, no less than in science, it is this basic horizon of conscious intentionality which grounds the circular self-correcting process of learning.[568] In concrete human praxis or performance the patterns are highly complex and variously differentiated according to the web of memories, habitual contexts of insights, judgments, beliefs,

---

[565]Cf. Insight, pp. 277-278.

[566]Cf. M.i.T., pp. 6-13; Insight, pp. 4, 9, 74, 220-222, 348-350, 380-381.

[567]Cf. Insight, pp. 324ff.; Collection, pp. 222-224.

[568]Cf. Insight, pp. 174f., 286-293, 300-304, 397f., 448f., 558, 622f., 713-718.

values, and patterns of action.

Insofar as this is the starting point and foundation
for meta-methodology it is eminently suited to avoid both
the extremes of empiricism and idealism. For it obviously goes
beyond the naive notions of awareness and knowing that have
been the bane of positivism.[569] And it does this without
falling into the identity patterns of Idealism by postulating
some absolute knowledge or starting point that cannot be
critically and empirically justified.[570] Lonergan indicates
how invariant these structures of consciousness are, how
they cannot be avoided in the critical self-mediation of
consciousness into knowledge. A fundamental illustration of
this is in the attempt to essentially revise or reject this
thematization of interiority. Such attempts would occur
inasmuch as someone's empirical attentiveness _experienced_
consciousness differently and _understood_ the experiences
differently, _judging_ his experience and understanding to
more adequately correspond to human consciousness than the
levels and structures thematized by Lonergan, and, on the
strength of this judgment, _deciding_ essentially to revise or
reject Lonergan's. In other words, he bears witness to the
invariance of the levels and structures in the very attempt
to deny them!

> Clearly, revision cannot revise its own presuppositions.
> A reviser cannot appeal to data to deny data, to his
> new insights to deny insights, to his new formulation
> to deny formulation, to his reflective grasp to deny
> reflective grasp.[571]

There is, then, in the givenness of formally conscious
dynamic structures a way out of the impasse created by
privatized notions of cognitional theory. For these structures and operations are present in any and all instances
of self-presence as experiencing, understanding, judging,

---

[569]Cf. Schnädelbach, Einfahrung, Begründung und
Reflexion: Versuch über den Positivismus (Frankfurt, 1971).

[570]On this dilemma in Hegel; cf. W. Becker, Hegels
Begriff der Dialektik und das Prinzip des Idealismus
(Stuttgart, 1969) and M. Riedel, Theorie und Praxis im Denken
Hegels (Stuttgart, 1965), pp. 204ff.

[571]Insight, pp. 336.

deciding, and acting. They are as present in common sense day-to-day activity as in the operations of scientific activity or scholarly pursuits. Undoubtedly the experiences, intelligence, rationality, and responsibility of each human person throughout the course of history has been unique. But this individuality of categorical achievement or failure does not militate against the universality of the experiencing, understanding, judging, and deciding as transcultural formally dynamic structures. One can, therefore, posit transcendental imperatives of human growth and development corresponding to the four levels of consciousness:

empirical⟵⟶be attentative
intelligent⟵⟶be intelligent
rational⟵⟶be critical
responsible⟵⟶be responsible

In the light of these transcendental precepts Lonergan can show the ultimate ground for either progress or decline:

The term, alienation, is used in many different senses. But on the present analysis the basic form of alienation is man's disregard of the transcendental precepts, Be attentative, Be intelligent, Be reasonable, Be responsible. Again, the basic form of ideology is a doctrine that justifies such alienation. From these basic forms, all others can be derived. For the basic forms corrupt the social good. As self-transcendence promotes progress, so the refusal of self-transcendence turns progress into cumulative decline.[572]

Here we see the unity of the subject as one of identity and non-identity. For the structures and levels of consciousness are not some identical object-structure. Even in their invariance they witness to the non-identity of human subjectivity. For while it is rather impossible, short of perpetual somnambulism, to avoid experiencing, understanding, judging, deciding, and acting, still they are structures of freedom. Human beings can just as easily (if not more so) be inattentative, stupid, irrational, and irresponsible. The negativity of alienation and decline, of inhumanity and decadence, is just as real in its non-identity as authenticity and progress, humanization and concern.

The transcendental imperatives are not, therefore, an

---

[572]M.i.T., p. 55.

imposition on freedom. Nor do they admit of an immediate
concrete application to particular dialectics operative in
personal or social living. They are instead meta-contextual
or transcultural imperatives capable of overcoming the extremes of either absolutizing a particular dialectic or
smothering any dialectic within the complete relativism of
a historicism or tyranny of tolerance.[573] Moreover,
these imperatives are also capable of interrelating the manifold of dialectics in process and thereby critically helping
them to avoid either fanaticization or trivialization.[574] For
the ultimate norm of any dialectical process is to extend the
frontiers of mankind's effective freedom in order that as many
as possible can actualize their essential freedom of becoming
more attentive, intelligent, critical and responsible.[575]

2. The Subject-as-Object

In the foregoing subsection on the subject-as-subject
the attentive reader will have noticed that it really dealt
with the subject-as-subject insofar as he or she experienced,
understood, judged, and decided regarding these same related
and recurrent operations of his or her own consciousness. For
I was presenting Lonergan's approach to the subject-as-subject
and that necessarily involved a transition from consciousness to
knowledge. Now such a transition is an instance of the self-
mediation of consciousness insofar as one appropriates, i.e.,
comes to know and acts according to, the structures of consciousness. For one _experiences_ the empirical, intelligent,
critical, and responsible levels of consciousness (or their
reverse) all the time of one's conscious living. Much
philosophical and psychological effort has been expended in
trying to _understand_ experiencing, understanding, judging,
deciding - and one such effort has been presented in the
previous pages. Specifically, one is asked to _judge_ on the
correctness of this previous understanding of experiencing,

---

[573]For the relevance of this, cf. Chapter One, pp. 46-49.
Chapter Two, pp. 82-92, 107-115, 175-195 and the references
given there.

[574]Cf. Chapter One, pp. 44-46.

[575]Cf. _Insight_, pp. 619-624.

understanding, judging, deciding. And finally, one must
decide whether or not it is worth the effort to begin the
task of elucidating the many consequences of such a knowledge
of consciousness. The self-mediation, then, is at the same
time a critical self-transcendence of consciousness. It
does not appeal to some absolute knowledge, nor to a noumenal
subjectivity, but to the experience of consciousness. This
goes beyond, and in this sense transcends self, in so far
as one's experiencing, understanding, judging, and deciding
is known, i.e., grasped in a judgment as virtually unconditioned. It could well have been differently, but de facto
the conditions for the correctness of the above description
of consciousness are fulfilled since I do experience, understand, judge and decide.[576] It is in judgment that the
subject-as-subject mediates the subject-as-object, if that
judgment concerns the structures of consciousness. The
experienced there-ness of empirical-intelligent-critical-
moral consciousness is known through correct judgments:·

> There exist subjects that are empirically, intellec-
> tually, rationally, morally conscious. Not all know
> themselves as such, for consciousness is not human
> knowing but only a potential component in the
> structured whole that is human knowing. But all can
> know themselves as such, for they have only to attend
> to what they are already conscious of, and understand
> what they attend to, and pass judgment on the
> correctness of their understanding.[577]

In order to explore some of the main elements in the
subject-as-object I shall first discuss objectivity, then go
into the isomorphism between knowing and known, emergent
probability, and finally aspects of a meta-anthropology.

A. Objectivity and Extroversion. For Lonergan any
adequate understanding of objectivity involves a recognition
of its ground in self-transcending subjectivity. The principal notion of objectivity lies in a patterned context of
judgments which, insofar as it is related to being as that
which is known through the totality of correct judgments,
includes an absolute moment in the grasp of a virtually

---

[576]Cf. Insight, pp. 217-316, 331, 340f., 343-345, 366,
372, 377f., 517-519, 549-552.

[577]Collection, p. 227; also Insight, pp. 319-347.

unconditioned, a normative moment in the unfolding of the
unrestricted desire to know open to all further relevant
questions and able to meet them, and an experiential moment
in the given data as the field of inquiry.[578] Thus one has
the proportional correlation:

$$\frac{\text{human consciousness}}{\text{(empirical:intelligent:critical)}} :: \frac{\text{objectivity}}{\text{(experiential:normative:absolute)}}$$

Lonergan has shown how both empiricism and idealism concur in
confusing objectivity with extroversion, where the former
tries to maintain the validity of extroversion, the latter
simply sees (as Kant did) that there can be no knowledge
in this fashion and so attempts to either posit a noumenal
thing-in-itself or to sublate all matter in mind à la
Hegel.[579] The fear of starting with the mind and never being
able to get outside it springs from the polymorphism of
human consciousness.

When the biological pattern blends with the intellectual,
things become real in the measure of their being bodies.
Objectivity becomes a disguised extroversion (empiricism) or
introversion (idealism); reality can only be known by taking
a noetic look (Anschauung) at it. Truth becomes the conformity of an impoverished mental image or concept with the out-
there-now or the in-here-now.[580] These extremes shatter,
however, under the pressure of the dilemmas they create. For
to judge that my knowing is similar to reality involves a

---

[578]Cf. Insight, pp. 375-384. On objectivity as self-
transcending subjectivity; cf. M.i.T., pp. 37, 338.

[579]Cf. Insight, pp. 372-374; also G. Sala, Das Apriori
in der menschlichen Erkenntnis: eine Studie uber Kants
Kritik der reinen Vernunft und Lonergans Insight (Meisenheim,
1972).

[580]Insight, pp. 250-254. This confusion of the realism
of empirical acts and the realism proper to understanding
is implicit in the "reality" referred to by Herbert Feigl in
his "Mind-Body, Not a Pseudoproblem" Dimensions of Mind, ed.
Sidney Hook (New York, 1961), p. 40. He wants the realities
which are the referents of physics to somehow be continuous
with our "direct experience." Notice how the intelligibility
immanent in all data, and the consequent interplay between
description and explanation, solves Feigl's problem of
relating scientific laws to empirical experience; and this
interplay would be impossible without central forms.

comparison between the knowing and the real, but either the real is known or it is not. If it is known then the comparison is between two items of knowledge (Hegel), or, if it is not known, no comparison is possible (Kant's noumenon), or one must analyze sensations in some faint hope of establishing a comparison (empiricists).[581]

Evidently, two types of realism exist. The unquestioning realism belongs to the animal whose extroverted attention is confined to the acts, contents, and derivatives of empirical awareness. The realism of intelligent inquiry and critical affirmation includes the acts and contents of empirical consciousness, but within a context where they are only the experiential or material component. For the proper object of the human mind is attained only when it knows the existence (grasp of virtually unconditioned) of the intelligibilities (insight) immanent in the empirically experienced and experiencing. Here reality is identified with being and not bodies - being as the objective of the unrestricted desire to know.

Intelligibility, then, is intrinsic to reality. The real is neither beyond the intelligible nor separate from it; otherwise no possibility of knowledge beyond unquestioning sensations could be found. Assuredly, our knowing by experience, insight, and judgment is extrinsic to the known - the knowing is not the known. But the above dilemma is created by a failure to grasp that such a distinction between knowing and known is within being (reality) and presupposes its intrinsic intelligibility. Otherwise our knowing would give knowledge of the intelligible but not of the real; the difference between knowing and known would be a distinction within the field of the intelligible but not a distinction of two beings.[582] Consciousness is oriented towards the concrete totality of the universe and so is impelled by the unrestricted desire to continue to raise ever more questions

---

[581]Cf. Verbum: Word and Idea in Aquinas, pp. viii, 47.

[582]Since intelligibility is intrinsic to being the differences of the potentially intelligible, formally intelligible, and actually intelligible are also intrinsic to being as potency, form, act. Cf. Insight, pp. 499-501.

in order to know being ever more fully.[583]

The transition from experiencing consciousness to knowing consciousness occurs because experienced consciousness itself is a dynamic intentional unity of experiencing-understanding-judging-deciding, and as such is a knowing and acting within the intention of being.[584] It was the oversight of this aspect of interiority which allowed Dilthey to acquiesce in the Kantian conception of knowing and its noumenal restrictions for the natural sciences. An oversight that led him to the impasse where he could not account for a true knowledge of the reality-itself of interiority. For reality and objectivity are not known as simply experienced in empirical consciousness, prior to all questions and answers. As the subject is a unity of experiencing-understanding-judging in the intention of knowing, so the object is a structured unity of material-formal-actual components:

> Empiricists have tried to find the ground of objectivity in experience, rationalists have tried to place it in necessity, idealists have had recourse to coherence. All are partly right and partly wrong, right in their affirmation, but mistaken in their exclusion. For the objectivity of human knowing is a triple cord; there is an experiential component that resides in the givenness of relevant data; there is a normative component that resides in the exigences of intelligence and rationality guiding the process of knowing from data to judging; there finally is an absolute component that is reached when reflective understanding combines the normative and experiential elements into a virtually unconditioned, i.e., a conditioned whose conditions are fulfilled.[585]

Because Dilthey had placed the normative in empirical rather than in intelligent and rational consciousness, he could not conceive of interiority as self-transcending and so could not account for the knowledge of the larger systems ("objektiver Geist") in history within his notion of re-experiencing ("Nacherleben"). He was coherent; as he had misplaced the normative, so he centered the structures of interiority around the emotive.

The fundamental problem in Dilthey - as in all

---

[583]Cf. _Insight_, pp. 348-374. [584]Cf. _Collection_, p. 228.
[585]_Ibid._, pp. 229f.

bifurcations of the phenomenon-noumenon type - originates in the polymorphism of consciousness and the above mentioned confusion of objectivity with extroversion or introversion. And any attempt to erect a defense against empiricism, positivism, or conceptualism cannot succeed on that confusion. For it admits the basic premise of its opponents. Lonergan, by going behind the procedures of even the natural sciences has, in this writer's opinion, most effectively criticized the premise and its consequences.

The progress of science is through the recurrent operations of observation and experiment, insights and hypothesis formations, verification and application. The drive for the ideal of complete explanation guarantees that science, both natural and human, will become involved increasingly with things as they are differentiated by classical laws and statistical probabilities. These complex intelligible relations of things among themselves cannot be verified in the common everyday empirical experiences proper to simple descriptions. This is illustrated in the specialized and refined operations proper to scientific research and verification.

This shift from imaginable descriptions to immanent intelligibilities has been dramatized in the progress of modern science. Einstein's Special Relativity, with its explanatory yet non-imaginable space-time, removed the imaginable framework in which imagined atomic elements were thought to move. Quantum Mechanics continues to puzzle scientists whenever they turn from their observing, understanding, and verifying to give laymen approximations of what scientific reality is supposed to look like. Darwin set the stage for an explanation in terms of probabilities which has sounded the death knoll for biological determinism. Freud's discovery of the notion of psychogenic disorders has extended the refutation of reductionism - however little Freud himself perceived it - into the domain of psychology.[586]

Modern science identifies reality and intelligibility to an extent few have appreciated. It indicates how no thing

---

[586]Cf. Insight, pp. 203-206, 132-134, 107, 131, 250-254.

as explained, no thing itself, can be imagined.[587] For
reality is known only when verification occurs, and the
complex relations of scientific explanation cannot be verified
in actual sensations. The images in which insight grasps
explanatory relations are not those of bodies, but complex
symbolic notations or models expressing possible intelligibilities to be verified through highly specialized acts of
measurement.[588] Insofar as the data are explained by the
understanding expressed in the symbols, to that degree the
understood intelligible relations are verified in wide ranges
of concrete, individual instances.[589] To limit reality to
the empirical is to deny the very practice of the empirical
sciences.

Hence the entire problematic of Dilthey concerning
outer and inner experience, the experiencing of outer reality
as impression and resistance, the puzzlement over how one
re-experienced larger systems in history not originally
experienced in anyone's individual interiority, the centrality
of the emotive structures - these are all traceable to a
misplaced notion of objectivity.[590] It is not to disparage
his studies of the central nervous system that the observation is made. One can most profitably analyse the physical,
chemical, neurological, and phenomenological components of
experiential objectivity. But in so doing one should be aware
that these experiential components are intrinsically related
to normative and absolute components, and that it is the
totality of these that is mediating and constituting the
objectivity of one's analysis of the experiential components.

---

[587]Cf. Insight, p. 250.

[588]Cf. P. Heelan, "Towards a Hermeneutic of Pure and Applied Science: An Essay in the Phenomenology of Scientific
Activity," in European Philosophy Today (Dublin, Sept., 1971).

[589]For the telling critique the implications of
relativity give to the widely accepted distinction between
primary and secondary qualities, cf. Insight, pp. 84-86, 99,
252-254, 388-389, 413. Descriptive and explanatory conjugates
are not other names for these qualities since both conjugates
are verifiable, indeed, descriptions mediate explanation,
ibid., pp. 247-345.

[590]Cf. G.S. V, p. 248 and compare with VII, p. 83.

Anyone claiming that intelligence and reason are merely subjective appearances of yet to be determined neural events, or that they are mere sublimations of unconscious drives, or merely a representational superstructure to emotion and conation - such a person is overlooking the very conscious processes of his or her own efforts at understanding and criticizing. For all the physiological, neurological, and psychological aspects of experience can be scientifically discovered and verified only by means of the related and recurrent operations of human consciousness as these are differentiated in the particular scientific methods.[591]

In one blow Lonergan's distinction of objectivity and extro- or introversion, as based on the polymorphism of consciousness, hits both the materialists and mechanists with their reductionisms, and the advocates of vitalism or meta-physical disquisitions on idealism. The latter, without going to the root of materialism, try to tack vital entelechies onto its imaginable elements which are meant to metaphysically explain life processes. They fail to realize that the material-formal-actual components do not explain any object but are the general structures in which any explanation would occur. Metaphysics is no surrogate for empirical science.[592]

B. The Isomorphism of Human Consciousness and Its Objects. Having established the context within which objec-tivity can be approached, I should now like to discuss, in outline form, how Lonergan's notion of the subject-as-subject is operative within the methods of science. These all have to do with the isomorphism between knowing and known. Six areas of this isomorphism will be handled.

First, there is the problem of just what facts are. There has been voluminous literature, especially in the Anglo-Saxon traditions of metascience, on the subject. One of the primary issues in the correspondence versus coherence debate

---

[591]Cf. M. Lamb, "Ascent from human consciousness to the human soul," in Insight, A Quarterly Review of Religion and Mental Health.

[592]Cf. Insight, pp. 431ff., esp. p. 498.

is that of fact. Positivistic correspondence tends to see
facts as given, irreducible, extra-mental realities. Idealistic coherence holds that facts and mental judgments or linguistic propositions are, for the purposes of verification,
the same thing.[593] Lonergan, however, seems to have exposed
where both are right and wrong by showing the isomorphism
between facts and consciousness. As with objectivity, so
here he shows the interrelations between experiential,
intellectual, and rational components in the reality of facts.

> Clearly, then, fact is concrete as is sense or con-
> sciousness. Again, fact is intelligible: if it is
> independent of all doubtful theory, it is not indepen-
> dent of the modest insight and formulation necessary
> to give it its precision and its accuracy. Finally,
> fact is virtually unconditioned: it might not have been;
> it might have been other than it is; but as things
> stand, it possesses conditional necessity, and nothing
> can possibly alter it now. Fact, then, combines the
> concreteness of experience, the determinateness of
> accurate intelligence, and the absoluteness of rational
> judgment. It is the natural objective of human cog-
> nitional process. It is the anticipated unity to
> which sensation, perception, imagination, inquiry,
> insight, formulation, reflection, grasp of the
> unconditioned, and judgment make their several,
> complementary contributions.[594]

We are committed to facts by the very dynamism of the subject-
as-subject. So one has the isomorphism expressed in the
formula:

$$\frac{\text{human consciousness}}{\text{(empirical:intelligent:critical)}} :: \frac{\text{facts}}{\text{(concrete:determinate:absolute)}}$$

Those familiar with the debate on the meaning of facts and
factual propositions will appreciate the neatness of
Lonergan's perspective.[595]

Second, Lonergan understands isomorphism as a unity of
identity and non-identity. "For the knowing and the known,
if they are not an identity, at least stand in some

---

[593] Cf. A. D. Woozley, Theory of Knowledge (London,
1959), p. 129. Gerard Radnitzky, Contemporary Schools of
Metascience, pp. 54, 72-92, 170f.

[594] Insight, p. 331.

[595] Thus Lonergan's position could critically clarify
the difficulty Karl Popper has in trying to elucidate the
objectivity of empirical facts. Cf. Popper, The Logic of

390

correspondence and, as the known is reached only through the knowing, structural features of the one are found to be reflected in the other."[596] The identity in this isomorphism may be found in the procedures of classical scientific methods and their isomorphic conjugates.[597] Propositions are expressions of relations and, in the general case, these state:

    (1)   the relations of things to empirical acts, and

    (2)   the relations of things to one another.

Propositions contain two types of terms whose modes of verifying are different. First is the term which may be referred to as the experiential or descriptive conjugate. These are correlatives whose meaning is grasped, in the final analysis, by appealing to the contents of some common sense human experience. Secondly, there are terms referred to by Lonergan as pure or explanatory conjugates. These are correlatives defined implicitly by classical scientifically established correlations, functions, laws, theories, systems. For example, the descriptive conjugates of color can be defined by appealing to visual experience. The explanatory conjugate of color, however, will define it in terms of the correlatives and measurements implicit in the equations dealing with electromagnetic wave-lengths and surface or pigment absorptivity.[598]

It is possible to show the difference between these two types of conjugates by adverting to the fact that every experience is a component of act and content. A series of experiences can be represented as AA', BB', CC',..., where the unprimed letters signify contents and the primed acts. Hence, in establishing the correlatives A, B, C,... it is a question of the contents among themselves and so of explanatory conjugates. In correlating A', B', C',... contents are

Scientific Discovery (New York, 1965), pp. 97-100.

[596]Insight, p. 115.

[597]Cf. Insight, pp. 33-53. Note that "classical" here does not refer to classical culture but to procedures of empirical method.

[598]Cf. Insight, pp. 79-82.

prescinded from and one is involved in psychological or cognitional theories about the acts. The combination of the primed and unprimed involve descriptive conjugates. As presenting the three basic alternatives, these enter into the broad heuristic principle of classical empirical method that states that similars are similarly understood.[599] There are similarities of things in relation to human empirical consciousness which form the basis of preliminary classifications. There also are the similarities of the things among themselves that are the proximate materials of insight into nature, which insight seeks to specify the unspecified correlation and determine the undetermined function by means of complex measurement.[600]

Because the formulations of descriptive conjugates are expressions of insights into the contents, correlatives and derivatives of empirical consciousness, they do admit of recourse to these latter, and so of verification as outlined in Figure Seven. Explanatory conjugates, on the other hand, do not have their verification in the contents and correlatives of empirical experience as such, but in vast combinations of these contents and derivatives as combined through insights. The formulations of these insights express the relations of things among themselves and so are the unifying functions, laws, theories, etc. which insight grasps in large aggregates of data. The verification outlined in Figure Seven still holds since it is a question of empirical science, but the fulfillment of conditions in empirical consciousness involve highly specialized and technical acts of measurement whereby it is determined if the functions, laws, theories, etc. adequately explain vast complexes of data. If so, any further pertinent questioning of these latter will have to have recourse to the former and the limits they assign and on which the aggregates of data converge.

Moreover, there is the canon of operations in empirical method by which such functions, laws, theories, etc. provide

---

[599] Insight, pp. 80f. The place of these conjugates in classical heuristic structures is treated on pp. 37f., 254-267.

[600] Cf. Insight, pp. 44-46.

the premises and rules for the guidance of human technological activity on sensible data, thereby bringing to light fresh data that raise new questions and stimulate further insights, and so contributing to the revision or confirmation of the previous functions, laws, etc.[601] All this implies that the verification process is not a simple matter of "looking" either outwards or inwards, but an intelligent and critical checking of the coherence of formulated insights (functions, laws, theories, etc.) with one another and their ability to describe experience or unify and explain vast combinations of data.

Third, the non-identity in isomorphism can be found in the heuristic structures of statistical method and their isomorphic events.[602] Classical laws, and the conjugates they explanatorily define, are abstract. Even in the physical sciences the determination of explanatory correlations and functions does not guarantee an exactly determinate and similar recurrence. The phrase "other things being equal" has to be continually expressed or implied when applying the abstract formulation to the concrete situation. The conjugates will give, as formulated in classical anticipation, the conditions (intelligible pattern) required if such and such a thing is to be or occur. But they do not determine how often one may expect the conditions to be fulfilled as realized possibilities. This shows the importance of events: "Without events, conjugates can be neither discovered nor verified. Without conjugates, events can be neither distinguished nor related."[603] In verification the statistical laws that deal with events and their frequency are complementary to the classical laws; while the latter determine what would happen if conditions were fulfilled, the former determine how often the conditions can be expected to be fulfilled. So one has the proportional relation of isomorphism where knowing is a compound of questioned data

---

[601] *Ibid.*, pp. 74-76.

[602] Cf. *Ibid.*, pp. 53-68, 86-102.

[603] *Insight*, p. 83.

(empirical), questions for intelligence, and questions for reflection; while the isomorphic known is a compound of underlying manifolds (empirical), conjugates, and events. This isomorphism is found in the methods of empirical investigation as a compound of the empirical residue, classical laws, and statistical laws.[604]

On determinist grounds, statistical laws are only a cloak for ignorance which the advent of complete knowledge of classical laws will render useless. An event is probable and not certain only because investigations of the classical type have not been pushed far enough. This overlooks the fact that classical laws are verified only in events, and events are not abstract but concrete. Concrete events make no effort at exactly measuring up to the abstract laws of classical heuristic methods, which must thereby set up refined techniques of measurement to determine systematic correlations between aggregates of data. They are verified as such, i.e., if a particular verification fails it may simply mean, not that the function, law, theory, etc. has been disproved, but that "other things were not equal." To put it another way, "what is verified is what can be refuted or revised. What can be refuted or revised, is the general, abstract formulation."[605] An event cannot be refuted or revised, it simply is.

This discloses the centrality of insight's pivotal role between the concrete and the abstract conceptions and propositions. It grasps in an event or series of events an intelligibility or pattern which it expresses as a function, law, theory, etc. the correlatives of which are conjugates. As long as the conditions expressed by the law are fulfilled, the type of event distinguished by the conjugates will recur. But the concrete recurrence is never exactly the same for the event takes place in the concrete continuum of space-time. The concrete insight has a fuller object than

---

[604]Cf. Insight, pp. 79-83.

[605]Ibid., pp. 90f. For a detailed account, cf. pp. 86-97. Notice how this incorporates K. Popper's notion of falsification; cf. his The Logic of Scientific Discovery.

the abstract law; it grasps that law in a determined situation which is the product of a concrete series of diverging conditions that do not come under the general law except in a general, indeterminate way. The concrete insight has to add further determinations when applying the classical law to concrete situations. These further determinations are capable of being understood and conceptually formulated; but the formulations do not reveal any further classical laws but simply an unmanageable infinity of cases in which these classical laws have triumphed, although such victories are not in accordance with any further classical laws.[606]

The random event indicates the non-identity present in statistical anticipations, and it can be handled only by inverse insight.[607] The non-systematic character of the concrete series of diverging conditions can only partially be overcome by statistical laws which formulate the ideal frequency of schemes of recurrence. These latter are recurrent events distinguished and related by classical laws. The probability expectations of statistics are not always realized in the actual unfolding of events; but they do assign norms from which the actual series diverge only in a random or non-systematic way. Should the divergence continue a new probability can be assigned and an investigation can proceed to look for the classical law (conjugates) which gives the events their systematic character. Such a new law, however, will only have an ideal frequency, i.e., the "other things being equal" of all classical laws. For all classical conjugates share in an indeterminacy that is the property of the abstract when it comes to applying them to, or verifying them in, the concrete series of events. Statistical procedures try to measure that uncertainty, pointing out the non-systematic divergencies observable within the concrete field of empirical observations. This is not a contradiction,

---

[606]Cf. Insight, pp. 105-111. Here I have only discussed the complementarity of classical and statistical laws in terms of verification. Lonergan also shows such complementarity in regard to procedures, formulations, modes of abstraction, and data explained.

[607]Cf. Insight, pp. 54-58.

for each <u>single</u> event is intelligible - otherwise there could be no insight into concrete processes - but when observed as within a series of events it may well be non-systematic or random, and so grasped by inverse insight.

The old determinists, with their insistence upon identity, overlooked the pivotal function of insight in moving from abstract systems to concrete aggregates of events. The new indeterminists, like J. Monod, commit the same oversight from the opposite direction when they insist upon interpreting classical laws concretely. The fact of randomness and divergence does not disprove classical method, they simply verify the position which states that such classical laws are not the whole of explanatory knowing but a necessary part which is to be complemented by statistical method. The complementarity in methods between the classical and statistical laws gives rise to emergent probability to be discussed below.

<u>Fourth</u>, in the light of the complementarity between classical and statistical methods and the isomorphism between consciousness and those methods, we can express the proportional relation:

$$\frac{\text{human consciousness}}{\text{(empirical:intelligent:critical)}} :: \frac{\text{methods of empirical knowing}}{\text{(emp. residue:classical:statistical)}}$$

This isomorphism is more concretely expressed by Lonergan in the chapter in <u>Insight</u> on the canons of empirical method. In it he shows how the heuristic structures of the classical and statistical type can be further defined through insight into the procedures of all empirical sciences. Space does not permit an extensive discussion of these, yet he aptly summarizes:

There is a canon of <u>selection</u>, for the empirical inquirer is confined to insights into the data of sensible experience. There is a canon of <u>operations</u>, for he aims at an accumulation of such insights, and the accumulation is reached, not in the mathematical circuit through insights, formulations, and symbolic images, but in the fuller circuit that adds observations, experiments, and practical applications. There is a canon of <u>relevance</u>, for pure science aims immediately at reaching the immanent intelligibility of data and leaves to applied science the categories of final, instrumental, and efficient causality. There is a canon of <u>parsimony</u>, for the empirical investigator may add to the data of experience only the laws verified

> in the data... There is a canon of <u>complete explana-</u>
> <u>tion</u>: ultimately science must account for all data, and
> the account must be scientific... Finally, there is a
> canon of <u>statistical residues</u>; though all data must be
> explained, one must not jump to the conclusion that
> all will be explained by laws of the classical type;
> there exist statistical residues and their explanation
> is through statistical laws.[608]

These canons disclose the intelligible unity that grounds the
diversity and multiplicty of rules of empirical method.
Lonergan is concerned to show why such a unity can emerge
in the light of the basic structures of human consciousness.

Fifth, since the objects known are reached only via
consciousness it is not surprising that the structure of
the known is isomorphic with that of the knowing. In a
proportional formula this may be expressed as:

$$\frac{\text{human consciousness}}{\text{(empirical:intelligent:critical)}} :: \frac{\text{the known objects}}{\text{(material:formal:actual)}}$$

This is the general form of isomorphism applicable to all
forms of knowing.[609] The material component of the known
object, or potency, corresponds to empirical consciousness.
As the latter consists in a flow of sensations, perceptions,
and images prior to any questions and answers, so potency
grounds the empirical residue of place and time, continua,
individuality. Empirical consciousness provides the data for
inquiry in which a succession of insights may emerge, in a
similar manner potency is oriented entirely to the forms it
individualizes; this orientation is indeterminate, enabling
it to provide for the emergence of a succession of forms.[610]

The formal component of the known object is correlative
to intelligent consciousness understanding things in their
interrelationships. The general ways in which we understand
things parallels the several types of forms or intelligibilities.[611] We have already seen how classical empirical methods
differentiate this formal component into descriptive and
explanatory conjugates. The general mode of isomorphism

---

[608]<u>Insight</u>, p. 70.   [609]Cf. <u>Insight</u>, pp. 431f.

[610]Cf. <u>Insight</u>, pp. 442-451.

[611]On things; cf. <u>Insight</u>, pp. 245-270.

understands things, however, as unities, identities, wholes.
Data not only are similar to other data but also are concrete
and individual; they can be understood as forming a concrete
intelligible unity. Understanding data in their concrete
individuality and in the totality of their aspects constitutes
the exact notion of a thing. For example, turning one's
attention to any given object, one finds it a unity containing
every datum within the unity; no datum within it can be
understood in the totality of the datum's aspects without
reference to the unity. Differentiated by experiential
conjugates it is a thing for us, a thing as described; as
differentiated by explanatory conjugates it is a thing itself,
a thing as explained. The forms isomorphic to understanding
concrete, intelligible unities-identities-wholes are central
forms.[612]

Scientific knowledge is impossible without the notion
of central forms constituting things as individual unities
differentiated by conjugates.

> For science advances through the interaction of
> increasingly accurate descriptions and ever more
> satisfactory explanations of the same objects. Unless
> the objects are the same, there is no relation between
> the description and the explanation and so no reason
> why explanation should modify description or description
> lead to better explanation. But the only object that
> is the same is the concrete and intelligible unity,
> identity, whole; for the explanatory conjugates
> change; and the descriptive or experiential terms
> undergo modifications and rearrangements. Accordingly,
> as long as science is developing, the notion of the
> intelligible unity is indispensable. But in their
> term no less than in their development, scientific
> conclusions need to be supported by evidence; the
> evidence for such conclusions lies in change; and with-
> out concrete and intelligible unities there is nothing
> to change, for change is neither the substitution of
> one datum for another nor the replacement of one concept
> by another; it consists in the same concrete, intelli-
> gible unity providing the unification for successively
> different data; and so without the unity there is
> no change and without change there is lacking a no-
> table part, if not all, of the evidence for scientific
> conclusions. Finally, science is applicable to
> concrete problems; but neither descriptive nor
> explanatory knowledge can be applied to concrete
> problems without the use of the demonstrative, this,
> and that demonstrative can be used only inasmuch as

---

[612]Cf. Insight, pp. 434-437, 511.

there is a link between concepts and data as individual;
only the notion of the concrete and intelligible
unity of data supplies such a link, and so that notion
is necessary for science as applied.[613]

Act is the third component of the object. Critical
consciousness affirms or denies the existence of the hypotheses formulated by intelligence; similarly, act is the existence of forms, thereby dividing into conjugate acts and
central acts. Potency to forms has a parallel division. Since
central form is the intelligible unity of data as individual,
central potency is the individuality of the residue; conjugate
potencies are the space-time continua, conjunctions and
successions of the empirical residue in which conjugate forms
are verified.

By sensitive experience, insight, and judgment we know
one and the same object; in like manner, one, identical thing
is constituted by potency, form, act. These are not objects
within objects but the principles by which one and the same
unity in multiplicity exists and is knowable, a unity by
central potency-form-act, differentiated by conjugate poten-
cies-forms-acts. The potencies and acts are specified only
through the forms, just as experiences and judgments are
specified by the insights. Finally, the above account of
potency, form, and act will cover any possible scientific
explanation since these are theories verified in instances.
As verified the explanation refers to act; as theory it refers
to form; as in instances it refers to potency.[614]

---

[613]Ibid., p. 436; also cf. pp. 247-248. Regarding the
application of abstract principles to concrete situations,
note the pivotal function of insight grasping the intelligibility in presentations of individual data and then formulating it in concepts and hypotheses applicable to all
instances of similar data. Both positivism and idealism overlook this role of insight between the concrete level of
empirical consciousness and the abstract level of concepts
and propositions. As a result each clings to one level,
ascribing to it the characteristics proper to the other
level.

[614]Cf. Insight, pp. 431-433. The instances in which
theories are verified are events. The abstractive procedure
of scientific generalization extends also to statistical
methods insofar as intelligence abstracts from the non-
systematic divergences among actual frequencies occurring in
the empirical residue, thereby constructing the ideal

Sixth, and finally, the distinction between central potency-form-act and conjugate forms and events enables Lonergan to correlate the several aspects of genetic scientific method.[615] These methods aim at understanding, not single schemes of recurrence, but flexible circles of ranges of schemes. The flexibility of these circles is constituted by the fact that random divergencies from the schemes of recurrence and their probabilities need not result in schemes of recurrence of the same generic type as those from which they emerged, but may actually initiate higher generic schemes of recurrence.

> Masses and electric charges, atoms and molecules, are statically systematic; their performance is not a function of their age; there is not a different law of gravitation for each succeeding century. In contrast, organic, psychic, and intellectual development involves a succession of stages; and in that succession the previously impossible becomes possible and the previously awkward and difficult becomes a ready routine. The infant can neither walk nor talk, and once we all were infants. Hence, where the physicist or chemist is out to determine single sets of conjugate forms and consequent schemes of recurrence, the biologist or psychologist or intellectual theorist is out to determine genetic sequences of conjugate forms and consequent sequences of flexible circles of schemes or recurrence.[616]

Thus genetic method is concerned with sequences in which correlations and regularities change and develop. As the heuristic structures of classical method aim at determining indeterminate functions in explanatory conjugates, and as heuristic structures of statistical method aim at determining the ideal frequency of schemes of recurrence from which there can only be random non-systematic divergencies, so the heuristic structures of genetic method aim at determining the general and particular elements of development.

Development involves seven general principles or

---

frequencies of probability expectations. On the complementarity of classical and statistical investigations once the structure of human consciousness is realized, cf. Insight, pp. 82-83, 103-115.

[615] Cf. Insight, p. 458f.

[616] Ibid., pp. 460-461.

functions. First, there is the principle of emergence whereby coincidental manifolds of lower conjugate acts invite higher integrations to be effected by higher conjugate forms. Second, the principle of correspondence implies that development take into account how significantly different underlying manifolds demand different higher integrations. The third function of development is finality inasmuch as the underlying manifold is not some static and inert mass, but an upwardly, although indeterminately, directed dynamism. Fourth, the principle of development itself aims at showing how there is a linked sequence of dynamic higher integrations until the possibilities of development along a given line are fully actualized and the relative stability of maturity is reached. The fifth function or principle is that of increasing explanatory differentiation. From the rather amorphous initial underlying manifold the successive stages of development through genera and species leads to ever more highly explanatory differentiations. Sixth, there is the principle of minor flexibility inasmuch as development toward the same goal can emerge along different roots. And, seventh, there is the function of a major flexibility whereby development shifts or modifies its ultimate objective. Major and minor flexibilities are functions of the relation between potency and form.

> In the light of the foregoing considerations, a development may be defined as a flexible, linked sequence of dynamic and increasingly differentiated higher integrations that meet the tension of successively transformed underlying manifolds through successive applications of the principles of correspondence and emergence.[617]

Lonergan goes on to illustrate these functions or principles of development in genetic method by discussing organic development, psychic development, intellectual development, and finally human development. He also succeeds in sharply differentiating his position from the views of the mechanists, vitalists, those who would reduce biology to chemistry or physics, the advocates of wholism or organicism, some of the crucial aspects of Darwin's understanding of

---

[617]Cf. Insight, p. 454.

evolution, and Kant's notion of formal purposiveness.[618]

C. Emergent Probability. Just as an exclusive acceptance of classical methods leads to determinism and a similar
acceptance of statistical methods leads to the relativism of
indeterminism, so an acknowledgment of the complementarity
between classical and statistical methods, and of the
isomorphism between knowing and the known, which in its
general form enables Lonergan to explicate the principles of
genetic methods - so the acknowledgment of these leads to
an affirmation of what Lonergan calls emergent probability.[619]
Here I should like to first summarize the essentials of
emergent probability and then show how they provide a framework for correlating the sciences.

Lonergan has summarized his rather extensive analysis
of the characteristics of emergent probability in nine
assertions.

1. An event is what is to be known by answering "Yes"
   to such questions as: Did it happen? Is it
   occurring? Will it occur?
2. World process is a spatio-temporal manifold of
   events. In other words, there are many events
   and each has its place and time.
3. Events are of kinds. Not every event is a new
   species, else there could be neither classical nor
   statistical laws.
4. Events are recurrent. There are many events of
   each kind, and all are not at the same time.
5. There are regularly recurrent events. This
   regularity is understood, inasmuch as combinations
   of classical laws yield schemes of recurrence.
   Schemes are circular relationships between events
   of kinds, such that if the events occur once in
   virtue of the circular relationships then, other
   things being equal, they keep on recurring
   indefinitely.
6. Schemes can be arranged in a conditioned series,
   such that the earlier can function without the
   emergence of the later, but the later cannot emerge
   or function unless the earlier already are functioning.
7. Combinations of events possess a probability, and
   that probability jumps, first when a scheme becomes
   concretely possible in virtue of the fulfillment of
   its prior conditions, and secondly when the scheme
   begins actually to function.

[618] Ibid., pp. 454-487.

[619] Ibid., pp. 103-139, 259-262.

8. The actual frequencies of events of each kind in each place and at each time do not diverge systematically from their probabilities. However, actual frequencies may diverge non-systematically from probabilities, and that non-systematic divergence is chance. Accordingly, probability and chance are distinct and are not to be confused.

9. Emergent probability is the successive realization in accord with successive schedules of probability of a conditioned series of schemes of recurrence.[620]

Lonergan then elaborates the characteristics of world process.[621] Every situation in world process will be characterized by the schemes of recurrence actually functioning, by the further schemes that have become concretely possible in virtue of the former, and by the current probability expectations for the survival of existing schemes and the emergence of possible schemes. Emergent probability is a completely open explanation of world process insofar as it consists in the succession of probable realizations of possibilities. It conforms neither to a rigid determinism nor to unintelligible chance precisely because it incorporates them both in a higher synthesis. In its view world process will become increasingly systematic, admitting of enormous differentiation. Since the schemes are only assigned a probability value, break-downs and blind alleys will also be characteristic of the process. These properties of world process, while assuming laws of the classical, statistical and genetic type, do not determine the contents of any of these laws.

Illustrations of the continuities, oscillations, rhythms, routines, alternations, circulations, regularities, etc. which compose schemes of recurrence might point to the planetary system, the geological cycle, the nitrogen cycle, the life cycle, generalized equilibria. The food chain and the Krebs cycle are good examples of the conditional character of the schemes. Yet these obvious illustrations must not lead one to overlook how this emergent probability enters into every scientific discovery of laws. For if events of a certain kind were not recurrent there could be no possibility

---

[620]Ibid., pp. 125f.   [621]Ibid., pp. 126-128.

of establishing any type of law. Nor is the uniqueness of
events slighted, along with the chance of random divergences,
since the recurrence means that the spatio-temporal factors
of difference and individuality are present in the concrete
unfolding of the scheme.

A correct recognition of Lonergan's cognitional analysis
is of the utmost importance in appreciating the flexibility
of emergent probability and what distinguishes it from other
world views. The pivotal nature of insight between accurate
observations and descriptive or explanatory formulations is
especially significant. If these cognitional factors are
not comprehended sufficiently, emergent probability will
appear to some as an idealistic-deterministic imposition of
a priori categories on empirical data; while others will
claim that it surrenders that data to a radical indeterminism.

How does emergent probability provide a framework for
the synthetization of the sciences? Obviously, the problem
would demand the highly specialized knowledge available in
group research to be solved in detail. However, following
up the hints given by Lonergan,[622] I have been able to sketch
some of the main lines according to which an open synthetization patterned on emergent probability would proceed.
Naturally, these make no pretension to exhaust all the possible patterns which could be utilized.

A key factor is Lonergan's distinction between chance
and probability.[623] It implies that what is non-systematic
for one kind of schema of recurrences can become systematic,
with a probability value attached to it, and thereby effect
a new scheme. This indicates that there can be successive
levels of scientific inquiry. The coincidental manifold of
non-systematic events on the level of physics can be
systematized by the higher chemical level without encroaching
on any physical laws. Coincidental manifolds on the level
of chemistry can be systematized by the higher biological
level without violating any chemical laws. What is non-
systematic on the level of biology can be brought under the

---

[622]Ibid., pp. 205f.; 256f.

[623]Ibid., pp. 58-62, 112-114.

404

higher psychological laws without in any way annulling the
biological schemes of recurrence.

In each of these progressions what is non-systematic
on one level of scientific inquiry is rendered systematic
by the higher level. A conditioned series of schemes of
recurrence is thus in function. The posterior or higher
schemes cannot exist without the prior ones whose coincidental
manifolds they systematize. Figure eight outlines these
progressions. As far as the laws of subatomic elements are

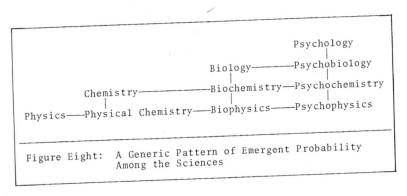

Figure Eight: A Generic Pattern of Emergent Probability
Among the Sciences

concerned, the behavior of atoms within chemical compounds are
patterns of happy coincidence. Yet each chemical compound
demands a specific combination of atoms if it is to exist,
the chemical level renders the combinations systematic.
Chemicals do not dispense with the physical manifolds they
systematize, so physical chemistry studies the interrelations
of these two levels.

From a strictly chemical viewpoint the combination and
interactions of chemicals occurring during the metabolism
and division of cells are mere patterns of happy coincidence.
But from the higher vantage point of biology which systematizes them, these complex chemical and physical activities
are necessary if the living cell is to exist, function and
multiply. In biochemistry and biophysics, the intelligible
patterns of the physical and chemical processes within
organisms are sought after in order to grasp the explanatory

biological laws which account for the chemical regularities lying beyond the range of strictly physical and chemical explanations.[624]

Remaining strictly within the field of biology, the behavior of animals appears to be no more than patterns of happy coincidence. Yet this behavior ceases to be thought of as coincidental once the correct correlations or laws are discovered by psychological investigation. ("Psychological" in Figure Eight refers primarily to the empirical or sensitive awareness and its concomitants shared to a greater or lesser extent by all animals, including man.) Psychobiology, psychochemistry, psychophysics and allied sciences study the complex neurological, organic, chemical and physical processes as they are affected by, and contribute to, the emergence of psychological schemes of recurrence which system-atize them for such functions as sensation, emotion, conation, imagination.

Because the higher emergent cannot survive without the underlying manifolds it systematizes does not mean that it can be deduced from, or reduced to, the lower. As Lonergan points out,[625] physics, chemistry, biology, and psychology can exist as autonomous sciences since in each prior science there are statistical residues, or coincidental manifolds, which remain to be regulated by the following science. Thus the higher level sciences could not be deduced from the lower by any strict necessity. The lower are related to the higher only insofar as they furnish the higher with the manifolds to be brought under the higher laws - this relationship also implies a limitation exercised by the lower on the higher. By the same token, the higher cannot be reduced to the lower; otherwise there would have been no non-systematic occurrences in the lower level sciences. No less obvious than their autonomy is the need each science will eventually experience for intercommunication, especially when studying deeply complex subjects which systematize one or several underlying manifolds.

The open quality of the generic pattern outlined in

---

[624]Ibid., pp. 463-467. [625]Ibid., p. 608.

Figure Eight is diagrammed in Figure Nine. There I have
inserted the physical and chemical schemes of recurrence
which have actually been realized on the geological scale.
The complex physical and chemical processes which specifically
are involved in the formation and conservation of this planet
are coincidental from a strictly physical or chemical viewpoint whereas geology systematizes them. The transition,
however, is not so great as those in Figure Eight. In the
latter the movement from one generic level to the next added
a new set of laws which define the level's own basic terms
by its own empirically established correlations.[626] In
moving from physics and chemistry to geology no radically new
set of explanatory laws is introduced. Moreover, the further
differentiations of Figure Nine admit of more inclusive
extensions or specific divisions. For example, instead of
geology one might insert cosmology, cosmochemistry and
cosmophysics to embrace the physical and chemical processes
actually realized on the universal scale. This in turn could
be divided into astronomy, astrochemistry, astrophysics, or
into geology which might be further specified into meteor-
ology, oceanology, etc.

The insertion of geology affects biology to the extent
of introducing the study of bionomics, biogeography, ecology,
etc. to investigate the environmental distributions and
influences on organisms and vice versa. In the realm of
psychology such sciences as psychonomics or environmental
psychology inquire into these correlations with regard to
psychological systems. Since the spatio-temporal similarity
of environment shared by plants and animals will also involve
interbiological and interpsychological manifolds, sociology
emerges. In the case of man this also brings in the study
of his cultures by ethnology or cultural anthropology. Here
again in the transposition from biology and psychology to
sociology and the anthropological sciences, societies and
cultures must not be reified into completely autonomous levels
of superorganic or superpsychic sui generis entities. Just
as geology is not a higher systematization of what would be

---

[626]Ibid., p. 255.

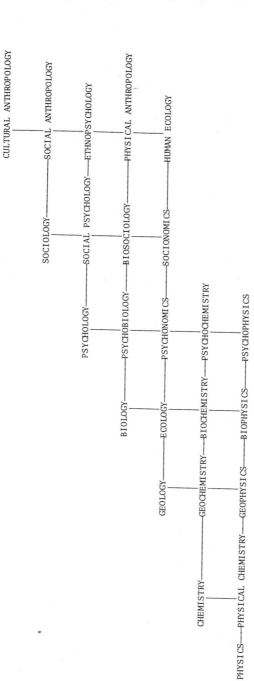

Figure Nine: Generic Illustrations of Emergent Probability among the Sciences

from an _explanatory_ viewpoint the lower manifolds of physical
and chemical laws, so also the emergence of society or
culture is not simply a happy set of coincidences from the
biological and psychological standpoints. With this strong
interdependence kept in mind, the degree of autonomy between
these sciences can be appreciated.[627]

Thus sciences such as socionomics and bioclimatology
investigate the distributions of societies and their interaction with their physical and chemical environment. With
man this brings in sciences like human ecology, anthropo-
geography, ethnography, and so on. Are there sciences which
inquire into the physical and chemical manifolds of societal
or cultural systems? As far as I can determine these are
studied only via the physical, chemical environment on the
one hand, and the biochemical-biophysical and/or
psychochemical-psychophysical manifolds of the individual
societal or cultural organisms on the other hand. Biosociol-
ogy, bioecology and allied sciences deal with the biological
manifolds as they are systematized from a sociological
standpoint; with man these manifolds are studies by physical
anthropology which sets them in their ethnic and sociocultural
perspectives. Social psychology and related disciplines study
the complex psychological factors and correlations effecting,
and affected by, social groupings and organizations; in the
case of man this will also be investigated by ethnopsychology,
macrolinguistics, etc., which take into account the interaction of human psychological and cultural processes.

The matter is still far from being settled, yet it
does seem necessary to distinguish sociology, with its
interests in societal relationships of wide generalization,
from social anthropology which views social systems as manifolds within a cultural context.[628] Another aspect of the
further differentiation is that social systems are not
specifically human whereas culture is. Even in the area of
human societies there cannot be an exact equation of it with

---

[627] Cf. D. Bidney, _Theoretical Anthropology_ (New York,
1960), pp. 140ff.

[628] _Ibid._, pp. 96-103.

its cultures. Sociologists tend to view cultural achievements as functions of the particular society while culturologists have tended to the opposite extreme in disregarding the partial dependence of culture on the individual and society. Nevertheless, different societies may have the same cultural attainments, and cultures are not necessarily integrated with their corresponding societies.[629]

Indeed, Bidney's concept of emergent evolution is very close to that of emergent probability, and the description he gives of the emergence of cultures fits in well with its approach to emergence:

> In the last analysis, we must fall back upon man in society in a given environment as the ultimate source of his culture. We do not, then, explain a given culture by deducing it from human nature or society, but by pointing out the probable or necessary and sufficient conditions for its emergence. When we say that culture constitutes a new level of phenomena, what we mean is that logically culture cannot be inferred or deduced; it can only be described as it is in itself and by reference to the conditions which brought it about.[630]

In this perspective, cultural anthropology or ethnology systematizes what would otherwise be coincidental from a strictly sociological point of view.

D. Anthropological Dimensions of Meta-Method. No treatment of subject-as-object would be complete without entering into the specifically anthropological dimensions of emergent probability and Lonergan's grounding of meta-method in the related and recurrent operations of human consciousness. The interrelating of the sciences according to emergent probability leads naturally into this problematic. Here I should like to treat, however briefly, three of the main problem areas in human development today and how Lonergan's method would go about offering solutions to them. This is a prolegomenon to the fuller treatment of Lonergan's approach to the problems in the following section on history.

i. Human consciousness and the crisis of will. We have already seen how the dialectic of the Enlightenment has led to a pluralism within the contemporary schools of metascience,

---

[629] Ibid., pp. 104ff.   [630] Ibid., p. 114.

and how the exigencies of meaning could lead to a sublation
of any irrationality resulting from such pluralism. But it
is not only on this level that a crisis of critical normativity to guide human action discloses itself. Recently the
eminent American psychologist, Rollo May, has indicated the
profound effects of a crisis of will within contemporary
industrialized societies.[631] He describes the personal
anguish and ambiguity human persons experience when there
seems so much to take into consideration, so much to know,
that they are never certain whether or not their decisions
are correct. The paralysis of will and action that results
creates a very unhealthy sense of powerlessness. The self
becomes the pawn of either the super-ego (parents, mentors,
etc.) or of the id (the instinctual drives welling up from
the unconscious).[632] How can we really discover ourselves
if we are continually pressured by forces that spring either
from the super-ego or the id? Are there no norms inherent
within the self which do not originate either in the contin-
gencies of our upbringing (super-ego) or in those of our
unconscious conditioning (id)? Are "self, freedom, person,
value, meaning" no more than illusions in a universe that is
either completely determined by laws totally beyond our control, or completely blind and haphazard in its ultimate
absurdity?

The personal crisis of will which May discusses does
not occur in a vacuum. It is part of the crisis of modern
men and the breakdown of the Enlightenment worldview. As
May indicates, the personal crisis is caused to a great extent
by the advance of psychiatry with Freud.[633] The insights of
Freud were reflections of the overall cultural crisis of
modern man. The industrial revolution led men to see themselves in the image of the machines they made. Freud
believed that if psychology was to be "scientific" then it

---

[631] Cf. R. May, Love and Will (New York, 1970) and his
Power and Innocence: A Search for the Sources of Violence
(New York, 1972).

[632] Cf. Love and Will, pp. 181-201.

[633] Cf. Love and Will, pp. 182-184, 196ff.

must reduce human behavior to "energy systems."[634]   The same
tendency to reductionism can be found in Marx's notion of
basing all social phenomena on the economic forces and relations of production; it can be found in the positivism
and behaviorism which interprets the entire scientific
enterprise as eventually having to control and manipulate
men "for their own good."[635]   Thus, just as the self is torn
in Freudian psychology between the powers of the superego
and the unpredictable impulses of the id, so in our contemporary world situation mankind is reduced to an unfree pawn
caught between the superego of a scientistic mechanomorphic
technocracy (cf. "Brave New World" and "1984") on the one
hand, and by the passions and biases of nationalist and
racist groupings or the vagaries of counter-cultures
(corresponding to the id) on the other hand.

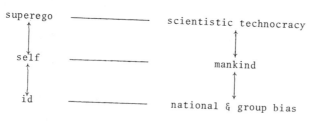

From what we have seen of Lonergan's grounding of meta-
method in the invariant levels and structures of consciousness, what he is aiming to do is expand the domain of the
self in its attentative-intelligent-critical-responsible
constitution of its own history. At the same time, this is
not a privatized concern. From those patterns of consciousness one can, through self-appropriation, begin the arduous
task of setting up the framework for both a radical critique
of scientism and bias, and a positive correlation of the
results of modern sicence. This is evident, not only in what
we have already seen of Lonergan's critique of empiricist
and idealist counter-positions and the resulting possibility

---

[634]Ibid., pp. 207ff., also C. Wilson, New Pathways in
Psychology (New York, 1973), pp. 88-100.

[635]Cf. F. Matson, The Broken Image, pp. 3-110.

412

of interrelating the sciences according to emergent probability, but will also become clear as we handle successive
issues in the following subsections. In contradistinction
from Freud, Lonergan has opened up the domain of consciousness
and self as the determining dimension capable of integrating
personal and social human development.[636]

ii. The unrestricted desire to know and fear. Coupled
with the crisis of will described by Rollo May are the phenomena of what Lonergan refers to as scotosis and what A.
Maslow refers to as a fear and flight from understanding.
The stories of Adam and Eve, of Prometheus and Oedipus,
illustrate the ambiguity of the quest for knowledge: "it
is precisely the god-like in ourselves that we are ambivalent
about, fascinated by and fearful of, motivated to and
defensive about."[637] Similar to his distinction of
deficiency-needs and growth-needs, Maslow distinguishes an
anxiety-reduction quest for knowledge and a growth-quest for
knowing. A child's spontaneous curiosity is primarily within
a growth pattern of knowing; questions abound, an over-
eagerness to explore is manifested. The child can be
thwarted in a growth pattern if he or she must direct the
knowing process toward "learning" those types of activity
which will assure him or her of gaining the pleasure and
esteem of parents, or the satisfaction of needs. In order
not to be rejected they conform to the wishes of their
parents; knowing is channelled into an anxiety-reducing
pattern. Within such a pattern it is painful to try to
face questions which the child would just as soon repress
in order to avoid conflict.

An analogous process can be traced in the aesthetic,
religious, intellectual, moral, and dramatic patterns of
experience with their traditions. In any of these patterns
there emerge men and women of creative insight who launch
the pattern of experience on a growth quest for understanding.

---

[636]For Lonergan on Freud, cf. Insight, pp. 456-458,
203-206.

[637]A. Maslow, Toward a Psychology of Being (New York,
1968), pp. 60-67.

Because such insights are necessarily partial, it is important that both the originator of the tradition and his or her followers remain open to further developments and changes. This, however, becomes increasingly difficult to the extent that the knowledge they have gained is assimilated in order to reduce anxiety. The latter is especially prevalent when the individuals and groups concerned are threatened from without (censorship, rejection because of the new insights they are trying to communicate, etc.) or from within (many are attracted to them who do not share in the creative thrust of the originating insights and so devaluate the tradition through mere conformity). Hence the tradition becomes sectarian and defensive, rather than open and inclusive.

This process, could be illustrated within the aesthetic pattern of experience (e.g., how art forms emerge, achieve recognition, and then decline because of cheap imitation), the religious pattern (e.g., a charismatic figure emerges who attracts a following, which sooner or later loses the charismatic spirit of the leader and insists upon the letter of observance rather than the spirit), and the moral pattern (where new insights into values and meanings degenerate into a conformism aimed at self-righteousness rather than growth).

Here I would like to illustrate the process in relation to the emergence of modern science. In his scholarly study The Myth of the Machine, Lewis Mumford traces the emergence of modern scientific technology, indicating how the brilliant genius operative in the discovery of new methods was soon translated into conservative traditions of research which took as "scientific" only quantifiable observations.[638] A similar point is made by Thomas Kuhn in The Structure of Scientific Revolutions, where he indicates how the conservative routines of normal science resist any revolutionary change in paradigms.[639] It was this narrowing of the horizons of

---

[638] This is also treated at greater length in the section on the Dialectic of the Enlightenment in Chapter Two, and that on historical typology of patterns of experience in Chapter Three.

[639] Cf. also A. Maslow, The Psychology of Science (New

science to an anxiety-reducing quest for knowledge that made it so easy for industry to coopt the modern scientific revolution and put technology at the service of exponential growth. Markets are competitive, so the technology was also directed toward the "pentagons of power" and the anxiety-reducing pattern is only too evident in the vast amount of money and research that go into "defense contracted programs."

But contemporary science is also experiencing the crisis of will outlined above. E. Neumann in his The Origins and History of Consciousness mentions how the mythological origins of science in alchemy and magic were a projection of inner complexes into the physical universe; now there is a reversal inasmuch as the in-scape of mind is being treated according to the projected laws of the physical universe.[640] A reversal of this objectivism is necessary if science is to find its proper norms for deciding how to effect the transformation of nature. For modern science is rapidly discovering that the "objective laws of nature" and the "mechanomorphic conception of reason" are not adequate guides for the transformative activity of science and technology.[641]

As the crisis of will is met in Lonergan by calling attention to the immanent norms of the transcendental imperatives (be attentive, be intelligent, be reasonable, be responsible), so the fear that leads to an anxiety-reducing quest for knowledge is met by Lonergan's notion of the unrestricted desire to know, where knowledge can occur within the context of growth and freedom.[642] This is especially relevant to the intellectual pattern within which science and technology function. For it is only in this commitment to all relevant further questions that the mechanomorphic misconception of intellect which underpins the industrial

---

York, 1967), pp. 20-39.

[640]E. Newmann, The Origins and History of Consciousness (New York, 1970), pp. 210ff.

[641]Cf. Chapter Two, pp. 115-209.

[642]Cf. the above subsection on Invariance and Freedom, pp. 378ff.

revolution, and has caused the schizoid condition of modern man, can be effectively overcome.[643]

 iii. The spirituality of man. Perhaps nowhere are the detrimental effects of mechanomorphic objectivism more evident than in the field of behavioristic human science. It is not surprising that Lonergan's analyses of classical, statistical, and genetic empirical methods have attempted to set the scientific understanding of consciousness and human self-hood within a new perspective. A mechanistic reductionism leads many to identify psychological conjugates with neural conjugates in the brain. Psychic development is intrinsically conditioned by neural development, yet it consists essentially in a sequence of increasingly differentiated sets of capacities for perception, aggressive or affective response, memory, imagination, and performance.[644] Köhler and Eccles have indicated the dilemma facing those who identify consciousness with brain events.[645] They must either predicate a consciousness present in all physical and chemical processes, in which case the sciences have gravely erred in their analysis of them; or, they must recognize that when these processes

---

[643]Cf. R. May, Love and Will, pp. 3-24; L. Mumford, The Transformations of Man (New York, 1972), pp. 36-56.

[644]The difference between psychic development and neural conjugates is seen in the abnormality of multiple personality where empirical consciousness interacts with its neural base strongly enough to cause incompatible integrations of capacities, cf. Insight, p. 456. Because of the principles of emergence and correspondence (ibid., pp. 451ff.) operative between the underlying manifolds and the higher integration, it is possible, not only for higher integrations, such as empirical consciousness, to initiate changes in the underlying conjugates, but also for significant changes in these lower conjugates to generate mutations in the higher integrations. In both cases explanatory research into the patterns and processes of the underlying manifolds can disclose how such mutations occur and how they are to be favored or reversed.

[645]Cf. W. Köhler, "The Mind-Body Problem," in Dimensions of Mind, p. 31; Sir John Eccles, The Understanding of the Brain (New York, 1973), pp. 188ff. Note how Lonergan's notion of emergent probability answers the objections of Köhler to emergent evolution (cf. Lonergan, Insight, pp. 134, 264-265), and would provide Eccles with a control of meaning in terms of conscious interiority (Eccles' World Two).

reach a certain level of complexity a phenomenal fact
emerges not present before, namely, empirical consciousness.

Freedom from domination by underlying manifolds
increases as the generic levels are ascended. Chemical
elements are given atomic weights and numbers explainable
by underlying subatomic elements. In the myriad chemical
compounds, a first degree of freedom is attained insofar as
the patterned aggregates of chemical elements greatly lessen
subatomic limitations. The multicellular plant offers a
second degree of freedom since not only is each cell a vast
aggregate of chemical compounds but the plant itself is a
patterned aggregate of these cells having its own laws of
development. In the animal, a third degree of freedom occurs
insofar as multicellular structures become the material basis,
through neural tissues, for the higher patterned aggregates
of empirical consciousness.[646]

With the intellectual conjugates of man, a fourth degree
of freedom occurs. Inquiry and insight, reflection and
judgment, deliberation and choice are generically different
from seeing, hearing, smelling and tasting, imagining and
feeling. The latter take place in correspondence[647] with
neural processes but the former emerge to integrate psychic
contents which otherwise would be coincidental.[648] Even
inquiry into one's own neural or chemical processes is
mediated by psychic contents. This shift from integrating
neural processes to integrating psychic contents themselves
means the materials to be systematized are not built into
man's organic constitution. As a result, the intellectual

---

[646]Cf. Insight, pp. 264-267.

[647]Correspondence is used here in the precise sense
mentioned in note 644 above.

[648]For example, in the act of reading this essay it
is purely coincidental from the viewpoint of perception and
imagination which order the sequence of marks on the papers
have; whatever their order, they can be perceived and
imagined, just as I can perceive and imagine and retain
in empirical memory, words of a language unknown to me.
But the sequence of marks is not coincidental to communicating
an understanding of what my thought processes are; understanding systematizes the symbolic notations to convey its
insights.

conjugates are not so much a higher system as a perennial source of higher systems.[649]

The censor, as defined by Lonergan, includes both the repressive aspects proper to Freud's endopsychic censorship and the constructive aspects of Jung's teleology of the unconscious - the   unconscious influence of intellectual conjugates in the selection and arrangement of psychic contents to facilitate or inhibit their emergence into consciousness.[650]

The freedom enjoyed by intellectual conjugates is emphasized further in the approach intelligent and critical consciousness take to psychic contents. As mentioned above, inquiry as a search for intelligibility is not satisfied with the sensible presentations of objects; it wants to know them in an inward aspect, to grasp their form. When insights occur, and what is relevant to understanding formulated, the irrelevancies of the empirical residue are left behind - an example of this is scientific generalizations. The residue is needed as the underlying manifold to be systematized through insights, but the empirical residue does not constitute the intellectual conjugates. Its influence is extrinsic   providing the materials for understanding, judgment, deliberation.

Here we touch on the main difference between intellectual conjugates and the lower level ones. The latter are intelligible, but it is an intelligibility conditioned intrinsically by the empirical residue. The activities of subatomic elements, chemical elements and compounds, cells,

---

[649]"For an animal to begin a new mode of living, there would be needed not only a new sensibility but also a new organism. An animal species is a solution to the problem of living, so that a new solution would be a new species; for an animal to begin to live in quite a new fashion, there would be required not only a modification of its sensibility but also a modification of the organism that the sensibility systematizes. But in man a new department of mathematics, a new viewpoint in science, a new civilization, a new philosophy, has its basis, not in a new sensibility but simply in a new manner of attending to data and of forming combinations of combinations of combinations of data." Insight, p. 266.

[650]Cf. ibid., pp. 190, 192, 194-196, 267, 457.

418

and empirical consciousness cannot reach out beyond the space-time limitations imposed by the empirical residue. Intellectual conjugates are _intelligible_ and _intelligent_; they abstract, through insights, from individualities, continua, actual frequencies the intelligible relations, laws, and ideal frequencies repeatedly recurring in the empirical residue.

Fresh light is thrown on the mind-body problem. Both dualism and monism are rejected for the same reason: their confusion of body with thing, of objectivity with extroversion. The correct distinction is not mind-body but intelligent-intelligible; and in man, this proves to be only an inadequate distinction since the intelligent is also intelligible, capable of self-analysis such as that sketched in the sub-section on the subject-as-subject. Intelligence is the escape of intelligibility from the limitations of the empirical residue. [651]

Another distinction is also put in proper perspective. The difference between the material and the spiritual is that the material is constituted or intrinsically conditioned by the empirical residue while the spiritual is not. This type spirituality is not mystery-mongering; on the contrary, it is what gives man his insatiable thirst for knowledge. It was because of this freedom of intellectual conjugates from the restrictions inherent in systematizing strictly organic processes and from the limitations of the empirical residue that Aristotle and Aquinas could refer to the potential omnipotence of the human mind; its "potens omnia fieri et facere"[652] which ultimately is content with nothing

---

[651]This in no way Platonizes the human intellect, its proper object is intelligibilities _in empirical data_ - Aquinas called it "quidditas in re materiali existens" - so that the intellect's extrinsic dependence on psychic contents is a real one while these, in turn, are intrinsically conditioned by neural processes. For adequate and inadequate distinctions, cf. _Insight_, p. 490.

[652]Cf. Aristotle, _Peri Psyches_, III, 5, 14-15. Potential is used here to distinguish it from actual omnipotence. For some of the many insights St. Thomas had on this native infinity of the human mind, cf. _Verbum_, pp. 70-72. An insight very relevant to the present discussion is not given

less than the complete explanation of the universe.

Their generically diverse conjugates do not leave
humans in fragments. By central potency they are individuals,
by central form they are unities-identities-wholes, and they
exist by central acts. Reductionism claims that, since
lower level laws can be verified in humans, the things defined
solely by these lower conjugates also exist in them. This
position is due again to the confusing of thing and body,
and the consequent failure to distinguish conjugate and
central forms.

A thing has been defined as a concrete unity differentiated by conjugates. Hence, things take in the totality of
the data considered in all of their aspects, whereas conjugates are reached through considering certain data in some of
its aspects. To say physical and chemical laws are realized
in humans, therefore, is to assert the obvious fact of
underlying manifolds. But to conclude that a human being
can be reduced from intellectual to neural to chemical to
subatomic _things_ is to forget that not all the aspects of the
lower conjugates are accounted for within the viewpoint
provided by the lower things. The intelligible patterns
which lower conjugates adopt when they become underlying
manifolds is strictly coincidental from the viewpoint of
their own levels and is necessary from that of the higher
conjugates systematizing them. Lower conjugates are necessary
for the existence of the higher. But central forms are

there. Aquinas holds that there are no limits to technology
because of this "virtus ad infinita" of the intellect and the
versatility of human hands, "...per eas homo potest sibi
praeparare _instrumenta infinitorum modorum, et ad infinitos
effectus_." Summa Theo. I, 76 5 ad 4; also 91, 3 ad 2. This
throws a fresh light on McCulloch and Pitts' boundary
theorem for cybernetics. Far from denying the theorem it
affirms it from a different perspective. For Aquinas
sees that no one machine, or finite set of machines, will
ever be able to exhaust every possible technological insight.
An unbridgeable gap exists between man and his machines. He
will never be satisfied with the machines he has constructed
since his insights into the future technological possibilities
will always outstrip his present accomplishments. An
infinite series of machines can only be invented by minds
possessing unlimited capacities for insight and so in
continual advance of their artifacts.

differentiated by conjugates of the lower and higher orders;
they unify the totality of data making no further intelligible,
concrete unity discernable in the same data and differentiated solely by conjugates of a lower level.[653]

Man is differentiated by both material and spiritual
conjugates. As an animal his psychological, biological,
chemical, and physical conjugates are conditioned intrinsically by the empirical residue. No less factual is the
above account of his intelligent, critical, and moral
consciousness with their abstraction from the residue to
attain understanding of the intelligibilities within it.
Is man's central form, his soul, material and spiritual?
An affirmative reply would contradict the unity of our
being and actions, the self differentiated intellectually,
emotively, organically, chemically, physically. Can we
follow the pattern of emergent probability so far outlined
and assert the central form of man to be of the same order
as the highest level conjugates differentiating him? No
alternative exists if we grant the confusion of objectivity
and extroversion to account for both the materialistic
monism of reductionism and the dualistic fragmentation of man
by metaphysical vitalists and animists.

If the material central form intelligibly unifying an
animal can ground the material conjugate forms of the sensitive, organic, chemical, and physical orders, could not a
spiritual central form, unifying man, ground his spiritual and
material conjugates? Since the spiritual and material in man
are only inadequately distinct in terms of the intelligent-
intelligible relationship, any imagined impasse between the
two, created by the mind-body dualism, is overcome. Human
consciousness as intelligent is capable of understanding
both its own spiritual intelligibility and the intelligibility
immanent in all material things.[654] In a similar fashion,

---

[653]Cf. Insight, pp. 258-259.

[654]This understanding does not result from an intuition
of what the soul is, but an understanding that the soul, as
central form exists and what necessary properties it must
have in order to ground man's intellectual and volitional
activites. Cf. Verbum, pp. 61-64.

the human central form as spiritual is capable of unifying
both its intellectual and moral conjugates as spiritual,
and its neurological, biological, chemical, and physical
conjugates as material:

> Were man's central form a material intelligibility,
> then it could not be intelligent and so could not be
> the center and ground of man's inquiry and insight,
> reflection and judgment. Inversely, though man's
> central form were a spiritual intelligibility, it
> could be the ground and center of his physical,
> chemical, organic, and sensitive conjugates; for the
> spiritual is comprehensive; what can embrace the whole
> universe through knowledge, can provide the center
> and ground of unity in the material conjugates of a
> single man.[655]

This affirmation of the spirituality of man is not, however,
simply an adaptation of a classicist concern with substance
to the more modern horizon of classical, statistical, and
genetic empirical methods. Rather, it is meant as a
prolegomenon to the task of meeting the exigencies of
historical consciousness. For Lonergan disagrees with those
transcendental Thomists, like E. Coreth, who try to place
metaphysics as the thematization of the total and basic
horizon. For that function can only be a "transcendental
doctrine of methods with the method of metaphysics just one
among many" - i.e., metaphysics as the integral heuristic
structure of proportionate being is no substitute for
meta-method.[656]

At the same time it is important to realize how
Lonergan's meta-method does not exclude the positive gains of
behaviorism, Freudian psychoanalysis, or structuralist
anthropology. For all of these are providing invaluable
knowledge of the conjugates in human living that affect, as
lower manifolds, man's intelligent, rational, and responsible
conscious living. What he rejects is any effort to reduce
the latter to the conjugates and events within the empirical

---

[655]Insight, p. 520. Instead of hemming in the drive for
complete explanation, a correct understanding and affirmation
of the spiritual opens the whole of material reality to man's
inquiring mind; boundless horizons to be explored by the
slow, steady advance of the recurrent structure of observations, understanding, verification.

[656]Cf. Collection, pp. 219f.

level. The reductionist versus idealist dilemma of either minimizing history in favor of nature or vice versa is sublated in the context of emergent probability.

3. From Interiority to History

Having moved in the thematization of the structures of meta-method from the related and recurrent operations of human consciousness in the subject-as-subject to how those operations yield cumulative and progressive results in the subject-as-object, as well as the dialectial tensions that result from their neglect in the confusion of objectivity and extroversion, it is time to see how the unity of identity and non-identity, in terms of both emergent probability and dialectics, functions in a mutual mediation of method and history.

We have seen how for Dilthey the understanding of history was possible because of a certain fundamental similarity of self-presence or interiority operative within the dynamic contexts of history as a complex interaction of meaning-systems, value-systems, operational-systems. History as an operational-system ("Wirkungszusammenhang") was constituted by the interplay of forces, values, purposes.[657] Yet Dilthey' incomplete notion of interiority made it difficult for him to interrelate these aspects of the historical process. It is not surprising that in his last period he almost entirely replaces the notion of historicality ("Geschichtlichkeit") with that of historical spontaneity ("Lebendigkeit").[658]

For Lonergan the basic related and recurrent structures of self-transcending interiority lead to the notion of reality as a compound of identity and non-identity where, in proportionate being, the self-correcting process of learning corresponds to emergent probability in world process.[659] As Lonergan differentiates the natural and human sciences in

---

[657]Cf. G.S. VII, pp. 158-188; also Diwald, op. cit., pp. 115-128; Bellnow, op. cit., pp. 114-166.

[658]Cf. Renthe-Fink, op. cit., pp. 120-130.

[659]Cf. Insight, pp. 448f; on emergent probability, cf. pp. 115-128, and how this is operative in history, pp. 209-211.

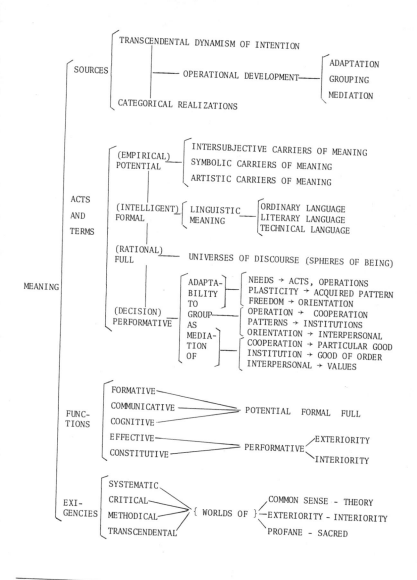

Figure Ten: The Unity of Subject and Object in Meaning

reference to mediated and constitutive meaning, so the transition from the subject-as-object to the unity of both
subject and object in history calls for a thematization of
intelligibility in terms of meaning and value, with the
basic related and recurrent operations providing the
meaning of meaning insofar as intelligibility in the
subject-as-subject is a self-constituting formally dynamic
intelligent intelligibility.[660]

In Figure Ten I have outlined some of the main
relationships between the subject-as-subject and the sources,
act and terms, functions and exigencies of meaning. Nor does
this neglect in any fashion the subject-as-object, for
"the all-inclusive term of meaning is being, for apart from
being there is nothing. Inversely, the core of all acts of
meaning is the intention of being."[661] Both the intentional
(object) and the conscious (subject) dimensions of interiority are present. There are four areas especially relevant
to a methodological concern with history which I shall
take up.

A. The Functions and Exigencies of Meaning. The
sources of meaning are in the related and recurrent operations
of the subject-as-subject as they intend being and so transcend themselves in actualizing their capacity to attend,
inquire, reflect, deliberate, act. The categorical realizations are the determinate images, concepts, judgments, actions,
reached through experiencing, understanding, judging, deciding.
This grounds the self-correcting process of learning as an
operational development in which the operator and integrator
of genetic method is differentiated into the notions of
adaptation, group, and mediation.[662] Lonergan himself
extrapolates from the notion of time as a unity in difference
to the reality of continuity in change underlying history.[663]

---

[660]Cf. Collection, pp. 223f.; Insight, pp. 319-324, 348-
364, especially 357-359 on being as the core of meaning.

[661]Insight, p. 358.

[662]Ibid., pp. 458-479; and Lonergan's unpublished De
Methodo Theologiae, p. 1-4.

[663]M.i.T., p. 177.

However one could just as easily discover the unity of identity and non-identity that is history in the unity-in-difference between the transcendental dynamisms and categorical realizations within the sources of meaning. It is this unity-in-difference that grounds all human experiencing and is especially evident in the experiencing of time and of history. Thus Lonergan can distinguish between historical experience and historical knowledge just as he distinguishes between consciousness and knowledge. Consciousness, or the subject-as-subject, is a formally dynamic unity differentiated by the related and recurrent operations of experiencing, understanding, judging, deciding and acting. Knowledge is the intentional orientation of this formal dynamism toward the experienced, understood, judged, and decided-upon activity. Hence the subject-as-subject cannot only transcend itself toward the objects and persons of its world, but also through a heightening of its consciousness appropriate its own formally dynamic structures and operations, as Lonergan has done in the knowledge grounding meta-method.

The categorical realizations through adaptation, group and mediation, involve not only isolated instances of experiencing, understanding, judging and deciding, but also the myriad contexts constituted by those operations. Historical experience is constituted by memory of past contexts and anticipations of future contexts. The self presence of the subject-as-subject is not an instant isolated in its own identity, but a unity of that identity within a non-identity whereby the subject reaches "into the past by memories, stories, history and into the future by anticipations, estimates, forecasts."[664] In order to show the constitutive function of memory Lonergan proposes a thought experiment:

> Suppose a man suffers total amnesia. He no longer knows who he is, fails to recognize relatives and friends, does not recall his commitments or his lawful expectations, does not know where he works or how he makes his living, and has lost even the information needed to perform his once customary tasks. Obviously, if he is to live, either the amnesia has to be cured, or else he must start all over. For our pasts have made us whatever we are and on that capital we have to live

---

[664] <u>M.i.T.</u>, p. 181.

426

> or else we must begin afresh. Not only is the individual an historical entity, living off his past, but the same holds for the group. For, if we suppose that all members in the group suffer total amnesia, there will be as total a collapse of all group functioning as there is in each individual in the group. Groups too live on their past, and their past, so to speak, lives on in them.[665]

The constitutive function of ancitipation of the future is grounded in the dynamism of an unrestricted desire to raise further questions regarding both meaning and value. No matter whether the underlying conception of history was cyclical or linear, men would only preserve their individual and group memories within the context of a present in its ongoing anticipation of a future.[666] So we have seen how the contextual aspect of judgment involves, for Lonergan, not only a relation of the present to the past, but also of the present to the future.

Just as consciousness by its own inner dynamism is orientated toward knowledge, so historical experience objectifies itself in historical knowledge. This process of objectification can be found in the pre-critical traditions embodied in the narrative stories and legends of a group, in the efforts of autobiography as diary, and biography as an objectification of another subject's history. The functions of such pre-critical historical knowledge are artistic, ethical, explanatory, apologetic and prophetic. Lonergan summarizes these functions of pre-critical history as follows:

> So it is never just a narrative of bald facts. It is artistic: it selects, orders, describes; it would awaken the reader's interest and sustain it; it would persuade and convince. Again, it is ethical: it not only narrates but also apportions praise and blame. It is explanatory: it accounts for existing institutions by telling of their origins and development and by contrasting them with alternative institutions found in other lands. It is apologetic, correcting false or tendentious accounts of the people's past, and refuting the calumnies of neighboring peoples. Finally, it is prophetic: to hindsight about the past there is joined foresight on the future and there are added the

---

M.i.T., p. 181; J. B. Metz, "Erinnerung," in H. Krings, H. M. Baumgartner (eds.) Handbuch philosophischer Grundbegriffe (München, 1973).

[666]M.i.T., pp. 134-136, 277f.

recommendations of a man of wide reading and modest wisdom.[667]

These functions of pre-critical history occur within the larger context of the functions of meaning. For the formative and cognitive functions of meaning are what moves individuals and groups from the world of immediacy to the world mediated by the meanings and values communicated by the tradition. This larger world mediated by meaning lies beyond any individual's immediate experience insofar as experiencing the drive of questions and the anticipations of value are not isolated acts but ongoing formal dynamisms. It is this larger world that defines what we mean when we speak of "the real world." It is not only open to the genetic development of higher viewpoints and authentic humanizing progress, but also to the dialectic of dishonesty, error, breakdown and cumulative decline.[668] The effective functions of meaning can be found in the phenomenon of human work whereby the formative and cognitive functions of meaning realize their own anticipations within the domain of the world. "Men work. But their work is not mindless. What we make, we first intend. We imagine, we plan, we investigate possibilities, we weigh pros and cons, we enter into contracts, we have countless orders given and executed. From the beginning to the end of the process we are engaged in acts of meaning; The whole of that added, a man-made artificial world is the cumulative, now planned, now chaotic, product of human acts of meaning."[669] As technologies emerge from the effective functions of meaning, so the cognitive functions issue in the constitutive functions of meaning whereby social institutions and human cultures with their myriad objectifications are the embodiment of such constitutive meaning. Not only do such objectifications within historical experience and pre-critical historical knowledge constitute themselves by meaning, they also communicate to others their meanings.[670] The communicative function of meaning is essential to meaning itself since we have seen how the core of meaning is the

---

[667]_M.i.T._, p. 185. [668]_M.i.T._, p. 77.

[669]_M.i.T._, pp. 77-78. [670]_M.i.T._, pp. 78-79.

intention of being and so transcends itself spontaneously.
A privatized meaning, incapable of communication is a
radical impossibility.

The transition from pre-critical historical knowledge
embodied in ongoing traditions, to critical history involves
the entire panoply of philosophical, exegetical, literary-
critical, archaeological, and socio-historical methods aimed
at determining the actual processes whereby historical experience has objectified itself down the ages. Critical history
is, therefore, an instance of the self-correcting process of
learning as applied, not to the world of nature through
scientific exploration of classical statistical or genetic
schemes of recurrence, but to the world of history with its
concrete and particular dialectical developments and break-
downs.[671] This process of developing a critical understanding
of history involves a whole series of different functions.
Lonergan identifies such functions and summarizes his rather
lengthy discussion of them as follows:

> It is heuristic, for it brings to light the relevant
> data. It is ecstatic, for it leads the inquirer out
> of his original perspectives and into the perspectives
> proper to his object. It is selective, for out of a
> totality of data it selects those relevant to the
> understanding achieved. It is critical, for it
> removes from one use or context to another the data
> that might otherwise be thought relevant to present
> tasks. It is constructive, for the data that are
> selected are knotted together by the vast and intricate
> web of interconnecting links that cumulatively came to
> light as one's understanding progressed.[672]

The transition from pre-critical historical knowledge
to critical historical knowledge occurs within the categorical
realizations of the exigencies of meaning. Just as the
systematic exigence is operative in the transition from
common sense meanings and descriptions to theoretical
explanatory constructions, so this same exigence accounts for
the shift from the artistic, ethical, explanatory, apologetic
and prophetic functions of pre-critical historical knowledge
to the heuristic, ecstatic, selective, critical and

---

[671]Cf. Insight, pp. 214-244, esp. pp. 233-234.

[672]M.i.T., pp. 188-189. cf. pp. 185-196.

constructive functions of critical history. Nevertheless, as the progress of critical history in the nineteenth and twentieth centuries has illustrated, this systematic differentiation between the worlds of historical experience and pre-critical historical knowledge and the worlds of critical historical knowledge - this differentiation gives rise to the critical exigence which asks whether or not the truth of history is to be found in the pre-critical world or the critical world of history.[673] The Historical School associated with Ranke attempted to find the truth of history through the methods of critical historical analysis, an attempt summed up in Ranke's perpetually quoted phrase "Wie es eigentlich gewesen war." Such an attempt, however, has led to the crisis of historicism whereby all traditions and institutions constituted by the formative, communicative, cognitive and effective functions of meaning are thrown into doubt inasmuch as the meanings and values communicated in a pre-critical fashion are, through critical history, seen to be relative and intrinsically conditioned by empirical and historical limitations. If the truth of history were the prerogative of critical history, then as Dilthey remarked, all the labors and efforts, the sufferings and achievements spread across the entire sweep of human history would have no other pupose than to provide data for the comfortably situated historian in his armchair or archives.[674] Hence it is not surprising that in our day philosophers such as Gadamer, relying on the existential hermeneutics of Heidegger, have attempted to reinstate or re-discover the truth embodied in pre-critical history. This has been accompanied by a revival of interest and appreciation for symbolism, myth, narrative and story.[675]

    Within the perspective of the exigencies of meaning, we

---

[673]Cf. Gadamer, Wahrheit und Methode, pp. 329f.

[674]Cf. Briefwechsel, p. 158.

[675]Cf. Van Austin Harvey, The Historian and the Believer (New York, 1972); W. Taylor Stevenson, History as Myth: The Import for Contemporary Theology (New York, 1969); Michael Novak, Ascent of the Mountain, Flight of the Dove (New York, 1971).

can see how critical history is primarily limited to the functions involved in the systematic differentiation of the common sense world of pre-critical history and the more theoretical world of critical history. The resolution of the crisis of historicism does not demand, therefore, an option for one over the other. As the differentiation led to the critical exigence, illustrated so well in the crisis of historicism, so this crisis should lead to attempts at realizing the methodical exigence whereby the truth of history is not placed in some absolute knowledge or unconditioned praxis but in the open and dynamic unity of identity and non-identity of experiencing, understanding, judging, deciding, and acting as transcendentally and categorically operative. Not only does this allow for the truths and errors of precritical and critical history to work themselves out through the self-correcting process of learning, it also prevents them from falsely absolutizing their methods by claiming that they alone have the truth of history.

The methodical exigence serves two closely related purposes. First, it effectively criticizes the inadequate attempts of the historicality philosophies to somehow isolate subjectivity from the vicissitudes of the criticalhistorical methods. For it shows how such an isolation is not only impossible but also unnecessary. It is impossible inasmuch as societies and institutions are de facto involved in the crisis of historicism and the consequent relativism of so many of the meanings and values they pre-critically communicate. It is unnecessary since the critical exigence is not an end in itself but leads to the methodical exigence capable of interrelating the meanings and values of precritical history with those of critical history. Second, the methodical exigence makes possible a post-critical appreciation of the functions of pre-critical history by showing how they are linked to the related and recurrent operations of the subject-as-subject, i.e., the very operations which have also given rise to the functions of critical history. Thus we are not limited to simply the study of history in hermeneutics and critical historical methods, but can also move on to the reflective making of history through dialectics to communications. The following subsections will expand on this.

B. Embodiments of Meaning and Value. Attention to the potential acts and terms of meaning, which correspond to the empirical level of consciousness, introduces the notions of carriers or embodiments of meaning. Such embodiments of meaning are an integral aspect of historical experience as well as pre-critical historical knowledge and they must necessarily be taken into account in any post-critically methodological integration, whereby the basic structures of conscious intentionality are applied to the patterns of experience. Such a return was only partially effected by Lonergan in Insight. The self-appropriation of the related and recurrent operations of consciousness occurs within the intellectual pattern of experience, and the return to the other patterns in meta-method would also be within the intellectual pattern.

In Insight Lonergan limited himself to a brief account of the central relevance of the basic structures of interiority to an elucidation of common sense, ethics, and religious belief; the main thrust of the book is concerned to work out the implications of meta-method for the sciences and metaphysics, attempting to set things in order within the intellectual pattern before moving on to the others. Even here Lonergan's work is only a beginning, an anticipation whose realization would require vast collaboration. Here I should like to briefly discuss how Lonergan has laid the groundwork for such collaboration within the context of his latest book, Method in Theology. His discussion there of intersubjectivity and community, and of symbolism and aesthetics as embodiments of meaning and value, as well as his discussion of the formal acts in terms of linguistic meaning, provide the basis for post-critically enlightening the relevance of pre-critical historical experience. There are four main areas which should be covered in this regard.

First, we have already seen the centrality of the dramatic pattern of experience within both historical experience and pre-critical historical objectifications of

of traditions.[676] The formation of community is a primary
concern within the world of persons and history. Lonergan
has shown how the conjunction of constitutive and communicative functions of meaning enter into the creation of community.
For community is not some type of automatic process but is
dependent upon the structures of freedom we have already seen
involved in the subject-as-subject. The dimensions of
community are the dimensions of human consciousness expressing
itself, not simply within the individual domain, but within
the intersubjective and social domains of human living. For
community involves, if it is to be genuine, a sharing of
experiences, meanings, judgments, and values. When any of
these is missing community is endangered. This sharing
need not be complete and total, but there must be some common
experiences, some common meanings, some common judgments,
and some common values if the community is to be existentially
authentic. Thus we have the correlation:

Consciousness	Community
empirical————————————	experiences
intelligent————————————	meanings
critical————————————	judgments
responsible————————————	values

On the empirical level occurs both the rather prosaic temporal
and spatial simultaneity which brings individuals into mutual
proximity. This of itself does not initiate community. Of
more dynamic implications for the experience of community are
the feelings and emotions that occur in intersubjectivity.
Lonergan develops a notion of feelings which can distinguish
non-intentional emotive states and trends from intentional
emotive responses.[677] Intersubjectivity is originally the
prior emotive communion between subjects, that is the prior
"we" that precedes the distinction of subjects. "Just as one
spontaneously raises one's arm to ward off a blow against
one's head, so with the same spontaneity one reaches out to

---

[676]Cf. Chapter Three, pp. 272ff.

[677]M.i.T., pp. 30ff.

save another from falling."[678] Within the context of this intersubjectivity Lonergan can enter into a discussion of community of feeling, fellow feeling, psychic contagion, and emotional identification. Moreover, he analyzes the communications of intersubjective meaning through bodily movements, especially in the myriad phenomena of facial expressions.[679]

Both intersubjective experiential activities, even when intentional, must be sublated in meanings, judgments and values if community is to emerge. For common meaning is potential within the common field of intersubjective experiences. One most certainly loses touch with community if one no longer shares in its experiences. But the experiences themselves, no matter how profound (even those of sexual intimacy) are not sufficient unless they are embodied within a larger context of meaning and mutual understanding. Common meaning is related to understanding, judging and deciding as follows:

> Common meaning is formal when there is common understanding, and one withdraws from that common understanding by misunderstanding, by incomprehension, by mutual incomprehension. Common meaning is actual inasmuch as there are common judgments, areas in which all affirm and deny in the same manner; and one withdraws from that common judgment when one disagrees, when one considers true what others hold false and false what they think true. Common meaning is realized by decisions and choices, especially by permanent dedication, in the love that makes families, in the loyalty that makes states, in the faith that makes religions.[680]

Such a notion of community applies as well to prehistoric cave dwellers, as to communities of scientific investigators. It is transcendental in the sense of being trans-culturally present throughout history. Nor is it an automatic process but rather an objectification of freedom and so is subject to minor and major inauthenticity. Minor inauthenticity occurs insofar as individuals within a community, while sharing similar experiences and symbols fail to understand

---

[678]Ibid., p. 57.

[679]Ibid., pp. 59-61; on symbols cf. pp. 64ff.

[680]Ibid., p. 79.

and evaluate them in accordance with the traditions of the community. Major inauthenticity occurs insofar as the increase of minor inauthenticity is augmented to the point where the community is no longer an expression of, but rather opposed to attentiveness, intelligence, reasonableness and responsibility. Hence it is that communal traditions themselves can become inauthentic, devaluated, distorted, and destined to extinction.[681]

As with community so one can also find in the phenomenon of human love the presence of the levels of consciousness. E. Fromm and R. May have called attention to the difference between the sexual dimension of love and the erotic dimension. In highly industrialized societies dominated by a mechano-morphic objectification of interpersonal relationships it is to be expected that the sexual would be approached in a mechanistic manner, as the flood of how-to-do-it books on human sexuality illustrates. For the erotic dimension of human love requires more than simply the empirical facticity of sexual differences. It demands the attention and sensi-tivity as an intelligent expression of sexual fantasy and imagination. Just as empirical sexual differentiation of itself leads to an attitude of promiscuity, so, as Eric Fromm has shown, do the intelligent expressions of erotic love find their fulfillment within the exclusivity of fulfilling intimacy. Human love, however, cannot remain limited to empirical and intelligent experiences, there must be that sharing of worlds and communication which constitutes the universality of friendship.[682] If friendship, however, is to survive the inevitable tensions and conflicts of mutual human growth and decline, it must responsibly open itself to that agapic love of other human beings that is grounded upon, and fascinated by, the mystery of human

---

[681]Erich Fromm, The Art of Loving (A Bantam Book. New York, 1956); R. May, Love and Will (New York, 1970); William A. Sadler, Existence and Love (New York, 1969); pp. 313-361; L. Kolakowsky, Traktat über die Sterblichkeit der Vernunft (München, 1967), pp. 33-50.

[682]On friendship, cf. Fromm, The Art of Loving, pp. 39ff.; W. Sadler, Existence and Love, pp. 332-338.

personality.[683] Thus we have the correlation:

Consciousness	Love	Attitudes
empirical————————sexual—————————promiscuity
intelligent———————erotic——————————exclusivity
rational——————friendship——————————universality
responsible——————agape————————————mystery

Second, the embodiment of meaning is not only evident within intersubjective carriers of meaning, but is also to be found in symbolic and artistic carriers of meaning. Symbols are operative within the dramatic pattern of experience insofar as they are images of real or imaginary objects evoking or being evoked by feelings.[684] They also provide the transition to the aesthetic pattern of experience where art is defined "as the objectification of a purely experiential pattern."[685] Without entering into an extensive discussion of the aesthetic it is possible to show how the distinction between consciousness and knowledge becomes a differentiation of aesthetic experience and aesthetic criticism. The artist functions so that his understanding, judging, and deciding is primarily geared toward an objectification of his experience as such. The artist thereby bears witness to the spontaneous symbolic intellectuality of the human imagination.[686] The art critic, on the other hand, is not concerned with creating art, but with understanding and criticizing it so that his experience and decisions are geared toward, not experience in itself, but understanding and judging.

It is also possible to show how the various art forms, as objectifications of the visual, tactile, sonic, symbolic and linguistic dimensions of human experience can be interrelated in a manner analogous to emergent probability. Such an interrelation of the aesthetic would be something like

---

[683] On mystery, cf. Insight, pp. 531ff.

[684] M.i.T., pp. 64-69.   [685] M.i.T., pp. 61ff.

[686] M.i.T., pp. 61-63.

the following:

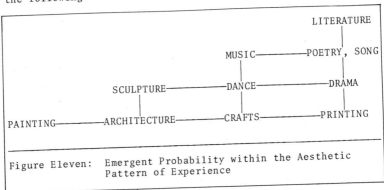

Figure Eleven: Emergent Probability within the Aesthetic Pattern of Experience

In Figure Eleven we see how the visual coordination of space and color provides the constitutive element in painting as well as the underlying manifolds for the remaining art forms. Sculpture objectifies the tactile dimension of experience and combines with the visual not only in its own activity but also in architectural objectifications. Music emerges beyond the tactile and visual realms of experience into the aural and sonic. Nevertheless, the sonic is combined with the tactile in dance and with the visual in crafts.[687] The emergence of linguistic symbols occurs in literature as an objectification of that experience. In poetry and song the linguistic objectification combines with the sonic, while in drama it combines with the tactilely sculptural, and in such forms as printing and film combines with the visual.[688]

Third, the emergence of linguistic symbolism leads into the formal acts and terms of meaning. In this embodiment meaning finds its greatest liberation insofar as conventional signs and symbols can be multiplied almost indefinitely. The importance of language can be seen in how "conscious

[687]On how dance is related to sculpture and music, cf. Susanne K. Langer, Feeling and Form (New York, 1953); Herbert Read, The Philosophy of Modern Art (New York, 1967).

[688]Jacques Maritain, Creative Intuition in Art and Poetry (New York, 1961); Werner Hofmann, Grundlagen der modernen Kunst (Stuttgart, 1966); Gustav René Hocke, Die Welt als Labyrinth (Hamburg, 1957); Herbert Read, The Philosophy of Modern Art.

intentionality develops in and is moulded by its mother
tongue."[689] As language develops, there emerges the differentiations of ordinary, literary, and technical languages.
Ordinary language is the carrier of meaning within the common
sense everyday world of human community pursuing its interests
and goals. Literary language is not as transient as ordinary
language; it is a fuller statement aimed at making good the
lack of mutual presence by evoking emotions and creating
intersubjective worlds linguistically. Technical language
arises with the emergence of the systematic exigence whereby
the world of common sense is left behind for the world of
craftsmen, experts, specialists who develop and communicate
their specialization through technical usage.[690]

We have already seen how the levels of consciousness
are operative as a meta-contextual framework for the science
of linguistics. Thus one is able to interrelate the four
general fields of semiotics as follows:

empirical	-	syntactics
intelligent	-	semantics
critical	-	sigmatics
responsible	-	pragmatics

The significance of this meta-contextual correlation has
already been discussed in Chapter Two and need not be
repeated here.[691] Notice however, how the full acts of meaning correlative to sigmatics open up those dimensions or
spheres of meaning where real being is known when the fulfilling conditions, grasped in the virtually unconditioned,
are data of sense or of consciousness and where restricted
spheres of meaning are known when the fulfilling conditions
are not data but some lesser requirement. Logic finds its
conditions fulfilled in clarity, coherence and rigor;
mathematics finds its conditions fulfilled when any freely

---

[689] M.i.T., p. 71.   [690] M.i.T., p. 72.

[691] Cf. Chapter Two pp. 177ff. Also Karl-Otto Apel,
"Sprache als Thema und Medium der transzendentalen Reflexion,"
Man and World, 1970, pp. 323-337.

chosen set of suitable postulates has its conclusions
rigorously drawn; hypothetical spheres of meaning are
instances of the logical that have some likelihood of being
relevant to an understanding of the data of sense or of
consciousness.[692]

Fourth, the emergence of technical language is not an
end in itself but rather through applied science and technology affects the everyday world of dramatic living. Thus
it is important to understand both how the scientific and
scholarly mediation of human social life occurs and how this
communication facilitates the development of a post-
scientific dramatic consciousness and literature.[693]
Lonergan's meta-methodology provides several avenues for
correlating the many scientific and scholarly disciplines
involved in this mediation of meaning within society.

Gibson Winter in his book Elements of a Social Ethics,
analyzes at length the four schools of sociology concerned
with social mediation and constitution. They are respectively:
the behaviorist, functionalist, intentionalist and
voluntarist trends or schools.[694] Where the behaviorist
is primarily concerned with regularities or laws governing
impulses and the balance of forces, the functionalist
concentrates more on the maintenance of the social system
with its variations of patterns in the fulfillment of needs.
The intentionalist trend zeroes in on meaning as that meaning
projects various horizons of possibility, while the voluntarist trend emphasizes the importance of interests in the
patterns of domination and compromise within societies.[695]
It would take too long to show how these trends are capable
of a meta-contextual correlation, yet it is significant
that Winter's description of the trends shows a marked
similarity to Lonergan's development of the levels of human

---

[692]Cf. Lonergan's A Second Collection (New York, 1974),
pp. 269ff.

[693]M.i.T., pp. 304f.

[694]Gibson Winter, Elements for a Social Ethic (New York,
1968), pp. 112ff.

[695]Ibid., pp. 114, 176.

consciousness.[696]

Levels of Consciousness	Schools of Sociology
empirical———————————	behaviorist
intelligent———————————	functionalist
rational———————————	intentionalist
responsible———————————	voluntarist

Sociology, however, is not the only science concerned with the mediation of meaning in socio-historical living. Of central importance, even within sociology, but more so within the practical domain of social living in a highly industrialized society, is the necessity of correlating in a critical way technology, economics and politics. Lonergan has shown how economy emerges from technology and polity from economy and technology.[697] If political decisions should not be left to social engineers or public managers it is crucial, not only to recover a lost political imagination, but also to correlate political science to economics and technology. I have attempted such a correlation in Figure Twelve. The basic pattern is one of emergent probability which would move from the technologies of engineering and cybernetics to the economic sphere and from there to the political. The emergence operative here can be seen in the fact that of the many technological possibilities only some are economically feasible, and of those that are economically feasible some are politically more important than others. Lonergan has

---

[696]Thus the behaviorist's dynamic structure is defined in terms of pleasure-pain impulses which is Lonergan's empirical level. Compare Winter, Elements for a Social Ethic, pp. 175f. and Insight, p. 596. The functionalist sees the given order as the true order, i.e., the intelligent good of order according to Lonergan; compare Winter, op. cit., p. 246 and Insight, p. 596. The intentionalist style of sociology stresses the world-constituting projects of the social self, and that is the function of judgment as knowledge of the real in Lonergan. The voluntarist is obviously related to the responsible or "moral" level of consciousness in Lonergan. Cf. Winter, op. cit., pp. 116ff.

[697]Cf. Insight, pp. 207ff.; also Barden and McShane, Towards Self Meaning, pp. 105ff.

440

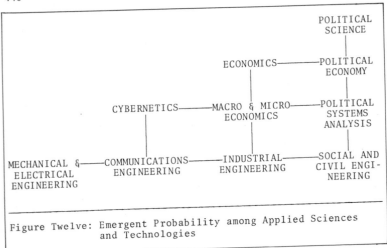

Figure Twelve: Emergent Probability among Applied Sciences and Technologies

shown in his unpublished Economic Manuscript (written in the late 30's and 40's) how prices cannot be regarded as ultimate norms guiding strategic economic decisions. Those decisions must be correlated with non-economic factors if the economic quest for systematic profits is not to become a short-sighted quest for windfall profits.[698] The destructive character of such short-sighted economic decision making can be illustrated in the military-industrial complex where economic interests are dictating the needs of technological research and are also controlling the political processes of decision and priority planning, rather than having a truly political open discussion of the issues involved. Recent American and Russian history has shown how this underlies both an inordinate demand for secrecy on the part of governments and the collusion between big business and government spending. It is all the more important therefore, that the applied

---

[698]The photocopy of the Economic Manuscript in the present writer's possession does not have any title page. It has always been referred to as such by those who have read it. Lonergan himself is now interested in revising it, in collaboration with some economists. He has certainly received encouragement to do so by those who have read it. Given the present alternatives in the sphere of economic theory, Lonergan's novel insights into economic processes could be of decisive importance.

sciences and technologies begin to articulate both their diversity and their interrelatedness. Figure Twelve indicates how engineering studies the applications of technology to society. Cybernetics emerges insofar as the systems operative within engineering and technology are open to systematic feedback applications involved in both the production process and the communication process.[699] Economics emerges in order to study not only the forces and relations of production but also how those processes are involved in monetary circulation.[700] Finally, political science introduces the dimensions of social interests, goals, and values which cannot be reduced to economic, cybernetic or technological processes. Notice however, how this pattern of emergence does allow for the proper interplay between political science and the schemes of recurrence studies by political economy, political systems analysis, and social engineering.

In order for such a development of political science to be effective, however, it is necessary to indicate how the human good and social praxis can creatively function within society.

C. Acts and Terms of Meaning as Praxis. We have already seen how the contemporary stage in human history might be defined by a mechanomorphic rationalism. In Lonergan's attempt to elaborate a meta-methodology that would break through such mechanomorphism he does not propose to belittle or reject the intellectual pattern of experience. Instead, as our long analyses have attempted to show, he tries to liberate the intellectual pattern of experience from the bias and scotosis occasioned by mechanomorphism, calling for an appropriation of the related and recurrent operations of the subject-as-subject. This liberation degrades neither technology nor science, but rather seeks to

---

[699]Norber Wiener, Kybernetik (Düsseldorf, 1968); for the more philosophical aspects cf. Georg Klaus, Kybernetik und Erkenntnis Theorie (Berlin, 1966) and F. J. Crosson and K. M. Sayre (eds.) Philosophy and Cybernetics (University of Notre Dame Press, 1968), esp. D. B. Burrell "Obeying Rules and Following," pp. 203-232.

[700]Cf. Lonergan's Economic Manuscript, pp. 1-23.

integrate them in a dynamic orientation toward genuine human growth and self-transcendence. The appropriation of the operations of conscious intentionality is not through any theory or system but only through the praxis of the subject heightening his or her own consciousness as subject. The very self-transcendence of consciousness indicates that such a self-appropriating praxis is anything but privatized subjectivity. In order to show the socio-historical dimensions of this praxis, I shall elaborate three structural models aimed at the social mediation of praxis. The first indicates how institutions and roles are oriented toward interpersonal values; the second indicates how this model has a feedback character, while the third shows how a purely formalist approach to roles and institutions excludes such an orientation, reducing praxis to technique.

First, we have seen how mechanomorphic rationalism reduces sociality to social engineering where a means/ends calculation leaves goals and purposes undiscussed and dehumanizes human persons into role-fillers. Human growth itself demands a differentiation of roles, but those roles have to be conducive to growth, not just of technology and economy, but of polity and humanity. We have seen how a meta-scientific feedback model could initiate such a liberation of the intellectual pattern of experience from mechanomorphism within the domain of science and the philosophy of science. Such a program must be complemented however by one that is more directly concerned with recovering the neglected and repressed subjectivity within the dramatic pattern of experience. Lonergan has shown how this might be done in his discussion of the structure of the human good.[701] Therein Lonergan uses the operational development of adaptability-group-mediation to implicitly define eighteen terms regarding individuals and their potentialities and actuations, cooperating groups, and the ends intended.

Lonergan has succinctly explained each of the terms involved and how they form the complex related and recurrent structures of the human good in society. Instead of repeating

---

[701] M.i.T., pp. 47-52.

his explanation, it might be more helpful to illustrate how this structure functions. It should be kept in mind, however, that this is not some "utopia, some theoretic ideal, some set of ethical precepts, some code of laws, or some super-institution."[702] It is rather the concretely functioning of "if - then" relationships within social relationships.

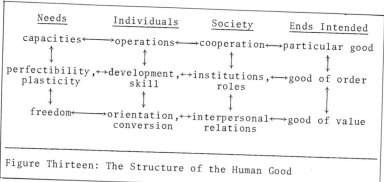

Needs	Individuals	Society	Ends Intended
capacities ←→	operations ←→	cooperation ←→	particular good
perfectibility, ↔ plasticity	development, ↔ skill	institutions, ←→ roles	good of order
freedom ←→	orientation, ↔ conversion	interpersonal ←→ relations	good of value

Figure Thirteen: The Structure of the Human Good

Take, for example, the need for food. It is a basic need and provided the structure of the human good is fully operative, can be transformed from a deficiency-need into a growth-need. I experience the <u>need</u> for food in hunger and this need presupposes a <u>capacity</u> to feel hunger (digestive tract) and to satisfy the need. I have acquired the <u>operations</u> required to fulfill the need through eating. Moreover, because I live in a society I do not myself have to go hunting or harvesting in order to obtain the food; others have done this and so <u>cooperated</u> toward the attainment of my <u>particular good</u> of eating. But such capacities are <u>perfectible</u> and have a certain <u>plasticity</u>: the operations of eating are not just the child's capacity to put food in its mouth, but also the <u>skills</u> of handling cultural instruments (knives, forks, spoons, chopsticks, automatic food dispensers, etc.) for the operations of eating. As societies become more complex the cooperation involved in attaining the particular good of eating is perfected into <u>roles</u> and <u>institutions</u>, such as farmers, fishers, cooks, restaurants, waiters, co-ops

---

[702]<u>M.i.T.</u>, p. 49.

supermarkets, etc. These roles and institutions are a good of order inasmuch as they fulfill the particular good of eating, not just in a random individual way, but recurrently for a large number of persons. My eating, moreover, is part of my total personality, my freedom. Routinely I can accept the orientation prevalent today and satisfy my need for food in a hurried, perfunctory fashion. If so the personal relations and good of value are minimal, since they are primarily oriented towards the satisfaction of a deficiency need. But more or less often, I can experience the orientation of freedom toward interpersonal relations and the good of value by enjoying a festive meal among friends, where the food and eating is integrated into the symbolism of sharing and communion. If my orientation to food is almost exclusively a mechanism of oral satisfaction, a conversion would be required to really enter into an orientation of growthful interpersonal relations. And it is only on such a basis that meals can take on a religious significance and value. Such a conversion, though not of a religious but of a moral character, is also required today insofar as wealthy societies are over-consuming food while underdeveloped countries suffer massive starvation. Communist China is a good example of how a country can undergo a full scale conversion of its institutions in order for everyone to be able to satisfy their need for food.

Second, there is a continual feedback relation between the components of the human good. When the level of freedom is suppressed, there results an atrophication of praxis into techniques aimed only at satisfying deficiency needs. Social cooperation then aims only at keeping its roles and institutions functioning, and the criterion for the good of order disappears, viz., the good of value. Little or no reflection is given to the goals which the social order is pursuing. "What's good for General Motors is good for the country." The main preoccupation becomes a preservation of the status quo. The essence of praxis for Lonergan is the transcendental imperatives (Be attentive, Be intelligent, Be rational, Be responsible) as that open dynamism whereby human freedom can progressively and cumulatively expand. Free praxis defines true progress, so its neglect or absence spells decline.[703] To indicate how this praxis of freedom can be integrated into the structures of the human good in a feed-back fashion is to indicate how one can have a social ethics of change.[704] There are eight components in the following feedback relationship:

(1) Freedom implies two elements: first there is the <u>essential</u> possibility of freedom inasmuch as human capacities are perfectible to the point where people can deliberate and choose their own orientations in a more or less attentive, intelligent, critical, and responsible fashion. Second, they are <u>effectively</u> free insofar as men actually do attentively, intelligently, critically, and responsibly decide and act. There is then a gap between essential and effective freedom in every instance of inattentiveness, stupidity, irrationality, irresponsibility.

(2) The first step in effectively actualizing essential human freedom is to perfect one's capacities through the acquisition of operations and skills which enable one to cooperate with others in fulfilling institutional roles. Such role competence is within institutions aimed at the recurrently ordered fulfillment of any of the needs within the various patterns of experience. E.g.

> dramatic: family and tribal groupings, the legal, economic, and political professions;
> biological: food, medical, clothing, housing, energy, transportation industries;

---

[703]<u>M.i.T.</u>, pp. 52-55.

[704]Cf. Metz, <u>Diskussion zur politischen Theologie</u>, pp. 279-284.

aesthetic: communication media, music, art, theater, museums, etc.

intellectual: research centers, schools, universities; moral: humanitarian institutions, consumer protection groups, peace movements, etc.

religious: churches, synagogues, sects, etc.

(3) But any of these institutional orders can easily become ends in themselves, tending to see good only in the preservation of their own order. This creates class animosity and war insofar as value is not within the totality of interpersonal relations but only within the narrow confines of the group, institution, or society. Atrophication of ends within biased social orders spreads.

(4) Commitment to freedom then calls for praxis aimed at conversion whereby the institutional good of order is oriented towards the higher good of value and freedom.

(5) Such praxis must seek to establish critical collaboration within the existing institutional orders in order to effectively analyse the particular situation.

(6) Priorities must then be established as to whether the praxis should aim at a conversion in terms of reform, i.e., change within the parameters of existing institutions, or of revolution, i.e., a complete change of institutional structures.

(7) The strategies for implementing the priorities are elaborated with reference to new operational and cooperational skills and roles to be acquired for the furtherance of value.

(8) Action and communication of the need for change leads to an enlargement of the effective freedom within the group, institution, or society through the changes effected. The process then begins again insofar as the new skills and roles and institutions are insufficient to meet the new possibilities of growth which the changes have created.[705] For the dynamisms of experience,

---

[705] For an extensive analysis of a somewhat different model, cf. Charles Hampden-Turner, _Radical Man_ (New York, 1971). On essential-effective freedom, cf. _Insight_, pp. 619-626.

understanding, judging, deciding and acting cannot be totally fulfilled in any existing social good of order.

Third, by way of contrast we can see how a mechano-morphically conceived good of order perverts the possibility of effective freedom by de facto excluding the possibility of conversion and change except within the confines of its own priorities. (1) In place of essential and effective freedom one has official policies, information, plans as the essential. The effective elements consist in roles, formal positions, and job descriptions. (2) Role competence is primarily seen as status, marks of privilege, and hier-archical levels within the group, institution, or society. (3) In place of a consciousness of the need for change there is only emphasis upon improvement of skills and roles to increase the efficiency of the existing order. Any reference to the deteriorating situation is taken as disloyalty, unpatriotism etc. (4) In place of commitment to freedom and the development of attentiveness, intelligence, critical reasonableness, and responsibility there is commitment to the goals of the group, institution, or society. (5) Collabora-tive praxis for change is supplanted by the degrees of differentiation required by the division of labor between various units or groups to be coordinated. (6) In place of rational priorities for change one only has the formal techniques for evaluation, recognition, and integration within the system. (7) Strategies for change are replaced by such stabilizing coordination procedures as collective bargaining, committee meetings, and official liaison activities. (8) In place of implementing plans for change and growth, one has periodic accounting, control, analyses of variance threatening the organization. This then is fed back into (1) and the formalist system grinds on.

Such formal systems, inasmuch as they are unable to adapt to the needs of growth and freedom, tend in the long run to decline and collapse, usually to be replaced by others that undergo similar cycles of decline. Lonergan speaks of the essential problem of liberation consisting in the incapacity of men for sustained development. And that incapacity sets problems for ethical and moral reflection,

448

as well as praxis, which cannot be met solely within the ethical or moral realm of meaning and value.[706] There can be no blissful affirmation of identity, nor any pessimistic resignation to non-identity, but only the commitment to the unity of identity and non-identity.

D. History and the Foundations of Collaboration. This sketchy presentation of the structures of Lonergan's meta-method and its approach to history through the sources, acts and terms, functions and exigencies of meaning has emphasized the resemblances and divergences from Dilthey. Similar to Dilthey, Lonergan approaches history from the perspective of the subject-as-subject. But this subject is not encapsulated in an empirical self-presence of privatized individuals requiring re-experiencing in order to be understood. The problem Dilthey had with the larger operational systems or contexts in history disappears once the self-transcending dynamisms of the subject-as-subject are properly thematized in the subject-as-object, i.e., once the transition from consciousness to knowledge has been effected within the context of human historical interiority. Relativism is overcome, not by appealing to timeless concepts, nor by invoking the authority of tradition, but by adverting to the virtually unconditioned normativity of the sources of all meaning and value in history.

Do these sources within the subject undergo radical historical change? Lonergan is primarily concerned with fact and not fiction. There can be little doubt that there has been enormous development (and decline) from primitive man to the present, not only in man's capacity to be attentive, intelligent, critical, and responsible but also in his biased inclination to put a highly differentiated intelligence to work for pervertedly irrational and irrespon-sible goals. Yet the misuse is such because of the presence of the sources; bias, scotosis, decline, nausea, and absurdity could never be experienced, let alone understood, were it not for the thrust of self-transcending interiority. If at any time in his history man did not experience, understand, judge,

---

[706]Cf. Insight, pp. 627-633.

decide, and act - then and only then would the conditions be fulfilled for the judgment that Lonergan's thematization of subject was incorrect.[707]

Historical understanding, no less than any science is possible only because of the related and recurrent operations of the subject. Much of the opposition of the Historical School to the claims of the sciences sprang from the classical necessitarianism and mechanistic reductionism of modern science.[708] History cannot be mastered with logic alone. Now we are beginning to see that science cannot be so mastered either. Since both scientific and historical consciousness arose within the intellectual pattern of experience, one would suspect that they are not as opposed as the romanticists would have us believe. The disputes over whether history was a science or an art seem cast in the shadow of the classicist conceptions of episteme and phronesis. Lonergan's meta-method, grounded in an appropriation of the basic structures of conscious intentionality, has formulated a control of meaning in terms of interiority which effectively sublates the classicist control.[709]

The problems associated with historicism are solved, not by trying to reintroduce normative ideas or values within the world of theory, nor by advocating a haphazard praxis within the world of common sense, but by critically moving to the sources of all meanings and values within the world

---

[707]On heuristic notions; cf. Insight, pp. 36-37, 63, 298, 312-313, 392, 461, 522-523, 577-578, 580-581, 586-587. In relation to being, pp. 356, 371-372, 394-642.

[708]Hence Dilthey's criticisms of "erklärende Psychologie" inasmuch as it reduces consciousness to causal relationships after the manner of the natural sciences, cf. G.S. V, pp. 158-168. Cf. also Matson, op. cit., for abundant illustrations; also R. G. Collingwood, The Idea of History, (Oxford, 1963), pp. 165-183.

[709]Cf. references in note 533 above, also Lonergan's "The Hellenization of Dogma," T.S. (1967), pp. 336ff. The curious fact is that Dewart in trying to separate or distinguish being and reality in fact seems to be attempting to avoid the classical control of meaning while not really confronting the obvious parallels such a distinction has with the noumenal-phenomenal bifurcation spoken above; cf. Dewarts' The Foundations of Belief (New York, 1969).

of the subject or interiority. Hence the new notion of wisdom found in Lonergan's meta-method attains its universal ability to order, not from abstract necessities, but from its capacity to elaborate heuristic structures anticipating the concrete historical process.[710] For all historical experience and all historical knowledge is grounded in the open and dynamic structures of human historical conscious intentionality. No less in the historical disciplines than in the natural and human sciences, or in the fields of common—sense dramatic living, the fundamental alienation of man is from the imperatives of his own self-transcending subjectivity:

> The term, alienation, is used in many different senses. But on the present analysis the basic form of alienation in man's disregard of the transcendental precepts, Be attentative, Be intelligent, Be reasonable, Be responsible. Again, the basic form of ideology is a doctrine that justifies such alienation. From these basic forms, all others can be derived. For the basic forms corrupt the social good. As self-transcendence promotes progress, so the refusal of self-transcendence turns progress into cumulative decline.[711]

Any fully adequate dialectic for both historical performance and historical knowledge must be grounded within the subject-as-subject, i.e., the dialectic must be based upon the sources of meaning and value if it is going to be fundamental. Within historical praxis one can thereby relate the relative dialectics in their concrete, dynamic, and contradictory interactions in terms of their furtherance of, or hinderance to, the historical unfolding of human attentiveness, intelligence, reasonableness, and responsibility. As bias and scotosis are the principles of alienated decline, so the expansion of effective freedom is the principle of progress.[712]

Similarly, the manifold efforts at historical knowledge can be set in a genetic and dialectic relationship through a dialectically conceived universal viewpoint.[713] This

---

[710]Cf. _Insight_, pp. 654-658.

[711]_M.i.T._, p. 55, also _Insight_, pp. 191-206, 214-244, 401-430, 558-562, 619-624.

[712]Cf. _Insight_, pp. 214-244; _Collection_, pp. 244-245.

[713]_M.i.T._, p. 153; _Insight_, pp. 562-594.

universal viewpoint is not some conceptualist absolute
knowledge, nor a formula for uncovering the necessary laws
of history, but an ordering of the manifold of attempts at
critical historical knowledge, i.e., it is a potential
totality of genetically and dialectically ordered viewpoints:

> The totality in question is potential. A universal
> viewpoint is not universal history. It is not a
> Hegelian dialectic that is complete apart from matters
> of fact. It is not a Kantian a priori that in itself
> is determinate and merely awaits imposition upon the
> raw materials of vicarious experience. It is simply
> a heuristic structure that contains virtually the
> various ranges of possible alternatives of inter-
> pretations; it can list its own contents only through
> the stimulus of documents and historical inquiries;
> it can select between alternatives and differentiate
> its generalities only by appealing to the accepted
> norms of historical investigation.[714]

The potential totality is actually determined only by the
totality of successful attempts at interpreting historical
events, movements, epochs.[715] In other words, we have here
a heuristic anticipation similar to that of K.-O. Apel's
revision of Pierce's "unlimited community of investigators."[716] It adds to that, however, the full range of just
what it means to experience, understand, judge, decide and
act, and how these anticipations enable one to articulate
methodologically (in terms of classical, statistical, genetic,
dialectic methods, emergent probability, meaning, value,
and functional specialization) what is implied in the control
of any investigation presupposed by the investigator. This
universality does not impose some extraneous system on history.
It is both empirically factual and critically normative.
Factually men are either attentive, intelligent, critical,
and responsible or they are not. The observance or

---

[714] Insight, pp. 564-565.   [715] Insight, pp. 565ff.

[716] Cf. Lonergan's unpublished lecture on Hermeneutics (1962), p. 14.   K.-O. Apel seeks a regulative
principle beyond Gadamer's Applikation.   Apel
finds this principle in the idea of an unlimited "Interpretative community which is implicitly presupposed as an
ideal control by anyone who argues or makes judgments."
cf. Hermeneutik und Dialektik I, pp. 140-144. Note how
Lonergan's universal viewpoint envisages this concrete
potential totality.

non-observance of the transcendental imperatives are facts with normative connotations.[717]

Lonergan's meta-method provides a possible foundation for both the hermeneutical-historical concerns with a critical historical knowledge, and the dialectical-critique-of-ideologies concern for the critical norms of historical praxis. For, as we have seen in this subsection, meta-method is able to ground both the procedures of historical experience, of pre-critical historical knowledge, of critical historical knowledge, of post-critical historical knowledge, of spontaneous historical praxis, and of reflective historical praxis. And it does this, not by the grand designs of some rigid system of theories or doctrines, but by adverting to the open and dynamic, related and recurrent operations that can yield cumulative and progressive results.

The very least one can say is that the structures of Lonergan's meta-method deserve some consideration if one is interested in an attentive, intelligent, critical, and responsible formulation of the foundations for ongoing collaboration both in man's hermeneutic and historical understanding of history and in his dialectical constitution of history through praxis.

E. Critical Appraisal. It is difficult to take exception to attentiveness, intelligence, reasonableness, and responsibility. Having spent years seeking to understand and verify Lonergan's notion of the subject-as-subject in terms of my own experience and knowledge, the present writer expresses his admiration for the power, depth, and breadth of meta-method. Inasmuch as meta-method is grounded, not on some theory, but on the praxis of self-appropriation, so the critical appraisal of its expansion into other domains of human knowing and doing, outlined in the previous pages, will be made by the actual praxis of implementing the correlation suggested. These implementations have already led to significant critical revisions and extensions of meta-method.[718] Perhaps the most significant has been a better

---

[717]Cf. Lonergan's "Hermeneutics," pp. 14-15.

[716]Cf. Philip McShane (ed.), Foundations of Theology and

understanding of the mediation of theory and praxis, which led Lonergan to show their interrelation within the structure of the human good in <u>Method in Theology</u> in a way he had not in <u>Insight</u>. I have incorporated those changes within this dialectical comparison since I am not primarily interested in an historical presentation of the development of Lonergan.

Moreover, if this dialectical comparison proves useful to the interdisciplinary collaboration operative within political theology, there will undoubtedly be many criticisms and alterations through that praxis. Meta-method is neither a school nor a cult, it is an effort to structure critical and creative collaboration in the furtherance of attentiveness, intelligence, critical rationality, responsibility.

CONCLUSIONS

The patient reader is entitled to a brief summary of such a long chapter. The guiding question of the chapter concerned the structures of history and method in Dilthey's critique of historical reason and Lonergan's methodology. In the first section we saw how Dilthey's proposal of new foundations for the cultural sciences, if they were to adequately meet the historical challenge of the Enlightenment, had to be found in the lived consciousness of human historical interiority. Because this reality is immediately and certainly experienced in the subject-as-subject, Dilthey differentiated the natural sciences from the cultural sciences in terms of introrsive and extrorsive experience. Lonergan also began from the notion of the subject-as-subject in attempting to ground his methodology. Instead of differentiating inner and outer experience, Lonergan, analyzed the various patterns of experience within the polymorphic variety of human consciousness.

The structures of Dilthey's critique of historical reason and Lonergan's methodology are somewhat similar insofar as both deal with the subject-as-subject, the subject-as-

---

Language Truth and Meaning.

object, and move from these to history. The comparison between these two approaches has not simply been historical but also dialectical, seeking notions relevant to the foundations for interdisciplinary collaboration. Lonergan's method seems to this writer to provide significant insights into the foundations for an ongoing collaboration inasmuch as it has succeeded in thematizing the related and recurrent operations or structures of human historical interiority. No sphere of human historical activity is foreign to its methodical interests. It has effectively appropriated the sources of both the scientific and historical revolutions in contemporary consciousness so that it is able to be both factually ongoing - not appealing to a now defunct classical normativity - and simultaneously critical. Where Dilthey sought to attain the creative sources of all historical objectifications in an experienced interiority which, despite his own intentions, could not ground scientific objectivity or a dialectic, Lonergan succeeds, by adverting to the self-transcending dynamisms of inner experience or human interiority. Dilthey had intended to work out a Selbstbesinnung which would issue in a Lebensphilosophie capable of doing justice to both theoretical and practical reason. In fact he seemed to tend more and more toward a passive contemplative stance toward history, unable to explicate a dialectic applicable to historical action.[719] Meta-method has uncovered the sources common to both theory and praxis and so is able to relate hermeneutics, history and dialectics. Dilthey's experiencing and re-experiencing was unable to offer the foundations of an extensive ongoing collaboration; meta-method's basic horizon offers a transcendental doctrine of methods proportionate to the requirements of such collaboration.

Unless I am mistaken, Lonergan's meta-method is definitely only a beginning, but a very necessary beginning. It correlates both the non-logical and the logical, the pre-systematic and the systematic. It provides for its

---

[719]Cf. Riedel, op. cit., in Hermeneutik und Dialektik; and Habermas, Erkenntnis und Interesse, p. 224.

own correction, implementation, differentiation, for these developments will occur in the measure that men are attentive, intelligent, reasonable and responsible. What is true of the method is no less true of the complexities of our historical situation. Lonergan offers no pat answers or ready-made solutions but an invitation to appropriate the sources of all one's historical activity in order, on such a foundation, to carry on the arduous task of effective collaboration.

CHAPTER FOUR

HISTORY AND METHOD IN THEOLOGY

> When the classicist notion of culture
> prevails, theology is conceived as a
> permanent achievement, and then one
> discourses on its nature. When
> culture is conceived empirically,
> theology is known to be an ongoing
> process, and then one writes on its
> method. Method is not a set of rules
> to be followed meticulously by a dolt.
> It is a framework for collaborative
> creativity. It would outline the
> various clusters of operations to be
> performed by theologians when they go
> about their various tasks. A
> contemporary method would conceive
> those tasks in the context of modern
> science, modern scholarship, modern
> philosophy, of historicity, collective
> practicality and corresponsibility.
>
> Bernard Lonergan

> If theology wants to uncover the
> relation between the christian faith
> and a contemporary world defined
> increasingly by science, and if it
> wants to express intelligently and
> cogently the traditions of this faith
> in that world as an unrealized,
> critical, and liberating memory, then
> for its part theology is always
> dependent upon the chance of a
> dialogue with the sciences.
>
> Johann B. Metz

CHAPTER FOUR

INTRODUCTION

This comparison of Dilthey and Lonergan's work has been guided by three basic questions. The first asked how each developed a metascientific methodology capable of providing more or less adequate alternatives to the scientistic claim as the sole legitimate representative of methodology. That question was answered in Chapter Two where we saw how Dilthey's study of the Enlightenment led to a critique of the Kantian, positivist, and empiricist philosophies of science in his day; and how Lonergan's appreciation of the contemporary crisis led from a cognitional theory to a meta-methodology capable of integrating critically the various trends in contemporary metascience. The second question asked how such alternative approaches to method would structure both history and method and to what extent such structures might provide possible foundations for a vast collaborative effort aimed at a critical mediation, not only from the past into the present but also from the present into the future. That question was taken up in Chapter Three where we saw how the structures of history and method in Dilthey's critique of historical reason, while providing a real breakthrough in terms of the subject-as-subject, still was unable to ground a truly dialectical approach capable of grounding collaboration; and how the structures of history and method in Lonergan's meta-methodology could very well provide the foundations for such a collaboration insofar as they explicate the subject-as-subject in its self-transcending movement from consciousness to knowledge - a movement as applicable to the natural sciences as to the cultural sciences and history.

The final question asked precisely how such approaches to history and method were also capable of mediating theological performance and if so, how the method of theology could be

structured to provide for interdisciplinary collaboration.
This third question is addressed in the present Chapter.
The first section will accordingly analyze the task of
theology within the context of Dilthey's critique of
historical reason, as that can be gleaned from the admittedly
fragmentary writings of Dilthey on the subject. That task
is seen as a shift from dogma to religious experience. The
second section will then show how Lonergan has succeeded
in thematizing a shift in theology from religious experience
to interdisciplinary collaboration.

The three guiding questions for this dialectical comparison of Dilthey and Lonergan were posed within the context of
political theology. The methodological presuppositions of
that context were set forth in Chapter One. The first section
of Chapter Two discussed the possible relevance of a dialectical comparison of Dilthey and Lonergan for the program of
political theology. The third and final section of the
present Chapter will examine the extent to which those anticipations were actually realized, especially in reference to
Lonergan's conception of method in theology.

THEOLOGY: FROM DOGMA TO RELIGIOUS EXPERIENCE

Dilthey's own personal development was a testimony to
his theoretical conviction that the Enlightenment posed a
radical critique of any and all theologies.[1] Leonhard von
Renthe-Fink has already indicated how Dilthey's efforts at
clarifying his understanding of historicality are closely
related to the problem of theology and religious experience.[2]
We have seen, moreover, how Dilthey's assertions of metaphysical consciousness had a religious dimension.[3] As with

---

[1] Cf. P. Hünermann, op. cit., pp. 137-148; J. -F.
Suter, op. cit., pp. 1-4. I am not concerned here with an
historical account of Dilthey's early theological training,
but instead with his conception of the task of theology
as paralleling that of metaphysics versus meta-physics.

[2] Cf. Renthe-Fink's Geschichtlichkeit, pp. 69, 91-114, 122-124.

[3] Cf. pp. 152ff. of Chapter Two and the references given;

metaphysics, however, his affirmations of this religious
dimension are tempered in the crucible of the Enlightenment.
He never did come up with a coherent, rounded-off theory on
religion and theology. But his approach to religious phenomena was typical of his approach to all other historical
objectifications. Here I should like to briefly outline
how Dilthey saw the challenge of the Enlightenment as
confronting theology, and by this I mean specifically
Christian theology, with the epochal problem of finding a
new control of religious meaning. Then I shall go on in
the second sub-section to discuss how Dilthey proposed to
find that new control of meaning. The final sub-section
will then indicate how Dilthey's quest for a new control of
religious meaning shares in the ambiguity of his critique
of historical reason. In this presentation I have only
minimally referred to Dilthey's study of Schleiermacher's
system as theology. For it is difficult to determine, except
in the references provided below, exactly what Dilthey's own
position vis-a-vis Schleiermacher was.

We shall see how Dilthey's conception of the task of
theology was similar structurally to his analysis of the three
schools of metascience in his day, insofar as they demanded
a transition from metaphysics to cognitional theory; and to
his analysis of philosophy as having to move, under the
pressure of the Enlightenment, from a critique of metaphysics
to an explication of meta-physical consciousness.[4] Thus it
is not surprising to find Dilthey advocating a shift in
theology from a traditional concern with objective historical
religious expressions, such as dogmas, rituals, sacraments,
etc., to a concern for religious experience.

1. The End of Conventional Christianity

For Dilthey one of the distinguishing characteristics of
the Enlightenment in Germany - as opposed to the English or

---

for Dilthey's rejection of religious categories for understanding history, cf. W. Kluback, W. Dilthey's Philosophy
of History (New York, 1956), pp. 17, 283.

[4]Cf. Chapter Two, pp. 142ff.

French Enlightenment - was its "theological" aspect.[5] German Protestantism showed a greater ability to accommodate itself to the new ideas than either French Catholicism or English Anglicanism. Yet Dilthey was convinced that the accommodation was basically a compromise which could not withstand the increasing success of the empirical sciences. These would "sever the heart artery of the German Enlightenment."[6] He illustrated this in his studies on the Enlightenment, especially in reference to the compromises Leibniz sought between the scientific ideals of the age and dogmatic faith. Compromises Dilthey saw as linked with national interest.[7]

He was less interested in this aspect, however, than in the effect on theology from the efforts of the Enlightenment thinkers to reconcile biblical faith and reason. For the accommodation led to a critical study of the Bible and attempts to integrate such doctrines as immortality into the rational natural philosophies of the time:

> A continuous development emerged from the religious spirit through the interaction of people, clerics, and the leadership of universities and churches. In this the christian worldview remained dominant as one was educated in the scientific mentality. What was left, however, after the dissolution of dogmas, was the teleological structure of the universe wherein man himself was a teleologically conditioned being. The critical study of the Bible also led to this.... The teachings on immortality were added to this teleological situation of man as determined by God. In this context belonged Melanchthon, Leibniz, Wolff, the common literature, and Kant.[8]

Such a "naturalist" approach was but an uneasy transition to Dilthey's way of thinking; it did indeed center the criterion of knowledge and belief in man and this world rather than in

---

[5] Cf. _L.S._, p. 84; also _G.S._ III, pp. 62-68, 142-147.

[6] _L.S._, p. 86; on the Catholic countries, cf. _G.S._ III, pp. 131ff.

[7] Cf. _G.S._ III, pp. 62-68; VII, pp. 335-345.

[8] _G.S._ VII, p. 337; also II, pp. 112ff.

462

God and the other-world.[9] But it was radically objectivistic and so, as with the "immediate truths" in metascience and the Leibnizean "fundamental proposition," the naturalist position here blunted the cutting edge of the Enlightenment critique of religion.[10]

What eventually overcame the accommodations in German Enlightenment thought, from Kant to Hegel and Schleiermacher, was the advance of the empirical natural and historical sciences. The notion of progress based upon a reconciliation of the old metaphysical religious positions with the new scientific reason was too obscurantist. Even when the church leadership tried to restore religious meanings and values by entering into social questions, the scientific mentality increased its dominance.

> The domination and control of reality through scientific reason arose from the feeling that the ideas of the churches were incapable of shaping the real order of things. At times this new orientation would attack religious ideas, at other times it would seek alliances with them. But everywhere it penetrated the real order, analyzing it, constructing it, finding its laws. It gained domination over nature and satisfied the immeasurable needs of the new industrial society through a new ordering of that society.[11]

Here too, Dilthey uncovered the pathos inability of scientific reason to ground a new order of

---

[9]Cf. G.S. I, p. 379: "In discussing how modern science has destroyed the theological and metaphysical views of society, we limit ourselves to the first phase, which closed with the eighteenth century and now lies behind us. First there arose the naturalist system of knowledge of human society, its structures and external organization, during the seventeenth and eighteenth centuries. It was no less imposing an effort than the grounding of the natural sciences, even if not as consistent as it. This naturalist system meant that from then on society would be understood as a product of human nature. And in this system the cultural sciences first found their center: human nature."

[10]On the naturalist positions, cf. G.S. I, pp. 379-386; II, pp. 90-245; on immediate truths, cf. pp. 127ff..of Chapter Two; on objectivism, cf. G.S. I, p. 379.

[11]G.S. II, p. 244. On the following page Dilthey delivers his condemnation of capitalism quoted on p. 131 of Chapter Two.

society after having destroyed the old:

> This entire development from the seventeenth to the
> nineteenth century was increasingly influenced by the
> concept of natural law. Every historical form that
> could not be assimilated by this concept was destroyed.
> ... And what was the result? The principles of natural
> law helped bring about the dismantling of the old
> society, but they were unable to build a new stable
> order. One cannot escape the strong evidence Comte
> has given for this process. The contemporary situation
> of society presents new evidence.[12]

And the proofs which Dilthey saw in respect to religion could
be found in the gradual disintegration of church affiliated
theologies.[13] Contrary to his friend, Graf Yorck von
Wartenburg, Dilthey could not accept any doctrinal position,
even that of Luther, as binding.[14] Dilthey acknowledged that
he was "not a christian in any specific sense" to Yorck.[15]
If the emergence and development of modern science had ended
the two thousand year old quest for an objective metaphysics,
so they also initiated a whole new attitude toward Christianity:

> Once and for all one should proceed from the realization
> that we moderns relate to Christianity in a completely
> different way than how they did in the sixteen hundred
> years before the establishment of the scientific
> mentality.[16]

There could be no evasion of the consequences of the scientific revolution in regard to the Christian faith. In an
unfinished statement entitled "Rechnungsabschluss der
Gegenwart," Dilthey mentioned that any designation of our
culture as Christian was no more than an empty "pastoral
phrase."[17]

---

[12]G.S. II, pp. 244f.

[13]On the "kirkliche Theologie" cf. G.S. II, pp. 110-115,
129ff. Also cf. Renthe-Fink, op. cit., pp. 100ff.

[14]Cf. Briefwechsel, p. 146.

[15]Ibid., p. 125.   [16]E.D., p. 219.

[17]G.S. XIV/2, p. 592. In his appreciation of the
centrality of the scientific revolution, Dilthey did not
succumb to the indictment H. Butterfield leveled against
later historians of ideas; cf. Butterfield's The Origins of

464

We have seen how for Dilthey the origins of metaphysics in the West can be found in the experience of interiority grounding religion.[18] Yet just as there was an unresolvable succession of antinomies within metaphysics and its concomitant shadow, skepticism, which eventually led to the demise of metaphyiscs, so Dilthey saw the progressive efforts at attaining an objectification of religion as necessarily involved in a succession of antinomies. These latter were between the conceptions of the divine intellect and the divine will, between the omnipotence of God and the freedom of men, between the positivity of Christianity and its claim to universality. They prepared the way for a new control of meaning that would be thoroughly secular.[19] The Enlightenment substituted natural law for divine law, material progress for providence, and the autonomy of reason in the empirical sciences for faith in revelation. This led to the typically modern stance toward reality.[20]

Dilthey's study of the life and writings of F. Schleiermacher- a study which extended throughout Dilthey's philosophical career- sprang from his conviction that Schleiermacher represented an epochal turning point in Christian theology. He began his <u>Leben Schleiermachers</u> with the bald statement:

> I write the life of a man who occupies the most distinguished place in the development of European religiosity since its transformation through the Enlightenment... down to our own day. There occurred in him a great lived experience of religion as originating out of the depths of our relationship to the universe. Completely free from all the encrusted belief in dogma, philosophy, or moral rules, his spirit grasped, in a unique way, the invisible nexus of reality in the interactions of the world and the human soul. This, and only this, is for him religion.[21]

In his study of Schleiermacher's theological system, he

<u>Modern Science</u> (London, 1957), pp. 175-190.

[18]Cf. Chapter Two pp. 152ff.

[19]<u>G.S.</u> I, pp. 274-290, 317-326.

[20]Chapter Two, pp. 142ff.   [21]<u>L.S.</u>, p. xxxv.

proclaims him as the Kant of theology.[22] Schleiermacher, in Dilthey's eyes, had articulated a transcendental standpoint from which it would be impossible to ground the objects of Christian religiosity in any objective fashion. As Kant had exposed the limits of reason vis-à-vis all metaphysical questions, and thereby initiated the "Wendung zur Subjekt," so Schleiermacher was a turning point within theology insofar as he initiated an awareness of the impossibility of any purely theoretical grounding of the doctrines and practices of religious subjectivity.[23]

Nevertheless Dilthey was by no means satisfied with the theology of Schleiermacher as an adequate response to the critique of religion initiated in the Enlightenment. Even in his very positive assessment of Schleiermacher's life and work one can find instances of a growing critical distance that Dilthey as biographer was taking to the positions of Schleiermacher.[24] In his posthumously published Schleiermachers System als Theologie, Dilthey criticizes Schleiermacher's dogmatic retention of the Christological positions of the Christian faith and his consequent inability to overcome the dualism between a universal religiosity and the positive historical doctrines of ecclesial theology. He sees the increasing "secularization of life" through an empirical science released from metaphysical and theological bonds, and historical-critical studies no longer subservient to dogmatic presuppositions, as inevitably leading to an extinction of Christian religiosity within the modern world. After graphically describing the withering of theology as a serious academic descipline, the sad state (indeed, almost the death) of any Christian art forms whether in music, painting, writing or architecture, and after showing how the political predominance of the Church was increasingly waning, Dilthey could conclude:

> Since christian religiosity is no longer the root of our living today, the christocentric standpoint, which is the indispensable presupposition of

---

[22] G.S. XLV/2, p. 535.   [23] G.S. XIV/2, pp. 531-538.

[24] L.S., pp. 427-432.

Schleiermacher's christology, dissolves.[25]
In Dilthey's view Schleiermacher had not sufficiently carried
through his concern for religious subjectivity. Had he done
so, he would have seen how the transcendence of consciousness, which constitutes the core of religion, has been
objectified into an illusory "presentational transcendence" (Vorstellungstranszendenz) in the dogmas, hier-
archies, and sacraments of the churchs."[26]

2. The Quest for a New Beginning

Dilthey did not agree with those who heralded the end
of Christianity or of religion. Just as he saw the need for
a critique of historical reason to renounce any objectivistic
science of metaphysics, while affirming meta-physical
consciousness, so he distinguished between an objectivistic
expression of religion in dogma and the interiority of religious experience. In a letter to Yorck he remarked how he
read the second volume of Harnack's Dogmengeschichte "with
deepest aversion." Cautiously, Dilthey suggests how the
particularity of Christianity is rooted in an experience
capable of critical grounding.[27] If one would identify the
Enlightenment with the naturalist systems, overlooking the
impetus it gave to empirical science, then one could say
that Dilthey opposed the naturalist, "scientific reason"
of that period with an "historical reason." For such a
naturalist world view:

> ...finds its limits in how it forced the infinite (das
> Unendliche) out of life into the beyond. For in life
> the infinite is only present as an emotive power that is
> vague and without boundaries. It thereby becomes an
> endless progression of the individual human spirit and
> of humankind. The world is emptied of gods, and pro-
> gress itself points towards the infinite. Thus a
> consciousness of the fullness of life in its many forms
> holds sway as a faith experience, as a mystical depth
> in every life relationship, as an interiority in nature.
> At the same time, however, the philosophical knowledge
> of understanding does not hold up to criticism.[28]

---

[25]G.S. XIV/2, p. 592.   [26]G.S. XIV, p. 593.

[27]Cf. Briefwechsel, p. 126; also G.S. VIII, p. 49; V,
p. 390. Also G. Misch, Lebensphilosophie und Phänomenologie,
p. 318.

[28]G.S. VII, pp. 336f (emphasis mine).

Dilthey believed the possibility of a critical grounding of
religion could only be in relation to meta-physical
consciousness:

> Cannot it be said that an unbiased comprehension,
> nay more, that lived experience and the need to
> experience factual interiority, carries with it a
> grasp of the structure of things compatible with
> religion. Although not by mathematical proof, this
> would occur on a factual basis, through preponderately
> enlightening conclusions which then, in life
> itself, would increasingly prove their correspondence
> with the nature of things. Is there not what I call
> in my book a meta-physical consciousness, in
> contradistinction to all scientific metaphysics;
> inner lived experience of processes that have no
> analogy with natural processes. If this is not so,
> then the uprooted particular datum of religion can
> only dry up and die away.[29]

Without religion then, the transcendence immanent in history
tends to latch onto some inner-wordly goal as with the notion
of unlimited progress.[30] Not only in the notion of unlimited
progress, but also in the efforts to construct a philosophy
of history and a unified ideal of science in sociology - in
both these attempts, Dilthey saw a manifestation of a repressed
(and so falsely secularized) religious consciousness.[31]
Whatever the position of Yorck, Dilthey did not see any future
in a restoration of theology to its Reformation status, any
more than he envisaged a restoration of metaphysics. Instead
he accepted the consequences of the shift toward historical
subjectivity as introducing a new epochal relation to
religion, just as it did in relation to science and
philosophy.[32]

---

[29]Briefwechsel, p. 126.

[30]Cf. Renthe-Fink, op. cit., pp. 95-99, 112 on how
Dilthey essayed a notion of transcendence that would
escape the objectivism of classical metaphysics. Also
G.S. IV, p. 359.

[31]Cf. G.S. I, p. 98 regarding the philosophy of history;
I, p. 112 on the Catholic background of Comte's sociological
scientism.

[32]Cf. reference in note 16 of this Chapter; also G.S.
XIV/2, pp. 476-478.

Dilthey interprets this shift to the subject within the context of the unity of identity and non-identity in his own efforts at articulating historical interiority, and so he could extend the transcendental philosophy and theology associated with that shift far beyond the Kantian limitations it usually received:

> The expression, transcendental philosophy, embraces all schools of thought that relate knowledge, and all other cultural achievements, to their ground in the creative nature of man. Similarly, one could designate as transcendental theology all those schools that strive to go behind the given formulae, histories, and dogmas to an always and everywhere operative human Divinity in the soul, which has produced all these forms of religious life.[33]

He realized that this would displace the center from a theological to an anthropological concern:

> It has its center outside of theology in the vast consciousness of creative human nature linked with the Invisible, as this nature has manifested itself in art, religion, and morality. The whole of history is its kingdom.[34]

As Dilthey understood this shift, it had three critical consequences. First, it respected the "depths of life" so central to his grounding of the human sciences, and was, therefore, also critical of the denigration of the human, which was occurring as a result of the objectivistic and scientistic transposition of the methods of the natural sciences to properly human studies.[35] Second, it meant that just as Dilthey could not accept the objectivistic intellectualism in the Kantian position on transcendental philosophy, so he rejected the theological variants of it in Hegel, Bauer, Ritschl, and Harnack. Cynically he remarked how comfortably situated professors were not about to replace the Apostles and Martyrs. He then continued, showing how he

---

[33] G.S. II, p. 109. [34] G.S. II, p. 109.

[35] Thus in Briefwechsel, p. 156, Dilthey links a "loss of faith" with the predominance given to reductionist natural scientific methods. On the "depths of life," cf. G. Misch, Lebensphilosophie und Phänomenologie, pp. 50, 55, 64f., 163, 237, 265.

interpreted the shift to the subject in relation to religion:

> But all dogmas must be related to their universal life-value for every human life (Lebendigkeit). They were first formulated in historically limited contexts. If they are to be freed from these, then they are, if you will, the consciousness of the supersensual and super-intelligent nature of historicality itself. In this statement I ally myself with that universal tendency that I call universal Theism or transcendental theology. But I reject their intellectual version of dogma. This prevails as much in the speculative interpretations of Hegel and Baur, as in the critiques by Ritschl and Harnack.[36]

Third, the shift of transcendental theology to an anthropo-logical standpoint enabled it to find its norm for practical theology within the process itself of Christian religiousness, in such a fashion that its concern for ecclesial praxis could find a fruitful collaboration in historical and phil-osophical positions. There would be an openness on the part of transcendental method in theology to incorporate the insights of psychology and historical sociological studies into its practical theological investigations.

> Practical theology refers back to the historical and philosophical. From the religious process itself, practical theology derives the notion of a perfection of the forms operative and realized in the process. The transcendental, philosophical standpoint of theology finds its completion when joined with the Historical School. Thus emerges, within this transcendental standpoint of theology, the methodical procedure for discovering in the psychology of religiosity the law by which religious forms develop. It can also show the stages of perfection in this development, so that, within the limits of the subjectivity of religious consciousness, a psychologically well grounded faith would be possible. So we would have a psychology of religiosity, a comparative history of religions, and grounded on that psychology an indication of the subjective, inner perfection of the present stage of christian religiosity. This is the required inner context that alone could provide a solution to contem-porary theological problems.[37]

Thus Dilthey remarks that Schleiermacher was able to correlate

---

[36]Briefwechsel, p. 158.   [37]G.S. XIV/2, p. 537.

more fruitfully and prudently transcendental philosophy with the historical school in his theology than Hegel was able to correlate philosophy and history, even though Hegel's achievement was more "genially unified."[38]

Dilthey's position is neither that of a rationalist, who would concentrate exclusively on the cognitive content of religious expressions, nor that of a moralist, who would only see the ethical implications of religion, nor that of a skeptic, who would reject religion. In a strange turn of phrase, Dilthey designated his position as one of "comparative historical religiousness."[38a] It was not simply an objective study of comparative religion; Dilthey did maintain a truth aspect in religious experience. The claim to universality could not be made for any particular historical religious expression, but only for its origin in the supra-sensible and supra-intellectual domain of historicality. This led to a theory of dogmas which would demythologize and de-confessionalize them. For the truth of religious experience could not be expressed dogmatically in any fully adequate way. To assert that would be to mistake the transcendence of conscious interiority for a "presentational transcendence."[38b]

There was an antinomy between religious experience and religious expression:

> Religious life contains an insoluble antinomy. The lived religious experience is sure of its power and truth. Yet it inevitably happens that these inner processes are bound up, in man, with images and concepts through which man elaborates his place and security in reality. Now this image language demands the same authority that rightfully belongs only to the lived experience itself. No work of theologians can sublate this contradiction, that such a language as dogma and confessional formulae demand an absolute authority which should only be given to [the inner experience] contained in them. Only with the passing of the last religious person can this contradiction disappear.[39]

---

[38]Ibid., p. 538.

[38b]G.S. XIV/2, p. 593.

[38a]Briefwechsel, p. 125.

[39]G.S. II, pp. 167, 205.

This religious antimony is but another manifestation of the metaphysical antinomies Dilthey studied in his _Einleitung_.[40] Like them, the religious antinomy was fated to necessary contradictions insofar as it was impossible "to grasp the transcendent within the nexus of concepts."[41] What the antinomies revealed was the necessity of a new control of meaning, a shift to interiority and the need to ground the human sciences as concerned with that interiority.[42] From a theological standpoint, Schleiermacher had initiated such an approach. But his dogmatic stance in Christology and failure to take full responsibility for a new form of Christianity (no longer finding its norm in Christ or in the Early Church) indicated for Dilthey the insufficiency of Schleiermacher's theology.[43] Yet such an insufficiency was to be remedied only by accepting the epochal shift in religious consciousness represented by Schleiermacher. For he sublated the opposition between the subjective methods of Kant and Fichte and the objective methods of Schelling and Hegel through his efforts at articulating the dialectic of identity and non-identity between subject and object.[44]

Theology was not dogmatically but critically grounded in the phenomenon of religious consciousness.[45] For dogmas are the symbolic expressions of "ungroundable life itself,"

---

[40]Cf. _G.S._ I, pp. 279-290, 318-327; also above, Chapter Two, pp. 142-155.

[41]_G.S._ II, p. 143.   [42]Cf. _G.S._ I, pp. 327f.

[43]Cf. _G.S._ XIV/2, p. 592; also M. Redeker's _Einleitung_ to this volume, pp. xliv-xlvi. Also _L.S._, p. 550: "Schleiermacher's uncommon position resulted from his preaching this pantheistic mysticism of an Eckardt and his disciples within the christian worship services, from his extending the parameters of the christian worship of God so far beyond what was customary in Protestantism. But for him the reality of God was absorbed in this mystical-religious experience (_Erlebnis_). And if we view this in its historical significance, then we cannot escape the conclusion: Early Christianity is not the norm of faith for the contemporary church. European religiousness advances toward newer, broader goals from the starting point it had in Early Christianity."

[44]Cf. _G.S._ IV, pp. 393-395.

[45]Cf. _G.S._ IV, pp. 397-399.

and in relating religion to that "ground" Schleiermacher
had shown the way to a proper reconciliation of religion
and modern science.[46] The root of his theology was a
cognitive explication of religion as a necessary function
of human historicality.[47] For Dilthey, however, this
involved a pantheistic interpretation of Christianity which
would sublate its dogmatic particularity in a religious
universalism.[48] Indeed, it has been suggested that the
reason why Dilthey never completed his work on Schleiermacher
was due to his efforts at coming to terms with Hegel and
"modern German pantheism."[49]

Although Dilthey never succeeded in carrying out his
projected theory of Dogma, it is possible to delineate how it
would have proceeded. It would have been marked by the
duality already discussed with regard to historicality
philosophies.[50] On the one hand there is the replacement
of dogmatic theology with historical method. As Dilthey
wrote in 1900:

> This analysis demands further, that the dogmatic
> methods still prevalent today be replaced with
> historical methods.[51]

Such a historical method would effectively destroy the claim
Church doctrines make regarding absolute validity. Religion
as historical spontaneity ("Lebendigkeit") expressed itself
in images and doctrines of the first degree, or first order
dogmas. Christianity increasingly had to come to terms with
the external world in the historical flux of many divergent
cultures. Groups arose which, while preserving the thrust of

---

[46]Cf. G.S. II, pp. 242f.; IV, p. 395, 397ff.; L.S.,
pp. 427ff.

[47]Cf. G.S. IV, p. 397.

[48]Cf. G.S. II, pp. 203ff., 210, 242f.; XIV/I, pp.
xli-xlv. Hence the possibility of Dilthey speaking of
"religious atheists" I, p. 401.

[49]Cf. Nohl's Introduction to G.S. IV, pp. v-vii; also
Renthe-Fink, op. cit., pp. 124f.

[50]Cf. Chapter One, pp. 32ff.

[51]G.S. II, p. 203.

religiousness, criticized the dogmas in the light of reason.
This critique Dilthey referred to as resulting in second
order doctrines that corresponded more to reason. In the
context of discussing the Socinians and Arminians, Dilthey
gives us an indication of how his critical theory of dogmas
would function:

> These symbols or images enter into the wider context of
> the external world. Here they are encountered by his-
> torical and natural laws, conceptual systems, causal
> knowledge. It is inevitable, at that point, that dogmas
> of the second order emerge, concepts that enter into a
> universal context of thought, since they are connected
> with the highest ideas. The interiority of religion
> lapses into a tragic fate. The most one can hope is
> that at least these concepts correspond to life....
> The great contribution of this critique is that it has
> once and for all destroyed the arrogant claim of these
> dogmas to an absolute validity. In spite of its
> limitations, even its superficial grasp of the religious,
> it was an event of tremendous significance due to its
> honesty, clarity of understanding, and inexorable
> veracity. What understanding had built up, it could
> destroy. Those dogmas, which understanding had elabor-
> ated over many centuries, would now be dismantled
> piece by piece by the same understanding operating
> under the aegis of a tragic necessity.[52]

There are several important aspects to this description of
the critique of doctrines.

First of all, Dilthey is revealing both his appreciation
for, and distance from, those who would criticize the expressions of religion from within the limits of reason alone.
The difference between the Socinians and Arminians on the one
hand, and historians like von Harnack on the other, is that
the former still had very strong ties to the spontaneity of
religiousness. Hence the happy coincidence when their
rational concepts do, at least, correspond to "Leben."
Secondly, Dilthey admits that the doctrines are products of
reason as "Verstand" and so he sees the presence of this
reason within the context even of his first order dogmas. The
antinomy of religion is another expression of the antinomy

---

[52] Ibid., p. 137. Although this is said in regard to the
critique of dogma by the Socinians and Arminians it allows
us, as Renthe-Fink has said, to see Dilthey's position; cf.
Renthe-Fink, op. cit., pp. 102f.

between historical spontaneity and knowledge or cognitive expressions. The great merit of a critical approach to doctrines is that it has the intellectual honesty to see this. Yet, finally, there is a tragic aspect to this. At the time Dilthey wrote the above he was also engaged in a thorough study of the young Hegel. Undoubtedly he was looking for a way to correlate "Leben" and "Begriff" that would offer some escape from the tragic dilemma of the Enlightenment's "search for truth." The fact that he sees the dogmas being criticized within the context of the "external world" and naturalist system indicates that an approach to them in terms of the subject-as-subject would be different. But how different, he was not able to determine.

He was unable to develop an appropriation of the subject-as-subject which would account for the phenomena of religious objectifications, yet insightful enough to understand that such objectifications were an essential and permanent concomitant of religious experience. Toward the end of his life, he sought within the pan-entheism of Hegel for that unity of identity and non-identity which would sublate the extremes of either a religious immediacy without criticism or a critical historical attitude without religious immediacy.[53]

3. Religion Within the Limits of Historical Reason

The death of Graf Yorck left Dilthey without the stimulation of their extensive correspondence on the significance of Dilthey's discovery of the subject-as-subject as a new control of religious meaning. In the Fall of 1897 Dilthey wrote of his work on Schleiermacher's dialectic and how philosophy and theology could be unified in a historical control of meaning and value.

> The worldview can only be developed through an analysis of the subject in its relationships with what affects it and is affected by it.... Philosophy is an action which raises to consciousness and thinks through to the end life itself, i.e., the subject in its relations of lived spontaneity.... The highest phenomena of history

---

[53]Cf. _G.S._ IV, pp. 50-190.

are to be understood in their inner relation to this context, and they then constitute the means of understanding. For him [Schleiermacher] these were represented in his Christ. What for us is history... that for him was Christ, and secondarily Socrates and Plato. And here lies the unity of his theology and philosophy: this theology is only the synthetic structure of that higher (i.e., where the lower... feelings are integrated in the ideal of a consciousness grounded in God) life, in the individual historical form of Christianity.[54]

With Yorck's death Dilthey turned to the young Hegel in his continuing quest for a control of religious meaning adequate to his insight into the subject-as-subject.

Perhaps in no other sphere of Dilthey's work on a critique of historical reason can we find such a clearly defined recurrence of the very pathos of the Enlightenment which Dilthey was seeking to overcome.[55] As he was unable to articulate his notion of the subject-as-subject in such a fashion as to critically integrate the method of the natural sciences and the cultural-historical sciences, as he was unable to further elaborate precisely what meta-physical consciousness would mean in the light of his telling critique of metaphysics, so in his treatment of theology and the historical objectifications of religion he was unable to articulate adequately that unity of identity and non-identity which would have enabled him to relate his affirmation of religious interiority to his hermeneutical and historical criticisms of religious objectification.

We have already seen how the philosphies of historical-ity, especially Heidegger's brilliant analysis of _Dasein_ were drawn upon by various criticomorphic theologies in order to relate the affirmations of religious faith to the historical-critical analyses of that faith's historical objectifications. The inability of such attempts, as we saw, to realize such an objective can be traced to a Kantian dichotomy or bifurcation between phenomenon and noumenon.[56]

---

[54]Cf. _Briefwechsel_ n. 57, p. 247.

[55]Cf. Chapter Two, pp. 115ff.

[56]Chapter One, pp. 32ff. ; Chapter Two, pp. 82ff.

The attentive reader has undoubtedly perceived how this problematic is at the heart of Dilthey's projected theory of dogma and his analysis, however fragmentary, of religious experience. On the one hand Dilthey was convinced of the necessity to find truly critical and introrsively empirical norms with which to meet the challenge the Enlightenment posed to religious thought. Such a conviction did not allow him simply to affirm the authority of tradition as, for instance, Gadamer would later do. Perhaps it was Dilthey's profounder appreciation of the centrality of the Enlightenment to an understanding of modernity that led him to distinguish clearly between historical presuppositions and historical prejudices. He could not, therefore, fault the Enlightenment for having a "prejudgment against prejudgments,": as Gadamer would.[57]

On the other hand, his acceptance of the Kantian affirmation of the noumenal thing-in-itself, within the domain of natural scientific methods, prevented him from truly overcoming the phenomenon-noumenon dichotomy within his grounding of the cultural sciences. As a result, he could merely affirm the _experience_ of the subject-as-subject, without being able to show how the certainty and there-ness of such experience could proceed to a critical objectification of itself. For Dilthey the reality itself of interiority is the given there-ness of "self-hood" or "interiority" and any statement about this experience is "objectively true" in so far as it utters the occurrence of the experience (_Erlebnis_). Any expression is true in so far as either through experience or re-experience (_Nacherleben_) it manifests the given there-ness of interiority. This meant that all expressions, insofar as they occur, must express some aspect of interiority and therefore be understandable through re-experience.[58]

Heidegger's ontological radicalization of understanding and disclosure reflects a similar pattern. The main concern

---

[57]Cf. Gadamer, _Wahrheit und Method_, pp. 256ff.

[58]Cf. Chapter Three, pp. 249-254, 352-356 and references given there.

of Being and Time is not how truth discloses but that it discloses, so that any manner of disclosure is related to truth, and the luminosity of Dasein is seen as "a primordial phenomenon of the truth." Yet when all understanding is characterized as truth one no longer inquires into the truth of understanding since as disclosure it already is true.[59]

Heidegger and Gadamer could appeal to this ontological radicalization of the there-ness of interiority. Theologians, such as Bultmann, could use such an ontology to preserve the dimension of religious commitment and experience as existential ("Geschichte") from the vicissitudes of historical-critical methods ("Historie"). But Dilthey's more foundational concern with a critical grounding of the historical-cultural sciences, and his discovery of the subject-as-subject as a unity of identity and non-identity, did not permit him to rest content with such an unmediated duality. Hence the tension which we have seen in Dilthey's struggles to relate his foundational Erlebnis to the larger historical contexts or systems, re-emerges in his handling of theology and religious objectifications. Because he was unable to find within Erlebnis a self-transcending dynamism that could be expressed in the experience of knowing, he could not adequately relate religious experience and its interiority to religious knowledge and its myriad objectifications. The dichotomy between historical consciousness and historical knowledge, which his notions of objective comprehension and objective possession exemplify, is extended into a dichotomy between historical religious experience and historical religious knowledge.[60]

---

[59] Cf. Tugendhat, op. cit., pp. 350, 356-362, 399. Compare Tugendhat's complaint that Heidegger gives no concrete formal regulatives (op. cit., pp. 360, 376, 399) with Diwald's remarks on the lack of criteria for veracity in Dilthey, op. cit., pp. 157, 69-71, 76-77, 156-158. There is the question of whether or not Gadamer, in taking over Heidegger's notion of truth (cf. op. cit., pp. 463-464), comes closer to Dilthey than he suspected; cf. Tugendhat, op. cit., p. 358 note 35; and C.V.Bormann, "Die Zweideutigkeit der hermeneutischen Erfahrung," Phil. Rundschau, 16 (1969), pp. 92-119.

[60] Cf. Chapter Three, pp. 249f., 256-260, 325-340 and references given there.

For Dilthey religion within the limits of historical reason meant there was no way by which he could appropriate the religious experience of pre-critical Christian tradition. His commitment to historical-critical methods tended to isolate him in a type of methodological conceptualism. One is not surprised therefore, that he would turn to Hegel and especially the young Hegel in order to break through that conceptualism in regard to the interiority of religious experience. Dilthey had, indeed, broken through such conceptualism in regard to history itself inasmuch as he understood how the subject-as-subject is not some extra-historical reality but rather the ground and constitutive reality, in its unity of identity and non-identity, of history itself.

His analysis of the Enlightenment and its continued effect upon modern history convinced him of the importance of a critique of historical reason which would overcome the ahistorical conceptualism common to Kantianism, French positivism, and British empiricism. Yet as he was unsuccessful in carrying through that project because of the noumenal residue within his subject-as-object, so he was unable to carry through an analysis of the subject-as-subject which would be capable of remaining within precritical religious traditions while moving through an historical-critical analysis of those traditions to a post-critical appropriation of the truth of those religious traditions.

Nor is this dilemma restricted to Dilthey's critique of historical reason. As we have already seen, the critico-morphic theologies dependent upon philosophies of historical-ity are caught in a similar predicament inasmuch as they are unable to provide a critical mediation between the results of the historical-critical methods and the actual experiential praxis of believing communities.[61] So the religious praxis of ecclesial tradition is left in a pre-critical dependence upon paleomorphic or fideomorphic theologies in order to provide some (largely uncritical) mediation between its religious experience and the religious knowledge objectified

---

[61]Cf. Chapter One, pp. 32ff. and the references given there.

in its institutional structures. Lacking such a critical mediation, the religious traditions and their theologies are necessarily prevented from seriously undertaking a critical mediation from the present into the future. For they cannot take religious experience except in a privatized and/or ontologized fashion, as in the criticomorphic theologies, or (in an even more radical way), in the neomorphic theologies which are only capable of explicating religious experience within the categories of some contemporary psychology or sociology of experience. No wonder that the great ecclesial traditions turn more toward paleomorphic or fideomorphic theologies in order to avoid the critical questions of religious experience within a world which, as Dilthey remarked, no longer draws its inspiration or meaning from traditional Christian religiousness.

THEOLOGY: FROM RELIGIOUS EXPERIENCE TO INTERDISCIPLINARY COLLABORATION

The structures of Lonergan's meta-method indicate how there is a progression of applications. Meta-method discloses the presence of the basic levels and operations of the subject-as-subject within the objective spheres of the sciences with their complementary classical, statistical, genetic, and dialectical methods. There it moves through emergent probability into a methodical appropriation of the biological, dramatic, aesthetic, intellectual, and moral patterns of experience and praxis. In discussing the religious pattern I shall emphasize the novelty of how Lonergan relates historical religious experience to historical religious knowledge. We have seen how the advantage of Lonergan's thematization of the subject-as-subject consists in the ability of the basic levels and operations of consciousness to be verified in the conscious praxis of self-appropriation.[62] As critically and empirically self-mediating, the subject is a unity of identity and non-identity

---

[62]Chapter Three, pp. 260-281, 388ff.

capable of not only mediating its own constitutive reality (identity) but also its intrinsic orientation to the totality of reality (non-identity).

Just as Lonergan was able to carry through the starting point of Dilthey's critique without its errors, so Lonergan can wholeheartedly agree to the positive results of the anthropological turn initiated in the Enlightenment, can insist upon the need for new methodological foundations within concrete theological performance, and yet avoid the extremes of a neomorphism (which tends to collapse religious experience into a psychology or sociology of experience) or a fideomorphic theology (which tends to isolate religious experience from human experience). And he avoids such extremes without having to construct a criticomorphic theology or theological method dependent upon an ontology of Dasein, or a metaphysics of vitalism, or a metaphysics of process.[63]

There are four main areas of Lonergan's transition within meta-method from human consciousness and its historical expressions to theology which are relevant to the present study. I shall take up each of these four in turn; first dealing with the limits of liberation, then showing how the transcendental exigence leads to an interrelation of conversions, so that it becomes possible to treat critically religious experience and the dialectics of religious expressions. These contexts allow, finally, an elaboration of how Lonergan's meta-method secures the foundations for a vast collaborative effort within theology, and between theology and the many other disciplines involved in the transition from consciousness to knowledge and action.

1. The Limits of Liberation

In our discussion of how Lonergan can move from the functions, exigencies, and embodiments of meaning and value to the acts and terms of meaning as praxis with its feedback structure of the human good, we briefly saw how the need for a constant liberating praxis is unavoidable insofar as human

---

[63]Cf. Chapter One, pp. 22f. and the references given there.

growth and effective freedom is continually involved in a
dialectical tension between the encroachments of formalist
institutional structures (with their tenacious tendency
toward self-preservation) on the one hand, and the encroachments of disparate particular goods of empirical consciousness
on the other. Such tendencies were anticipated in the sub-
section dealing with the contemporary crisis of will. That
crisis, we saw, is the result of a mechanomorphic proliferation of institutional relations within society, whereby persons are reduced to the mechanisms of role-filling, and the
rather amorphous revolt against such a conceptualist reductionism by a re-affirmation of the demands of empirical
spontaneity on the part of the counter-culture. We saw how
the anthropological significance of Lonergan's meta-method
consisted in his efforts to expand the dimensions of the
effective freedom of the self so that the structures of that
freedom might extend ever further into the realms of empirical
consciousness on the one hand, and into the realms of socio-
historical objectifications on the other.[64]

If it is true that Lonergan sees historical progress
as the extension of mankind's effective freedom, just as he
sees historical decline as the result of bias and scotosis,
nevertheless he would by no means agree with those advocates
of human liberation who believe in humankind's innate ability
for unlimited progress or in an unending advance towards
human maturity. Lonergan would not agree with them, not
so much for what they advocate as for what they omit. For
they seem oblivious to the fact that effective freedom is
restricted "not in a superficial fashion that results from
external circumstance or psychic abnormality, but in the
profound fashion that follows from incomplete intellectual
and volitional development."[65] This incomplete intellectual
and volitional development is genetic as well as dialectical.
It is genetic insofar as the totality of any one man's knowledge, as well as the totality of mankind's common knowledge,

---

[64]Cf. Chapter Three, pp. 409ff., 441ff., with the
references given there.

[65]Insight, p. 627.

does not exhaust the unlimited questions which men either in their individuality, or as a totality can and do raise. At any given time in history there will only be a finite assemblage of knowledge, and such finite assemblages will always be outstripped by the imperative of human inquiry and questioning. The same applies to volitional development. Even granted a continuous genetic development of the realization of human projects of value within history, those projects would never fully satisfy the human demand for value. There would always be a recognition that the advance of knowledge had outdated previous volitional achievements of value and so would require a willingness to revise the projects incorporating those values so that man's doing might be in accord with his knowing.

Besides such, admittedly ideal, genetic incompleteness of intellectual and volitional development, there is also the all too evident dialectical incompleteness. For just as individuals have to contend not only with the demands of their own intelligent questioning continually moving them beyond their present intellectual achievements, so also they must contend with the at least equally imperative demands of their own biased flight from attentiveness, intelligence, reasonableness and responsibility. Just as individual bias prohibits a genetic intellectual and volitional development, so group bias and the longer cycles of general bias guarantee that any genetic intellectual and volitional development within mankind has, is, and always will be a concrete historical impossibility.[66]

Thus the profounder problem of human liberation consists in the human incapacity for sustained development. Lonergan outlines the elements of this problem in rather simple fashion:

> Man's intelligence, reasonableness and willingness
> 1. proceed from a detached, disinterested, unrestricted desire to know,
> 2. are potentialities in process of development toward a full, effective freedom,
> 3. supply the higher integration for otherwise coincidental manifolds on successively underlying

---

[66]_Insight_, pp. 222-224.

4. psychic, organic, chemical and physical levels, stand in opposition and tension with sensitive and intersubjective attachment, interest, and exclusiveness and

5. suffer from that tension a cumulative bias that increasingly distorts immanent development, its outward products, and the outer conditions under which the immanent development occurs.[67]

Not only does the genetic incompleteness of man's development involve a tension between desire and fulfillment, but also the dialectical disorientation of his understanding and willing lead to the social surd whereby attentiveness, intelligence, reasonableness and responsible action seem to become ever more irrelevant to a biased and alienated population.

Lonergan goes on to discuss how this problem of the limits to liberation is radical, permanent, not primarily social, and yet real. It is radical for it has to do with the dynamic structures of cognitional, volitional, and social praxis. It is not only a particular error or deviation but a continued recurring scheme of decline. The problem is permanent because, even supposing that bias and scotosis were miraculously abolished tomorrow, the day after tomorrow men would still realize the genetic limitations and so the tension and opposition, between their unrestricted desire to know and their very restricted knowledge itself. No doubt if the underlying manifolds of physical, chemical, biological, neurological conjugates and events were otherwise, men would experience different tensions in their higher cognitional and volitional integrations. But the tensions would still be there. Thus the problem is not primarily social. For if one could change all social structures tomorrow in order to assure an equal distribution of the planet's resources there would still be the problem the day after tomorrow not only of making mankind's intelligent and responsible consciousness commensurate to the structural changes, but also of seriously meeting the further questions and desires that such a change of social structures and social consciousness would demand.

---

[67]Insight, p. 630.

Those who see the problem of human liberation as primarily social are caught in the dilemma of force or violence. Lonergan while admitting the possibility and even the necessity of force to achieve worthwhile social change, points out how such a use by no means solves the deeper problem of human liberation:

> The problem is not met by setting up a benevolent despotism to enforce a correct philosophy, ethics or human science. No doubt, if there is to be the appeal to force, then it is better that the force be directed by wisdom than by folly, by benevolence than by malevolence. But the appeal to force is a counsel of despair. So far from solving the problem, it regards the problem as insoluble. For if men are intelligent, reasonable, and willing, they do not have to be forced. Only in the measure that men are unintelligent, unreasonable, unwilling, does force enter into human affairs. Finally, if force can be used by the group against the wayward individual and by the larger group against the smaller, it does not follow that it can be used to correct the general bias of common sense. For the general bias of common sense is the bias of all men and, to a notable extent, it consists in the notion that ideas are negligible unless they are reinforced by sensitive desires and fears. Is everyone to use force against everyone to convince everyone that force is beside the point?[68]

The problem therefore is real, and Lonergan warns against a misconception of his meta-method as trying to transpose that problem into some theoretical realm, "on the contrary, its dimensions are the dimensions of human history, and the fourth, fifth, and sixth volumes of Arnold Toynbee's Study of History illustrate abundantly and rather relevantly the failure of self-determination, the schism in the body social, and the schism in the soul that follow from an incapacity for sustained development."[69] The very real question arises as to whether or not these inherent limitations on human development and liberation lead only to either a cynical resignation and pessimism or to a determination to work for the expansion of effective freedom, even though this determination is admitted to be ultimately a revolt against an absurd and meaningless universe of nature and history.[70]

---

[68]Insight, p. 632.

[69]Insight, p. 632.

[70]Cf. Sartre's interview - Der Spiegel, 12. Februar 1973, pp. 84-98.

Neither of these alternatives do justice to the inherent dynamism of the subject-as-subject with its open and dynamic orientations toward experiencing, understanding, judging and deciding upon responsible action. Thus Lonergan sees in the problem of human liberation the need for a still higher integration of human living. Such a higher integration takes people and their histories just as they are, it does not suppress the problem but seeks to work through human attentiveness, intelligence, reasonableness and freedom in order to redeem mankind from the bias and scotosis that has scarred and destroyed so much of human life on this planet.[71] Such a higher integration does not redeem mankind by any automatic process, nor does it eliminate the reality of human suffering and death. Rather, it redeems by revealing a higher meaning and value that is capable of transforming the suffering and evil into a redemptive good.

It is at this point that Lonergan introduces the notions of general and special transcendent knowledge in <u>Insight</u> in order to show the possibility of a higher integration of human development that would be in accord with the actual processes of individual and social history.[72]

2. The Transcendental Exigence and Conversion

We have already seen how the exigencies of meaning are fourfold. There is a systematic exigence whereby human knowing and doing moves from the worlds of common sense with their ordinary and literary languages to the worlds of scientific explanations and theories with their technical languages. This in turn provides the materials for the critical exigence which asks which of these diverse worlds is real and how judgments about reality are to be critically grounded. We have seen how this exigence functions both within the contemporary crisis of metascience and how it was present in the crisis of historicism.[73] These two exigencies

---

[71] <u>Insight</u>, p. 632, 633; also Metz, "Erlösung und Emanzipation," <u>Stimmen der Zeit</u> (March, 1973), pp. 171-184.

[72] <u>Insight</u>, pp. 634-730.

[73] Cf. Chapter Two, pp. 158ff.; Chapter Three, pp. 424ff., and the references given there.

are further sublated in the methodical exigence which seeks to
relate all of the processes and products of the previous two
exigencies in terms of the subject-as-subject in its self-
transcending interiority. We also saw how the methodical
exigence, by its very nature, gives rise to the transcendental
exigence.[74]

Transcendence is initially the very obvious experience
of simply raising further questions. As the questions for
understanding arise out of the data of empirical consciousness
and go beyond (transcend) them, as questions for reflection
arise out of hypothetical formulations and go beyond
(transcend) them by asking if they are true or false, as
deliberation arises out of knowledge and goes beyond
(transcends) knowledge by responsible decision and action, so
the entire sweep of human knowing and doing gives rise to the
question of God which arises out of that knowing and doing
and goes beyond (transcends) it by religious experience
and faith. Such transcendence is not extraneous to but
immanent within human experience. Lonergan has been able
to show how the transcendental exigence is not simply tacked
on to the methodical, the critical, and the systematic
exigencies but implicit within them. Not only is it
implicit within those cognitive exigencies, but also within
the moral exigencies of an attentive, intelligent, critical
and responsible quest for an actualization of values.

We have already seen how the problem of human liberation
demands a transcendental dimension if it is not to end in
either a cynical pessimism or an equally cynical resolution
to struggle for meaning and value in a meaningless and
valueless universe. In Insight, Lonergan raised the question
of God wihin the context of the unrestricted desire to know
and the intrinsic and complete intelligibility that desire
presupposed.[75] He has recently remarked how his proof for
the existence of God in Chapter 19 of Insight was within a
classical context rather than within a historical context,
which would indicate the experiential dimensions of the God

---

[74]Cf. Chapter Two, pp. 185-194.

[75]Insight, pp. 657-677.

question. The incongruity was that, while the entire
movement of _Insight_ was based upon a long and methodical
appeal to experience, in contrast his account of God's
existence made no appeal to religious experience.[76]

In _Method in Theology_ Lonergan indicates how the
question of God is adequately formulated by a transcendental
exigence which, as we have seen, does not cut short the
systematic, critical, and methodical exigencies of meaning.[77]

And it is only when those exigencies are critically
appropriated that the transcendental exigence can critically
raise the issue of God _as_ a question:

> It is not a matter of image or feeling, of concept
> or judgment. They pertain to answers. It is a
> question. It rises out of our conscious intentionality,
> out of the _a priori_ structured drive that promotes us
> from experiencing to the effort to understand, from
> understanding to the effort to judge truly, from
> judging to the effort to choose rightly. In the
> measure that we advert to our own questioning and
> proceed to question it, there arises the question
> of God.[78]

The transcendental exigence with its question of God moves us
beyond the world of common sense, the world of theory, and
the world of interiority into the world of the sacred.[79]
But this world is within man's horizon:

> Man's transcendental subjectivity is mutilated or
> abolished, unless he is stretching forth towards
> the intelligible, the unconditioned, the good of value.
> The reach, not of his attainment, but of his intending
> is unrestricted.[80]

This immanent source of transcendence does not break into the
autonomy of human experiencing, understanding, judging,
deciding and acting. I have already outlined this exigence
in Chapter Two and need not repeat it here.[81]

It could be asked, however, how Lonergan could

---

[76]Cf. _Philosophy of God and Theology_ (New York, 1973),
pp. 11ff.

[77]Cf. Chapter Two, pp. 185ff.

[78]_M.i.T._, p. 103.   [79]_M.i.T._, p. 84.

[80]_M.i.T._, p. 103.

[81]Cf. Chapter Two, pp. 185-194 and the references
given there.

488

simultaneously affirm both God and the free autonomy of man
in history. That takes us back to his doctoral dissertation
on Grace and Freedom: Operative Grace in the Thought of
St. Thomas Aquinas where, in the medieval context of metaphysics he very effectively resolved the Molinist versus
Banezian debate by showing how the conceptuality of Thomas
was within the world of theory where universal instrumentality
asserts that God governs the entire universe and so governs
each event.[82] God governs each event because He governs the
whole, and not vice versa. The eternal Divine Mind and Will
knows and wills the universe in each and every detail, from
the galaxies to the smallest subatomic particle in each of
their movements, but the truth of this statement is one of
contingent predication which, for its truth, depends not only
on the eternal Divinity but also on the actual occurrence
of the universe in all of its spatio-temporal events -
including the myriad events of human history. Hence, the
Divine efficacy

> does not impose necessity upon its consequents. In
> the light of divine efficacy it is quite true
> that if God understands or affirms or wills or effects
> this or that to exist or occur, then it impossible for
> this or that not to exist or not to occur. Still, the exist-
> tence or occurrence is a metaphysical condition of the
> truth of the antecedent, and so the consequence merely
> enunciates the principle of identity, namely, if there
> is an existence or occurrence, then there is the
> existence or occurrence. To recall Aquinas' repreated
> illustration, "Socrates, dum sedit, necessario sedit,
> necessitate tamen non absoluta sed conditionata."[83]

The divine and eternal transcendence, then, lets the
universe and human freedom be since contingent predication
involves not only an identity but also the non-identity of
the created and contingent conditions.[84]

---

[82]Grace and Freedom (Notre Dame, 1971), especially
pp. 72-91, 97-116, 143-145.

[83]Insight, p. 662.

[84]Grace and Freedom, pp. 143-144: "Remove this key
position and it becomes impossible to reconcile human
instrumentality with human freedom: one can posit a
praedeterminatio physica to save instrumentality, or one can
posit a concursus indifferens to save self-determination;
one cannot have a bit of both the antecedents and the whole

In the contemporary context of method Lonergan allows
the created sources, acts and terms, functions and exigencies
of meaning to autonomously operate in complete freedom.
The transcendent exigence is not identified with the systematic, critical, or methodical but is seen as   dynamically
related to them in the unity of identity and non-identity
that is human freedom. The God-question is not one that
abrogates or minimizes the manifold of unending human
questions but underpins those questions arising from the
unrestricted desire for meaning and value.

As the transcendental exigence critically arises
only within the context of the systematic, critical, and
methodical exigencies, so religious conversion is integrated
within the context of intellectual and moral conversion. The
horizontal freedom in human empirical consciousness going
beyond (transcending) neurological underlying manifolds,
in intelligence going beyond (transcending) experiential
data, in rationality going beyond (transcending) intelligent
hypotheses, in responsbility going beyond (transcending)
judgments in action - this horizontal freedom is within a
vertical freedom that implicitly or explicitly selects
the basic stance or horizon of the subject-as-subject.[85]

Intellectual conversion occurs implicitly in the
manifold shifts of paradigms in science whereby the accepted
paradigms of normal science are overthrown by new paradigms
more consonant with a probable explanation of the data.
Thomas S. Kuhn has illustrated this process in his The
Structure of Scientific Revolutions.[86] But the critical

---

of both the consequents. There is a material resemblance
between the Molinist gratia excitans and the Thomist gratia
operans, but the resemblance is only material, for the
Molinist lacks the speculative acumen to make his grace
leave the will instrumentally subordinate to divine activity.
But the Banezian has exactly the same speculative blind spot:
because he cannot grasp that the will is truly an instrument
by the mere fact that God causes the will of the end, he goes on
to assert that God also brings in a praemotio to predetermine
the choice of the means.

[85]Cf. M.i.T., p. 40.

[86]T. S. Kuhn, The Structure of Scientific Revolutions;
also Imre Lakatos & Alan Musgrave (eds.), Criticism and the
Growth of Knowledge (Cambridge University Press, 1970).

questions that this recognition implies calls for the
explicit intellectual conversion of method whereby the polymorphic character of human consciousness is recognized
in human knowing of objectivity and reality. Such an
intellectual conversion is precisely what Lonergan has been
trying to promote in terms of self-appropriation of the
related and recurrent operations of human consciousness:

> Intellectual conversion is a radical clarification and,
> consequently, the elimination of an exceedingly stubborn
> and misleading myth concerning reality, objectivity,
> and human knowledge. The myth is that knowing is like
> looking, that objectivity is seeing what is there to be
> seen and not seeing what is not there, and that the real
> is what is out there now to be looked at. Now this myth
> overlooks the distinction between the world of immediacy,
> say, the world of the infant and, on the other hand, the
> world mediated by meaning.... The consequences of the
> myth are various. The naive realist knows the world
> mediated by meaning but thinks he knows it by looking.
> The empiricist restricts objective knowledge to sense
> experience; for him, understanding and conceiving,
> judging and believing are merely subjective activities.
> The idealist insists that human knowing always includes
> understanding as well as sense; but he retains the
> empiricist's notion of reality, and so he thinks of
> the world mediated by meaning as not real but ideal.
> Only the critical realist can acknowledge the facts of
> human knowing and pronounce the world mediated by
> meaning to be the real world; and he can do so only
> inasmuch as he shows that the process of experiencing,
> understanding, and judging is a process of self-
> transcendence.[87]

It was the lack of such an intellectual conversion that
led Dilthey to remain within the confines of an experienced
noumenal subject-as-subject. The religious antinomy between
religious experience and its constant objectifications in
religious doctrines, rites, etc. was not a religious antinomy
at all. It was the antinomy of Dilthey's critique of historical reason which could not move from historical experience
to historical knowledge and so ended in a worldview of the
idealism of freedom or dualistic idealism.[88] Just as his
critique could not handle the larger systems or contexts of
historical meaning because they could not be found in the

---

[87]M.i.T., pp. 238f.

[88]Cf. Chapter Three, pp. 249-253, 349-356 and the
references given there.

Erlebnis of any individual, so his critique could not handle religious expressions as related to religious experience.[89] This finds its roots in Dilthey's notion of objective mental comprehension, where he was unable to move from experience to concepts through insight.[90]

A critically methodical understanding of history is impossible without an intellectual conversion breaking through the horizons of empiricism and idealism that prevent one from moving from historical experience to historical knowledge in a critical fashion.

> What are historical facts? For the empiricist they are what was out there and was capable of being looked at. For the idealist they are mental constructions carefully based on data recorded in documents. For the critical realist they are events in the world mediated by true acts of meaning.[91]

We have seen how Dilthey came very close to a critical realist position insofar as he acknowledged the subject-as-subject. Yet his inability to hit upon the self-transcending operations of _Erlebnis_ meant that he ended up in an interiorized form of experiential idealism.

We have also seen how this dilemma was shared by the historicality philosophies and the theologies dependent upon them. Here too, Lonergan insists on the need for an intellectual conversion to enable them to overcome the false dichotomy between religious experience and its expressions, on the one hand, and, on the other, the methods of a properly conducted science and scholarship. Thus he points out how both Barth and Bultmann, in different ways, tried to respond to the crisis of historicism by calling attention to the need for moral and religious conversion. Yet they paid too little attention to the need for intellectual conversion in order to liberate science and scholarship from the hold of a mechanomorphic rationalism and empiricism. This in turn had an effect on their theologies.

---

[89] Cf. Chapter Three, pp. 345ff; Chapter Four, pp. 470ff, and the references given there.

[90] Cf. Chapter Three, pp. 326-333 and the references given there.

[91] _M.i.T._, p. 239.

> Only intellectual conversion can remedy Barth's fideism.
> Only intellectual conversion can remove the secularist
> notion of scientific exegesis represented by Bultmann.
> Still intellectual conversion alone is not enough. It
> has to be made explicit in a philosophic and theological
> method, and such an explicit method has to include a
> critique both of the method of science and of the
> method of scholarship.[92]

It is such a critique that is operative in the structures of
Lonergan's meta-methodology. Obviously much remains to be
done, but it is only on the basis of the subject-as-subject
in its self-transcending dynamisms explicitly appropriated
in intellectual conversion that the program is a concrete
historical possibility.

As intellectual conversion is explicit in the recognition of the polymorphism of human consciousness and the
attendant difference between body and thing, so moral conversion is the change that occurs when one's criterion for
decision and action shifts from satisfactions to values. It
is to move beyond the libidinal impulses of empirical
consciousness, with its emotive criteria of pleasure and pain,
as the main determinants of decision and action. It is also
to adopt a critical attitude vis-à-vis the pressures of
conformity and routine inculcated by the superego, where the
motivation is one of security and acceptance.

> So we move to the existential moment when we discover
> for ourselves that our choosing affects ourselves no
> less than the chosen or rejected objects, and that it
> is up to each of us to decide for himself what he is
> to make of himself.[93]

Such a conversion to values is not some automatic process.
It involves painful struggles to discern real from apparent
values, to uncover continually the effects of individual,
group, and general bias on one's own behavior, and to be
consistently open to learn from others.

We have already seen how the acts and terms of meaning
as praxis involve such a moral dimension of freedom. The
particular goods of empirical consciousness, along with the
good of order of intelligent cooperation, are oriented
toward the good of values, and the orientation of one's

---

[92]_M.i.T._, p. 318.   [93]_M.i.T._, p. 240.

freedom towards other persons.[94] In his treatment of ethics,
Lonergan shows how the good is related to the basic levels
and operations of human consciousness.[95] So one has the
correlation:

Consciousness	Good of:
empirical————————————	particular
intelligent————————————	order
rational————————————	critique
responsible————————————	value

Here I have referred to the good of critique in what Lonergan
discusses as judgments of value. For such judgments are
clearly within the moral order of praxis and mediate between
the good of order, with its institutions and roles, and the
good of value.[96] Critique is involved in judgments of value
insofar as the moral achievement of value will always, as
we saw in the limits of liberation, lag behind the human
thrust towards value. It is the good of critique that is
operative in the functions of cosmopolis as exposing the
consequences of general bias, just as it was the good of
critique that was operative in the feedback structure of the
human good.[97] For critique, or judgments of value, must
unite a knowledge of human realities with an intentional
response to value that transcends the present achievements of
order towards new worthwhile possibilities.[98]

As we saw in the previous subsection, moral conversion
is not sufficient for human praxis in history due to the

---

[94]Cf. Chapter Three, pp. 441-448 and references given
there.

[95]Cf. Insight, pp. 595-607; also D. Johnson, "Lonergan
and the Redoing of Ethics." Continuum (1967), pp. 211-220.

[96]Cf. M.i.T., pp. 36-41. So, for example, Critical
Theory seeks to reintroduce reflection on values and interests
into modern science.

[97]Cf. Chapter Two, pp. 195-208, Chapter Three, pp. 441-
448; Chapter Four, pp. 480-485 and references given there.

[98]Cf. M.i.T., p. 38.

limitations posed by liberation. There is a moral impotence in historical experience that cannot be remedied by utopian plans or calls for enlightened maturity alone.[99] If intellectual conversion moves us beyond the familiar sights and sounds of common sense reality to a world of intelligible correlations, and if moral conversion moves us beyond the warm security of pleasure and flight from pain into the quest for worth and value commensurate with the growth of our freedom, then religious conversion moves us beyond the limitations of our finite world. We are grasped by an ultimate concern that assures us that the meaning and value of freedom are not met by the cold indifference of a spatio-temporal universe, but by an infinite understanding and love.

> Religious conversion is being grasped by ultimate concern. It is other-wordly falling in love. It is total and permanent self-surrender without conditions, reservations, qualifications. But it is such a surrender, not as an act, but as a dynamic state that is prior to and principle of subsequent acts. It is revealed in retrospect as an under-tow of existential consciousness, as a fated acceptance of a vocation to holiness, as perhaps an increasing simplicity and passivity in prayer. It is interpreted differently in the context of different religious traditions.[100]

Here again we notice the unity of identity and non-identity. Intellectual, moral, and religious conversions find their correlation in the unity of the subject-as-subject, but they are different. To stifle the religious dimension of the subject is to get caught in the dilemma of human liberation, to fail to acknowledge the thrust of human questioning. It is to end in a trivialization or fanaticization of some inner-wordly objective which is then loved without conditions even though it is conditioned. For the love of God experienced in religious conversion brings a fulfillment beyond the vicissitudes of human success or failure:

> That fulfillment bears fruit in a love of one's neighbor that strives mightily to bring about the kingdom of God on this earth. On the other hand, the absence of that fulfillment opens the way to the trivialization of human life in the pursuit of fun, to the harshness of human life arising from the ruthless exercise of power, to despair about human welfare

---

[99] Cf. *Insight*, pp. 627-630.   [100] *M.i.T.*, pp. 240ff.

springing from the conviction that the universe is absurd.[101]

The unity in difference between intellectual, moral and religious conversions is thematized by Lonergan in dependence upon Karl Rahner's notion of <u>Aufhebung</u>, as meaning

> that what goes beyond what is sublated, introduces something new and distinct, puts everything on a new basis, yet so far from interfering with the sublated or destroying it, on the contrary needs it, includes it, preserves all the proper features and properties, and carries them forward to a fuller realization within a richer context.[102]

So moral conversion goes beyond the value of truth to values generally, establishing the subject as an originating value. But this does not derogate from his devotion to the value of truth but makes him all the more aware of the presence of values and interests within the quest for knowledge.

So religious conversion goes beyond moral and intellectual values to the love of God that enables the subject to experience the boundless joy and peace of infinite love and surrender even to the point of that self-sacrificing love that through suffering seeks to undo the effects of decline. But far from stifling intellectual concern for truth, or moral concern for value, these are strenghtened by inclusion within a transcultural and cosmic context and purpose.[103]

Nor can religious conversion do without moral and intellectual. For the expressions of religious experience demand theologies, and those, as we have seen, call for an intellectual conversion in a time of highly differentiated and specialized consciousness like our own. So also, the sorry performance of ecclesial communities in society indicates the need for moral conversions that will keep a check on the biased tendency to use (and thereby devalue) religious expressions - with a minimum of religious experience - to

---

[101]<u>M.i.T.</u>, p. 105; also Chapter Two, pp. 185ff.

[102]<u>M.i.T.</u>, p. 241; cf. K. Rahner, <u>Hörer des Wortes</u> (Munich, 1963), p. 40.

[103]<u>M.i.T.</u>, p. 242.

legitimatize repressive social orders.[104]   At the same time, religion will not pretend to be a new and more efficacious ground for the pursuit of intellectual and moral ends.   For the autonomy of the intellectual and moral are realized in the unity of identity and non-identity of the sublation. Thus, the religious notion of sinfulness is not to be equated with moral evil:

> Holiness abounds in truth and moral goodness, but it has a distinct dimension of its own. It is other-worldly fulfillment, joy, peace, bliss. In Christian experience these are the fruits of being in love with a mysterious, uncomprehended God. Sinfulness similarly is distinct from moral evil; it is the privation of total loving; it is a radical dimension of lovelessness. That dimension can be hidden by sustained superficiality, by evading ultimate questions, by absorption in all that the world offers to challenge our resourcefulness, to relax our bodies, to distract our minds. But escape may not be permanent and then the absence of fulfillment reveals itself in unrest, the absence of joy in the pursuit of fun, the absence of peace in disgust - a depressive disgust with oneself or a manic, hostile, even violent disgust with mankind.[105]

Those who would equate moral and religious conversion not only have a difficulty with Stoicism but, more recently, with the accounts of Paul Tillich's personal life.[106]

Finally, Lonergan has succeeded in relating his notion of religious conversion as a being-in-love in an unrestricted manner to the seven common areas of the world religions described by F. Heiler.[107]   He thereby provides a very fruitful basis for a much needed dialogue and dialectic between the world's varying religious traditions that will sublate the hostility and incomprehension that has so discredited religion. If Lonergan is correct in his treatment of the systematic, critical, methodical, and transcendental exigencies

---

[104]Cf. _M.i.T._, pp. 358-367; _Insight_, pp. 724-729.

[105]_M.i.T._, pp. 242-243.

[106]Cf. Charles Curran, "Christian Conversion in the Writings of Bernard Lonergan," in McShane (ed.) _Foundations of Theology_ pp. 41-59; Hannah Tillich, _From Time to Time_ (New York, 1973).

[107]Cf. _M.i.T._, p. 109; also the unpublished lecture on _Faith and Beliefs_ (1969).

with the attendant intellectual, moral and religious conversions, then not only is there a critical and methodical
foundation for collaboration between the sciences, humanisms,
and theology, but also between the manifold religious
traditions as well.

3. Religious Experience and Expressions

Just as Lonergan was able to move from consciousness to
knowledge in a critically methodological fashion, just as he
was able to move from historical experience to historical
knowledge, so meta-method can move from religious experience
to religious expressions. We have seen how Dilthey's
religious antinomy was in reality the antinomy of his critique
of historical reason in its inability to critically move from
Erlebnis to knowledge in objective mental comprehension. We
have also seen how Dilthey's theological dilemma was not
limited to him but influenced subsequent theological efforts
to handle the problem of how to relate the traditions of
religious expressions to religious experience in such a
way that, while the former would be under the tutelage of
historical-critical methods, the latter would be preserved.[108]

Now, Lonergan does provide a rather novel, and to this
writer fruitful, alternative to criticomorphic theological
efforts. For he shows how such problems arise from the
polymorphism of human consciousness and so must be met, not
by some form of fideism (fideomorphic theologies), nor by
a retreat into past theological systems (paleomorphic
theologies), nor by an uncritical acceptance of contemporary
scientific or socio-political systems (neomorphic theologies),
nor by a dualist concordism that would distinguish concrete
history from an existentialist historicality (criticomorphic theologies). The problem is met by an intellectual
conversion commensurate with the differentiations of
consciousness operative within the intellectual pattern of
experience today. Such a conversion is a self-appropriation
of the related and recurrent operations operative within all

---

[108]Cf. Chapter One, pp. 10-41, Chapter Three, pp. 249-253,
352-356; Chapter Four, pp. 466-478 and the references
given there.

of the patterns of experience, and so does not lock the
intellectual pattern in some ivory tower of conceptualism.
There can be no subsuming of experience into concepts; and
one is able to move from a critical historical knowledge to
a post-critical appreciation of the patterns. The self-
transcending character of intellectual patterns assures that
the most rigorous scientific and scholarly disciplines will
not negate the realities of human consciousness itself.
They are activities of that consciousness. Thus Lonergan
avoids any half-hearted immunizing of religious experience
from the historical-critical methods.

Lonergan returns from the subject-as-subject through
the subject-as-object to the patterns of experience operative
in history.[109] How does such a return operate in regard to
the religious pattern of experience? If the account of the
progressions from the systematic, through the critical and
methodical, to the transcendental exigence is correct, then
the problems associated with religious expressions (such as
dogmas) and critical historical knowledge should be met,
not by some extreme of denying any validity to the expressions
because they are historical, nor by trying to immunize them
from critical historical investigation, but by showing to
what extent the doctrines proceed from authentic religious
conversion. In order methodologically to effect such a
foundation for this distinction, it is necessary for Lonergan
to distinguish between, as a unity in identity and non-
identity, religious experience and religious expressions.

The basic pattern of religious experience is being
in love with God in an unrestricted fashion. Lonergan
points out how all love is a self-surrender to the one
loved.[110] Yet any human love has conditions and is bounded
by the limits of the persons involved. There is present in
love a desire for unrestricted communion, but that desire
can never be fully achieved in a purely human fashion. For
in love there is present a transcendental notion or intimation

---

[109]Cf. Chapter Three, pp. 422ff.

[110]Cf. M.i.T., pp. 105f., also Chapter Three, pp.
434-435.

of unrestrictedness that brings to any achievement a sense
of disenchantment if that achievement was sought in an
unconditioned manner.

> That disenchantment brings to light the limitation
> in every finite achievement, the stain in every
> flawed perfection, the irony of soaring ambition
> and faltering performance. It plunges us into the
> height and depth of love, but it also keeps us aware
> of how much our loving falls short of its aim. In
> brief, the transcendental notion of the good so in-
> vites, presses, harries us, that we could rest only
> in an encounter with a goodness completely beyond
> its powers of criticism.[111]

Being in love with God is the unlocking of the transcendental
intimation, the fulfillment that knows no limitation. Yet it
need not be known as such, and often is not. But it is
experienced as a dynamic state:

> To say that this dynamic state is conscious is not to
> say that it is known. For consciousness is just
> experience, but knowledge is a compound of experience,
> understanding, and judging. Because the dynamic state
> is conscious without being known, it is an experience
> of mystery. Because it is being in love, the mystery
> is not merely attractive but fascinating; to it one
> belongs; by it one is possessed. Because it is an
> unmeasured love, the mystery evokes awe. Of itself,
> then, inasmuch as it is conscious without being
> known, the gift of God's love is an experience of
> the holy, of Rudolf Otto's mysterium fascinans et
> tremendum. It is what Paul Tillich named being
> grasped by ultimate concern. It corresponds to St.
> Ignatius Loyola's consolation without a cause, as
> expounded by Karl Rahner.[112]

This experience is caught in the interstices of human living
and is the utter fulfillment of the responsible dimensions of
human consciousness.

As this experience has expressed itself in the many
historical forms of the world religions one can find a
certain structural similarity, according to F. Heiler.[113]
Those common features are: (1) they exhibit an orientation to
a transcendent reality; (2) this transcendent reality is
immanent in human hearts; (3) he is supreme beauty, truth,

---

[111] M.i.T., p. 36.   [112] M.i.T., p. 106.

[113] Cf. F. Heiler, "The History of Religions as a
Preparation for the Cooperation of Religions," in The History
of Religions edited by M. Eliade and J. Kitagawa (Chicago,
1959), pp. 142-153.

righteousness, goodness; (4) he is love, mercy, compassion; (5) the way to him is one of repentance, self-denial, and prayer; (6) that that way is also one of love for one's fellow men, even one's enemies; and (7) that this way is a love of God, so that supreme happiness is conceived of as a knowledge of God, a communion and even a dissolution in him. Lonergan succinctly shows how these seven common features of religion can be found as rooted dynamically in the notion of religious experience as a being in love with God.

> To be in love is to be in love with someone. To be in love without qualifications or conditions or reservations or limits is to be in love with someone transcendent. When someone transcendent is my beloved, he is in my heart, real to me from within me. When that love is the fulfillment of my unrestricted thrust to self-transcendence through intelligence and truth and responsibility, the one that fulfills that thrust must be supreme in intelligence, truth, goodness. Since he chooses to come to me by a gift of love for him, he himself must be love. Since loving him is my transcending myself, it also is a denial of the self to be transcended. Since loving him means loving attention to him, it is prayer, meditation, contemplation. Since love of him is fruitful, it overflows into love of all those that he loves or might love. Finally, from an experience of love focused on mystery there wells forth a longing for knowledge, while love itself is a longing for union; so for the lover of the unknown beloved the concept of bliss is knowledge of him and union with him, however they may be achieved.[114]

This, however, seems to be a highly idealistic description of religious experience. Any acquaintance with the histories of religion will indicate how sorely the achievement matches the intention.

Accordingly, Lonergan introduces the notion of how religious development is _dialectical_ in its expressions. Attentiveness, intelligence, reasonableness, and responsibility are structures of freedom that in concrete living can just as well define the root alienation of biased inattentiveness, stupidity, irrationality, and irresponsibility.[115] So also with religious experience. The dialectic is a concrete one, etched across the pages of human history, of religious

---

[114]_M.i.T._, p. 109.

[115]Cf. Chapter Three, pp. 381ff.

persons and groups and institutions faced with the imperatives of transcending themselves in love or not. The dialectic is not one of propositions but of persons in their concrete religious living, it is not one to be deduced a priori, but only from the careful discernment of history. Lonergan outlines how such a discernment might function in terms of the seven common features of religious experience.[116] There are three main elements to consider.

First, there is the dialectical process itself. In the earlier stages of religion, transcendence can be so powerful, and immanence so minimal, that God is "remote, irrelevant, almost forgotten."[117] Or immanence can be so stressed, and transcendence forgotten, that the hierophantic expressions in shrines, statues, rituals will become idols, magic, myth.[118] This can also happen at a later stage of development: the transcendence of God in Buddhism is not the expression of a love for a person, there is no notion of being as the to-be-known, so that transcendent mystery becomes named nothing at all; or in the manifold forms of pantheism and panentheism, the immanence of the divine is so stressed and identified with universal process that transcendence is minimized.[119]

When the love of God is not joined with a self-transcendence to truth, value, and goodness, there emerges the facile re-inforcement by "the erotic, the sexual, and the orgiastic."[120] Or it may be that an immanent experience

---

[116] Cf. M.i.T., pp. 110-113.

[117] Cf. M.i.T., p. 110 where Lonergan refers to F. M. Bergounioux and J. Goetz, Prehistoric and Primitive Religions, Faith and Fact Books 146, London: Burns and Oates, 1965, pp. 82-91.

[118] Cf. M.i.T., p. 111 where Lonergan refers to A. Vergote, Psychologie religieuse, Bruxelles: Dessart, 1966, p. 55.

[119] Cf. M.i.T., p. 110 where Lonergan, on Buddhism, refers to E. Benz, op. cit., p. 120 and F. Heiler, op. cit., p. 139; M.i.T., p. 111 where Lonergan refers to Bergounioux and Goetz, op. cit., pp. 117-126.

[120] Cf. M.i.T., p. 111 where Lonergan refers to A. Vergote, op. cit., p. 56.

of transcendence is felt, but it is not seen as compassion and mercy; then the awe is easily turned into the terrifying and daimonic, "an exultant destructiveness of oneself and others," as is so evident in the "religious" practices of human sacrifice and "religious" wars.[121] The self-transcendence of repentance, self-denial and prayer can easily slip into a false pharisaism when the other elements are not present, so that a Superego God is the sham substitute for real self-transcendence. A contemplative stance can so dominate that it becomes an excuse for socio-political or economic compromise. Or love of neighbor can be reduced to a "Golden Rule" do-goodism that fails even to touch the mystery of one's brothers and sisters. Finally, the desire for ultimate communion and knowledge of God can be so strong that it topples over into a quietism, a neglect of loving service and mission to the world; or the ultimate goal may be so lost sight of that religious fervor is enlisted in the quest for utopia in the best of all possible worlds.

All of these moments in the dialectic of development and decline in religious experience and its myriad historical expressions indicate how Lonergan is striving to articulate a unity of identity and non-identity comparable to his articulations for intellectual conversion and moral conversion. The unity is seen in the non-identity of transcendence and the identity of immanence. The unity can easily disintegrate and decline set is when the tensions of immanence-transcendence, birth rituals-death rituals, action-contemplation, incarnational-eschatological counterpoints imperil their own unity by overemphasis.

Second, within this dialectic there is operative not only a human religiosity but also a divine love. That love finds its primary expression in the love that is poured into our hearts, that gifts the religious experience as a being in love with God. To that divine expression of love we respond as to a word in faith, as a knowledge born of religious

---

[121]Cf. M.i.T., p. 111 where Lonergan refers to A. Vergote, op. cit., p. 57 and R. May, Love and Will, (New York, 1969), Chapters Five and Six.

love.[122] Such a word and faith are within the world of religious immediacy, the realm of a transcendent value beyond vital, personal, cultural, and social values. Yet all immediacy of experience tends to a self-transcendence from the subject-as-subject to the subject-as-object, and religious experience is no exception. If religious conversion occurs, it can recur, can spread to become a scheme of recurrence within social and cultural contexts. Communities are formed, religious traditions emerge in which religious meanings and values are objectified: as the inner word of religious conversion is preached within the many socio-historical contexts of the world of common sense, as the words of this preaching are reflected upon and systematized in worlds of theory, and as "its foundations, its basic terms and relationships, its method are derived from the realm of interiority."[123]

Here too the dialectic is operative, preaching can be set against theological speculation, the lack of intellectual conversion can lead to endless theological controversies. Even when that conversion is present, there can emerge a tension between the pre-critical "commonsense apprehension instinct with feeling and the new theoretical apprehension devoid of feeling and bristling with definitions and theorems. So the God of Abraham, Isaac, and Jacob is set against the God of the philosophers and theologians."[124] This dialectic can only be met by moving into the world of interiority which can, in differentiating consciousness, explain the "nature and complementary purposes of different patterns" of experience.[125]

Faith, as a knowledge born of religious love, goes beyond the knowledge to be gained by empirical, intelligent, and rational consciousness to the knowledge gained through the discernment of value and the judgments of value of a person in love with God.[126] The many community expressions

---

[122]M.i.T., pp. 112-118.   [123]M.i.T., p. 114.

[124]M.i.T., pp. 114-115.   [125]M.i.T., p. 115.

[126]M.i.T., p. 115. Lonergan makes this analysis in the context of a commentary on Pascal's "le coeur a ses raisons

of this faith in religious beliefs indicate how faith through
beliefs is social and historical. For those beliefs may,
as expressions of a knowledge gained through the discernment
of persons in love with God, be expressed in imperatives,
narratives, ascetical and mystical treatises, or theoretical
doctrines and systems. Such expressions as beliefs stand
within the dialectical unity of identity and non-identity
with faith, so that

> we have secured a basis both for ecumenical encounter
> and for an encounter between all religions with a basis
> in religious experience. For in the measure that
> experience is genuine, it is orientated to the mystery
> of love and awe; it has the power of unrestricted love
> to reveal and uphold all that is truly good; it remains
> the bond that unites the religious community, that
> directs their common judgments, that purifies their
> beliefs. Beliefs do differ, but behind this difference
> there is a deeper unity. For beliefs result from
> judgments of value, and the judgments of value relevant
> for religious belief come from faith, the eye of
> religious love, an eye that can discern God's self-
> disclosures.[127]

There is, then, the possibility of a truly critical and
methodological collaboration within the religious traditions.

Third, but this religious faith and its beliefs and
practices are not introrsive but are within the overall
historical process. The transcendent values revealed by the
discernment of persons in love with God are not unrelated
to the vital, personal, social and cultural values operative
within the other patterns of experience. For "in the light
of faith, originating value is divine light and love, while
the terminal value is the whole universe."[128] Hence there
is a new energy and resolve that holiness adds to human
purpose and commitment, one that does not allow human expectation to stop at the grave.

> To conceive God as originating value and the world as
> terminal value implies that God too is self-transcending
> and that the world is the fruit of his self-
> transcendence, the expression and manifestation of his
> benevolence and beneficence, his glory.[129]

---

que la raison ne connaît pas."

[127] M.i.T., p. 119.   [128] M.i.T., p. 116.

[129] Ibid.

We have seen how, for Lonergan, moral conversion and judgments of value comes up against the limits of liberation. It is now possible to see how those limits can be met by the praxis of religious faith. For faith experiences freedom as gift and so imparts a higher integration in the struggle for expending mankind's effective freedom. "So faith is linked with human progress and it has to meet the challenge of human decline."[130]

It is linked with human progress inasmuch as both are rooted in man's cognitive and moral self-transcendence, so that to advance one is to advance indirectly the other. It dispels the cynicism and disgust that confronts the task of liberation within a closed and dead-end universe. Faith, moreover, is a powerful resource in overcoming the forces of decline:

> Decline disrupts a culture with conflicting ideologies. It inflicts on individuals the social, economic, and psychological pressures that for human frailty amount to determinism. It multiplies and heaps up the abuses and absurdities that breed resentment, hatred, anger, violence. It is not propaganda and it is not argument but religious faith that will liberate human reasonableness from its ideological prisons. It is not the promises of men but religious hope that can enable men to resist the vast pressures of social decay. If passions are to quiet down, if wrongs are to be not exacerbated, not ignored, not merely palliated, but acknowledged and removed, then human possessiveness and human pride have to be replaced by religious charity, by the charity of the suffering servant, by self-sacrificing love. Men are sinners. If human progress is not to be ever distorted and destroyed by the inattention, oversights, irrationality, irresponsibility of decline, men have to be reminded of their sinfulness. They have to acknowledge their real guilt and amend their ways. They have to learn with humility that religious development is dialectical, that the task of repentance and conversion is life-long.[131]

Religious faith can, therefore, offset the limits of liberation insofar as it opens the possibility of a total self-transcendence as gift that is not bound to the limitations of present sorry achievement. Men crave such an actualization of their desires, and if they do not find it in authentic religious conversion, they tend too easily to bestow upon a

---

[130]_M.i.T._, p. 117.   [131]_M.i.T._, pp. 117-118.

limited objective the drive that can only come from God. Hence the extremes of trivializing human life or fanaticizing some project are the constant reminder of a lost transcendence. The death of God would be the death of mankind. Perhaps now it is clear why theology was included in the foundational articulation of a humanizing metascience.[132]

Lonergan's distinction between faith and beliefs puts the distinction Dilthey drew between religious _Erlebnis_ and dogmas within a context that overcomes the privatized problematic of Dilthey. Yes, the dogmas are expressions within particular social, cultural, and historical contexts of a religious tradition. But they are expressions of experience, and so once that experience is grasped as truly self-transcending not only can there be the validity of a virtually unconditioned in the dogmas or doctrines, but one can, in the light of faith, discern to what extent the doctrines are the expressions of religious conversion, i.e., to what extent they do express communities in love with a transcendentally immanent God, to what extent those doctrines do promote true progress and undo decline. An antinomy between religious experience and expression would only exist insofar as the beliefs did not express such self-transcendence, or insofar as they were studied by one who had not gone through the processes of religious, moral, and intellectual conversions.

4. Functional Specialties

If it true that religious conversion and faith profoundly unite all religious traditions, if it is true that religious conversion sublates moral and intellectual conversion in the manner of Rahner's _Aufhebung_, then how would a theology based upon Lonergan's notion of meta-method actually function? We might anticipate that Lonergan would not try to limit his method in theology to any one particular religious tradition. For if faith and religious conversion are the foundations of any genuine religious expression, then they are the foundations of theology also. And as faith is distinct from, yet

---

[132]Cf. Chapter Two, pp. 195-208.

related to, beliefs, so theological method founded on religious conversion would be applicable to the doing of theology in any religious tradition. We can also anticipate that insofar as the sublation of the moral and intellectual conversions by the religious means that the latter still needs and includes and preserves the former, then the method in the doing of theology would, structurally, be applicable to moral and intellectual reflections as well as to religious. Such is indeed the case with Lonergan's notion of functional specialties in theology:

> Clearly functional specialties as such are not specifically theological. Indeed, the eight specialties we have listed would be relevant to any human studies that investigated a cultural past to guide its future. Again, since the sources to be subjected to research are not specified, they could be the sacred books and traditions of any religion. Finally, while there is a theological principle assigned, still it is not placed in authoritative pronouncements but in the religious conversion that turns men to transcendent mystery; and while I believe such a turn always to be God's gift of grace, still it becomes specifically Christian conversion when the gift of the Spirit within us is intersubjective with the revelation of the Father in Christ Jesus.[133]

As Lonergan remarks in reply to Rahner, "in our day of ecumenism, of openness with non-Christian religions, of dialogue with atheists, there is not a little advantage in a theological method that with slight adjustments can be adapted to related yet quite different investigations."[134]

My purpose here is not to enter into a detailed discussion of the functional specialties, that has already been done in Lonergan's own Method in Theology. Instead I shall briefly outline how this method is related to the basic structures of his meta-method discussed in the previous Chapter. There are three main areas to cover: first I shall go into the need of such an approach to theology and the types of specialization involved. Then I will show how it is related to the basic structures of meta-method; and, finally, take up each of the eight specialties in summary fashion.

---

[133]Foundations of Theology, p. 233.

[134]Ibid. For Rahner's objections, cf. ibid., pp. 190-196.

508

First of all, the need for some type of methodological correlation of the theological specializations is apparent both from the many types of special disciplines now operative within theology and from the need for theology to enter into an effective collaboration with other disciplines and sciences. We have already seen, in Chapter Two, how the dialectic of the Enlightenment can only be met by an extensive interdisciplinary collaboration.[135] Such an interdisciplinary collaboration cannot be effective if it only consists in correlating the results of the many disparate fields of inquiry. For those results are continually open to revision and new discoveries. Thus in Chapter Two we also saw how Lonergan's notion of a functional feedback correlation could be applied to the vast problems in contemporary meta-science. The feedback quality of the functional relations insures that the correlation will be ongoing and open to all further relevant questions.

Now this is no less true for the many specializations within theology. Karl Rahner has recently called attention to the estrangement ("Befremdung") in theology arising from the impossibility to come anywhere near providing an adequate overview of all the relevant theological positions within the many fields.[136] Lonergan has indicated how there are three general types of specialization. First there is the specialization that arises by dividing and subdividing the field of the data investigated. This _field specialization_ is rampant in theology. No one can keep abreast of all the periodicals, monographs, books within their own field; subdivisions occur more rapidly than librarians can catalogue them. The Old and New Testaments, Patristics, Councils, Middle Ages, Renaissance, Reformation and Counter-Reformation, Enlightenment, Modern fields of theological inquiry are here divided and subdivided so rapidly that work aimed at providing comprehensive introductions to any one of them are outdated before they come off the presses.[137]

---

[135]Cf. Chapter Two, pp. 93-114.

[136]Cf. K. Rahner, _Schriften_ IX, pp. 81ff.

[137]Cf. _M.i.T._, pp. 125f.; also D. Tracy, _op. cit._, pp. 238ff.

Hence there arises the <u>subject</u> <u>specializations</u> that divide up the data, not according to fields of investigation, but according to the results of those investigations to be taught in the various departments, subjects, and courses. There are courses divided up into, for example, Biblical, Historical, Systematic, Dogmatic, Moral, Mystical and Ascetical, Pastoral subject specialties.[138] Professor David Tracy has rather tellingly described how such subject specialties are no adequate answer to the problem of estrangement:

> Indeed, in any theological school the alert student very quickly learns the "strong" points of the curriculum and the "weak" ones. In general, then, it is fair to say that ... the student is left with the disconcerting impression that somehow it is up to himself alone to relate and integrate all these disciplines. Nor will he ordinarily find too much encouragement for that task from most of his professors. For he also soon discovers that most of them are so wedded to their own particular disciplines that their lack of interest in other disciplines borders on the patronizing. He may, for example, find exegetes decrying the use of any "profane" philosophy as a intrinsic violation and distortion of the pure word of God. Or he may find systematic theologians blithely using scriptural texts whose scientific exegesis has no connection at all with the systematic issue in question. Or he may find "pastoral" theologians, innocent of exegesis, history or systematics alike, insist that the sole concern of the theologian at present must be to find ways to become "relevant" to the prevailing <u>Zeitgeist</u>. Or he may find exegetes or systematic theologians contemptuous of any attempt to communicate their "purely scientific" results in a fashion relevant to the needs of any and especially contemporary culture.[139]

Lonergan proposes the third form of specialization, <u>functional</u>. It is not concerned only with the data to be investigated nor only with the results of the investigation. Rather it concerns the process from data to results. Functional specialization does not mean adding more specialists to already crowded departments, nor does it introduce new theological data or results into the already heavy curriculum. The functional specialties are aimed at correlating what is already in process now, only doing it in a critically methodical manner. Already there are the tasks performed by

---

[138]Cf. <u>M.i.T.</u>, p. 126.

[139]Tracy, <u>op. cit.</u>, pp. 240-241.

textual criticism and the manifold of archaeological research methods aimed at critically assembling the data relevant to religious traditions. Already there are the manifold exegetical methods aimed at interpreting the data so assembled. Already there are the historical methods involved in showing what was going forward in the data so interpreted. Already. there are concerns with more or less opposed histories such as the apologetic and ecumenical concerns and methods. Already there are fundamental theologies attempting to articulate the horizons within which the divergent histories and their contradictions can be sublated. Already there are doctrinal and dogmatic theologies concerned with the truths consonant with the various religious traditions. Already there are systematic theologies attempting to provide a creative under-standing of doctrinal tenets. Already there are the many specialties of pastoral, literary, and communication orien-tated theologies aimed at transmitting to the vastly divergent societies and cultures what religious traditions affirm.

This, then, is the process from data to results that Lonergan's notion of functional specialization explicates. "It arises, not to divide the same sort of task among many hands, but to distinguish different tasks and to prevent them from being confused. Different ends are pursued by employing different means, different means are used in different manners, different manners are ruled by different methodical precepts."[140] Unless such a differentiation (non-identity) and correlation (identity) of the specialties in theology are carried out, there is a constant tendency on the part of specialists to give one-sided "totalitarian" views of theology: "from such one-sidedness theology has suffered gravely from the middle ages to the present day. Only a well-reasoned total view can guard against its continuance in the present and its recurrence in the future."[141] One has only to think of how paleomorphic theologies tend to see all of theology as serving the interests of dogmatic theology.[142]

---

[140]M.i.T., pp. 136-137.   [141]M.i.T., p. 137.

[142]Cf. M. Sechler, "Die Theologie als Kirchliche Wissen-schaft nach Pius XII und Paul VI," in Tübingen Theologische

Or how neomorphic theologies reduced everything to history as mediated by historical-critical methods; or more recently, how uncritically Marxist inspired theologies tend to reduce all theology to forms of socio-political legitimatization.[143] Introducing functional specialization would also guard against the tendency upon the part of ecclesial authorities, students, and laypeople to put excessive demands on theologians. They are, after all, specialists and cannot answer all questions within theology; nor should they be expected immediately to tie in their discoveries with all their ramifications for the other areas of theology.[144]

Figure Fourteen outlines the eight functional specialties. There are three main points to discuss in relation to them before taking each of them up in turn. First there is the evident correlation between the specialties and the levels of consciousness. This is not a naive one-to-one correlation, for obviously the specialties of research and communications, for instance, demand not only an attentiveness of empirical consciousness, but also intelligence, critical reason, and responsibility. The correspondence is functional, where all four levels operate in each of the specialties for a goal or end defined primarily by the level of consciousness in question.

> In a scientific investigation the ends proper to particular levels may become the objective sought by operations on all four levels. So the textual critic [level of research] will select the method (level of decision) that he feels will lead to the discovery (level of understanding) of what one may reasonably affirm (level of judgment) was written in the original text (level of experience). The textual critic, then, operates on all four levels, but his goal is the end proper to the first level, namely, to ascertain the data.145

A similar functional specialization occurs when the exegete pursues his different goal of understanding the text. For that hermeneutical understanding (intelligent) demands

---

Quartalschrift 149 (1969), pp. 209-234.

[143]Cf. Chapter One, pp. 17-19, and references given there.

[144]Cf. M.i.T., pp. 137-138.   [145]M.i.T., p. 134.

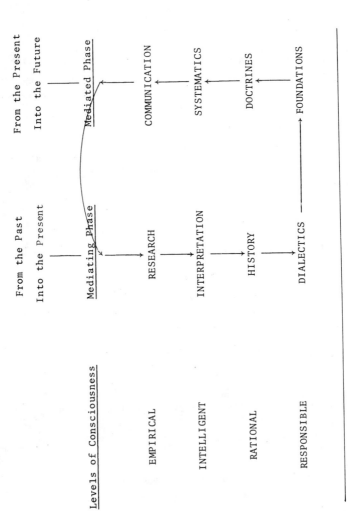

Figure Fourteen: Functional Specialties in Theology

that he accurately apprehend the text (empirical), that he decide which methods of interpretation are most suitable (responsible) to understanding the text, and that he be capable of judging (rational) whether or not he has correctly understood the text. The historian aims at a critical understanding of historical process (rational); but this involves not only his selective decision regarding the methods for that goal (responsible), but also that he accurately apprehend all the relevant data (empirical) and properly understand them (intelligent). The dialectician is concerned primarily with the decisions (responsible) that account for the contradictory movements both in the history written about and in the written histories. Yet this implies that he apprehend all of the relevant data (empirical), that he understand that data (intelligent), and that he be capable of critically judging if that understanding is correct (rational).[146]

This is the mediating phase of theology from the past into the present. It finds its classical counterpart in the lectio divina and oratio obliqua that is concerned with appropriating all the relevant documents and monuments from the past of a religious tradition.[147] It corresponds to what P. Ricoeur has called the archaeological dimension of history applied to religious tradition.[148]

Classically the lectio prepared for the questio, oratio obliqua had to give way to oratio recta, wherein theologians, enlightenend by the past, must confront the problems of their own day. This is formulated by Ricoeur as the teleological dimension of history, and it finds its christian counterpart in the eschatological orientation of the christian message.[149] This dimension leads political theology to critize a facile ontologizing of historicality on the part of the critico-morphic theologies and to seek norms expressive of a unity

---

[146] Ibid.   [147] Cf. M.i.T., p. 153.

[148] Cf. P. Ricoeur, De l'interprétation (Paris, 1965), pp. 407-443.

[149] Cf. M.i.T., p. 133; also Ricoeur, ibid., pp. 444-475.

514

of identity and non-identity capable of a critical mediation
from the present into the future. It is also here that the
present study has attempted to show the relevance of Dilthey
and Lonergan toward such a project.[150] For such a move will
be critical to the extent that it develops methods capable
of handling the question of the social surd and of distinguishing between progress and decline.[151]

In foundations, fundamental theologians aim at explicating the critical categories capable of deciding which of the
contradictory decisions, and their accompanying horizons,
uncovered by dialectics are most suitable to religious
conversion (responsible). But this demands that they properly
apprehend the data supplied by dialectics (empirical), that
they are able to understand dialectical realities (intelligent), and can correctly judge, both factually and evaluatively, their understanding (rational). Doctrinal or
dogmatic theology aims at explicating doctrinal truths of the
religious tradition (rational); but this demands not only the
decisions regarding the horizon of conversion and the methods
suited to it (responsible), but also that the historical
processes involved in the emergence of doctrines are understood (intelligent) and an attentiveness to the results of
foundational data (empirical). Systematic theologians not
only aim at providing a systematic understanding of doctrinal
truths (intelligent), but must do so my deciding on the best
methods for such understanding (responsible) and be able to
properly apprehend the doctrinal data (empirical) and judge
if their understanding is appropriate (rational). Finally,
the many specialties involved in communicating the christian
message to varying societies and cultures must not only
appropriate the symbols and meanings of those audiences
(empirical), but must decide on the best methods of communication (responsible) and judge (rational) if their understanding (intelligent) of both the theological message and

---

[150]Cf. Chapter One, pp. 30-53; Chapter Two, pp. 57-92,
pp. 157-209 and references given there.

[151]Cf. Chapter Three, pp. 358-452 and references given
there.

the relevant socio-cultural context is correct.[152]

The feedback quality of functional specialization is seen in how communications then affect the religious communities and traditions and so provide more data for research, intepretation, history, dialectics, doctrines, systematics, and a new communications. Nor does Lonergan claim that specialists can only function in one of the eight; many range through several of the specialties. He is only asking that they be aware of the different aims they are pursuing.[153]

The meta-methodological character of the functional specialties should also be evident. Lonergan is not trying apriori to decide for specialists which particular methods they should use. He is simply providing a meta-contextual correlation of whatever methods they choose. While the meta-context is open, it is also critical. For a false choice of particular methods will lead to conflicts that can be revealed in dialectics and resolved in foundations. The mediating phase from the past into the present incorporates the methods used in field specialization, while the mediated phase from the present into the future incorporates the methods of subject specialization.[154]

The differentiation of the eight functional specialties is a formally dynamic unity-in-difference.[155] The tasks of the eight are distinct but interdependent. W. Pannenberg has criticized Lonergan's functional specializations on two counts. First, Lonergan's intentional approach (like Husserl's) cannot account for the totality of meaning which precedes individual intentional consciousness. Thus, Pannenberg asserts, the interpreter has to refer to history when exegeting a particular text.[156] On this score, however, I have already shown how Lonergan's approach to meaning and

---

[152]M.i.T., pp. 130-133.   [153]M.i.T., pp. 136-137.

[154]Cf. M.i.T., p. 140.

[155]On a formally dynamic unity-in-difference, cf. Lonergan, Collection, pp. 221-224.

[156]Cf. W. Pannenberg, "History and Meaning in Lonergan's Approach to Theological Method," Irish Theological Quarterly 40 (1973), pp. 105-106, 110-111.

knowledge mediates the objective totality through the unrestricted desire to know as raising ever further questions. Here Lonergan provides a more critically mediated account of the heuristic of total meaning than, for example, Dilthey, to whom Pannenberg appeals.[157]

Acknowledging that Lonergan stresses the interdependence of the functional specialties, Pannenberg's second criticism is to ask: "why, then, is such a division needed at all?"[158] This can be answered in two levels. First, there is an interdependence precisely because the very notion of functional specialization demands that all four levels of consciousness are functioning, though for different goals. Pannenberg, as most historicality theologians, seems hesitant to discuss goals, except in very broad terms such as the goal of history. On a deeper level, however, Pannenberg's question reveals his own reluctance to face up to the demands of history in critical terms, when those demands are not a question of only a mediation from the past into the present but of the present into the future.[159] For the purpose of the differentiations in functional specialization is aimed at showing how a critical methodological mediation is possible, not only from the past into the present, but also from the present into the future. The only alternative to the differentiation is the rather vague undifferentiated status of so much hermeneutical and historical ontologizing of historicality, against which Metz has so effectively protested.[160]

For the demands of our contemporary historical situation cannot be met by either the systematic exigence or the critical

---

[157]Cf. Chapter Three, pp. 422-453 and references given there.

[158]Pannenberg, op. cit., p. 111; on the interdependence, cf. M.i.T., pp. 141-144.

[159]On this flaw in Pannenberg, cf. Geyer, Janowski, and Schmidt, Theologie und Soziologie (Stuttgart, 1970), pp. 63-65: "Historical criticism loses its critical cutting-edge if it does not make use of the limited capabilities of methods aimed at historical critiques of ideologies, and instead overextends itself into a universal-historical hermeneutic."

[160]Cf. Chapter One, pp. 30-53.

exigence functioning on the levels of metaphysics or epistemology.[161] To assert otherwise is to overlook the dialectic of the Enlightenment and its contemporary consequences. That dialectic has impelled us to seek means of establishing an open, yet critical, ongoing collaboration.[162] Certainly, Pannenberg would not dispute the differentiation of theology, as a critical religious knowledge, from religious experience. Yet, as Lonergan has shown, a proper thematization of the relation between religious experience and its cognitive expressions does not separate the two.[163] Would Pannenberg say that, because they are interdependent, the division or differentiation should be suppressed! Lonergan can write:

> Development is through specialization but it must end in integration. Nor is integration to be achieved by mere regression. To identify theology with religion, with liturgy, with prayer, with preaching, no doubt is to revert to the earliest period of Christianity. But it is also to overlook the fact that the conditions of the earliest period have long since ceased to exist. There are real theological problems, real issues that, if burked, threaten the very existence of Christianity. There are real problems of communication in the twentieth century, and they are not solved by preaching to ancient Antioch, Corinth, or Rome. So it is that we have been led to the conclusion of acknowledging a distinction between the Christian religion and Christian theology and, at the same time, of demanding an eighth functional specialty, communications.[164]

The long range issues, so often discussed in ontological categories in historicality theologies, must be cast in methodological terms open to collaboration if those real issues - emergent in the dialectic of the Enlightenment - threatening the very existence of Christianity are to be theologically met. While the interdependence of the eight specialties is guaranteed when one specialist is performing several of them, still, as the specialties develop that becomes

---

[161]Cf. M.i.T., pp. 135-138; Chapter Two, pp. 157-209, and references given there. On the exigences of meaning, cf. Chapter Three, pp. 424-431 and its references.

[162]Cf. Chapter Two, pp. 93-114.

[163]Cf. this Chapter, pp. 497-506 and references given there.

[164]M.i.T., p. 140. Emphasis is mine.

518

less and less feasible, so that a critically methodological
differentiation and integration is necessary in order for
theology to become a truly collaborative venture.[165]

The following outline of each specialty as Lonergan
develops it is no more than a rough sketch. A series of
workshops at Boston College is planned over the coming years
to explore their wide-ranging implications and possible
applications.[166]

Research makes available the data relevant to the
investigations of theology. It is either special or general.
Special research is directed at particular areas of theological inquiry, whereas general research involves the total
assemblage of relevant data. As such it includes the whole
array of archaeological and linguistic methods aimed at
deciphering monuments and documents of the past apropos of
a religious tradition. "It composes indices, tables,
repertories, bibliographies, abstracts, bulletins, handbooks,
dictionaries, encyclopedias. Some day, perhaps, it will give
us a complete information-retrieval system."[167]

Interpretation aims at understanding the data so collected. It includes the more general problems of the basic
exegetical operations. Lonergan enters into them as understanding the object, the words, the author, one's own horizon,
judging the correctness of the understanding, and stating
the meaning of the data.[168] The problems of interpretation
are many, and they have been heightened by the emergence of
historical consciousness on a world scale, by the pursuit
of the human sciences in which meaning is a fundamental
category, and by the confusion this has generated in philosophical and cultural circles still uncertain about just
what knowing is. Hence we experience a modernity wherein
humans have critically cast off the authority of traditions

---

[165]Cf. M.i.T., pp. 141-142.

[166]Cf. also D. Tracy's new book, soon to be published,
Blessed Rage for Order: The New Pluralism in Theology. (New
York, 1975).

[167]M.i.T., p. 127; also pp. 149-151.

[168]Cf. M.i.T., pp. 127, 153-173; also Insight, p. 562-594.

and gone about the independent constitution of their worlds
of meaning. In reference to the tendency to treat all these
issues in hermeneutics, Lonergan remarks:

> Embedded in the problem of hermeneutics, then, there are
> quite different and far profounder problems. They are to
> to be met neither by a wholesale rejection of modernity
> nor by a wholesale acceptance of modernity. In my
> opinion, they can be met only by the development and
> application of theological method. Only in that fashion
> can one distinguish and keep separate problems of
> hermeneutics and problems in history, dialectic, founda-
> tions, doctrines, systematics, and communications. In
> fact the most striking feature of much contemporary
> discussion of hermeneutics is that it attempts to treat
> all these issues as if they were hermeneutical.
> They are not.[169]

The differentiation of hermeneutics from the critique
of ideologies in Germany at the present time indicates how
interpretation cannot handle all of the relevant issues.[170]
For just as that shows the need to distinguish hermeneutics
and dialectics, so H. -D. Bastian's writings have called
attention to the detrimental effect on an all-encompassing
hermeneutic tied to kerygma has had on the efficacy of
preaching itself.[171] Gadamer has called attention to the
errors of attempting to see history as the interpretation of
a text; while both Metz and Moltmann have shown how theology
cannot rely solely on a hermeneutics that is oriented
towards the past but must develop foundations capable of
critically moving from the present into the future.[172] This
has led Metz to a very fruitful distinction, not only of
interpretation from foundations, but also from doctrines. For
these are not only of hermeneutical interest vis-à-vis their
past, but also are "subversive memories" relevant to the
present's future-constituting praxis.[173] Finally, K. Rahner's

---

[169]_M.i.T._, p. 155.

[170]Cf. _Hermeneutik und Ideologiekritik_ (Frankfurt, 1971).

[171]Cf. H. -D. Bastian, _Theologie der Frage_ (Munich,
1969), and his _Verfremdung und Verkündigung_ (Munich, 1967).

[172]Cf. F. Lawrence, "Self-Knowledge in History according
to Gadamer and Lonergan," in _Language Truth and Meaning_, pp.
167-217; on Metz and Moltmann, cf. Chapter One, pp. 30ff.

[173]Cf. Metz, "Erinnerung," in _Handbuch philosophischer_

later writings have emphasized how any future theology cannot
content itself with offering a hermeneutics of past confessional formulae but must seek a systematic understanding of
doctrines commensurate with the mystery of the future.[174]

If, then, interpretation as a functional specialty is
concerned with the general exegetical operations of understanding the text (which involve the fourfold understanding
of the object, words, author, and the exegete's own horizon),
judging the correctness of the understanding (often only more
or less probable), and stating the meaning of the text,
then one could go into the more special exegetical methods
such as literary criticism, form criticism, redaction criticism, and structural criticism.[175] These, and many methods
yet to be discovered and developed, pertain to the functional
specialty of interpretation.

History as a functional specialty is concerned with the
basic, special, and general histories that are written and
their methods.[176] Lonergan does not go into these at any
length since, as with interpretation, he is interested in
the more methodological questions that have plagued the
application of particular methods. Thus he discusses the
emergence of historical knowledge from historical experience,
the necessary perspectivism involved in the historian's
horizon, and the heuristic structures of doing historical
work.[177] These methodological reflections aim at showing
how meta-method can illuminate the work of historians insofar
as they become aware of their own experiencing, understanding,
judging, and deciding. He is careful to point out the difference between historical data and facts, as well as how
the historian in his critical appropriation of history does

Grundbegriffe (Munich, 1973).

[174]Cf. K. Rahner, Schriften IX (Cologne, 1970),
pp. 11-159.

[175]Cf. H. Zimmerman, Neutestamentliche Methodenlehre
(Munich, 1968).

[176]Cf. M.i.T., p. 128.

[177]Cf. M.i.T., pp. 175-234.

not destroy pre-critical history but, through the remaining
functional specialties, is committed to the communication
of a post-critical historical knowledge to the believing
community.[178] Discussions about a value-free history are
put in proper perspective once history is seen as related to
dialectics where there are criteria in terms of the sources,
acts, exigencies, and functions of meaning and value in
history for overcoming the irrationalism of historicism.
As I have pointed out, meta-method can do this without having
to appeal to any absolute knowledge system or set of beliefs
which would constrict historical knowledge to an identity
thought pattern.[179] It is thus able to bring a methodologically formulated unity of identity and non-identity to bear
on the problems of history.

   Dialectics as a functional specialty is concerned with
the concrete, contradictory, and dynamic; and there is
abundant material for this in the history of religious movements. Its primary object centers about the conflicting
movements themselves and the value-judgments and decisions
operative in them. But it is also concerned with the
contradictions that arise from those movements in the writing
of history, and the conflicting interpretations of the data
that result.[180] It is here that an encounter with the past
in a manner that calls for critical self-appropriation occurs.
Indeed, this entire study has been concerned with elaborating
some of the many aspects involved in dialectics and the norms
that must be found therein to overcome the avoidance of the
dialectical issue. Lonergan mentions how the natural and,
to a lesser extent, the human sciences can skirt the dialectical problem. "But a theology can be methodical only if
these issues are met head on."[181] Inasmuch as the unity of
identity and non-identity is operative, the structure of
dialectic will consist of an operator and the materials to be

---

[178]Cf. _M.i.T._, pp. 201-203, 230-233.

[179]Cf. Chapter Three, pp. 422ff.

[180]Cf. _M.i.T._, pp. 128-130; 235-266.

[181]_M.i.T._, p. 249.

522

operated on. The operator will develop positions and reverse
counter-positions, where the positions are all materials
compatible with intellectual, moral, and religious conversion,
and the counter-positions are those incompatible with such
conversions; and they are reversed by removing those elements
incompatible with the conversions.[182] An example of this
can be found in the present study's analysis of Dilthey's
move from dogma to religious experience and how the validity
of the move can be affirmed once the grasp of religious
experience is adequately articulated.[183] More generally, the
same structure of dialectic can be applied to the conflicts
in metascience, as well as to the problems of liberation.[184]

K. Rahner has criticized Lonergan's method in theology
as being neither specifically Christian, nor even specifically
theological.[185] It is undoubtedly true as regards its ability,
especially evident in dialectics, to be applicable to all
theologies and human sciences concerned with man's past in the
light of his future. We have already seen how Lonergan concedes this willingly.[186] Yet its applicability to the human
sciences does not mean it is a-religious, for Lonergan has
rather convincingly shown how the problem of liberation
demands religious conversion just as the methodical exigence
leads into the transcendent exigence.[187] This aims, therefore,
at showing how crucial it is for theology to enter actively
into interdisciplinary collaboration with the sciences. As
for its lack of specificity regarding Christianity, Rahner
himself has had difficulty with his notion of the anonymous
christian. While that notion is understandable within the

---

[182]Cf. M.i.T., pp. 249-250.

[183]Cf. pp. 459-478 of this Chapter.

[184]Cf. Chapter Two, pp. 157-208; Chapter Four, pp. 480-485

[185]Cf. K. Rahner, "Some Critical Thoughts on Functional Specialties in Theology," in Foundations of Theology, pp. 194-196.

[186]Cf. note 134 above.

[187]Cf. Chapter Two, pp. 175-195; Chapter Four, pp. 480-485.

Christian tradition, still it can be made dialectically operative only by seeking to elaborate a method capable of being true to the exigencies of meaning operative in all religious traditions. Insofar as those exigencies will structure each religious tradition's theological reflection, a vast dialectical encounter can gradually occur whereby the differences will be clear and can be resolved in the light of intellectual, moral, and religious conversions. As Lonergan states regarding the aim of dialectics:

> This is high and distant. As empirical science aims at a complete explanation of all phenomena, so dialectic aims at a comprehensive viewpoint. It seeks some single base or some single set of related bases from which it can proceed to an understanding of the character, the oppositions, and the relations of the many viewpoints exhibited in conflicting Christian movements, their conflicting histories, and their conflicting interpretations.[188]

Lonergan is not asking that any religious tradition abandon its claim to universality; rather he is asking them to deepen their own appreciation of that universality and to determine how it has and has not been lived out in praxis. To the extent that the praxis has not been in accord with intellectual, moral, and religious conversion, to that extent the tradition has not been in accord with the universality of its religious faith.[189] And as that praxis is historically brought into accord with intellectual, moral, and religious conversion, to that extent the dialectic will tend towards a unification, first of religious faith, and then of religious beliefs expressive of that faith.[190]

Foundations as a functional specialty objectifies the religious conversion that is basic to religious living. It takes its data from dialectics and seeks to determine which of the conflicting movements, or which elements within them, truly objectifies religious conversion as being in love with God. If in dialectics theology encounters the past in

---

[188] M.i.T., p. 129. On the comprehensive viewpoint; cf. Insight, pp. 564-568.

[189] Cf. pp. 485ff. of this Chapter.

[190] Cf. pp. 497ff. of this Chapter.

the present, in foundations it struggles to articulate the meaning and value of being in love with an immanently transcendent God. Inasmuch as Lonergan has shown the interdependency of religious conversion to moral and intellectual conversion, the task of foundations is not by any means to simply collect statements about conversion but to provide a critical thematization of the general and special categories of religious conversion.[191] The general categories would entail extensive reflections on the conversions correlative to the basic related and recurrent operations of the subject-as-subject, while the special categories will elaborate the models suitable to differentiating the general categories.[192]

However, this is not to be interpreted as any deductive set of logically first propositions. Rather it is the ongoing, developing process that admits of detours and breakdowns, that is as concrete and real as the myriad quest-ionings and searchings of men and women for ultimate meaning and value, their discovery of such ultimate meaning and value, and their transformations when they are grasped by an ultimate concern, a being in love with God.[193] We have already discussed some of the general aspects of foundations when dealing with the transcendental exigence and conversion, with religious experience and expression. It should be pointed out how this notion of foundations in theology is not an appeal to Scripture, Councils, or other authoritative instances. If foundations were for a theology conceived of along classicist lines - as in the paleomorphic theologies - then indeed one could make the foundations such authoritative articulations of the religious community. From them one could then deduce the implications and applications. Yet not everyone who says Lord, Lord will enter the Kingdom of Heaven. The authoritative pronouncements have their authority only for those minds and hearts open to hear and obey. The foundations of theology, accordingly, have to be the formulation of converted religious praxis in the present as that is orientated towards the future. Just as religious conversion is a religious faith linked with

---

[191]Cf. _M.i.T._, pp. 267-293.   [192]Cf. _M.i.T._, pp. 281-293.

[193]Cf. _M.i.T._, pp. 268-271.

the struggles of human progress and decline, so foundations must thematize precisely this link.[194]

Nor does this leave foundations to some merely subjective factor, for we have seen how the transcendental exigence is a dynamic unity-in-difference with the methodical, critical, and systematic exigencies. Far from foundations being solely in the fideomorphic type, they indicate how such fideomorphism is an incomplete thematization of what it means to believe.[195] At the expense of repetition, it must be kept in mind that Lonergan's explicitation of the foundational reality of theology is through his meta-methodological formulation of a unity of identity and non-identity. If either of those is missing, the unity is gone. Then one falls into either an "objectivist" insistence upon the objective contexts of faith as some understanding of historical or world process, or upon definitive pronouncements, or one takes a "subjectivist" stance that cuts off decision from cognitive and moral self-transcendence and is unable objectively to mediate ones faith.

Doctrines express judgments of fact and judgments of value. Hence they include not only what is commonly known as dogmatic theology - for theology is not limited to theory divorced from praxis - but also such judgments of the moral, ascetical, and mystical branches of theology.[196] The functions of doctrines is the realization in religious knowledge of the general functions of meaning. The authority and normativeness of doctrines derives from dialectics and foundations as they discern the values and disvalues of religious experience and expression.

> For the functional specialty, dialectic, deploys both
> the truth reached and the errors disseminated in the
> past. The functional specialty, foundations, discrim-
> inates between truth and error by appealing to the
> foundational reality of intellectual, moral and religious
> conversion. The result of such discrimination is the
> functional specialty, doctrines, and so doctrines, based

---

[194]Cf. pp. 504-506 above and references.

[195]Cf. Chapter One, pp. 19-22; Chapter Four, pp. 497-506.

[196]Cf. M.i.T., p. 132.

> on conversion, are opposed to the aberrations that
> result from the lack of conversion.[197]

This, of course, does not mean that doctrines have always
been formulated in such a critically methodical manner.
Lonergan goes into the differentiations of consciousness in
terms of the exigencies of meaning. How the systematic
exigence emerges in theology to distinguish the common sense
world from the world of theory; how that raises the critical
exigence seeking to relate the two; and how this is accomplished only in the methodical exigence. From this he shows
how in the Catholic history of doctrines such an ongoing
discovery of mind was operative.[198]

He then discusses the permanence and historicity of
doctrines. But he does this not by appealing to the differences
between religious faith and religious beliefs directly, but
by discussing the decrees of Vatican I on those subjects.[199]
It appears that Lonergan skirts the issue of a critique
of doctrines which his own discussion of the ongoing discovery
of mind calls for.[200] Both David Tracy and Charles Davis
have called attention to this inconsistency. Nevertheless,
Lonergan's understanding of Vatican I is definitely not in any
paleomorphic context of static permanence; rather he formulates
a praxis-unity of permanence (identity) and historicity (contextual non-identity).[201] This will not mean a rejection of
the magisterium, any more than the establishment of the
Sacred Congregations after Trent was a rejection of the
previous tradition. Rather it is a critical appreciation of
the context within which Roman Catholic doctrines have been
formulated. An appreciation definitively endorsed by Vatican
II. A critical formulation of doctrines, suitable to its

---

[197] M.i.T., p. 299.

[198] Cf. M.i.T., pp. 302-320.

[199] Cf. M.i.T., pp. 320-326.

[200] Cf. M.i.T., pp. 314-320.

[201] Cf. D. Tracy, "Lonergan's Foundational Theology, an
Interpretation and Critique," in Foundations of Theology, pp.
197-222; also Charles Davis, "Lonergan and the Teaching
Church," ibid., pp. 60-75. M.i.T., pp. 311, 323, 326-330.

future-constituting praxis, can be found in Metz's notion of
the "subversive memory" expressed in church doctrines.[202]   Just
as religious faith is linked to the struggle between progress
and decline, so doctrines are linked to the proclamation of
redemption within the concrete historical struggles of personal
and social living.

   Systematics recognizes that the facts and values
expressed in doctrines may be figurative, symbolic, descriptive. Thus it attempts to meet the further questions that
arise by searching for that fruitful understanding of
religious doctrines that reveals their inner coherence and
their analogies with more familiar domains of human experience.[203]   It is within this context that Lonergan shows how
such analogies can no longer be drawn in terms of classical
metaphysics and faculty psychologies. Metaphysical terms
are not basic but derived from meta-method, so that they
can become critical only in that derived condition.[204]   The
use of mystery as central to systematics can be critically
grounded because of the reality of the subject's orientation
into the known unknown and the transcendental exigence.[205]
Moreover, systematics must not be made to do the work of
doctrines. It is not concerned with articulating truths in
the light of foundations, but of searching for a probable
understanding of such truths. One should not, therefore,
condemn theologians for trying. Indeed, as Lonergan remarks:

> Now it may be thought that one endangers the authority
> of church officials if one acknowledges that theologians
> have a contribution of their own to make, that they
> possess a certain autonomy, that they have at their
> disposal a strictly theological criterion, that they have
> grave responsibilities that will all the more effectively
> be fulfilled by adopting some method and working
> gradually towards improving it. But I think the
> authority of church officials has nothing to lose and
> much to gain from the proposal.[206]

---

[202]Cf. Chapter One, pp. 30-53.

[203]Cf. M.i.T., p. 132.

[204]Cf. M.i.T., pp. 340-344 on "Closed Options" of
metaphysics.

[205]Cf. M.i.T., pp. 344-347.   [206]M.i.T., p. 332.

This autonomy of theologians applies to all of the eight functional specialties, but it is especially operative in systematics done in the contemporary context which, as Lonergan has shown and we have discussed above, has created a scientific enterprise based not upon certain and immutable principles but upon probable verification of hypothetical formulations of understanding.[207]

Communications as a functional specialty indicates how the entire thrust of theology as a movement from data to results is not some introrsive activity for the sole benefit of theologians, but is rather at the service of the believing community and all of humankind. Communications is involved in three types of external relationships. First, there are interdisciplinary relations with art, language, literature, other religions, with the natural and human sciences, with socio-political experience and knowledge, with philosophy and history.[208] This type of relationship is capable of critical and methodological articulation in terms of functional specialization and meta-method. We have seen how Lonergan's notion of functional specialization can be applied to the massive problems of metascience.[209] We have also seen how meta-method is able to formulate the critical thrust of hermeneutical, historical, and dialectical methods without severing such critical knowledge from the pre-critical experience they objectify. This means that a post-critical communication of religious meaning and values is not only possible but necessary.

Lonergan sees the second type of external relation to be the development of an identity and non-identity commensurate with the vast diversity of societies, cultures, and classes spread across the dimensions of human history.[210] Such communication is possible in collaboration with the arts, languages and literatures of those diverse cultures and

---

[207]Cf. Chapter Two, pp. 157ff.

[208]Cf. M.i.T., p. 132; also pp. 358ff.

[209]Cf. Chapter Two, pp. 195ff.

[210]Cf. M.i.T., pp. 132-133.

societies because in all of them there is present the related and recurrent operations of the subject-as-subject. This implies, as Lonergan points out, that the pluralist multiplicity of cultural traditions is entirely respected without falling into a radically uncritical or irrational relativism.[211]

Finally, the functional specialty of communications has to develop those methods which could make use of the diverse media of communication available at any given time or place. Such a development is necessary in order that the dialectical, foundational, doctrinal and systematic specializations, with their multiple methods, lead effectively into policy making, planning and the execution of the plans in order that the praxis of the believing community effectively incarnate meanings and values of religious conversion in a redemptively significant fashion within the many socio-political contexts. Thus Lonergan can conclude the section on the Church and its contemporary situation by calling attention to the demand for interdisciplinary collaboration proportionate to the "ever-increasing change due to an ever-increasing expansion of knowledge."[212] So he also calls for a correlation of theology with scholarly and scientific disciplines in order to achieve an effective critique of evil and decline as well as an effective promotion of good and progress. I have already indicated how such an integration could be carried out within the context of meta-science.[213]

It would be appropriate to close this discussion of how Lonergan's meta-method moves theology from religious experience to interdisciplinary collaboration with the following rather lengthy quotation:

> We have been indicating a method, parallel to the method of theology, for integrating theology with scholarly and scientific human studies. The aim of such integration is to generate well-informed and continuously revised policies and plans for promoting good and undoing evil both in the church and in human

---

[211]Cf. M.i.T., pp. 362-364.

[212]M.i.T., p. 367; also pp. 132-133.

[213]Cf. Chapter Two, pp. 195ff.

society generally. Needless to say, such integrated
studies will have to occur on many levels, local,
regional, national, international. The principles
of subsidiarity will require that at the local levels
problems will be defined and, in so far as possible,
solutions worked out. Higher levels will provide
exchange centers, where information on successful and
unsuccessful solutions is accumulated to be made available to inquiries and so prevent the useless duplication
of investigations. They will also work on the larger
and more intricate problems that have no solution at
the lower levels, and they will organize the lower levels
to collaborate in the application of the solutions to
which they conclude. Finally, there is a general
task of coordination, of working out in detail what
kinds of problem are prevalent, at what level they are
best studied, how all concerned on any given type of
issue are to be organized for a collaborative effort.

I have been speaking mainly of the redemptive action of
the church in the modern world. But no less important
is its constructive action. In fact, the two are
inseparable, for one cannot undo evil without also
bringing about the good. Still one will be taking a
very superficial and rather sterile view of the
constructive side of Christian action, if one thinks
only of forming policies, planning operations and
carrying them out. There is the far more arduous
task (1) of effecting an advance in scientific knowledge,
(2) of persuading eminent and influential people to
consider the advance both thoroughly and fairly, and
(3) of having them convince practical policy makers
and planners both that the advance exists and that it
implies such and such revisions of current policies
and planning with such and such effects.[214]

CONCLUSIONS WITHIN THE CONTEXT OF POLITICAL THEOLOGY

Throughout his Method in Theology, Lonergan calls attention to the fact that he is primarliy engaged in articulating
a method for theology and, as a methodologist, leaves to
theologians the task of explicating the theological significance
of such a critically methodological theologizing.[215] Indeed,
although Lonergan has devoted most of his teaching career to
theology, nevertheless he has had to do it within a context
which he found increasingly inadequate. Thus he states

---

[214] M.i.T., pp. 366-367.

[215] Cf. M.i.T., pp. 119, 312.

concerning his own Latin works <u>De Deo Trino</u> and <u>De Verbo</u> <u>Incarnato</u>, the results of his lectures at the Gregorian University, that these works indicate how a methodologically sophisticated theology should <u>not</u> be done.[216]   In these works Lonergan had to conform to the rather privatized theological research-through-communication syndrome of a classically structured Roman Catholic theology curriculum. He was unable to form that type of interdisciplinary collaboration which he saw as essential for the proper doing of theology today.[217]

I have conceived the present dialectical comparison of Dilthey's critique of historical reason and Lonergan's metamethodology within the context of Metz's political theology for the following reasons. These reasons indicate both the conclusions this study has reached as well as the tasks those conclusions demand if they are to regard not only theory but praxis.

<u>First</u> of all, there are minor and major similarities between Metz and Lonergan in their theological developments. The minor similarity can be seen in how both began their theological development with a re-appropriation of St. Thomas Aquinas. Both had found that such a re-appropriation had provided them with a clearer understanding not only of St. Thomas but also of modernity.[218] Both, however, once they had entered into the complexities of the contemporary situation, came to realize how St. Thomas' medieval context, with its dependence upon metaphysical and faculty-psychological categories, was insufficient for the tasks of theology today. This minor similarity led to their major similarity, which consists in the fact that both find the need for theology to be based upon interdisciplinary collaborative praxis. Such

---

[216]Cf. "An Interview With Fr. Bernard Lonergan," edited by Philip McShane, <u>The Clergy Review</u>, LVI (1971).

[217]In a conversation with the present writer Fr. Lonergan narrated how he had hoped to collaborate with a New Testament scholar and a Patristics specialist in preparing his course on Christology, but that this proved to be impossible within the context of the Gregorian University at that time.

[218]Cf. Metz, <u>Christliche Anthropozentrik</u> (Munich, 1962); Lonergan, <u>Grace and Freedom</u>; Lonergan, <u>Verbum - Word and Idea</u> <u>in Aquinas</u>.

532

a concern for interdisciplinary collaboration is not simply
a rather perfunctory call for teamwork but a critical coming
to terms with the dialectic of the Enlightenment. Thus both
have seen how the crisis of historicism has led in our day
to a crisis of pluralism. This latter crisis is not to be
overcome by any appeal to some abstract or universal identity
system. Nor is the crisis to be met with a rather half-
hearted resignation to a complete non-identity and relativism.
Interdisciplinary collaboration for both Lonergan and Metz
requires a profound and penetrating re-formulation of the
foundations of theology themselves.

Secondly, one can see how Metz's criticisms of those
theologies I have typified as paleomorphic, neomorphic,
fideomorphic and criticomorphic occur within the context of
methodological presuppositions that touch upon the very foundations of the theological enterprise.[219] Metz's critique of
the privatization and ontologization of historicality philosophies and theologies has significance for a critical understanding of the aspirations of Dilthey's critique of historical
reason and, more importantly, of the limitations which that
critique was necessarily involved in due to Dilthey's noumen-
anlly privatized misunderstanding of Erlebnis. Such limitations should not lead us to overlook the positive contributions
Dilthey's critique offers in its attempts to ground the
human sciences. For it was precisely the retreat from such an
attempt that led phenomenological and existential thought into
its ontological affirmation of the non-identity between
sciences and authenticity, thereby leaving unchallenged the
scientistic monopoly on method.

If my articulation of the methodological presuppositions
of political theology is correct, then Lonergan's move from
cognitional theory to meta-method may prove extremely useful
to the tasks of political theology.[220] This usefulness might
be articulated according to the four areas mentioned in
Chapter Two.[221]

---

[219]Cf. Sacramentum Mundi III, p. 1234.

[220]Cf. Chapter One, pp. 41-53.

[221]Cf. Chapter Two, pp. 56-93.

First, Lonergan, insofar as he carried through a thematization of the related and recurrent operations of the subject-as-subject capable of handling not only subjective acts of meaning but also the objective contexts, may have provided a type of transcendental reflection extremely necessary for the methodological interests of political theology. For such reflection is not an epistemological Erkenntnis-metaphysik or a metaphysical Fundamentalontologie which, as Metz has seen, fall behind the critical demands posed by the dialectic of the Enlightenment. The transcendental reflection of Lonergan, on the contrary, exposes the uncritical character of epistemology and metaphysics and is able, through its articulation of the exigencies of meaning in history, to meet the critical exigencies that have emerged since the Enlightenment with a methodical exigence that takes seriously the entire scope of human historical theory and praxis.

Secondly, such a methodical exigence is not formulated according to an exclusive identity nor an exclusive non-identity pattern. The unity of identity and non-identity so central to Metz's own foundational reflections is just as central to meta-method. There is no monopoly or universalization of some particular method aimed at regulating the entire flow of interdisciplinary collaboration. Meta-method exhibits a unity of identity and non-identity between its level of reflection and appropriation and the level of particular methods. Lonergan does not, for instance, enter into a debate concerning the usefulness or validity of any particular methods of research, interpretation, history, dialectics, foundations, doctrines, systematics or communications. The goal of functional specialization is the exact opposite of any one-sided totalitarian imposition. Instead it seeks only to create an open yet critical meta-context where the manifold of particular methods can function most creatively. This open meta-context is critical because it does foster a framework for creative collaboration that can in praxis distinguish between attentiveness and inattentiveness, intelligence and stupidity, critical reasonableness and irrationality, responsibility and irresponsibility.

Thirdly, Metz's concern with narrative and story is not

534

some pious afterthought to his foundational methodological position. Rather, if my interpretation is correct, this concern with post-critical narrative is to assure that the critical tasks of argument and reflection do not fall into that abstract conceptualism against which both Dilthey and Lonergan, and Lonergan more effectively than Dilthey, have argued. We have seen how despite his intentions, Dilthey could not account for a pre-critical experience capable of moving to objective critical knowledge, so that he was theologically constrained to reject doctrine in order to preserve experience. Lonergan, on the other hand, has rather convincingly shown how one can move - and how de facto the exigencies of meaning in history have occurred - from pre-critical experiencing, understanding, judging and deciding to a critical appropriation of that pre-critical experience. A methodological unity in difference exists between the pre-critical and the critical. This movement from consciousness to knowledge, from historical consciousness to historical knowledge, from religious experience to religous expression indicates how effectively Lonergan has removed an understanding of method from the Cartesian and consequently scientistic monopoly of method. Lonergan can account without difficulty, indeed is impelled to by his very method, for the unity in difference between narrative and argument.

Finally, Metz's concern with the foundations of theology demanded, as we saw in Chapter One, that those foundations be found in the praxis of the present as that praxis appropriates its past and confronts the eschatological demands of the future.[222] The above discussion of functional specialization with its two phases of mediation from the past into the present and the present into the future might prove valuable to political theology's concern. More importantly, Lonergan's articulation of the foundational reality as one of intellectual, moral and religious conversion could be of immense value in political theology's task not only of relating argument and narrative, but, on a broader scale, of

---

[222]Cf. Chapter One, pp. 41ff.

articulating theological foundations for interdisciplinary collaboration. Just as Metz has called for a new mediation of theory and praxis, so Lonergan's notion of intellectual, moral and religious conversions are realities and not simply theories. Yet they are realities that depend upon freedom. Insofar as they are present, real human progress is assured; and insofar as they are absent, real human bias, scotosis and decline become cumulative. Moreover, foundations as the objectification of religious conversion understood as the discernment of values by persons and communities in love with God, demands a new mediation of theory and praxis.

Thirdly, and in conclusion, if the present dialectical comparison between Dilthey's critique of historical reason and Lonergan's meta-methodology has provided rather insightful methodological clarifications of the presuppositions of political theology, it is no less true that political theology has provided many crucial theological clarifications regarding methodological issues. Lonergan's statement that the Church must be and promote self-transcendence finds a much more articulated theological treatment in the ecclesiology of political theology. Metz's understanding of the Church and religious life as instances of social-critical freedom is able to clarify, in a way Lonergan has not, how the eschatological orientation of Christian praxis toward the kingdom of God must find its institutional expression within the Church.

Of equal importance is the concrete theological praxis Metz has been engaged in in setting up the interdisciplinary Theological Research Center at the State University in Bielefeld.[223] The significance of such a venture can only be fully appreciated within the context of the dialectic of the Enlightenment. It could offset the contemporary consequences of the dialectic, such as a mechanomorphic rationalism and scientism threatening to "solve" the problems of pluralism through social engineering and a demise of the political. The tasks of political theology are many, for to

---

[223]Cf. Metz und T. Rendtorff (ed.), Die Theologie in der interdisziplinären Forschung (Düsseldorf, 1971).

attempt the arduous theoretical issues involved in transforming the ecclesial institutions into instances of self-
transcending social criticism has significance, not only
for the church, but also for society at large. Where Lonergan
has had to extrapolate from his own praxis at self-
appropriation to the dynamic functions of the human good,
Metz has actually initiated the praxis of interdisciplinary
collaboration within an institutional framework. Perhaps
political theology is more theologically aware of the
dialectics involved in relating religious experience and
expression.

The aim of this dialectical comparison of Dilthey and
Lonergan was to explore the methodological contributions they
could make to the program of political theology. Undoubtedly,
there would be many criticisms of Lonergan's functional
specialization arising from the actual theological praxis
of interdisciplinary collaboration called for by political
theology. The feedback character of functional collaboration
demands such criticism and revision. The present work of
application is, I trust, sufficiently detailed and lengthy
to present in itself.